OFFICIALLY NOTED

Stain on Front page
& Color on 44 & 45. CSC

FIJI

WEEDED

DAVID STANLEY

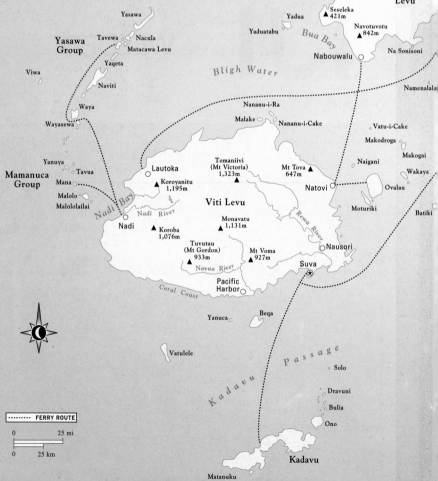

Rotuma

To Viti Levu
(Approx 600 km)

SOUTH PACIFIC OCEAN

Kia

Macuata-i-Wai

Yaqaga

Yalewa Kalou

Vanua Levu

Yasawa

Seseleka
421m

Navotuvotu
842m

Tavewa
Nacula

Yadua

Bua Bay

Yasawa Group

Matacawa Levu

Yaduatabu

Nabouwalu

Na Sonisoni

Yaqeta

Bligh Water

Namenalala

Viwa

Naviti

Nananu-i-Ra
Malake
Nananu-i-Cake

Vatu-i-Cake

Waya

Makodroga

Wayasewa

Makogai

Yanuya

Tavua

Lautoka

Tomaniivi
(Mt Victoria)
1,323m

Mt Tova
647m

Naigani

Wakaya

Mamanuca Group

Koroyanitu
1,195m

Natovi

Ovalau

Mana

Viti Levu

Moturiki

Batiki

Malolo
Malololailai

Nadi

Nadi River

Nadi Bay

Koroba
1,076m

Monavatu
1,131m

Rewa River

Tuvutau
(Mt Gordon)
933m

Mt Voma
927m

Nausori

Navua River

Suva

Pacific Harbor

Coral Coast

Yanuca

Beqa

Kadavu Passage

Vatulele

Solo

Dravuni

Bulia

Ono

····· FERRY ROUTE

0   25 mi

0   25 km

Kadavu

Matanuku

© DAVID STANLEY

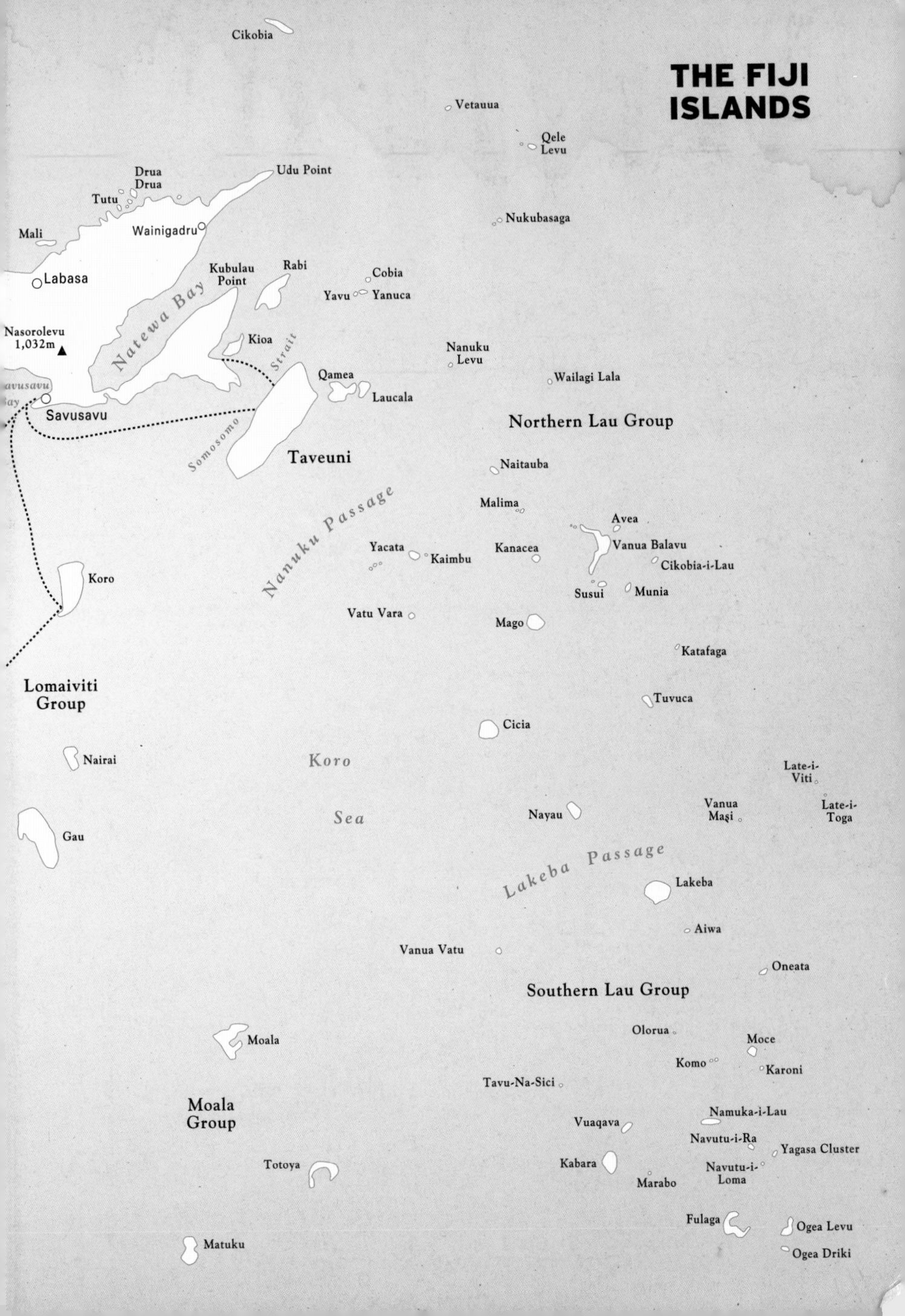

THE FIJI ISLANDS

Cikobia

Vetauua

Qele
Levu

Nukubasaga

Drua
Drua

Tutu

Udu Point

Mali

Wainigadru

Labasa

Kubulau
Point

Rabi

Cobia

Yavu Yanuca

Nasorolevu
1,032m ▲

Natewa Bay

Kioa

Nanuku
Levu

Wailagi Lala

avusavu
Bay

Savusavu

Qamea

Laucala

Northern Lau Group

Somosomo Strait

Taveuni

Naitauba

Malima

Avea

Nanuku Passage

Yacata Kaimbu

Kanacea

Vanua Balavu

Cikobia-i-Lau

Susui Munia

Koro

Vatu Vara

Mago

Katafaga

Lomaiviti
Group

Tuvuca

Cicia

Nairai

Koro

Late-i-
Viti

Gau

Sea

Nayau

Vanua
Masi

Late-i-
Toga

Lakeba Passage

Lakeba

Aiwa

Vanua Vatu

Oneata

Southern Lau Group

Moala

Olorua

Moce

Komo

Karoni

Tavu-Na-Sici

Moala
Group

Vuaqava

Namuka-i-Lau

Navutu-i-Ra

Yagasa Cluster

Totoya

Kabara

Navutu-i-
Loma

Marabo

Fulaga

Ogea Levu

Matuku

Ogea Driki

VITI LEVU

Yasawa Group

Waya Island

Wayasewa Island

Kuata Island

White Rock

Navadra Island

Vomolailai Island

Vomo Island

Nacilau Point

Bligh Water

Vatia Point

Tavua

Vatukoula

Ba

Nadarivatu

Mount Evans Range

Saweni Beach

Lautoka

BA

Navala

Nagatagata

Koro

Nadrau

Yanuya Island

Beachcomber Island

Treasure Island

Abaca

Koroyanitu 1,195m

Navilawa

Ba River

Mana Island

Anchorage Beach

Navini Island

Castaway Island

Nadi Bay

Mamanuca Group

SHERATON RESORT

✕ NADI AIRPORT

Nadi

VATURU DAM

Bukuya

Nanoko

Nubutautau

Malolo Island

Malololailai Island

Nadi River

Nadrau

Tavarua Island

Nausori Highlands

Keiyasi

Plateau

Koroba 1,076m

Naihehe Cave ✝

Monavatu 1,131m

Momi Bay

SEASHELL COVE RESORT

Tau

Lomawai

Robinson Crusoe Island

Naduri

Sigatoka River

Viti

Levu

Island

Tuvutau (Mt Gordon) 933m

NADROGA

Natadola Beach INTERCONTINENTAL FIJI GOLF RESORT

SHANGRI-LA'S FIJIAN

Cuvu

Sigatoka

Korotogo

Navua River

Nabukelevu

Navua Gorge

SERUA

QUEENS

TAMBUA SANDS

THE NAVITI

HIDEAWAY RESORT

THE WARWICK

Korolevu

BEACHOUSE

RD

CRUSOE'S RETREAT

WAIDROKA BAY RESORT

Serua Island

Coral Coast

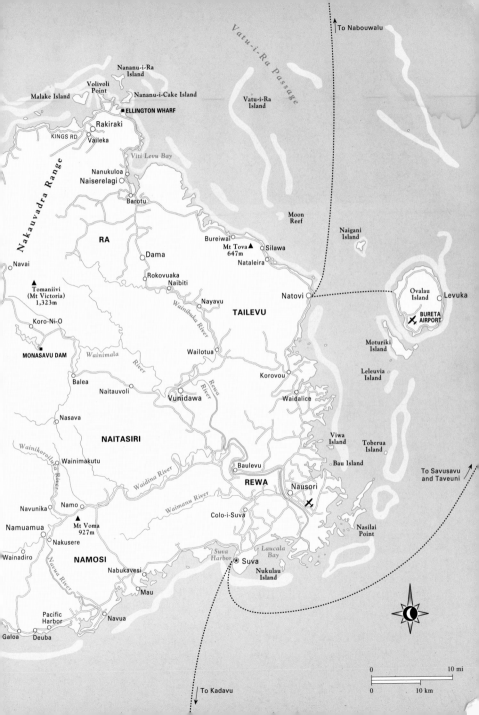

Contents

Discover Fiji

Once notorious as the "Cannibal Isles," Fiji is now the colorful crossroads of the South Pacific. Of the 322 islands that make up the Fiji group, more than 100 are inhabited by a rich mixture of Melanesians, Indo-Fijians, Polynesians, Micronesians, Chinese, and Europeans, each group with a cuisine and culture of its own. Here Melanesia mixes with Polynesia, ancient India with the Pacific, and tradition with the modern world. Fijians preserve an amazing variety of traditional customs and crafts, such as the presentation of the whale's tooth, fish driving, turtle calling, tapa beating, and pottery making.

The landforms and seascapes of Fiji are just as diverse – and just as dramatic. The cartoon-shipwreck sandbars of the Mamanucas, the grassy volcanic hilltops of the Yasawas, and the impenetrable rainforests of Taveuni are all concentrated in a relatively small area. The two main islands, Viti Levu and Vanua Levu, are among the largest in the region. Strewn like a halo around these giants are scattered island chains, which require time and effort to visit.

Most visitors experience Fiji through the resorts and aquatic activities of the Mamanuca and Yasawa islands, and many Coral Coast resorts have a family-friendly reputation. Fiji's intriguing history comes alive in the old colonial capital, Levuka, where the main street recalls the whaling days of

a bygone century. Savusavu on Vanua Levu is an old coconut plantation town with the feel of the American Deep South, while the big sugar mill towns, Lautoka and Labasa, are rough and ready. Suva, the capital, is the stage on which the country's modern history is acted out.

Fiji is a traveler's country par excellence. You'll meet vibrant, outgoing people whose knowledge of English (one of two official languages, the other being Fijian) makes communicating a breeze. Unlike areas where you're a mere spectator, in Fiji you're encouraged to participate. You'll be able to swim along reefs rich in marine life and coral, hike over grassy ridges with half of Fiji at your feet, and surf waves meeting land for the first time since Antarctica. The bite of spicy Indian curries will awaken your taste buds, while Fijian specialties like diced raw tuna marinated in lime juice or whole reef fish baked in coconut cream will make you feel you've arrived in heaven.

Bula, welcome to Fiji, everyone's favorite South Pacific country.

Planning Your Trip

▶ WHERE TO GO

Nadi and the Mamanucas

As the site of Fiji's main international airport, Nadi is the country's gateway city, with numerous shopping and dining possibilities. The beaches around Nadi leave a lot to be desired, however; for the white sandy beaches of the travel brochures, you must hop over to the enticing Mamanuca Group. Nearly half of Fiji's island resorts are there, and the clear waters, golden sands, dazzling reefs, and good facilities make this a popular destination.

The Yasawa Islands

The long, narrow Yasawa Group off northwestern Viti Levu is wilder, mightier, and less developed than the Mamanucas: the beaches are longer, the jungle-clad mountains higher, and the accommodations rougher. These islands rank high for their spellbinding environment and activities include scuba diving, snorkeling, and hiking. The *Blue Lagoon* and *Captain Cook* mini cruise ships ply these

IF YOU HAVE . . .

- **ONE WEEK:** Visit the Mamanuca or Yasawa Islands from Nadi.
- **TWO WEEKS:** Fly to Taveuni and return via Savusavu and Suva.
- **THREE WEEKS:** Add the Yasawa Islands to Taveuni and Savusavu.
- **FOUR WEEKS:** Add Kadavu, Levuka, and Nananu-i-Ra.

waters, which are named for Captain William Bligh.

Southern Viti Levu

The southern flank of Fiji's mainland, Viti Levu, is the Coral Coast with a series of large hotels. Visitors looking for more than beach life often pick these resorts for the numerous

a clownfish taking refuge among a sea anemone's tentacles in the Beqa Lagoon, south of Viti Levu

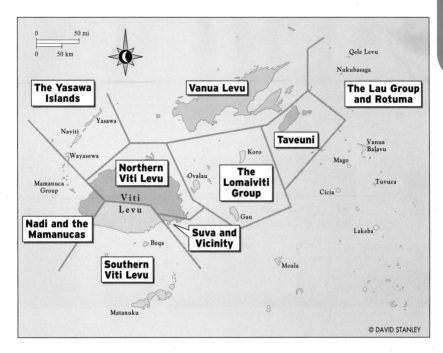

tours and sporting activities they offer. South of Viti Levu are Beqa Island with upscale scuba resorts and Yanuca Island with budget surfing camps. Farther south, Kadavu is another mecca for scuba divers.

Wainibuka River through the heart of Viti Levu. Nananu-i-Ra Island off Rakiraki is a favorite of scuba divers, windsurfers, and backpackers. Sugar city Lautoka offers good facilities and a lot to see. Roads into the

Suva and Vicinity

Fiji's capital, Suva, has the country's finest cinemas, monuments, museums, discos, restaurants, stores, and all of the excitement of the South Pacific's largest town. Ships, buses, and planes depart Suva for every corner of the republic. City slickers won't bore easily in Suva. Much of the country's history has unfolded here, and for the nature lover, the nearby hill station of Colo-i-Suva is of interest.

Northern Viti Levu

Viti Levu's northern half is often neglected by travelers, though Kings Road follows the

cinemas in Suva

the Church of the Sacred Heart on Levuka's waterfront, on Ovalau Island in the Lomaiviti Group

interior of the island begin in Lautoka, Ba, and Tavua.

The Lomaiviti Group

Anyone with an interest in Fiji's vivid history won't want to miss Ovalau Island and the time-worn old capital, Levuka. The town's long row of wooden storefronts looks like the set of a Wild West film, set below towering volcanic peaks. Just south of Ovalau are several small islands with backpacker camps, while the very rich and famous are flown into Wakaya Island.

Vanua Levu

Across the Koro Sea from Ovalau is Fiji's second island, Vanua Levu, heart of the "friendly north." Savusavu is a picturesque town set along a splendid wide bay. Two spectacular highways sweep away from Savusavu. One travels through the mountains to the mill town of Labasa, and another snakes east along the verdant coast to Buca Bay.

Taveuni

Taveuni's high spine is draped in impenetrable rainforest, with huge coconut plantations tumbling to the west coast and magnificent waterfalls pouring down the steep eastern slopes. Several lovely nature reserves are at Bouma and Lavena on the east side of Taveuni. The fabulous soft corals of the Rainbow Reef and Great White Wall are just across Somosomo Strait from western Taveuni.

The Lau Group and Rotuma

The little-known isles of the Lau Group are seldom visited, largely due to their distance from Viti Levu. Only two islands in the Lau Group, Lakeba and Vanua Balavu, have regular accommodations, effectively limiting where you can go. Rotuma Island, far to the north, is about as far as you can go without actually leaving Fiji.

▶ WHEN TO GO

The seasonal climatic variations in Fiji are not extreme. There's a hotter, more humid season November–April, and a cooler, drier time May–October. March is the hottest and rainiest month and July is the coolest and driest. Hurricanes occur during the rainy season, but they only last a few days a year.

In Fiji, location is as important as the time of year in determining the weather. The southeast sides of the main islands face the prevailing winds, and as the clouds are forced up over the mountains, they discharge much of their moisture. The northwest sides of Viti Levu and Vanua Levu are a rain shadow. Suva gets nearly twice as much rain as Nadi at any time of year.

If you're a scuba diver, it's useful to know that the best diving conditions are April–October, with the calmest seas in April and May. Visibility is tops June–October, then slightly worse November–March due to river runoff and plankton growth. The marine life is most bountiful July–November. There's surf for surfing throughout the year, with the best swells out of the south March–October. May–October is the yachting season, with the trade winds blowing reliably out of the southeast.

▶ BEFORE YOU GO

Visas and Officialdom

A passport valid at least three months ahead is required of everyone, but visitors from 101 countries do not need a visa. Your airline may ask to see a ticket to leave Fiji as you are checking in.

Getting There

Thirteen international airlines either fly to Fiji or have code share agreements, with frequent service from Auckland, Brisbane, Guam, Honolulu, Los Angeles, Melbourne, Seoul, and Sydney. In addition, Air Pacific flies to most western Pacific destinations but there are no direct flights to Fiji from Rarotonga or Tahiti.

Getting Around

Fiji's domestic airline, Pacific Sun, flies from Nadi to Kadavu, Labasa, Malololailai, Mana, Savusavu, Suva, and Taveuni, and from Suva to Kadavu, Labasa, Lakeba, Levuka, Savusavu, Taveuni, and Vanua Balavu. Fast catamarans link Nadi to islands in the Mamanuca and Yasawa Groups, and larger car ferries leave Suva for Ovalau, Taveuni, and Vanua Levu. Public bus service is frequent around Viti Levu, across Vanua Levu, and up and down Taveuni. Rental cars and taxis are plentiful.

Explore Fiji

▶ THE 10-DAY BEST OF FIJI

Ten days are enough to see a good cross section of Fiji, provided you start moving immediately upon arrival. You can shorten this itinerary to seven days by leaving out Levuka and booking your Mamanuca or Yasawa day cruise directly from your Coral Coast resort (connecting shuttle buses are available). To include the smaller outer islands, extend your stay and turn to the next itinerary, the *Island-Hopper Special.*

Day 1

You'll probably arrive at Nadi International Airport in the middle of the night. Change a good chunk of money at the exchange office in the arrivals hall, then walk over to the departures hall to await the morning flight to Taveuni. To be sure of getting on the plane, book ahead online through Pacific Sun (www .pacificsun.com.fj). Spend the rest of the day relaxing at your Taveuni resort or join an afternoon tour.

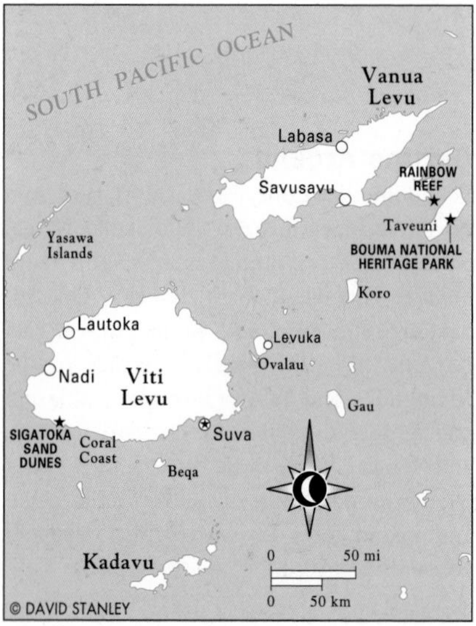

Day 2

Go to Bouma National Heritage Park today for the wonderful hiking and swimming. Unless you stay overnight in one of the small guesthouses at Bouma and Lavena, you won't be able to do this on public transportation. Instead, hire a taxi or join an organized tour arranged through your resort.

Day 3

Explore the south end of Taveuni today or go scuba diving on the Rainbow Reef.

Day 4

Catch the morning flight to Suva (book ahead online). If you're a little adventurous, there are overnight ferries from Taveuni to Suva three times a week. In Suva, visit the Fiji Museum and nearby colonial monuments in the afternoon and enjoy a night on the town.

Day 5

Catch the morning flight to Levuka on Ovalau Island. Levuka is the picturesque old capital of Fiji with many historic sites to explore.

Day 6

Today you could go scuba diving or join an organized hiking or island tour of Ovalau.

Day 7

Catch the bus to Suva, which leaves Levuka

SOUTH PACIFIC OCEAN

Vanua Levu

Labasa

RAINBOW REEF ★

Savusavu

Taveuni ★

BOUMA NATIONAL HERITAGE PARK

Koro

Yasawa Islands

Lautoka

Levuka
Ovalau

Nadi   Viti Levu

Gau

SIGATOKA SAND DUNES ★   Coral Coast

⊗ Suva

Beqa

Kadavu

0   50 mi
0   50 km

© DAVID STANLEY

traditional boat on display at the Fiji Museum in Suva

shortly before dawn five days a week. Of course, you can also fly, but the bus/boat trip is easy to do and worth it. In Suva connect with another bus to the Coral Coast resort of your choice. In the evening, you might be able to catch a Fijian firewalking show.

Day 8

After a morning swim at your resort, catch a bus back toward Nadi. If hiking and nature appeal to you, ask the driver to drop you off at the Sigatoka Sand Dunes visitor center just west of Sigatoka town. Some fine coastal scenery is available to those who hike up onto the dunes. Later flag down another bus to Nadi. Alternatively, hire a taxi from your resort to Nadi, which will allow you to visit the Kula Eco Park, Sigatoka town, the sand dunes, Natadola Beach, the Momi guns, and anything else you'd care to see along the way (ask for a fixed price with all the stops).

Day 9

For a glimpse of some of Fiji's most spectacular outer islands, take a day cruise to Botaira

Beach Resort on Naviti Island in the Yasawa Islands today. Cruising to Monuriki Island on the schooner *Seaspray* is another possibility. Otherwise, the tour desks at all the main hotels can book various excursions and recreational activities around Nadi.

Fijian firewalking performance

a South Pacific sunset at Port Denarau, Nadi

Day 10

If you're leaving Fiji today, your flight will probably depart late at night. Store your luggage at your hotel or take it to the 24-hour airport luggage office. Then go on a tour or spend part of the day exploring the upscale resorts of Denarau Island. After shopping and dinner in downtown Nadi, catch a bus back to the airport for your flight.

▶ ISLAND-HOPPER SPECIAL

If you only follow our *10-Day Best of Fiji* itinerary to Taveuni and back, you'll miss out on many of the smaller outer islands that have far better beaches than those on the main islands. Transportation is more of an issue here, as none of the outer islands have bus services or car rental agencies. Some are accessible by small plane, but most can be reached only by boat. Awesome Adventures offers a seven-day "Bula Pass" for a round-trip on the daily catamaran from Nadi to the Yasawa Islands with unlimited stopovers. That's a great way to spend a week, and if you have a few more days, add Nananu-i-Ra.

Day 1

If your flight arrives at Nadi International Airport in the middle of the night, you should still be able to catch the 0830 sailing of the high-speed Awesome Adventures catamaran from Port Denarau to Nacula, Tavewa, or Nanuya Lailai (choose one). You can book ahead online (www.awesomefiji.com) or at any Nadi Airport travel agency upon arrival. By cruising straight through to the vessel's last stop, you'll get extra mornings at the beach on your way back to Nadi. The beaches, reefs, scenery, snorkeling, scuba diving, and hiking in this area are among the best in Fiji.

Day 2

A day of relaxation, hiking, or activities on Nacula, Tavewa, or Nanuya Lailai. The resorts offer excursions to neighboring islands, so you won't be limited to the one you chose.

The fabulous Blue Lagoon is between Nanuya Lailai and Tavewa.

Day 3
Catch the afternoon catamaran to Naviti Island and enjoy the beach.

Day 4
Choose a day of relaxation or activities on Naviti. Scuba diving is possible, and there's good hiking in the hills behind the resorts.

Day 5
Catch the afternoon catamaran to Waya, Wayasewa, or Kuata for more of the same.

Day 6
Spend the day on Waya, Wayasewa, or Kuata. The snorkeling is good off all of these islands, and you'll be exposed to traditional Fijian culture.

Day 7
The afternoon Awesome Adventures catamaran will take you back to Nadi. Rather than spend the night in Nadi itself, stay on the shuttle bus to Lautoka to be better positioned for the next day's trip.

Day 8
Take the 0815 Sunbeam express bus from Lautoka to Vaileka market at Rakiraki, a 2.5-hour ride. Shuttle boats from the resorts on Nananu-i-Ra Island pick up from Ellington Wharf, a F$15 taxi ride from Vaileka. Make resort reservations ahead of time.

Day 9
Spend the day snorkeling, scuba diving, windsurfing, or hiking on Nananu-i-Ra.

Day 10
If you're leaving Fiji tonight, return to Vaileka in the morning and catch a bus back to Lautoka. Nadi Airport is nearby. If you have another day, do a trip from Nadi to one of the tiny Mamanuca islands on your last day. To extend your trip to Kadavu Island (daily flights from Nadi) would require another three or four days.

▶ FIJI'S FINEST BEACHES

Fiji has many fabulous beaches but few of them are on the three largest islands, Viti Levu, Vanua Levu, and Taveuni. The gray beaches around Nadi and Lautoka are lapped by murky, coral-free waters. Some Nadi-area resorts have dumped white sand onto their beaches to enhance their visual appeal. To find the beaches featured in the travel brochures you must head for the outer islands. One thing you'll seldom encounter anywhere

THE REAL FIJI

Fiji's culture is rich and many large resort hotels around Nadi and along the Coral Coast offer cultural performances for visitors, which could include Fijian firewalking over hot stones or a traditional song and dance performance called a *meke*. The **Arts Village** at Pacific Harbor on Viti Levu's south coast presents Fijian firewalking Wednesday–Saturday and offers village tours that re-create and interpret Fiji's traditional culture.

FIJIAN CULTURE

Few living Fijian villages are considered tourist attractions, but most warmly welcome visitors with a genuine interest in learning about or experiencing the Fijian way of life. There's a certain etiquette involved in visiting a Fijian village. A formal presentation of kava roots called a *sevusevu* is the focal point of all such visits.

Fiji's best-preserved traditional village is **Navala,** inland from Ba on Viti Levu's northwest coast. All of the houses in Navala are thatched, and sightseers are welcomed in exchange for a community admission fee. Rosie Holidays in Nadi organizes guided hiking tours to remote villages in central Viti Levu upon request if as few as two people want to go.

INDIAN CULTURE

Nearly half of Fiji's population is of East Indian descent, with traditions and culture different from those of indigenous Fijians. Indian culture isn't marketed in Fiji the way Fijian culture is promoted, and Indo-Fijian firewalking over hot embers is performed only at religious festivals.

For visitors, the easiest way to connect with Indian culture is to have a meal at an Indian vegetarian restaurant or to visit a Hindu temple. The most visited temple by far is the colorful **Sri Siva Subrahmaniya Swami Temple** in Nadi. However, there are less-known temples and mosques all around the larger islands, and visitors willing to remove their shoes are welcome inside. For a more engaged experience, there's the Sunday prayer session and vegetarian feast at the **Sri Krishna Kaliya Temple** in Lautoka.

detail of Sri Krishna Kaliya Temple in Lautoka

LIVING HISTORY

Considerable information on Fiji's history and culture can be found at the **Fiji Museum** in Suva. **Jack's Handicrafts** outlets around Viti Levu and most markets sell woodcarvings and other handicrafts, though many of the items displayed there are only of souvenir quality.

To really relive Fiji's history, a visit to the old capital, **Levuka,** on Ovalau Island, can't be beat. The **Levuka Community Center** has the second-best museum in Fiji, and there are numerous century-old colonial buildings around town. The scenery and laid-back atmosphere are also great.

in Fiji is surf crashing on the shore as coral reefs stand in the way.

Mamanuca Group

Picture-postcard white sand beaches are easy to find on the small islands of the Mamanuca Group off Nadi. Resort islands like Beachcomber, Bounty, Castaway, Matamanoa, Navini, South Sea, and Tokoriki have lovely beaches with excellent snorkeling in their lagoons, especially at high tide. The larger Mamanuca Islands also have good beaches. Mana Island has them on the northern, southern, and western sides. The best beach on Malololailai Island is in front of Plantation and Lomani resorts. The western beach on Vomo Island is superb.

Yasawa Islands

There are many fine beaches in the Yasawa Islands, beginning with the ones on Kuata and Wayasewa Islands. The southern beaches of nearby Waya Island are also good, but the high white beach in front of Octopus Resort on the northwest coast is the best. On Naviti Island, farther north, the beach at Botaira Resort is better than one at Korovou and Coconut Bay. The famous Blue Lagoon Beach on Nanuya Levu Island has the azure waters and white sands dreams are made of, and Long Beach on nearby Nacula Island is certainly one of Fiji's finest. Tavewa Island also has a nice beach and there are many more, including the long sandy beach up the western coast on Yasawa Island.

Southern Viti Levu

Viti Levu may be an island of few fine beaches, but Natadola Beach south of Nadi is the exception with its long white sands and clear waters. The Coral Coast beaches along the southern coast of Viti Levu are only nice at high tide, and even then you must beware of deadly currents draining the lagoon. The Wellesley Resort sits on one of the Coral Coast's finest sandy beaches. The beach at Pacific Harbor is similar to those at Nadi— nice to stroll along, but with few fish and no corals for snorkelers.

As usual, the best beaches are on the smaller offshore islands, starting with tiny Robinson Crusoe Island off Natadola. Vatulele and Yanuca off southern Viti Levu have good beaches, and Lawaki Beach on Beqa is also excellent. The large island of Kadavu has a nice long beach beside Matana Resort, but

a serene South Seas beach on Matamanoa in the Mamanuca Group

Lawaki Beach on the south side of Beqa Island

Kadavu's smaller neighbor Ono has better beaches.

Northern Viti Levu

Northern Viti Levu is not known for its beaches, with the exception of the one at Volivoli near Rakiraki. For long white sands and crystal clear waters you must cross over to Nananu-i-Ra Island, which boasts a choice of seven or eight white sandy beaches.

Lomaiviti Group

Ovalau is another disaster island as far as beaches go, but the smaller neighboring islands of Leleuvia and Naigani boast fine beaches and good snorkeling. Farther afield, Koro and Wakaya also have great beaches.

Vanua Levu

You won't find many good beaches on Vanua Levu. Labasa has none, but several small offshore islands have the type of beaches hyped in the brochures, such as Nukubati and Namenalala on opposite sides of Vanua Levu. The only good beach around Savusavu is at Lesiaceva Point—just ask Jean-Michel Cousteau. A few upscale resorts east of Savusavu, including Namale and Savasi, squat on excellent if diminutive beaches. Vanaira Bay at far eastern end of Vanua Levu has good beaches, most easily accessed from Taveuni.

Taveuni

Like Fiji's other large islands, Taveuni is no great shakes for beaches. One of the best is Prince Charles Beach west of Matei Point near the airport. The beaches east of Matei Point are mud flats most of the time. Surprisingly, Taveuni's top resorts aren't on Prince Charles Beach but high on a plateau above it. Lavena on the eastern side of Taveuni has another good beach. Once again, the small offshore islands have the finest beaches: Matagi, Qamea, and Laucala all offer good options.

▶ DIVING AND SNORKELING IN FIJI

Fiji has been called "the soft coral capital of the world," and seasoned divers know well that Fiji has some of the finest diving in the South Pacific. You won't go wrong choosing Fiji for underwater adventure. The worst underwater visibility conditions here are the equivalent of the finest off the Florida coast. In the Gulf of Mexico, you've about reached the limit if you can see for 15 meters; in Fiji the visibility begins at 15 meters and increases to 40 meters in some places. Many fantastic dives are just 10–15 minutes away from the resorts by boat (whereas at Australia's Great Barrier Reef, speedboats often have to travel more than 60 kilometers to get to the dive sites).

Scuba Diving

Facilities for scuba diving exist at most of the resorts in the Mamanuca and Yasawa Groups; along Viti Levu's Coral Coast and at Pacific Harbor; on small resort islands off Viti Levu; at Levuka, Nadi, and Savusavu; and on Taveuni and adjacent islands. When choosing a place to stay, pick somewhere as close as possible to the sites you wish to dive, as scuba operators generally resist spending a lot of money on fuel to commute to distant reefs.

If you've never dived before, Fiji is an excellent place to learn. Most scuba operators offer Open Water Diver certification courses lasting four or five days. For children, Subsurface Fiji at several Mamanuca resorts specializes in teaching diving to kids as young as eight! Many of the scuba operators listed in this guide also offer introductory "resort courses" for those who want only a taste of scuba diving.

Snorkeling

While scuba diving quickly absorbs large amounts of money, snorkeling is free and you can do it as often as you like. Some dive shops take snorkelers out in their boats for a nominal fee, but there are countless places around Fiji, mostly on smaller outer islands, where you can snorkel straight out to the reef. The Mamanuca Group owes its popularity to its excellent snorkeling.

Best Dive Sites

· Gotham City, Mamanuca Group: Corals and reef fish abound around these pinnacles in a passage through the Malolo Barrier Reef. The soft corals are especially colorful here. This is an easy dive for beginners.

· Great Astrolabe Reef, Kadavu: The eastern side of this huge barrier reef features spectacular walls of hard corals, with caves, canyons, and abundant marine life. A variety of dive sites of differing levels of difficulty are available.

· Namena Barrier Reef, south of Savusavu: Big fish such as tuna, barracuda, mantas, and sharks patrol this largely unexplored reef, which is also known for its soft

scuba divers exploring a reef in the Beqa Lagoon, south of Viti Levu

FOR NATURE LOVERS ONLY

Fiji's most beautiful natural attractions can be neatly divided into mountains, coastlines, and reefs. The forested mountain areas are accessible to most hikers, and there are fine coastlines near roads and resorts. Many reefs can be seen with only a mask and snorkel, but to visit the most spectacular sea reefs, a boat and scuba gear are usually necessary. A few areas are officially protected as national parks and reserves.

MOUNTAINS

Commercial hiking tours from Nadi are offered to the **Nausori Highlands** toward Bukuya, but **Koroyanitu National Heritage Park,** inland from Lautoka, is more spectacular. There are waterfalls near the village of Abaca, but it's the huge trees and views from Mount Batilamu overlooking Nadi that beckon serious hikers. Fiji's highest mountain, Tomaniivi, can be climbed from **Nadarivatu** above Tavua in central Viti Levu.

A more accessible hiking area is **Colo-i-Suva Forest Park,** just 11 kilometers from Suva. Quiet walks through a mahogany forest lead to waterfalls where you can swim, and the mountain climate here is much cooler than in sultry Suva.

On Vanua Levu, there's the **Waisali Nature Reserve** just off the main highway between Savusavu and Labasa. This park is still being developed, but many native tree species including giant kauri trees can be seen from the trails.

Fiji's most visited nature reserve is **Bouma National Heritage Park** on the east side of Taveuni. At Bouma you can hike in to three swimmable waterfalls, the first of which is only a 10-minute stroll from the road. Hikes into the Vidawa Rainforest here are organized by local guides.

COASTLINES

A hike along the coast from any of Fiji's outer island resorts is usually a fascinating experience. On the main islands, mangrove forests often get in your way, but on most of the western offshore islands, you can keep going as far as you want (or until you reach coastal cliffs).

There are great views of coastal scenery at the **Sigatoka Sand Dunes National Park** between Nadi and Sigatoka, which has a visitor center easily accessible by public bus. Some of the dunes are 50 meters high, and the sea crashes directly onto this shore unhampered by any offshore reefs.

On Taveuni, the **Lavena Coastal Walk** in Bouma National Heritage Park continues beyond the end of the road to a river with another waterfall. A boat is necessary to reach even more spectacular sections of coastline where waterfalls plunge over cliffs directly into the sea.

Other islands with excellent (but unnamed) coastal walks include Beqa, Kadavu, Nananu-i-Ra, Naviti, Vanua Balavu, and Waya, and there are many more.

REEFS

Fiji's only official marine conservation areas are a stretch of fringing reef off Ono Island near Kadavu, and the **Waitabu Marine Park,** part of the Bouma National Heritage Park project off northeastern Taveuni. Since fishing is prohibited at Waitabu, the marine life is profuse. A few resorts such as Beachcomber, Navini, and Namenalala have also banned fishing on their fringing reefs and these places are ideal for beach-based snorkeling.

Some of Fiji's finest reefs accessible only by boat are the **Great Astrolabe Reef,** Kadavu (caves, marine life); **Namena Barrier Reef,** south of Savusavu (giant clams); **Rainbow Reef,** west of Taveuni (crevices, soft coral); **Sidestreets,** Beqa Lagoon (soft corals, sea fans); **Supermarket,** west of Mana Island (shark feeding); and **Wakaya Passage,** east of Levuka (rays, hammerheads).

protected coral in Beqa Lagoon

lionfish

accessed through a tunnel. The soft corals are unparalleled here. Some experience is required to dive safely here.

- **Sidestreets, Beqa Lagoon:** A maze of pinnacles covered with red and purple soft corals give you the sensation of swimming through a city. Large schools of fish are encountered in this reef passage. This and several other Beqa Lagoon sites are accessible to beginners.

- **Shark Reef, south of Pacific Harbor:** Swimming with bull and tiger sharks is the attraction here. Divemasters feed these big sharks, plus a half dozen other smaller shark species. This dive is supposed to be for experienced divers only, but in practice novice divers are taken, too.

- **Wakaya Passage, east of Levuka:** The marine life is the thing here, including rays, hammerheads, bronze whalers, schools of barracuda, lionfish, snappers, and silver jacks. Dives here are rated from novice to intermediate.

corals and giant clams. The dives vary from easy to advanced.

- **Rainbow Reef, west of Taveuni:** This 32-kilometer fringing reef includes more than a dozen named dive sites, including the Great White Wall, a bottomless wall

▶ THE LIFE AQUATIC

Sports and recreational activities are well developed and available in many parts of Fiji. They're offered by almost every medium to large resort in Fiji, except those in urban Suva.

Surfing

A growing number of surfing camps are off southern and western Viti Levu. The most famous is Tavarua Island in the Mamanuca Group, accessible only to surfers on prepackaged tours. Other mortals can also use speedboats from Seashell Cove and Rendezvous resorts to surf nearby reef breaks at far less expense, or try to get a booking at the top-end surf resort on Namotu Island right next to Tavarua. The surf resort at Nagigia Island just off west Kadavu is mid-priced. You'll find the Batiluva Beach Resort on Yanuca

Island more budget-oriented and an ideal base for surfing at Frigate Passage on the Beqa Barrier Reef. Surfing is the main activity at the Waidroka Bay Resort and Matanivusi Surf Resort on the Coral Coast. The new Maqai Beach Eco Resort on Qamea Island off Taveuni is a budget-oriented surf camp. Beach break surfing (as opposed to more challenging reef break surfing) is possible at the mouth of the Sigatoka River.

Few of Fiji's waves are for the beginner, especially the reef breaks, and of course, you should bring your own board(s). One of the few companies actively renting surfboards is the Fiji Surf Shop in Nadi.

Fijian clans control traditional fishing rights (*qoliqoli*) on their reefs, and on many islands they also claim to own the surfing rights. This

windsurfing in Fiji

can also apply at breaks off uninhabited islands and even ocean reefs. In the past, upscale surf camps like Tavarua and Namotu have paid big bucks to try to corner the rights to surf famous waves like Cloudbreak, and they often tried to keep surfers from rival resorts away. None of this was ever enshrined in law, and in July 2010 the Fiji Government issued a decree giving the Director of Lands full authority over surfing areas. The government said the intention was to allow greater competition and all existing surfing licenses were cancelled. How this will play out is still unknown but it seems that surfing in Fiji will become much easier to arrange.

Windsurfing

Windsurfing is possible at a much wider range of locales than surfing, and many upmarket beach hotels off southern and western Viti Levu include equipment in their rates. Windsurfing is possible at most of the Mamanuca resorts, including Castaway, Musket Cove, Malolo Island, Plantation Island, Tokoriki, and Treasure Island. Other offshore resorts around Fiji offering windsurfing are Matana Resort, Naigani Island, Qamea Beach, Toberua Island, Turtle Island,

and Vatulele. Windsurfing tours to Nananu-i-Ra are well promoted, with the best conditions June–August. Almost all of the surf camps also offer windsurfing. The mouth of the Sigatoka River is said to be Fiji's finest windsurfing spot.

Boating

Exciting white-water rafting on the cliff-hugging rapids of the Upper Navua River is offered by Rivers Fiji at Pacific Harbor. Also in southern Viti Levu, villagers will pole you down the Lower Navua River on a bamboo raft. More white-water rafting is available on the Ba River below Navala.

In the past, organized ocean kayaking expeditions have been offered among the Yasawa Islands, around Beqa and Kadavu, in Vanua Levu's Natewa Bay, and off Taveuni and Vanua Balavu. Those who only want to dabble can hire kayaks at Kadavu, Taveuni, Savusavu, and a number of other places. Several upmarket Mamanuca resorts loan kayaks to their guests.

You can get in some sailing by taking one of the day cruises by yacht offered from Nadi and Savusavu. Yacht charters are available at Musket Cove Resort in the Mamanuca Group.

NADI AND THE MAMANUCAS

At 10,531 square kilometers, Viti Levu is the second largest island in the South Pacific, about the same size as the Big Island of Hawaii. This island, with an elevation of 1,323 meters at its highest point, accounts for more than half of Fiji's land area. The town of Nadi (NAN-di) is the main gateway to the South Pacific region.

Nadi International Airport faces Nadi Bay in the center of an ancient volcano, the west side of which has fallen away. A small airstrip existed at Nadi even before World War II, and after Pearl Harbor the Royal New Zealand Air Force began converting it into a fighter strip. The U.S. military arrived in 1942 to construct a major air base with paved runways for transport aircraft supplying Australia and New Zealand. In the early 1960s, Nadi Airport was expanded to accommodate jet aircraft, and today the largest jumbo jets can land here. This activity has made Nadi what it is.

The area's Indo-Fijian population works the cane fields surrounding Nadi. There aren't many sandy, palm-fringed beaches on this western side of Viti Levu—for that you have to go to the nearby Mamanuca Group, where a string of sun-drenched resorts soak up vacationers in search of a place to relax. The long gray mainland beaches near Nadi face shallow murky waters devoid of snorkeling possibilities, but okay for windsurfing and waterskiing. Fiji's tropical rainforests are on the other side of Viti Levu, not on this dry side of the island.

In recent years, Nadi has grown into Fiji's fourth-largest town, with a population of 42,000. The town center's main feature is a long stretch of restaurants and shops with

© VALERY SHANIN/123RF.COM

HIGHLIGHTS

(Sri Siva Subrahmaniya Swami Temple: This is easily the largest and most colorful Hindu temple in the South Pacific. Visitors are welcome to enter (after removing their shoes) and take photos (upon payment of a small fee). Devotees perform intriguing religious ceremonies here throughout the day (page 29).

(Denarau Island: Denarau Island has more in common with Hawaii than Fiji, but it's fun to tour the lavish resorts and maybe sneak a swim in one of the five-star pools. A shopping center is next to the marina with its fleet of tourist boats, and you can visit the clubhouse of the region's top golf course. An interesting half-day can be spent exploring here (page 30).

(Momi Battery Historic Park: The British six-inch guns installed here in 1941 are of some historical interest, but the view of the offshore islands and surrounding landscape is even more appealing. If you've hired a car, it's worth carrying on to the nearby Marriott Fiji Resort for more sightseeing (page 55).

(Cloudbreak: Fiji's most famous surfing wave, Cloudbreak, is next to Tavarua and Namotu islands, straight out from the Momi guns. The surf resorts on these islands are accessible only on package tours, but you can surf Cloudbreak any Saturday morning by boat from Seashell Cove Resort (page 65).

(Beachcomber Island: Beachcomber was the first large island resort in Fiji to offer all-inclusive dormitory accommodations for single travelers. Today the clientele has grown a little older, and visits by families with young children are encouraged, but the beach, reef,

water sports, and lunch buffet are as good as ever. You can do it as a day trip from Nadi (page 65).

(Monuriki Island: Anyone who has seen the Tom Hanks movie *Castaway* will be familiar with uninhabited Monuriki. The high white beach, emerald lagoon, and high grassy hill are the very image of paradise. Day cruises from Nadi and some Mamanuca resorts bring Monuriki within range of everyone (page 70).

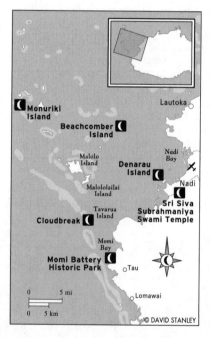

LOOK FOR **(** TO FIND RECOMMENDED SIGHTS, ACTIVITIES, DINING, AND LODGING.

high-pressure sales staffs peddling luxury goods and mass-produced souvenirs. It's easily the most tourist-oriented place in Fiji, yet there's also a surprisingly colorful market, and the road out to the airport is flanked by an excellent variety of places to stay.

PLANNING YOUR TIME

A huge selection of day cruises, sightseeing tours, and adventure activities are offered around Nadi, and the city makes a convenient base for exploring this part of Fiji. From Nadi, there are bus tours to gardens, valleys, mountains, and beaches. You can go scuba diving, golfing, and fishing as often as you like. You could cruise to a different Mamanuca resort every day, returning to your inexpensive Nadi hotel room at dusk.

To get true feeling for the outer islands, however, you'll want to spend a couple of days on one or more of them. If you're a beach person, a tiny island with an active water-sports operation (such as Beachcomber, Bounty, Castaway, Treasure, Matamanoa, or Tokoriki) may be all you need. If you want activities but also legroom, pick a somewhat larger island (Malolailai, Malolo, or Mana). If you're more of a sightseer than a swimmer, you'll get bored after a few days at any of these islands.

Just about every form of transportation in Fiji is available here. Fast catamarans leave from Nadi's Port Denarau Marina to the Yasawa Islands every day, and to almost every island in the Mamanucas two or three times a day. Frequent local buses make day trips to Lautoka and Sigatoka extremely cheap and easy. Within Nadi, taxis are quite affordable.

Keep in mind, however, that Nadi is Fiji's "border town," and to experience real Fijian life you have to get beyond it. Nearby Lautoka is far less foreigner-oriented, though it doesn't have as wide a choice of activities or places to stay. A few days in Nadi town are probably enough. And since you'll have to come back here anyway to catch your flight out of Fiji, it's probably better to leave your explorations around Nadi until the end of your trip.

© TOURISM FIJI

approaching a small island at the west end of the Mamanuca Group

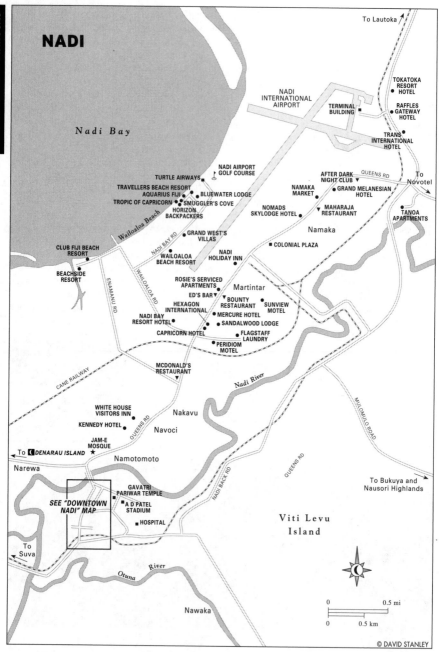

NADI

To Lautoka

Nadi Bay

NADI INTERNATIONAL AIRPORT

TERMINAL BUILDING

TOKATOKA RESORT HOTEL

RAFFLES GATEWAY HOTEL

TRANS INTERNATIONAL HOTEL

To Novotel

NADI AIRPORT GOLF COURSE

QUEENS RD

AFTER DARK NIGHT CLUB

GRAND MELANESIAN HOTEL

TURTLE AIRWAYS
TRAVELLERS BEACH RESORT
AQUARIUS FIJI
TROPIC OF CAPRICORN
BLUEWATER LODGE
SMUGGLER'S COVE
HORIZON BACKPACKERS

NAMAKA MARKET

NOMADS SKYLODGE HOTEL

MAHARAJA RESTAURANT

TANOA APARTMENTS

Wailoaloa Beach

Namaka

CLUB FIJI BEACH RESORT

NADI BAY RD

GRAND WEST'S VILLAS

WAILOALOA BEACH RESORT

NADI HOLIDAY INN

COLONIAL PLAZA

BEACHSIDE RESORT

ENAMANU RD

WAILOALOA RD

ROSIE'S SERVICED APARTMENTS

Martintar

ED'S BAR

HEXAGON INTERNATIONAL

BOUNTY RESTAURANT

SUNVIEW MOTEL

NADI BAY RESORT HOTEL

MERCURE HOTEL

SANDALWOOD LODGE

CAPRICORN HOTEL

FLAGSTAFF LAUNDRY

PERIDIOM MOTEL

CANE RAILWAY

MCDONALD'S RESTAURANT

Nadi River

MULOMULO ROAD

WHITE HOUSE VISITORS INN

Nakavu

KENNEDY HOTEL

QUEENS RD

Navoci

JAM-E MOSQUE

To **DENARAU ISLAND**

Namotomoto

Narewa

GAVATRI PARIWAR TEMPLE

A D PATEL STADIUM

SEE "DOWNTOWN NADI" MAP

HOSPITAL

NADI BACK RD

QUEENS RD

To Bukuya and Nausori Highlands

Viti Levu Island

To Suva

Otuna River

Nawaka

0   0.5 mi

0   0.5 km

© DAVID STANLEY

Sights

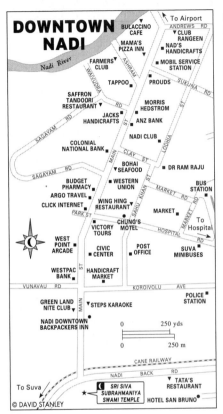

DOWNTOWN NADI

Nadi River

BULACCINO CAFE
To Airport
ANDREWS RD
CLUB RANGEEN
MAMA'S PIZZA INN
NAD'S HANDICRAFTS
ASHRAM RD
MOBIL SERVICE STATION
FARMERS CLUB
SUKUNA RD
WAVUVAU
TAPPOO
PROUDS
SAFFRON TANDOORI RESTAURANT
MORRIS HEDSTROM
RD
JACKS HANDICRAFTS
ST
ANZ BANK
SAGAYAM RD
NADI CLUB
COLONIAL NATIONAL BANK
CLAY ST
LODHIA ST
MAIN ST
BOHAI SEAFOOD
DR RAM RAJU
SAGAYAM RD
BUDGET PHARMACY
WESTERN UNION
BUS STATION
ARGO TRAVEL
MARKET RD
SAHU KHAN ST
CLICK INTERNET
PARK ST
WING HING RESTAURANT
MARKET
VICTORY TOURS
CHUNG'S MOTEL
MARKET RD
To Hospital
HOSPITAL RD
WEST POINT ARCADE
CIVIC CENTER
POST OFFICE
SUVA MINIBUSES
WESTPAC BANK
HANDICRAFT MARKET
VUNAVAU RD
KOROIVOLU AVE
POLICE STATION
GREEN LAND NITE CLUB
MAIN ST
STEPS KARAOKE
NADI DOWNTOWN BACKPACKERS INN
0   250 yds
0   250 m
CANE RAILWAY
NADI BACK RD
To Suva
TATA'S RESTAURANT
SRI SIVA SUBRAHMANIYA SWAMI TEMPLE
HOTEL SAN BRUNO
© DAVID STANLEY

streets (observe what the others are having and order the same). It's all quite a contrast to the tourist scene along Main Street!

◖ SRI SIVA SUBRAHMANIYA SWAMI TEMPLE

Nadi's only other substantial sight is the Sri Siva Subrahmaniya Swami Temple (open during daylight hours, photography permit F$3.50, admission free), off Queens Road at the south entrance to town. It's easily the largest and finest of its kind in the South Pacific. The local Hindus erected this colorful South Indian–style temple in 1994 with the help of skilled workers flown in from India. The entire brick and concrete building is painted in basic colors with intricate sculpture on the towers. This temple is dedicated to Muruga (also known as Subrahmaniya), the mythical general who led the devas (divinities) to victory over the demons, and on the ceiling outside the three-story main sanctum is a fresco of a six-faced Lord Muruga riding a peacock. Visitors may enter

NADI MARKET

To get a glimpse of the "real Fiji," visit Nadi Market, off Hospital Road between downtown Nadi and the bus station. It's open daily, except Sunday, but busiest on Saturday when city folk and villagers mix to buy and sell the week's produce. One corner of the market is assigned to *yaqona* (kava) vendors, and it's possible to order a whole bowl of the root beverage for about a dollar (the locals will gladly help you finish the bowl, so don't worry about having to drink more than you want). Some market stalls also sell a few homemade souvenirs, and there are lots of cheap places to eat in the surrounding

© DAVID STANLEY

Sri Siva Subrahmaniya Swami Temple, Nadi

this consecrated place of worship, but shoes must be removed at the entrance, and you must cover bare shoulders or legs with a *sulu*.

◖ DENARAU ISLAND

The upscale resorts, golf course, and marina on Denarau Island, six kilometers west of downtown Nadi, may seem to be an unlikely sightseeing attraction, but there's nothing quite like it anywhere else in Fiji. The resorts themselves are impressive, with imposing lobbies, shops, restaurants, bars, and swimming pools. Each resort has its own unique character, and it's fun to wander through a few enjoying the soft seating, artworks, gardens, and views.

You're welcome to use the beach anywhere along the strip (and maybe sneak a dip in one of the sprawling hotel pools). A good plan is to catch a bus or taxi to the Radisson Resort and walk back along the road or beach toward the Port Denarau Marina. Have a look around the fancy clubhouse of the Denarau Golf & Racquet Club opposite the Sheraton, and don't miss the view from the lobby of the Sofitel. The cubical Hilton is strikingly different from the other resorts and worth a side trip.

You could end your tour at the marina, which has a shopping mall and many places to eat. It's amusing to have a beer on a terrace here and watch the tour groups embarking or

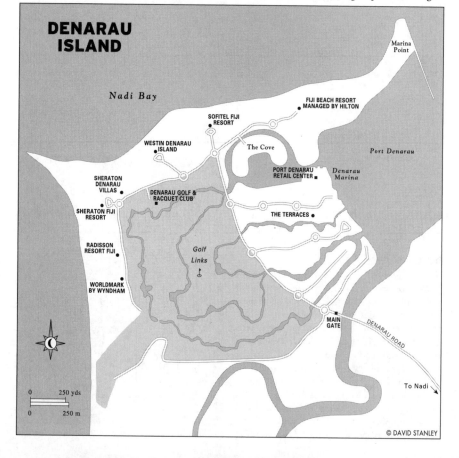

DENARAU ISLAND

Nadi Bay

Marina Point

FIJI BEACH RESORT MANAGED BY HILTON

SOFITEL FIJI RESORT

WESTIN DENARAU ISLAND

The Cove

Port Denarau

PORT DENARAU RETAIL CENTER

Denarau Marina

SHERATON DENARAU VILLAS

DENARAU GOLF & RACQUET CLUB

SHERATON FIJI RESORT

THE TERRACES

RADISSON RESORT FIJI

Golf Links

WORLDMARK BY WYNDHAM

MAIN GATE

DENARAU ROAD

To Nadi

0   250 yds
0   250 m

© DAVID STANLEY

Some of Fiji's largest resorts face this beach on Denarau Island.

disembarking from their catamarans and cruise vessels. When you've seen enough, walk back out to the main road and flag down any empty taxi returning to Nadi; drivers should be happy to take you for a few dollars. There are better places to stay than Denarau Island, but this mecca of industrial tourism is always worth a look.

Touts around Denarau Island offer free shopping, meals, and activities if you'll sit through a 90-minute sales pitch for a time-share at the WorldMark resort. If you're a backpacker, dress up and name an expensive hotel when they ask where you're staying. If you say you're from anywhere other than Australia or New Zealand, the touts may not be interested in you.

Entertainment and Shopping

BARS AND CLUBS
Green Land Nite Club (38 Main St., Mon.–Sat. 1800–0100, admission free), opposite the Nadi Downtown Backpackers Inn, is a rougher place than **Steps Karaoke Nite Club,** upstairs across the street. Both of these cater to local Fijians rather than tourists.

Club Rangeen (Thurs.–Sat. 2030–0100, admission F$5), on Andrews Road at the north end of town, is a predominately Indo-Fijian disco.

The **Nadi Farmers Club** (tel. 670-0415, Mon.–Thurs. 1000–2200, Fri. and Sat. 1000–2300, Sun. 0900–2100), just up Ashram Road from the Mobil station in Nadi town, is a relatively safe male drinking place where tourists are welcome. There's billiards but no music or dancing. Simple Indian meals (F$5–6) are provided by Anals Fastfood in the back courtyard.

You're also welcome to drink at the **Nadi Club** (tel. 670-0126, Mon.–Thurs. 1000–2200, Fri. and Sat. 1000–2300, Sun. 0900–2100) on Lodhia Street. **Felix Fastfood** (Mon.–Thurs. 0700–2200, Fri. and Sat. 0700–2300, Sun. 1000–2100), attached to the Club, serves tasty Indian meals (chicken, lamb, duck, goat, and fish) for around F$5. The Indian-style chop suey is substantial.

© DAVID STANLEY

Ed's Bar is one of the most popular eating and drinking places around Nadi.

© TIM PARKINSON/FLICKR.COM/TIMPARKINSON

fire dancing at the Westin Denarau Island

The best choice, though, is **Ed's Bar** (tel. 672-4650), a little north of the Mercure Hotel in Martintar. You'll enjoy chatting with the friendly staff and meeting the trendy locals and surfers who hang out here. Happy hour is daily 1200–2100. It's a colorful spot that you'll want to visit again. There are three pool tables in a section that opens at 1700.

After Dark Night Club (daily 2000–0100), near Morris Hedstrom at Namaka, just northeast of Morris Hedstrom and not far from the Grand Melanesian Hotel, hosts a mostly indigenous Fijian crowd. They play newly released music. You may be viewed as a source of beer by some of the other clients here.

A safer place to go is the nightclub at the **Novotel** (tel. 672-2000) toward the airport, which has a live band Friday and Saturday from 2030.

CULTURAL SHOWS FOR VISITORS

The **Sofitel** (tel. 675-1111) has a *meke* (traditional song and dance show) on Thursday at 1730 (F$75 pp). Also on Denarau Island, the **Seafront Restaurant** (tel. 675-0722) at the WorldMark has a *meke* Tuesday at 2000 (F$55 including the buffet) and a Polynesian show Friday at 1830 (F$55). The **Radisson Resort Fiji** has a *meke* in the Nautilus Restaurant on Monday, Wednesday, and Saturday at 1900 (F$34–46 for the buffet).

You can also enjoy a *meke* at the **Mercure Hotel** (tel. 672-2255) in Martintar on Saturday (F$35).

A fire dancing show is presented at the **Westin Denarau Island** (tel. 675-0000) Tuesday, Friday, Saturday, and Sunday at 1800. The **Fiji Beach Resort Managed by Hilton** (tel. 675-6800) has fire dancing on Monday and a *meke* or kava ceremony on Friday.

SHOPPING

The **Nadi Handicraft Market,** opposite the Nadi Hotel just off Main Street, provides you with the opportunity to buy directly from handicraft producers. Several large curio emporia are along Main Street, including **Jack's Handicrafts** (tel. 670-0744, www.jacksfiji

© DAVID STANLEY

The Nadi Handicraft Market offers a wide selection and prices are negotiable.

.com), opposite Morris Hedstrom, and **Nad's Handicrafts** (tel. 670-3588), closer to the bridge. Visit a few of these before going to the market to get an idea of what's available and how much your preferred items should cost.

Prouds and **Tappoo** on Main Street sell the kind of imported luxury goods usually seen in airport duty-free shops. The **Post Fiji Philatelic Sales Center** (weekdays 0800–1300 and 1400–1600, Sat. 0800–1200, www.stampsfiji.com.fj) is just outside Prouds.

If you have an interest in world literature, you can purchase books on yoga and Indian classics at the **Sri Ramakrishna Ashram** (tel. 670-2786), across the street from the Farmers Club. There's a prayer session in the Ashram on Sunday morning, followed by a vegetarian feast.

Beware of the friendly handshake in Nadi, for you may find yourself buying something you neither care for nor desire. Lots of visitors get conned in Nadi: Don't let anyone lead you around. Most shops in Nadi are closed on Sunday.

Recreation

SCUBA DIVING

Dive Adrenalin (tel. 675-0061, www.adrenalinfiji.com) at many Denarau Island resorts charges F$140/220 for one-/two-tank dives, plus F$25 for gear. Their Open Water certification course is F$695. Call for free bus transfers from all Nadi hotels.

SURFING

The **Fiji Surf Shop** (tel. 670-5960, www.fijisurfshop.com), above Victory Tours at the corner of Hospital Road and Main Street in downtown Nadi, organizes three-hour surfing lessons and surf trips (F$200/175/150 pp for one/two/three people including transfers, guide, surfboards, and reef booties). Surfboards are available for rental.

FISHING

Sportfishing operators based at Port Denarau include **SeaFiji** (tel. 675-0611 or 672-5961,

www.seafiji.net) and **Sundancer** (tel. 672-0786, www.sundancerfiji.net).

Adrenalin Fiji (tel. 675-0061, www.adrenalinfiji.com) at Denarau Island offers fishing charters aboard the four-angler *Katchalot* at F$590/990 for four/seven hours. On the six-angler *Synergy,* it's F$990/1,600, while the more luxurious six-angler *Opulence* is F$2,900/4,500.

GOLF

The 18-hole, par-70 **Nadi Airport Golf Club** (tel. 672-2148, www.nadigolffiji.com) is pleasantly situated between the airport runways and the sea at Wailoaloa Beach. Greens fees are F$30, plus F$20 for clubs and F$10–15 for a caddy. There's a bar and billiard table in the clubhouse (and tourists are welcome). The course is busy with local players on weekends but quiet during the week. World champion

International pro golfer Vijay Singh got his start at the Nadi Airport Golf Club.

© DAVID STANLEY

golfer Vijay Singh got his start here a quarter century ago.

The 18-hole, par-72 course at the **Denarau Golf & Racquet Club** (tel. 675-9710), opposite the Sheraton, was designed by Eiichi Motohashi. This fabulous course features bunkers shaped like a marlin, crab, starfish, and octopus, and water shots across all four par-three holes (the average golfer loses four balls per round). Greens fees are F$85/125 for 9/18 holes. Golfers are not allowed to walk around the course, and the electric cart runs F$40 extra. Clubs can be rented at F$45 a set. Call ahead for a starting time, and be aware of the strict dress code: collared shirt and dress shorts for men, smart casual for women, and golf shoes for all (no jeans, bathing suits, or metal spiked shoes). Ten tennis courts (four floodlit) are available here at F$22/30 per hour day/night. Rackets and shoes can be rented at F$27, and a can of balls is F$8.

LOCAL TOURS

Numerous day cruises and bus tours operating in the Nadi area are advertised in the free tourist brochures you see everywhere. Reservations can be made through Rosie Holidays or ATS Pacific, with several offices around Nadi. Bus transfers to/from your hotel are included in the price, though some trips are canceled when not enough people sign up.

The "road tours" offered by **Rosie Holidays** (tel. 672-2755, www.rosiefiji.com), at Nadi Airport and numerous resorts, are cheaper than those of other companies because lunch isn't included (though lunch is included on all the cruises and river trips). Rosie's day trips to Suva (F$70) involve too much time on the bus, so instead go for the Sigatoka Valley/Kula Eco Park full-day tour (F$100 including entry fees). If you're looking for a half-day tour around Nadi, sign up for the four-hour Vuda Lookout/Viseisei Village/Garden of the Sleeping Giant tour, which costs F$67, including admission to the garden (the lookout and garden are not accessible on public transport). These trips operate only Monday–Saturday, but on Sunday morning Rosie offers a half-day drive to the Vuda Lookout and the Garden of the Sleeping Giant only, also F$67 per person. There's a tour to Pacific Harbor (F$131) that includes firewalking and a *meke*. Also ask about the full-day hiking tours to the Nausori Highlands (Mon.–Sat., F$74 including lunch), the easiest way to see this beautiful area.

ATS Pacific (tel. 672-2811, www.atspacific.com) is in the office marked Accommodation Information near the public toilets in the airport's arrivals terminal, to the left beyond the cafés. Other airport tour operators, including **Coral Sun Fiji** (tel. 672-3105, www.coralsunfiji.com) and **Great Sights/Tourist Transport Fiji** (tel. 672-3311, www.tourist transportfiji.com), offer the same kind of day tours as Rosie, such as a half-day Discover Nadi Tour (F$75) to Viseisei and the Garden of the Sleeping Giant.

Victory Tours (tel. 670-0243, www.tour istinformationfiji.com), also known as the Tourist Information Center, offers "Adventure Jungle Treks" with stays in different Fijian villages for one or two nights (minimum of two persons). The hiking trips offered by **Adventure Fiji** (tel. 672-5598), a division of Rosie Holidays, are more expensive than these, but the quality is more consistent.

Should you not wish to join an organized bus tour from Nadi, you can easily organize your own **self-guided day tour** by taking a local bus to the Sigatoka Sand Dunes National Park visitor center on Queens Road. After a hike over the dunes, catch another bus on to Sigatoka town for lunch, some shopping and sightseeing, and perhaps a taxi visit to the Tavuni Hill Fort. Plenty of buses cover the 61 kilometers from Sigatoka back to Nadi until late in the evening. All of this will cost you far less than the cheapest half-day tour, and you'll be able to mix freely with the locals.

If there are two or three people in your group, it's much cheaper to hire a taxi for the day than to take an organized city sightseeing tour.

FLIGHTSEEING
Turtle Airways (tel. 672-1888, www.turtleair ways.com) at Wailoaloa Beach offers scenic overwater flights in their Cessna floatplanes at F$100 per person for 20 minutes (minimum of four persons weighing not over 350 kg together).

Island Hoppers (tel. 672-0410, www.heli copters.com.fj), in a separate terminal behind the airport post office and in the Port Denarau Retail Center, runs 20-minute helicopter tours around Nadi and the Mamanucas starting at F$275 per person (minimum of two).

In 2009, **Adrenalin Fiji** (tel. 675-0061, www.adrenalinfiji.com), at the Port Denarau Retail Center and several resorts, began operating a one-hour hot air balloon ride over Nadi every morning. Pickups are at 0445 from all Denarau and some Nadi hotels for the sunrise champagne breakfast (F$390).

OTHER RECREATION
Thirty-minute jet-boat rides around the mouth of the Nadi River are offered by **Jet Fiji** (tel. 675-1288, www.jetfiji.com) about every half hour daily 0830–1500 from Port Denarau (adults F$85, children under 16 years F$45, hotel transfers included). It's fairly certain the birds and fish of this mangrove area are less thrilled by these gas-guzzling, high-impact craft than the tourists seated therein. Also, snorkeling from a jet boat can be risky.

Skydive Fiji (tel. 672-8166, www.sky divefiji.com.fj), opposite the Hexagon International in Martintar, offers tandem skydiving jumps from a small plane every two hours daily 0800–1600. It's F$350–500 per person depending on the height from which you wish to jump, plus F$175 for photos and videos, if desired. Packages that combine skydiving with a Jet Fiji ride, scuba diving with AquaBlue, or whitewater rafting with Rivers Fiji are available. Call for a free transfer.

Babba's Horse-Riding at Wailoaloa Beach offers one-hour beach rides at F$30. Longer rides can be arranged.

You can watch rugby or soccer on Saturdays at the A. D. Patel Stadium, near Nadi Bus Station. You might also see soccer on Sundays.

Accommodations

Most of Nadi's hotels offer free transport from the airport, which is lucky because only a couple lodgings are within walking distance of the terminal. As you exit the customs area at the airport, you'll be met by uniformed tour guides. If you already know which hotel you want, tell them the name, and if a driver from that hotel is present, you should get a free ride (ask).

Repeat visitors know that many medium-priced hotels along Queen's Road regularly discount their official rack rates for walk-in bookings, and you could pay considerably less than the full undiscounted prices quoted herein (in this guidebook, we provide the published rates).

DOWNTOWN
Under US$25

The **Nadi Downtown Backpackers Inn** (Main St., tel. 670-0600, www.showmefiji.com) is above PVV Tours opposite the BP service station in the center of Nadi. Its main attraction is the price: F$53 single or double with fan, F$71 with air-conditioning, both with private bath. The four-/eight-bed dormitory is F$19/14 per person, and basic rooms with shared bath are F$39. These rates include a toast-and-coffee breakfast and are easily reduced with bargaining. This place looks seedy from the outside, but some of the rooms upstairs are okay. A cozy little 24-hour bar is in back. The adjacent Steps Karaoke Nite Club projects a steady disco beat on the northern side of the inn well into the morning.

Chung's Motel (Hospital Rd., tel. 670-7522), on the corner of Sahu Kahn Street near the market, has six rooms with private bath at F$40 single or double (plus F$10 for air-conditioning) and four rooms with shared bath at F$30. The rooms are also available by the hour, an indication of what to expect here.

Just off Queens Road half a block north of the Kennedy Hotel is the two-story **White House Visitors Inn** (40 Kennedy Ave., tel. 670-0022). The 12 fan-equipped rooms are F$25/30 single/double with shared bath, F$35/50 with private bath, or F$15 per person in the dorm. Rooms with air-conditioning cost F$5 extra. The beds are comfortable, and a weight-watchers' toast-and-coffee breakfast is included in the price. You can cook your own meals in the communal kitchen.

US$25-50

The mid-priced, two-story **Hotel San Bruno** (Nadi Back Rd., tel. 670-0444, www.sanbruno .com.fj) is east of the Sri Siva Subrahmaniya Swami Temple. The 10 fan-cooled rooms are F$50 single or double, while the 10 with air-conditioning are F$60. The one-/two-bedroom family "villas" are F$100 each. A miniature swimming pool is in front of the billiard room. The San Bruno can be rather noisy with some local guests partying all night.

The aging, three-story **Kennedy Hotel** (Queens Rd., tel. 670-1703) is a 10-minute walk north of central Nadi. The 16 air-conditioned rooms with private bath are F$59 single or double, tax included. Apartments with cooking facilities are F$120. Beds in the 10-bed dormitory blocks cost F$15 per person with air-conditioning. Some of the rooms are small and shabby, so have a look before committing yourself.

TOWARD THE AIRPORT
Under US$25

The nicest backpacker place in Martintar is the two-story, 18-room **C Sunview Motel & Hostel** (14 Gray Rd., tel. 672-4933, hsunview motel@connect.com.fj), 300 meters beyond the Bounty Restaurant. A room for a single or couple is F$45/65 with fan/air-conditioning. The two six-bed dorms are F$25 per person. Breakfast is included, cooking facilities are available, and it's clean, quiet, and friendly.

The tatty, single-story **Nadi Holiday Inn** (67 Cawa Rd., tel. 672-5076), on Queens Road just north of Martintar, has a dubious reputation (and no connection with the Holiday Inn

© DAVID STANLEY

Sunview Motel & Hostel at Martintar is the low-budget backpacker's best choice around Nadi.

chain). Rooms with private facilities are F$45 single or double (plus F$10 for air-conditioning). A bar is on the premises, and there's a lot of in/out action late at night.

US$25-50

A few hundred meters off the main highway at Martintar is the flashpacker-style **Nadi Bay Resort Hotel** (Wailoaloa Rd., tel. 672-3599, www.fijinadibayhotel.com), a two-story concrete edifice enclosing a swimming pool. The 44 rooms are F$70 single or double with shared bath and fan (plus F$10 for air-conditioning) or F$100 with private bath and air-conditioning. An air-conditioned apartment with cooking facilities is F$160. Beds in the 12-bed dorms are F$30 per person. Breakfast is included with the rooms but not the dorms. The Nadi Bay Resort Hotel is something of a staging point for young tourists on "Feejee Experience" packages or headed for the backpacker resorts in the Yasawas. You'll meet other travelers lounging by the pools or in the slow-service restaurant and bar. Videos are shown nightly in a hall below the games room. In the morning,

everyone lines up to board the tour buses. The airport flight path passes right above the Nadi Bay, which is a blast.

Peridiom Motel Accommodation (Northern Press Rd., tel. 672-2574, www.peridiommotelfiji.com), down the road from Daikoku Japanese Restaurant, Martintar, is worth considering if you want cooking facilities. The three units with a double bed are F$69, while the two with one double and one single are F$98. The family room is F$110 for up to five people. All units are in a long, single-story block and have air-conditioning.

Next door to the Capricorn International Hotel in Martintar is **Travelers Holiday Apartments** (Queens Rd., tel. 672-4675), a three-story hotel containing 31 rooms with bath in two buildings. Those in the two-story block are F$55/75 single or double with fan/air-conditioning. Self-catering apartments in the main three-story building are F$65/85. Hidden surveillance cameras cover all entrances.

The **Hexagon International** (Queens Rd., tel. 672-0044, www.hexagonfiji.com), formerly known as The West's Motor Inn, is near

Jetpoint Supermarket in Martintar. This place was completely redeveloped in 2008 and lost some of its character in the process. Hexagon International is now a sprawling complex of two- and three-story blocks with three semi-rectangular swimming pools. The 27 standard air-conditioned rooms with private bath and fridge are F$66 double, the 54 larger deluxe rooms F$97, the four family rooms and four studio apartments F$115, and the 24 two-bedroom apartments with kitchen F$159. You may be charged more if you book ahead. Features include a courtyard swimming pool, bar, restaurant, conference room, and ATS Pacific tour desk. Internet access is F$4.50 a half hour.

Above the Bounty Restaurant in Martintar is overpriced **Mountainview Apartments** (Queens Rd., tel. 672-1880), also known as Bounty Apartments, with air-conditioned rooms with bath at F$65 single or double.

The respectable **Hotel Martintar** (22 Kennedy St., tel. 628-3745, hotelmartintar@ connect.com.fj), around the corner from Ed's Bar in Martintar, has three rooms with bath and fan at F$50 single or double, four air-conditioned rooms at F$60, and an air-conditioned two-bedroom flat at F$100. It's a good value.

Rosie's Deluxe Serviced Apartments (Queens Rd., tel. 672-2755, www.rosiefiji .com), near Ed's Bar in Martintar, offers functional studio apartments accommodating four at F$79, one-bedrooms for up to five at F$105, and two-bedrooms for up to eight at F$135. All 18 air-conditioned units have cooking facilities, fridge, and private balcony. You may use the communal washer and drier for free. The Rosie Holidays office at the airport books this place and arranges free airport transfers at any time of night or day.

One kilometer farther along toward the airport is the **Nomads Skylodge Hotel** (Queens Rd., tel. 672-2200, www.nomadsskylodge.com. fj), which was constructed on spacious grounds in the early 1960s while Nadi Airport was being expanded to take jet aircraft. Today it's inconsistently managed by Tanoa Hotels (www .tanoahotels.com). The 12 standard rooms without towels are F$78 single or double, the 23

superior rooms with towels and TV are F$128, and the six rooms with cooking facilities are F$153. There are also 183 dorm beds in rooms of ten and eight beds (F$27), six beds (F$29), and four beds (F$31). All rooms other than the dorms have air-conditioning and private bath, and they vary considerably. If you're catching a flight in the middle of the night, there's a F$64 "day use" room rate valid noon–2000. Scheduled airport transfers are free. Gordy's Restaurant has main dishes for F$10–18. Happy hour at the bar is 1730–1830. A swimming pool is on-site. Young flashpacker tourists on soft adventure tours usually stay in the dorms, while middle-aged couples book the more expensive rooms. Some like it, some hate it.

The **Grand Melanesian Hotel** (Queens Rd., tel. 672-2438, www.hexagonfiji.com) is in an unappealing commercial area at Namaka, two kilometers south of the airport. The two wings are separated by a swimming pool, bar, and restaurant. The old wing in back has 11 standard rooms with shared bath at F$50/55 single/ double and eight deluxe rooms with air-conditioning at F$60 single or double. The new wing beside the highway has 18 air-conditioned rooms with TV at F$62/68/70 single/double/ triple, two six-bed air-conditioned dorms at F$25 per person, and two deluxe family rooms at F$110 for up to five people.

US$50-100

The nondescript **Capricorn International Hotel** (Queens Rd., tel. 672-0088, www.capri cornfiji.com), a bit south of the Mercure Hotel in Martintar, consists of two-story blocks surrounding a swimming pool. The 62 small air-conditioned rooms with fridge begin at F$105 single or double. The 17-bed dorm here is F$35 per person. Cooking facilities are not provided, but there's a restaurant/bar on the premises. ATS Pacific has a tour desk here.

The **Mercure Nadi** (Queens Rd., tel. 672-2255, www.mercure.com), at Martintar halfway between the airport and town, is one of Nadi's nicest large hotels. This appealing three-story building was built in 1973 and joined Accor Hotels in 2004. The 85 air-conditioned

© DAVID STANLEY

The Trans International Hotel is within walking distance of Nadi International Airport.

rooms with balcony or terrace are F$179 single or double, plus F$40 extra if you want a "deluxe" with a TV and a bathtub instead of a shower, plus F$44 for a third person. A walk-in rate is available at F$109 single or double superior without breakfast. The F$91 late check-out rate allows you to keep your room until 1800. Even if you're paying in cash, a credit card must be presented upon arrival. Lots of well-shaded tables and chairs surround the swimming pool. On Saturday night, you can take in a *meke* (F$35). There's a Rosie Holidays desk, a spa, and a taxi stand. The tennis court is free for guests (day use only).

(Sandalwood Lodge (Ragg St., tel. 672-2044, www.sandalwoodfiji.com), behind the Mercure Hotel and 250 meters inland, has 33 air-conditioned rooms with bath, Sky TV, fridge, and cooking facilities at F$87/99/111 single/double/triple. The two-story blocks face the swimming pool. There's no restaurant here, but several are within walking distance. Sandalwood is ideal for those in search of a quiet, respectable place to stay.

Hans Travel Inn (Queens Rd., tel. 672-8384, www.hansmotel.com), opposite the Mercure Hotel, has five studio apartments at F$110 double and one two-bedroom penthouse apartment with four beds at F$350. You may be able to get a lower walk-in price.

The three-story **Trans International Hotel** (Queens Rd., tel. 672-8633, www.transint hotel.com.fj), next to the Raffles Gateway Hotel and opposite the airport, opened in October 2008. The 48 air-conditioned, non-smoking rooms with bath, TV, and fridge are F$135 superior, F$155 deluxe (including a hot tub), or F$280 for a suite. Reduced walk-in rates are available. A rectangular swimming pool faces the rooms, and a restaurant, bar, and bottle shop are on the premises.

The two-story, colonial-style **Raffles Gateway Hotel** (Queens Rd., tel. 672-2444, www.rafflesgateway.com), directly across the highway from the airport, is within easy walking distance of the terminal. Despite this location, it's quiet enough and not overpriced. It has 22 standard rooms without TVs at F$98 single or double, 46 larger deluxe rooms at F$155, and four suites at F$210. Only the

The Raffles Gateway Hotel is just across the highway from Nadi International Airport.

© DAVID STANLEY

deluxe rooms can be reserved through the hotel's website. There are two swimming pools. The Gateway's bar is worth checking out if you're stuck at the airport waiting for a flight but the restaurant is pricey. A Rosie Holidays desk is here.

US$100-150

Tanoa Apartments (tel. 672-3685, www.tanoahotels.com) is off Votualevu Road, on a hilltop overlooking the surrounding countryside. The 20 self-catering apartments begin at F$270 (weekly and monthly rates available). Local rate reductions to as little as F$100 are possible for walk-in bookings. Facilities include a swimming pool and tennis courts. First opened in 1965, this property was the forerunner of the Tanoa hotel chain owned by local businessman Yanktesh Permal Reddy. For those who get the discount, Tanoa Apartments is a top pick for its comfort and location—close to the action but secluded from the commercial strip.

A few hundred meters inland from Tanoa Apartments is the **Novotel Nadi** (Votualevu Road, tel. 672-2000, www.novotel.com), a sprawling two-story hotel with mountain views from the spacious grounds on Namaka Hill. Until the Accor chain took over in 2006, it was known as the Mocambo Hotel, The 127 air-conditioned rooms with patio or balcony and fridge begin at F$200 single or double (or considerably less when booked through the Novotel website). Walk-in discounts are also possible. Two children under 16 are accommodated free when sharing their parents' room. A swimming pool is available, and there's a par-27, nine-hole executive golf course on the adjacent slope. A Rosie Holidays desk is here.

People on brief prepaid stopovers in Fiji are often accommodated at the two-story **Tanoa International Hotel** (tel. 672-0277, www.tanoahotels.com), formerly the Nadi Travelodge Hotel, across Votualevu Road and inland from the Novotel. The 146 superior air-conditioned rooms with fridge are F$164/194 standard/executive single or double. They also have a day-use rate of F$105, which gives you a room from noon until 1800 (airport transfers are free). Children under 12 stay free. A swimming pool and fitness center, floodlit tennis courts, and an ATS Pacific tour desk are on the premises. The Tanoa International is a cut above the Novotel, but no non-hotel shops or restaurants are within walking distance of either hotel.

The **Tokatoka Resort Hotel** (Queens Rd., tel. 672-0222), a short walk north from the airport terminal, caters to families with young children. The 116 air-conditioned villas and rooms with cooking facilities, mini-fridge, and video begin at F$153/189 walk-in/rack rate single or double. The housekeeping and maintenance here are poor. The large swimming pool with a water slide is usually full of noisy kids. Happy hour by the pool is daily 1700–1900. A Jack's Handicrafts outlet is on the premises.

WAILOALOA BEACH

Wailoaloa Beach (also known as New Town Beach) is for flashpackers what Denarau Island is for rich tourists on upscale package tours. A half-dozen reasonably priced places to stay are near the seaplane base and golf club on the opposite side of the airport runway from Queens Road, a three-kilometer hike from the Nadi Bay Resort Hotel. Ask for a free shuttle bus at the airport or take a taxi. The Shahabud Dean Transport bus (F$1.15) to Wailoaloa New Town leaves from beside the toilet block at Nadi Bus Station Monday–Saturday at 0715, 0815, 1115, 1500, 1600, and 1700, on Saturday also at 1045 and 1210 (no service on Sun.). It leaves the beach to return to town about 20 minutes after these times. Be aware that only Tropic of Capricorn Resort, Smugglers Cove Beach Resort, Aquarius Fiji Resort, and Travelers Beach Resort are right on the beach. In 2010 Warwick International Hotels announced that they would build a 250-room hotel on Wailoaloa Beach at a cost of F$30 million, the first large development of its kind in this area.

Wailoaloa is probably your best bet on the weekend, and sporting types can play a round of golf on the public course or go jogging along the brown sands (the swimming in the knee-deep, murky water is poor). You can also ride a horse. Remain aware of your surroundings if you stroll far down this lonely beach, as muggings of tourists have occurred.

US$25-50

The **Wailoaloa Beach Resort** (Nadi Bay Rd.,

© DAVID STANLEY

Nadi's Wailoaloa Beach, with the Mount Evans Range in the background

tel. 672-6633, wailoaloabeachresort@yahoo.com.au), near Grand West's Villas, is far from the beach, though there is a swimming pool. It has 10 fan-cooled rooms at F$55/65 double/triple, 10 air-conditioned rooms at F$75/85, and one six-bunk dorm at F$15 per person. All rooms are with bath and fridge. Breakfast is included. **Grand West's Villas** (Nadi Bay Rd., tel. 672-4833, www.hexagonfiji.com), near Wailoaloa Beach between Nadi Bay Road and the airport runway, opened in 2001. The 10 studios at F$80, 10 one-bedroom apartments at F$100 single or double, and 20 two-bedroom apartments at F$140 double are in several two-story blocks. These spacious, self-catering apartments are a reasonable value, but unfortunately the location is poor as the beach is too far away and the airport runway is too close. Some of the units are rented to locals on a long-term basis, raising noise and security issues. Two tennis courts, a swimming pool with waterslide, and an ATS Pacific desk are on the grounds. New Town Shopping Center (daily 0630–2100), next to Grand West's Villas, sells alcohol and groceries at normal prices.

The two-story **(New Town Beach Motel** (5 Wasawasa Rd., tel. 672-3339, newtownbeach@connect.com.fj), 100 meters inland from the beach, is a good choice if you're on a budget yet want to avoid the backpacker brigade. The seven clean rooms with fan are F$40/50/60 single/double/triple. There's no cooking area, but this relaxed hostel does have a small TV lounge. A nice protected swimming pool is in the backyard.

The **Horizon Backpackers** (10 Wasawasa Rd., tel. 672-2832, www.horizonbeachfiji.com) is a large wooden two-story building just across a field from the beach. The 14 rooms with bath begin at F$50 single or double with fan or F$65–80 with air-conditioning. Horizon's 10-bed dormitory is F$15 per person (or F$22 pp with air-conditioning) including a cup of tea and a piece of toast for breakfast. No cooking facilities are provided, but there's a mid-priced restaurant/bar and a miniature swimming pool. To use the washer/drier is F$10 a full load. A tour desk and Internet café are on the premises. It's popular among low-budget backpackers unwilling to pay the higher prices at Smugglers Cove and Aquarius resorts.

The **Tropic of Capricorn Resort** (11 Wasawasa Rd., tel. 672-3089, www.mamasfiji.com), right next to Horizon Beach Resort, is a pleasant, welcoming place. The manager, Mama Selena, has traveled the world and is a lot of fun to meet. The old building facing the figure-eight swimming pool contains six-bed and 10-bed dorms with fan at F$18 per person, plus a four-bed family room at F$55 (plus F$15 for air-conditioning) and an air-conditioned double at F$60. The new three-story building erected between the pool and beach in 2009 has an eight-bed dorm on the ground floor and 10-bed dorm in the middle floor, both F$24 per person. Also on the middle floor are two doubles at F$89 or F$105. On the top floor are five deluxe doubles at F$165 and two deluxe singles at F$130. The deluxe rooms have a fridge, TV, and balcony. All rooms in this building are air-conditioned. Breakfast is included.

Between Smugglers Cove and Travelers Beach Resort is the **Aquarius Fiji** (17 Wasawasa Rd., tel. 672-6000, www.aquariusfiji.com), a flashpacker paradise. This large mansion contains four standard rooms at F$85 double and four oceanview rooms at F$105. A third person pays an extra F$25. Otherwise there are two two-bed dorms at F$30 per person, plus six- and 12-bed dorms at F$28 per person. All rooms are air-conditioned. Breakfast is included with the dorms but not with the rooms. Aquarius has a swimming pool right on the beach and a party atmosphere.

Edgewater Backpackers Accommodation (33 Wasawasa Rd., tel. 672-5868, edgewater@connect.com.fj), opposite Aquarius, is an older wooden building with an eight-bed dorm at F$13 per person, one single at F$40, and a four-bed family room for F$50. Breakfast is included and the restaurant serves meals at F$6–12 with beer for F$3. Camping without breakfast is F$8 per person (own tent). Though basic, it's the cheapest option around here.

A few minutes' walk north along the beach from Aquarius is **Travelers Beach Resort**

(Wasawasa Rd., tel. 672-3322, beachvilla@ connect.com.fj). The five air-conditioned ocean wing rooms in the old building are F$65/70 single/double, while the two beachfront rooms facing the pool are F$85/90. However, most of the rooms are in several two-story buildings across the road and a block back from the beach. The eight rooms with private bath are F$55/60 single/double with fan. The two 16-bed dorms cost F$21 per person. A four-bed family room is F$80 for up to five people. All rates include a light breakfast and tax. There's a restaurant/bar and swimming pool near the beach with a Polynesian show on Fridays.

Beach Escape Villas (tel. 672-4442, www .beachescapefiji.com) occupies a noisy compound tightly packed around a swimming pool two blocks back from Travelers Beach Resort. The eight large air-conditioned villas are F$75/90 double/triple. There are also six rooms with fan in a shared villa at F$46 single or double, and one six-bed air-conditioned dorm at F$18 per person. To use the cooking facilities in the villas costs another F$20 a day. Add 5 percent tax to all rates.

The **Beachside Resort** (Wailoaloa Beach Rd., tel. 999-3840, www.beachsideresortfiji .com), at the end of a potholed road beyond Club Fiji, is a misnomer as it has no beach access at all. To swim in the ocean you must walk back to Club Fiji. The swimming pool partly compensates for this and Beachside's rooms are a better value than those at Club Fiji. The 15 air-conditioned rooms in the main block are F$95/105 single/double on the bottom and middle floors or F$106/114 on the top floor. In 2007, three two-story blocks were added to the resort with eight mountain-view rooms in two blocks at F$78/88 and six studios in another block at F$68/76. All rooms have a fridge and tea/coffee, but no cooking facilities. A blackboard menu in the dining area lists dinner dishes priced around F$20–25.

US$50-100

A kilometer southwest of the other places hotels on Wailoaloa Beach is **Club Fiji Resort** (Wailoaloa Beach Rd., tel. 672-0150, www

.clubfiji-resort.com). It's three kilometers off Queens Road from McDonald's down a dusty back road. The 24 thatched duplex bungalows, all with veranda, private bath, solar hot water, and fridge, are priced according to location: F$94 single or double for a garden unit, F$129 ocean view, or F$152 on the beach. The eight so-called "beachfront villas" in a two-story building are F$180 double with air-conditioning. Cooking facilities are not provided and food and drink costs quickly add up, with main plates at the Club's restaurant costing F$18–33. Special events include the beach barbecue on Sunday night (F$22–34). JB's On The Beach adjacent to Club Fiji has a nice view from its deck. The only other eating option within easy walking distance is at the Beachside Resort. Horseback riding is F$30 an hour, but windsurfing and paddleboats are free. The day tour to Natadola Beach costs F$55 with lunch. At low tide, the beach here resembles a tidal flat, but there's a small, clean swimming pool.

Three-story **Nadi Bay Beach Apartments** (tel. 672-7700, www.nadibaybeachapartments .com), adjacent to New Town Beach Motel and two blocks from the beach, opened in 2007. The one/two/three-bedroom apartments are F$130/160/200 with air-conditioning, cooking facilities, and Internet. Weekly (from F$450) and monthly rates are available.

The focal point for young business-class backpackers is ◖ **Smugglers Cove Beach Resort** (Wasawasa Rd., tel. 672-6578, www.smugglers beachfiji.com), diagonally opposite Horizon Beach Resort (which is owned by the same company). The four garden-view rooms are F$115 single or double, the 12 oceanview suites F$155, the four oceanfront suites F$185, and the one 32-bed dorm F$33 per person. The rooms and the dorm include a light continental breakfast. Tax is included, but there's a 5 percent surcharge if you pay by credit card. Self-catering facilities are not provided. There's an evening activity every night except Monday at the trendy Ghostship Bar and Grill (fire dancing three times a week). Ten Internet-equipped computers, laundry facilities, a convenience store, tour desk, and snazzy swimming pool are available.

© DAVID STANLEY

Smugglers Cove on Wailoaloa Beach is one of Nadi's top flashpacker resorts.

Bluewater Lodge (tel. 672-8858) is in an attractive two-story house across the street from Beach Escape Villas. The two rooms with bath are F$96 single or double while the three three-bed dorms are F$28 per person. A light breakfast is included. There's a pool, restaurant, and bar. Bluewater Lodge is okay for a brief stopover.

DENARAU ISLAND

Nadi's big transnational resorts are on Denarau Island (www.denarau.com) opposite Yakuilau Island, seven kilometers west of the bridge on the north side of Nadi town. It's a 15-minute drive from the airport. The murky waters lapping Denarau's gray sands aren't the best for swimming, but all of the resorts have pools. There'd be no point in snorkeling here, but windsurfing, waterskiing, and sailing are better choices. If you came to Fiji mainly for the beach, you should skip Denarau Island entirely and head for a resort in the Mamanuca Group.

Sidestepping the Waikiki syndrome, none of the Denarau resorts is taller than the surrounding palms, although the manicured affluence has a dull Hawaiian neighbor-island feel. In 1993, a championship golf course opened on the site of a former mangrove swamp adjacent

to the Sheraton. Two-thirds of the resort staff and all of the taxi drivers based here belong to the landowning clan.

Almost all of the tourists staying at the Denarau Island resorts arrive on package tours, and they pay far less than the rack rates quoted in this book. The hotel restaurants are pricey, but the new Port Denarau Retail Center contains many alternatives. Bring insect repellent, unless you want to be on the menu yourself, and have something warm to wear in your room, as the air-conditioning is strong enough to give you pneumonia in this climate. Romantic couples should be prepared for lots of kids everywhere. If your travel agent booked you into any of these resorts, you'll be wrapped in North American security and sheltered from the real Fiji. Otherwise, these resorts make interesting sightseeing attractions if you've got some time to kill around Nadi.

A local bus marked "Westbus" operates between Nadi and Denarau Island about every hour (F$0.70). It leaves Nadi Bus Station Monday–Saturday at 0645, 0700, 0730, 0800, 0830, 1015, 1230, 1330, 1430, 1545, 1600, 1700, and 1800, Sunday at 0800, 0900, 1200, 1300, and 1700. For the departure times from Denarau Island, add about 15 minutes to these times (which could change). Resort receptionists sometimes pretend not to know about this bus. The taxis parked in front of the resorts ask a firm F$12 to/from Nadi town or F$24 to the airport. Walk down the road a short distance and stop any returning taxi headed for Nadi—most will take you for F$3. A "Bula Bus" shuttle links the resorts to the Port Denarau Retail Center 0730–2330 (F$6 day pass). Budget Rent-a-car (tel. 675-0888) has an office in the Port Denarau Retail Center.

US$150-250

The Terraces (tel. 675-0557, www.the terraces.com.fj), near the Port Denarau Marina, overlooks the third hole of the golf course on Denarau Island. The 41 self-catering apartments in a series of three-story blocks are F$400/667/800 for one/two/three bedrooms, plus 17.5 percent tax. There's a swimming pool but the beach is far away.

The F$93 million **(Radisson Resort Fiji** (tel. 675-6677, www.radisson.com/fiji), between Sheraton Fiji and the Trendwest Resort, opened in May 2007. It's the first major investment in Fiji by the Minneapolis-based Carlson Group. The 270 sizable rooms and suites are in three-story blocks around a huge swimming pool open to the beach. Rooms start at F$370 single or double and increase to F$1,005 for a two-bedroom suite, plus 17.5 percent tax. The Radisson often has very attractive specials (such as two nights for the price of one). An impressive waterfall pool faces the reception, the Harmony Retreat day spa is on an island in the pool, and six food outlets are scattered around the Radisson. Extensive children's facilities are provided at this family-oriented resort. Rosie Tours and Adrenalin Fiji have activities desks in the lobby.

A bit south of the Radisson, the **WorldMark By Wyndham** (tel. 675-0442, www.wyndham vrap.com), formerly the Trendwest Resort, features a series of two- and three-story blocks between the reception and a large beachside pool (which compensates for the poor beach). Most of the 136 spacious self-catering apartments in this "vacation ownership resort" have been sold to individual buyers under a timeshare arrangement with WorldMark. All stays are prebooked and walk-in guests are not accepted. The Seafront Restaurant is near the pool. Food and drink is expensive here, so bring along your duty free bottles. There's a Rosie Holidays desk at the reception. Adrenalin Watersports runs the scuba concession here.

Over US$250

The F$270 million **Fiji Beach Resort Managed by Hilton** (tel. 675-6800, www.fijibeachresort byhilton.com), occupying the north end of a peninsula, has more of an outer-island feel than nearby mega-resorts like the Sofitel and Sheraton. Striking rectangular swimming pools flank an artificial white beach with picturesque island views. The Hilton consists of a series of 23 two-story white cubes. The first 219 rooms of the 540-room project opened in 2006, starting at F$600 for a studio and rising to F$2,150 for a three-bedroom. Room prices are slashed for walk-ins. Breakfast is included but the 17.5

© DAVID STANLEY

Virtually all of the large resorts on Denarau Island have flashy swimming pools, such as those at the Fiji Beach Resort Managed by Hilton.

percent tax is extra. Lepicier Coffee Shop at the Hilton has sandwiches for F$11 and pizza at F$21–35. Rosie Tours has a desk in the small lobby. In late 2009, the resort's New Zealand–based owners were facing bankruptcy and expansion plans put on hold, but the unfinished hotel remained open and Hilton was not affected. Depending on what happens next, you may experience construction work in this area.

Air Pacific owns a 35.9 percent interest in the F$80 million **Sofitel Fiji Resort** (tel. 675-1111, www.sofitelfiji.com.fj), which opened in 2005. The Sofitel consists of a series of three-story blocks with a long swimming pool winding down the artificial beach. The 186 oceanview rooms are F$600 single or double, the 100 superior rooms F$729, and the 10 suites from F$931, all plus 17.5 percent tax. The exact rates vary daily depending on what the market will bear and there are sometimes discounts for Internet bookings and walk-ins. A 600-seat conference center flanks one side of the lobby, tourist shops the other. Mandara Spa (tel. 675-7870, www.mandaraspa.com) runs a nine-*bure* spa village, but the Sofitel is best viewed as a large family-friendly resort rather than a hideaway

for romantic couples. Adrenalin Watersports (tel. 675-0061, www.adrenalinfiji.com) offers parasailing, personal watercraft rentals, banana boat rides, and the like. Rosie Tours and the Colonial Bank are also here.

The **Westin Denarau Island** (tel. 675-0000, www.westinfiji.com) opened in 1975 as The Regent of Fiji. Later it was the Sheraton Royal Denarau, and it closed for several years after the May 2000 coup in Suva. In 2006, it was relaunched as a Westin. This sprawling series of two-story clusters contains 271 spacious rooms from F$700 single or double, plus 17.5 percent tax but including breakfast. Facilities include a thatched swimming pool, spa, kids club (extra charge), Rosie Holidays tour desk, and Westpac Bank ATM. Adrenalin Watersports handles nautical activities here. The Westin's lobby is rather dark and this resort is less lively than the Sheraton. It could use a facelift. Fire dancing and *meke* dancing are offered irregularly on the "Coco Palms" grounds beside the lawn bowling green.

Between the Sheraton and the Westin and opposite the golf club is a cluster of two-story buildings called the **Sheraton Denarau Villas**

swimming pool at the Sofitel Fiji Resort

© DAVID STANLEY

(tel. 675-0777, www.sheraton.com/denarau villas), which opened in 1999. The 82 condos with one, two, or three bedrooms have kitchenettes, washer/dryer, TV, and lounge, starting at F$1,025 plus tax for a family of two adults and two children. Aside from families, two couples traveling together might find this chain hotel to their liking. The swimming pool and bar face the beach.

Next along the Denarau resort row is the modern-style **Sheraton Fiji Resort** (tel. 675-0777, www.sheraton.com/fiji). The 292 rooms begin at F$700 single or double, plus 17.5 percent tax. For the presidential suite it's F$1,800. Almost everyone here is on some sort of discount package tour. This two-story hotel opened in 1987, complete with a shopping arcade and an 800-seat ballroom. The pool is conveniently situated if you'd like to pose for those seated in the adjacent overpriced restaurant and café. The Adrenalin Fiji beach hut looks after watersports, including scuba diving. The Sheraton's flashy shopping arcade features Prouds, Tappoo, and Jacks stores. Budget Rent-a-Car and ATS Pacific have counters at the Sheraton Fiji.

Food

DOWNTOWN

Several places along Sahu Khan Street near the market serve a good cheap breakfast of egg sandwich with coffee. The **Wing Hing Restaurant** (tel. 670-1766) is the best of these.

A real find if you like Indian food is **Tata's Restaurant** (tel. 670-0502, weekdays 0730–1700, Sat. 0730–1600), on Nadi Back Road between the Siva Temple and the Hotel San Bruno. The curries are a great value at F$5–7, and most dishes are listed on a blackboard. Though this place is surrounded by automotive workshops, the seating is outside on a pleasant terrace.

⬤ Bohai Seafood Restaurant (tel. 670-0178, daily 1000–2200), upstairs from the Bank of Baroda on Main Street, offers a large selection of Chinese dishes, curries, and seafood at good prices (entrées F$6–18). Plenty of local Asians eat here—a recommendation.

Just down Sagayam Road are the adjacent **Corner Café** (Mon.–Sat. 0800–1430 and 1730–2130, Sun. 1730–2130) and **⬤ Saffron Tandoori Restaurant** (tel. 670-3131, Mon.–Sat. 1100–1430 and 1730–1930, Sun. 1730–1930), both owned by Jack's Handicrafts. At dinner, the seafood and meat entrées average F$39, or you can order something from the grill. The food and service at Saffron Tandoori are better than anything you'll find at the resort restaurants of Denarau Island, for less money. The selection of Indian dishes is large and you can also get fish and chips for the kids.

Mama's Pizza Inn (tel. 670-0221, daily 1000–2300), opposite the Mobil service station on Main Street at the north end of Nadi town, serves good pizza at F$8–28. Mama's has a second location in Colonial Plaza halfway out toward the airport but the downtown branch is better. It's a good choice if you're with a group and want to keep your costs down.

Bulaccino (tel. 672-8638, www.bulaccino.com, weekdays 0800–1630, weekends 0800–1500), next to the bridge, is a European-style coffee and cake place with a nice terrace overlooking the Nadi River. It's good for breakfast. Other meals run F$12–20. There's a computer with Internet access on-site that costs F$3 a half hour.

TOWARD THE AIRPORT

Only resort restaurants are available at Wailoaloa Beach, and for a non-hotel eating-out possibility, you must take a bus or taxi three kilometers to Martintar on Queens Road between downtown Nadi and the airport.

The atmospheric **Daikoku Japanese Restaurant** (tel. 670-3623, Mon.–Sat. 1200–1400 and 1800–2130, www.daikokufiji.com), at the corner of Queens Road and Northern

The Nadina Authentic Fijian Restaurant at Martintar is a good place to sample the local cuisine.

Press Road in Martintar, is the place to splurge on teppanyaki dishes (F$26–33) cooked right at your table. The sashimi and sushi are also good. Ask for the special seafood sauce. **Restaurant 88** (tel. 672-7799), just down Northern Press Road, serves huge portions of Southeast Asian–style seafood.

Sitar Restaurant (tel. 672-7722, daily 1100–1500 and 1800–2200), at the corner of Queens Road and Wailoaloa Road, serves Indian *thalis* at F$9–13, curry dishes at F$16–19, and Thai dishes at F$17–20.

The 🄲 **Nadina Authentic Fijian Restaurant** (tel. 672-7313, daily 1100–2200), opposite the Capricorn International Hotel, features traditional Fijian chicken, fish, and prawn dishes at F$10–17 for lunch and F$19–27 for dinner. The *kokoda* (marinated raw fish) is especially good. Seating in thatched pavilions is available outside.

The **Bounty Restaurant** (tel. 672-0840, www.bountyfiji.com), located a little north of the Mercure Hotel in Martintar, has Chinese and Fijian dishes and hamburgers for lunch, steaks and seafood for dinner. Lunch specials

here start at F$12, while dinner plates are F$16–33. Lobster is F$45. The dining room has lots of local color and the terrace is very popular during happy hour (daily 1600–1900).

It's a sure sign that a location has arrived as an international tourism center when Thai restaurants appear, and the **Royale Thai Restaurant** (tel. 672-8940), beside Bounty Restaurant, offers Thai curries from F$14, seafood from F$16, and Thai dinners from F$17–23.

The cheapest place in Martintar to eat is the **Masala Restaurant** (tel. 672-3758, Mon.–Sat. 0730–1830), up the road from Royale Thai. It's good for an egg sandwich and coffee for breakfast or an Indian plate lunch from the warmer (F$5–10).

Tu's Place (tel. 672-2110), across the street from Masala, is more upscale but still reasonable. If you like pancakes, come for breakfast. For lunch, try the *kokoda*. **The Curry Haven** next door is similar.

The **Ed's Bar** complex (tel. 672-4650) in Martintar is a fun place. You can dine on appetizers at the bar, such as a plate of six big, spicy barbecued chicken wings for F$6.50.

Otherwise, go through the connecting door into the adjacent **Choc Bar** (Mon.–Sat. 1200–2300, Sun. 1630–2300) or "Chocolate Bar," which serves lunch for F$6.50 (try the sui beef bone soup). At dinnertime there are blackboard specials, such as a pot of garlic prawns for F$29 or a T-bone steak for F$32. Otherwise you can get burgers at F$8–9.50, curries at F$12–15, and fish and chips at F$15.

The **Maharaja Restaurant** (tel. 672-2962, Mon.–Sat. 1000–1500 and 1800–2200, Sun. 1700–2200), out near the Nomads Skylodge Hotel, is popular with flight crews who come for the spicy Indian curries, tandoori dishes, and local seafood. It's one of Fiji's finest Indian restaurants (dinner is generally better than lunch here).

The **Outer Reef Seafood Café** (tel. 672-7202, daily 1100–2300), near the Maharaja Restaurant, has a blackboard menu priced F$10–25 (sandwiches F$10–14). The outdoor seating in back is nice, though the food can be hit or miss. A live band starts playing in the Sand Bar back behind the restaurant Friday–Sunday at 1800.

DENARAU ISLAND

Golf courses always seem to have good, inexpensive restaurants and the breezy **Clubhouse Restaurant** (tel. 675-9705) at the Denarau Golf & Racquet Club is no exception. Lunch is offered daily 1100–1500 for F$19–32 and the service is good. Even if you're not a golfer, it's an ideal place for a lunch out if you're staying at the Sheraton or Westin.

The **Port Denarau Retail Center** (www.portdenarau.com.fj), a flashy shopping mall near the outer island shipping docks, opened in 2007. Among the various eating options are sandwiches and meat pies (F$4) from the **Hot Bread Kitchen,** fried chicken meals (F$6–12) at **Chicken Express,** pizza (F$10–30) at **Mama's Kitchen,** fine dining at highly rated **Chef's Restaurant,** and expensive meals at **Amalfi Restaurant Italiano** (www.amalfifiji.com) and **Indigo Indian Restaurant.**

The longstanding favorite at Port Denarau is **Cardo's Steakhouse & Cocktail Bar** (tel. 675-0900, daily 0700–2300), behind the overpriced Hard Rock Café. Cardo's offers charbroiled steaks for F$28–49. Other meals from prawns to pizza cost F$17–49, and cheaper Chinese meals are sometimes available. You'll have a good view of Nadi's bustling tourist port from the terrace. The Denarau beach resorts are a 15-minute walk away.

Jee's Supermarket (daily 0700–1900) in the Port Denarau Retail Center is pricey but there if you need it.

Information, Services, and Transportation

INFORMATION

Tourism Fiji (tel. 672-2433, www.fijime.com) has a marketing office in Suite 107, Colonial Plaza, Namaka, but it's not really set up to deal with the general public. There's no official tourist information office in Nadi, and the private travel agencies masquerading as such give biased information.

Travel Agents

Argo Travel (269 Main St., tel. 670-2308), next to Budget Pharmacy, can book flights around the region.

Fiji's Finest Tours (tel. 675-0611, www.fijisfinesttours.com), at the Port Denarau Retail Center, books most activities and tours around Fiji.

Rosie Holidays (tel. 672-2755, www.rosiefiji.com), at Nadi Airport and many resorts, is an in-bound tour operator that books somewhat upmarket tours, activities, and accommodations. They'll often give you a discount on their day tours and trekking if you book directly with them. **Adventure Fiji** (tel. 672-5598), two offices down from Rosie at the airport, is a branch of the same company oriented toward backpackers.

Coral Sun Fiji (tel. 672-3105, www.coralsunfiji.com) and **ATS Pacific** (tel. 672-2811,

SPELLING AND PRONUNCIATION

When early British missionaries created a system of written Fijian in the middle of the 19th century, they established a unique set of orthographic rules followed to this day. In an attempt to represent the sounds of spoken Fijian more precisely, they rendered "mb" as *b*, "nd" as *d*, "ng" as *g*, "ngg" as *q*, and "th" as *c*. Thus Beqa is pronounced *Mbengga*, Nadi is *Nandi*, Sigatoka is *Singatoka*, Cicia is *Thithia*, etc. In order to be able to pronounce Fijian names and words correctly, visitors must take a few minutes to learn these pronunciation rules.

www.atspacific.com), both at the airport and several hotels, are similar to Rosie and quite reliable. **Sun Vacations** (tel. 672-4273, www.sunvacationsfiji.com) at the airport can book almost any hotel or tour in Fiji.

Great Sights Fiji/Tourist Transport Fiji (tel. 672-3311, www.touristtransportfiji.com), next to the washrooms in the arrivals area at Nadi Airport, handles the "Feejee Experience" backpacker bus tours around Viti Levu. They should have information on the Abaca day tours to Koroyanitu National Heritage Park.

Many smaller travel agencies upstairs from the arrivals concourse at Nadi Airport book budget resorts in the Yasawa Islands and elsewhere around Fiji. For example, there's **Western Travel Services** (tel. 672-3612) in office No. 4 and **Sunset Tours** in office No. 21. **Rabua's Travel Agency** (tel. 672-1377 or 672-3234, dreammakertravel@yahoo.com) in office No. 23 represents Wayalailai Resort on Wayasewa. Other backpacker resorts with offices of their own upstairs at the airport are Ratu Kini of Mana Island in office No. 26 and David's Place of Tavewa Island in office No. 31. The Turtle Island office (tel. 672-2921), downstairs in the arrivals terminal, handles Oarsman's and Safe Landing resorts. Be aware that all of the backpacker travel agencies around Nadi will want to send you to the resort that pays them the

highest commission, not necessarily the place most suitable for you. Getting a refund is difficult if you decide to change your plans.

The largest backpacker-oriented travel agency is **Victory Tours** (tel. 670-0243, www.touristinformationfiji.com, daily 0730–2000) with an office at the corner of Main Street and Hospital Road in downtown Nadi. Their signpost reads Tourist Information Center, but this is purely a commercial operation. Victory sells a variety of four-wheel-drive and trekking "inland safari" excursions into the Nausori Highlands, as well as booking low-budget beach resorts on Mana, Malolo, Tavewa, and Waya islands. Their prices are not fixed and you may feel hustled here.

Better known as PVV Tours, **Pacific Valley View Tours** (tel. 670-0600, www.showmefiji.com), at the Nadi Downtown Backpackers Inn, is similar. Their specialty is discounted prices at upscale resorts near Nadi (including Sonaisali and Shangri-La's Fijian Resort). Prices vary here and bargaining might work.

You can often get a better deal by booking directly with a resort over the phone. The Nadi agents collect commissions as high as 30 percent, and the resort owners are often willing to pass along some of their savings to those who call. Always keep in mind that the Nadi travel agents only promote properties that pay them commissions. If they warn you not to go somewhere, it may be because they don't get an adequate commission from the place.

Airline Offices

Reconfirm your flight, request a seat assignment, or check the departure time by calling your airline: Aircalin (tel. 672-2145), Air New Zealand (tel. 672-2870), Air Pacific (tel. 672-0888), Korean Air (tel. 672-7775), Qantas Airways (tel. 672-2880), and Solomon Airlines (tel. 672-2831). All of these offices are at the airport. Pacific Blue (Oneworld Flight Center, tel. 670-8157) is next to Mama's Pizza on Main Street.

SERVICES
Money

The Westpac Bank opposite the Nadi

Handicraft Market, the ANZ Bank near Morris Hedstrom, and the Colonial National Bank between these, are open Monday–Thursday 0930–1530, Friday 0930–1600. The ANZ Bank and the Westpac Bank charge F$5 commission, whereas Colonial National does not. If you need a Visa/MasterCard ATM, go to the ANZ Bank branches in downtown Nadi, at Namaka toward the airport, and at the airport itself. McDonald's also has an ATM and there's a Westpac Bank ATM at the Port Denarau Marina.

Money Exchange (tel. 670-3366, Mon.–Fri. 0700–1700, Sat. 0800–1600), between the ANZ Bank and Morris Hedstrom, changes cash and travelers checks without commission at a rate comparable to the banks (and without the line).

Just Exchange (tel. 670-5477), inside Prouds, and **GlobalEX Western Union** (tel. 670-7213, weekdays 0800–1645, Sat. 0800–1245), on Main Street near Big Bear, are similar.

City Forex Money Exchange (daily 0800–2000) and the **Westpac Bank** (weekdays 0830–1600, Sat. 0830–1300) are in the Port Denarau Retail Center. The Westpac Bank at Denarau has an ATM.

City Forex/Western Union has a 24-hour exchange counter in the arrivals concourse at Nadi International Airport.

Post

There are two large post offices, one next to the market in central Nadi, and another between the cargo warehouses directly across the park in front of the arrivals hall at Nadi Airport. Check both if you're expecting general-delivery mail. Both post offices are open Monday–Friday 0800–1600, Saturday 0800–1300.

Internet Access

If you're headed for the Yasawa resorts, Nadi offers your last chance to check email, and prices are competitive. Unfortunately Nadi's Internet cafés close early and there's no 24-hour café of the kind you find in Suva.

Click Internet and Game (Mon.–Sat. 0800–1930, Sun. 1000–1800), located at Main Street at Park Street in the center, has lots of computers available at F$1.90 an hour.

Nadi is a convenient, inexpensive place to check email.

Kidanet Internet (tel. 670-6496, www .kidanet.com.fj, Mon.–Thurs. 0815–1615, Fri. 0815–1600), Main Street near the bridge, charges F$1 for 20 minutes.

Planet Net Café (tel. 672-8460, weekdays 0800–2030, Sat. 0900–2030, Sun. 0930–1800), in the strip mall opposite Ed's Bar, charges F$3 an hour.

Biloccino Coffee Lounge (tel. 675-0065), at the Port Denarau Retail Center, offers Internet access at F$7 a half hour.

Immigration Office

Visa extensions can be arranged at the Immigration office (tel. 672-2263, Mon.–Fri. 0830–1230), upstairs near the Pacific Sun check-in counter in the departures hall at Nadi Airport.

Laundrettes

Flagstaff Laundry (tel. 672-3061, Mon.–Sat. 0800–1700), at the end of Northern Press Road beside Sunny Travelers Inn, charges F$3.50 a kilogram to wash, dry, and fold your laundry. Ironing is F$2–3 a piece.

Toilets

Free public toilets are at the corner of Nadi Market closest to the post office, at the bus station, and in the Nadi Civic Center.

Health

The outpatient department at **Nadi District Hospital** (tel. 670-1128), inland from Nadi Bus Station, is open Monday–Thursday 0800–1630, Friday 0800–1600, and Saturday 0800–1200.

You'll save time by visiting Dr. Ram Raju (2 Lodhia St., tel. 670-1375, Mon.–Fri. 0830–1630, Sat. 0830–1230), at the DSM Center. Dr. Raju is a family doctor specializing in travel health.

Dr. Adbul Gani (tel. 670-3776) has his dental surgery downstairs in the mall at the Nadi Civic Center near the post office. (Dr. Gani is a former mayor of Nadi.)

The **Namaka Medical Center** (tel. 672-2288) is on Queens Road near the Grand Melanesian Hotel. After hours, press the bell for service.

At Wailoaloa Beach, Dr. Sarat Naidu (tel. 670-0202) is at Nadi Bay Beach Apartments.

Budget Pharmacy (tel. 670-0064) is on Main Street in town.

GETTING THERE AND AROUND

Nadi's bus station adjoining the market is an active place. **Pacific Transport** (tel. 670-0044) has express buses to Suva via Queens Road daily at 0720, 0750, 0900, 1300, 1640, and 1820 (188 km, four hours, F$15.10). The 0900 bus begins its run at Nadi (all of the others arrive from Lautoka). **Sunbeam Transport** (www.sunbeamfiji.com) express buses to Suva (F$15.70) leave at 0930, 1020, 1100, 1200, 1335, 1505, and 1610 daily. Collective taxis and minibuses parked in a corner of Nadi Bus Station take passengers nonstop from Nadi to Suva in three hours for F$17 per person.

Coral Sun Fiji (tel. 672-3105, www.coral sunfiji.com) at Nadi Airport operates the air-conditioned Fiji Express luxury coach to Suva via the Coral Coast resorts, departing Nadi Airport daily at 0730 and 1300 (F$22 to Suva). In Nadi town, it stops outside Prouds.

Local buses to Lautoka (33 km), the airport, and anywhere in between pick up passengers at a bus stop on Main Street opposite Morris Hedstrom.

Unmarked white "Viti Mini" minibuses shuttle frequently between the bus stop on the highway outside Nadi Airport and Nadi town at F$1 a ride. Collective taxis cruising the highway between the airport and Nadi do the same for about what you'd pay on a bus (ask first).

Taxis around Nadi are quite cheap provided the driver uses the meter. Many Nadi hotels offer free airport transfers, although sometimes it's only the trip *from* the airport that is free. Ask before getting in.

North of Nadi

SIGHTS
Viseisei Village

A popular legend invented in 1893 holds that Viseisei village, on the old road between Lautoka and Nadi, was the first settlement in Fiji. It's told how the early Fijians, led by Chiefs Lutunasobasoba and Degei, came from the west, landing their great canoe, the *Kaunitoni,* at Vuda Point, where the oil tanks are now. A Centennial Memorial (1835–1935) in front of the church commemorates the arrival of the first Methodist missionaries in Fiji, and opposite the memorial is a traditional Fijian *bure*—the official residence of Tui Vuda. Fiji's former president, Ratu Josefa Iloilo, holder of the Tui Vuda title, lives in the green-roofed house behind this central *bure.*

Near the back of the church is another monument, topped by a giant war club, the burial place of the village's chiefly family. The late Dr. Timoci Bavadra, the prime minister of Fiji deposed during the 1987 Rabuka coup, hailed from Viseisei and is interred here. Dr. Bavadra's traditional-style home faces the main road near

© ANDREW GOULD

orchid in the Garden of the Sleeping Giant

the church. His son currently lives there, and with his permission you'll be allowed to enter to see the photos hanging on the walls.

All this is only a few minutes' walk from the bus stop, but you're expected to have someone accompany you through the village. Most visitors arrive on sightseeing tours, and if you come on your own, you should ask permission to visit of anyone you meet at the bus stop. They'll probably send a child along with you, and as you part, you should give the child a pack of chewing gum or a similar item (give something else if your escort is an adult). There's a fine view of Nadi Bay from Viseisei, and the bus tours often stop here, as the souvenir vendors in the village indicate. In any case, don't come on a Sunday. A bypass on Queens Road avoids Viseisei, and only local buses between Lautoka and Nadi take the back road past the village.

British Guns

A couple of kilometers from the village on the airport side of Viseisei, just above Lomolomo Public School, are two British six-inch guns set up here during World War II to defend the north side of Nadi Bay. Between 1939 and 1941, coastal defense batteries were established at five points around Viti Levu. It's a fairly easy climb from the main highway, and you'll get an excellent view from on top.

Garden of the Sleeping Giant

Many tours visit the Garden of the Sleeping Giant (Mon.–Sat. 0900–1700, Sun. 0900–1200, admission F$12/6 adult/child), 2.5 kilometers down Wailoka Road off Queens Road north of the airport. It's also known as Perry Mason's Orchid Garden because American actor Raymond Burr established the garden in 1977. The brochure claims that 2,000 kinds of orchids are kept in these gardens at the foot of the hills, though that figure may be a slight overstatement.

ACCOMMODATIONS

The **Stoney Creek Resort** (Sabeto Rd., tel. 672-2206, www.stoneycreekfiji.net) is six kilometers east of Queens Road, about 11 kilometers northeast of Nadi Airport. There are two *bure* with indoor hot tubs at F$145 double, two rooms with balcony behind the restaurant at F$110 double, and a beautifully designed hilltop dormitory with a splendid mountain view at F$33 per person. The 16 dorm beds are divided among four cubicles, plus two private "love shack" rooms at FJ$50/75 single/double, and there are hammocks from which to take in the scene. Continental breakfast in the restaurant/bar is included and there's a swimming pool. Activities include easy walks around this rural neighborhood, river swimming during the rainy season, waterfall visits, and kayaking. Bicycles are F$25 a day. You can soak up in the Sabeto natural hot springs (F$10 pp), a 25-minute walk from resort. Situated above the Sabeto River and below the scenic Sleeping Giant Mountain Range, this is an animal-friendly spot with local birds, butterflies, flora, and fauna. The Sabeto bus runs to Stoney Creek five times a day from Nadi (F$2.40) or you could arrive by taxi from the airport for around F$7 (ask the driver to use his meter).

The **Mediterranean Villas Hotel** (tel. 666-4011, www.villas.com.fj), on Vuda Hill overlooking Viseisei village near Vuda Point Junction on Queen's Road, has six individually decorated self-catering villas with fridge priced from F$99/140 single/double. There's a pool, but the beach is far from here. The view of Nadi Bay is good. Local buses between Lautoka and Nadi stop nearby.

Two kilometers down Vuda Road from Mediterranean Villas is the **Anchorage Beach Resort** (tel. 666-2099, www.anchoragefiji.com). It's on a hilltop just before the descent to First Landing Resort, a 15-minute walk along the cane railway line or beach from Viseisei. Anchorage has 10 mountain-view rooms at F$195 single or double, 10 ocean-view rooms at F$208, 20 oceanfront rooms at F$269, 12 beachside villas at F$370, eight one-bedroom apartments at F$350, and eight two-bedroom apartments at F$410. All units are air-conditioned, and each has a fridge and balcony. Only the apartments have cooking facilities (other guests must use the restaurant). Even though continental breakfast and tax are included, the Anchorage is a poor value. The shoreline below Anchorage isn't as good for swimming as the beach at nearby First Landing Resort, but the views across Nadi Bay are nice and there's a swimming pool. The Anchorage can be noisy when local guests are present.

First Landing Resort (tel. 666-6171, www.firstlandingfiji.com) is next to the Vuda Point Yacht Marina, three kilometers down Vuda Road from Mediterranean Villas. The 14 aging duplex units facing the swimming pool are F$185 single or double, while the 18 duplex beachfront units go for F$270 (extra persons F$48). All these units have fully screened porches and are equipped with a fridge and coffeepot (but no cooking facilities). Connecting doors make the units ideal for large families or small groups. Three units are wheelchair accessible. One beach villa opposite the reception has its own kitchen and pool at F$520 double. Prices are negotiable. A cooked breakfast is included in all rates. The large garden restaurant on the premises bakes pizza (F$16–26), seafood (including lobster at F$65), and bread in a wood-fired stone oven. Menu items average F$25–38 at dinner (ask about the day's special). The café in the adjacent Vuda Point Marina (daily 0700–1500, also Tues., Thurs., and Sat. until 2100) is far less expensive and recommended. The beach here is much better than those in and around Nadi, but you'd only call it good at high tide. The snorkeling is poor. Subsurface Fiji offers scuba diving. Airport transfers are F$30/45 single/double one-way. First Landing is okay for a night or two, but you'd be making a mistake to plan your whole vacation around it.

YACHTING FACILITIES

The **Vuda Point Marina** (tel. 666-8214, www.vudamarina.com.fj) is between Lautoka and Nadi, three kilometers down Vuda Road off Viseisei Back Road. Here yachts moor Mediterranean-style in a well-protected oval anchorage blasted through the reef. The excellent facilities include a yacht club, chandlery, workshop, general store (daily 0730–1900), inexpensive café (daily 0700–1500, and Tues., Thurs., and Sat. until 2100), fuel depot, laundry, showers, and sail repair shop. Subsurface Fiji (tel. 666-6738, www.fijidiving.com) will pick up scuba divers here upon request.

South of Nadi

SONAISALI BEACH RESORT

Opened in 1992, this greenwashed resort (tel. 670-6011, www.sonaisali.com) is on Naisali, a long, low island surrounded by mangrove flats in Momi Bay, just 300 meters off the coast of Viti Levu. The turnoff is 10 kilometers south of Nadi, then it's three kilometers down Nacobi Road to the landing. The 32 air-conditioned rooms with fridge in the two main two-story buildings are F$427 single or double, and there are 91 duplex units at F$504–612 including tax and breakfast (no cooking facilities). The lunch and dinner meal package is F$84 per person. It's necessary to make dinner reservations, and you may have difficulty arranging a convenient time (like everything here, the food and drink is overpriced). The water pressure at Sonaisali is low, and it takes ages to fill the tiny spa baths built into some of the units. The resort features a marina, large swimming pool (which could use a cleaning), tennis courts, a children's program, and free non-motorized water sports, but the snorkeling off the black sand beach is mediocre. Scuba diving and noisy personal watercraft are available. For F$85, you can "test your combat skills" by donning protective paramilitary clothing and firing paintballs at members of an opposing team! Airport transfers are F$48 per person one-way, and unless you're alone it would be much cheaper to take a taxi. Non-guests wishing to take the "free" shuttle boat across to the island must first pay F$30/15 per adult/child for a non-refundable food credit (not valid for drinks). In short, look for somewhere else to go.

SURF & DIVE RENDEZVOUS

In 2001, Ben and Naoko Seduadua established a backpacker camp (tel. 603-0211, www.surfdivefiji.com) on Uciwai Beach north of Nabila village, right next to the landing for Tavarua and Namotu islands. Accommodations include one room with private bath (F$110/150 single/double), four rooms with shared bath (F$80/100 single/double), a five-bed dorm (F$42 pp), and camping space (F$30 pp). The lunch and dinner plan is F$40 per person or you can cook your own food in a communal kitchen. There's a swimming pool. Scuba diving is F$160/240 for one/two tanks including gear. Ben's three- to four-day Open Water certification course is F$720. Surfing trips for experienced surfers to the reefs off Namotu and Malolo islands are F$65 per person. Surfboard rental, sale, and repair are available. Other activities include surfing lessons, fishing, and horseback riding. The beach is okay for Viti Levu. The turnoff to Rendezvous is at Uciwai Junction, 15 kilometers south of Nadi town on Queens Road, then it's another six kilometers west on a rough gravel road. Get there on the Dominion Transport "Uciwai" bus from Nadi (F$2.40) weekdays at 0815, 1330, and 1730 or Saturdays at 0700, 1300, and 1700 (or pay F$45 for a taxi from Nadi).

◖ MOMI BATTERY HISTORIC PARK

On a hilltop overlooking Momi Bay, 28 kilometers from Nadi, are two British six-inch guns named Queen Victoria (1900) and Edward VII (1901). Both were recycled from the Boer War and set up here by the New Zealand Army's 30th Battalion in 1941 to defend the southern approach to Nadi Bay. The only shots fired in anger during the war were across the bow of a Royal New Zealand Navy ship that forgot to make the correct signals as it entered the passage. It quickly turned around, made the proper signals, and reentered quietly. You get a great view of the Mamanuca Group, reefs, and surrounding countryside from the guns. This historic site is managed by the National Trust for Fiji (daily 0900–1700, admission F$6/3/1 family/adult/student). To reach the battery, catch the bus at the Nabila Bus Station at 0900, 1600, and 1715 (only the 0900 bus returns to town the same day). The turnoff from Queens Road is at Nawai Junction, 17 kilometers south of Nadi town, then it's another nine kilometers along a gravel road to the guns. Seashell Cove Resort is nine kilometers south.

MOMI BAY

Momi Bay, 29 kilometers southwest of Nadi, is not an especially scenic or accessible area. The beaches are as poor or poorer than those around Nadi. Yet in 2005, construction began on the 250-room **JW Marriott Fiji Resort & Spa** at a cost of US$200 million. The plan called for 22 units to be built on concrete pilings over the lagoon, plus 61 two- and three-bedroom villas with full kitchens and individual plunge pools. An 18-hole golf course, underground nightclub, lavish pools, and sporting facilities were to have rounded out the resort. A separate development by Ritz Carlton was envisioned for a nearby site. Construction was running 12 months behind schedule in 2007 when the Fiji Islands Revenue and Customs Authority suddenly changed its taxation policies and demanded an advance assessment from hundreds of individual overseas owners who had purchased freehold residential lots sold to finance the project. The New Zealand Securities Commission became involved after receiving complaints about false statements by the developers and funding quickly dried up. New Zealand–based Bridgecorp Limited and its Australian subsidiary Matapo Limited are said to have lost F$100 million at Momi Bay. In June 2009, the Fiji National Provident Fund conducted an auction of movable assets to recover the F$74 million it had invested on behalf of its 300,000 members in Fiji but F$18 million had to be written off. In May 2010, several Fiji-based investment trusts auctioned off the freehold land to cover mortgage arrears. For better or worse, it's now highly unlikely the half-finished Marriott will ever be completed. No winners, only losers here.

Seashell Cove Resort (tel. 670-6100, www.seashellresort.com), just down from the defunct Marriott on Momi Bay, has been around since the 1980s. Even though it's now part of the Hexagon Group of Hotels (www.hexagonfiji.com), you should not expect a fancy resort. There are six duplex *bure* with fans, fridge, and cooking facilities at F$165 single or double, and 17 lodge rooms with lumpy beds and shared bath at F$50/74 single/double. Six larger units near the restaurant are available for families at F$260 for up to six, and babysitters can be provided. The two honeymoon suites attached to a lodge are also F$240. Not all of the rooms face the water. The dormitory above the bar includes three five-bed rooms at F$90 per bed including three meals. Otherwise, pitch your own tent beside the volleyball court for F$15 per tent.

Cooking facilities are not provided for campers or lodge guests; the meal plan is F$75 per person, and there's a small grocery store just outside the resort. A *meke* and Fijian feast (F$25) occurs on Saturday. Baggage storage is available free of charge. Internet access on the one computer at the office is F$10 an hour or F$0.30 a minute.

A small saltwater swimming pool is near the shore, but there's no beach here, only a concrete seawall. At low tide, it's a 10-minute trudge across the mudflats to the water. Amenities and activities include a swimming pool, day trips to Natadola Beach (F$45 including lunch), tennis, and volleyball. There's a horse that's used to walk tots under 10 around the resort, but the free kayaks leak and become unstable after 20 minutes.

Seashell Cove deserves a top-pick recommendation for the many sporting activities offered. Daily at 0700, the Seashell boat shuttles surfers out to the reliable left at Namotu Island breakers or long hollow right at Wilkes Passage (F$60 pp, minimum of four). The boat also goes to Swimming Pools, Desperations, and Mini Cloudbreak, staying with the surfers while they surf. Since July 2010, the famous Cloudbreak lefthander at Navula Reef between Wilkes and Seashell can be visited every day (F$60 pp). Expect crowds of 25 guys in the water—all other spots are less crowded. There's also an offshore break near the Momi Bay Lighthouse. This type of reef break surfing can be dangerous for the inexperienced.

Seashell Cove's scuba-diving operation, **Scuba Bula** (tel. 628-0190, www.scubabula

.com), can handle to up to 24 divers at a time from beginners to advanced. The cost is F$125/185 for one/two tanks, and F$745 for a PADI certification course (minimum of two). Seashell divers experience lots of fish/shark action at Navula Lighthouse, and there's great drift diving at Canyons (the guides really know their spots). When there's space, snorkelers are welcome to go along at F$45 per person.

The turnoff to Seashell Cove is at Nawai Junction, 17 kilometers south of Nadi town on Queens Road, then it's another 12 kilometers to the resort. Airport transfers arranged through the resort are F$25 per person each way (minimum of two). A taxi from Nadi Airport will cost F$60, from Nadi town F$40, from Sigatoka F$65. Dominion Transport has buses direct to Seashell from the position marked "Sigatoka" at Nadi Bus Station Monday–Saturday at 0800, 1000, 1215, 1600, and 1700, Sunday at 0830 only (F$2.40). From Sigatoka Bus Station, Dominion Transport buses to Seashell leave Monday–Saturday at 1100 (F$5).

The Mamanuca Group

The Mamanuca Group (www.fijiresorts.com) is a paradise of eye-popping reefs and sand-fringed isles shared by traditional Fijian villages and jet-age resorts. The white coral beaches and super snorkeling grounds attract visitors aplenty; boats and planes arrive constantly, bringing folks in from nearby Nadi. These islands are in the lee of big Viti Levu, which means you'll get about as much sun here as anywhere in Fiji. Some of the South Pacific's finest scuba diving, surfing, game fishing, and yachting await you, and many nautical activities are included in the basic resort rates.

Middle-aged vacationers from Australia and New Zealand have been coming to the Mamanucas for decades, and more recently,

© MARK HEARD / WWW.FLICKR.COM/HEARDSY

on Matamanoa Island in the Mamanuca Group

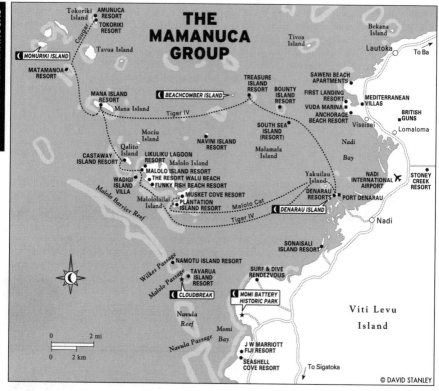

© DAVID STANLEY

younger travelers have pioneered the Yasawa Islands. The Mamanucas are fine for a little time in the sun, though much of it is a tourist scene irrelevant to Fiji life. If the beach is your main focus, you won't mind staying on a tiny coral speck like Beachcomber, Bounty, Matamanoa, Namotu, Navini, Tavarua, and Treasure, but if hiking and land-based exploring are also on your agenda, you'll do better on the larger of the Yasawas.

GETTING THERE

Pacific Sun discontinued scheduled flights from Nadi to Malololailai and Mana Islands in July 2010, and only charter flights are now available.

Turtle Airways (tel. 672-1888, www.turtle airways.com), next to the golf course at Wailoaloa Beach in Nadi, runs a seaplane shuttle to the main Mamanuca resorts at F$235 per person one-way (minimum of two passengers). Baggage is limited to one 15-kilogram suitcase plus one carry-on, or 185 kilograms maximum body weight and luggage per couple.

South Sea Cruises (tel. 675-0500, www .ssc.com.fj), owned by Fullers of New Zealand, operates a high-speed catamaran shuttle to the offshore island resorts on the 27-meter, 150-seat *Tiger IV.* The boat leaves Nadi's Port Denarau daily at 0900, 1215, and 1515 for Bounty (F$65 each way), Treasure (F$75), Malolo (F$85), Castaway (F$85), and Mana (F$89). Interisland hops between the resorts themselves are F$60 each. Children under 16 are half-price on all trips (under five free). Be prepared to wade on and off the boat in ankle-deep water at all islands except Mana. If all you want is a glimpse of the lovely Mamanuca Group, a four-island, three-hour, nonstop round-trip cruise is F$75. Connections from Port Denarau to Matamanoa and Tokoriki are available at 1515 on the 145-seat catamaran *Cougar* (F$110).

The daily catamaran *Yasawa Flyer II* operated by **Awesome Adventures** (tel. 675-0499, www.awesomefiji.com) calls at South Seas Island on its way from Nadi to the Yasawa islands, with immediate connections available to/from Beachcomber and Bounty islands. The *Flyer* also serves Vomo Island.

A separate catamaran service operates to Malololailai island on the *Malolo Cat.* Catamaran bookings can be made at any travel agency around Nadi, and bus transfers to the wharf from the main Nadi hotels are included.

Day Cruises

Food and accommodations at the Mamanuca Group resorts are expensive, and a cheaper way to enjoy the islands—for a day, at least—is by booking a day cruise from Nadi to Castaway (F$145), Malolo (F$145), Mana (F$135), or Treasure (F$139) on the fast catamaran *Tiger IV,* operated by **South Sea Cruises** (tel. 675-0500, www.ssc.com.fj) and departing from Port Denarau. The price includes lunch (but not drinks) on the island of your choice, non-motorized sporting activities, and a day at the beach (children under 16 are half-price). South Sea Cruises also has day trips to the outer Mamanuca islands (including Monuriki, the island from the Tom Hanks movie *Castaway)* on the two-masted schooner *Seaspray* (F$185 with lunch and drinks).

Several companies offer day cruises to sunny specks of sand such as Bounty Island, Malamala Island (tel. 670-5192, www.mala malaisland.com), and South Sea Island (tel. 675-0500), costing F$95–115, usually including drinks (ask) and non-motorized sporting activities. Children under 16 are often half price. These trips are fine if all you want is a day at the beach; otherwise you'll find them a colossal bore. Any hotel tour desk can book them. Ask about reduced early-bird prices, if you're willing to arrive and leave early.

Storck Cruises (tel. 675-1101, www.storck cruises.com) offers a day trip to Savala Island

on the MV *Oolala* Monday–Saturday at 1000. It's F$165 per adult or F$50 for children under 16, with food, soft drinks, and snorkeling gear included.

Youthful travelers will enjoy a day cruise to **Beachcomber Island Resort** (tel. 666-1500, www.beachcomberfiji.com), Fiji's unofficial Club Med for the under-35 set. Operating daily, the F$105 fare includes the return boat ride and a buffet lunch (alcohol not included). Families should consider Beachcomber because children under 16 are half price and infants under five are free. Beachcomber has an office in the arrivals terminal at Nadi Airport, or you can book through any Rosie Holidays, ATS Pacific, or Coral Sun Fiji desk.

Sailing Adventures (tel. 623-2001, www .sailingadventuresfiji.com) operates day trips to Malololailai Island (F$135) on the 15-meter yacht *Pelorus Jack.* They also do three-day Yasawas cruises for backpackers at F$600 per person.

Captain Cook Cruises (tel. 670-1823, www .captaincook.com.fj) runs day cruises to tiny Tivua Island on the sailing vessel *Ra Marama* for F$139 including a buffet lunch, drinks, and non-motorized water sports. One child under 10 is allowed aboard free for each paying adult. Two bungalows on Tivua host those who'd like to stay overnight at F$299 per person all-inclusive. Three-hour sunset dinner cruises on the ship *City of Nadi* are F$99.

Every day the Oceanic Schooner Co. (tel. 670-2443, funcruises@connect.com.fj) does an upscale "taste of the islands cruise" on the 30-meter schooner *Whale's Tale,* built at Suva's Whippy Shipyard in 1985. You get a champagne breakfast and gourmet lunch served buffet style aboard ship, an open bar, and cocktails in the company of a limited number of fellow passengers at F$179 per person (F$89 for children under 17). *Whale's Tale* is a nicer vessel than the *Seaspray,* but both cruises take you to the unspoiled isles at the outer edge of the Mamanuca Group in relative comfort.

Virtually all of the day cruises include free bus transfers from most Nadi hotels and from Coral Coast hotels at additional cost. Verify the pickup time carefully as you'll miss your cruise if you miss the bus. Be aware that several buses may be picking up from your resort at the same time and they may look confusingly similar. Be sure to get on the right one. At Port Denarau, you'll have to line up to exchange your voucher for the cruise ticket, and although it seems chaotic, the employees are usually efficient and will point you in the right direction. In the afternoon, be prepared to wait a while for the bus back to your resort to depart as the last passengers straggle aboard.

Most of the cruises include free snorkeling gear, but they do run out occasionally so don't be slow to select yours. Hope for high tide as snorkeling at low tide can be uncomfortable.

SCUBA DIVING

Subsurface Fiji (tel. 666-6738, www.subsurfacefiji.com) is represented at a dozen offshore Mamanuca resorts and will pick up divers at the Port Denarau Marina upon request. They charge F$110/199/540 for one/two/six tanks plus F$25 a day for gear. Ask about their multiresort dive pass. They visit 36 dive sites in the Mamanuca Group, and unlimited diving is available at F$850. Their three-day PADI certification course is F$740 (minimum of two persons). Children eight years and up are accepted at their scuba school.

Reef Safari (tel. 675-0566, www.reefsafari.com.fj) books scuba diving day trips from Nadi to South Sea Island in the Mamanuca Group. For beginners, it's F$220 per person for the tour, lunch, drinks, and an introductory dive. Certified divers pay the same for two dives. Reef Safari also handles diving at Amunuca Island Resort and Bounty Island Resort.

Aqua Trek Mana (tel. 666-9309, www.aquatrekdiving.com) serves guests at Mana Island Resort, while **Viti Watersports** (tel. 670-2413, www.vitiwatersports.com) is based at Matamanoa Island Resort, and **Tokoriki Diving** (www.tokorikidiving.com) is at Tokoriki Island Resort.

Dive Sites

Some of Fiji's most exhilarating scuba diving is on the Malolo Barrier Reef and the passages around tiny **Namotu,** or "Magic Island," where nutrients are swept in by strong currents. Both pelagic and reef fish abound in the canyons, caves, and coral heads around Namotu, but in some places the action has been distorted by scuba operators who regularly feed the fish. The outer slopes of Namotu, where the reef plunges 1,000 meters into the Pacific abyss, feature turtles, reef sharks, and vast schools of barracuda, with visibility up to 50 meters. Dolphins also frequent this area.

Bigger fish, manta rays, and ocean-going sharks are often seen at **The Big W** on the outer edge of the Malolo Barrier Reef. Susie, a friendly bronze whale shark, happens by from time to time. Vertical walls drop 70 meters at this spectacular site.

In another passage in the outer barrier reef are the pinnacles of **Gotham City,** so called for the batfish seen here, along with brilliantly colored soft corals and vast schools of tropical fish.

One of the world's most famous reef shark encounter venues is **Supermarket,** a 30-meter wall just west of Mana Island. Grays, white tips, and black tips are always present, and you might even see a tiger shark. Divemasters hand-feed sharks more than two meters long on this exciting dive.

Shallow Kaka Reef north of Mana Island is known as **The Circus** for the myriad clown fish and colorful corals. Eagle rays sometimes frequent the **South Mana Reef** straight out from the island's wharf. Other well-known Mamanuca dive sites include Japanese Gardens, Lobster Caves, the Pinnacles (near Malolo), Sunflower Reef, The Barrel Head, The Fingers, Jockie's Point, a B-26 bomber dating from World War II, and the wreck of the *Salamanda,* a decommissioned Blue Lagoon cruise ship.

MALOLOLAILAI ISLAND

Malololailai, or "Little Malolo," 22 kilometers west of Nadi, is a 216-hectare island eight kilometers around (an interesting walk). In 1880, an American sailor named Louis Armstrong purchased Malololailai from the Fijians for one musket; in 1964, Dick Smith bought it for many muskets. You can still be alone at the beaches on the far side of the island, but with three growing resorts, a marina, a nine-hole golf course, and projects for lots more time-share condominiums in the pipeline, it's becoming overdeveloped. An airstrip across the island's waist separates its two resorts; inland are rounded, grassy hills.

Plantation Island

Plantation Island Resort (tel. 666-9333, www.plantationisland.com), on the southwest side of Malololailai, is one of the largest resorts off Nadi. It belongs to the Raffles Group, which has another large hotel in Nadi. The 142 rooms are divided between 41 air-conditioned hotel rooms in a two-story building and 101 individual or duplex *bure*. Rates start at F$281 single or double for one of the 26 garden hotel rooms and increase to F$606 for a deluxe beachfront *bure*. The rooms have a fridge but no cooking facilities, so add F$89 per person for all meals. A supermarket is at the airport end of the resort. Plantation Island Resort tries hard to cater to families, with two children under 16 accommodated free when sharing with their parents and a children's meal plan at F$50 for guests under 16. Crèche and babysitting services are available, and there's a 20-meter waterslide and two pools.

Free activities here include snorkeling gear, windsurfing, paddle boats, leaky kayaks, and Hobie cat sailing, and daily snorkeling and fishing trips are offered at no charge. Scuba diving is extra. Greens fees at Plantation Island's golf course toward the airport are reasonable and clubs and cart are for hire. Just don't drive their golf cart anywhere other than on the course, unless you're looking for trouble! Plantation Island has a better beach than neighboring Musket Cove and is much more of an integrated resort. Musket Cove is a do-it-yourself kind of place.

Lomani Island

Near the west end of Malololailai, **Lomani Island Resort** (tel. 666-8212, www

.lomaniisland.com) is more intimate and upscale than Plantation, with eight deluxe suites in a two-story building at F$630 double and four duplex suites at F$690. The five beachfront *bure* are F$740. Tax and a full American breakfast are included, and for F$99 per person extra, lunch and dinner are also served. Children under 16 are not accepted here (although there are hordes of them at nearby Plantation Island). The pool and gardens are lovely, but at these prices. . . .

Musket Cove

Also on Malololailai Island is **Musket Cove Island Resort** (tel. 666-2215, VHF 68, www .musketcovefiji.com), which opened in 1977. This is one of the few Mamanuca resorts that provide cooking facilities for its guests, but these vary according to the class of accommodations. Full kitchen facilities are provided in the 16 two-bedroom villas, costing F$742 double, plus F$35 per extra adult to a maximum of six. The 21 garden and lagoon *bure* have breakfast bars at F$495 single or double. The 12 beachfront *bure* (from F$604 single or double) also have breakfast bars. The six air-conditioned rooms (F$318 single or double) upstairs in the resort's administration building have no cooking facilities at all. Add 17.5 percent tax to these rates. You can tell that Musket Cove has been patched together over time, as the accommodations are so dissimilar.

Musket Cove's well-stocked grocery store sells fresh fruit and vegetables (but no alcohol), and a coin laundry is near the store. A F$92/110 per-person plus tax two-/three-meal plan is available at Dick's Place Restaurant by the pool (children under 12 are half price). Entertainment is provided every night, except Sunday. The bar on Ratu Nemani Island, a tiny coral islet connected to the marina by a floating bridge, is popular among yachties off the many boats anchored here. The resort also includes Mandara Spa (tel. 666-2215, www .mandaraspa.com).

Activities such as snorkeling, windsurfing, canoeing, kayaking, and line fishing are free for Musket Cove guests. Paid activities include the Hobie cats and waterskiing. The launch *Anthony Star* is available for deep-sea game-fishing charters at F$560 for four hours (up to four persons). The 10-meter cruiser *Dolphin Star* can be chartered for longer fishing trips at F$1,100 for four hours (up to eight persons). The 14-meter catamaran *Take a Break* (www.takeabreakcruises.com) does cruises to Castaway Island (F$85 pp without lunch), dolphin-watching trips (F$85 pp), and sunset viewing (F$75 pp).

Subsurface Fiji (www.subsurfacefiji.com) runs the scuba-diving concession at the Musket Cove marina, and many famous dive sites are less than 15 minutes away. It's F$110/199 for one/two tanks including equipment. **Musket Cove Yacht Charters** has a small fleet of charter yachts stationed here. The *Merlin* yachts can do a five-day crewed cruise to the Yasawas.

Malololailai is a favorite stopover for cruising yachts, with water and clean showers provided at the marina. Fuel and groceries are also available. Yachts can use the Musket Cove marina moorings or moor stern-to Mediterranean-style at a daily rate. There is a restriction of 1.8 meters draft at low tide at the entrance to the marina. The marked anchorage is protected and 15 meters deep, with good holding.

Most of the boats in the Auckland-to-Fiji yacht race in June end up here just in time for the President's Cup, Fiji's prestige yachting event. In mid-September, there's a yachting regatta week at Musket Cove.

Getting There

Malololailai's grass-and-gravel airstrip is the busiest in the Mamanuca Group and serves as a distribution point for the other resorts. Pacific Sun discontinued scheduled flights to Malololailai's grass-and-gravel airstrip in July 2010, and only charter flights are now available. The catamaran *Malolo Cat* leaves Nadi's Port Denarau for Malololailai at 0730, 1030, 1400, or 1730 (50 minutes, F$60 one-way). A F$60 same-day return fare is also offered. Discounts are available for children under 16. Only two bottles of liquor per person are allowed. From Malololailai, the *Cat* departs at

0845, 1215, and 1515. Free pickups are offered from any Nadi-area hotel.

MALOLO ISLAND

At low tide, you can wade from Malololailai to nearby Malolo Island, largest of the Mamanuca Group. Yaro, one of two Fijian villages on Malolo, is known to tourists as "shell village" for what the locals offer for sale.

The **◖ Funky Fish Beach Resort** (tel. 628-2333, www.funkyfishresort.com) on the south coast is a flashpacker place. The 16-bed dorm is F$35 per person, or it's F$105 for a double room with shared bath in the dorm. A small thatched beach *bure* with private bath is F$160 double, or F$320 for a two-bedroom, self-catering beach *bure* for up to four people. Add 17.5 percent tax to these rates, plus another 5 percent if you pay by credit card, and F$60 per person for the three-meal plan. Even with the extras, it's still good value compared to the other places on Malolo Island. Funky Fish has a pool as well as a fine beach, and it makes a good base for surfing and scuba diving. The three-hour round-trip hike to the old Fijian fort provides a 360-degree view. The boat transfer from the *Malolo Cat* to Funky Fish is F$5 per person each way.

A 30-minute walk from Funky Fish at low tide is **The Resort Walu Beach** (tel. 665-1777, www.walubeach.com), a party resort with two bars that stay open late. The 14 beach *bure* with fridge are F$290/370/450 with one/two/three bedrooms. The meal plan applicable to beach *bure* guests is F$60 per person extra. In addition, Walu Beach has six three-bedroom hillside lodges divided into a double with private bath at F$190 and two singles with shared bath at F$95, breakfast and dinner included. The 60-bed bunkhouse dorm is F$82 per person including breakfast and dinner. All the usual water sports are offered here, plus there's a swimming pool, fitness center, games room, tour desk, etc. Subsurface Fiji arranges scuba diving at both Walu Beach and Funky Fish.

Malolo Island Resort (tel. 666-9192, www.maloloisland.com) is at Malolo's western tip, a 20-minute walk from Walu Beach at low

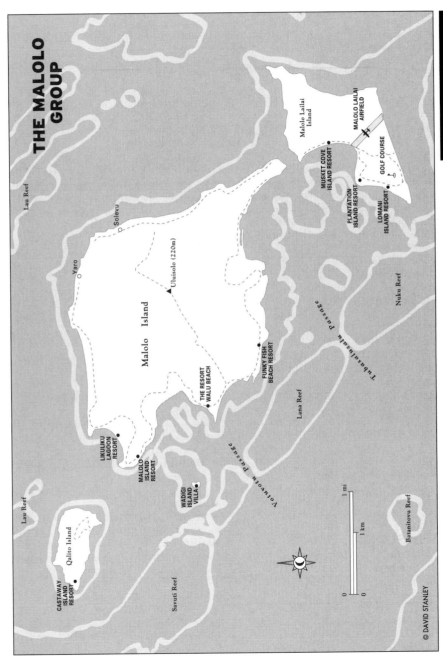

THE MALOLO GROUP

Lau Reef

Solevu

Yaro

Uluisolo (220m)

Malolo Island

Lau Reef

Qalito Island

CASTAWAY ISLAND RESORT

Savuti Reef

LIKULIKU LAGOON RESORT

MALOLO ISLAND RESORT

WADIGI ISLAND VILLA

THE RESORT WALU BEACH

FUNKY FISH BEACH RESORT

Lana Reef

Volivoli Passage

Malolo Lailai Island

MUSKET COVE ISLAND RESORT

PLANTATION ISLAND RESORT

LOMANI ISLAND RESORT

MALOLO LAILAI AIRFIELD

GOLF COURSE

Tubasilaila Passage

Nuku Reef

Batanitovu Reef

1 mi

1 km

© DAVID STANLEY

tide. The resort is owned by the Whitton family of Nadi, which also runs Rosie Holidays. No backpacker dormitories here! Malolo Island Resort offers 30 oceanview bungalows at F$625 double, 18 deluxe oceanview bungalows at F$730, and one family bungalow at F$1,176 for up to seven persons. All but the family bungalow are duplexes so don't expect much privacy, despite the price. Up to two children under 12 can stay with their parents for free and there's a kids club on-site. The meal plan costs F$118 per person (half price for children under 12). Malolo Island Resort has a two-tier freshwater swimming pool, and most non-motorized water sports are free. Scuba diving with Subsurface Fiji costs extra.

Even more upscale is the couples-only **Likuliku Lagoon Resort** (tel. 666-3344, www.likulikulagoon.com), which opened just over the point from Malolo Island Resort in 2007. It's also owned by Rosie Holidays. The tightly packed accommodations here cost F$1,444 double for the 18 air-conditioned garden *bure,* F$1,734 for the 18 beachfront *bure,* and F$2,426 for the 10 Tahitian-style over-water *bure* with glass floors. Included are taxes, meals (drinks extra), and non-motorized water sports. Children under 17 are not permitted. The lagoon has been partly dredged to provide deeper swimming areas but at low tide the over-water bungalows are over mud. Likuliku Lagoon Resort is off limits to non-guests.

The *Tiger IV* catamaran arrives from Nadi's Port Denarau three times a day at F$85 each way. Malolo Island to Mana Island costs F$60. South Sea Cruises offers a day trip to Malolo Island Resort at F$145 including lunch and snorkeling gear (children half price).

THE SURFING CAMPS
Tavarua Island

Tavarua Island Resort (tel. 670-6513, www.tavarua.com), just south of Malololailai, is the South Pacific's most famous surfing resort. It caters to more affluent and mature surfers than the places on Viti Levu, Yanuca, and Kadavu. Although you can sometimes surf the same waves as the Tavarua crowd

from budget resorts like Seashell Cove and Rendezvous on the mainland, you won't have the constant immediate access to world-class breaks like Cloudbreak and Restaurants that you have here.

Guests are accommodated in 14 beach *bure* with hot showers and private bath, plus two larger family *bure.* The facilities have been upgraded, with a lagoon-style swimming pool and a large hot tub.

Tavarua formerly had exclusive access to some of Fiji's finest waves, including Cloudbreak, but this all changed in July 2010, when the Fiji Government allowed unrestricted use. Although other surfers are now able to use Cloudbreak on a daily basis, Tavarua still has the advantage of being located right next to the best waves. There are both lefts and rights in Malolo Passage at Tavarua, although the emphasis is usually on the lefts. When the swell is high enough, you'll have some of the best surfing anywhere in the world. On the off days you can get in some deep-sea fishing, windsurfing, snorkeling, or scuba diving (extra charge). Surfing guests are expected to have had at least three years of experience in a variety of conditions.

Bookings must be made six months in advance through **Tavarua Island Tours** (U.S. tel. 805/686-4551, www.tavarua.com) in Santa Barbara, California. The minimum stay is one week. Local bookings from within Fiji are not accepted, and they're usually sold out anyway, as Tavarua has become *the* place to go for top U.S. surfers.

Namotu Island

Just across Malolo Passage from Tavarua Island on tiny Namotu Island is **Namotu Island Resort** (tel. 670-6439, www.namotuisland fiji.com), a "Blue Water Sports Camp" for surfers. It's similar to Tavarua but slightly more accessible. They have one double *bure,* three triple *bure,* one villa with two double rooms, and two "VIP" dorm-style *bure* with six single beds in each. Children under 12 are generally not accepted.

All guests arrive on seven-night package

tours from Los Angeles, costing from US$3,703 per person including airfare, accommodations, meals (drinks extra), and unlimited access to the local surf breaks. All reservations must go through Waterways Travel in Santa Monica, California (www.waterwaystravel.com). Local bookings from within Fiji are possible only in January and February, if space happens to be available. However, Namotu is usually sold out.

You must bring your own surfboards, sailboards, and kite sails as none are available on the island. Snorkeling gear, kayaks, outrigger canoes, and wakeboards are loaned free of charge. Fishing is also included, although lost lures must be paid for. Scuba diving is arranged with Subsurface Fiji at F$110 per dive including gear. Massage also costs extra.

As at Tavarua, Namotu's market is mostly American water-sports enthusiasts who fly from the United States to ride Fiji's spectacular waves. Namotu Left is a world-class reef break that's more forgiving than its fearsome, famous neighbor Cloudbreak. The powerful right barrels of Wilkes Passage are good anywhere from one to three meters. Rounding out the scene is Swimming Pools, a playful, full wraparound right break on the leeward side of Namotu that, with its crystal-blue water and sheltered position, has to be one of the world's most remarkable breaks.

C Cloudbreak

Fiji's most famous surfing spot is Cloudbreak, a hollow left-breaking wave on the Navula Reef at the south end of the Mamanuca Group. At five meters, Cloudbreak is the thrill of a lifetime; at two meters, it's a longboarder's paradise. Cloudbreak barrels best in a southwest offshore wind, with tube rides of up to 200 meters possible. In summer (Dec.–Feb.), it can be flat, but otherwise Cloudbreak is consistently perfect. A few caveats are in order. First, Cloudbreak is an exposed reef break for experienced surfers only. Second, Tavarua Island Resort formerly had exclusive access to the wave through an agreement with the Fijian clan that claims *qoliqoli* (traditional fishing) rights in the area. In July 2010, the Fiji Government cancelled this agreement and opened Cloudbreak to surfers from other resorts (such as Seashell Cove and Surf & Dive Rendezvous on Viti Levu). This has led to overcrowding and you should seek the advice of other surfers who have used Cloudbreak recently or your resort operator.

THE TINY ISLANDS
C Beachcomber Island

Since the 1960s, Beachcomber Island (tel. 666-1500, www.beachcomberfiji.com), 18 kilometers west of Lautoka, has been "Club Med on a budget" for thousands of young travelers. Beachcomber still has its trademark sand-floor bar, dancing, and floor shows four nights a week, but the average guest has become a little older in recent years and the prices have crept up. These days, the bar closes and the music goes off at 0100. The island is so small that you can stroll around it in 10 minutes, but there's a white sandy beach and buildings nestled among coconut trees and tropical vegetation. A beautiful coral reef with well-fed fish extends far out on all sides, and scuba diving is available with Subsurface Fiji (F$130/230 for one/two tanks including gear; PADI Open Water certification F$740). A full range of other sporting activities is available at an additional charge (parasailing F$90, waterskiing F$80, Jet Skis F$80 for 15 minutes). If you don't enjoy water sports and the beach, you will quickly run out of things to do here.

Accommodations include all meals served buffet style. Most young backpackers opt for the big, open mixed dormitory where the 42 double-decker bunks (84 beds) cost F$119 each a night. Secure lockers are provided. The 16 simple lodge rooms at F$275/365 single/double (fridge and fan provided) are a good compromise for slightly older, budget-conscious couples. You can also get one of 16 thatched oceanview *bure* with ceiling fan, fridge, and private facilities for F$399/479/598 single/double/triple (plus F$50 for the six beachfront units). The *bure* are okay for young families, as children under 12 enjoy slightly reduced rates. Drinks at the bar are pricey, so a duty-free bottle purchased upon arrival at the airport will come in handy here.

Of course, there's also the F$150 round-trip boat ride from Nadi or Lautoka to consider. You can make a day trip to Beachcomber for F$105 if you only want a few hours in the sun. There's a free shuttle bus from all Nadi hotels to the wharf; the connecting catamaran leaves from Port Denarau daily at 0900, 1215, and 1515. From Lautoka, the pickup is daily at 1030 except Tuesday and Thursday. The *Yasawa Flyer II* picks up passengers for the Yasawas every morning at 0915, and it can also drop you off here on the way back to Nadi.

Bounty Island

Bounty Island Resort (tel. 666-6999, www .fiji-bounty.com), a poor cousin of nearby Treasure Island Resort, imitates the Beachcomber Island formula with 54 bunks in three dorms at F$44/48 per person without/with air-conditioning. The 22 fan-cooled beachfront *bure* are F$217/255 budget/deluxe. The meal plan (F$53 per person per day) is extra. At 20 hectares, Bounty is much larger than Beachcomber,

with more nature to explore; otherwise, most of the information for Beachcomber also applies here. Choose Bounty over Beachcomber if you like to party now and then but don't wish to be part of a 24-hour circus. Young British and European travelers on round-the-world tours often stay here, but Bounty Island might also suit families. The scuba diving is with Reef Safari. The snorkeling here is amazing, with lots of marine life. Transfers are via the Vuda Point Marina and cost F$65 per person each way including hotel pickups. The South Sea Cruises catamarans from the Denarau Marina at 0900, 1215, and 1500 will drop you here for F$65, and you can also transfer to the *Yasawa Flyer* at South Sea Island.

Castaway Island

Castaway Island Resort (tel. 666-1233, www.castawayfiji.com) sits on a sandy point at the western end of 174-hectare Qalito Island, just west of Malolo. This was Fiji's first outer-island resort, created by Dick Smith in 1966. Today it's owned by Geoff Shaw, who also owns the Outrigger on the Lagoon on the

the jetty at Bounty Island

Coral Coast. It has always been one of Fiji's most popular resorts. The 66 closely packed thatched *bure* sleep four at F$805 and up. No cooking facilities are provided, but the generous all-meal plan is F$99 per person (or F$49 for children under 13). The *lovo* and *meke* are on Wednesday night, the beach barbecue on Saturday.

Among the free non-motorized water sports are sailing, windsurfing, paddleboats, tennis, and snorkeling, but scuba diving and fishing are extra. There's a swimming pool. Many Australian holidaymakers return to Castaway year after year, and you should reserve far in advance. Castaway is marketed to families with small children but only four persons are allowed per *bure*—and infants count. A 10-person family *bure* will cost F$2,332. A free kids club operates daily 0900–2100 with lots of fun activities for those aged 3–12.

The catamaran *Tiger IV* calls here three times a day from Nadi's Port Denarau (F$85 each way). South Sea Cruises offers day trips to Castaway at F$145 including lunch and snorkeling gear (children F$105). Only 15 persons a day are allowed to book the day cruises, so inquire early.

Navini Island

🅒 **Navini Island Resort** (tel. 666-2188, www .navinifiji.com.fj) is a secluded eco-resort on a 2.5-hectare coral isle with just 10 beachfront *bure* nicely ensconced in the low island's shrubbery. If you're willing to risk being spoiled, Navini is the perfect first stop in Fiji. Rates vary from F$555 double for a fan-cooled unit with a motel-like bathroom and small beds to F$695 for the deluxe honeymoon *bure* with a bathtub and enclosed courtyard. Discounts are available for stays of more than a week and for children. The compulsory two-/three-meal package is F$98/110 per person a day; it's excellent food, and you have a choice. Everyone gets to know one another during pre-dinner cocktails and by eating together at long tables at fixed times. In the evening, you can also request private candlelit dining on the beach in front of your *bure*. Navini is ideal for couples

and families looking for a quiet holiday—those interested in an intense social life or lots of organized activities might get bored. Free morning boat trips are offered, as are snorkeling gear, paddleboats, sailboats, and kayaks. Scuba diving with Subsurface Fiji can be arranged, and the snorkeling right off the beach is good at high tide (there's abundant marine life, as fishing has been banned here for many years). Car/boat transfers from Nadi via the Vuda Point Marina are arranged anytime upon request (F$230 pp round-trip, or free if you stay a week). Only overnight guests are accepted (no day-trippers).

South Sea Island

South Sea Island (tel. 651-0506, www.ssc.com .fj) is a party island for young backpackers. This is one of the smallest Mamanuca islands, a sandbank reminiscent of the shipwreck cartoons. Thirty-two people are packed into a thatched dormitory upstairs in a two-story building at F$92 per person, with good buffet meals and lots of water sports included. Even though the beach is fine, the developers have constructed a tacky little swimming pool in the center of the island. Boat transfers from Nadi on the *Tiger IV* are F$55 each way, but many guests use the free stopover allowed here on *Yasawa Flyer* tickets to the Yasawa Islands. Awesome Adventures and South Sea Cruises deliver as many day-trippers to this tiny island as they possibly can. It's overcrowded and not as clean as it could be, but fine if swimming and socializing are the things you like most to do.

Treasure Island

Beachcomber's little neighbor, **Treasure Island Resort** (tel. 666-1599, www.treasureisland-fiji .com), is popular among packaged vacationers from New Zealand and Australia. The resort is half owned by the Tokatoka Nakelo landowning clan, which also supplies most of the workers, although the management is European. The 66 air-conditioned units, each with three single beds (F$570 single or double), are contained in 33 functional duplex bungalows packed into the greenery behind the island's white sands. Geckos control the insect population. Cooking facilities are not provided, so add F$119 per person daily for the meal plan (F$40 for children under 12). Otherwise, the food and drink available on the island is overpriced. A kids club attends to young guests under 15. Some nautical activities such as windsurfing, sailing, and canoeing are included and there's a swimming pool. Scuba diving with Subsurface Fiji (www .subsurfacefiji.com) is F$110/199 for one-/two-tank boat dives. Guests arrive on the shuttle boat *Tiger IV*, which departs Nadi's Port Denarau three times a day (F$75 each way, half price under age 16).

Wadigi Island

In 1998, **Wadigi Island Villa** (tel. 672-0901, www.wadigi.com) opened on the isle of the same name off the western end of Malolo. Each group of visitors gets exclusive use of the entire three-suite resort, costing F$4,300 per couple up to six persons maximum (minimum stay three nights). Included in the tariff are all meals, drinks, and sporting equipment

such as kayaks, windsurfers, spy boards, fishing rods, and snorkeling gear. Only deep-sea fishing, surfing trips, and scuba diving (with Subsurface Fiji) cost extra. Transfers to the island from Nadi are also not included.

MANA ISLAND

The only resort islands in the Mamanuca Group also inhabited by Fijian villagers are Mana and Malolo. Mana Island, 32 kilometers northwest of Nadi, is well known for its scuba diving and luxury resort, and over the past decade a whole slew of low-budget backpacker hostels have sprouted in the Fijian village on the eastern side of the island. There's much bad blood between the Japanese investors who run the resort and the Fijian villagers who accommodate the backpackers, and a high fence has been erected down the middle of the island to separate the two ends of the market. Uniformed security guards patrol the perimeter and shoestring travelers are most unwelcome anywhere in the resort, including the restaurants, shop, bars, and dive shop. In contrast, tourists from the resort are quite welcome

© DAVID STANLEY

Mana Island's South Beach is shared by a Fijian village, backpacker camps, and an upscale resort.

to order cheap drinks or meals at the backpacker camps.

Although this situation does poison the atmosphere on Mana Island slightly, there are lots of lovely beaches all around the island, most of them empty because the packaged tourists seldom stray far from their resort. The long white beach on the northeast side of the island is deserted. At the resort, the snorkeling is better off South Beach at low tide, off North Beach at high tide, but the nicest beach is Sunset Beach at the western end of Mana. There's a great view of the Mamanucas and southern Yasawas from the highest point on the island, a 10-minute hike from the backpacker camps, and splendid snorkeling on the reef. The Mana Main Reef is famous for its dropoffs, with visibility never less than 25 meters. You'll see turtles, fish of all descriptions, and the occasional crayfish.

The presence of the resort supports the frequent air and sea connections from Nadi, and the budget places allow you to enjoy Mana's stunning beauty at a fraction of the price tourists at the Japanese resort are paying. But to be frank, the backpacker facilities on Mana are rather squalid and the places in the Yasawa Islands offer better accommodations for only a bit more money.

Sports and Recreation

Resort guests may patronize **Aqua Trek Mana** (tel. 666-9309, www.aquatrekdiving.com), which offers boat dives at F$90 for one tank plus gear, or F$500 for a six-dive package. Night dives are F$120. They run a variety of dive courses, beginning with a four-day PADI Open Water certification course (F$700). Underwater shark feeding is Aqua-Trek Mana's specialty, usually every Wednesday and Saturday at 0830. Be prepared for lengthy briefings in Japanese. Aqua Trek doesn't accept divers from the backpacker camps, who must dive with Ratu Kini's dive operation (F$160/230 for a one-/two-tank dive).

Awesome Adventures (tel. 675-0499, www.awesomefiji.com) operates the water-sports concession on South Beach at the resort, offering waterskiing, Jet Skiing, water scooters, knee boarding, wakeboarding, sky riding, banana riding, and parasailing. Like Aqua-Trek, it discriminates against backpackers and only tourists from Mana Island Resort may use their services.

The Backpacker Camps

Right up against the security fence near an enclosed sentry box are the reception and dining areas of **Ratu Kini Backpackers** (tel. 672-1959, www.ratukini.brock.vg). The large accommodations buildings are 100 meters back in the village. The concrete main house has a 22-bunk dorm downstairs and a 26-bunk dorm upstairs, plus another four-bunk dorm in the corridor. Nearby are two thatched dormitory *bure* with seven and 14 bunks, all costing F$28 per person. The main house also contains three double rooms with shared bath at F$100, and six better rooms with private bath at F$130. A thatched four-bed family *bure* in the backyard is F$170 double. Have a look around before committing yourself, as all of the rooms are different. Breakfast is included but other meals cost extra (on Wednesdays or Thursdays, they prepare a *lovo*). Full-day boat trips and two-hour snorkeling trips can be arranged if four people want to go. Ratu Kini works out of office No. 26 upstairs from arrivals at Nadi Airport. There's an electricity generator but expect water shortages, occasional overcrowding, nocturnal animal sounds, mediocre meals, a party atmosphere, and a lack of privacy in the mixed dorms. Unattended gear may disappear from the beach.

Rara Cava's █ **Mana Lodge** (tel. 993-4177, manalodge2@yahoo.com) is on the beach nearby. There's an 18-bed dorm at F$60 per person, four fan-cooled beach *bure* with private bath at F$160 double, and one six-person family *bure* at F$200. All rooms have ceiling fans and meals are included. Camping with your own tent is F$40 per person including meals. Mana Lodge has a large beach bar where a *lovo* meal is served on Friday nights (F$10). The food and accommodations are a step up from Ratu Kini.

Mana Lagoon Backpackers (tel. 929-2337)

nearby offers dorm beds at F$55 and rooms with shared bath for F$130, meals included. Their beachfront dining area has picnic tables on a sandy floor.

Mana Island Resort

Juxtaposed against the backpacker camps is Mana Island Resort (tel. 665-0423, www .manafiji.com), by far the biggest of the tourist resorts off Nadi, with numerous tin-roofed bungalows clustered between the island's grassy rounded hilltops, white sandy beaches, and crystal-clear waters. A spa was added in 2007. The 53 "island bungalows" are F$320 single or double, while the 52 "deluxe oceanview bungalows" are F$400. The 12 "executive oceanview bungalows" are F$480. Thirty newer "oceanfront suites" in a hotel section near the wharf are F$600. Then there are the six "beachfront bungalows" with hot tub at F$680 and seven "honeymoon bungalows" west of the airstrip at F$800. Flashpackers who find Ratu Kini's too basic can get a third off these rates by requesting the walk-in special. Mana Island Resort caters to people of all ages and has a daily kids club program. Children under 13 sleep free if sharing with one or two adults. About half the guests here are Japanese. Some non-motorized water sports are included, but add 17.5 percent tax. Cooking facilities are not provided, so you'll need to patronize the resort restaurants (entrées F$28 and up). Live entertainment is presented nightly, and there's a Fijian *meke* on Tuesday and a Polynesian show on Friday.

Getting There

In July 2010, Pacific Sun discontinued scheduled service between Nadi and the airstrip on Mana, and only charter flights now service the island. The terminal is a seven-minute walk west of the resort (to get to the backpacker camps, head for the wharf, from which the security fence will be visible).

The *Tiger IV* catamaran operates three times a day between Port Denarau and Mana Island (F$89 each way including Nadi hotel pickups). Otherwise, South Sea Cruises runs a day trip from Nadi, including lunch at Mana Island

Resort for F$135 (children under 16 half price). The ferry ties up to a wharf at South Beach. In fact, Mana is the only Mamanuca island with a wharf, so you don't need to take off your shoes when you disembark.

Ratu Kini's own shuttle boat leaves Wailoaloa Beach daily at 1100, costing F$50 one-way including bus transfers from Nadi hotels. Mana Lodge and Mana Lagoon guests use the *Mana Flyer*, which departs Wailoaloa Beach daily at 1030 (F$55 one-way). The agent at Wailoaloa Beach is the Tropic of Capricorn Resort, which also handles accommodations bookings. Other Nadi travel agencies and hotels can also book these transfers.

THE OUTER ISLANDS
Matamanoa Island

To the northwest of Mana Island, **Matamanoa Island Resort** (tel. 672-3620, www.mata manoa.com) has 13 air-conditioned motel-style rooms at F$425 single or double, and 20 fan-cooled *bure* at F$685, tax included. Children under 16 are not accepted. The full American breakfast included in the basic price is okay, but the same cannot be said of the lunch and dinner (limited choice, same all the time, too much deep-frying). Even so, the meal plan costs F$98 per person extra. Complimentary afternoon tea is served at the bar, followed by snacks during happy hour 1730–1830. Bring along a few packets of instant soup and some freeze-dried food, so you can spare yourself the meals! Loud cruise-ship-style entertainment is laid on at meal times and during the evening. The tiny island's beach is complemented by a small swimming pool and spa. Scuba diving is with Viti Watersports (tel. 670-2413, www .vitiwatersports.com), although the snorkeling is better than the diving.

Boat transfers from Nadi on the high-speed catamaran *Cougar* cost F$110 per person each way. The ferry departs Port Denarau at 1515.

◖ Monuriki Island

Matamanoa is the closest resort island to Monuriki, the uninhabited island seen in the Tom Hanks film *Castaway*. On this paradise

CASTAWAY, THE MOVIE

In early 2001, moviegoers worldwide got a taste of the savage beauty of Fiji's westernmost islands from Robert Zemeckis' film *Castaway*. The story revolves around a FedEx employee (Tom Hanks) who is stranded on an uninhabited tropical isle after his plane goes down in the Pacific. The plane-wrecked air courier eventually spends four years on the island, and to achieve the desperate look needed to play his role, Hanks had to lose 40 pounds and grow a ragged beard. Thus *Castaway* was filmed in two stages eight months apart, with the second portion shot on location in the western Mamanucas in early 2000. For this event, about 100 members of the film crew descended on tiny **Monuriki Island,** between Matamanoa and Tokoriki.

At the time, concerns were raised that there might be a repeat of the damaging controversy surrounding the filming of *The Beach* in Thailand, when the producers were accused of inflicting environmental damage on Maya Beach in Krabi's Phi Phi Islands National Park. To avoid this, Zemeckis was careful to have veteran naturalist and author Dick Watling do an environmental-impact assessment before the filming, and the film crew followed Watling's recommendations carefully. Later, when naturalists from the World Wide Fund for Nature in Suva investigated the affair, they gave Zemeckis and his team high marks.

Ironically, 50-odd feral goats have long ravaged the vegetation on Monuriki, threatening the island's rare crested iguanas with extinction. The filmmakers offered to pay the Fijian landowners a bounty of F$100 per goat to remove the beasts, but their offer was refused.

To Monuriki's customary owners on nearby Yanuya Island, a steady supply of goat meat is worth more than money or iguanas. Although no Fijians appear in *Castaway*, it conveys well the spellbinding scenery of this exotic region. To see the island off-screen, day cruises to Monuriki, such as the one offered by **South Sea Cruises** (tel. 675-0500, www.ssc.com.fj) on the two-masted schooner *Seaspray* (F$185 with lunch and drinks), can be booked through hotel tour desks in Nadi.

© MARK WHATMOUGH

Monuriki Island

island, green volcanic slopes fall to a high white beach facing a broad lagoon perfect for snorkeling. You'd probably need a guide to find the rare crested iguanas that dwell high up in the island's trees. The endangered hawksbill turtle is often seen in the lagoon off Monuriki. Sheer cliffs on the back side of the island make it impossible to walk right around Monuriki.

The schooner *Seaspray* (tel. 675-0500, www

.ssc.com.fj) operates all-inclusive day cruises to Monuriki, and passengers have a chance to go ashore for snorkeling or exploration. You can board the *Seaspray* at Matamanoa (F$150) or Mana (F$150), or do it as a day trip from Nadi (F$185), departing the Denarau Marina at 0900. Lunch and drinks are included, and any Nadi tour desk can book the trip (Nadi hotel transfers are also included).

Tokoriki Island

Tokoriki Island Resort (tel. 672-5926, www.tokoriki.com) is the farthest Mamanuca resort from Nadi and the most private and secluded. There are 29 spacious fan-cooled *bure* from F$922 single or double (no cooking facilities). Some units are better than others (beware of generator noise). The five new honeymoon villas with private pools are F$1,267. The three-meal plan is F$140 per person (the food and service are inconsistent, so bring along some snack food). To appeal to romantic couples, children under 12 are not accepted. Instead, there's a wedding chapel. Unfortunately the house band seems to specialize in non-Fijian music and the compulsory group welcomes and farewells are rather embarrassing. There are two pools. This upscale resort faces west on a seaweed beach with good swimming. Non-motorized water sports such as reef fishing, windsurfing, and Hobie cats are free (sportfishing available at additional charge). Scuba diving with Tokoriki Diving (www.tokorikidiving.com) also costs extra. At the center of the island is a 94-meter-high hill offering good views of the Yasawa and Mamanuca groups.

Separated from Tokoriki Island Resort by a barbed wire fence is the less expensive **Amunuca Island Resort** (tel. 664-0640, www.amunuca.com), which opened on Tokoriki Island in 2007. Construction deficiencies have already led to maintenance problems. The 98 air-conditioned rooms range from rainforest studios (F$253) to beachfront suites (F$664 single or double) with a few other categories crowded in between. A meal plan is not available at Amunuca Island Resort and all meals must be ordered à la carte. Amunuca attempts to cater both to families with children and romantic couples who would rather not see or hear children. A separate adults-only swimming pool and restaurant are provided, in addition to the "general" restaurant and pool.

There's a kids club accepting those aged 3–12 (when operating), so parents may also be able to escape their offspring. Adults can repair to the reasonably priced bamboo spa. Reef Safari (www.reefsafari.com.fj) arranges scuba diving at Amunuca.

The fast catamaran *Cougar* leaves Port Denarau for Tokoriki daily at 1515 (F$110 pp each way). Pacific Island Seaplanes (tel. 672-5644, www.fijiseaplanes.com) and Island Hoppers (tel. 672-0410, www.helicopters.com.fj) offer air transfers to Tokoriki and Matamanoa.

Vomo Island

Standing alone midway between Lautoka and Wayasewa Island, 87-hectare Vomo is a triangular high volcanic island with a white beach around its western side. The view from the top of the hill is spectacular. Since 1993, the coral terrace and slopes behind this beach have been the site of the high-priced **Vomo Island Resort** (tel. 666-7955, www.vomofiji.com), managed by Sofitel. The 29 air-conditioned duplex and freestanding villas with individual hot tubs range in price from F$1,250–3,500 single or double, including all meals (but not drinks) and non-motorized activities, plus 17.5 percent tax (minimum stay three nights). Families with children are welcome—romantic couples take note. Individual units are advertised for sale as timeshares on www.vomovillas.com. Once part of the Sheraton chain, Vomo Island Resort offers swimming and snorkeling infinitely better than anything at Denarau. The nine-hole pitch-and-putt golf course is free to guests. South Sea Cruises operates the fast catamaran *Yasawa Flyer II* from Nadi's Port Denarau to Vomo Island daily at 0830 (F$145 one-way). You can also arrive by air on Pacific Island Seaplanes (tel. 672-5644, www.fijiseaplanes.com) or Island Hoppers (tel. 672-0410, www.helicopters.com.fj).

THE YASAWA ISLANDS

The Yasawas are a chain of 16 large volcanic islands and dozens of smaller ones, stretching 80 kilometers in a north-northeast direction, roughly 35 kilometers off the west coast of Viti Levu. In the lee of Viti Levu, the Yasawas are dry and sunny, with beautiful, isolated beaches, cliffs, bays, and reefs. The waters are crystal clear and almost totally shark-free. The group was romanticized in two movies about a pair of child castaways who grow up and fall in love on a deserted isle. The 1949 version of *The Blue Lagoon* starred Jean Simmons, while the 1980 remake featured Brooke Shields. (A 1991 sequel starring Milla Jovovich, *Return to the Blue Lagoon,* was filmed on Taveuni.)

It was from the north end of the Yasawas that two canoe-loads of cannibals sallied forth and gave chase to Captain William Bligh and

his 18 companions in 1789, less than a week after the famous mutiny. More than two centuries later, increasing numbers of ferries and mini cruise ships ply the islands, but there are still few motorized land vehicles or roads. The $2,000-a-day crowd is whisked straight to Turtle Island by seaplane, while most backpackers arrive from Nadi on the high-speed catamaran.

Super-exclusive Turtle Island Resort and the backpacker camps on Tavewa Island have coexisted for decades, but only since 2000 have the Yasawans themselves recognized the moneymaking potential of tourism. Now a bumper crop of low-budget "resorts" has burst forth, up and down the chain, as the villagers rush to cash in. The **Nacula Tikina Tourism Association** (tel. 672-2921,

THE YASAWA ISLANDS

HIGHLIGHTS

◖ Vatuvula Peak: The invigorating hike up this towering volcanic plug provides a superb view of Wayasewa and Kuata islands with Viti Levu on the horizon (page 80).

◖ Waya Island: The mountains and cliffs of Waya are picturesque from sea, and there are great beaches, good hiking, and welcoming villages for those who stay in any of the island's small resorts (page 80).

◖ Tavewa Island: Tavewa was the first of the Yasawa Islands to be developed for backpacker tourism, and the swimming and snorkeling are still good. The natural beauty of the Blue Lagoon spreads before hikers who climb to Tavewa's highest peak (page 84).

◖ Nacula Island: Nacula has everything the Yasawa traveler could desire, including Long Beach with excellent snorkeling just off its high white sands, optimum hiking along the grassy hillsides of Nacula's interior, and some of the most appealing small resorts in the chain (page 87).

◖ Sawa-i-Lau Island: Swimmers can pass through an underwater opening between the two portions of the island's limestone sea cave featured in legend and film (page 90).

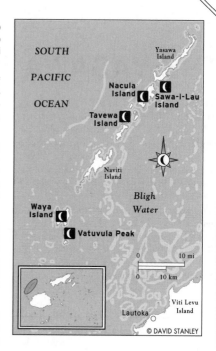

LOOK FOR ◖ TO FIND RECOMMENDED SIGHTS, ACTIVITIES, DINING, AND LODGING.

www.fijibudget.com) coordinates the development of locally owned backpacker resorts on the central islands around the Blue Lagoon. Thankfully, the resorts associated with the scheme have committed to a code of conduct to preserve and protect the natural environment. Some of the backpacker resorts are better than others, but shared bathrooms, a lack of electricity, water shortages, and variable food are to be expected. What you pay for is the superb natural beauty of this region. The sun-drenched beaches, blue lagoons, panoramic open hillsides, and dazzling reefs are truly magnificent.

PLANNING YOUR TIME

Considering the expense involved in just getting to the Yasawa Islands, the recommended minimum stay is one week. With two or three nights at several different resorts, you can easily visit two or three islands in that time. A fast ferry links the main islands (Kuata, Wayasewa, Waya, Naviti, and Nacula) every day. From Nacula or Tavewa, you can visit several other islands around the Blue Lagoon.

A good plan is to go straight through from Port Denarau to Nacula on your first day, then slowly work your way back down to Nadi. This has two advantages. First, you'll get an idea where you want to stop on the southbound trip from what you see on the way north. Second, since the return boat passes in the afternoon, you'll get an extra morning on the beach at all stops. There will be no need to get up early to catch the northbound boat and everyone who is leaving will have left by the time you get to your resort (you won't have to hang around waiting for someone to vacate their room).

The Yasawas are on the dry side of Fiji, so travel is comfortable throughout the year. Even so, it's risky to schedule a return to Nadi on the same day you must catch an international flight, as bad weather can lead to the cancellation of all boat trips. This does happen at times, and even allowing two days' leeway won't be sufficient if a hurricane warning has been issued. December–April is the official hurricane season, but hurricanes can also occur in November, May, and June.

RESORT BOOKING TIPS

At Nadi Airport, the **Turtle Island Resort office** (tel. 672-2921, nacula@hotmail.com),

on the left in the arrivals concourse, should be able to provide information about the Yasawa Islands resorts. Other booking agents at Nadi Airport include **Western Travel Services** (tel. 672-3612) in office No. 4 upstairs from arrivals, **Sunset Tours** in office No. 21, and **Rabua's Travel Agency** (tel. 672-1377 or 672-3234, dreammakertravel@yahoo.com) in office No. 23. There are also resort-specific booking offices.

Only book your first two nights if you wish to allow yourself the flexibility of moving elsewhere after arrival or bargaining for a lower rate. The Nadi travel agents take 30 percent commission, so you can often get a better deal by booking directly over the phone. Many of the Yasawa backpacker resorts have radio telephones. Dial 666-6644, listen for two beeps, then key in the extension. Only one party can speak at a time over these connections. If you don't mind sleeping in a dorm or are packing a tent, you could just show up without reservations.

Most of the rates quoted in this chapter

Bure such as these await backpackers traveling to the Yasawa Islands.

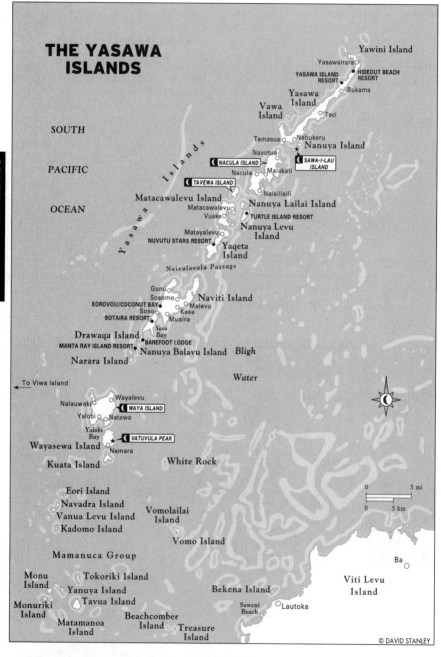

THE YASAWA ISLANDS

Yawini Island

Yasawairara

YASAWA ISLAND RESORT
HIDEOUT BEACH RESORT

Bukama

Yasawa Island

Vawa Island

Teci

SOUTH

Tamasua
Nabukeru

Navotua

Nanuya Island

PACIFIC

NACULA ISLAND

SAWA-I-LAU ISLAND

Nacula
Malakati

TAVEWA ISLAND

OCEAN

Naisilisili

Matacawalevu Island

Nanuya Lailai Island

Matacawalevu

Yasawa Islands

Vuake

TURTLE ISLAND RESORT

Nanuya Levu Island

Matayalevu

NUVUTU STARS RESORT

Yaqeta Island

Naivalavala Passage

Gunu

Sosomo

Naviti Island

KOROVOU/COCONUT BAY
Malevu

Soso
Kese

BOTAIRA RESORT
Muaira

Soso Bay

Drawaqa Island
BAREFOOT LODGE

MANTA RAY ISLAND RESORT
Nanuya Balavu Island
Bligh

Narara Island
Water

← To Viwa Island

Wayalevu

Nalauwaki
WAYA ISLAND

Yalobi
Natawa

Yalobi Bay
VATUVULA PEAK

Wayasewa Island
Namara

Kuata Island
White Rock

Eori Island

Navadra Island

Vanua Levu Island
Vomolailai Island

Kadomo Island

Vomo Island

Mamanuca Group

Ba

Monu Island
Tokoriki Island

Yanuya Island
Tavua Island

Monuriki Island
Viti Levu Island

Matamanoa Island
Beachcomber Island
Saweni Beach
Lautoka

Treasure Island

Bekena Island

0   5 mi
0   5 km

© DAVID STANLEY

THE YASAWA ISLANDS

include all meals and taxes (although some have adopted the practice of quoting rates with meals and tax additional). Virtually all of the resorts have mixed dormitories, where you pay per person and *bure* are intended for two persons. Singles who don't wish to sleep in the dormitory are at a disadvantage, as many resorts charge the same single or double for their *bure,* even though they only have to feed one person instead of two. The Yasawas backpacker resorts are ideal for campers, as most have unlimited tent space. Campers with their own tents pay slightly less than people in the dorm.

You shouldn't expect gourmet cuisine at any of the backpacker resorts, and at times the meals can be pretty basic. A vegetarian meal is often simply the standard plate with the meat removed. At times, it seems like the numerous vegetarian requests have resulted in plates of cabbage and rice being served to one and all! You should ask other travelers for their opinion of the food at the places where they stayed—just keep in mind that the person's standards and expectations may be different from yours, as impressions vary considerably. All too often, what you pay for isn't what you get.

MONEY

Don't expect to be able to use your credit card in the Yasawas (although Oarsman's Bay Lodge on Nacula accepts *only* credit cards). Changing foreign currency is also usually not possible. Thus it's important to bring along sufficient Fijian currency in cash. Even if you've prepaid all your food, accommodations, and inter-island transportation, you'll still need a minimum of F$25 per person extra per day to cover alcoholic drinks, bottled water, excursions, equipment rentals, and the like (take snack foods with you). The more optional activities you plan to book, the more cash you'll need. Failure to accurately budget for your expenses may force you to return to Nadi early or miss out on some activities. Also, take care where you leave your money while at lunch or on the beach as theft from the rooms is not unheard of. Always lock your bags when going out.

Prices continue to creep up in the Yasawas,

and on a visit of a week or less, you'll spend at least F$125 per person a day on transportation, food, and dormitory accommodations alone. On stays of more than a week, the transportation component falls exponentially and long-stay discounts kick in.

GETTING THERE AND AROUND

Turtle Airways (tel. 672-1888, www.turtleair ways.com) charges F$299 per person one-way (minimum of two travelers) to the Yasawas, plus a 10 percent surcharge if you pay by credit card. The total body weight for two passengers plus luggage should not exceed 175 kilograms, as the Cessna seaplane carries four passengers and has a weight maximum of 350 kilograms. It only takes 30 minutes by air from Turtle's Nadi base at Wailoaloa Beach to go all the way to the seaplane landing area off Nacula Island. The emerald lagoons and colorful reefs are truly dazzling when seen from above.

The vast majority of visitors arrive on the fast 25-meter catamaran *Yasawa Flyer II* operated by **Awesome Adventures** (tel. 675-0499, www.awesomefiji.com), a subsidiary of South Sea Cruises. The *Yasawa Flyer II* zips up and down the Yasawa chain daily, leaving Nadi's Port Denarau at 0830 and arriving at Bounty Island at 0905, Beachcomber Island at 0915, Kuata at 1030, Waya at 1045, Naviti at 1155, and Nacula at 1300. The return trip leaves Nacula at 1300, with stops at Naviti at 1420, Waya at 1530, Kuata at 1545, Beachcomber Island at 1700, and reaching Port Denarau at 1745. Fares from Nadi are F$100 one-way to Kuata or Waya, F$110 to Naviti, and F$120 to Nacula or Tavewa, bus transfers in Nadi and Lautoka included. Inter-island fares within the Yasawas vary between F$35 from Kuata to Octopus Resort, F$60 from Waya to Naviti, or F$75 from Kuata to Nacula.

Awesome Adventures also offers a "Bula Pass," which includes one round-trip transfer between Nadi and Nacula on the *Yasawa Flyer II,* with unlimited stops at Kuata, Wayalailai, Waya, Naviti, or anywhere else along the route. The Bula Pass costs F$391/535/628 for 7/14/21

THE YASAWA ISLANDS

© TIM PARKINSON/FLICKR.COM/TIMPARKINSON

Yasawa Flyer II at Naviti

consecutive days, and is worth considering if you plan to make a stop or two on the way to Nacula. The main limitation is that only one trip back to Nadi is included. The moment you disembark at Port Denarau your pass becomes invalid even if there are still days left on it. The pass can also be used on the South Sea Cruises shuttle to South Sea Island, Bounty, Beachcomber, Mana, and Malolo, although you may connect only to/from the *Yasawa Flyer II* at South Sea Island and not at Port Denarau. Though there are 250 seats on the ferry, reservations are sometimes necessary. Each individual trip segment can be booked at the time you buy your pass, so it's a good idea to work out an itinerary in advance. Reservations can also be made by phone 24 hours in advance.

Expect to come under serious pressure to pre-book your Yasawa accommodations from airport touts and Awesome Adventures staff. The easiest option is the Awesome Adventures "Bula Combo Pass" which includes transportation, accommodations, and (sometimes) meals at F$781/1,380/1,928 for 7/14/21 consecutive days in dormitories or F$871/1,575/2,228 per

person double occupancy in rooms or *bure*. Meals are included at the cheaper properties but cost extra at the more upscale places. You select where you want to stay from the resorts on their list. Other packages include scuba diving. The packages carry heavy cancellation penalties if not used exactly as specified but they're quite convenient if you're willing to go with the flow. If you don't like being herded, consider changing your plans and going to Taveuni instead. Skip the packages, which include all sorts of add-ons you can purchase for the same price once you're there.

The "yellow boat" (as people call the *Yasawa Flyer II*) is the safest and most comfortable way to go and any travel agency in Fiji can book Awesome Adventures services. There are no refunds on unused tickets. Outboards from the backpacker resorts pick up passengers from the *Yasawa Flyer II*'s rear deck and transfer them to the beach. A few resorts do this for free, but most will charge you F$10 or so per person each way to go ashore (none of the islands has a wharf). Know where your backpack is at *Yasawa Flyer II* stops, as cases of people grabbing the wrong pack in the rush to disembark do occur. Stock up on bottled water every time you're on the *Flyer* as it's half the price you'll pay on land.

If you only want a brief taste of the Yasawas, **South Sea Cruises** (tel. 675-0500, www.ssc .com.fj) sells quickie day trips from Nadi to a village on Waya Island (F$130), Octopus Resort (F$150), and Botaira Beach Resort on Naviti Island (F$145). You leave Port Denarau on the *Yasawa Flyer II* at 0830 and have 4.5 hours on Waya or 2.5 hours on Naviti. Lunch is included.

A few of the Yasawa backpacker camps have boats of their own from Lautoka, and when booking with them, it's best to avoid prepaying your return boat fare. Safety can be an issue on some of the smaller resort and village boats, which often carry more passengers than life jackets (if any). One traveler reported that the local boat he was on ran out of gas a kilometer short of Lautoka and ended up drifting in high seas until it bumped into a container ship that radioed for help. Cases of local boats being lost at sea are not unknown. There are few government controls over the village boats, and they aren't that much cheaper than the perfectly safe *Yasawa Flyer II*.

KUATA ISLAND

Kuata is the *Yasawa Flyer II*'s first stop in the Yasawa Islands. Like neighboring Wayasewa and Waya, it's a scenically spectacular island, though without any Fijian villages. You can climb to the island's summit (171 m) for a great view. With a buddy, you could also snorkel across the open channel to Wayasewa in half an hour, although this activity involves obvious risks, and we cannot recommend it.

The **Kuata Island Resort** (tel. 651-0504), on a nice beach on the side of the island facing Wayasewa, is a backpacker place with dormitories of 10 or 20 beds at F$65 per person and 15 basic thatched *bure* with private bath at F$160 double. Camping is F$45 per person. Three meals of average quality are included. There's no electricity and fussy travelers should look elsewhere, but the location is great. An optimum snorkeling area is just across the point on the southwest side of Kuata. Look for the cave near the seagull rocks at the point itself. You'll pay F$10 per person for the transfer from the *Yasawa Flyer II*.

WAYASEWA ISLAND

Wayalailai Resort (tel. 651-2292, www.way alailairesort.com) is spectacularly situated on the south side of Wayasewa opposite Kuata Island. It's directly below Wayasewa's highest peak, Vatuvula (349 m), with Viti Levu clearly visible behind Vomo Island to the east. Photos don't do this place justice.

This large backpacker camp is built on two terraces, one 10 meters above the beach and the other 10 meters above that. The lower terrace has the double, duplex, and dormitory *bure*, while the upper terrace accommodates the restaurant/bar and the former village schoolhouse of Namara village, now partitioned into 14 tiny double rooms. Simple rooms with shared bath and open ceiling in the school building are F$60 per person (a good option for singles), while the five individual *bure* with private bath and a small porch are F$150 double. A beach cottage is F$180. One duplex *bure* with four beds on each side serves as an eight-bed dormitory or *burebau* at F$60 per person. The camping space nearby is F$45 per person. The minimum stay is three nights. Upon arrival, ask the staff to change the sheets, if they haven't already done so.

Three meals are included in all rates (but drinks cost extra). Wednesday evening, a *lovo* is prepared. An electric generator is used in the evening, and there's no shortage of water. Informal musical entertainment occurs nightly, and because this resort is collectively owned by the village, the staff is like one big happy family. The pleasant atmosphere more than makes up for the rather basic rooms and *bure*.

There's lots to see and do at Wayalailai, with hiking and scuba diving the main activities. Aside from scuba and snorkeling trips, the resort's dive shop, Dive Trek Wayasewa, offers a PADI Open Water certification course. For groups of six or more, there are snorkeling trips to a reef halfway to Vomo.

Naqalia Lodge (tel. 624-0532 or 672-4274, www.naqalialodge-yasawa.com) is a friendly new place to stay that opened near the southeast tip of Wayasewa Island in 2009. The five beachfront *bure* with private bath are F$200 double and there's a 10-bed dorm at F$75 per person. Camping is F$55 per person in a set tent or F$45 per person with your own tent. Meals and afternoon tea are included in all rates. The beach is good and there's an even better one with great snorkeling over the ridge.

CANNIBALISM

It has been said that the Fijians were extremely hospitable to any strangers they did not wish to eat. Native voyagers who wrecked on their shores, who arrived "with salt water in their eyes," were liable to be killed and eaten, since all shipwrecked persons were believed to have been cursed and abandoned by the gods. Many European sailors from wrecked vessels shared the same fate. Cannibalism was a universal practice, and prisoners taken in war, even women seized while fishing, were invariably eaten. Most of the early European accounts of Fiji emphasized this trait to the exclusion of almost everything else; at one time, the island group was referred to as the "Cannibal Isles." By eating the flesh of the conquered enemy, one inflicted the ultimate revenge. One chief on Viti Levu is said to have consumed 872 people and to have made a pile of stones to record his achievement. The leaves of a certain vegetable (*Solanum uporo*) were wrapped around the human meat, and it was cooked in an earthen oven. Since the fingers and lips of chiefs and priests were taboo, and the attendants who normally fed them were banned from the spirit house during cannibal feasts, the chiefs used wooden forks to feed themselves, and these objects themselves became taboo as a result and were kept as relics (the notion that the forks were used because Fijian cannibals didn't wish to touch human flesh is false).

The Awesome Adventures shuttle from Nadi is F$100 one-way. Passengers on the *Yasawa Flyer II* are picked up by a boat from Wayalailai at Kuata (F$10 each way). Rabua's Travel Agency (tel. 672-1377 or 672-3234, dreammakertravel@yahoo.com), in office No. 23 upstairs at Nadi Airport, takes Wayalailai bookings.

Vatuvula Peak

The most popular hike on Wayasewa is to the top of Vatuvula Peak, the fantastic volcanic plug hanging directly over the Wayalailai Resort. The well-trodden path circles the mountain and comes up the back, taking about 1.5 hours total excluding stops from the resort (a guide really isn't necessary). From the top of Vatuvula, you get a sweeping view of the west side of Viti Levu, the Mamanucas, and the southern half of the Yasawa chain—one of the scenic highlights of the South Pacific. From Vatuvula, you can trek northwest across the grassy uplands to another rock with a good view of Yalobi Bay (also known as Alacrity Bay).

WAYA ISLAND

The high island clearly visible to the northwest of Lautoka is Waya, closest of the larger Yasawas to Viti Levu and just 60 kilometers away. At 579 meters, it's also the highest island in the chain. Waya is an excellent choice for the hyperactive traveler, as the hiking possibilities are unlimited. The beaches are very nice, and it's a great place to experience unspoiled Fijian culture. So if you can live with a few rough edges, Waya is *the* place to go.

Four Fijian villages are sprinkled around Waya: Nalauwaki, Natawa, Wayalevu, and Yalobi. The rocky mass of Batinareba (510 m) towers over the western side of Yalobi Bay, and in a morning or afternoon you can scramble up the mountain's rocky slope from the western end of the beach at Yalobi. Go through the forested saddle on the south side of the highest peak, and follow the grassy ridge on the far side all the way down to Loto Point. Many wild goats are seen along the way. An easier hike from Yalobi leads southeast from the school to the sandbar over to Wayasewa.

One of the most memorable walks in the South Pacific involves spending two hours on a well-used trail from Yalobi to Nalauwaki village. Octopus Resort is just a 10-minute walk west over a low ridge, and from there it's possible to hike back to Yalobi down Waya's west coast and across Loto Point in another two or three hours. Due to rocky headlands lapped by the sea, you can only go down the west coast at low tide, thus one must set out from Yalobi at high tide and from Octopus at low tide. It's a great way to fill a day.

Accommodations

The **Sunset Waya Resort** (tel. 672-4274, www.sunsetwaya resort.com) is right next to the sandbar that links Waya to Wayasewa. The five simple *bure* are F$250 double and the 20-bed dorm F$60 per person, basic meals included. Camping is also possible. The staff is friendly and the food okay. Scuba diving is available, and there's good snorkeling right offshore anytime. At low tide it's possible to cross to Wayasewa without removing your shoes, and two villages, Naboro and Yamata, are nearby. It's even possible to hike over the mountains to the Wayalailai Resort in about three hours. However, the vast majority of guests headed for the three backpacker places in this area, Sunset, Bayside, and Adi's, arrive on the *Yasawa Flyer II,* which stops nearby (transfers ashore F$10).

A 30-minute walk northwest toward Yalobi village is the **Bayside Resort** (tel. 672-2600, www.baysideresortfiji.com), run by a guy named Manasa, the brother of Adi Sayaba of Adi's Place. Count on paying about F$90/140 single/double, including meals, to stay in one

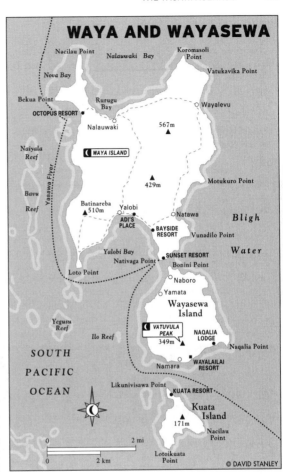

WAYA AND WAYASEWA

Nacilau Point · Nalauwaki Bay · Koromasoli Point · Vatukavika Point · Nova Bay · Bekua Point · Rurugu Bay · OCTOPUS RESORT · Wayalevu · Nalauwaki · 567m · Naiyala Reef · WAYA ISLAND · 429m · Motukuro Point · Bavu · Batinareba · 510m · Yalobi · ADI'S PLACE · BAYSIDE RESORT · Natawa · *Bligh* · Vunadilo Point · Yalobi Bay · SUNSET RESORT · *Water* · Nativaga Point · Bonini Point · Loto Point · Naboro · Yamata · Yegusu Reef · **Wayasewa Island** · Ilo Reef · VATUVULA PEAK · 349m · NAQALIA LODGE · Naqalia Point · **SOUTH PACIFIC OCEAN** · Namara · WAYALAILAI RESORT · Likunivisawa Point · KUATA RESORT · **Kuata Island** · 171m · Nacilau Point · 0 — 2 mi · 0 — 2 km · Lotoikuata Point · © DAVID STANLEY

of the two simple *bure* here. Expect nothing more than a beautiful beach and you won't be disappointed.

Adi's Place (tel. 665-0573, www.wayais land.com), at Yalobi village on the south side of Waya, is a small family-operated resort in existence since 1981. Although rather primitive, it still makes a good hiking base, with prices designed to attract and hold those on the barest of budgets. The accommodations consist of one eight-bunk dorm at F$55 per person and four *bure* at F$130. Lighting is by kerosene lamp. The rates include three meals of variable quality. The beach looks good from shore, but it's hard to swim here due to the corals (and you shouldn't leave valuables unattended on this beach). It's all a little messy and shouldn't be your first choice.

On a high white-sand beach in Likuliku Bay on northwestern Waya is **Octopus Resort** (tel. 666-6337, www.octopusresort.com). This popular flashpacker resort from way back tries hard to cater to both ends of the market. The 14 comfortable but not luxurious *bure* come in seven different categories. There are five bungalows with shared bath at F$319 double. The four beachfront "point" *bure* are F$589–639. The three suites in a triplex go for F$619. One garden *bure* has been converted into a deluxe dorm at F$140 per person. There's also a 15-bed dorm at F$110 per person. The minimum stay is two nights and a generator provides electricity. All rates include tax and the compulsory meal plan (choice at lunch, if you arrive early). Drinks are served at the large restaurant/bar (extra charge). Octopus has its own dive shop, which offers PADI certification courses. The snorkeling here is best at high tide (beware of getting cut on coral at low tide). Watch out if you're only swimming, as the bottom drops off fast. Lots of other activities are arranged. The Awesome Adventures ferry *Yasawa Flyer II* from Nadi is F$100 each way. Some readers have reported confusion over their reservations and bills at Octopus, so be sure to review all charges.

VIWA ISLAND

Viwa Island sits alone, 30 kilometers west of the main Yasawa chain. Most of the 258 inhabitants of Viwa live in Naibalebale village at the southwest end of the island. In November 2008, the upscale **Viwa Island Resort** (tel. 603-0066, www.viwaislandresort.com) opened on a fabulous beach near the village. The eight deluxe *bure* are F$598 single or double, while three two-bedroom *bure* are F$685. All units are air-conditioned and come with coffee maker and fridge. Continental breakfast is included but lunch and dinner are F$80 per person extra. You can also order à la carte.

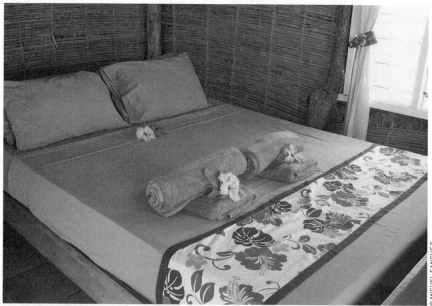

bure at Octopus Resort on Waya Island

© MIGUEL SANCHEZ

Children under 12 are not accepted, so this is a good option for romantic couples. Aside from the beach, there's a swimming pool. Transfers from the *Yasawa Flyer* at Octopus Island Resort cost F$71 per person each way (one hour).

NANUYA BALAVU AND DRAWAQA

From March to November, huge manta rays frequent the channel between Nanuya Balavu and Drawaqa islands just south of Naviti. The strong current here calls for caution on the part of snorkelers, who should also remain at a safe distance from the rays.

The (**Manta Ray Island Resort** (tel. 664-0520, www.mantarayisland.com), on Nanuya Balavu Island between Waya and Naviti, sits on a point between two nice white beaches. A "jungle" *bure* with private bath is F$195 single or double, and there's a small "treehouse" *bure* with shared bath for F$128. The 32-bed dorm is F$49 per person, camping F$36 per person. The compulsory buffet meal package is F$59 per person extra. All the usual parties and activities are laid on for the youthful backpacking guests. The focus here is on water sports rather than land-based activities like hiking. From July to September, you can snorkel with manta rays here at high tide. Scuba diving is with Reef Safari (www.reefsafari.com.fj).

Barefoot Lodge (tel. 670-1823, www.fiji sailing.com.fj) on the beach at Drawaqa, the next island north of Nanuya Balavu, is used mostly by passengers on Captain Cook Cruises. Barefoot Lodge isn't promoted by Awesome Adventures and your fellow guests are likely to be a little older and the atmosphere quieter than at Manta Ray. The 20 simple thatched beach *bure* with shared bath and no electric lighting are F$149/198 single/double including meals (minimum stay two nights). Snorkeling gear and kayaks are free, but you should bring your own towel.

NAVITI ISLAND

Naviti, at 33 square kilometers, is the largest of the Yasawas. All of Naviti's villages are on the east coast, including Soso, residence of one of the group's highest chiefs. Soso's church houses fine wood carvings, and on the hillside above the village are two caves containing the bones of ancestors. Yawesa, the secondary boarding school on Naviti, is a village in itself. The Awesome Adventures shuttle from Nadi (F$100 one-way) cruises right up the west side of Naviti, where most of the resorts are found.

Natuvalo Bay

Three backpacker resorts—Coconut Bay, Korovou, and White Sandy Beach—share a rather poor beach on Natuvalo Bay directly across Naviti from Kese village. You can swim here at high tide, but there isn't much coral for snorkelers to see. From the beach, a huge mango tree is visible atop the ridge to the southeast. A shady, well-trodden path leaves the beach 20 meters before the first rocky headland south of Coconut Bay Resort and climbs to the tree, a 40-minute walk. Go south along the ridge a few hundred meters to a grassy hill with great views as far as Wayasewa. The trail continues to Kese village. Do this hike right after breakfast while it's still relatively cool.

A much easier walk is to Honeymoon Point, the peninsula overlooking the north end of Natuvalo Bay. The trail begins next to White Sandy Beach Dive Resort and takes only 15 minutes. You'll have a view of the entire west side of Naviti, plus the long low island of Viwa at the 1100 o'clock position on the horizon, far to the west. For better swimming and snorkeling than what's available right in front of the resorts, carry on to Honeymoon Beach.

The **White Sandy Beach Dive Resort** (tel. 666-4066) on Natuvalo Bay does one-/two-tank dives at F$90/170, with the price varying slightly depending on the site. They can also take you snorkeling at a plane wreck in three meters of water or with manta rays. A boat trip around the island with stops at both of these sites is also possible. Snorkeling gear is for rent.

Reef Safari (tel. 675-0566, www.reefsafari .com.fj), based at the Manta Ray Island Resort on Nanuya Balavu Island, provides scuba diving services to all of the resorts on Naviti (F$110/205 one/two tanks including gear).

Accommodations

The **Botaira Beach Resort** (tel. 603-0200 or 603-0198, www.botaira.com), on the southwest side of Naviti, faces one of the island's best beaches. Botaira has 15 upscale *bure* with bath at F$443 double including tax, meals, and some sporting activities. The snorkeling is great, with manta rays in June and July. South Sea Cruises sells hurried day trips to Botaira from Nadi at F$145, including lunch (drinks extra).

On Natuvalo Bay, a few kilometers north of the Botaira Beach Resort, is the **Coconut Bay Resort** (tel. 666-6644, ext. 1300). The 10 thin-walled duplex units with private bath are F$120/150 single/double. The two large 20-bed dorms are F$65 per person (camping with your own tent also costs F$65 per person). The meals are served in an enclosed building with no view, but the food is good, with a buffet dinner nightly. Water shortages happen here.

The **Korovou Eco-Tour Resort** (tel. 665-1001, korovoultk@connect.com.fj), a few minutes on foot from the Coconut Bay Resort, also caters to the backpacking masses. The 14 *bure* with private bath are F$200 double while the 32-bed dorm is F$80 per person. The *bure* come in a variety of thatched and duplex styles, so you might ask to see a couple before deciding. All prices include three basic meals. Korovou is the largest resort in this area, and has a spacious restaurant with a large deck right above the beach and a swimming pool. Frankly, there isn't anything "Eco-Tour" about Korovou. Activities include snorkeling and manta rays (F$25) and an evening fire-dancing show. A generator provides electricity in the evening.

The **White Sandy Beach Dive Resort** (tel. 666-4066), on the beach next to Korovou, has only a handful of neat little bungalows with tin roofs at F$150 double, including very good meals. The dorm is F$65 per person. All three resorts just mentioned include afternoon tea in their prices and provide free transfers from the ferry to shore. Drinking water is scarce, and you'll be expected to buy bottled water.

You can also stay in the home of Toye Momonikese in Malevu village on the east side of Naviti. This should be arranged in advance through www.fijibure.com/malevu, which charges F$80 per person including meals. A *sevusevu* of kava roots should be presented. Many village activities are possible, and it's a great alternative to the backpacker camps. You transfer from the *Yasawa Flyer II* at the Manta Ray Resort on Nanuya Balavu Island (F$50 per group of three each way to Malevu).

YAQETA ISLAND

The upscale **Navutu Stars Resort** (tel. 664-0553, www.navutustarsfiji.com) on the west side of Yaqeta is attempting to fill the niche between top-end Turtle Island Resort and backpacker-accessible properties like Oarsman's Bay Lodge. The architecture of the nine thatched *bure* is a mix of Mediterranean and Fijian. The units face three small bays but the muddy tidal beach is poor. At least there's a swimming pool. Non-motorized sporting activities are included in the basic rates, which ranges F$500–850 single or double. Continental breakfast is also included, but the à la carte lunch and dinner are F$90/115/170 vegetarian/light/gourmet per person extra. Add 17.5 percent tax to these prices. This resort's rates are based on U.S. dollars and you'll save about 10 percent by paying in U.S. cash rather than Fiji dollars for meals, drinks, and incidentals. The target clientele is romantic couples, and children under 16 are not usually accepted. Massage is offered, with the first massage free. From Nadi, you can get there on the Awesome Adventures catamaran at F$110 per person each way.

◖ TAVEWA ISLAND

Tavewa is much smaller and lower than Waya and twice as far from Nadi, yet it's strikingly beautiful, with excellent bathing in the warm waters off a picture-postcard beach on the southeast side, as well as a good fringing reef with super snorkeling. Tall grass covers the hilly interior of this two-kilometer-long island.

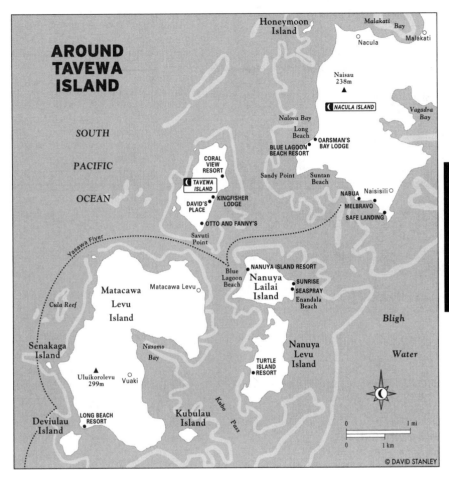

AROUND
TAVEWA
ISLAND

SOUTH

PACIFIC

OCEAN

Honeymoon
Island

Malakati
Bay

Nacula

Malakati

Naisau
238m ▲

◖ NACULA ISLAND

Vagadra
Bay

Nalova Bay

Long
Beach

● OARSMAN'S
　BAY LODGE

BLUE LAGOON ●
BEACH RESORT

Sandy Point

Suntan
Beach

NABUA ●　Naisisili ○

● MELBRAVO

SAFE LANDING ●

CORAL
VIEW
RESORT

◖ TAVEWA
ISLAND

DAVID'S ●
PLACE

● KINGFISHER
　LODGE

● OTTO AND FANNY'S

Savuti
Point

Yasawa Flyer

Blue
Lagoon
Beach

● NANUYA ISLAND RESORT

Nanuya
Lailai
Island

● SUNRISE

● SEASPRAY

Enandala
Beach

Bligh

Matacawa
Levu
Island

Matacawa Levu ○

Cula Reef

Senakaga
Island

Nasomo
Bay

Nanuya
Levu
Island

Water

TURTLE
ISLAND
● RESORT

▲
Uluikorolevu
299m

○
Vuaki

Deviulau
Island

LONG BEACH
RESORT

Kubulau
Island

Kubo
Pass

0　　　　　　　　1 mi

0　　　　1 km

© DAVID STANLEY

Tavewa is in the middle of the Yasawas, and from the summit, you can behold the long chain of islands stretching out on each side, with Viti Levu in the background. The summit offers the best view of the adjacent Blue Lagoon, and the sunsets can be splendid.

There's no chief here, as this is freehold land. In the late 19th century, an Irishman named William Doughty married a woman from Nacula who was given Tavewa as her dowry. A decade or two later, a Scot named William Bruce married into the Doughty family, and some time thereafter, beachcombers called Murray and Campbell arrived on the scene and did the same, with the result that some 50 Doughtys, Bruces, Murrays, and Campbells comprise the population of Tavewa today. William Doughty died in 1926 at the ripe age of 77.

The islanders are friendly and welcoming; in fact, accommodating visitors is their main source of income. Coral View, David's, and Otto's have been operating since the 1980s, long before the current crop of backpacker resorts appeared on Naviti, Nacula, and Nanuya Lailai, and their experience shows in better

© TIM PARKINSON/FLICKR.COM/TIMPARKINSON

volcanic rocks on the beach of Tavewa Island

food, accommodations, and tours. Most of their guests are backpackers who stay six nights, and most are sorry to leave. It's idyllic, but bring along mosquito coils, toilet paper, a flashlight, bottled water, and a *sulu* to cover up. Be prepared for water shortages.

Accommodations

(Coral View Island Resort (tel. 666-2648 or 925-8341, www.coral.com.fj), nestling in a cozy valley on a secluded beach with high hills on each side, is one of the nicest low-budget places to stay in Fiji. It has 14 deluxe *bure* with private bath and fridge at F$210 double and three 20-bunk dorms at F$70 per person. Discounts are offered for children under 14. Mosquito nets are supplied and there's 24-hour electricity. Included in the price are three decent meals and transfers to/from the *Yasawa Flyer II*. Coral View's beach isn't that great, but boat trips to Blue Lagoon Beach are F$15 (minimum of five). The boat trip to the Sawa-i-Lau caves requires a minimum of five people willing to pay F$50 per person. Snorkeling gear

is F$10 extra. Dive Yasawa Lagoon (www.dive yasawalagoon.com) based at Coral View charges F$110/165 for one/two tanks and gives PADI certification courses for F$600. Although there are lots of organized activities, Coral View is also a place people come to relax and socialize, and most guests tend to be under 35. You'll be touched as the genuinely friendly staff gathers to sing "Isa Lei," the Fijian song of farewell, when the time comes for you to go.

Kingfisher Lodge (tel. 666-6481), next to David's Place, offers one self-contained beach bungalow at F$100 double plus meals. Bookings are through Otto and Fanny's Place.

David's Place Resort (tel. 672-1820) stands in a coconut grove near a small church on the island's longest beach. There are seven thatched *bure* with shared bath, two larger bungalows with private bath, and a 26-bed dorm. Camping with your own tent should be possible. The minimum stay is two nights. Prices are similar to those at Coral View, but David's *bure* aren't as good and the communal toilets and showers are inadequate when the place is full. Three meals are included in the price (opinions about the food vary). If you're a fun-loving backpacker, you may like the atmosphere here. Bookings can be made through David's Travel Service in office No. 31 upstairs in the arrivals concourse at Nadi Airport.

Otto and Fanny's Place (tel. 666-6481, www.ottoandfanny.com), on spacious grounds near the south end of the island, caters to a more mature clientele less interested in activities and partying. There are two large bungalows with toilet, cold-water shower, and sink at F$90 single or double. Three thatched *bure* with private bath cost the same. The deluxe *bure* is F$100. The single 12-bed dormitory is F$40 per person. Camping is not allowed. Three good buffet-style meals served at a common table are F60 per person. The generator is on until 2300, but the light is dim. The *bure* are nicely scattered through the plantation, but they don't overlook the beach. MasterCard, Visa, and cash are accepted. Yachties anchored at the nearby Blue Lagoon are welcome to order dinner here, so long as 24 hours notice is given. From 1500–1630, afternoon tea is served to both guests and non-guests at Aunty Fanny's Tea House, featuring some of the richest banana or chocolate cake in Fiji. It's an island institution. Ice cream is also available.

Getting There

Most visitors arrive from Nadi on the Awesome Adventures catamaran *Yasawa Flyer II* at F$120 one-way. An island hop from Tavewa to Kuata on the catamaran is F$75. Outboard transfers from Tavewa to Nacula or Nanuya Lailai are around F$10 per person each way.

◖ NACULA ISLAND

Ten-kilometer-long Nacula, between Tavewa and Yasawa islands, is the third largest in the chain. From its contorted coastline rise hills like Naisau (238 m) and Korobeka (258 m). Of the four villages, Naisisili and Nacula are the most important, and the Tui Drola, or chief of the middle Yasawas, resides on the island. Some of Fiji's best snorkeling is just off the high white sands of **Long Beach,** in the southwest corner of Nacula opposite Tavewa. Since 2000, several small resorts have been built on Nacula. Meals are included in most of the rates quoted here, but be aware that water-taxi transfers to/from the *Yasawa Flyer II* cost F$10 per person.

On a good beach on the southeast side of Nacula is **Nabua Lodge** (tel. 666-9173, www .nabualodge-yasawa.com) with nine thatched *bure,* six with shared bath at F$140 double and three with private bath at F$180. The seven-bed dorm is F$60 per person. Tax and meals are included but only Fijian cash is accepted. Great sunsets can be seen from the hill just above the lodge, and you can hike along the ridge right to the center of the island (take water).

Melbravo Lodge (tel. 665-0616 or 666-6644, ext. 7472, melbravoresort@yahoo.com), right next to Nabua Lodge, has six thatched *bure,* two with private bath at F$160 double and four with shared bath at F$130 including meals. The eight-bed dorm is F$65 per person. If you call direct rather than booking through a Nadi travel agent, these prices are reduced.

There's electricity in the dining area, but none in the rooms. The food can be monotonous and the portions small, but drinking water is free. Activities here include a Sawa-i-Lau cave tour, Blue Lagoon snorkeling, village entertainment, and snorkeling gear rental.

Safe Landing Resort (tel. 623-2984, www .safelandingfiji.com) is on a white-sand beach tucked between two dark headlands, on the next bay over from Melbravo. Unlike Melbravo and Nabua Lodge, which are mostly for backpackers, Safe Landing tries also to cater to middle-aged tourists. The three well-constructed deluxe *bure* with private bath are F$300 double, while two duplexes with four interconnecting rooms with bath are F$260 double. Children under 13 are half price in these units. The 10-bunk dorm is F$95 per person and camping (own tent) F$90 per person. All rates include three meals with lots of fish. It's a nice spot with good swimming at high tide, though the beach at Oarsman's Bay Lodge is much better. Safe Landing is owned by the Vola Vola family of nearby Naisisili village. Guests staying at Nabua, Melbravo, and Safe Landing are welcome to attend the Sunday service in Naisisili. The snorkeling isn't that great in this area, however, as there's little coral.

Oarsman's Bay Lodge (tel. 628-0485, www.oarsmansbay.com) is on fabulous Long Beach, at the southwest end of Nacula. There's a 13-bed dormitory above the restaurant/bar at F$25 per person, six self-contained bungalows with solar panels at F$183 double, and two large family bungalows sleeping six at F$289. Camping with your own tent costs F$27 per person. The compulsory meals plan is F$67 per person extra. Paddleboats, kayaks, and snorkeling gear are loaned free. Most of the workers hail from Nacula village on the north side of the island, and resort profits go to village projects. If you're staying at Safe Landing or one of its neighbors and wish to visit Oarsman's for the day, it takes a bit more than an hour to walk along a shortcut trail across the island to/from Suntan Beach. It's easy to walk there along the beach only at low tide—at high tide, you'll need to wade part of the way.

Oarsman's and Safe Landing have many things in common. Both were built in 2000 with interest-free loans provided by the owner of Turtle Island Resort. To ensure that the loans are repaid, both resorts are now managed by Turtle Island, and bookings are controlled by the Turtle Island office (tel. 672-2921, nacula@hotmail.com) at Nadi Airport. To further control finances, all accounts at Oarsman's must be paid by credit card (cash not accepted anywhere, not even at the bar). The transfer fees from the *Yasawa Flyer II* are F$10 per person each way at both, and both resorts operate on "Bula Time" (one hour ahead of Fiji time) to give guests an extra hour of daylight. Compared to the rest of the Yasawa backpacker resorts, Oarsman's and Safe Landing are rather expensive, yet compared to Mamanuca resorts like Malolo, Castaway, and Matamanoa, they're cheap. Unfortunately, both places are getting a little tired.

The new trendy place to stay on Nacula is **(Blue Lagoon Beach Resort** (tel. 666-9452, www.bluelagoonbeachresort.com.fj), launched in 2009 by the owners of Octopus Resort on Waya Island. It's adjacent to Oarsman's Bay Lodge on Nalova Bay and both resorts share the same glorious beach. The seven well-constructed beachfront villas range in price from F$189 to F$349 double. To sleep in one of the six set tents costs F$99 double, or pay F$40 per person in the two six-bed dorms. The compulsory three-meal plan at the restaurant/bar is F$70 per person (or F$45 for children under 13). All reports to date are good.

AROUND THE BLUE LAGOON
Sports and Recreation

Westside Watersports (tel. 666-1462, www.fiji-dive.com), also known as Yasawa Dive, has a dive center on the beach at Nanuya Island Resort on Nanuya Lailai Island. The price gets cheaper the more diving you do (F$110/165 for one/two dives, subsequent dives F$65 each). Open-water scuba certification is F$625. Credit cards are accepted for diving. Their two dive boats, *Absolute II* and *Aftershock,* go out

CAPTAIN WILLIAM BLIGH

In 1789, after being cast adrift by the mutineers on his HMS *Bounty*, Captain Bligh and 18 others in a seven-meter longboat were chased by two Fijian war canoes through what is now called Bligh Water. His men pulled the oars desperately, headed for open sea, and managed to escape the cannibals. They later arrived in Timor, finishing the most celebrated open-boat journey of all time. Captain Bligh did some incredible charting of Fijian waters along the way.

at 0900 and 1330, and where you'll dive depends upon the wind. Aside from the spectacular underwater topography, encounters with sea turtles, reef sharks, and eagle rays are fairly common. Free pickups are offered from most nearby resorts.

Nanuya Lailai Island

Nanuya Lailai, between Tavewa and Nanuya Levu islands, is best known for **Blue Lagoon Beach** on the island's west side. The snorkeling here is about the finest in the area, and this beach is often visited by cruise-ship passengers. Many yachts anchor just offshore. You can tell the fish have been fed at the Blue Lagoon from the way they swim straight at you. Unfortunately, much of the coral is now dead.

Since 2000, the island's seven families, related to the Naisisili people on Nacula, have established a half-dozen small backpacker resorts along Enandala Beach on Nanuya Lailai's east side. Expect water shortages (bring bottled water), a lack of electricity (this could change), and no credit cards accepted (all prices include meals). Transfers from the *Yasawa Flyer II* to Nanuya Lailai are F$10 per person each way. It's only a 10-minute walk across the island from the backpacker camps to Blue Lagoon Beach. To avoid conflicts with the powerful tour operators, your hosts may ask you to stay away from the groups of cruise-ship passengers swimming in the Blue Lagoon—the beach is long enough for everyone.

With transportation and Blue Lagoon tourism increasingly concentrated on Nanuya Lailai, some of the backpacker camps there have become overcrowded, and it's increasingly common for people with *bure* reservations to be shoved into a dormitory due to overbooking. Feedback on the food and accommodations at the backpacker places is mixed. For this reason alone, you might consider staying on another island and visiting on a day trip unless you're willing to shell out for the Nanuya Island Resort.

Sunrise Lagoon Resort (tel. 666-6644, ext. 9484, or 651-1195, rosalinimeri@yahoo. com), at the north end of Enandala Beach, charges F$160 double in 10 thatched *bure* with shared bath and F$210 in one garden *bure* with private bath. Both the seven-bed family beach *bure* and a 14-bed dorm are F$65 per person. At last report, Sunrise Lagoon was the only backpacker resort on Nanuya Lailai with electricity, but opinions about the place vary considerably. One reader called it "basic, ugly, unfriendly, noisy, dirty, bad beach, windy, horrible." This resort is well promoted by the Nadi travel agents, so it's usually overflowing with young guests.

On a long stretch of beach next to Sunset Lagoon is **Seaspray Resort** (tel. 666-8962) with two simple *bure* with shared bath at F$120 double, plus a 10-bed dorm at F$70 per person. Lighting is by kerosene lamp, but the outdoor eating area is nice and the food okay. Sadly, we've heard reports of petty theft from the dorm at Seaspray.

The **Gold Coast Inn** (tel. 665-1580, gold coastinn@connect.com.fj), on the beach right next to Seaspray, has seven *bure* with private bath at F$150. It's less crowded than the other places and the rooms and food are also better.

At the south end of the strip is **Kim's Place** (tel. 666-6644, ext. 1019), with six basic thatched *bure* with shared bath at F$140

double and one four-bed dorm at F$70 per person, meals included. You can buy souvenirs or have afternoon tea and banana cakes here. At low tide, you can easily walk across the sandbar behind Kim's Place to Nanuya Levu Island, though you'll be most unwelcome there.

The **(Nanuya Island Resort** (tel. 666-7633, www.nanuyafiji.com), right on the famous Blue Lagoon Beach, is the pearl of Nanuya Lailai. It's one of the nicest beach resorts in Fiji and far more upscale than the places just mentioned. The eight small hillside *bure* are F$260 double, while the four deluxe beach *bure* F$410. All units have private bath and 24-hour electricity. The rates include a light breakfast, but all other meals are à la carte (mains F$20–34) and no meal plan is available. The food is excellent. There are numerous activities. Westside Watersports has a dive shop here, which is great if you're a diver. If you're not, the comings and goings of speedboats can be a nuisance. There's a lovely reef just 30 meters offshore, but few large fish, probably due to over-fishing. Another drawback is the shortage of beach chairs (you almost have to be there at 0700 to reserve one). The staff here are great, and excellent musicians to boot.

Nanuya Levu Island

In 1972, an eccentric American millionaire named Richard Evanson bought 200-hectare Nanuya Levu Island in the middle of the Yasawa Group for US$300,000. He still lives there, and his **Turtle Island Resort** (tel. 672-2921 or 666-3889, www.turtlefiji.com) has gained a colorful reputation in Fiji. Only 14 fan-cooled, two-room *bure* grace Turtle, and Evanson swears that there will never be more. That's all very fine, but the small size also leaves less money to invest in necessary renovations and five-star amenities like a swimming pool, fitness room, and spa.

The 28 guests pay F$4,500 per couple per night and that includes meals, drinks, and activities (17.5 percent tax is extra). Sports such as sailing, snorkeling, scuba diving, canoeing, windsurfing, deep-sea fishing, horseback riding, guided hiking, and moonlight cruising are all included in the tariff. Resort staff will even do your laundry at no additional charge (only Lomi Lomi massage costs extra).

If you want to spend the day on any of the dozen secluded beaches, just ask, and you'll be dropped off (if the beaches aren't already booked). Later, someone will be back with lunch and a cooler of wine or champagne (or anything else you'd care to order over the walkie-talkie). Otherwise, use the beach a few steps from your door. Meals are served at remote and romantic dine-out locations, or taken at the community table. Same-sex couples may not feel entirely comfortable at this resort.

Aside from the per diem, it's another F$1,900 per couple for round-trip seaplane transportation to the island from Nadi. There's also a six-night minimum stay. You can often find all-inclusive packages to Turtle Island Resort, which work out less expensive than the rack rates quoted here. (Turtle Island is off-limits to anyone other than hotel guests.) The 1980 Hollywood production *The Blue Lagoon* starring Brooke Shields was filmed on Nanuya Levu.

Matacawa Levu Island

Matacawa Levu, west of Nanuya Levu, is less developed touristically. **Long Beach Resort** (tel. 672-2600, www.longbeachfiji.com) stands on a point at the end of the long white beach on Matacawa Levu's south side. It has four simple *bure* with shared bath at F$180 double, including meals. A much better unit with private bath is F$250. A mattress on the mat-covered floor of the eight-bed dorm costs F$70 per person with meals. At low tide, you can walk across to nearby Deviulau Island, and good snorkeling is available.

A more recent arrival is **Bay of Plenty Lodge** (tel. 902-3739 or 933-1027, bayofplentylodge@yahoo.com) at the south end of Matacawa Levu. The five *bure* with private bath are F$160 double or it's F$65 per person in a dorm with five or 10 beds, meals included. Ask for the five-bed dorm overlooking the sea.

Free activities include cooking lessons, coconut demonstration, basket weaving, volleyball, touch rugby, *sulu* tying, and farm visits. An extra charge applies for cave trips, deep-sea fishing, reef jumping, village trips, and a trip to the Blue Lagoon. Passengers are transferred from the *Yasawa Flyer II* at the south end of Matacawa Levu at F$15 per person each way.

It's also possible to stay in Matacawa Levu village for F$80 per person, including meals. Details are available on www.fijibure.com/matacawalevu.

SAWA-I-LAU ISLAND

On Sawa-i-Lau is a large limestone cave illuminated by a crevice at the top. There's a clear, deep pool in the cave where you can swim, and an underwater opening leads back into a smaller, darker cave (bring a light). A Fijian legend tells how a young chief once hid his love in this cave when her family wished to marry her off to another. Each day, he brought her food until they could both escape to safety on another island. In the 1980 film *The Blue Lagoon,* Brooke Shields runs away to this very cave. Many cruise ships stop at the cave, and the backpacker resorts on Tavewa and Nacula also run tours. Yachties should present a *sevusevu* to the chief of Nabukeru village, just west of the cave, to visit.

YASAWA ISLAND

The Tui Yasawa, highest chief of the group, resides at Yasawairara village at the north end of Yasawa, northernmost island of the Yasawa Group.

For many years, the Fiji government had a policy that the Yasawas were "closed" to land-based tourism development, and it was only after the 1987 coups that approval was granted for the construction of **Yasawa Island Resort** (tel. 666-3364 or 672-2266, www.yasawa.com). This Australian-owned resort opened in 1991 on a creamy white beach on Yasawa's upper west side and most of the resort's employees came from Bukama village, which owns the land. On Christmas Eve 2009, the resort's restaurant and offices were destroyed in a major fire, and at press time it was uncertain if/when they would reopen. The spacious accommodations consist of six air-conditioned duplexes, which, before the fire, cost F$1,700 double, 10 one-bedroom deluxes F$2,000, one two-bedroom F$2,565, and a honeymoon unit F$3,420, all plus 17.5 percent tax. Meals of variable quality were included, but, unlike at most other resorts in this category, alcoholic drinks were not. Scuba diving, game fishing, and massage also cost extra. Guests arrived on a chartered flight (F$500 pp plus 17.5 percent tax each way), which landed on the resort's private airstrip. Children under 12 were admitted only in January.

A less extravagant choice is **Hideout Beach Resort** (www.hideoutfiji.com), a 10-minute walk south of Yasawa-i-rara, the northernmost village on Yasawa Island. This locally run place, formerly known as Cagini-wasalima Eco-Tour Resort, opened on a long white beach in 2005. Of the five individual *bure,* two have private bathrooms (F$200 double) and three have shared bath (F$160). There are two dorms with eight or 10 single beds (not bunks) at F$80 per person. To encourage longer stays, the seventh night is free. All prices include boiled fish and cassava meals. Ocean kayaking and horseback riding are popular activities here. It takes most of the day to get there from Nadi. The two-hour water taxi ride from the *Yasawa Flyer II* at Nanuya Lailai Island is F$150 each way, which is shared between all passengers (F$75 pp for two, F$25 pp for six, F$150 for one, etc.). Guests staying five nights or more get this transfer for half price.

THE YASAWA ISLANDS

SOUTHERN VITI LEVU

The southwest side of Viti Levu along Queens Road is known as the Coral Coast for its fringing reef. Sigatoka (sing-a-TO-ka) and Navua are the main towns in this area, with most accommodations at Korotogo, Korolevu, and Pacific Harbor. This shoreline is heavily promoted as one of the top resort areas in Fiji, largely because of its convenient location along the busy highway between Nadi and Suva, but to be honest, the beaches here are second-rate, with good swimming and snorkeling conditions only at high tide. Much of the coral has been destroyed by hurricanes, and beaches have been washed away. To compensate, most of the hotels have swimming pools, and in some places you can go reef walking at low tide.

Top sights include Natadola Beach, the Sigatoka Sand Dunes, Sigatoka town, and the impressive Navua River Gorge. Organized tours often go to the Tavuni Hill Fort, Kula Bird Park, and Pacific Harbor's Arts Village. There are many dive shops all along the Coral Coast, and some of Fiji's best river trips begin or end in Navua. Rivers Fiji, based at Pacific Harbor, is the South Pacific's finest whitewater rafting operation.

Off southern Viti Levu are a number of islands with accommodations for visitors. Yanuca and Beqa Islands are usually reached by boat from Pacific Harbor, Yanuca for its surfing camps and Beqa for its upscale boutique resorts. Many people go to Beqa to dive the Beqa Lagoon, but it's worth noting that the famous dive sites like Golden Arch and Sidestreets are almost as far from Beqa as they are from Pacific Harbor (where the diving costs a lot

© IAN SUTTON / KULA BIRD PARK

HIGHLIGHTS

◖ **Natadola Beach:** Natadola is easily the finest white-sand beach on the Viti Levu mainland. Its clear waters are great for swimming and snorkeling, and you can go horseback riding. The Inter-Continental Resort Fiji and adjacent golf course are worth a sightseeing visit (page 94).

◖ **Sigatoka Sand Dunes:** Hiking trails climb and cross these dunes, offering excellent views of the coast and local vegetation. Archaeological remains uncovered here and the ecology of the area is explained in the visitor center on Queens Road (page 97).

◖ **Tavuni Hill Fort:** This is one of Fiji's only accessible archaeological sites, with excellent views of the Sigatoka River Valley from the hill. You'll hear the story of a Tongan invasion of this area hundreds of years ago. Tavuni Hill is easily reached from Sigatoka by taxi, or you can hike along the cane railway (page 98).

◖ **Kula Bird Park:** Most visitors have few opportunities to see Fiji's fauna in the wild, but this eco-park just off Queens Road presents the birds, bats, and iguanas in a pleasing tropical setting (page 102).

◖ **Arts Village:** This impressive cultural center at Pacific Harbor is a good place to witness the spectacle of Fijian firewalking and learn about Fiji's traditional culture. Tours are offered daily except Sunday, and for those with less time, a lot can be seen for free from the Village's marketplace (page 114).

◖ **Frigate Passage:** Frigate Passage off Yanuca Island attracts surfers for its fast left-hander and scuba divers for the prolific marine life. The dive shops of Pacific Harbor organize daily scuba trips to Frigate Passage and the reefs of the Beqa Lagoon, while surfers are served by the Batiluva Beach Resort on Yanuca (page 115).

◖ **White-Water Rafting:** The best river trips in Fiji are on the Navua River inland from Pacific Harbor. The Upper Navua is white-water country where the rubber raft rules, while the quieter Lower Navua is a place for bamboo rafting. Village visits are often included in these tours (page 116).

◖ **Great Astrolabe Reef:** This major barrier reef off eastern Kadavu is famous for its walls and caves. Several east Kadavu resorts offer scuba diving here, and sea kayaking is possible in adjacent protected waters (page 129).

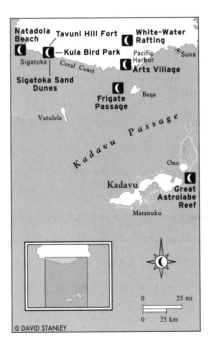

LOOK FOR ◖ TO FIND RECOMMENDED SIGHTS, ACTIVITIES, DINING, AND LODGING.

SOUTHERN VITI LEVU

less). Kadavu Island is also noted for its scuba diving, plus the surfing at Nagigia Island. Unlike Beqa, Kadavu can only be reached by ship from Suva or by air from Suva or Nadi.

PLANNING YOUR TIME

Many tourists spend their entire Fiji vacation on the Coral Coast. All of the large resorts offer a wide range of nautical activities and entertainment, and they're better positioned for land-based sightseeing than the Mamanuca resorts off Nadi. Many of Fiji's largest resort hotels are along the Coral Coast, but there are also budget properties for backpackers and independent travelers. A night or two at a couple of these is worth the time. For variety, chose one resort in Korotogo and another in Korolevu.

The possibility of rainfall and the lushness of the vegetation increase as you move east. Pacific Harbor is wetter than Korotogo. If you're a scuba diver, golfer, or sightseer, there's enough to see and do at Pacific Harbor to keep you busy for a few days. Your stays on Yanuca and Beqa will also depend on personal interests.

Frequent buses link all of the places just mentioned, but getting to Kadavu is more of a challenge. And even after you've flown to Vunisea Airport from Suva or Nadi, there's usually a long outboard boat ride to your Kadavu resort. There wouldn't be much point in going to Kadavu for less than three days, and the usual stay is one week.

GETTING AROUND

An easy way to get between the Coral Coast resorts and Nadi/Suva is on the air-conditioned **Fiji Express** shuttle bus run by Coral Sun Fiji (tel. 672-3105, www.coralsunfiji.com). The bus leaves the Holiday Inn in Suva at 0715 and 1530, calling at The Pearl South Pacific at 0810 and 1625, at the Beachouse at 0845 and 1700, at the Warwick hotel at 0855 and 1710, at The Naviti Resort at 0910 and 1725, at Rydges Hideaway Resort at 0920 and 1735, at Tambua Sands at 0930 and 1745, at the Outrigger on the Lagoon at 0945 and 1800, at the Fijian Resort at 1010 and 1830, and arriving at Nadi International Airport at 1130 and 2000. It leaves Nadi Airport for Suva at 0730 and 1300 and returns along the same route, reaching the Holiday Inn in Suva at 1200 and 1715. The through fare from Suva to Nadi is around F$22, and bookings can be made at hotel tour desks. At Nadi Airport, contact Coral Sun Fiji in the arrivals area.

Many less expensive non-air-conditioned Pacific Transport and Sunbeam express buses pass on the highway.

The Coral Coast

NATADOLA AND ROBINSON CRUSOE

Viti Levu's southeast corner is blessed with the island's finest beach, which has only recently been developed for first-world tourism. Queens Road crosses rolling, pine-clad hills near here, but to see the sands one must leave the highway. This area is popular among day-trippers who arrive by rental car or aboard a converted cane train. However you come, you're likely to meet people from the large Fijian village at the end of the beach and to see the isolated farmhouses of Indo-Fijian residents inland. Offshore, a small resort island caters to young travelers.

◖ Natadola Beach

The long, white sandy beach here is easily the best on Viti Levu. Natadola has long been a popular picnic spot with day-trippers arriving on the sugar train from Shangri-La's Fijian Resort on the Coral Coast. Local villagers on the beach offer passengers and resort guests horseback riding to a cave. Unfortunately, Natadola is one of the few beaches in Fiji where horse riders, shell peddlers, coconut cutters, and kids can be a constant nuisance and valuables should not be left unattended. Care should also be taken while swimming in the ocean here, as the waves can be unexpectedly strong. The small left point break at Natadola is good for beginning surfers, but one must always be aware of the currents and undertow. The left-hand breaks outside the reef are only for the experienced. For hikers, the three-hour walk along the coastal railway line from Natadola to a point opposite Shangri-La's Fijian Resort at Cuvu is interesting and you can always catch a taxi back. Local buses from Sigatoka arrive four times a day.

One of the largest tourism development projects in Fiji was focused on this area. The Natadola Marine Resort (www.natadolabay resort.com) partnered with the 300,000-plus members of the Fiji National Provident Fund to erect five international hotels and 600 residential units here before 2017. In 2003, the Fiji Government built a modern highway from Queens Road directly to Natadola Beach and the InterContinental Fiji Golf Resort opened on a sandy point in June 2009. A 125-room Four Seasons boutique hotel and 100 luxury villas were envisioned for Navo Island facing the InterContinental site with a 160-meter causeway linking Navo to Viti Levu. A number of factors have put these projects on hold, not least among them the collapse of the US$200 million JW Marriott Fiji Resort & Spa development at Momi Bay just north of Natadola, which has spooked investors. In early 2010, the Fiji National Provident Fund wrote off F$327 million from failed tourism investments at Natadola, Momi Bay, and other locations.

The three-star **Yatule Resort** (tel. 672-8004) was originally built in 2006 to house key staff working on the InterContinental construction project. The 50 villas are now rented to the general public at F$150/250 standard/deluxe. A self-catering family villa is F$300 for up to four persons.

The dusty, Santa Fe-style **Natadola Beach Resort** (tel. 672-1001, www.natadola.com), beside Yatule and across the road from the public beach, has been around since the mid-1990s. It offers nine suites in several motel-style blocks at F$185 single or double, plus a "sandcastle" villa at F$245 including tax. Honeymooners are the target clientele, and children under 16 are not accepted. In practice, this place is usually deserted. Each of the 10 fan-cooled units has a fridge, but no cooking facilities are provided and guests are expected to patronize the resort's pricey restaurant. A long swimming pool meanders between huge native trees in a garden setting.

The flashy **InterContinental Fiji Golf Resort** (tel. 673-3300, www.intercontinen tal.com) at Natadola has 216 spacious rooms and suites with cable TV, mini-fridge, bathtub, and terrace or balcony. The rooms are F$625/675/725 garden/lagoon/beachfront, while the suites go for F$825/925 lagoon/beachfront. Discounts are available through the hotel website. Perched high on the hill with sweeping views of Natadola Bay, the 55 villas of Club InterContinental feature plunge pools or spa baths and cost somewhat more. Among the many general facilities are four swimming pools, three restaurants, two bars, kids club, gym, spa, dive shop, and business center. Five hundred people can sit down to dinner in the resort's conference center. At the par-72 Natadola Bay Championship Golf Course (tel. 673-3500, www.natadolabay.com), on the rolling hills next to the resort, 15 of the 18 holes hug the coast. Be prepared for strong winds, especially in the afternoon.

Some residents of Sanasana village at the south end of the beach rent thatched huts to backpackers. The only budget resort in the area is **Namuka Bay Lagoon** (tel. 651-1550) on a nice beach at Naidiri, a 45-minute walk east of Sanasana along the cane railway. Namuka Bay is six kilometers off Queens Road via a dirt access road. The basic Fijian *bure* rent for F$150/175 single/double, and the dorm *bure* go for F$45–75 per person. Meals are included.

Likuri Island

The most popular offshore resort in this area is 🏝 **Robinson Crusoe Island** (tel. 651-0200, www.robinsoncrusoeislandfiji.com), on

Likuri Island, a small coral isle just north of Natadola. Not to be confused with Crusoe's Retreat on the Coral Coast toward Pacific Harbor, Robinson Crusoe caters to a more active and younger crowd. The 16 simple thatched *bure* with shared bath start at F$103 per person (F$252 double with private bath), while the dorm *bure* with 20 beds upstairs and 38 downstairs is F$89 per person. The 5 percent hotel tax is additional. Prices include three good meals, handline fishing, kayaks, snorkeling, and evening entertainment in the Pirates Night Club. Scuba diving with Reef Safari is F$110/205 for one/two tanks including gear or F$600 for a PADI Open water certification course (minimum of two persons). Boat transfers at 1000 and 1630 from the Tuva River Jetty near Natadola are F$89 per person roundtrip, bus transfers from Nadi included. Day tours to Robinson Crusoe Island are offered on Tuesday, Thursday, and Sunday, costing F$119 per person including Nadi hotel transfers and a *lovo* lunch. The beach here is great, and this is a good alternative to the better-known Mamanuca resorts for the young at heart.

THE FIJIAN AND VICINITY

Shangri-La's Fijian Resort (tel. 652-0155, www.shangri-la.com) occupies all 40 hectares of Yanuca Island (not to be confused with another island of the same name west of Beqa). The Fijian (as it's often called) is connected to Viti Levu by a causeway 10 kilometers west of Sigatoka and 61 kilometers southeast of Nadi Airport. Opened in 1967, this Malaysian-owned complex of three-story Hawaiian-style buildings was Fiji's first large resort, and it's still Fiji's biggest hotel. The 442 air-conditioned rooms start at F$480 single or double in the "lagoonview wings," F$520 in the "oceanview wings," F$573 for a family room, or F$793 for a suite, plus 17.5 percent tax. Included is a buffet breakfast for two people per room. A third adult is F$75, but two children 18 or under who share their parents' room stay free (kids 12 and under also eat for free). This makes Shangri-La's Fijian an ideal choice for families and you should expect hordes of kids. Shangri-

La's Fijian often has wonderful accommodations specials, then they sock it to you with the overpriced food and drink. Australians on cheap packaged holidays are the usual clientele. The resort offers a well-designed nine-hole golf course (par 31), five tennis courts, numerous restaurants and bars, a lovely wedding chapel, and three swimming pools (which close at sunset). Avis Rent A Car and Coral Sun Fiji have desks in the Fijian, and an ANZ Bank ATM and Nads Handicrafts shop are available.

Reef Safari (tel. 675-0566, www.reefsafari .com.fj) has the diving concession at Shangri-La's Fijian Resort. Dive sites such as Nabaibai Passage, Barracuda Drift, The Wall, Golden Reef, and The Pinnacles are within a few minutes of the resort jetty.

Gecko's Resort (tel. 652-0200, www.fiji culturalcentre.com), at the Kalevu Cultural Center on Viti Levu across the highway from the entrance to Shangri-La's Fijian Resort, has 23 rooms at F$125 double. A swimming pool compensates for the lack of a beach. An evening show with Samoan fire dancing is performed in the frog-infested restaurant a couple of times a week.

Malaqereqere Villas (tel. 652-0704, www .malaqerevillas.com), 500 meters off Queens Road, 2.5 kilometers east of Shangri-La's Fijian Resort, stands on a hill overlooking Cuvu Bay. The four deluxe villas, each with three bedrooms, kitchen, fridge, and lounge, are F$365 single or double, F$536 for three to six persons, plus 17.5 percent tax (minimum stay three nights). The local walk-in rate is about 40 percent lower than this. There's a swimming pool. The location is good, but the furnishings are rather worn-out for an upscale place like this.

Attractions near the Fijian

Train buffs won't want to miss the *Fijian Princess,* a restored narrow-gauge railway originally built to haul sugarcane. It now runs 16-kilometer day trips along the coast to Natadola Beach daily at 1000. The station is on the highway opposite the access road to Shangri-La's Fijian Resort, and the ride costs F$95 per person (children under 12 are half price)

FIREWALKING VENUES

Fijian firewalking over hot stones originated on Beqa and Yanuca Islands off southern Viti Levu, but it's now performed at resort hotels along the Coral Coast. **Shangri-La's Fijian Resort** west of Sigatoka presents firewalking together with a *meke* (traditional Fijian dance show) on Friday nights. The package also includes a *lovo* (underground oven) meal. The other resorts all charge a flat F$15-20 admission fee to witness their firewalking performances, which generally begin around 1830. It happens at the **Warwick Fiji** on Mondays and Fridays, at the **Outrigger Reef Resort** on Tuesdays, at **The Naviti Resort** on Wednesdays, and at **Rydges Hideaway Resort** on Thursdays. Perhaps the best place to witness firewalking is at Pacific Harbor's **Arts Village,** where you also get handicraft demonstrations and a tour of a re-created Fijian village for your F$60 day pass, Wednesday-Saturday. Check the dates at the hotels, as these things do change.

COURTESY WARWICK INTERNATIONAL HOTELS

firewalking at The Naviti Resort at Korolevu

including a barbecue lunch. Otherwise there's a trip that combines Natadola with Robinson Crusoe Island. For information about hotel pickups, call the **Coral Coast Railway Co.** (tel. 652-0434).

Across the road from the train station is the **Kalevu Cultural Center** (tel. 652-0200, Tues.–Sun. 0900–1700), a re-created Fijian village dispensing instant Fijian culture to tourists. The basic one-hour tour is F$20 per person. For groups of 25 or more, a full day at the center costs F$75, and includes tours of the Fiji, Samoa, Tonga, Rotuma, New Zealand, and Kiribati villages; a dance show; and a *lovo* lunch, upon request. This place has a slightly deserted feel.

◖ SIGATOKA SAND DUNES

From the mouth of the Sigatoka River westward, five kilometers of incredible 20-meter-high sand dunes separate the cane fields from the beach. These dunes were formed over millennia as sediments brought down by the river were blown back up onto the shore by the southeast trade winds. The winds sometimes uncover human bones from old burials, and potsherds lie scattered along the seashore—these fragments have been carbon-dated at up to 3,000 years old. Now and then, giant sea turtles come ashore here to lay their eggs.

It's a fascinating, evocative place, protected as a national park since 1989 through the efforts of the National Trust for Fiji. The **Visitors Center** (tel. 652-0243, www.nation altrust.org.fj, daily 0800–1800, admission F$20/8/3 family/adult/student) is on Queens Road, about seven kilometers east of Shangri-La's Fijian Resort and four kilometers west of Sigatoka. Exhibits outline the ecology of the park and archaeological findings. The mahogany forest here was planted in the 1960s to prevent sand from blowing onto Queens Road, and there are also dry beech and casuarina forests here. It takes about an hour to cover the loop trails over dunes that reach as high as 50 meters in one area. It's well worth a visit to experience this unique environment. Most buses between Nadi and Sigatoka will drop you right in front of the Sand Dunes Visitors Center on the main highway (though some express buses won't stop here).

KULUKULU

Fiji's superlative surfing beach is near Kulukulu village, five kilometers south of Sigatoka, where the Sigatoka River breaks through Viti Levu's fringing reef to form the Sigatoka Sand Dunes. The surf is primarily a river-mouth point break with numerous breaks down the beach. It's one of the only places for beach-break surfing on Viti Levu, and unlike most other surfing locales around Fiji, no boat is required here. The windsurfing in this area is fantastic, as you can either sail "flat water" across the river mouth or do "wave jumping" in the sea (all-sand bottom and big rollers with high wind). The surfing is good all the time, but if you want to combine it with windsurfing, it's good planning to surf in the morning and windsurf in the afternoon when the wind comes up. You can also bodysurf here. Be prepared, however, as these waters are treacherous for novices. There's a nice place nearby where you can swim in the river and avoid the ocean's currents. The beach itself looks like an elephant graveyard, covered with huge pieces of driftwood.

There's no regular hotel here but a couple of backpacker places behind the dunes, three kilometers off Queens Road, offer basic accommodations for surfers and nature lovers. **Club Masa**, also known as Oasis Budget Lodge, has a 10-bed dormitory and a couple of rooms. If it's closed (as is often the case), **Sand Dunes Inn** (tel. 650-0550, chrishwork@connect. com.fj), a bit closer to the Sand Dunes Visitor Center, has a dorm at F$30 plus tax, which includes breakfast. Leave your valuables behind before going out for an evening stroll, however, as this is an isolated area.

Sunbeam Transport has buses (F$0.75) from Sigatoka to Kulukulu village eight times a day Monday–Saturday, but none on Sunday and holidays. Taxi fare to Club Masa should be around F$6, and later you may have to pay only F$1 for a seat in an empty taxi returning to Sigatoka. Due to a land dispute with the local village, taxis cannot drive right up to Club Masa, and you must walk the last 10 minutes.

SIGATOKA

Sigatoka is the main business center for the Coral Coast and headquarters of Nadroga/Navosa Province. The racially mixed population numbers about 9,500. The Melrose Bridge over the Sigatoka River opened here in 1997, replacing an older bridge damaged during a 1994 hurricane. The town has a picturesque riverside setting and is pleasant to stroll around. The ostentatious palace on the hillside above Sigatoka belongs to supermarket owner V. L. Naidu.

Upriver from Sigatoka is a wide valley known as Fiji's "salad bowl" for its rich market gardens beside Fiji's second-largest river. Vegetables are grown in farms on the western side of the valley, while the lands on the eastern bank are planted with sugarcane. Small trucks use the good dirt road up the west side of the river to take the produce to market and you can drive right up the valley in a normal car. The locals believe that Dakuwaqa, shark god of the Fijians, dwells in the river.

◖ Tavuni Hill Fort

Near Sigatoka, five kilometers up the left (eastern) bank of the river from the bridge, is the Tavuni Hill Fort on a bluff at Naroro village. The fort was established by the 18th-century Tongan chief Maile Latemai and destroyed by native troops under British control in 1876. The Sigatoka Valley was always a main contact corridor between the coastal dwellers and the hill tribes of the interior, hence the strategic importance of this fort. The nearby village is still inhabited by persons of Tongan descent. An interpretive center and walkways have been established here, and admission is F$12 for adults or F$6 for children under 12 (closed Sun.). There's an excellent view of the river and surrounding countryside from this site. Those

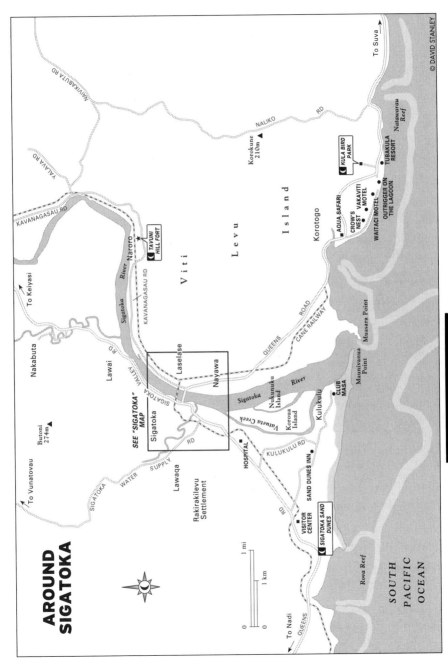

© DAVID STANLEY

To Suva

NALIKO   RD

Konokune
210m ▲

KULA BIRD
PARK   TUBAKULA
            RESORT

Natawawau
Reef

AQUA SAFARI   VAKAVITI
              MOTEL
CROW'S   OUTRIGGER ON
NEST   THE LAGOON
        WAITACI MOTEL

Island

Korotogo

V i t i   L e v u

MAIVIKABUTA RD

YALAVA RD

KAVANAGASAU RD

River Naroro
Sigatoka River

**TAVUNI
HILL FORT**

To Keiyasi

QUEENS   ROAD
        CANE RAILWAY

Muasara Point

Nakabuta

Lawai

RD

Laselase

SIGATOKA VALLEY RD

Nayawa

Sigatoka   River
                        Maunivanua
Natunuku   Point
Island
Koroua
Island   Kulukulu

**CLUB
MASA**

Vaiuela Creek

Butoni
274m ▲

Sigatoka

*SEE "SIGATOKA"
MAP*

To Vunatovau

Lawaqa

RD

KULUKULU RD

HOSPITAL

SIGATOKA   WATER   SUPPLY

Rakirakilevu
Settlement

SAND DUNES INN

**VISITOR
CENTER**

**SIGATOKA SAND
DUNES**

**AROUND
SIGATOKA**

1 mi

1 km

SOUTH
PACIFIC
OCEAN

Rova Reef

To Nadi

QUEENS

0
0

SIGATOKA

Viti

Levu

Island

© DAVID STANLEY

without transport can take a taxi from Sigatoka to the reception area (about F$20 round-trip including a one-hour wait). Otherwise, the occasional Mavua bus will bring you here from Sigatoka. To hike there from Sigatoka takes about an hour or so each way, and it's more pleasant to walk along the former cane railway line than on the dusty road.

River Tours
Sigatoka River Safari (tel. 650-1721, www .sigatokariver.com), with a desk in Tappoos Sigatoka Store, runs 3.5-hour jet boat trips 60 kilometers up the Sigatoka River. Tours operate daily except Sunday at 0800 and 1300 (F$210 pp including lunch and transfers from most

Coral Coast resorts) and visit a different Fijian village every day to lessen the impact. This trip offers an easy way of seeing a bit of the river and meeting local residents while enjoying an exciting speedboat ride.

Eva Eco Tours and Free Information Center (tel. 998-0499), next to the Indigenous Women's Handicraft Center on the riverside, books river tours.

Shopping
Sigatoka has ubiquitous souvenir shops and a colorful local market with a large handicraft section (especially on Wednesday and Saturday). **Jack's Handicrafts** (tel. 650-0810, www.jacksfiji.com) facing the river sells the

© DAVID STANLEY

Sigatoka's population has great ethnic and religious diversity.

traditional handmade Fijian pottery made in Nakabuta and Lawai villages near Sigatoka.

The **Sigatoka Indigenous Women's Handicraft Center,** beside the river opposite Morris Hedstrom, is also worth a look.

For quality snorkeling gear and Internet access, try **Nats** (tel. 650-0064), upstairs between the Colonial National Bank and Big Bear on the street facing the river.

Accommodations

The **Riverview Hotel** (tel. 652-0544), facing the highway bridge in town, has six rooms with bath and balcony at F$35/45 single/double, plus F$5 for air-conditioning. A large public bar is downstairs, so be prepared for noise.

Also try **Aarame Manzil Backpackers Accommodations** (tel. 864-1682) above Raj's Curry House, if open.

The **True Blue Hotel** (Queens Rd., tel. 650-1530, www.truebluehotel.com), above the Sigatoka Club across the traffic circle from the Riverview, has nine air-conditioned rooms with private bath at F$89 for up to three

people, breakfast included. There's also a four-bed dorm at F$25 per person.

Sirelii Kurivitu, manager of the Tavuni Hill Fort, runs the **Naroro Guest House** (www.fijibure.com/naroro), behind the reception to the historic site. It's F$80 per person including meals. Horseback riding (F$12) and many other village activities are possible. The sunsets from here are amazing.

Food

A number of snack bars around the bus station and market dispense greasy fast food and sandwiches to bus passengers during their 15-minute stops here.

Café.com (tel. 652-0877, Mon.–Fri. 1000–1600), next to Jack's Handicrafts, offers lunch specials for F$6–7 (pizzas F$14–17). It's also a good breakfast place.

For Indian dishes, there's **Raj's Curry House** (tel. 650-1470, Mon.–Sat. 0800–2200), on Queens Road next to the Riverview Hotel. There are two sections here: a cheap fast food side and an overpriced regular restaurant. The curries listed on the restaurant menu cost F$8–19, plus an additional 15 percent tax. A couple of vegetarian dishes are available.

The restaurant downstairs at **Sigatoka Club** (tel. 650-0026, Mon.–Sat. 1000–2300, Sun. 1000–2200), across the street from the Riverview Hotel, serves good meals priced F$7–8 daily from 0900–2200 (see the printed menu). The Club's bar is always fine for a beer or a game of pool (three tables). The picnic tables outside next to the river are especially good. A more expensive tourist restaurant is upstairs.

Services

There are several banks in Sigatoka. The ANZ Bank opposite the bus station and the Westpac Bank have Visa/MasterCard ATMs outside their offices. At last report, the Colonial National Bank beside the Westpac Bank changed cash and travelers checks without commission (both Westpac and ANZ take F$5 commission).

Western Union Currency Exchange (weekdays 0800–1800, Sat. 0800–1600), between Jack's Handicrafts and the Riverview Hotel, changes money at rates similar to the banks, without commission.

T-Wicks Net-Cafe (tel. 652-0505), on Sigatoka Valley Road, offers Internet access.

Public toilets are available at the bus station.

Health

The **District Hospital** (tel. 650-0455) is 1.5 kilometers southwest of Sigatoka, out on the road to Nadi.

Dr. Rudy Gerona and Dr. Aida Gerona (tel. 652-0327) work out of an office on Sigatoka Valley Road, facing the river near the old bridge. They're open weekdays 0830–1600, Saturday 0830–1300. A dentist is next door.

Patel Chemist (tel. 650-0213) is behind the market.

Getting There and Around

Pacific Transport (tel. 650-0088) express buses leave Sigatoka for Suva at 0845, 0910, 1025, 1425, 1800, and 1945 (127 km, 3.5

hours, F$10.70), and for Nadi Airport at 0935, 1115, 1220, 1500, 1800, and 2020 (70 km, 1.5 hours, F$5.65). **Sunbeam Transport** (tel. 927-2113) has express buses to Suva (F$11.25) at 0640, 0800, 1050, 1130, 1220, 1320, 1500, 1645, and 1720, and to Nadi (F$5.80) at 1025, 1110, 1245, 1350, 1610, 1715, and 1825. Many additional local services also operate to/from Nadi (61 km). Beware of taxi drivers hustling for fares at the bus station who may claim untruthfully that there's no bus going where you want to go. A taxi from Sigatoka to Korotogo should cost F$7.

Paradise Transport (tel. 650-0028) has a bus up the west side of the Sigatoka Valley to Keiyasi and back. A ride up and back on the morning bus (about four hours in all) provides a good introduction to the valley. Carriers to places farther up the valley like Korolevu and Namoli leave weekday afternoons, returning the next day. They park near the market.

Budget Rent-a-Car (tel. 650-0986, www .budget.com.fj) is at Niranjan's, opposite the Mobil service station at the west entrance to town. **Coastal Rental Cars** (tel. 652-0228, www.coastalrentalcars.com.fj) is next to the Riverview Hotel. Sharmas Rent-a-Car near the Total Service Station in Sigatoka is not recommended.

KOROTOGO

A cluster of inexpensive places to stay and one large American-run resort are at Korotogo, eight kilometers east of Sigatoka, with only the Outrigger on the Lagoon, Sandy Point Beach Cottages, and Tubakula Beach Resort right on the beach itself. Most of the places to stay farther east at Korolevu are more upmarket. East of Korotogo, the sugar fields of western Viti Levu are replaced by coconut plantations with rainforests creeping up the green slopes behind. The swimming and snorkeling at Korotogo are only good at high tide.

◀ Kula Bird Park

A road almost opposite the Outrigger on the Lagoon leads to Kula Bird Park (tel. 650-0505, www.fijiwild.com, daily 1000–1630, admission

F$20, children under 12 half price). It's your only chance to get a close look at the *kula* lorikeet, the Kadavu musk parrot, the goshawk, flying fox fruit bats, and others in near-natural settings. From the reception pavilion, a shaded walkway passes a half dozen aviaries and displays in the valley, then loops back through the hillside forest with several additional aviaries. Numerous small bridges cross the seasonal stream that winds through the park, and if you pause, the call of the barking pigeon, the shrill cry of the honeyeater, and songs from a host of other unseen creatures may reach your ears. Aside from the birds, 140 floral species have been identified in this verdant park. Kula Bird Park has a captive breeding program for the endangered crested iguana and peregrine falcon, and the park's educational program provides free environmental awareness instruction to visiting school groups. It's a beautiful place to stroll around for a couple of hours.

Sports and Recreation

Aqua Safari (tel. 652-0901, aquasafari@con nect.com.fj), on the traffic circle at Korotogo, does two-tank dives each morning at F$149. In the afternoon, there's a snorkeling trip costing F$37 per person, including gear. Their four-day PADI certification course is F$595. **Diveaway Fiji** (tel. 652-0100, www.diveaway-fiji.com) picks up from all hotels in this area.

You can arrange horse riding on the beach next to the Outrigger at the end of Sunset Strip. The Outrigger books horses at F$30 for half an hour or F$50 for an hour, but you'll do much better than that if you pay direct.

SNORKELING SAFETY TIPS

When snorkeling on a fringing reef, beware of deadly currents and undertows in channels that drain tidal flows. Observe the direction the water is moving before you swim into it. If you feel yourself being dragged out to sea through a reef passage, try swimming across the current, rather than against it. If you can't resist the pull at all, it may be better to let yourself be carried out. Wait until the current weakens, then swim along the outer reef face until you find somewhere to come back in. Or use your energy to attract the attention of someone onshore.

Snorkeling along the outer edge of a reef at the drop-off is thrilling for the variety of fish and corals, but attempt it only on a very calm day. Even then, it's wise to have someone standing onshore or paddling behind you in a canoe to watch for occasional big waves, which can take you by surprise and smash you into the rocks. Also, beware of unperceived currents outside the reef – you may not get a second chance. Avoid touching the reef or any of its creatures, as contact can be very harmful to both you and the reef. Take only pictures and leave only bubbles.

snorkeling on a coral reef in Fiji

© ANDREW JALBERT / 123RF.COM

Accommodations
US$25-50

The **Vakaviti Motel and Dorm** (Sunset Strip, tel. 650-0526, www.vakaviti.com), next to The Crow's Nest, has four self-catering units facing the pool at F$80 single or double. The five-bed family *bure* with one double and three single beds is F$90 double. Children under 12 are free. The six-bed backpacker dorm is F$20 per person. Stay a week and the eighth night is free. Facilities include a swimming pool and a large lending library/book exchange at the reception. Day trips to Natadola Beach are arranged.

The **Casablanca Hotel** (Sunset Strip, tel. 652-0600), next door to Vakaviti, is a two-story hillside building on the inland side of Sunset Strip. Its eight rooms with cooking facilities and arched balconies begin at F$50/65 single/double. Have a look at a few rooms as they do vary.

Just west of the Outrigger on the Lagoon at Korotogo is the **Waitaci Motel** (tel. 650-0278), with three large A-frame bungalows and two rooms below the reception in the main building. Cooking facilities are provided. The swimming pool and charming management add to the allure. Prices are similar to those at Vakaviti.

A bit east of the Outrigger and right on the beach, **(Tubakula Beach Resort** (Queens Rd., tel. 650-0097, www.fiji4less.com) offers a holiday atmosphere at reasonable rates. The 22 pleasant A-frame bungalows with fan, cooking facilities, and private bath—each capable of sleeping three or four—start at F$126 double near the highway. Renovated bungalows are F$139 double poolside, F$153 garden, or F$180 beachfront (extra persons F$24 each, with a maximum of five). One self-catering house has three rooms with shared bath at F$63/69 single/double. The "Beach Club" dormitory consists of eight rooms, each with five or six beds at F$28 a bed (small discount for students and HI card holders). The units are not new or fancy, but they are a good value. Late readers will like the good lighting. Tubakula caters to independent travelers rather than people on "Feejee Experience"–style packages. A communal kitchen is available to all, plus there's a swimming pool, restaurant, game room, nightly videos, and a mini-mart. To allow the lagoon coral to regenerate undisturbed, motorized water sports are not offered. Tubakula's conference building can host conferences, meetings, and seminars for up to 250 people (it's often used

Tubakula Beach Resort offers inexpensive Coral Coast accommodations.

© DAVID STANLEY

by NGOs). Ask about the Tuesday-night *lovo* (underground-oven feast) at Malevu village, 500 meters east of Tubakula. The snorkeling here is good, there's surfing and scuba diving nearby, and bus or taxi excursions are available. What more do you want? Basically, Tubakula is a quiet, do-your-own-thing kind of place for people who don't need lots of organized activities. Seated on your terrace, watching the sky turn orange and purple behind the black silhouettes of the palms along the beach, a bucket of cold Fiji Bitter stubbies close at hand, you'd swear this was paradise! It's one of the most popular backpacker resorts on the Coral Coast and well worth a couple of nights.

US$50-100

The Crow's Nest (Sunset Strip, tel. 650-0230, www.crowsnestfiji.com), a few hundred meters southeast of the traffic circle, has 18 split-level duplex bungalows with cooking facilities, veranda, and thin walls. The eight "executive" units are F$135 single or double, while the 10 self-catering units are F$145, plus F$25 per extra adult to four maximum. The restaurant up on the hill faces the swimming pool. The nicely landscaped grounds are just across the road from the beach, and good views over the lagoon are obtained from The Crow's Nest's elevated perch.

The well regarded **Bedarra Inn** (77 Sunset Strip, tel. 650-0476, www.bedarrafiji.com), a bit west of the Outrigger on the Lagoon, has 21 spacious air-conditioned rooms with fridge in a two-story block at F$167/180 standard/deluxe double. It's all tastefully decorated but only three rooms have microwaves. A swimming pool, video room, and lounge round out the facilities.

◖ Sandy Point Beach Cottages (Queens Rd., tel. 650-0125, www.sandypointfiji .com) shares the same beach with the adjacent Outrigger. Three fan-cooled beachfront units and one garden bungalow with full cooking facilities are F$90/110 single/double and a five-bed cottage is F$160. Set in spacious grounds right by the sea, Sandy Point has its own freshwater swimming pool. The owner, Bob Kennedy, has erected 10 huge satellite dishes on his lawn to allow you to pick up 12 channels on the TV in your room. It's a good choice for families or small groups, but it's often full, so you must reserve well ahead. Check-out time is 1000.

OVER US$250

The 254-room **Outrigger on the Lagoon Fiji** (Queens Rd., tel. 650-0044, www.outrig ger.com/fiji) plunges down the hillside from Queens Road to a sandy beach. A great view of this Fijian village-style complex can be had from the reception. The spa and wedding chapel crowning an adjacent hill provide an even better view. The main highway was rerouted away from the coast when this property was being redeveloped in 2000, blocking the old highway (now called Sunset Strip). Entry to the resort is from the Queen's Road side only. The four-story main building on the hill has 167 air-conditioned rooms with ocean views and balconies, beginning at F$567 single or double plus 17.5 percent tax. Scattered around the grounds are 47 regular thatched *bure* with fan from F$820 plus tax, and five big duplex *bure* at F$1,640 plus tax for a family of up to six. Most guests book ahead through the Outrigger website and pay a lot less than this, so ask for a discount. Wheelchair-accessible rooms are available. Romantic couples and throngs of children share the huge million-liter swimming pool beside the ho-hum beach. A free kids club operates irregularly 0900–2100. Even if you're not staying here, it's worth coming for the Fijian firewalking Tuesday at 1830 (F$19), followed by a *meke* and buffet in the restaurant. There's a small shopping mall, Thrifty Car Rental and Rosie Holidays have desks just off the lobby, and wireless Internet is available at fair prices. A tunnel under the highway near the tennis courts leads to Kula Bird Park.

Food

Facing the beach just west of the Outrigger is the **Beach Side Restaurant** (tel. 652-0584, daily 0800–2300) with chicken, meat, and seafood dishes of variable quality for F$8–17. Pizza is available for dinner only. A mini-mart and handicraft shop adjoin the restaurant. To get there from the Outrigger, go down onto the beach and walk west.

Le Café Garden Restaurant (tel. 652-0877, daily 1000–2200) is between the Beach Side Restaurant and the Waitaci Motel. Pizzas are F$9–19, mains F$16, specials F$7. Happy hour is 1700–1900. Under Swiss management, this place has class.

At **The Crow's Nest Restaurant** (tel. 650-0230, daily 0700–2200), the menu ranges from fish and chips at F$11 to a lobster dish for F$48, but the food isn't highly rated. A much better bet for a meal out along this way is the **Bedarra Inn** (tel. 650-0476, daily 0700–1500 and 1800–2200), with main dishes ranging from pasta puttanesca at F$18 to lobster for F$65. The specialty is seafood curry (F$25). The **Sinbad Pizza Restaurant** (tel. 652-0600) at the Casablanca Hotel isn't as nice. **Tubakula Beach Resort** (tel. 650-0097) has a good-value restaurant open to the public.

Getting There

Local buses on Queens Road stop at the doors of the Outrigger on the Lagoon and Tubakula Beach Resort. For the Crow's Nest, Vakaviti, Casablanca, Bedarra, and Waitaci, get off the bus at the traffic circle on the coast, just where the highway turns inland and heads east toward the Outrigger. From there, follow the old highway (Sunset Strip) south along the beach to your hotel.

Car Rentals and Tours

Thrifty Car Rental (tel. 652-0242) has a desk in the lobby of the Outrigger on the Lagoon.

Coastal Rental Cars (tel. 652-0228, www.coastalrentalcars.com.fj), on Korotogo Back Road near the traffic circle at Korotogo, rents cars from F$80/480 for one/seven days including tax and insurance.

Several other places, including the Beach Side Restaurant and the Bedarra Inn, rent cars for a negotiable F$65 a day plus insurance. It's also easy to arrange a taxi tours to Natadola (F$100), Pacific Harbor (F$135), or Suva (F$135) for up to four passengers. This is much cheaper than the tours sold at the Outrigger.

Adventures in Paradise (tel. 652-0833, www.adventuresinparadisefiji.com) operates tours to

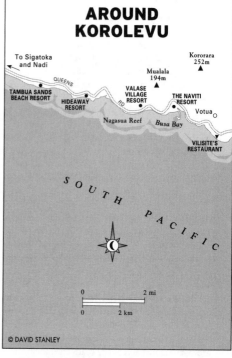

Biausevu Falls and the Naihehe Cave. Each tour costs F$109 per person, including transfers from Coral Coast hotels, lunch, drinks, and guides. From Nadi hotels, they're F$129. Book through your hotel tour desk (and wear disposable shoes on the falls hike). These trips are highly rated.

Vatukarasa

This small village between Korotogo and Korolevu is notable for its quaint appearance and **Baravi Handicrafts** (tel. 652-0364), 7.5 kilometers east of the Outrigger on the Lagoon. Baravi carries a wide selection of Fijian handicrafts at fixed prices, and it's worth an outing if you're staying at one of the Coral Coast resorts. Two other Vatukarasa handicraft shops are just west of Baravi.

KOROLEVU

At Korolevu, east of Korotogo, the accommodations tend to cater to a more upscale crowd,

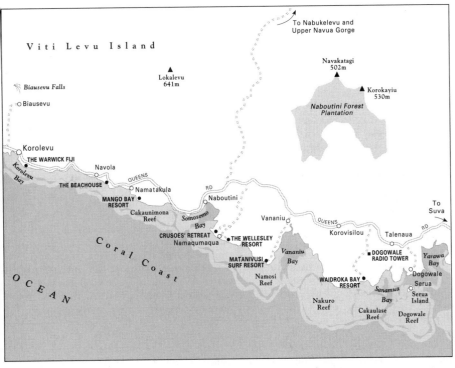

Viti Levu Island

Biausevu Falls

Biausevu

Lokalevu
641m

Navakatagi
502m

Korokayiu
530m

Naboutini Forest
Plantation

To Nabukelevu and
Upper Navua Gorge

Korolevu

THE WARWICK FIJI

Korolevu Bay

Navola

THE BEACHOUSE

Namatakula

MANGO BAY RESORT

Cakaunimona Reef

Somosomo Bay

CRUSOES' RETREAT

Namaqumaqua

Naboutini

Vananiu

Korovisilou

Talenaua

QUEENS RD

To Suva

THE WELLESLEY RESORT

MATANIVUSI SURF RESORT

Vananiu Bay

Namosi Reef

WAIDROKA BAY RESORT

Nakuro Reef

DOGOWALE RADIO TOWER

Sanamua Bay

Cakaulase Reef

Yarawa Bay

Dogowale

Serua Island

Serua

Dogowale Reef

OCEAN

Coral Coast

and cooking facilities are usually not provided for guests. These places are intended primarily for Australians and New Zealanders on packaged beach holidays who intend to spend most of their time unwinding. Distances between the resorts are great, so for sightseeing you'll be dependent on your hotel's tour desk. Exceptions are The Beachouse, the Mango Bay Resort, and Waidroka Bay Resort farther east, which cater to the flashpacker market. If you swim anywhere along this coast, beware of dangerous currents in channels draining the fringing reef.

Sports and Recreation

Diveaway Fiji (tel. 650-1124, www.diveaway-fiji.com), at Rydges Hideaway Resort and the Mango Bay Resort, is small enough to give personalized service. Their favorite dive sites are named Gunbarrel, Bigfoot and Sundance, Purple Haze, Stingray, and Bordello (F$95/160 for one/two tanks, plus F$25 for gear). If you don't dive and want an excuse to hang out on the Coral Coast, consider the PADI Open Water certification course at F$725 per person for one or two, F$675 per person for three or more. An outer reef snorkeling trip is F$45 per person.

South Pacific Adventure Divers (tel. 653-0055, www.spadfiji.com), based next to the pool at the Warwick resort, also handles diving at The Naviti and Tambua Sands (free pick-ups). They frequent the top dive sites in the Beqa Lagoon, 40 minutes away by boat, as well as colorful sites closer to home. For Coral Coast dives, it's F$95/155 for one/two tanks, plus F$35 for gear. Dive excursions to the Beqa Lagoon or Vatulele are F$230 for two tanks including gear (six-person minimum). SPAD's PADI four-day Open Water course is F$680.

Tropical Fishing and Watersports (tel. 653-0069, www.sportfishingfiji.com), based at the Mango Bay Resort, offers game fishing from the *Mango Princess,* an eight-meter open boat, at F$1,080/1,440 a half/full day (six anglers).

Several companies offer tours to **Biausevu Falls,** a 25-minute hike from Biausevu village, itself just less than three kilometers inland from Queens Road between the Warwick and Vilisite's Restaurant. The trail to the falls zigzags across the river a half dozen times (expect to get your feet wet), but you'll enjoy a refreshing swim in the pool at the foot of the cascading waterfall. The village charges F$10 per person admission to the area. Call Adventures in Paradise (tel. 652-0833) in Korotogo for information on tours.

Accommodations
US$25-50
The **Valase Village Resort** (Queens Rd., tel. 650-7001, www.valasebeachresort.com), at Tagaqe village just west of The Naviti Resort, offers a six-bed family *bure* at F$105, two double *bure* at F$85, and an eight-bed dorm at F$30 per person. All rooms have a toilet, shower, and fridge, and breakfast is included. Meals can be ordered. It's a good choice for families that don't require luxury, as children under 16 stay free if sharing a room with their parents. The beach here is good.

US$50-100
One of the South Pacific's best budget resorts, **❰ The Beachouse** (Queens Rd., tel. 653-0500, www.fijibeachouse.com), is on a palm-fringed white beach just off Queens Road, between Navola and Namatakula villages, five kilometers east of the Warwick. It's 35 kilometers east of Sigatoka and 43 kilometers west of Pacific Harbor. The slogan here is "low-cost luxury on the beach," and the whole project was painstakingly designed to serve the needs of backpackers (and not as a dormitory tacked onto an upmarket resort as an afterthought). The eight six-bed dorms are F$35 per person, or F$40 per person in a four-bed dorm. One dorm is women-only. In addition, 12 neat little units in a quadrangle at the heart of the

property are F$110 single or double, F$130 triple. Campers are allowed to pitch their tents on the wide lawn between the rooms and the beach for F$25 per person. Tax, breakfast, and afternoon tea are included in all rates. Stay six nights and the seventh night is free. Separate toilet/shower facilities for men and women are just behind the main buildings, and nearby is a communal kitchen and dining area. It's all very clean and pleasant. Meals in the restaurant (open until midnight) consist of fish and chips, burgers, and vegetarian fare. The closest grocery store is in Korolevu (there's only a tiny cooperative store in Namatakula). The British reality-TV series *Celebrity Love Island* spent much of 2006 filming here, and left behind the new swimming pool and Fijian-style movie set by the beach. Not only is the ocean swimming good at high tide (unlike the situation at many other Coral Coast hotels, where you could end up using the pool), but they'll take you out to the nearby reef in their launch for snorkeling. However, do ask about the currents before going far off on your own—tourists have drowned after being swept out through the reef passage here. Sea kayaks are loaned free. A wooden building near the highway contains the reception, a lending library, free SkyTV, Internet connections, and a travel center. A shopping shuttle to Suva can be arranged. There's a bush track up into the hills behind the resort. Or you can join a vigorous four-hour round-trip hike to Navola Falls.

You can stay in Namatakula village at **Batibasaga Guest House** (www.fijibure.com/namatakula), operated by Judith and Simon Batibasaga. It's F$95 per person including meals, and many village activities are possible. A *sevusevu* of kava roots should be presented upon arrival.

The **Waidroka Bay Resort** (tel. 330-4605, www.waidroka.com) is up the steep, rough gravel road leading to the Dogowale Radio Tower between Korovisilou and Talenaua, four kilometers off Queens Road. Operating since 1995, Waidroka has earned a reputation as one of Fiji's top surfing resorts. More recently, the Waidroka Bay has tried to mitigate the surf-camp atmosphere by adding a swimming pool, outdoor bar, yoga cabana, and spa, but non-surfers and non-divers may still feel somewhat out of place. Accommodations include a four-bed dormitory at F$120 per person including meals, and five little oceanfront bungalows with private bath, fan, bamboo walls, and covered deck at F$170/220 double/triple without meals. The two superior bungalows are F$255/316/357 double/triple/quad. The optional meal plan is F$68 per person a day (cooking facilities are not provided). Videos are shown in the jungle bar at night. The surfing crowd loves this place, and it's the only "mainland" resort habitually surfing Frigate Passage and six other local breaks. Three breaks are just a five-minute boat ride from the resort, and they'll ferry you out there at F$50 per person for two hours, provided the boatman is around. Waidroka's beach is mediocre but snorkeling trips can be arranged. Waidroka's dive boats have powerful engines that enable them to reach Frigate Passage in just 20 minutes (surfers pay F$85 pp including lunch, with a F$340 minimum charge for the boat). Scuba diving is F$105/185 for one/two tanks, plus F$40 for equipment. Sport fishing is also offered. Call ahead, and they'll pick you up at Korovisilou village on Queens Road at F$20 for the car. Reservations are necessary, as the Waidroka Bay Resort is often full.

US$100-150

The good-value **Tambua Sands Beach Resort** (Queens Rd., tel. 650-0399, www .tambuasandsfiji.com), in an attractive location facing the sea about 10 kilometers east of the Outrigger on the Lagoon, conveys a feeling of calm and peace. The 31 beach bungalows are F$255 double garden or F$266 beachfront (third persons F$40). No cooking facilities are provided. Though the restaurant is nothing special, there's a swimming pool, excellent live music most evenings, and a *meke* on Saturday night if enough guests are present.

The 100-room **Rydges Hideaway Resort** (Queens Rd., tel. 650-0177, www.hideaway fiji.com) at Korolevu, is three kilometers east of Tambua Sands and 20 kilometers east of Sigatoka. Set on a palm-fringed beach before

© CHRISTIAN HAUGEN

Rydges Hideaway Resort

a verdant valley, the 30 garden *bure* are F$199 double, while the 58 oceanview *bure* go for F$230. The 10 beachfront villas are F$317. Four larger family units suitable for up to six people go for F$403. Children under 12 stay and eat free. Be prepared for the lively holiday camp atmosphere, especially around the resort's huge oceanside pool. Some rooms get a lot of disco noise from the bar or traffic roar from the adjacent highway. A full buffet breakfast is included in all rates. The lunch-and-dinner plan, which also covers drinks, is F$120 per person a day (minimum of three days). This big resort provides zany cruise ship–style entertainment nightly, including a *meke* on Tuesday and Friday (free), and firewalking on Thursday (F$15, kids under 12 half price). The all-you-can-eat Fijian feast is also on Thursday night (F$32). From January to May, surfing is possible on a very hollow right in the pass here (not for beginners). Scuba diving is offered by Diveaway Fiji (tel. 652-0100, www .diveaway-fiji.com), based here. Beware of unperceived currents, and expect dead coral if you snorkel here (possible at high tide only). The Rosie Holidays desk arranges other trips and Thrifty Car Rental bookings.

In 2006, the **((Mango Bay Resort** (tel. 653-0069, www.mangobayresortfiji.com) opened on lovely grounds behind a sparkling white beach near Namatakula village. There are 10 thatched beachfront *bure* with private bath at F$275 double and 10 three-person safari tents with attached bath at F$195 triple. Much cheaper is the 16-bunk dorm at F$36 per person, while the open eight-bed dorm is F$45 per person. Tax and a light breakfast are included, but other meals are extra. Children under 12 are usually not accepted. Mango Bay styles itself "Fiji's first flashpacker resort," and there are loads of parties and activities for the young traveler provided sufficient guests are present. By day, there's snorkeling (high tide only), kayaking, water sports, game fishing, tours, hiking, rafting, horseback riding, and scuba diving (with Diveaway Fiji, www .diveaway-fiji.com); by night, it's happy hour,

bonfires, full-moon parties, DJ dancing, and outdoor cinema. The lagoon-shaped pool has a swim-up bar. Feejee Experience groups often stay here.

((Crusoe's Retreat (tel. 650-0185, www .crusoesretreat.com), by the beach four kilometers off Queens Road from Naboutini, is the most isolated place to stay on the Coral Coast. The 29 large *bure* each have two double beds, an antique fridge, and a porch. The 11 "seaside" *bure* are from F$321 double, while the 17 "seaview" bungalows on the hillside are from F$234. Only units Nos. 1–6 have thatched roofs (No. 1 is the closest to the beach). Prices include a buffet breakfast, afternoon tea, and non-motorized sports such as kayaks, sailboards, and paddleboards. It's cheaper to order from the menu at the restaurant than to buy a meal plan. The on-site dive shop charges F$250 for one/two tanks including gear, but don't worry: This isn't a dive resort. The resort's name refers to Daniel Defoe's novel *Robinson Crusoe,* and the footprint-shaped freshwater swimming pool symbolizes Man Friday.

The overrated **Wellesley Resort** (tel. 603-0664, www.wellesleyresort.com.fj) is near Namaqumaqua village, 4.5 kilometers off Queens Road down the same bumpy access road as Crusoe's Retreat. The Wellesley is set in a narrow valley that opens onto a lovely white beach (one of the Coral Coast's best) facing a protected lagoon. There's also a large swimming pool. The 15 spacious rooms aligned in a long block well back from the beach start at F$219 double including a light breakfast and tax (free airport transfer with minimum three-night stay). Walk-in discounts are possible. Meals are extra. Reservations mix-ups are common here and the service is poor. An easy way to get to either The Wellesley or Crusoe's Retreat is by taking a public bus to the Warwick Fiji at Korolevu and a taxi from there (about F$10 for the car).

OVER US$250

In early 2007, the **((Matanivusi Surf Resort** (tel. 360-9479, www.surfingfiji.com) opened on a fine white sand beach five kilometers off Queens Road from Vananiu village. Matanivusi charges F$400 per person twin share in the eight attractive duplex units (minimum three-night stay). Included are three meals and boat rides to selected surfing and snorkeling spots. A swimming pool is near the restaurant. Most of the 16 guests come to surf at Frigate Passage (F$80 pp extra charge) or on three smaller waves closer by. Transfers from Nadi Airport are F$340 for two persons round-trip.

The Naviti Resort (Queens Rd., tel. 653-0444, www.warwicknaviti.com), five kilometers east of Rydges Hideaway Resort and 100 kilometers from Nadi Airport, has 220 spacious air-conditioned rooms and suites in a series of two- and three-story blocks beginning at F$610/780 single/double (garden view), plus 17.5 percent tax. The price includes all meals with unlimited wine or beer, plus many activities. Stay here only if you're willing to pay the all-inclusive price. Bed and breakfast alone are F$485 double plus tax and you'll be charged dearly for everything on top of that (check your bill carefully line by line). This place is popular among Australian families as kids under 13 stay and eat free when sharing with parents who are on The Naviti's comprehensive all-inclusive plan. The Naviti is also one of the more wheelchair-accessible resorts on this coast. There's a *lovo* (F$55) on Tuesdays and firewalking (F$16) on Wednesdays. The five tennis courts are floodlit at night. Scuba diving is with South Pacific Adventure Divers. Other facilities include two swimming pools, mini fitness center, nine-hole golf course, beauty center, Internet access (F$0.30 a minute), ATM in the lobby, and a boutique. Rosie Holidays has a desk at The Naviti Resort, and Avis has a car rental office across the road.

The **Warwick Fiji** (Queens Rd., tel. 653-0555, www.warwickfiji.com), on Queens Road six kilometers east of The Naviti Resort, is one of the largest hotels on the Coral Coast. Erected in 1979 and part of the Hyatt Regency chain until 1991, it's now owned by the same Hong Kong–controlled company as The Naviti Resort, and there's a

COURTESY WARWICK INTERNATIONAL HOTELS

guest room at the Warwick Fiji

© DAVID STANLEY

The Wicked Walu restaurant is on a point just off the main beach at the Warwick Fiji resort.

shuttle bus between the two. The Warwick has a livelier atmosphere than the somewhat depressed Naviti and is better managed. The 250 small air-conditioned rooms are in three-story wings running east and west from the soaring Hyatt-style lobby. It's F$482 double for the 51 rooms with mountain views, F$552 for the 166 with ocean views, F$600 for the 23 club rooms, and F$928 for the 10 suites, buffet breakfast and taxes included. Two children 12 and under sleep and eat free when sharing with their parents. The Wicked Walu seafood restaurant, on a small offshore islet connected to the main beach by a causeway, serves large portions but is expensive (dinner only). The other hotel restaurants can be crowded with Australian families and you could easily end up waiting in line. The F$85 per-person meal plan includes the pool grill lunch and buffet dinner but not the Wicked Walu or drinks. There's live music in the Hibiscus Lounge Wednesday–Saturday until 0100 and nightly

disco dancing. The firewalking is on Monday and Friday at 1830 (F$15, children under 13 half price). The South Pacific Adventure Divers' dive shop is next to the pool and there's a sports and fitness center. Most water sports are extra unless you're on some sort of all-inclusive deal. Thrifty Car Rental and ATS Pacific have desks on-site.

Food

⟨ Vilisite's Restaurant (Queens Rd., tel. 653-0054, daily 0800–2200), by the lagoon between the Warwick and The Naviti resorts at Korolevu, is better known as "Felicity's place." The favorite lunch dish is fish and chips, otherwise there's chop suey or curries. Dinner consists of a choice of six set seafood menus costing F$20–45. The champagne sunsets here 1800–1900 are unforgettable. Vilisite's gift shop has good prices on handicrafts and there are rooms for rent. It's worth the taxi ride if you're staying at the Warwick or The Naviti.

Pacific Harbor and Vicinity

Southeastern Viti Levu from Deuba to Suva is wetter and greener than the coast to the west, and the emphasis changes from beach life to cultural and natural attractions. Pacific Harbor satisfies sporting types, while Fiji's finest river trips begin at Navua. In this area, scattered Indo-Fijian dwellings join the Fijian villages that predominate farther west.

Pacific Harbor is a sprawling South Florida–style condo development and instant culture village, 148 kilometers east of Nadi Airport and 49 kilometers west of Suva. It was begun in the early 1970s by Canadian developer David Gilmour (the current owner of Wakaya Island) and his father, Peter Munk, and good paved roads meander between the landscaped lots with curving canals to drain what was once a swamp. Many residents have boats tied up in their backyards, and if it weren't for the backdrop of deep green hills you'd almost think you were in some Fort Lauderdale suburb. Many of the 180 individual villas are owned by Australian or Hong Kong investors.

Until recently, Pacific Harbor was eclipsed by the sunnier Denarau area near Nadi, and after the May 2000 coup, tourism to Pacific Harbor dropped to nearly nothing. Things began turning around in mid-2003 when Columbia Pictures filmed *Anacondas: The Hunt for the Blood Orchid* here, injecting millions of dollars into the local economy. Then in 2005, Eric Roberts took over the moribund Pacific Cultural Center and renamed it the Arts Village. A two-story building in the

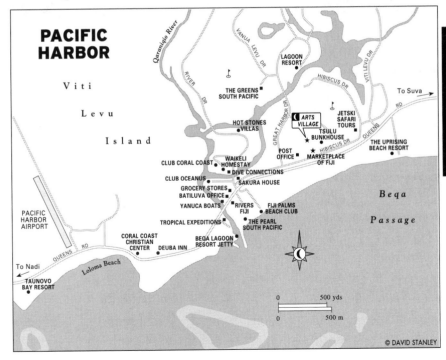

© DAVID STANLEY

bure at the Arts Village in Pacific Harbor

Arts Center was relaunched as Tsulu Beach Bunkhouse & Apartments in 2006, and new shops and restaurants opened in the old marketplace. Around the same time, Pacific Harbor's golf course and main resort changed hands and were upgraded, breathing new life into the area.

Pacific Harbor offers lots to see and do, varied accommodations and food, and convenient transportation. Where Pacific Harbor really sparkles is in the excellent scuba diving in the Beqa Lagoon to the south and the river trips into the interior to the north. The beach here is the last reasonable beach before Suva. Trips to the surfers' camps on Yanuca Island are easily arranged.

SIGHTS
◖ Arts Village

Pacific Harbor's imposing Arts Village (tel. 345-0065) presents tours and shows Wednesday–Saturday. The one-hour Island Temple Tour (F$20) visits a re-created Fijian village, featuring a small "sacred island"

dominated by a 20-meter-tall *Bure Kalau* (Spirit House). In the Vale Levu (Chief's *Bure*), you get to meet a pagan priest. On the Island Boat Tour (F$25), a tour guide "warrior" carrying a spear gives a spiel to visitors seated in a double-hulled *drua,* and Fijians attired in jungle garb demonstrate traditional canoe making, weaving, *tapa,* and pottery at stops along the route. The highlight of the day is a performance of Fijian firewalking (F$35). A combined ticket (F$60 or F$80 including lunch) is available for all three activities, and you should arrive by 1030 if you want to see and do everything. The adjacent marketplace (open daily) mixes mock-colonial boutiques with assorted historical displays, and even if you don't take any of the tours, you'll be able to see quite a few of the Arts Village's attractions for free from the catwalk. The Arts Village may sound like a mini-Disneyland but this should not discourage you from visiting as the introductions to all aspects of Fijian life are authentic and the guides are both entertaining and informative.

© DAVID STANLEY

dive boats moored at the mouth of the Qaraniqio River

SPORTS AND RECREATION

The 65 kilometers of barrier reef around the 390-square-kilometer Beqa Lagoon south of Pacific Harbor features multicolored soft corals and fabulous sea fans at Sidestreets, and an exciting wall and big fish at Cutter Passage. Sulfur Passage on the east side of Beqa is equally good. The top dive sites just north of Yanuca Island, such as Sidestreets, Soft Coral Grotto, Caesar's Rocks, and Coral Gardens, are easily accessible from Pacific Harbor.

◖ Frigate Passage

Fiji's most underrated surfing wave could be the left-hander in Frigate Passage southwest of Yanuca Island. This consistently fast and hollow tube is like Cloudbreak near Nadi but without the crowds. It breaks on the western edge of the Beqa Barrier Reef and isn't for beginners. Surfers from budget resorts on Yanuca Island and the Coral Coast arrive here daily by boat.

Aside from its surfing potential, Frigate Passage is one of the top scuba-diving sites near Suva. A vigorous tidal flow washes in and out of the passage, which attracts big schools of fish, and there are large coral heads. However, it's rather far from the dive shops of Pacific Harbor and Beqa Island, so get a firm commitment from your operator if you want to dive here. If it can't be done, there are numerous other dive sites closer in to Pacific Harbor, including Shark Reef, one of the top shark diving venues in the world.

Scuba Diving

Dive Connections (16 River Dr., tel. 345-0541, diveconn@connect.com.fj), just across the bridge from the Sakura House Oriental Restaurant, visits all the best dive sites off Yanuca Island on their spacious 12-meter dive boat, *Scuba Queen*. They charge F$155 for two-tank dives. Night dives are F$80. You can rent gear at F$30 a day, but it's better to bring your own. Four-day PADI Open Water certification is F$600 (medical examination not required), or there's an introductory two-dive package for F$180. Snorkelers are welcome to

© CRASHDIVER

scuba diving in the Beqa Lagoon

go along on their daily dive trips at F$60 per person, including a nice lunch and snorkeling gear (they'll drop you off on Yanuca for snorkeling). The dive boat is also available for fishing charters. Kayaks are for rent. Ask about the self-catering flat next to their office, which they rent to clients. They'll pick up anywhere within eight kilometers of the Pacific Harbor bridge.

Aqua-Trek Beqa (tel. 345-0324, www .aquatrek.com) at The Pearl South Pacific's marina is an efficient operation with good rental equipment. They send their 11-meter boat, the *Aqua-Sport,* to the Beqa Lagoon twice daily. A two-tank soft coral diving excursion costs F$200. Shark diving is F$210, plus a F$15 park fee. A night dive is F$120. Some of Fiji's top shark diving is on offer here: You may see several three-meter bull sharks, plus gray reef, black-tip, white-tip, lemon, and nurse sharks. They only do the shark dive a couple of times a week, so call ahead. If the boat isn't crowded, they'll take along non-divers for snorkeling at about F$65 per person.

Shark diving is also a specialty of **Beqa Adventure Divers** (tel. 345-0911, www .fijisharkdive.com), based at the Lagoon Resort. They regularly hand-feed eight species of sharks, including bull sharks, on the "Big Fish Encounter" (F$120/210 for one/two tanks, plus gear and F$20 Shark Reef Marine Reserve levy). This is one of Fiji's most spectacular dives.

Tropical Expeditions (tel. 345-0666, www .tropical-expedition.com) operates the 18-meter live-aboard *Beqa Princess,* based near the bridge across the river from The Pearl South Pacific Resort. Two-tank day trips are F$150 per person including lunch, or the boat may be chartered for overnight trips (six berths). A compressor is on board.

Fishing

Xtasea Charters (tel. 345-0280, www.xtasea charters.com) at Club Oceanus in Pacific Harbor offers game fishing from the 12-meter cruiser *Wai Tadra.* A full-day charter is under F$2,000 for up to eight persons. Xtasea offers a package including fishing, accommodations, and meals at F$700 per person per day (minimum of four anglers for four days).

Jet Ski Tours

Jetski Safari Tours (158 Kaka Place, Pacific Harbor, tel. 345-0933, www.jetski-safari .com) operates half-day Jet Ski excursions from Pacific Harbor to Beqa Island at F$215 per person, provided you're willing to share a Jet Ski with someone else. If you want to be sure to have one to yourself, it's F$400. Usually, four or five Jet Skis cross to the island together, leaving at 0830 and returning around 1330. You must book one day in advance.

◖ White-Water Rafting

Exciting white-water rafting trips on the Upper Navua River west of Namuamua are offered by **Rivers Fiji** (tel. 345-0147, www.riversfiji .com), with an office on the grounds of The Pearl South Pacific at Pacific Harbor. You're driven over the mountains to a remote spot near Nabukelevu, where you get in a rubber raft and shoot through the fantastic Upper Navua Gorge (inaccessible by motorized boat). Experienced paddlers can do the same on their own in an inflatable kayak, upon request. Due to the Class III rapids involved, children under eight are not accepted, but for others it's F$295 including lunch. This trip is offered on Monday, Wednesday, and Friday.

On Tuesday, Thursday, and Saturday, Rivers Fiji does a less strenuous run down the Wainikoroiluva River north of Namuamua, on which it's possible to paddle your own inflatable kayak. This costs F$240. Two days of kayaking on the Wainikoroiluva is F$590. If you're really keen, ask about overnight camping expeditions on the Upper Wainikoroiluva. These trips conclude with a motorized punt ride down the Lower Navua Gorge from Namuamua to Nakavu village, where you reboard the van to your hotel. A minimum is six bookings is required to run a tour.

Rivers Fiji also offers one-day sea-kayaking trips to Beqa Island (F$265 pp, minimum of eight). You cross to Beqa by catamaran, then explore a tiny uninhabited island and paddle into Malumu Bay. Deep inside this cliff-lined bay, hundreds of fruit bats cling to the trees. A secret mangrove tunnel provides an escape south to the great blue beyond. A different trip takes you along the coast of Viti Levu from Pacific Harbor in a two-person sea kayak at F$120 per person. It's a great way to explore the mangroves or glide across the reefs. All prices above include pick-ups around Pacific Harbor.

Zip Fiji

Zip 200 meters along a zip line at speeds of up to 60 kph with **ZipFiji** (tel. 930-0545, www.zip-fiji.com) near Wainadoi village, between Pacific Harbor and Suva. You fly from tree to tree through the rainforest at treetop level, crossing a mountain stream. Guided tree climbs, rappelling, and sleeping in the upper reaches of the jungle canopy are also offered. Rosie Holidays in the Arts Village marketplace books Zip Fiji at F$140 per person, including pickups. Most people enjoy this activity and leave wishing it had lasted longer.

Golf

Pacific Harbor's sporting focal point is the 18-hole, par-72 championship **The Greens South Pacific** (tel. 345-0905), also known as the Pearl Championship Golf Course and Country Club, designed by Robert Trent Jones, Jr. Greens fees are F$24/47 for 9/18 holes, electric-cart rental is F$24/41 for 9/18 holes, and club hire is a further F$20/40. The course is owned by The Pearl South Pacific, and hotel guests get one complimentary round during their stay. The clubhouse is a couple of kilometers inland off Queens Road. Persons dressed in jeans, bathing suits, or shoes with metal spikes are not allowed on the course. Men must wear a shirt with a collar, dress shorts, and golf shoes.

ACCOMMODATIONS
Under US$25

One kilometer west of the bridge at Pacific Harbor is the friendly **C Coral Coast Christian Center** (Queens Rd., tel. 345-0178, www.christiancampfiji.org). They offer four five-bed Kozy Korner rooms with a good communal kitchen and cold showers at F$15/28/41 single/double/triple. The four adjoining motel units go for F$40/55 single/double, complete with private bath, kitchen, fridge, and fan. The two family units are F$45/62/77 single/double/triple (plus F$10 for air-conditioning). Camping costs F$9 per person. A small selection of snack foods is sold at the office. No alcoholic beverages are permitted on the premises. The camp is just across the highway from long golden Loloma Beach, the closest public beach to Suva. Watch your valuables if you swim there (place everything in the trunk if you have a rental car). The snorkeling is good in calm, dry weather. Just avoid arriving on a weekend, as it's often fully booked by church groups from Friday afternoon until Sunday afternoon.

US$25-50

Adjacent to the Coral Coast Christian Center west of Pacific Harbor is the **Deuba Inn** (Queens Rd., tel. 345-0544, theislander@ connect.com.fj). They have eight small rooms with shared bath at F$45/50 single/double, and five self-catering units at F$80/90 for four/five people. Camping space costs F$15 per person. The restaurant serves good meals, and the Sand Bar (closed Mon.) is handy if you're staying at the "dry" Christian Center next door.

The 10-room **Club Oceanus** (Atoll Place, tel. 345-0498, www.cluboceanus.com), formerly known as the Pacific Safari Club, is just down from Sakura House Oriental Restaurant. A bed in a clean 24-bed dorm here is F$25 per person, otherwise it's F$30 per person in a four-bed dorm, both with communal cooking facilities and fridge. The 10 rooms in a long block are priced F$65–130 single or double with bath, fan, TV, and full cooking facilities (use of the air-conditioning is F$10 extra). The manager can organize scuba-diving discounts for you. It's quite pleasant, with a pool and bar on the riverside.

Club Coral Coast (12 Belo Cir., tel. 345-0421, clubcoralcoast@connect.com.fj) is past Dive Connections. There are seven air-conditioned rooms with fridge and a small kitchen at F$90–120 double, plus F$10 per additional person. The three small non-air-conditioned rooms in the main building are F$45 double with shared kitchen and bath. Amenities include a 20-meter swimming pool, tennis, and a gym.

Tsulu Beach Bunkhouse & Apartments (tel. 345-0065) occupies the top floor of a mock-colonial two-story building at the Arts Village. You've got a choice of apartments, rooms, and air-conditioned dorms, but don't expect luxury of any kind. The 24-bed bunkroom is F$25 per person, while smaller four- to 10-bed dorms are F$30 per person. Tsulu also has nine individual rooms for rent in apartments, beginning at F$63 single or double with shared bath or $85 with private bath. Self-catering apartments are F$96/126/285 with one/two/four bedrooms. The private apartments are suggested for families, as children under 16 are not allowed in the bunkrooms. Guests have access to a communal kitchen and lounge. The Ritz Kona Café opposite the reception serves breakfast. The Tiki Pool behind

the building has an 18-meter waterslide, hot tub spa, and swim-up bar. To swim in the sea, cross the highway from Tsulu and walk west a hundred meters till you're opposite the post office. A lane to the beach will be on your left.

US$50-100

◖ Nanette's Accommodation Villa 108 (108 River Dr., tel. 331-6316 or 345-2041, www.nanettes.com.fj or www.nanettespacific harbour.com), beside Dive Connections, has four rooms with private bath at F$150 double, including continental breakfast. Communal cooking facilities and fridge are provided. There's a large sitting room in the center of the building and a nice sheltered swimming pool out back. This building was built in 2006 and everything is clean and fresh. It's one of Pacific Harbor's best buys.

◖ Waikeli Homestay (Belo Circle, tel. 345-0328, www.waikeli.com), right next to Club Coral Coast, has three rooms at F$160 double, including a cooked breakfast and laundry facilities. It's very upscale with a modern lounge and garden, and Mrs. Cakau Cockburn is a delightful host.

Harbor Property Services Ltd. (tel. 345-0959, www.fijirealty.com), with an office at the Arts Village, rents out 22 of the Pacific Harbor villas at F$180–300 for up to six persons. All villas have kitchens, lounge, and washing machine, and some also have a pool. The minimum stay is three nights, and there's a reduction after a week. A one-time cleaning fee of F$50 is charged, and F$5 a day for electricity plus F$4 for gas are extra. It's a good value and well worth considering for a longer stay. **Resort Homes** (tel. 345-0034, www.resorthomesfiji.com), also at the Arts Village, is considerably more expensive at F$1,000 a week and up.

◖ The Uprising Beach Resort (Queens Rd., tel. 345-2200, www.uprisingbeachresort.com) is a flashpacker resort that opened in early 2007. Unlike Tsulu, it's right on the beach, just a little east of the Arts Village. There's a good view of Beqa Island from this long beach, which stretches west to the mouth of the Qaraniqio

© DAVID STANLEY

The dormitory *bure* at The Uprising Beach Resort provides budget accommodations for up to 24 persons.

River. The six attractive thatched beachfront *bure* are F$180 single or double, while the six garden-view *bure* are F$160 double. These spacious units accommodate up to four and extra persons are F$20 per person. Families are welcome. The 24-bed dormitory at the back of the property is F$35 per person. You can pitch your own tent near the dorm or on the sandy beach at F$20 per person. A light breakfast is included. Facilities include a swimming pool, open-air restaurant/bar, laundry service, free Internet computers at the reception. Kiteboarding is possible when there's wind but you'll need to bring your own gear. Feejee Experience tour groups often stay here and lots of locals come to drink at the bar.

US$100-150

Pacific Harbor's top hotel is **The Pearl South Pacific** (Queens Rd., tel. 345-0022, www.the pearlsouthpacific.com), a three-story building launched as a Travelodge in 1972 and later known as the Centra Resort and the Pacific Harbor International Hotel. It's at the mouth of the Qaraniqio River, between Queens Road and a long sandy beach, on attractive grounds and with a nice deep swimming pool. The 36 spacious garden-view rooms are F$248 single or double, the 36 oceanview rooms F$314, the three garden penthouses F$582, and the three oceanview penthouses F$666. Add 17.5 percent tax to these rates. You're better off paying the extra for the oceanview rooms, as the garden-view rooms sometimes receive a dank smell from the nearby mangroves. Even if you're not staying, it's worth a sightseeing visit.

Most of the units at the **Fiji Palms Beach Club and Resort** (Queens Rd., tel. 345-0050, fijipalms@connect.com.fj), right next to The Pearl South Pacific, have been sold as part of a timeshare scheme with the "Holiday Club." Only club members are allowed to stay in the 12 new units, but the 14 older two-bedroom apartments with cooking facilities are sometimes available on a casual basis at F$200/1,200 a day/week (Sat.–Sat.) for up to six people. You should call ahead as walk-ins are not usually accommodated.

swimming pool at The Pearl South Pacific

© DAVID STANLEY

The **Lagoon Resort** (tel. 345-0100, www
.lagoonresort.com), inland a couple of kilometers behind the Arts Village, is beautifully set
on Fairway Place between the river and the golf
course, a 10-minute walk from the clubhouse.
The 21 plush rooms with marble bathrooms
and TV are a good value at F$190 double. This
hotel started out in 1988 as the Atoll Hotel
and was later known as the Korean Village.
It's a little secluded, and VIP parties often
stay here. In 2003, the Hollywood crew filming *Anacondas* spent 24 weeks here, and a few
props from the film are on the resort grounds.
Many of the guests come to shark dive with
Beqa Adventure Divers.

In 2007, **Tiri Villas** (50 Rovodrau Rd., tel.
345-0552, www.tirivillas.com) opened among
the mangroves near the mouth of the Deuba
River, four kilometers east of Pacific Harbor.
The adjacent mangrove forest may interest
birdwatchers. The six well-constructed beach
villas are F$340 double, the five garden vil-
las F$245, and the three group villas F$204.
Meals, activities, and 17.5 percent tax are extra.

Happy hour at the Pacific Breeze restaurant/
bar overlooking Rovodrau Bay is 1700–1900
daily. Tiri Villas is three kilometers down a
gravel road off Queens Road from Moti Lal
and Sons. A taxi from the highway will charge
F$6.

US$150-250

Hot Stones Villas (37–38 River Drive, tel.
345-0045, www.hotstones.com.fj) rents luxury
villas in a tropical garden along the Qaraniqio
River. These cost F$400 plus 17.5 percent
tax for a two-bedroom or F$600 for a three-
bedroom (minimum stay three nights). A full
breakfast is included.

Over US$250

Just west of Pacific Harbor, **Taunovo Bay
Resort and Spa** (Queens Rd., tel. 999-2227,
www.taunovobay.com) is a beautifully situated upscale resort that opened in 2008. The
18 units range from a one-bedroom beachfront
suite at F$1,330 to a four-bedroom grand villa
at F$4,750, including tax, breakfast, and non-

motorized water sports. Exclusive use of the four-bedroom "heaven" tree house is F$11,500 a night. Despite the high prices, small size, and flashy website, the service may not satisfy the more demanding guest. Don't count on gourmet food, flawless maintenance, or being able to get a massage. Taunovo Bay charges in U.S. dollars and you should assume that all food and drink prices are also in that currency. The nearby Pacific Harbor airstrip has been reopened to allow direct Pacific Sun flights daily from Nadi (F$107) and Suva (F$150) using a six-seater Islander aircraft.

FOOD

The Refreshment Counter (Mon.–Fri. 0600–1900, Sat.–Sun. 0600–1700) at the Pic'n Pac Supermarket in the Arts Village marketplace serves sandwiches at F$2, chicken or fish and chips for F$4.80. This is also a good place to buy ice cream.

The longstanding **Oasis Restaurant** (tel. 345-0617, daily 0930–1430 and 1800–2130), in the Arts Village marketplace, has a sandwich (F$6–14), salad, and burger (F$9–14) menu at lunchtime, and more substantial main courses for dinner (F$16–40). Internet access here is F$0.20 a minute. A large selection of paperbacks is for sale at F$2 a book. It's pleasant sitting at the tables next to the pond outside.

The **Water's Edge Bar and Grill** (tel. 345-0145, Mon.–Thurs. 0930–1600, Fri.–Sat. 0930–2030), between Tsulu and the marketplace, has a large terrace overlooking the front pool. They serve Indian dishes (F$14–24) including curries (F$16), pizza (F$19), and pasta (F$18–28).

Perkins Pizza (tel. 345-2244, daily 0930–2100), on the side of the Arts Village marketplace facing the highway, has 20 varieties of pizza priced F$19–27.

For more upscale dining, try the **Sakura House Oriental Restaurant** (tel. 345-0256, Mon.–Sat. 1600–2200), just off River Drive from near the bridge.

Pacific Harbor's most exclusive restaurant is the **Mantarae Restaurant** (tel. 345-0022) at The Pearl South Pacific, specializing in fish and beef dishes (F$33). Come for the *lovo* (F$35) on Monday 1700–2200 to try all the island specialties with live entertainment. Formal or smart casual dress is required.

There are five small grocery stores near the bridge and a supermarket at the Arts Village marketplace. For fruit and vegetables, you must go to Navua.

INFORMATION AND SERVICES

Rosie Holidays (tel. 345-0655) in the Arts Village can make any required hotel or tour bookings, and they also represent Thrifty Car Rental. Call ahead if you want to pick up a car here.

Coral Sun Fiji has a tour desk at The Pearl.

The **Batiluva Beach Resort** of Yanuca Island has a booking office (tel. 992-0019) near the bridge at Pacific Harbor. If you're a surfer, this is where to go.

Both ANZ Bank and Colonial National Bank have ATMs in the Arts Village marketplace. The Colonial National Bank also has a branch open weekdays 0930–1600.

The main Pacific Harbor post office (with two card phones) is next to the Arts Village.

Soap 'n Surf Laundromat (Mon.–Fri. 0900–1700, Sat. 0900–1600), at the Arts Village, charges F$5 to wash, F$1.50 to dry.

GETTING THERE AND AROUND

Pacific Harbor's airstrip at Taunovo Bay receives daily flights from Nadi (F$203) and Suva (F$185). Arriving by bus is a lot cheaper and more convenient as all of the Queens Road express buses stop here. The express bus to Pacific Harbor from Suva stops on the highway opposite the entrance to The Pearl South Pacific, a kilometer from the Arts Village. The slower Galoa buses and some other local buses will stop right in front of the Arts Village itself (advise the driver beforehand).

The air-conditioned Fiji Express leaves from the front door of The Pearl South Pacific for Suva at 1050 and 1615 (F$10) and for Nadi at 0810 and 1625 (F$20). Cheaper and almost as

SOUTHERN VITI LEVU

fast are the regular Pacific Transport express buses, which stop on the highway: to Nadi Airport at 0750, 0930, 1035, 1315, 1605, and 1835 (148 km, three hours, F$12); to Suva at 1015, 1100, 1155, 1555, 1930, and 2115 (49 km, one hour, F$4.85). Sunbeam Transport buses to Lautoka stop here at 0830, 1100, 1210, 1415, and 1515.

NAVUA

The bustling riverside town of Navua (pop. 4,500), 39 kilometers west of Suva, is the market center of the mostly Indian-inhabited rice-growing and dairy cattle-ranching delta area near the mouth of the Navua River. It's also the headquarters of Serua and Namosi provinces. Many of the large buildings in the town center date back to the early 20th century, when this was an important sugar milling town.

For visitors, Navua town is only important as the gateway to the fabulous Navua River. The lower Navua below Namuamua is navigable in large outboard motorboats, while rubber rafts are used on the much faster upper Navua through the narrow **Navua River Gorge.** Either way, a river trip will give you a memorable glimpse of central Viti Levu.

Getting There and Around

All buses between Suva and Nadi stop at Navua. Large village boats leave from the wharf beside Navua market for Beqa Island south of Viti Levu daily except Sunday, but more depart on Saturday (F$30 pp one-way). Be aware that safety equipment is usually absent on such boats. Regular flat-bottomed punts carry local villagers 25 kilometers up the Navua River to Namuamua village Monday to Saturday afternoons, and they'll probably agree to take you along for F$20. You can charter an outboard from Navua wharf to Namuamua almost any time at F$100 for the boat round-trip. The hour-long ride takes you between high canyon walls and over boiling rapids with waterfalls on each side. Above Namuamua is the fabulous **Upper Navua,** accessible only to intrepid river-runners in rubber rafts. It's also possible to reach the river by road at Nabukelevu.

River Tours

An easy way to experience the picturesque lower Navua is with **Discover Fiji Tours** (tel. 346-0830 or 346-0480, www.discoverfijitours.com), which has operated here since 1988. Their office is on the riverside in Navua. They offer a "Jewel of Fiji Day Tour" up the Navua River by motorized canoe, leaving Navua at 1030 daily and returning at 1630. You have a choice of any two of three activities: a swim at a waterfall, a visit to a Fijian village with a welcoming kava ceremony, or a float down the river on a bamboo raft or canoe (no village visits on Sunday). The cost is F$133 per person from Suva (minimum of two), lunch included. Call to arrange a pick-up. They also organize overnight trekking into central Viti Levu for anywhere from one to seven nights at F$150 per person a night. You must call ahead, as they don't hang around in Navua waiting for customers to appear.

In addition, **Mr. Sakiusa Naivalu** (tel. 346-0641) of Navua organizes upriver boat trips to Namuamua village with the possibility of spending the night there. These trips depart Navua at 1000, returning at 1600. Readers have found Sakiusa's tour enjoyable.

If you'd like to spend some time exploring

A waterfall tumbles into the Navua River.

© TOURISM FIJI

© DAVID STANLEY

village boats from upriver and Beqa Island at the wharf beside Navua Market

the area, consider **Navua Upriver Lodge** (tel. 336-2589 or 925-9026, navrest05@yahoo.com), between Melita and Wainadiro villages, a two-hour hike from Namuamua. Double rooms with shared bath are F$90 per person or pay F$65 per person in a dorm, meals included.

THE LEGEND OF MAU

Long ago, a group of mountain warriors moved down to a coastal flatland. They built bure and called their new home Mau. The warriors brought with them many things, such as mountains, birds, springs, prawns, and a natural pool with a waterfall. Blessed by Mother Nature, they developed their culture. Today, Mau is still set amid tall mountains and thick jungles. The forests are full of tropical birds and beautiful flowers. A river flows to mangroves by the sea. The people of Mau will reveal their ancient totems to guests, and take them fishing and snorkeling on the coral reefs. Visits that begin with a kava ceremony always end with a heartfelt farewell.

Boat transfers from Navua are extra. The website www.fijibure.com arranges village stays in Namuamua and Nukusere at F$80 per person including meals.

Adre Sunika runs **Namuamua Village Stays** (adresunika@yahoo.com) at Namuamua. Mattress accommodations in one giant *bure* at the fork of the rivers is F$20 per person a night. Breakfast is F$5; other meals served to you while seated on floor mats are F$10. Horseback riding can be arranged at around F$20 per person depending on the length of the ride. *Bilibili* rafting, fishing, hiking, and swimming at the waterfall a 10-minute walk upstream are free. Boat transfers from Navua are F$40 per person round-trip.

Namosi

Carriers from the landing opposite Namuamua to Suva go via Namosi, spectacularly situated below massive Mount Voma (927 m), with sheer stone cliffs on all sides. You can climb Mount Voma in a day from Namosi for a sweeping view of much of Viti Levu. It's steep, but not too difficult. Allow at least four hours up and down (guides can be hired at Namosi village). Visit the old Catholic church at Namosi.

There are low-grade copper deposits estimated at 500,000 tons at the foot of the Korobasabasaga Range, which Rupert Brooke called the "Gateway to Hell," 14 kilometers north of Namosi by road. No mining has begun, due to depressed world prices of copper and high production costs, though feasibility studies continue. A 1979 study indicated that an investment of F$1 billion would be required.

Islands off Southern Viti Levu

VATULELE ISLAND

This small island, 32 kilometers south of Viti Levu, reaches a height of only 34 meters at its north end; there are steep bluffs on the west coast and gentle slopes facing a wide lagoon on the east. Both passes into the lagoon are from its north end. Five different levels of erosion are visible on the cliffs from which the uplifted limestone was undercut. There are also rock paintings, but no one knows when they were executed. Vatulele today is famous for its tapa cloth (*masi*).

Other unique features of 31-square-kilometer Vatulele are the sacred **red prawns,** which are found in tidal pools at Korolamalama Cave at the foot of a cliff near the island's rocky north coast. These scarlet prawns with remarkably long antennae are called *ura buta* ("cooked prawns") for their color. The red color probably comes from iron oxide in the limestone of their abode. It's strictly taboo to eat them or remove them from the pools. If you do, it will bring ill luck or even shipwreck. The story goes that a princess of yesteryear rejected a gift of cooked prawns from a suitor and threw them in the pools, where the boiled-red creatures were restored to life.

In 1990, Vatulele got its own luxury resort, the **Vatulele Island Resort** (tel. 672-0300, www.vatulele.com) on the island's west side. The 19 futuristic villas in a hybrid Fijian/New Mexico style sit about 50 meters apart on a magnificent white-sand beach facing a protected lagoon. The emphasis is on luxurious exclusivity: Villas start at F$2,300 per couple per night, including meals and tax. "The Point," a two-story unit on a low cliff over the ocean, is F$5,500 with private pool.

This extreme pricing creates high expectations—that are not always met. The minimum stay is two nights, and to make the resort more attractive to honeymooners and other romantics, children under 13 are accepted only at Christmastime. Weddings are arranged—bring your own partner. This trendy resort cleverly markets the lack of motorized water sports, a general swimming pool, phones, and TVs as environmental consciousness, yet there's still a lot to do, including sailing, snorkeling, windsurfing, paddling, fishing, tennis, and hiking, with guides and gear provided at no additional cost. Other than airfare to the island, about the only things you'll be charged extra for are scuba diving, fishing, massage, and alcohol. Vatulele's desalination plant ensures abundant fresh water.

The 990 inhabitants of the island live in four villages on the east side of Vatulele. Village boats from Viti Levu leave Paradise Point near Korolevu Post Office on Tuesday, Thursday, and Saturday if the weather is good. Resort guests arrive on a daily charter flight from Nadi, which costs F$940 per person round-trip (or F$3,350 one-way for a special four-person flight). The charters are operated by **Pacific Island Seaplanes** (tel. 672-5644, www.fijiseaplanes.com), which uses a four-seat Beaver seaplane able to land on the lagoon near the resort. If weather conditions prevent use of the seaplane, a Twin Otter aircraft is sent. It lands on the island's small private airstrip near the villages, six kilometers from Vatulele Island Resort. **Island Hoppers** (tel. 672-0410, www.helicopters.com.fj) offers helicopter transfers from Nadi Airport to Vatulele.

YANUCA ISLAND

This island west of Beqa should not be confused with the Yanuca Island on which Shangri-La's Fijian Resort is found. This Yanuca is a surfer's paradise best known for the left-hander in Frigate Passage southwest of the island.

In a coconut grove tucked below the jungly green peaks on the northwest side of Yanuca is the **(Batiluva Beach Resort** (tel. 992-0021 or 345-0384, www.batiluva.com), one of Fiji's top surf resorts. Americans Sharon Todd and Dan Thorn opened this place in 1998. The two four-bed dorms, two double *bure,* and one family *bure* are all F$175 per person—an excellent value compared to places like Nagigia, Namotu, and Tavarua. Included are gourmet meals, appetizers, kayaks, surfing, snorkeling, village tours, and 24-hour generator electricity. Fishing and scuba diving are available at additional cost. Transfers from Pacific Harbor are F$50 per person. This is the closest resort to Frigate Passage (30–40 minutes away), and Batiluva's surfing boats go there every day. Several top dive sites, including Three Nuns, Sidestreets, Soft Coral Grotto, and Gilligan's Tower, visited daily by the dive boats from Pacific Harbor, are only a kilometer straight out from this beach. Batiluva has a booking office near the bridge at Pacific Harbor where you can obtain full information.

Not far from Batiluva is the village-operated **Yanuca Island Resort** (tel. 336-1281, www.frigatesreef.com), also known as Frigate Surfriders Surf Camp or Frigates Reef Resort. Shared accommodations in a 12-bunk dormitory *bure* or a private *bure* are F$150 per person including meals and Frigate Passage boat trips. Boat transfers from the mainland are F$50 per person round-trip or F$120 for groups of 3–8 persons. The snorkeling right off the beach is great.

All surfing is banned on Sunday. Yet even without the surfing, Yanuca is still well worth a visit for the great beach-based snorkeling. The resorts are across the island from Yanuca's single Fijian village, a 30-minute walk. Shells, mats, and necklaces can be purchased from the locals. And as on neighboring Beqa, Fijian firewalking is a tradition here. Village boats to the one Fijian village

on Yanuca depart on Monday and Saturday afternoons from the highway bridge at Pacific Harbor. Contact Batiluva for direct transfers.

BEQA ISLAND

Beqa (MBENG-ga) is the home of the famous Fijian firewalkers; Rookwa, Naceva, and Dakuibeqa are firewalking villages. Nowadays, they perform mostly at hotels on the Coral Coast, although the local resorts occasionally stage a show. At low tide, you can hike part of the 27 kilometers around the island: Rookwa to Waisomo and Dakuni to Naceva are not hard, but the section through Lalati can be difficult. Malumu Bay, between the two branches of the island, is thought to be a drowned crater. Climb Korolevu (439 m), the highest peak, from Waisomo or Lalati. Kadavu Island is visible to the south of Beqa.

It's possible to arrange stays at Raviravi and Naiseuseu villages on Beqa through the website www.fijibure.com (F$80 pp including meals). The **(Lawaki Beach House** (tel. 992-1621 or 368-4088, www.lawakibeachhousefiji.com) faces the golden sands of Lawaki Beach west of Naceva village. This backpacker resort has two double *bure* at F$116/198 single/double and one six-bed family *bure* or dormitory at F$81 per person, all meals included (reduced rates for children under 12). To camp (with your own tent) is F$66

BEQA ISLAND

Waisomo
Malumu Bay
LALATI RESORT
Korolevu 439m
Raviravi
Lalati
Suliyaga
BEQA LAGOON RESORT
Rookwa
Beqa Island
Vaga Bay
Dakuni
Moturiki Island
Dakuibeqa
KULU BAY RESORT
LAWAKI BEACH HOUSE
Naceva

0   2.5 mi
0   2.5 km
© DAVID STANLEY

per person, including meals (no self-catering facilities). Credit cards are not accepted. There's a spacious lounge in the main house and good snorkeling right offshore. Hiking trips, fishing, and scuba diving can be arranged. Boat transfers from Navua are F$160 one-way for the first and second persons together, or F$60 per person for three or more. You can also get there on village boats departing the wharf beside Navua market weekdays around noon (F$30 pp one-way). Ask for the Naceva boat (Sam or Christine can arrange this for you).

In 2003, the **Kulu Bay Resort** (tel. 603-0617, www.kulubay.com) opened on the south side of Beqa a bit closer to Naceva. The seven spacious beachfront *bure* are F$3,800 double for seven nights, including variable meals, kayaking, and guided hikes. Skip the village visit as you'll be pestered for "donations." Drinks and transfers to Beqa are extra. Scuba diving is available at an additional charge and good snorkeling is nearby. Take insect repellant.

The Australian-run **Beqa Lagoon Resort** (tel. 330-4042, www.beqalagoonresort.com), formerly known as Marlin Bay Resort, on the west side of Beqa between Raviravi and Rookwa villages, dates back to 1991. The gardens and central pond are lovely, and there's an infinity swimming pool near the restaurant. An open-air spa was added in 2009. Scuba diving in the Beqa Lagoon and surfing runs to Frigate Pass are the main reasons people come here—non-high-end surfers and divers should look elsewhere. Each of the 12 beachfront *bure* has a private courtyard and plunge pool, starting at around F$650 double plus F$165 per person for meals (three-night minimum). Drinks, surfing, and scuba diving are extra. The Beqa Lagoon Resort boat picks up guests at Pacific Harbor (F$190 pp round-trip).

The upscale **Lalati Resort** (tel. 368-0453, www.lalatifiji.com), at the north opening of Malamu Bay, has five two-bedroom oceanfront *bure,* three hillside *bure,* and three honeymoon villas, starting at $F523/618 single/double. Meals, non-motorized water sports, and taxes are included (drinks and motorized activities extra). Boat transfers from Pacific Harbor are free with a three-night minimum stay, otherwise they're F$180/250 single/double round-

Beqa Lagoon Resort garden

© ERIK HANNON

© MARK HEARD / WWW.FLICKR.COM/HEARDSY

breakfast at the Royal Davui Island

trip. Scuba diving is extra (shark dive F$145). There's a swimming pool and spa. Lalati's muddy tidal beach is poor but you can snorkel out to a reef from the end of their pier.

Royal Davui Island (tel. 330-7090, www .royaldavui.com), on tiny Ugaga Island (aka Stuart Island), just southwest of Beqa, opened in 2004. The lagoon waters off Ugaga's white beaches have been declared a marine sanctuary, so the sealife is profuse. Each of the 16 two-room villas perched on the cliffs of Ugaga has its own plunge pool and spa. Meals are served in an open-air restaurant below a huge banyan tree. The exclusivity is reflected in the nightly tariff of F$1,786 double for the nine deluxe villas, F$2,214 for the four premium villas, and F$2,575 for the three honeymoon villas, including tax, set meals, and non-motorized activities. Lower rates may be available to residents of Australia. Upscale couples are the target market, and three people are not allowed to share a villa. Children under 17 are banned. Scuba diving, spa treatments, sport fishing, and semi-submersible rides all cost extra. Transfers from Nadi Airport are another F$1,800 round-trip per couple.

Kadavu

This big, 50-by-13-kilometer island 100 kilometers south of Suva is the third largest in Fiji (450 square km). A mountainous, varied island with waterfalls plummeting from the rounded rainforested hilltops, Kadavu is outstanding for its vistas, beaches, and reefs. The three hilly sections of Kadavu are joined by two low isthmuses, with the sea biting so deeply into the island that on a map its shape resembles that of a wasp. Just northeast of the main island is smaller Ono Island and the fabulous Astrolabe Reef, stretching halfway to Suva. A process is now underway to have Ono's fringing reefs declared a marine conservation area.

The **birdlife** is rich, with some species of honeyeaters, fantails, and velvet fruit doves

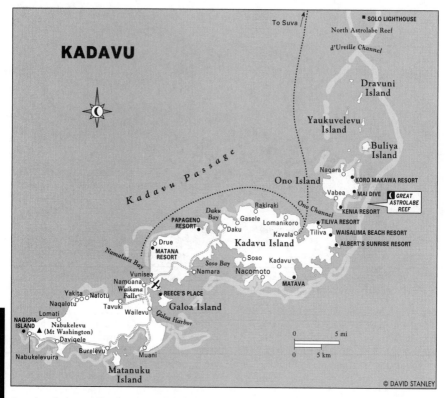

KADAVU

To Suva

North Astrolabe Reef

■ SOLO LIGHTHOUSE

d'Urville Channel

Dravuni Island

Yaukuvelevu Island

Buliya Island

Naqara

Ono Island

Kadavu Passage

Vabea   ● MAI DIVE

KORO MAKAWA RESORT

GREAT ASTROLABE REEF

Ono Channel

KENIA RESORT

Daku Bay   Rakiraki

Gasele   Lomanikoro

● TILIVA RESORT

PAPAGENO RESORT

Drue

Daku

Kavala

Tiliva   ● WAISALIMA BEACH RESORT

MATANA RESORT

Namalata Bay

Kadavu Island

● ALBERT'S SUNRISE RESORT

Soso Bay   Soso   Kadavu

Vunisea   Namara   Nacomoto

Namuana

Waikana Falls

Yakita   Nalotu

MATAVA

Naqalotu   Tavuki

★ REECE'S PLACE

Lomati   Wailevu

Galoa Harbor

NAGIGIA ISLAND   Nabukelevu

Galoa Island

▲ (Mt Washington)

Daviqele

Nabukelevuira   Burelevu   Muani

0   5 mi

0   5 km

Matanuku Island

© DAVID STANLEY

found only here. The famous red-and-green Kadavu musk parrots are readily seen and heard. But Kadavu really stands out for what it lacks. There are not only no mongoose, but also no mynahs, or bulbuls, or cane toads. Few islands of this size anywhere in the Pacific have as much endemic biodiversity left as Kadavu.

In the 1870s, steamers bound for New Zealand and Australia would call at the onetime whaling station at Galoa Harbor to pick up passengers and goods, and Kadavu was considered as a possible site for a new capital of Fiji. Instead, Suva was chosen, and Kadavu was left to lead its sleepy village life; only in the past two decades has the outside world made a comeback with the arrival of roads, planes, and just less than a dozen small resorts, many of them on the channel between Kadavu and

Ono. Some 10,000 indigenous Fijians live in 60 remote villages scattered around Kadavu.

SIGHTS

The airstrip and wharf are each a 10-minute walk, in different directions, from the post office and hospital in the small government station of **Vunisea,** the largest of Kadavu's villages and headquarters of Kadavu Province. Vunisea is strategically located on a narrow, hilly isthmus where Galoa Harbor and Namalata Bay almost cut Kadavu in two.

Just two kilometers south of the airstrip by road and a 10-minute hike inland is **Waikana Falls.** Cool spring water flows over a 10-meter-high rocky cliff between two deep pools, the perfect place for a refreshing swim on a hot day. A good beach is at **Muani** village, eight kilometers south of Vunisea by road.

© DAVID STANLEY

Headed for Kadavu's market, shoppers from outlying villages land on the beach near Vunisea.

West of Vunisea

A road crosses the mountains from Namuana to **Tavuki** village, seat of the Tui Tavuki, paramount chief of Kadavu. The provincial office is also at Tavuki. A couple of hours west on foot is the **Yawe District,** where large pine tracts have been established. In the villages of Nalotu, Yakita, and Naqalotu at Yawe, traditional Fijian pottery is still made. Without a potter's wheel or kiln, women shape the pots with a paddle and fire them in an open fire. Sap from the mangroves provides a glaze.

Another road runs along the south coast from Vunisea to **Nabukelevuira** at the west end of Kadavu. There's good surfing at Cape Washington in this area, and a deluxe surf camp on Denham Island just off the cape caters to the needs of surfers. The abrupt, extinct cone of **Nabukelevu,** or Mount Washington (838 m), dominates the west end of Kadavu. Petrels nest in holes on the north side of the mountain. This dormant volcano erupted as recently as 2,000 years ago.

◖ Great Astrolabe Reef

The Great Astrolabe Reef stretches unbroken for 100 kilometers along the south and east side of Kadavu. One kilometer wide, this reef is rich in coral and marine life, and because it's so far from shore, it still hasn't been fished out. The reef surrounds a lagoon containing 10 islands, the largest of which is 30-square-kilometer Ono. The reef was named by French explorer Dumont d'Urville, who almost lost his ship, the *Astrolabe,* here in 1827.

There are frequent openings on the west side of the reef, and the lagoon is never more than 20 meters deep, which makes it a favorite of scuba divers and yachties. The Astrolabe Reef also features a vertical drop-off of 10 meters on the inside and 1,800 meters on the outside, with visibility up to 75 meters. However, only the hard and soft corals on the outer side of the reef are truly spectacular, as most of the corals inside the reef are dead. This barrier reef is also famous for its caves, crevices, and tunnels.

The Astrolabe is exposed to unbroken waves

generated by the southeast trade winds, and diving conditions are often dependent on the weather and tides. Currents are to be expected in places like Naiqoro Passage, but they're not as strong as those at Taveuni. Surfing is possible at Vesi Passage (boat required).

Many possibilities exist for ocean kayaking in the protected waters around Ono Channel, and there are several resorts at which to stay. Kayak rentals are available and several companies offer kayaking tours to Kadavu.

ACCOMMODATIONS
Under US$25

Reece's Place (tel. 333-6097 or 362-6319), on Galoa Island just off the northwest corner of Kadavu, was the first to accommodate visitors to Kadavu. It's a 15-minute walk from the airstrip to the dock, then a short launch ride to Galoa itself. It's become run-down but there's always a chance it will be upgraded, so call for an update. The view of Galoa Harbor from Reece's Place is nice, but snorkeling in the murky water off the so-so beach is a waste of time. There's good anchorage for yachts just off Reece's Place.

For many years, Kadavu's other low-budget standby was **Albert's Sunrise Resort** (tel. 333-7555), a family operation at Lagalevu at the east end of Kadavu. In the past, they offered six *bure* with kerosene lighting and a three-bed dorm, and scuba diving could be arranged. Call ahead to ask if they're operating.

US$25-50

Manueli and Tamalesi Vuruya run **Biana Accommodation** (tel. 333-6010 or 368-1270), on a hill overlooking Namalata Bay near the wharf at Vunisea. The three rooms with cold showers are F$45/65 single/double, including breakfast, plus F$5 each for lunch or dinner. They ask that you call ahead before coming.

US$50-100

Kenia Resort (tel. 360-7951, www.keniafijiresort.com), formerly known as Jonas Paradise Resort, is at Vabea at the southern tip of Ono Island opposite Kadavu. The accommodations are good with two deluxe *bure* (private bath) at F$75 per person, three standard *bure* (shared bath) at F$60 per person, two four-bed dorm *bure* at F$25 per person, and camping space at F$15 per person. Three tasty meals a day are F$60 per person extra, but you'd be wise to bring a few snack foods with you. Kenia's generator goes off at 2300. This small, family-style resort has a steep, non-tidal white sand beach that is always right for swimming and very safe for kids (no current or big waves). The snorkeling is great (hundreds of clownfish in crystal clear water), and the gorgeous Great Astrolabe Reef is only a five-minute boat ride away. Turtles, sharks, and big fish are seen on most channel dives, and the fish and coral on the reefs are first rate, too. Scuba diving is with Viti Watersports (www.vitiwatersports.com).

US$100-150

The **Waisalima Beach Resort** (tel. 738-9236, www.waisalima.com) faces a one-kilometer beach on the north side of Kadavu, between Albert's and Kavala Bay. The three standard *bure* with shared bath are F$170/262 single/double, while the six "ensuite" units with private bath are F$200/357. Taxes, meals, and the boat transfer from Vunisea Airport are included. The minimum stay is four nights. Conditions have improved here since a change in ownership in 2008 and electricity is supplied. Kayaks are loaned free. Scuba diving is with **Viti Watersports** (www.vitiwatersports.com) at F$170 for a two-tank dive, plus F$15 for gear. A four-day Open Water certification course costs F$605.

US$150-250

Not to be confused with the more expensive Matana Resort is **Matava** (tel. 333-6222, www.matava.com), a 30-minute walk east of Kadavu village and almost opposite tiny Waya Island on the southeast side of the island. Opened in 1996, Matava styles itself as "Fiji's Premier Eco Adventure Resort." The managers have installed solar electricity and water heating, an organic vegetable garden, and a spring water system. There's no beach in front of Matava, but the snorkeling in the marine reserve off

Waya is fine. The 11 thatched oceanview *bure* with solar lighting start at F$380/490 single/double. Meals served at communal tables are included, as are airport transfers and taxes. Most guests come to scuba dive with Mad Fish Diving on the nearby Great Astrolabe Reef, which costs F$140/230/1,020 for 1/2/10 tanks, plus F$50 for equipment. The manta dive is exceptional. PADI Open Water certification is F$820. Kayaks and snorkeling gear are free. Game fishing is F$1,850 a day. It's rustic and remote, but just fine for the diehard diver.

The 16-room **Papageno Resort** (tel. 603-0466, www.papagenoresortfiji.com) is on the north side of Kadavu, 15 kilometers east of Vunisea and accessible only by boat. The *bure* start at F$342/485 single/double including meals, airport transfers, and tax. Garden rooms in a long block are F$250/420. The main house on this 140-hectare property is used as the resort's dining room. The beach is poor but scuba diving and a combined village/wildlife trip can be arranged.

The **Tiliva Resort** (tel. 333-7127, www.tilivaresortfiji.com), near Tiliva village between Kavala Bay and Waisalima on east Kadavu, faces a ho-hum beach with a nice view of Ono. Tiliva has one honeymoon beachfront bungalow at F$580 double, and five spacious fan-cooled twin bungalows at F$280/475 single/double. All meals in the restaurant/bar overlooking the resort are included. There's 24-hour electricity. Scuba diving with local divers is F$190 for two tanks, and sportfishing can be arranged. Airport transfers are included in the rates (minimum stay three nights).

Mai Dive Astrolabe Reef Resort (tel. 603-0842, www.maidive.com) is a new place on the east side of Ono Island with a three-room lodge and one luxury beach bungalow. Meals in the restaurant are served at a common table. Mai Dive caters to scuba divers, well-to-do families, and romantic couples. Everyone arrives on a package, starting at F$1,612/2,306 single/double for five nights including accommodations, meals, taxes, and airport transfers. Packages with scuba diving are more expensive.

The **Koro Makawa Resort** (tel. 603-0782, www.koromakawa.com.fj) is on a long white beach on the northeast side of Ono Island. The modern two-bedroom cottage surrounded by a large deck is F$475 double, plus 17.5 percent tax (five-night minimum stay). The price includes meals with wine served in the dining room of the main house of this large estate. Airport transfers are also included. Scuba diving and game fishing can be arranged at additional cost. Only one couple or family at a time is accepted here.

Over US$250

The **Matana Beach Resort** (tel. 368-3502, www.matanabeachresort.com) at Drue, six kilometers north of Vunisea, caters mostly to scuba divers who have booked from abroad with Dive Kadavu (www.divekadavu.com). The two oceanview *bure* on the hillside, six larger beachfront units, and two two-bedroom units are F$333/589/770/950 single/double/triple/quad (local rates or last-minute discounts are often available). All rates include three meals of variable quality, taxes, and transfers from Vunisea Airport (three-night minimum stay). Windsurfers, kayaks, and paddleboards are free. The morning two-tank boat dive is F$180 without gear. The snorkeling off Matana's golden beach is good, and the Namalata Reef is straight out from the resort (the east end of the Great Astrolabe Reef is an hour away).

In 2000, a surfing camp called **Nagigia Island Resort** (tel. 603-0454, www.nagigia-island.com) opened on tiny Denham Island off Cape Washington at the west end of Kadavu. The seven little bungalows perched on a limestone cliff are F$384/715 single/double deluxe or F$358/669 single/double oceanfront. A bed in a six-bed dorm is F$268 per person. Meals and some boat trips are included, but you'll need to add 17.5 percent tax to these rates. The food served here is pretty poor—come for the surfing. Surfers are changed an additional F$19 per person per day wave-use fee. Scuba diving and fishing also cost extra. There's good swimming directly below the units and at nearby sandy beaches. The traditional surfing season is April–November, but this resort has excellent surf during the other months as well, due to its outer reefs' curving 270 degrees. Boat transfers to Vunisea Airport F$95 per person each way, or you could pay F$6,650 per person round-trip to arrive by helicopter from Nadi.

OTHER PRACTICALITIES

Vunisea has no restaurants, but a coffee shop at the airstrip opens for flights, and a half-dozen small general stores sell canned goods. Vunisea Market is open Monday–Saturday 0800–1600 and offers cooked meals, hot coffee, and stacks of fruit. A woman at the market sells roti, pies, and juice.

The small Colonial National Bank agency at the post office in Vunisea doesn't deal in foreign currency, so change enough money before coming (and don't leave it unattended in your room).

Occasional carriers ply the rugged, muddy roads of west Kadavu, but there are no buses.

GETTING THERE

Pacific Sun has daily flights to Kadavu from Suva (F$147) and Nadi (F$165). Be sure to reconfirm your return flight immediately upon arrival. Boat pickups by the resorts on east Kadavu and Ono should be prearranged. The speedboats to east Kadavu are often without safety equipment or roofs, and in rough weather everything could get wet. Have sunblock and a hat ready if it's sunny, rain gear if it's not, as it's a one- to two-hour ride to east Kadavu or Ono. There's no road from Vunisea to east Kadavu.

Ships like the *Sinu-i-wasa* ply between Suva and Kadavu once a week (usually leaving Suva Tuesday at 2200), calling at villages along the north coast. These vessels are only of interest to low-budget travelers headed for Waisalima who can disembark at Kavala Bay (where the *Sinu-i-wasa Dua* might call around noon on Wednesdays). Take seasickness precautions before boarding.

The car ferry *Sinu-i-wasa* connects Suva to Kadavu once a week.

© DAVID STANLEY

SUVA AND VICINITY

The pulsing heart of the South Pacific, Suva is the largest and most cosmopolitan city in Oceania. The port is always jammed with ships bringing goods and passengers from afar, and busloads of commuters and enthusiastic visitors stream constantly through the busy market bus station. In the business center, there are Indo-Fijian women in saris, expatriate Australians and New Zealanders in shorts, indigenous Fijians in *sulus,* Asian seamen, and Polynesians from Rotuma and Tonga.

Suva squats on a hilly peninsula between Laucala Bay and Suva Harbor in the southeastern corner of Viti Levu. The verdant mountains north and west catch the southeast trade winds, producing damp conditions year-round. Visitors sporting sunburns from Fiji's western sunbelt resorts may appreciate Suva's warm tropical rains (which fall mostly at night). In 1870, the Polynesia Company sent Australian settlers to camp along mosquito-infested Nubukalou Creek on land obtained from High Chief Cakobau. When efforts to grow sugarcane in the area failed, the company convinced the British to move their headquarters here, and since 1882 Suva has been the capital of Fiji.

Today this exciting multiracial city of 173,000—a fifth of Fiji's total population and nearly half the urban population—is a brash, up-to-date city with American-style food courts and a few of the best restaurants and bars in the country. It's about the only place in Fiji where you'll see a building taller than a palm tree. Growing numbers of high-rise offices and business hotels overlook the compact

HIGHLIGHTS

◖ **Suva Municipal Market:** Suva's bustling marketplace is just the place to check out the local produce, examine a kava pyramid, or have a whole fish in coconut milk for lunch. It's almost exciting to be among the mass of island people moving between the bus station, market, and town (page 136).

◖ **Fiji Museum:** Surrounded by lovely tropical gardens, the outstanding exhibits in this important museum bring Fiji's history and culture to life. Adjacent Albert Park was the heart of the British Empire in the South Seas, and it still shows (page 140).

◖ **Parliament of Fiji:** Fiji's legislative building is significant for its striking modern architecture, its place in history as the scene of the May 2000 coup, and its sweeping mountain and sea views (page 141).

◖ **University of the South Pacific:** The university's attractive campus at Laucala Bay is enjoyable to walk around, and there's an art gallery, bookstore, library, good architecture, and lush vegetation (page 142).

◖ **Colo-i-Suva Forest Park:** Colo-i-Suva offers some of the most accessible rainforest hiking in the South Pacific. The trees, birds, and pools are all inviting, and a good restaurant is nearby. It's all just a short bus or taxi ride from Suva (page 143).

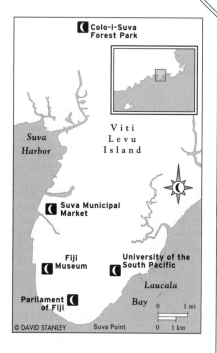

LOOK FOR ◖ TO FIND RECOMMENDED SIGHTS, ACTIVITIES, DINING, AND LODGING.

downtown. Yet despite the banks, boutiques, and Internet cafés, Suva still has a small-town feel, thanks largely to its friendly vibe.

South Suva retains the atmosphere of the long-gone British raj, with its lawn bowling, parliament, palaces, botanical garden, museum, and historic sites. The British left behind imposing colonial buildings, wide avenues, and manicured parks as evidence of their rule. The Fiji School of Medicine, the University of the South Pacific, the Fiji Institute of Technology, the Pacific Theological College, the Pacific Regional Seminary, and the headquarters of many regional organizations and diplomatic

missions have been established here. In addition, the city offers some of the hottest nightlife between Kings Cross (Sydney) and North Beach (San Francisco), plus shopping, sightseeing, and many good-value places to stay and eat. About the only thing Suva lacks is a beach.

The lovely "Isa Lei," a Fijian song of farewell, tells of a youth whose love sails off and leaves him alone in Suva, smitten with longing.

PLANNING YOUR TIME

Although you can see all of Suva's main sights in a single busy day, it's preferable to spend

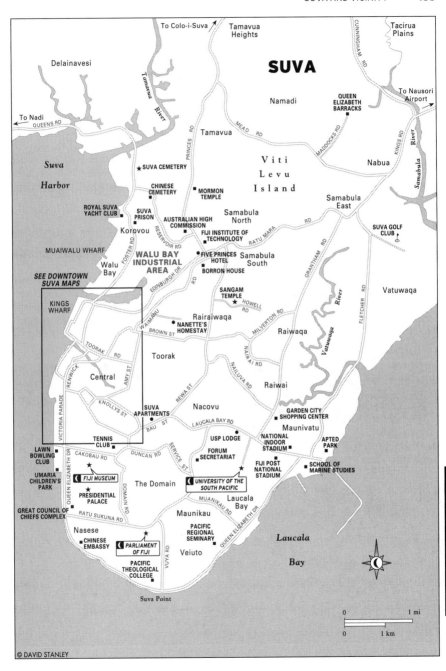

SUVA AND VICINITY

two or three days here to soak up the lively atmosphere. Suva Market and the downtown area, the Fiji Museum, South Suva and the University of the South Pacific, and Colo-i-Suva Forest Park could each fill half a day. There are the many eating and drinking venues, 24-hour Internet cafés, and people-watching spots to occupy your time.

Everything from the market to the museum is best visited on foot, and you can easily get to all of the other attractions by city bus or taxi. Remember that this is the rainy side of the island, and from December to April you must be prepared for at least some rain.

Be aware that on Sunday most of the shops will be closed, restaurants will open for reduced hours (if at all), and fewer taxis or buses will be on the road. In short, the city is very quiet on Sunday—so it's a good time to wander around in relative peace. If you decide to catch a boat or flight to Levuka and spend the weekend there, you should book your ticket a couple of days in advance. Otherwise, it's worth dressing up and attending church to hear the marvelous choral singing. Most churches have services in English, but none compare with the 1000 Fijian service at Centenary Methodist Church on Stewart Street.

Sights

CENTRAL SUVA
◖ Suva Municipal Market

The largest retail produce market in the Pacific, Suva's colorful municipal market off Rodwell Road next to the bus station is a good place to dabble. If you're a yachtie or backpacker, you'll be happy to hear that the market overflows with fresh produce of every kind. Don't miss the bundles of kava roots sold upstairs in the market. On the street outside, Fijian women sell fresh pineapple and guava juice from glass "fish tank" containers.

fruit and vegetable vendors at the Suva Municipal Market

© DAVID STANLEY

Other Sights

From the market, walk south on Scott Street to the **Government Information Center** in a former customs house (1912) opposite Suva's General Post Office. On the corner of Thomson and Pier Streets opposite the Information Center is the onetime **Garrick Hotel** (1914), with wrought-iron balconies upstairs. Go east on Thomson to the picturesque colonial-style arcade (1919) along **Nubukalou Creek,** a campsite of Suva's first European settlers. The arches are all that remain from the original building destroyed by fire in 1998, and in 2007 the four-story **Morris Hedstrom City Center** (MHCC) shopping complex on the site.

Cumming Street, Suva's oldest shopping area, runs east from the bridge over the creek. Suva's original vegetable market was here until it moved to its present location just prior to World War II. During the war, Cumming Street became a market of a different sort as Allied troops flocked here in search of evening entertainment. Since the early 1960s, Cumming has served tourists and local shoppers alike in its present form. Duty free electronics shops used to dominate here, but it's now mostly clothing stores. To continue your walk, turn right on Renwick Road and head back into town.

At the junction of Renwick Road, Thomson Street, and Victoria Parade is a small park known as **The Triangle** with five concrete benches and a white obelisk bearing four inscriptions: "Cross and Cargill first missionaries arrived 14th October 1835; Fiji British Crown Colony 10th October 1874; Public Land Sales on this spot 1880; Suva proclaimed capital 1882." Inland a block on Pratt Street is the **Catholic Cathedral** (1902), built of sandstone imported from Sydney, Australia. Between The Triangle and the cathedral is the towering **Reserve Bank of Fiji** (1984), which is worth entering to see the currency exhibition (Mon.–Fri. 0900–1600, www.rbf.gov.fj).

Return to Suva's main avenue, Victoria Parade, and walk south past **Sukuna Park,** a favorite site for political protest demonstrations. Farther along are the colonial-style **Fintel Building** (1926), nerve center of Fiji's

the Catholic Cathedral in Suva

HANNAH DUDLEY'S LEGACY

One of the few Methodist missionaries to achieve lasting success proselytizing among Fiji's Indian community was an Englishwoman named Hannah Dudley, who had previously worked in India, where she learned Hindustani. An individualist unwilling to follow the usual rules for white evangelists laid down by the male-managed mission of her day, "our Miss Dudley" (as her fellow missionaries called her) worked in Suva among the indentured Indian laborers from 1897 to 1913. Hannah adopted vegetarianism as a step toward godliness, and she visited the Hindu and Muslim women in their own homes, as only a woman could. Through the women and men she made contact with, and her Bible classes, she soon created a circle of Indian converts in Suva.

Although conditions for the Indians of her day were harsh, Hannah didn't protest to the colonial authorities, as some other Methodist missionaries had, but gathered the needy and lost around her. Her own home became an orphanage, and her Indian contacts and converts soon came to know her as *mataji*, the little mother. When Hannah returned to Calcutta in 1905 to work with the Bengali Mission, she took her orphans along. In 1934, members of the Indian Methodist congregation in Suva erected the Dudley Memorial Church on the spot where Hannah first preached. The cream building, strongly influenced by Hindu architecture with its domes and central Moorish arch, can still be seen at the corner of Toorak Road and Amy Street, just up the hill from downtown Suva.

Dudley Memorial Church's South Asian architectural touches suggest the building's role as the main place of worship for Suva's Indo-Fijian Methodists.

© DAVID STANLEY

The Grand Pacific Hotel, erected by the Union Steamship Company in 1914, awaits restoration.

international telecommunications links; the picturesque **Queen Victoria Memorial Hall** (1904), later Suva Town Hall and now a restaurant complex; and the **City Library** (1909), which opened in 1909, thanks to a grant from American philanthropist Andrew Carnegie (one of 2,509 public library buildings Carnegie gave to communities in the English-speaking world). All of these sights are on your right.

SOUTH SUVA
Around Albert Park

Continue south on Victoria Parade past the headquarters of the **Native Land Trust Board,** which administers much of Fiji's land on behalf of indigenous landowners. Just beyond and across the street from the Holiday Inn is Suva's largest edifice, the imposing **Government Buildings** (1939), once the headquarters of the British colonial establishment in the South Pacific. A statue of Chief Cakobau stares thoughtfully at the building. Here on May 14, 1987, Colonel Sitiveni Rabuka carried out the South Pacific's first

military coup, and for the next five years, Fiji had no representative government. The chamber from which armed soldiers abducted the parliamentarians is now used by Fiji's high court, accessible from the parking lot behind the building. Prime Minister Timoci Bavadra and the others were led out through the doors below the building's clock tower (now closed) and forced into the back of army trucks waiting on Gladstone Road.

The main facade of the Government Buildings faces **Albert Park,** where aviator Charles Kingsford Smith landed his trimotor Fokker VII-3M on June 6, 1928, after arriving from Hawaii on the first-ever flight from California to Australia. (The first commercial flight to Fiji was a Pan Am flying boat, which landed in Suva Harbor in October 1941.) Facing the west side of the park is the elegant, Edwardian-style **Grand Pacific Hotel,** built by the Union Steamship Company in 1914 to accommodate its transpacific passengers. The 75 rooms were designed to appear as shipboard staterooms, with upstairs passageways

SUVA AND VICINITY

surveying the harbor, like the promenade deck of a ship. For decades, the Grand Pacific was the social center of the city, but it has been closed since 1992. In 2002, the Government of Fiji purchased the building's empty shell. In 2006, plans were announced to renovate and expand the property, which was to have been rebranded as the Grand Pacific Crowne Plaza, part of the InterContinental chain. These plans flopped and at last report the Grand Pacific was being used for military staff housing.

◖ Fiji Museum

South of Albert Park are the pleasant **Thurston Botanical Gardens** (admission free), opened in 1913, where tropical flowers such as cannas and plumbagos blossom. The original Fijian village of Suva once stood on this site. On the grounds of the gardens is a clock tower dating from 1918, and the Fiji Museum (tel. 331-5944, www.fijimuseum.org.fj, Mon.–Sat. 0900–1630, admission F$7, children under 13 and students F$5), founded in 1904 and the

oldest in the South Pacific. The first hall deals in archaeology, with much information about Fiji's unique pottery. The centerpiece is a double-hulled canoe made in 1913, plus five huge *drua* steering oars, each meant to be held by four men, several large sail booms, and a bamboo house raft *(bilibili)*. The cannibal forks near the entrance are fascinating, as are the whale-tooth necklaces and the large collection of Fijian war clubs and spears. The history gallery beyond the museum shop has a rich collection of 19th-century exhibits, featuring items connected with the many peoples who have come to Fiji, including Tongans, Europeans, and Solomon Islanders. Notice the rudder from HMS *Bounty*. An air-conditioned room upstairs contains an exhibition of tapa cloth and displays on Indo-Fijians.

Palace and Seawall

South of the gardens is the Presidential Palace, formerly called Government House, the residence of the British governors of Fiji. The original building, erected in 1882, burned

The Fiji Museum in Suva is the oldest museum in the region.

© DAVID STANLEY

The Presidential Palace was once the seat of Fiji's British governor.

after being hit by lightning in 1921. The present edifice, which dates from 1928, is a replica of the former British governor's residence in Colombo, Sri Lanka. The grounds cannot be visited. The changing of the guard is on the last day of each month.

From the seawall south of the palace, you get a good view across Suva Harbor to Beqa Island (to the left) and the dark, green mountains of eastern Viti Levu punctuated by Joske's Thumb, a high volcanic plug (to the right). Follow the seawall south to the **Great Council of Chiefs Complex** on Queen Elizabeth Boulevard. The main building here was erected in the form of a traditional Fijian *bure* in 2003. Turn left onto Ratu Sukuna Road, the first street after the Police Academy.

🌒 Parliament of Fiji

About a kilometer up Ratu Sukuna Road from the Great Council of Chiefs Complex is the 1992 Parliament of Fiji (www.parliament.gov.fj), an impressive, traditional-style building with an orange pyramid-shaped roof. From May 19 to July 13, 2000, Fiji's prime minister and several dozen members of parliament were held hostage in the parliamentary complex by a gang of rebel soldiers and assorted thugs led by bankrupt businessman George Speight, who claimed his coup attempt was in defense of indigenous Fijian rights. The gatekeeper at the main entrance around the corner off Vuna Road will give you a visitors pass to go inside. Huge tapa banners hang from the parliament's walls, and skillfully plaited coconut-fiber ropes from the Lau Group highlight the decor. The parliamentary mace is Chief Cakobau's historic war club, once presented to Queen Victoria and later returned to Fiji by Britain. It's only brought out when Parliament is in session. The location is spectacular, with scenic sea and mountain views.

Suva Point

Both Protestants and Catholics have their most important regional training facilities for ministers and priests in South Suva, and the **Pacific Theological College** is just down Vuna Road from Parliament. From Suva Point nearby, you get a good view of **Nukulau,** a tiny reef island southeast of Suva. This was the site of the residence of the first U.S. consul to Fiji, John Brown Williams, and the burning of Williams's house on July 4, 1849, set in motion a chain of events that led to Fiji becoming a British colony. Later, Nukulau was used as the government quarantine station, and most indentured Indian laborers spent their first two weeks in Fiji here. Before the May 2000 coup, Nukulau was a public park. From 2000 to 2006, coup master George Speight was held in a jail there, serving his life sentence. After the December 2006 coup, Speight was moved to a high-security prison on Viti Levu and Nukulau became a park again.

From Suva Point, it's a good idea to catch a taxi to the University of the South Pacific (F$3). The Nasese bus does a scenic loop through the beautiful garden suburbs of South Suva: Just flag it down if you need a ride back to the market. In the other direction, catch it from the southwest corner of the bus station.

◖ University of the South Pacific

A frequent bus from in front of the Vanua Arcade opposite Sukuna Park on Victoria Parade brings you directly to the University of the South Pacific (get off when you see a McDonald's on the left). Founded in 1968, this beautiful 72.8-hectare campus on a hilltop overlooking Laucala Bay is jointly owned by 12 Pacific countries. Although more than 70 percent of the 11,500 students here are from Fiji, the rest are on scholarships from every corner of the Pacific. The site of the USP's Laucala Campus was a Royal New Zealand Air Force seaplane base before the land was turned over to the USP.

From Laucala Bay Road, follow the main walkway to the **University Library,** erected in 1988 with Australian aid. Across a wooden bridge behind the library, past the ANZ Bank and university bookstore, is a traditional Fijian *bure* called the Vale ni Bose, which is used for workshops and seminars. To the left of the *bure* is the **Oceania Center for Arts and Culture,**

The Vale ni Bose at the University of the South Pacific is a good example of a chiefly *bure*.

© DAVID STANLEY

© DAVID STANLEY

The colonial-era prison opposite the Royal Suva Yacht Club bears the slogan "Giving a Second Chance."

the university's art gallery (free), with a curvilinear mosaic floor.

NORTHWEST OF SUVA

The part of Suva north of Walu Bay accommodates much of Suva's shipping and industry. Carlton Brewery on Foster Road cannot be visited. About 600 meters beyond the brewery is the vintage **Suva Prison** (1913), a sinister colonial structure with high walls and barbed wire. Plans to replace this anachronism with a more modern facility have been on the back burner for years. Despite the colorful murals along Foster Road, one look at this place and you'll be a law-abiding citizen for the rest of your stay in Fiji! Opposite the prison is the **Royal Suva Yacht Club,** where the security guard may be able to suggest someone willing to sign you in. Remove your hat as you enter the building. The club's restaurant and bar are good, you'll meet some yachties, and maybe you'll find a boat to crew on.

In the picturesque **Suva Cemetery,** just north, the Fijian graves are wrapped in colorful *sulus* and tapa cloth, and make good subjects for photographers. Gangs of inmates from the nearby jail are often assigned to dig the graves, a common practice in Fiji.

Catch one of the frequent Shore, Lami, or Galoa buses west on Queens Road, past **Suvavou** village, home of the Suva area's original Fijian inhabitants, to the **Novotel Suva** beyond Lami town, seven kilometers from the market. Many cruising yachts tie up at the marina here, and the view of the Bay of Islands from the hotel's floating restaurant is excellent.

Colo-i-Suva Forest Park

This lovely park (tel. 332-0211, daily 0900–1600, admission F$5), at an altitude of 122–183 meters, offers 6.5 kilometers of trails through the lush forest flanking the upper drainage area of Waisila Creek. The mahogany trees you see here are natives of Central America and were planted after the area was logged in the 1950s. The park first opened in 1973. A half-kilometer nature trail begins near the Upper Pools,

SUVA AND VICINITY

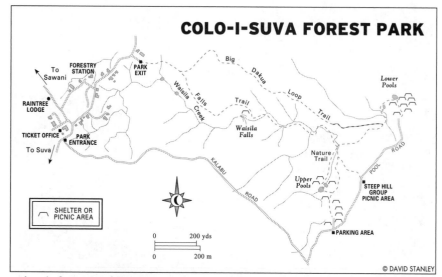

COLO-I-SUVA FOREST PARK

© DAVID STANLEY

and aside from waterfalls and natural swimming pools, there are thatched pavilions with tables at which to picnic. With the lovely green forests behind Suva in full view, this is one of the most breathtaking places in all of Fiji, and you may spot a few native butterflies, birds, reptiles, and frogs. The park is so unspoiled, it's hard to believe that you're only 11 kilometers from Suva.

Security has improved since a police post was set up opposite Raintree Lodge, but you must still keep an eye on your gear if you go swimming in the pools—and muggings are not unknown in this park (non-essential bags can be left at the park office). Colo-i-Suva is

easily accessible on the Sawani or Serea buses (F$1.15), which leave from the westernmost lane at Suva Bus Station every hour (Sunday every two hours). The last bus back to Suva leaves at about 1800. A taxi will be F$9. Make a circle trip of it by catching a bus from the park on to Nausori, rather than returning directly to Suva. And try to come on a dry day, as it's even rainier here than in Suva and the creeks are prone to flooding.

Also consider spending the night at Raintree Lodge, 50 meters from the entrance to the park. Lunch and drinks can be ordered at the lodge's attractive restaurant/bar (tel. 332-0562), which overlooks a small lake.

Entertainment and Shopping

In 1996, **Village Six Cinemas** (tel. 330-6006, www.damodarvillage.com.fj) opened on Scott Street, next to Nubukalou Creek, giving you a choice of six Hollywood films several times a day. Regular admission is F$5.50, reduced to F$4.50 on Tuesday. The air-conditioning is a relief on a hot day.

The best time to be in Suva is in August

during the **Hibiscus Festival** (www.hibiscus fiji.com), which fills Albert Park with stalls, games, and carnival revelers.

NIGHTCLUBS

There are numerous nightclubs in Suva, all of which have F$3–5 cover charges on weekends and require neat dress (no shorts or flip-flops).

By law, public nightclubs and bars in Fiji can only open weekdays 1700–0100, Saturdays 1700–midnight, although some take a risk and stay open later. Registered clubs and hotel bars are allowed to open 0900–0100 daily. Nothing much happens at the clubs until after 2200.

Women shouldn't enter these places alone. After dark, it's wise to take a taxi back to your hotel. Suva is still a very safe city, but nasty, violent robberies do occur.

The Ranch (54 Carnarvon St., closed Mon.) is a popular country-and-western club with live entertainment and a cover charge from 2100. The crowd here is a bit older than in some of the other clubs and it's something of a hangout for Rotumans.

The recently renovated **Downunder Bar** (54 Carnarvon St.), next to The Ranch, is more upscale the neighboring clubs, with Australian-theme decor and two pool tables. Happy hour is 1700–2100, after which a F$5 cover charge kicks in. There's live music some nights.

The **Golden Dragon** (379 Victoria Parade, tel. 331-1018) is frequented by university students and islanders from other parts of the Pacific (such as Samoa and Tonga).

Bar 66 (tel. 870-6071, closed Sun. and Mon.), above Dolphins Food Court (entrance off Loftus Street), is the hottest hip-hop rave club in town with the best DJ music, theme nights, and drink specials. It's very popular among USP students and is reasonably safe.

Signals Night Club (255 Victoria Parade, tel. 331-3590), opposite the Suva City Library, is popular among Asian seamen. Gay travelers will feel comfortable here.

Bourbon Bluez, across the street from O'Reilly's Pub, caters to an older, Fijian crowd.

Birdland R&B Club (6 Carnarvon St., tel. 330-3833), up and around the corner from O'Reilly's Pub, has outstanding live jazz from 2000 on Sunday. On other nights, there's recorded music. It's a late-night place where people come after they've been to the other clubs.

Bojangles Night Club, adjacent to Birdland, is a disco where Fijian students come to dance (cover charge after 2200).

Deep Sea, downstairs in the large warehouse-style building next to Birdland on Carnarvon Street, is another popular university student hangout. There's a pool table.

Purple Haze Night Club (closed Sun.–Tues.), Butt and MacArthur Streets (above

Village Six Cinemas next to Suva's Nubukalou Creek offers the latest films on six screens.

The Merchants Club), just up the hill from O'Reilly's Pub, is a predominately Indo-Fijian disco. It's one of the few places in town where you'll see men dancing with each other.

Liquids Night Club (tel. 330-0679), upstairs in the Harbor Center (access from beside Wishbone outside on the Nubukalou Creek side of the building), is crowded with local sports teams on weekends.

Be aware that the places north of Nubukalou Creek are considerably rougher than those just mentioned. **Friends Bar and Niteclub** (38 Cumming St., tel. 330-0704) has a happy hour 1700–2000. Security is tight.

Ritz Niteclub, at Usher and Scott Streets near the market, supplies cheap mugs of beer. Happy hour is 1600–2000. Show no fear if you go in there.

El Paso Night Club (194 Rodwell Rd.), located north of the bus station, was formerly known as the Club Bali Hai, one of the roughest places in town. Now there are dances Thursday–Saturday nights, with live music on one side and karaoke on the other. It's dead other nights.

BARS

O'Reilly's Pub (5 MacArthur St., tel. 331-2322), just off Victoria Parade, has a happy hour daily 1700–2000. It's a nice relaxed way to kick off a night on the town, and the big sports screen, two pool tables, and canned music are tops.

A block up from O'Reilly's at MacArthur is **The Merchants Club** (15 Butt St., tel. 330-4256, Mon. and Tues. 1700–2130, Wed. and Thurs. 1630–2230, Fri. 1630–2300, Sat. 1100–2230, Sun. 1100–1900). Properly dressed overseas visitors are welcome in this classic South Seas bar with a largely male clientele. Meals are available from a kitchen to the rear.

Next to a service station, **Traps Bar** (305 Victoria Parade, tel. 331-2922, weekdays 1700–0100, Sat. 1700–midnight) is a groupie Suva social scene with a happy hour until 2000 (drunks are unwelcome here). There's live music from 2200 on Mondays, and a DJ on Thursdays and Fridays, *the* nights to be there.

The Club at Garrick (tel. 330-8746, Mon.–Sat. 1100–2100), upstairs in an old colonial

building at the corner of Pier Street and Renwick Road, is a public bar with a rather rowdy Fijian clientele. There's a pool table and long Wild West–style bar, and interesting views of downtown Suva from the balcony.

Those in search of more subdued drinking should try the **Piano Bar** in the lobby at the Holiday Inn (tel. 330-1600), which often presents rather good jazz singers, or the **Rooftop Garden Bar** at the Town House Apartment Hotel (tel. 330-0055), which has a happy hour Mon.–Sat. 1700–1900.

The bar at the **Suva Lawn Bowling Club** (tel. 330-2394, Mon.–Sat. 0900–2100, Sun. 0900–1700), facing the lagoon opposite Thurston Botanical Gardens and just off Albert Park, is a very convenient place to down a large bottle of Fiji Bitter—the perfect place for a cold one after visiting the museum. You can sit and watch the bowling, or see the sun set over Viti Levu. Henry's Kitchen at the club serves snacks and meals (F$8.50–14.50) throughout the day.

SHOPPING

The large **Curio and Handicraft Market** (Mon.–Sat. 0800–1700) on the waterfront behind the post office is a good place to haggle over crafts, so long as you know what is really Fijian (avoid masks and "tikis"). Unfortunately, many of the vendors are rather aggressive, and it's not possible to shop around in peace. Never come here on the day when a cruise ship is in port—prices shoot up. And watch out for the annoying "sword sellers," as they could accost you anywhere in Suva.

Jack's of Fiji (38 Thomson St., tel. 330-8893, www.jacksfiji.com) has a good selection of shiny Fijian handicrafts and fashions.

Delta Cappuccino (161 Victoria Parade, tel. 330-9808) sells high-quality South Pacific music CDs.

Procera Music Shop (5 Greig St., tel. 331-4911), upstairs in the Harifam Center, has cassettes and CDs of local Indian and Fijian music.

Aladdin's Cave (tel. 330-1005, www.cavefiji .com), facing the Palm Court Bistro in the mall behind Air New Zealand, has one-of-a-kind jewelry, purses, and scarves for women, plus pillow covers and wind chimes. Prices are reasonable considering that everything is handmade.

Cumming Street is Suva's busiest shopping street. Expect to obtain a 10–40 percent discount at the "duty-free" shops by bargaining, but *shop around* before you buy. Be especially wary when purchasing gold jewelry, as it might be fake. Commission agents may try to show you around and get you a "good price." If the deal seems too good to be true, it probably is.

The **Suva Flea Market** on Rodwell Road opposite the bus station features a large selection of island clothing and souvenirs, and several good little places to eat. This is probably the cheapest place in Fiji to buy a *sulu*. The pandanus mats and tapa are other items to consider. You won't be hassled here.

For more upmarket apparel, examine the fashionable hand-printed clothing and beachwear at **Sogo Fiji** (tel. 331-5007), at 45 Cumming Street and on Victoria Parade next to Air New Zealand. You could come out looking like a real South Seas character for a reasonable price.

Bob's Hook Line & Sinker (14 Thomson Street, tel. 330-1013), on in an outside corner of the Harbor Center, sells good-quality snorkeling and fishing gear.

Wai Tui Surf (tel. 330-0287, www.waitui .com), Parade Arcade, Victoria Parade opposite McDonald's, carries surfing paraphernalia, including stylish bathing suits and trendy beachwear.

The **Philatelic Bureau** (1 Edward St., tel. 321-8209, www.stampsfiji.com.fj), next to the General Post Office, sells the stamps of Pitcairn, Solomon Islands, Tonga, Tuvalu, and Vanuatu, as well as those of Fiji.

Fuji Film in the Vanua Arcade, opposite Sukuna Park on Victoria Parade, does one-hour photo finishing and can burn memory cards onto CDs.

Recreation

HIKING

For a bird's-eye view of Suva and the entire surrounding area, spend a morning climbing to the volcanic plug atop **Mount Korobaba** (429 m), the highest peak around. Take a Shore bus to the cement factory beyond the Novotel at Lami, and then follow the dirt road past the factory up into the foothills. After about 45 minutes on the main track, you'll come to a fork just after a sharp descent. Keep left and cross a small stream. Soon after, the track divides again. Go up on the right and look for a trail straight up to the right where the tracks rejoin. It's a 10-minute scramble to the summit from here. The route can be confusing, so rather than try to find the way on your own, you should hire a local guide.

There's a far more challenging climb to the top of **Joske's Thumb**, a volcanic plug 15 kilometers west of Suva. Take a bus to Naikorokoro Road, and then walk inland 30 minutes to where the road turns sharply right and crosses a bridge. Follow the track straight ahead and continue up the river till you reach a small village. It's necessary to request permission of the villagers to proceed, and to hire a guide. From the village to the Thumb will take just less than three hours. The last bit is extremely steep, and ropes may be necessary. Even Sir Edmund Hillary took two tries to climb the Thumb.

SCUBA DIVING

Suva has no regular dive shops, although **Dive Center Ltd.** (tel. 330-0599), facing the Royal Suva Yacht Club at Walu Bay, fills scuba tanks. They don't rent equipment or offer diving.

OTHER RECREATION

At the 18-hole, par-72 **Fiji Golf Club** (15 Rifle Range Rd., Vatuwaqa, tel. 338-2872) the course record is 65. Visitors are welcome, and clubs and a pull trolley can be hired. Call ahead to ask if any competitions are scheduled,

SUVA AND VICINITY

as the course may be closed to the public at those times. Don't carry large amounts of cash or valuables with you around the course.

The **Olympic Swimming Pool** (224 Victoria Parade) charges F$2 admission. April–September, it's open weekdays 1000–1800, weekends 0800–1800; October–March, hours are weekdays 0900–1900, weekends 0700–1900. Lockers are available.

The **Suva Lawn Tennis Club** (tel. 331-1726, closed Sun.), Cakobau Road opposite the Fiji Museum, charges F$6 an hour to use their courts during the day or F$7 1800–2100. You can order drinks here.

The Fijians send champion rugby and soccer teams far and wide in the Pacific. You can see rugby (Apr.–Sept.) and soccer (Feb.–Oct.) on Saturday afternoons at 1400 at the **Fiji Post National Stadium** near the University of the South Pacific. Rugby and soccer are played at Albert Park on Saturday, and you could also see a cricket game here (mid-Oct.–Easter). Soccer is also played on Sunday (but rugby is only on Saturday).

Accommodations

Suva offers a wide variety of places to stay, and the low-budget accommodations can be neatly divided into two groups. The places on the south side of the downtown area near Albert Park are mostly decent and provide communal cooking facilities to bona fide travelers. However, some of the lodgings northeast of downtown are dicey and cater mostly to "short-time" guests; few of these bother providing cooking facilities. Many of the mid-priced hotels and self-catering apartments are along Gordon Street and its continuation, MacGregor Road. If you want to spend some time in Suva to take advantage of the city's varied activities, look for something with cooking facilities and weekly rates.

SOUTH SUVA
Under US$25
The 42-room 【 **South Seas Private Hotel**

The low-budget traveler's best headquarters in Suva is the South Seas Private Hotel.

© DAVID STANLEY

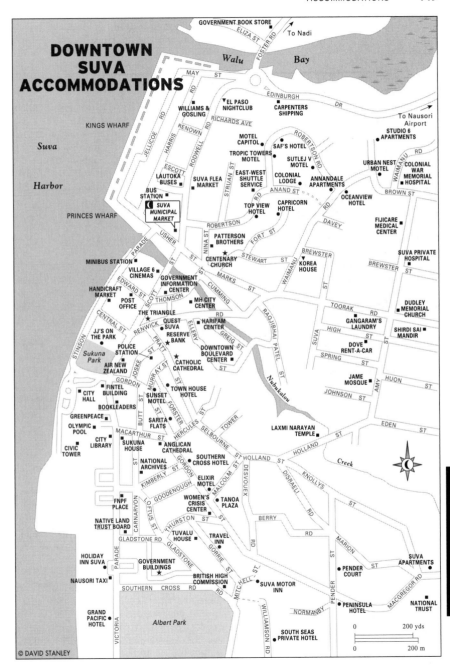

DOWNTOWN SUVA ACCOMMODATIONS

GOVERNMENT BOOK STORE
ELIZA ST
FOSTER RD
To Nadi

Walu **Bay**

MAY ST
EDINBURGH

WILLIAMS & GOSLING
EL PASO NIGHTCLUB
CARPENTERS SHIPPING

KINGS WHARF

RICHARDS AVE
RENOWN RD
HARRIS RD
RODWELL RD
JELLICOE RD

ROBERTSON RD

MOTEL CAPITOL
SAF'S HOTEL
SUTLEJ V MOTEL

STUDIO 6 APARTMENTS

Suva

TROPIC TOWERS MOTEL

URBAN NEST MOTEL
WAIMAN RD
COLONIAL WAR MEMORIAL HOSPITAL

ESCOTT
EAST-WEST SHUTTLE SERVICE
COLONIAL LODGE
ANNANDALE APARTMENTS

Harbor

LAUTOKA BUSES
SUVA FLEA MARKET
ANAND ST
OCEANVIEW HOTEL
BROWN ST

BUS STATION
SUVA MUNICIPAL MARKET
TOP VIEW HOTEL
CAPRICORN HOTEL
DAVEY

PRINCES WHARF
FORT ST
FIJICARE MEDICAL CENTER

ROBERTSON
NINA ST
STRIAN ST
STEWART ST
BREWSTER

PATTERSON BROTHERS
CENTENARY CHURCH
WAIMANU ST
KOREA HOUSE
BREWSTER ST
SUVA PRIVATE HOSPITAL

MINIBUS STATION
VILLAGE 6 CINEMAS
MARKS ST
CUMMING ST

GOVERNMENT INFORMATION CENTER
THOMSON
TOORAK RD
DUDLEY MEMORIAL CHURCH

HANDICRAFT MARKET
POST OFFICE
MH CITY CENTER

THE TRIANGLE
QUEST SUVA
HARIFAM CENTER
RENWICK
GANGARAM'S LAUNDRY
SHIRDI SAI MANDIR

JJ'S ON THE PARK
PRATT
RESERVE BANK
ELLERY ST
GREIG ST
SUVA HIGH ST
DOVE RENT-A-CAR

POLICE STATION
DOWNTOWN BOULEVARD CENTER
SPRING ST

Sukuna Park
AIR NEW ZEALAND
CATHOLIC CATHEDRAL

JOSKE
GORDON
Nubukalou
RAOJIBHAI PATEL ST
JAME MOSQUE
HUON

CITY HALL
FINTEL BUILDING
TOWN HOUSE HOTEL
JOHNSON ST

BOOKLEADERS
SUNSET MOTEL
FORSTER ST
TOWER ST

GREENPEACE
SARITA FLATS
MURRAY ST
BUTT ST

OLYMPIC POOL
MACARTHUR ST
HERCULES ST
SELBOURNE ST
LAXMI NARAYAN TEMPLE
EDEN ST

CIVIC TOWER
CITY LIBRARY
SUKUNA HOUSE
ANGLICAN CATHEDRAL
HOLLAND ST
HOLLAND ST
Creek

NATIONAL ARCHIVES
SOUTHERN CROSS HOTEL
KNOLLYS ST

KIMBERLY ST
ELIXIR MOTEL
MALCOLM ST
DESVOUEX
DISRAELI RD

FNPF PLACE
GOODENOUGH ST
WOMEN'S CRISIS CENTER
TANOA PLAZA

NATIVE LAND TRUST BOARD
OTTIS ST
THURSTON ST
BERRY
RD

GLADSTONE RD
TUVALU HOUSE
TRAVEL INN
MARION ST
SUVA APARTMENTS

HOLIDAY INN SUVA
CARNARVON ST
GORRIE ST
PENDER COURT

NAUSORI TAXI
GOVERNMENT BUILDINGS
BRITISH HIGH COMMISSION
MITCHELL ST
SUVA MOTOR INN
MACGREGOR RD
NATIONAL TRUST

SOUTHERN CROSS RD
PENDER ST
PENINSULA HOTEL

GRAND PACIFIC HOTEL
VICTORIA PARADE
Albert Park
WILLIAMSON RD
NORMANBY RD
SOUTH SEAS PRIVATE HOTEL

0   200 yds
0   200 m

To Nausori Airport

© DAVID STANLEY

(6 Williamson Rd., tel. 331-2296, www.fiji4 less.com), one block east of Albert Park, really conveys the flavor in its name. The building originally housed workers involved in laying the first telecommunications cable across the Pacific, and until 1983 it served as a girls' hostel. Things changed when backpackers took over the dormitories (and break-ins through the floorboards by amorous young men came to an end). Today, backpackers and independent travelers can get a bed in a five-bed dorm for F$19, a fan-cooled room with shared bath at F$35/45 single/double, or a better room with private bath at F$58 double (only one available). The owners have decided to keep their costs down by not paying commissions to the Nadi travel agencies—the only reason they aren't promoted by those outfits. You won't find the Feejee Experience crowd here either. Instead, you'll receive a F$1 discount if you have a youth hostel, VIP, or Nomads card. This quiet hotel has a pleasant veranda and a large communal kitchen. For a refundable F$10 deposit, you may borrow a plate, mug, knife, fork, and spoon, but there's a longstanding shortage of pots and pans. It's possible to leave excess luggage at the South Seas for free while you're off visiting other islands, but you should lock your bag securely. The staff changes money at bank rates. It's worth it to catch a taxi here from the bus station the first time (F$3).

US$25-50

Several apartment hotels on the hill behind the Central Police Station are worth a try. The congenial **Town House Apartment Hotel** (3 Forster St., tel. 330-0055, townhouse@con nect.com.fj) is a five-story building with panoramic views from the rooftop bar (happy hour 1700–1900). The 15 air-conditioned standard rooms with cooking facilities and fridge are a good value at F$60 single or double. A suite here is F$70/80 double/triple.

Nearby and under the same ownership is the four-story **Sunset Apartment Motel** (tel. 330-1799), at the corner of Gordon and Murray Streets. Avoid the four rooms without cooking facilities that go for F$60 single

or double, and instead ask for one of the 10 two-bedroom apartments with kitchens and fridge at F$70. The two-bedroom apartments cost F$15 per additional person. Some of the cheaper rooms are noisy and have uncomfortably soft beds.

The Town House reception also handles bookings at nearby **Sarita Flats** (39 Gordon St., tel. 330-0084), where a one-bedroom apartment with sitting room and cooking facilities will be F$89 single or double. A two-bedroom apartment with bathroom, kitchen, living room, TV, and telephone is F$108. This two-story building lacks the balconies and good views of the Town House, but it is well maintained. It might be a good choice for families or two couples traveling together.

Four-story **Elixir Motel Apartments** (77 Gordon St., tel. 330-3288, plantworld@con nect.com.fj), on the corner of Malcolm Street, has 15 two-bedroom air-conditioned apartments with cooking facilities and private bath at F$98 for up to three people, or F$135 deluxe. The six standard studios here are F$88.

Travel Inn (19 Gorrie St., tel. 330-4254, www.fiji4less.com), a two-story building opposite the Fiji Red Cross, is owned by the same company as the South Seas Private Hotel. There are 16 fan-cooled rooms with shared bath at F$37/50 single/double, all with access to communal cooking facilities (shortage of utensils), and four self-contained apartments for F$63 triple daily. There are plenty of blankets and good locks on the doors. Visitors from other Pacific islands often stay here, as this is one of Suva's better buys.

Pender Court (31 Pender St., tel. 331-4992) has 19 rooms beginning at F$50 single or double. It's sometimes a little noisy, and maybe sleazy.

Twenty self-catering units owned by the National Olympic Committee are available at **Suva Apartments** (17 Bau St., tel. 330-4280, fasanoc@fasanoc.org.fj), a few blocks east of Pender Court. The 10 fan-cooled units in this new four-story building are F$74/93 double/triple, while the 10 air-conditioned apartments are F$90/108. If you pay six nights, the seventh night is free. By staying here, you help support organized sports in Fiji!

Anyone with any sort of business at the University of the South Pacific should consider staying at **USP Lodges** (Laucala Bay Rd., tel. 321-2614, usplodges@usp.ac.fj). The accommodations here are in two clusters. The Upper Campus Lodge, overlooking the Botanical Garden on the main campus, has six small flats with TV and cooking facilities at F$66/75 single/double. Down beside Laucala Bay near the School of Marine Studies is Marine Lodge, with five self-catering units with TV at F$72/85 single/double. The reception for Marine Lodge is at Upper Campus Lodge. Rooms in both sections of USP Lodges are often occupied by students on a semi-permanent basis, so it's best to call or email ahead to check availability.

US$50-100

Quest Serviced Apartments (Renwick Rd., tel. 331-9119, www.questsuva.com) opened in 2005 on the sixth and seventh floors of the Suva Central building. The entrance is off Renwick Road opposite Jack's Handicrafts. Although it's right in the center of town, there's little traffic noise. The 22 studios are F$139, the one-bedrooms F$191, and the two executive studios F$192. Two units can be combined to form a two-bedroom apartment at F$330. All units have a fridge but the TVs may only pick up local stations.

The **Southern Cross Hotel** (63 Gordon St., tel. 331-4233, southerncross@kidanet.net.fj) is a high-rise concrete building. The 32 air-conditioned rooms accommodating up to three people start at F$135 for a standard room on the fourth floor, or a bit more for the deluxe rooms on the second, third, and fifth floors. Ask for a walk-in discount. The hotel restaurant on the sixth floor serves Korean dishes.

The 10-story **Tanoa Plaza Hotel** (Gordon St., tel. 331-2300, www.tanoahotels.com), formerly known as the Berjaya Hotel, at the corner of Malcolm and Gordon Streets, is the tallest hotel in Fiji. The 48 superior rooms are

© DAVID STANLEY

The 10-story Tanoa Plaza is Fiji's tallest hotel.

F$164 single or double, eight deluxe rooms F$182, and four penthouse suites F$327. All rooms have a fridge, TV, and uncomfortable beds, and all face the harbor. The air-conditioning helps drown out the noise from inside and out. The Tanoa Plaza has a business center and conference facilities for groups of up to 200 people, plus a swimming pool behind the building.

The **(€ Suva Motor Inn** (Gorrie St., tel. 331-3973, www.hexagonfiji.com), a three-story complex near Albert Park at the corner of Mitchell and Gorrie Streets, has 36 air-conditioned studio apartments with kitchenette at F$117 single, double, or triple (10 percent discount by the week). The nine two-bedroom apartments capable of accommodating five persons are F$183. A courtyard swimming pool with waterslide and cascade faces the restaurant/bar (happy hour 1800–1900). The house band is good. This building (erected in 1996 by the Hexagon Group of Hotels) is well worth considering by families who want a bit of comfort.

The **Peninsula International Hotel** (MacGregor Rd., tel. 331-3711, www.peninsula.com.fj), at the corner of MacGregor Road and Pender Street, is a four-floor building with a swimming pool. The 100 air-conditioned rooms start at F$80/90 single/double (the eight suites with kitchenettes run F$130).

US$100-150

JJ's on the Park (tel. 330-5005, www.jjsfiji.com.fj), in the former YWCA building on Sukuna Park, is now an upscale six-story hotel. The seven deluxe rooms are F$261 single or double, the nine premier rooms F$325, the six suites F$483, and the two executive suites F$735. Prices are negotiable and a 20 percent discount is easily obtained. Ask for a room on the park side of the building. JJ's caters to business travelers, and there's a 24-hour butler on every floor. There are meeting rooms for up to 150 people on the second floor. Coral Sun Fiji has a tour desk here.

Suva's largest hotel is the 130-room **Holiday Inn Suva** (501 Victoria Parade, tel. 330-1600, www.holidayinn.com), on the waterfront opposite the Government Buildings. Formerly a Travelodge, the Holiday Inn is a big American-style place with 76 air-conditioned standard rooms with fridge and TV beginning at F$228 single or double, 34 renovated superior garden rooms at F$289, and 20 superior seaview rooms at F$329. The swimming pool behind the two-story buildings compensates for the lack of a beach, and the view of Viti Levu from here is splendid. An ATS Pacific tour desk is at the hotel, and there's a brasserie-style restaurant, bar, lounge, fitness center, and three conference rooms. International phone calls from the rooms and Internet charges are extremely expensive.

NORTH SUVA
Under US$25

The four-story **Top View Motel** (58 Robertson Rd., tel. 331-2612), a six-minute walk up the hill from the market bus station, has 10 rooms with shared bath on the first floor at F$35 single or double, five rooms with private bath on the second floor at F$50, and eight VIP rooms with private bath on the top floor, also F$50. It's basic but okay for one night.

Tropic Towers Apartment Motel (86 Robertson Rd., tel. 330-4470, www.tropictowers.com) has 34 air-conditioned apartments with cooking facilities, fridge, and TV in a four-story building, starting at F$64/78 single/double downstairs and F$76/92 upstairs. The airy upstairs rooms are much better value than those downstairs and some are quite large and luxurious. The 13 "budget" units in the annex are F$43 single or double with shared bath. A bar and coffee lounge are on the premises and a swimming pool is available for guests.

Saf's Apartment Hotel (100 Robertson Rd., tel. 330-1849), between the Crossroad and Capitol, has a mixed clientele. The 40 rooms with bath in this three-story concrete building are F$30 single or double downstairs, F$40 upstairs, or F$50 with TV and cooking facilities (F$10 extra for air-conditioning).

The colorful, 44-room **Oceanview Hotel** (270 Waimanu Rd., tel. 331-2129) is slightly overpriced, with two singles at F$30, 33 doubles at F$35, and nine four-person family rooms at F$45. All rooms have shared bath. The Oceanview has a pleasant hillside location, and it's one of the only "lowlife" hotels in this area with any atmosphere.

US$25-50

Colonial Lodge (19 Anand St., tel. 330-0655, www.coloniallodge.com.fj) is an old wooden house on a side street just off Waimanu Road. The five backpacker dorms (F$30 pp) with 4–6 beds are all different; those in the two rear buildings are quieter and more airy than the three dingy dorms in the basement. There are also two double rooms downstairs with private bath and fan, but these are overpriced at F$70–75. A room with two beds is F$38/60 single/double. All rates include a good cooked breakfast. The large sitting room and terrace upstairs are nice and it's convenient to the bus station and city center.

An alley at the end of Anand Street leads straight up to **Annandale Apartments** (265

Waimanu Rd., tel. 330-9766), opposite the Oceanview Hotel. The 11 smaller rooms downstairs with a fridge and private bath are F$55 single or double, while the 12 spacious one-/two-bedroom apartments upstairs with balcony, TV, air-conditioning, and cooking facilities are F$80–90 for up to three or four people.

In 2008, the old Harbor Light Hotel was demolished and completely rebuilt as the three-story **Sutlej V Motel** (124 Robertson Rd., tel. 330-5495). The 15 double rooms with private bath and TV are F$60/65 with fan/air-conditioning. The four family rooms accommodating four are F$80/85 with fan/air-conditioning. There's a F$10 key deposit.

Studio 6 Apartments (1 Walu St., tel. 330-7477, www.studio6.com.fj), off Waimanu Road, is one of Suva's best deals. The 24 clean, comfortable standard rooms with fridge are F$80 single or double; the 47 seaview rooms with a balcony, cooking facilities, and a separate bedroom and the nine garden rooms are both F$110; and the eight super-deluxe rooms are F$140. Nine self-catering units facing the car park are F$99. All rooms have air-conditioning and SkyTV. There's a swimming pool, and some of the balconies have an excellent view of Walu Bay. Breakfast is included, but you can ask for a discount if you'll take the room without breakfast.

◖ Raintree Lodge (tel. 332-0562, www.raintreelodge.com), near the entrance to Colo-i-Suva Forest Park, 11 kilometers north of Suva, caters well to both ends of the market. The 20-bed split-level dormitory (F$25 pp) shares toilet, cooking, and bathing facilities with the 13 double rooms (F$65). More upscale are the five lodges or bungalows in another section just up the hill. These cost F$165 single or double, and are quite luxurious, with a sitting room, TV, fridge, private bath (warm showers), and a deck overlooking a small lake (but no cooking facilities). If you'll be using the cooking facilities in the dorm, bring groceries from Suva, as there's no store here. Raintree's large thatched restaurant/bar overlooks a former rock quarry, which has been converted into a lovely lake teeming with

tiny tilapia. You can spend F$50 on a three-course dinner or take one of the backpacker specials for about F$10. At breakfast, try the pancakes. Happy hour is 1700–1900 and they show movies later.

Raintree Lodge can be reached on the Sawani or Serea buses (F$1.15), which leave from Suva Bus Station. A taxi will cost F$8. Call ahead, as Raintree Lodge does fill up some nights with Feejee Experience groups.

US$50-100

Just up the hill from downtown, the **Capricorn Apartment Hotel** (7 St. Fort St., tel. 330-3732, www.capricornfiji.com) has 34 spacious, air-conditioned units with cooking facilities, fridge, and local TV beginning at F$115 single or double. A room upstairs is F$15 more, a one-bedroom flat another F$10. The three- and four-story apartment blocks edge the swimming pool, and there are good views of the harbor from the individual balconies. It's a good choice for families.

◖ Nanette's Homestay (56 Extension St., tel. 331-6316, www.nanettes.com.fj), off Waimanu Road just down the hill from the Outpatients Department at Colonial War Memorial Hospital, is an upscale bed-and-breakfast run by an Australian-Fijian couple. The four upstairs rooms (F$99 single or double) share a kitchen and lounge area. Downstairs are three self-catering apartments (F$145–170). All rooms have private bath and air-conditioning, and breakfast is included in the price. It's an excellent value.

The **Five Princes Hotel** (5 Princes Road, tel. 338-1575, www.fiveprinceshotel.com) is housed in an elegant colonial mansion (1920) in Samabula South. Aviator Harold Gatty bought the property in 1949 and later it became a bed-and-breakfast known as Tanoa House. In 2005, the property was renovated and re-launched. The three air-conditioned rooms in the main building are F$160 double, while the four self-catering cottages in the garden go for F$190. A two-bedroom villa beyond the swimming pool is F$310.

The **Novotel Suva** (Queens Rd., tel. 336-2450,

www.novotelsuva.com.fj), at Lami on the Bay of Islands seven kilometers west of Suva, includes a 600-seat convention center, waterside swimming pool, and floating seafood restaurant (try the marinated raw fish). Formerly the Raffles Tradewinds Hotel, the building was completely renovated when Novotel took over in 2009. The 108 rooms with private bath, limited TV, fridge, and air-conditioning in this tasteful two-story building are from F$184/219 double standard garden/oceanview or F$254 superior oceanview. Two children under 16 can share a parent's room for free. Many cruising yachts anchor here, and the location is the most picturesque of any Suva hotel. Though this property is far from the center, bus service into Suva is good and the taxis are inexpensive.

Food

FAST FOOD

If you're arriving in Suva by bus or boat and need breakfast or lunch, food vendors such as **Tui's Takeaway** in the food court at the Suva Flea Market can't be beat. Prices are low and they have wooden picnic tables in a covered courtyard.

On Marks Street are cheap Chinese snack bars, such as **Kim's Café** (128 Marks St., tel. 331-3252), where you can get a toasted egg sandwich and coffee for about F$2.50. Kim's has been there for ages, and Lum's Tea Room, Joe Wong's Café, and Soon King Café across the street from Kim's are similar. There are scores more cheap milk bars around Suva, and you'll find them for yourself as you stroll around town.

Daily 1700–0500, **BBQ vendors** on Edward Street opposite the post office sell takeaway chicken, chops, sausages, and eggs hot from their grills at around F$5 a meal. You'll see a steady stream of cars and taxis stopping here to pick up dinner.

An inexpensive **snack bar** (tel. 330-1443, weekdays 0800–1730, Sat. 0800–1530) with outdoor concrete picnic tables is at the back side of the Handicraft Market facing the harbor. Dishes like chop suey, chow mein, fried rice, long soup, and rump steak cost F$4–6 and the portions are gargantuan. This place is packed with locals around lunchtime.

Joji's Takeaways (tel. 331-1958, Mon.–Sat. 0900–1800, Sun. 0900–1600), accessed through an unmarked door on the back side of the City Hall building directly behind the Fintel Building, sells huge chicken, beef, pork, fish, and vegetarian meals priced F$4–6. There's counter space in the entry room where you can eat.

Jackson Takeaway (tel. 330-3986, Mon.–Sat. 0700–1800, Sun. 0900–1700), in the old town hall next to the Vine Yard Restaurant on Victoria Parade, serves Chinese lunches at F$4–6 or fish and chips at F$3. It's also good for a quick cup of coffee.

Familiar, easy eating is available in the American-style food courts in the **Harbor Center** (daily 0700–1800), along Nubukalou Creek between Scott and Thomson Streets; the top floor of **MHCC Department Store** (tel. 331-0683, daily 0900–2100) on Thomson Street; the **Downtown Boulevard Center** (weekdays 0800–1800, Sat. 0800–1500), on Ellery Street; and **Dolphins Food Court** (tel. 330-7440) at FNPF Place, Victoria Parade and Loftus Street. **Superfresh Supermarket** (daily 0900–2100) inside MHCC is Suva's largest.

FIJIAN

A popular place to sample Fijian food is the **Old Mill Cottage Café** (49 Carnarvon St., tel. 331-2134, Mon.–Sat. 0700–1700, mains F$5–12), located on the street behind the Dolphins Food Court. Government employees from nearby offices descend on this place at lunchtime for the inexpensive curried freshwater mussels, curried chicken livers, fresh seaweed in coconut milk, taro leaves creamed

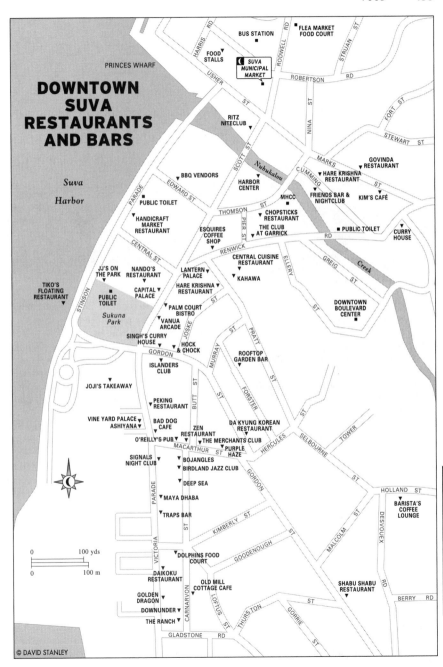

DOWNTOWN SUVA RESTAURANTS AND BARS

PRINCES WHARF

Suva

Harbor

BUS STATION

FLEA MARKET
FOOD COURT

FOOD
STALLS

SUVA
MUNICIPAL
MARKET

ROBERTSON RD

RITZ
NITECLUB

GOVINDA
RESTAURANT

BBQ VENDORS

HARBOR
CENTER

HARE KRISHNA
RESTAURANT

MHCC

FRIENDS BAR &
NIGHTCLUB

KIM'S CAFÉ

PUBLIC TOILET

CHOPSTICKS
RESTAURANT

THE CLUB
AT GARRICK

PUBLIC TOILET

CURRY
HOUSE

HANDICRAFT
MARKET
RESTAURANT

ESQUIRES
COFFEE
SHOP

Nubukalou

Creek

CENTRAL CUISINE
RESTAURANT

JJ'S ON
THE PARK

NANDO'S
RESTAURANT

LANTERN
PALACE

KAHAWA

DOWNTOWN
BOULEVARD
CENTER

TIKO'S
FLOATING
RESTAURANT

PUBLIC
TOILET

CAPITAL
PALACE

HARE KRISHNA
RESTAURANT

*Sukuna
Park*

PALM COURT
BISTRO

VANUA
ARCADE

SINGH'S CURRY
HOUSE

HOCK
& CHOCK

ISLANDERS
CLUB

ROOFTOP
GARDEN BAR

JOJI'S TAKEAWAY

PEKING
RESTAURANT

VINE YARD PALACE

ASHIYANA

BAD DOG
CAFE

ZEN
RESTAURANT

DA KYUNG KOREAN
RESTAURANT

O'REILLY'S PUB

THE MERCHANTS CLUB

PURPLE
HAZE

SIGNALS
NIGHT CLUB

BOJANGLES

BIRDLAND JAZZ CLUB

DEEP SEA

MAYA DHABA

HOLLAND ST

BARISTA'S
COFFEE
LOUNGE

TRAPS BAR

DOLPHINS FOOD
COURT

DAIKOKU
RESTAURANT

OLD MILL
COTTAGE CAFE

SHABU SHABU
RESTAURANT

BERRY RD

GOLDEN
DRAGON

DOWNUNDER

THE RANCH

GLADSTONE RD

0   100 yds

0   100 m

© DAVID STANLEY

The Old Mill Cottage Café serves Fijian curried specialties.

in coconut milk, and fish cooked in coconut milk. It's also very good for breakfast.

INDIAN

The **【 Hare Krishna Vegetarian Restaurant** (16 Pratt St., tel. 331-4154, closed Sun.), at the corner of Joske Street, serves ice cream (14 flavors), sweets, and snacks downstairs, main meals upstairs (available Mon.–Fri. 1130–1400). If you want the all-you-can-eat vegetarian *thali* (F$9.50), just sit down upstairs and they'll bring it to you. You can also select individual dishes from the warmer. No smoking or alcohol is allowed. Hare Krishna also has a smaller branch at 29 Cumming Street with sweets, snacks, and ice cream.

A cheaper Indian place is the very popular **Curry House** (44 Waimanu Rd., tel. 331-3756, Mon.–Fri. 0900–1730, Sat. 0900–1530). The special vegetarian *thali* (F$5) makes for a good lunch, and they also have meat curries from F$5.50. Try the takeaway *rotis.*

Govinda Vegetarian Restaurant (97 Marks St., tel. 330-9587, weekdays 0900–1730, Sat. 0900–1500) has an outstanding combination *thali* for F$10.50, plus sweets, ice cream, milkshakes, and masala tea. It's always jammed with people from nearby shops and offices, and highly recommended.

Singh's Curry House (tel. 330-6600, Mon.–Sat. 0930–2100, Sun. 1030–2000), Gordon Street off Victoria Parade, serves spicy South Indian dishes (including meat options) in the F$4–8 range. Choose from the warmer on the counter. It's nothing fancy but the portions are large.

A more upscale Indian restaurant is **Ashiyana** (tel. 331-3000, Tues.–Sat. 1130–1430 and 1800–2200, Sun. 1800–2130), in the old town hall next to the Vine Yard Restaurant on Victoria Parade. Their hot and spicy dishes are prepared in a tandoori clay oven by a chef from India. Curries are around F$10.

Trendy **Maya Dhaba** (281 Victoria Parade, tel. 331-0045, daily 1100–1500 and 1730–2200) serves a good variety of spicy South Indian dishes priced F$10–18. *Thalis* are F$10–12. Vegetarians will have no difficulty ordering here. It's a yuppie place compared to Singh's.

ASIAN

Not many Indian restaurants in Suva are open evenings or on Sunday, so this is when you should turn to Suva's many excellent, inexpensive Asian restaurants. Most serve beer, whereas the Indian restaurants are usually "dry."

⟨ Chopsticks Restaurant (68 Thomson St., tel. 330-0968, daily 1030–1430 and 1800–2200), upstairs in the Honson Building, is a bit hard to find. It's in the front part of the same building as Lamtec Services above J. Maneklal and Sons Ltd. near the Government Information Center. Don't confuse it with the more expensive Shanghai Seafood House nearby. Chopsticks serves some of the best Chinese food in Suva at very reasonable prices. All meals are individually prepared and you can eat well for under F$10.

Central Cuisine Restaurant (tel. 330-6491, Mon.–Sat. 0930–2100), upstairs in the Colonial Arcade at the Suva Central building with an entrance off Renwick Road, is an upscale self-service Chinese place. They have a good selection of meals (F$5.50–6.50) in the warmer daily 1100–1500. There's ample seating.

Two unpretentious Chinese places are adjacent to one another on Pratt Street near Hare Krishna Vegetarian Restaurant. Dishes in the glass-covered steam table at the **Lantern Palace Cafeteria** are F$5. If you're not in a hurry, the **Lantern Palace Restaurant** (10 Pratt St., tel. 331-4633, Mon.–Sat. 1130–1430 and 1700–2100) next door offers individually prepared dishes priced F$7–17.

The popular **Peking Restaurant** (195 Victoria Parade, tel. 331-2714, daily 1130–2200) is only a bit more expensive than the self-service Chinese places, but the meals are individually prepared (averaging F$7–20).

Suva's most imposing Chinese restaurant is the 300-seat **Vine Yard Palace** (tel. 331-5546, Mon.–Sat. 1130–1430 and 1800–2200, Sun. 1730–2200) in the old town hall next to the public library on Victoria Parade. Weekdays 1130–1430, there's a lunch buffet for F$14 (dinner entrées are F$8–48).

For upscale Japanese food, it's **Daikoku** (359 Victoria Parade, tel. 330-8968, www .daikokufiji.com, Mon.–Sat. 1200–1400 and 1800–2200), upstairs in FNPF Place. The teppanyaki dishes are artistically prepared right at your table (F$10–58 menu). Reservations are suggested.

The **Zen Restaurant** (tel. 330-6314, weekdays 1130–1430 and 1730–2130, Sat.

© DAVID STANLEY

Restaurants Ashiyana and Vine Yard Palace share Suva's old town hall building on Victoria Parade with Greenpeace.

1130–1430), in Pacific House, Butt and Gordon Streets, has mains at F$15–35. Photos of dishes are in the menu. The food is good but uninspired.

The **Da Kyung Korean Restaurant** (43 Gordon St., Mon.–Sat. 1100–1500 and 1730–2200, Sun. 1600–2200) also has a nifty photographic menu depicting dishes like *bulgogy* (F$15–17), steak barbecue, and vegetarian tofu soup. Mains average F$12–50 and a variety of side dishes are included with each order. The open dining room is in an old colonial house.

You could also try **Shabu Shabu Japanese Restaurant** (91 Gordon St., tel. 331-8350, Mon.–Sat. 1130–1500 and 1730–2200, Sun. 1730–2200) in Ra Marama House. The menu here includes sushi, tempura, teriyaki, and tonkatsu. The interior is chic and cozy.

INTERNATIONAL CUISINE

Tiko's Floating Restaurant (tel. 331-3626, Mon.–Fri. 1130–1400 and 1730–2200, Sat. 1800–2200) is housed in the MV *Lycianda,* an ex–Blue Lagoon cruise ship launched at Suva in 1970 and now anchored off Stinson Parade

behind Sukuna Park. Steaks (F$35) and seafood mains (F$18–45) are good. Lobster or a real mountain of crabs will run F$55–60. There's a salad bar. It's a romantic spot, and you can feel the boat rock gently in the waves.

Nando's Restaurant (tel. 330-1040, Mon.–Wed. 1100–2100, Thurs.–Sun. 1100–2200), in Regal Lane opposite JJ's on the Park, is a branch of an international chain famous for its spicy Portuguese-style flame-grilled chicken (F$12–18 a quarter-/half-chicken meal). The cold Nando's agua and peri-peri sauce are free. It's a giant step up from KFC on Victoria Parade. There's a second Nando's location at 237 Laucala Bay Road opposite the Fiji Post National Stadium out near the university.

JJ's on the Park (tel. 330-5005, www.jjs fiji.com.fj, daily 0730–2200), on Sukuna Park, is a casual restaurant of quality, with daily specials listed on blackboards. If you don't want any of the main courses (F$18–25), order a couple of appetizers (F$8–14), such as the sashimi (F$9–14) or mussels (F$10). Otherwise, there are hamburgers (F$18) and catch of the day. The desserts are special. You'll like the genteel

the elegant dining room of Tiko's Floating Restaurant

© DAVID STANLEY

atmosphere and harbor views. Coup master George Speight once owned a small stake in JJ's, and you never know who you'll meet at JJ's classic long wooden bar (which stays open until 0100). There's a pianist Monday–Thursday and a live band from 1800 Fridays.

The whimsically named ◖ **Bad Dog Café** (219 Victoria Parade, tel. 331-2455, Mon.–Sat. 1200–2300, Sun. 1700–2300), next door to O'Reilly's, is a trendy bar serving wine, margaritas, sangria, and 26 different brands of beers. You can order a jug of sangria for F$18. The eclectic menu features seven varieties of pizza (F$13–18), burgers (F$13), pasta (F$12–14), steaks (F$25), and other mains (F$12–21). The food has a reputation for being good, which is something we can confirm. A back door from Bad Dog leads into O'Reilly's.

At Gordon and Joske Streets, **Hock and Chock Fish and Chips** (tel. 368-1071, Mon.–Sat. 0830–2000, Sun. 0830–1400) serves upscale fish and chips (F$4.50/8 small/large). Chicken and chips is F$8/13, steaks are F$22. This place is also good for breakfast.

CAFÉS

One of the few places serving a Western-style cooked breakfast (F$10.80) is the **Palm Court Bistro** (tel. 330-4662, Mon.–Fri. 0700–1630, Sat. 0700–1330), in the Queensland Insurance Arcade behind Air New Zealand on Victoria Parade. Their burgers and sandwiches are good.

The **Focaccia Café** (weekdays 0700–1700, Sat. 0800–1500), in the Vanua Arcade on Victoria Parade opposite Sukuna Park, serves lunch in the F$5–7 range. Smoothies are F$4.50–6, coffees F$3–4.50. You can get a cooked breakfast here at F$5–7, including coffee.

The city's trendy youth congregate at **Esquires Coffee House** (9 Renwick Rd., tel. 330-0828), formerly the Republic of Cappucino. Another Esquires location (tel. 330-0333, Mon.–Sat. 0700–2100, Sun. 0700–1900) is in Dolphins Food Court at FNPF Place, Victoria Parade and Loftus Street. Both serve a variety of teas and coffees (F$4.50–6.50).

Baristas Coffee Lounge (8 Disraeli Road, tel. 331-8270, weekdays 0730–1600, Sat. 0730–1500, Sun. 0800–1500), on Holland Street opposite The Playhouse of the Fiji Arts Club, is an upscale café for breakfast, lunch, coffee, cakes, and juice. Try the apple crumb muffins. The entrance is from the rear and upstairs. You can sit outside and watch the buses careening around the corners. It's a WiFi hotspot.

Out at the University of the South Pacific, the **Treetop Café** (tel. 323-1000, weekday lunches only), across the bridge from the library and upstairs, serves hamburgers, fish and chips, and the like. There's a balcony where you can have a coffee as the world goes by.

Information and Services

INFORMATION

The **Government Information Center** (Mon.–Fri. 0800–1600, Sat. 0800–1300), at Thomson Street across from the General Post Office, used to be a Tourism Fiji outlet and they still have a few brochures and can answer simple questions.

Brochures are also available from the **Ministry of Tourism** (tel. 330-2060, www .tourism.gov.fj), Level 3, Civic Tower, behind the City Library.

The **South Pacific Tourism Organization** (FNPF Plaza, 343–359 Victoria Parade, 3rd Fl., tel. 330-4177, www.south-pacific.travel) provides information on the entire South Pacific.

The library of the **Bureau of Statistics** (tel. 331-5822, www.statsfiji.gov.fj, weekdays 0800–1300 and 1400–1600), on the fifth floor of the Ratu Sukuna House at Victoria Parade and MacArthur Street, has many interesting technical publications on the country. Ask for a free copy of "Fiji Facts and Figures."

© DAVID STANLEY

The Suva office of the Government Information Center is housed in the former Customs House erected in 1912.

The **Maps and Plans Shop** (tel. 321-1395, www.lands.gov.fj, Mon.–Fri. 0800–1300 and 1400–1500) of the Lands and Survey Department, on the ground floor within the Government Buildings, sells excellent topographical maps of Fiji.

Carpenters Shipping (22 Edinburgh Rd., tel. 331-2244, www.carpship.com.fj), across from the BP service station, sells British navigational charts of Fiji at a whopping F$104 each (buy these overseas). The **Fiji Hydrographic Office** (tel. 331-5457, Mon.–Fri. 0800–1630), top floor, Amra Street, Walu Bay, sells navigational charts of the Yasawas, Kadavu, eastern Vanua Levu, and the Lau Group at F$23 a sheet (all other areas are covered by the British charts).

Bookstores

Suva's number-one bookstore is the **USP Book Center** (tel. 323-2500, www.uspbookcentre .com, Mon.–Fri. 0800–1800, Sat. 0830–1300),

THE STOCK EXCHANGE

Investment-oriented visitors might like to visit the South Pacific Stock Exchange (Level 2, Provident Plaza One, 33 Ellery St., www.spse.com.fj), accessible from Downtown Boulevard Center. Sixteen of Fiji's largest companies are listed here, and everyone is welcome to attend the trading session, which begins every weekday at 1030 sharp. It only lasts around 15 minutes, so arrive a bit early. Nonresidents can buy shares in most of the companies by opening an account at one of the four local brokerages, and many of the companies pay handsome dividends in Fiji dollars. Electronic trading may be introduced here soon, bringing the live session to an end.

next to the ANZ Bank branch at the main Laucala Bay university campus. Not only do they have one of the finest Pacific sections in the region, but they stock the publications of several dozen occasional publishers affiliated with the university, and you can turn up some truly intriguing items.

Bookleaders Book Center (173 Victoria Parade, tel. 330-4394) has many hard-to-find books on Fiji and the South Pacific.

The **Fiji Museum** shop sells a few excellent books at reasonable prices.

The **Coconut Frond,** at the back of the Suva Flea Market on Rodwell Road, has a large stock of used paperbacks.

The **Government Bookstore** (tel. 331-5504, Mon.–Fri. 0800–1600, Sat. 0800–1300), on Foster Road, Walu Bay, sells Fijian dictionaries, history, and grammar texts at low prices.

Libraries

The **Suva City Library** (196 Victoria Parade, tel. 331-3433, Mon.–Fri. 0930–1800, Sat. 0900–1300) allows visitors to take out four books upon payment of a refundable F$22 deposit.

The **National Archives of Fiji** (25 Carnarvon St., tel. 330-4144, www.info.gov.fj, Mon.–Fri. 0800–1300 and 1400–1600) has an air-conditioned library upstairs with a large collection of local newspapers.

The excellent **Fiji Museum Library** (tel. 331-5944, www.fijimuseum.org.fj, Mon.–Fri. 0830–1300/1400–1600) is directly behind the main museum in a separate building. They charge F$1 to use the air-conditioned facilities.

The library at the Laucala Campus of the **University of the South Pacific** (tel. 323-2322, www.usp.ac.fj) is open year-round Monday–Friday 0800–1600. During semesters, it's also open Saturday, Sunday afternoon, and in the evening. You'll find a reading room with international newspapers downstairs. Tourists can buy a 10-day "external borrower" card for F$30, which allows limited access to the Pacific Collection. Only staff and graduate students may browse the Pacific Collection; all others must request specific titles at the counter and are only allowed to look at them for three hours. Prior to entering the building, bags must be left in a cloakroom behind and below the library.

© DAVID STANLEY

SUVA AND VICINITY

A century ago American philanthropist Andrew Carnegie financed the construction of Suva's public library.

Ecology Groups

The **Greenpeace Pacific Campaign** (tel. 331-2861) is above the Vine Yard Palace Restaurant in the old town hall on Victoria Parade. The library is accessible weekdays if they're not having a meeting.

Four NGOs are side by side in a Suva suburb. The **National Trust for Fiji** (3 Ma'afu St., tel. 330-1807, www.nationaltrust.org.fj) manages several nature reserves and historic sites around Fiji. Their neighbor, the **World Wide Fund for Nature** (4 Ma'afu St., tel. 331-5533, www.wwfpacific.org.fj) assists various projects for the support of wildlife and wild habitats. Next door is the Regional Office for Oceania of the **International Union for Conservation of Nature** (5 Ma'afu St., tel. 331-9084, www.iucn.org) and the South Pacific Country Program of the **Wildlife Conservation Society** (11 Ma'afu St., tel. 331-5174, www.wcs.org). If you'd like to spend some time in Fiji volunteering, you could inquire in these offices.

Travel Agents

Hunts Travel Service (tel. 331-5288), upstairs from the Dominion House arcade behind the Government Information Center, is the place to pick up air tickets. They often know more about Air Pacific flights than the Air Pacific employees themselves! The lines are much shorter too.

Rosie Holidays (46 Gordon St., tel. 331-4436, www.rosiefiji.com), near Sarita Flats, books tours, transfers, and accommodations all around Fiji. The **ATS Pacific** tour desk (tel. 331-2287, www.atspacific.com) in the lobby of the Holiday Inn Hotel and **Coral Sun Fiji** (tel. 322-8099) at JJ's on the Park do the same. Coral Sun Fiji books the twice daily Fiji Express bus from the Holiday Inn to Nadi Airport (F$22).

Airline Offices

Reconfirm your onward flight reservations at your airline's Suva office: **Air New Zealand** (tel. 331-3100) in the Queensland Insurance Center, 9 Victoria Parade; **Air Pacific** (tel. 330-4388) in the Colonial Building on Victoria Parade; **Pacific Blue** (tel. 330-4656), in the Oneworld Flight Center, Cumming Street and Waimanu Road; **Pacific Sun** (tel. 330-4237), in the Air Pacific office on Victoria Parade; and **Qantas Airways** (tel. 331-3888) on Victoria Parade next to Air Pacific. While you're there, check your seat assignment.

SERVICES

Money

The ANZ and Westpac banks charge a F$5 commission to change travelers checks. ANZ and Westpac branches on Victoria Parade near The Triangle have ATMs outside. Other ANZ Bank ATMs are at the 51 Renwick Road branch, outside Village Six Cinemas, at the food court in Downtown Boulevard Center on Ellery Street, at the ANZ Bank branch in Lami, and at many other locations around Suva.

The **Colonial National Bank** (tel. 331-4400, www.colonial.com.fj, weekdays 0900–1600, Sat. 0900–1400) has a commission-free Bureau de Change on Renwick Road at Pier Street.

You can avoid the long lines at the banks and get a better rate for your travelers checks without commission by changing money at a private exchange office like **Money Exchange** (50 Thomson St., tel. 331-1857, Mon.–Fri. 0830–1730, Sat. 0830–1500), Thomson and Pier Streets opposite the Government Information Center. **Lotus Foreign Exchange** (30 Thomson St., tel. 331-7755, Mon.–Fri. 0830–1700, Sat. 0830–1300) opposite the Westpac Bank and **UAE Exchange** (53 Waimanu Rd., tel. 331-8133) are similar.

If you need a quick infusion of funds, **GlobalEX** (tel. 331-4812, weekdays 0800–1730, Sat. 0800–1400), Victoria Parade at Gordon Street, is a Western Union agent. Money can be sent to you here from almost anywhere in world through the Western Union network.

On Sunday and holidays, changing money is a problem (try your hotel if you get stuck).

Telecommunications

Fintel, the **Fiji International Telecommunications** office (158 Victoria Parade, tel. 331-2933, www.fintelfiji.com, Mon.–Fri. 0830–1700, Sat. 0900–1700) is the best place in Suva to make long-distance calls. Their Kidatalk (www .kidatalk.com.fj) system allows you to phone many countries at F$1 for five minutes, then F$0.19 for each additional minute. No phone card is required. You can also send faxes here.

Telecom Fiji (tel. 330-4019, www.tfl.com .fj) operates a telephone center on Scott Street next to Village 6 Cinemas.

Internet Access

Several places around Suva offer Internet access, including the upstairs **Cyber Zone** (107 Victoria Parade, open 24 hours) opposite Sukuna Park. You can pay F$7 to surf the Web all night here. The noisy cyber games being played by kids are a drawback at Cyber Zone.

SkyNet Café, Gordon Street near Victoria Parade, has 40 computers available at F$3 an hour, and they're open around the clock.

Fintel (158 Victoria Parade, tel. 331-2933) provides very fast Internet access in a comfortable air-conditioned room at F$1 for 20 minutes.

Connect Internet (10 Thomson St., tel. 330-0777, www.connect.com.fj, weekdays 0800–1900, Sat. 0800–1600), near the Westpac Bank, provides Internet access in air-conditioned comfort at F$3 an hour.

The **Kahawa Café** (tel. 330-9671), upstairs from the Colonial Arcade, Renwick Road and Pratt Street, provides free Unwired Fiji wireless Internet access to anyone buying a coffee or fruit shake. Their sandwiches are made fresh for lunch and the cheesecake and chocolate cake are great.

At last report, the cheapest Internet access in Suva was F$2 an hour, available at **Lamtec Services** (tel. 331-5719, Mon.–Sat. 0730–1700) on the third floor of the Honson Building at 68 Thomson Street (across the street from the Government Information Center).

Immigration

The **Immigration Office** (tel. 331-2622, Mon.–Fri. 0830–1230, www.immigration .gov.fj) for extensions of stay (F$93), etc., is in

the Civic Tower behind the library on Victoria Parade.

Consulates

The following countries have diplomatic missions in Suva:

- **Australia:** 37 Princes Road, Samabula, tel. 338-2211, www.fiji.embassy.gov.au
- **Chile:** Asgar & Co. Optometrists, Queensland Insurance Building behind Air New Zealand, Victoria Parade, tel. 330-0433
- **China:** 147 Queen Elizabeth Drive, Suva Point, tel. 330-0215
- **European Union:** Development Bank Center, 360 Victoria Parade, 4th floor, tel. 331-3633
- **Federated States of Micronesia:** 37 Loftus Street, tel. 330-4566
- **France:** Dominion House, 7th floor, Scott Street, tel. 331-2233
- **Germany:** Williams and Gosling Ltd., 82 Harris Road, tel. 323-6350
- **India:** LICI Building, 5th floor, Butt Street, tel. 330-1125
- **Indonesia:** Ra Marama House, 6th floor, 91 Gordon Street at Thurston, tel. 331-6697
- **Japan:** Dominion House, 2nd floor, Scott Street, tel. 330-4633
- **Kiribati:** 36 McGregor Road, tel. 330-2512
- **Korea:** Vanua House, Victoria Parade, tel. 330-0977
- **Malaysia:** Pacific House, 5th floor, Butt and MacArthur Streets, tel. 331-2166
- **Marshall Islands:** 41 Borron Road, Samabula, tel. 338-7899
- **Nauru:** Ratu Sukuna House, 7th floor, Victoria Parade and MacArthur Street, tel. 331-3566

- **Netherlands:** Cromptons, Queensland Insurance Building behind Air New Zealand, Victoria Parade, tel. 330-1499

- **New Zealand:** Reserve Bank Building, 10th floor, Pratt Street, tel. 331-1422

- **Papua New Guinea:** 18 Ratua Street, Raiwai (off Nailuva Road), tel. 330-4244

- **Solomon Islands:** 34 Reki Street, tel. 331-0355

- **South Africa:** 16 Kimberly Street, tel. 331-1087

- **Taiwan:** Pacific House, 6th floor, Butt and MacArthur Streets, tel. 331-5922

- **Tuvalu:** 16 Gorrie Street, tel. 330-1355

- **United Kingdom:** 47 Gladstone Road, tel. 322-9100

- **United States:** Tamavua Heights, tel. 331-4466, suva.usembassy.gov

The U.S. embassy relocated to Tamavua Heights in early 2011. The former downtown location had created problems for the city as the entire block of Loftus Street in front of the old embassy was closed to traffic in 1999. The new 4.3-hectare compound is the largest U.S. diplomatic mission in the Pacific Islands, used by around 25 American and 75 local staff.

Everyone other than New Zealanders needs a visa to visit Australia, and these are available at the Australian High Commission weekdays 0830–1200. To get there, it's probably easier to go by taxi, then return to town by bus. Canada is represented by Australia.

Launderettes
Gangaram's Laundry (126 Toorak Rd., tel. 330-2269, Mon.–Fri. 0730–1800, Sat. 0730–1400) offers same-day cleaning services.

Public Toilets
Public toilets are just outside the Handicraft Market on the side of the building facing the harbor; in the Thurston Botanical Gardens; in Downtown Boulevard Center on Ellery Street;

on the food court level at the Harbor Center (F$0.30); at MHCC Food Court (F$0.20); beside Nubukalou Creek off Renwick Road; and between the vegetable market and the bus station.

The public toilets in Sukuna Park (Mon.–Sat. 0800–1535) cost F$0.80; you can have a shower here for F$1.30.

Yachting Facilities
The **Royal Suva Yacht Club** (tel. 331-2921, VHF channel 16, www.rsyc.org.fj), on Foster Road between Suva and Lami, offers visiting yachts such amenities as mooring privileges, warm showers, laundry facilities, restaurant, bar, email, and the use of club services. There have been reports of thefts from boats anchored here, so watch out. Many yachts anchor off the Novotel Suva on the Bay of Islands, a recognized hurricane anchorage.

Health
Suva's **Colonial War Memorial Hospital** (tel. 331-3444), about a kilometer northeast of the center, is available 24 hours a day for emergencies. You can see a doctor in the Outpatients Department on Extension Street off Waimanu Road weekdays 0800–1530 for a F$16 nonresident fee, but you'll have to line up, as there will be many locals waiting for free service. Built in 1914, this hospital may be an interesting sightseeing attraction, but if you actually need medical attention, you're better off seeing a private doctor.

CWM Hospital hosts the **Fiji Hyperbaric Unit** (tel. 321-5525) with an entrance off Waimanu Road. It's open weekdays 0700–1700 and on call for emergencies 24 hours.

Suva Private Hospital (120 Amy St., tel. 330-3404, www.sph.com.fj), at Brewster, which opened in 2001, offers state-of-the-art facilities. The medical center here is open 24 hours a day (F$24/61 to see a general practitioner/specialist) and provides service vastly superior to Colonial War Memorial for the same price (if you're a foreigner). There's an excellent pharmacy here.

The **FijiCare Medical Center** (123 Amy St., tel. 331-3355, Mon.–Fri. 0830–1300 and

© DAVID STANLEY

Built in 1914, Suva's massive Colonial War Memorial Hospital overlooks much of the city.

1400–1800, Sat. 0830–1130) has several foreign doctors (one female) on their roster. Consultations are F$25.

A dentist is **Dr. Abdul S. Haroon** (Epworth House, Ste. 12, tel. 331-3870), off Nina Street (just down the hall from Patterson Brothers).

Suva City Pharmacy (10 Thomson St., tel. 331-7400, Mon.–Fri. 0830–1730, Sat. 0930–1400) is in the post office building at the head of Victoria Parade.

The **Fiji Women's Crisis Center** (88 Gordon St., tel. 331-3300 answered 24 hours, www.fijiwomen.com, Mon.–Fri. 0830–1630, Sat. 0900–1200), opposite the Tanoa Plaza Hotel, offers free and confidential counseling for women and children.

Getting There and Around

Although nearly all international flights arrive at Nadi, Pacific Sun flies to many of Fiji's islands from Suva's Nausori Airport. Interisland shipping crowds the harbor, and if you'd rather go by boat, make the rounds of the shipping offices listed in this chapter, then head over to Walu Bay to check the information. Compare the price of a cabin and deck passage, and ask if meals are included. Keep in mind that all of the ferry departure times mentioned in this guide are only indications of what was true in the past. It's essential to check with the company office for current departure times during the week you wish to travel. Quite a few ships leave Suva on Saturday, but they rarely depart on Sunday. A few of these ships seem to be nearing the end of their working lives—use them at your own risk.

A solid block of buses awaits your patronage at the market bus station near the harbor, with continuous local service, and frequent long-distance departures to Nadi and Lautoka. Many

© DAVID STANLEY

Suva's city buses are frequent, inexpensive, and fun to ride.

points of interest around Suva are accessible on foot, but if you wander too far, jump on any bus headed in the right direction, and you'll wind up back in the market. Taxis are also easy to find and relatively cheap.

Suva's bus station can be a little confusing, as there are numerous companies, and timetables are not posted. Most drivers know where a certain bus will park, so just ask.

BY SEA
Ferries to Ovalau Island

The Suva to Levuka service is operated by **Patterson Brothers Shipping** (tel. 331-5644, patterson@connect.com.fj), based in the Epworth Arcade off Nina Street (Ste. 1, 1st Fl.). Patterson's "Sea-Road" bus leaves from the bus station opposite the Suva Flea Market daily except Wednesday and Sunday at 1300 (F$30). At Natovi (67 km), it drives onto the ferry *Spirit of Harmony* for Buresala on Ovalau, then continues to Levuka, where it should arrive around 1745. For the return journey, you leave the Patterson Brothers office in Levuka

at 0500, arriving in Suva at 0800. Bus tickets must be purchased in advance at the office, and on Saturdays and public holidays, reservations should be made at least a day ahead. These trips should take 4–5 hours right through, but can be late if the ferry connection is delayed.

Venu Shipping Ltd. (14 Kaua Rd., tel. 339-5000), Laucala Bay, operates the car ferry *Sinu-i-wasa* from Suva to Levuka irregularly.

Ships to Northern Fiji

Patterson Brothers Shipping (Epworth Arcade off Nina Street, Ste. 1, 1st Fl., tel. 331-5644, patterson@connect.com.fj) takes reservations for the Suva–Natovi–Nabouwalu–Labasa "Sea-Road" ferry/bus combination, which departs the bus station opposite the Suva Flea Market on Monday, Tuesday, Thursday, Friday, and Saturday at 0530. Fares from Suva are F$52 to Nabouwalu or F$55 right through to Labasa, an interesting 10-hour trip. The schedule varies each week. Patterson Brothers also has offices in Labasa, Lautoka, and Levuka.

Consort Shipping Line (tel. 331-3344,

© DAVID STANLEY

The Patterson Brothers ferry *Spirit of Harmony* links Suva to Ovalau and Vanua Levu Islands via Natovi.

www.consortshipping.com.fj), in the Dominion House arcade on Thomson Street, operates the MV *Spirit of Fiji Islands* or *"Sofi,"* an old Greek ferry with 182 airline-style seats in two video rooms, plus numerous long wooden benches outside on deck. First class consists of 20 four-berth cabins. The ship leaves Suva on Tuesday at 1700 for Koro (nine hours, F$48/70 deck/cabin), Savusavu (14 hours, F$50/85), and Taveuni (23 hours, F$58/95). Fridays at 1800 the *Sofi* leaves Suva for Savusavu and Taveuni only. The snack bar on board sells basic meals, but you're better off taking along your own food. Consort Shipping's main office is on Matua Street, Walu Bay.

The MV *Suilven* of **Bligh Water Shipping Ltd.** (tel. 331-8247, www.blighwatershipping.com.fj) leaves Suva on Monday, Wednesday, and Friday at 1800. The ship arrives in Savusavu at 0500 the next day, leaving Savusavu 0600, arriving Taveuni 1030, leaving Taveuni 1430, arriving Savusavu 1830, leaving Savusavu 2000, arriving Suva 0700. The *Suilven* spends Saturday night at Taveuni and leaves there for Suva at

1400. The schedule varies at Christmas and holidays. Fares from Suva to Savusavu are F$55 economy, F$95 first class with a bed in a 42-bed dorm, two-person cabin F$136 per person and up. From Suva to Taveuni it's F$65 and up. Taveuni–Savusavu is F$28 economy. The Prime Minister's cabin aboard the *Suilven* features a sitting room, bathroom with shower, bedroom with king-size bed, and outdoor dining verandah, costing F$359 for two people to Taveuni, breakfast and dinner included. *Suilven* offices are upstairs in the South Mall Center opposite the bus station and on Matua Street, Walu Bay, at the entrance to Muaiwalu Wharf.

Ships to Kadavu, Lau, and Rotuma

Venu Shipping Ltd. (14 Kaua Rd., tel. 339-5000), Laucala Bay, operates the *Sinu-i-wasa* to Kadavu once a week (F$55 deck, F$75 in the six-bed bottom lounge or the six-bed air-conditioned top lounge). It leaves Suva Tuesday at 2300 for Vunisea, departing Vunisea for Suva on Wednesday at 1100 with a stop at Kavala Bay around 1500.

ISA LEI (THE FIJIAN SONG OF FAREWELL)

Isa, isa vulagi lasa dina,
Nomu lako, au na rarawa kina?
Cava beka, ko a mai cakava,
Nomu lako, au na sega ni lasa.

Isa, isa, you are my only treasure,
Must you leave me so lonely and forsaken?
As the roses will miss the sun at dawning,
Every moment, my heart for you is yearning.

Isa lei, na noqu rarawa,
Ni ko sana vodo e na mataka.
Bau nanuma, na nodatou lasa,
Mai Suva nanuma tikoga.

Isa lei, the purple shadows falling,
Sad the morrow will dawn upon my sorrow.
Oh! Forget not, when you are far away,
Precious moments beside Suva Bay.

Vanua rogo, na nomuni vanua,
Kena ca, ni levu tu na ua.
Lomaqu voli, me'u bau butuka,
Tovolea, ke balavu na bula.

Isa lei, my heart was filled with pleasure,
From the moment I heard your tender greeting.
'Mid the sunshine, we spent the hours together,
Now so swiftly those happy hours are fleeting.

Isa lei, na noqu rarawa,
Ni ko sana vodo e na mataka.
Bau nanuma, na nodatou lasa,
Mai Suva nanuma tikoga.

Isa lei, the purple shadows fall,
Sad the morrow will dawn upon my sorrow.
Oh! Forget not, when you are far away,
Precious moments beside Suva Bay.

Domoni dina, na nomu yanuyanu,
Kena kau, wale na salusalu,
Mocelolo, bua, na kukuwalu,
Lagakali, baba na rosidamu.

O'er the ocean your island home is calling,
Happy country where roses bloom in splendor,
Oh, I would but journey there beside you,
Then forever my heart would sing in rapture.

Isa lei, na noqu rarawa,
Ni ko sana vodo e na mataka.
Bau nanuma, na nodatou lasa,
Mai Suva nanuma tikoga.

Isa lei, the purple shadows fall,
Sad the morrow will dawn upon my sorrow.
Oh! Forget not, when you are far away,
Precious moments beside Suva Bay.

Maritime Shipping Line (tel. 357-2972) in a green container on Muaiwalu Wharf operates the barge *Sea-Link* from Suva to northern or southern Lau every fortnight.

Western Shipping (tel. 331-4467, western shipping@connect.com.fj), in a yellow container on Muaiwalu Wharf, operates the *Cagi Mai Ba* to the Lau and Lomaiviti groups.

Bligh Water Shipping Ltd. (tel. 331-8247, www.blighwatershipping.com.fj) operates the *Suilven* from Taveuni to Vanua Balavu and Cicia on the first Saturday of every month.

Also check **Seaview Shipping Services** (tel. 330-9515, www.seaviewshippingfiji.com), in the side of the yellow building between the Consort Shipping and Bligh Water Shipping offices on Matua Street. They sometimes have a ship to Lau.

The small wooden copra boat *Adi Lomai* runs to Lomaiviti, Lau, and Rotuma. Other small boats operate from Suva to Lau every week or two. Ask the crews of vessels tied up at Muaiwalu Jetty, Walu Bay, for passage to Nairai, Gau, Koro, Lau, etc. Don't believe the first person who tells you there's no boat going where you want—*keep trying*.

Food is usually included in the price, and on the outward journey it will probably be okay, but on the return don't expect much more than rice and tea. If you're planning a long voyage by interisland ship, a big bundle of kava roots to captain and crew as a token of appreciation for their hospitality works wonders.

Ships to Other Countries

The Wednesday issue of the *Fiji Times* carries a special section on international shipping, though most are container ships that don't accept passengers. Most shipping is headed for Tonga and Samoa—there's not much going westward. Ships from neighboring countries sometimes come to Suva for repairs, and they carry passengers back on their return. It's often easier to sign on as crew on a yacht, and they'll probably be heading west. Try both yacht anchorages in Suva: Put up a notice, ask around, etc.

Williams & Gosling Ltd. Ships Agency (82 Harris Rd., tel. 331-2633, www.wgfiji.com .fj), near the market bus station, handles the monthly departures of the *Nivaga II* or *Manu Folau* to Funafuti, but the dates are variable. Fares in Australian dollars are A$291 one-way first class, A$224 second class, or A$73 deck, meals included. Unless you have an onward plane ticket from Funafuti, you'll be required to pay for a round-trip. Williams & Gosling will only know about a week beforehand approximately when the ship may sail. After reaching Funafuti, the ship cruises the Tuvalu Group.

BY LAND
Long-Distance Taxis and Minibuses

Minibuses from the Viti Minibuses Cooperative Limited park at the **Stinson Parade Mini Bus Station** on the waterfront behind Village Six Cinemas. Service to Nadi (F$17) and Lautoka (F$19) is throughout the day until 1900. The regular buses from the bus station are slower and safer, and you see more.

The **East-West Shuttle Service** on Robertson Road, up the hill from the market, offers taxis direct to long-distance Nadi at F$20 a seat or F$80 for the whole four-seat car. The trip takes only three hours but you can make a full day of it by hiring the car to Nadi for around F$150 with lots of stops along the way. Write out a list of the places you might like to stop, and show it to the driver beforehand, so he can't demand more money later on.

Taxis

All taxis in Suva are required to have working meters so using them is easy. Taxi meters are set at level one daily 0600–2200 with F$1.50 charged at flag-fall and F$0.50 a kilometer. From 2200–0600, the flag-fall is F$2 plus F$0.50 a kilometer. Waiting time costs F$0.10 a minute. Always ask the driver to use the meter. Fares average F$2 in the city center or F$3 to the suburbs. Drivers are not obliged to use their meters for trips over 16 kilometers and a negotiated fare will be required. To hire a taxi for a city tour might cost about F$25 an hour.

Nausori Taxi (tel. 347-7583), based at the taxi kiosk in the parking lot at the Holiday Inn, offers a shuttle service from Suva to Nausori Airport at F$10 per person. Trips are scheduled daily at 0445, 0845, 1300, 1530, and 1645, but only if bookings have been made. Thus it's important to reserve the day before.

Car Rentals

Car rentals are available in Suva from **Avis** (at Nabua, tel. 337-8361, www.avis.com .fj), **Budget** (123 Foster Rd., Walu Bay, tel. 331-5899, www.budget.com.fj), **Carpenters Rentals** (Foster Rd. across from the Mobil station, tel. 331-3644, www.carpenters.com .fj), **Central** (295 Victoria Parade, tel. 331-1866), **Dove** (42 High St., Toorak, tel. 331-1755, doverentals@connect.com.fj), **Hertz** (56 Grantham Rd., Raiwaqa, tel. 338-0981, www .hertzfiji.net), and **Thrifty** (46 Gordon St., tel. 331-4436, www.rosiefiji.com).

Parking

The parking machines on Suva streets must be fed F$0.20 every 15 minutes weekdays 0800–1630, Saturdays 0800–1230.

SUVA AND VICINITY

NORTHERN VITI LEVU

Northern Viti Levu has landscapes just as spectacular as the southern side of the island, and you haven't seen Viti Levu until you travel the northern route between Suva and Lautoka. Kings Road is now paved from Suva north to Korovou, then again from Nayavu to Lautoka, but between Korovou and Nayavu is a winding, 45-kilometer gravel stretch. Roadwork from both ends should have extended the pavement a bit by the time you get there, but at the present rate it will be many years before the asphalt reaches Korovou. If driving, check your fuel before heading this way. In June 2010, a Malaysian bank announced that it would loan Fiji US$40 million to complete the paved road around Viti Levu, so the work may speed up.

Since Kings Road follows the Wainibuka River from Wailotua village almost all the way to Viti Levu Bay, you get a good glimpse of the island's lush interior. In years gone by, the Fijians would use bamboo rafts to transport bundles of bananas down the Wainibuka to markets in Vunidawa and Nausori, and the road is still called the "Banana Highway."

The rugged north coast west of Rakiraki is marketed as the "Sun Coast" or "Sunshine Coast" for its relatively dry climate. Many visitors stop for a sojourn on Nananu-i-Ra Island near Rakiraki. The beaches, snorkeling, and hiking are all excellent on Nananu-i-Ra, and some of Fiji's best scuba diving is in this area. A number of dive shops are based at resorts around Nananu-i-Ra.

Tavua is a base for visiting the site of the gold

© MARK HEARD / WWW.FLICKR.COM/HEARDSY

HIGHLIGHTS

◖ Nananu-i-Ra Island: This inviting small island off northern Viti Levu features fine beaches, good snorkeling and diving, and an abundant supply of inexpensive resorts (page 178).

◖ Sri Krishna Kaliya Temple: The architecture of this Hindu temple is pleasing, and visitors are welcome to enter to see the gods. The Sunday prayer meeting and feast is worth attending if you're in Lautoka that day (page 190).

◖ Koroyanitu National Heritage Park: This mountain park behind Lautoka offers spectacular hiking and climbing. There are trails and waterfalls for the day-tripper, plus a small guest house in which to stay (page 197).

◖ Nausori Highlands: This favorite mountain trip takes you up into the grassy highlands behind Nadi for some hiking and village visits. The views are superb (page 198).

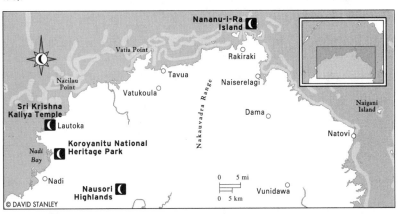

© DAVID STANLEY

LOOK FOR ◖ TO FIND RECOMMENDED SIGHTS, ACTIVITIES, DINING, AND LODGING.

mine at Vatukoula, and Ba is a starting point for many trips into Viti Levu's interior. The scenery between Tavua and Ba is breathtaking, with sweeping vistas across the grassy countryside to the mountains beyond. Kings Road ends in Fiji's sugar city, Lautoka, a gateway to the Yasawa Islands. The jagged mountains behind Lautoka are now part of Koroyanitu National Heritage Park.

PLANNING YOUR TIME

Although express buses take only six hours to cover Kings Road from Suva to Lautoka, a stopover of several days on Nananu-i-Ra Island or at a nearby mainland resort is recommended. Tavua or Ba is only worth a night if you want to experience small-town life in Fiji. There's enough to see in Lautoka to keep you occupied for a full day.

Nausori and the Rewa Delta

NAUSORI

The Rewa River town of Nausori, 19 kilometers northeast of Suva, is Fiji's third-largest town and the headquarters of Central Division and Rewa Province. The population of 47,500 is predominantly Indo-Fijian. There are several banks and a bustling market here. Nausori is best known for its large airport three kilometers southeast, built as a fighter strip to defend Fiji's capital during World War II.

In 1881, Nausori was chosen as the site of Fiji's first large sugar mill, which operated until 1959. In those early days, it was incorrectly believed that sugarcane grew better on the wetter eastern side of the island. Today, cane is grown only on the drier, sunnier western sides of Viti Levu and Vanua Levu. The old sugar mill is now a rice mill and storage depot, as the Rewa Valley has become a major rice-producing area. Chicken feed is also milled here.

The Rewa is Fiji's largest river, and in 1937 the nine-span **Rewa River Bridge** was erected here. In August 2006, the old bridge was replaced by Fiji's longest and widest bridge, 425 meters long and four lanes wide, built with F$30 million in European Union aid money. The historic old bridge is now closed to vehicular traffic and may eventually have to be removed, as it's a potential threat to the new bridge during flooding.

The **Syria Monument** (1983), at the end of the old Rewa bridge, commemorates the wreck of the iron sailing ship *Syria* on Nasilai Point in May 1884. Of the 439 indentured Indian laborers aboard ship at the time, 57 drowned. The monument tells the story of the rescue of the others.

Accommodations

Riverside Accommodation (tel. 861-6444), behind Big Bear and down the alley near the Nausori Club, has seven rooms with shared bath in the old building at F$15/35 an hour/day for one or two people. Better are the three

The old Rewa River Bridge, built in 1937, is now only used for foot and bicycle traffic.

© DAVID STANLEY

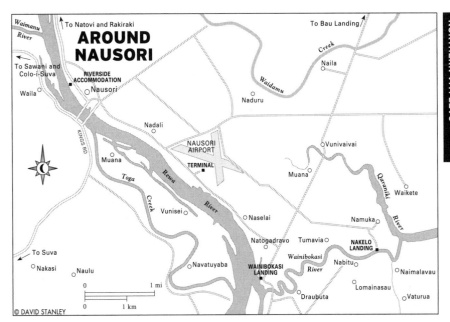

"master bedrooms" in an adjacent building at F$45 or F$50 double with private bath and shared cooking facilities.

Food
Krishna Vegetarian Restaurant (3 Ross St., closed Sun.) is down from the Westpac Bank and on the right. You can get Indian dishes, samosas, sweets, and flavored masala tea.

The **Whistling Duck Pub,** around the corner from Krishna Vegetarian Restaurant, is rough and you may prefer **KB's Bar and Night Club** (tel. 340-0115, Fri. and Sat. 1900–0300, F$5 admission) or **Dolphins Night Club** (tel. 347-5533) across the street. The **Nausori Club** (tel. 347-8287), on the river behind Big Bear, is a safer drinking place.

Getting There and Around
Local buses to the airport (F$0.70) and Suva (F$2.l0) are fairly frequent, with the last bus to Suva at 2200. A taxi to the airport is F$3.50. You can catch Sunbeam Transport express buses from Nausori to Lautoka at 0635, 0715,

0855, 1240, 1405, and 1745 (246 km, 5.5 hours, F$19.40).

Fast minibuses direct to Suva (F$1.50) leave from the end of the bus station closest to the Syria Monument.

EAST OF NAUSORI
Rewa Delta
Take a bus from Nausori to Nakelo Landing to explore the heavily populated Rewa River Delta. Many outboards leave from Nakelo to take villagers to their riverside homes, and they might agree to take you along for a few dollars. Larger boats leave Nakelo sporadically for Levuka, Gau, and Koro, but finding one would be pure chance. Some also depart from nearby Wainibokasi Landing. At **Naililili** in the delta, French Catholic missionaries built St. Joseph's Church (1905) of solid limestone with stained-glass windows.

Bau Island
Bau, a tiny, eight-hectare island just east of Viti Levu, has a special place in Fiji's history, as this

was the seat of High Chief Cakobau, who used European cannons and muskets to subdue most of western Fiji in the 1850s. At its pinnacle, Bau had a population of 3,000, hundreds of war canoes guarded its waters, and more than 20 temples stood on the island's central plain. After the Battle of Verata on Viti Levu in 1839, Cakobau and his father, Tanoa, presented the bodies of 260 men, women, and children to their closest friends and allied chiefs for gastronomical purposes. Fifteen years after this slaughter, Cakobau converted to Christianity and prohibited cannibalism on Bau. In 1867, he became a sovereign, crowned by European traders and planters desiring a stable government in Fiji to protect their interests.

The great stone slabs that form docks and seawalls around much of the island once accommodated Bau's fleet of war canoes. The graves of the Cakobau family and many of the old chiefs lie on the hilltop behind the school. The large, sturdy stone church near the provincial offices was the first Christian church in Fiji. Inside its nearly one-meter-thick walls, just in front of the altar, is the old sacrificial stone once used for human sacrifices, today the baptismal font. Now painted white, this font was once known as King Cakobau's "skull crusher," and it's said that a thousand brains were splattered against it. Across from the church are huge ancient trees and the thatched Council House on the site of the onetime temple of the war god Cagawalu. The family of the late Sir George Cakobau, governor-general of Fiji from 1973–1983, has a large traditional-style home on the island. You can see everything on the island in an hour or so.

To get to Bau, take the Bau bus (five daily) from Nausori to Bau Landing, where there are outboards to cross over to the island. Be aware that Bau is not considered a tourist attraction, and from time to time visitors are prevented from going to the island. It's important to get someone to invite you across, which they'll do willingly if you show a genuine interest in Fijian history. Like most Fijians, the inhabitants of Bau are generally friendly to outsiders. Bring a big bundle of *waka* for the *turaga-ni-koro*,

TANOA: CANNIBAL KING OF BAU

Tanoa was about 65 years old in 1840 when the U.S. Exploring Expedition, under Liutenant Charles Wilkes, toured Fiji. His rise to power threw the island into several years of strife, as Tanoa had to do away with virtually every minor chief who challenged his right to rule. With long, colorful pennants hung from the mast and thousands of *Cypraea ovula* shells decorating the hull, his 30-meter outrigger canoe was the fastest in the region. One of Tanoa's favorite sports was overtaking and ramming smaller canoes at sea. The survivors were then fair game for whoever could catch and keep them. At feasts where most nobles were expected to provide a pig, Tanoa always furnished a human body.

and ask permission very politely to be shown around. There could be some confusion about who's to receive the *sevusevu*, however, as everyone on Bau is a chief! The more respectful your dress and demeanor, the better your chances of success. If you're told to contact the Ministry of Fijian Affairs in Suva, just depart gracefully, as that's their way of saying no. After all, it's up to them.

Viwa Island

Before Cakobau adopted Christianity in 1854, Methodist missionaries working for this effect resided on Viwa Island, just across the water from Bau. Here the first Fijian New Testament was printed in 1847; Reverend John Hunt, who did the translation, lies buried in the graveyard beside the church that bears his name.

Viwa is a good alternative if you aren't invited to visit Bau itself. To reach the island, hire an outboard at Bau Landing. If you're lucky, you'll be able to join some locals who are going. A single Fijian village stands on the island.

Toberua Island

Created in 1968, **Toberua Island Resort** (tel. 347-2777, www.toberua.com), on a tiny reef island off the east tip of Viti Levu, was one of Fiji's first luxury outer-island resorts. The 15 thatched *bure* are designed in the purest Fijian style, and the small size means peace and quiet. The tariff is F$635 single or double standard, F$755 deluxe, including tax, good meals, and launch transfers from Nakelo Landing (five-night minimum stay). Discounts are available for children under 16 sharing with adults. Toberua is outside eastern Viti Levu's wet belt, so it doesn't get a lot of rain as does nearby Suva,

and weather permitting, meals are served outdoors. There are no mosquitoes.

Don't expect tennis courts or a golf course at Toberua, though, believe it or not, there's tropical golfing on the reef at low tide! The par-32 course has nine holes from 90–180 meters, and clubs and balls are provided free. Scuba diving is F$110/210 for one/two tanks. Most other activities are free, including snorkeling, sailing, windsurfing, and boat trips to a bird sanctuary or mangrove forest, and there's a swimming pool. It's a unique experience to snorkel among the inoffensive sea snakes just offshore.

Northeastern Viti Levu

KOROVOU

A good paved highway runs 31 kilometers north from Nausori to Korovou, a small town of about 350 souls on the eastern side of Viti Levu. Korovou is at the junction of Kings Road and the road to Natovi, terminus of the Ovalau and Vanua Levu ferries, and this crossroads position makes it an important stop for buses

plying the northern route around the island. Sunbeam Transport express buses leave Korovou for Lautoka at 0725, 0800, 0940, 1325, 1500, and 1830 (215 km, five hours, F$17.35), with local westbound buses departing at 0920 and 0950 (7.5 hours). (Be aware that because *korovou* means "new village," there are many places called that in Fiji—don't mix them up.)

fruits and vegetables for sale in Korovou

© DAVID STANLEY

© DAVID STANLEY

the Waibula River at Korovou

Korovou is the headquarters of Tailevu Province, and the district officer's office is in Waimaro House on the south side of town. The Seventh-Day Adventist Church operates Fulton College, a large Bible college just south of Korovou. Coup master George Speight hails from near Korovou, and a rather unpleasant atmosphere hangs over the town.

The dilapidated **Tailevu Hotel** (Kings Rd., tel. 343-0028), on a hill overlooking the Waibula River just across the bridge from Korovou, has three double rooms in an old building at F$50 double, or F$65 for a four-person family room. Better are the six new air-conditioned units in a long block facing an unfinished swimming pool at F$65 double. Two basic single rooms in a nearby cottage are F$35 double. This rustic colonial-style hotel features a large bar and restaurant, and a rowdy disco opens on Friday and Saturday nights.

THE TAILEVU COAST

North of Korovou is Natovi, terminus of ferry services from Vanua Levu and Ovalau. The **Natalei Eco-Lodge** (tel. 881-1168) at Nataleira village, up the coast beyond Natovi, offers dormitory accommodations at F$80 per person and *bure* at F$180 double, meals included. Horseback riding, hiking, waterfall visits, snorkeling, and cultural activities can be arranged.

Between Nataleira and Silana villages, 40 kilometers northwest of Korovou, is **Takalana Bay Beach Resort** (tel. 991-6338, takalana. blogspot.com). The two-bedroom homestead of this large country estate stands on a hilltop overlooking Vatu-i-Ra Passage with good views of Ovalau, Naigani, Wakaya, and Vanua Levu. The rate is F$95 per person, including hot showers, meals, and some activities. Dolphin watching at Moon Reef can be arranged at additional cost.

Both Takalana Bay Beach Resort and Natalei Eco-Lodge make ideal bases from which to climb **Mount Tova** (647 m) for its sweeping view of the entire Tailevu area. You can start from Silana village, or Nataleira a couple of kilometers southeast, and it will take about three hours to go up and another two to come back down. An experienced hiker might be able to find the way on his or her own, but it's better to hire a guide in one of the villages. This area also has waterfalls, Fijian villages, and coral reefs to explore.

Buses to Nataleira leave Suva bus station weekdays at 1330, 1430, and 1630 (F$12). These buses stop at Bureiwai village and return to Suva the next morning. A normal car can drive on from Bureiwai to Kings Road, but there's no bus service. A taxi from Nataleira to Barotu on Kings Road will cost F$60.

KINGS ROAD TO VITI LEVU BAY

The large dairy farms along the highway west of Korovou were set up after World War I. **Dorothy's Waterfall** on the Waimaro River, a kilometer east of Dakuivuna village, is 10 kilometers west of Korovou. Now managed by Dorothy's son Ulupeni, it's a nice picnic spot (admission F$2) if you have your own transportation.

At Wailotua No. 1, 20 kilometers west of Korovou, is a large **"snake cave"** (admission F$10) right beside the village and easily accessible from the road. One stalactite in the cave is shaped like a six-headed snake. Feejee Experience groups are taken *bilibili* rafting on the Wainibuka River here and you may also spot locals using such rafts. At Nayavu, the paved road starts again and continues 63 kilometers northwest to Rakiraki.

The old Catholic Church of St. Francis Xavier at **Naiserelagi,** on a hilltop above Navunibitu Catholic School, on Kings Road about 25 kilometers southeast of Rakiraki, was beautifully decorated with frescoes by Jean Charlot in 1962–1963. Typical Fijian motifs, such as the *tabua, tanoa,* and *yaqona,* blend together in the powerful composition behind the altar. Father Pierre Chanel, who was martyred in 1841 on Futuna Island between Fiji and Samoa, appears on the left holding the weapon that killed him, a war club. Christ and the Madonna are portrayed in black. Charlot had previously collaborated with the famous Mexican muralist

Diego Rivera, and his work (restored in 1998) is definitely worth stopping to see. Flying Prince Transport (tel. 669-4346) runs buses from Vaileka to Naiserelagi eight times a day; otherwise, all the local Suva buses stop there. A taxi from Vaileka might cost F$30 round-trip with waiting time. At **Nanukuloa** village just north of here is the headquarters of Ra Province.

NEAR ELLINGTON WHARF

The upscale **Wananavu Beach Resort** (tel. 669-4433, www.wananavu.com) is beautifully situated on a point facing Nananu-i-Ra Island, four kilometers off Kings Road. There are 31 air-conditioned bungalows costing F$293–440 single or double—reasonable value for the quality. No cooking facilities are provided, but each room does have a fridge. Adjacent to the resort are three two-bedroom villas with kitchens starting at F$464 for up to four persons. Honeymoon *bure* start at F$640 double. A buffet breakfast is included but add 17.5 percent tax to all rates. Local-rate discounts are possible. A lunch and dinner meal plan is F$82 per person but the food doesn't match the standard of the rooms. The resort has a swimming pool, tennis court, and muddy brown beach. A variety of water sports are available but the snorkeling here isn't good. Many people come to dive with Ra Divers.

In 2005, a self-catering villa called **Starfish Blue** (tel. 999-6746, www.starfishblue.com) opened on a hill next to Wananavu Beach Resort. The three air-conditioned rooms with bath are F$475 double, F$525 for up to four, or F$575 for up to six for the whole house with a minimum stay of four nights. Stay six nights and the seventh is free. You can cook your own meals or ask the maids to do so (extra charge). The maids will also do laundry or babysit for a small fee. A small oceanfront pool is in front of the building and guests may use the facilities of the Wananavu Resort. Suncoast Taxis and Tours (tel. 669-4366) will pick up Starfish Blue guests at Nadi Airport for F$150/180 by car/van.

◀ Volivoli Beach (tel. 669-4511, www.volivoli.com) is on sandy Volivoli Point at the northernmost tip of Viti Levu, about four kilometers beyond Wananavu Beach Resort. Beds in the eight-bed dorm rooms are F$25 per person (or F$27 pp in the females-only dorm, plus F$2 for a towel or sheet), while lodge rooms with shared bath are F$100 double. A self-catering studio room is F$320 double. Add 5 percent hotel tax to these rates. You can cook your own food or order reasonable meals at the restaurant/bar. Volivoli Beach is an ideal place to stay if scuba diving is a priority, as it's run by Ra Divers. Fishing charters can be arranged. The snorkeling, kayaking, and hiking are all good here and there's a pool with swim-up bar. Feejee Experience tour groups often use Volivoli. A taxi from Vaileka to either Wananavu or Volivoli will cost F$15.

Adventure Water Sports (tel. 669-3333, www.safarilodge.com.fj) on Ellington Wharf offers a variety of activities, often with a minimum of two persons. The Coconut Café serves coffee and meals. You can use their phone to call the island at F$1 a call or check your email at F$5 an hour. Boat transfers and day trips to Nananu-i-Ra can be arranged.

C NANANU-I-RA ISLAND

This small (355-hectare) island, three kilometers off the northernmost tip of Viti Levu, is a good place to spend some quality time amid tranquility and beauty. The climate is dry and sunny, and there are great beaches, reefs, snorkeling, walks, sunsets, and moonrises over the water—only roads are missing. Seven or eight separate white sandy beaches lie scattered around the island, and it's big enough that you won't feel confined. In the early 19th century, Nananu-i-Ra's original Fijian inhabitants were wiped out by disease and tribal warfare, and an heir sold the island to Europeans whose descendants now operate a few small family-style resorts.

Most of the northern two-thirds of Nananu-i-Ra Island was once owned by Procter & Gamble heiress Louise Harper of Southern California, who bought it for a mere US$200,000

© DAVID STANLEY

windsurfers off Nananu-i-Ra's Mile Long Beach

in 1968. Until Harper's death in 2005, her cattle grazed beneath coconuts on the 219-hectare Harper Plantation and the land was largely untouched. Several hotel and marina development projects have been proposed for this site, but as yet nothing much has been done.

It's possible to hike all the way around Nananu-i-Ra, as the entire coastline is public—but only as far as the high-tide line. Thick mangroves on the western side of the island make that stretch difficult to cover. A good plan is to hike up the eastern side of the island, trying to get as far as deserted One Beach on the still-unspoiled northern side of the island and then return the same way. This is the easiest and most beautiful part of the hike around the island. It's best to do it at low tide, but even then, at some point you'll probably have to take off your shoes and wade through water just over your ankles or scramble over slippery rocks. Avoid becoming stranded by high tide.

Ed and Betty Morris own five hectares on

Nananu-i-Ra known as Sunset Point, next door to MacDonald's Nananu Beach Cottages. On the top of their peninsula is the **Sunset Point Labyrinth,** the only labyrinth in Fiji. Ed is a past international president of the International Brotherhood of Magicians, and he enjoys showing visitors how to meditate while walking the 15-meter-diameter labyrinth.

Scuba Diving

Ra Divers (tel. 669-4511, www.volivoli.com), based at Volivoli Beach and Wananavu Beach Resort, has been diving the waters around Nananu-i-Ra since the 1980s. They offer scuba diving at F$90/160 for one/two tanks (gear extra). Night diving is F$90. Ra Diver's resort course costs F$140; full four-day PADI or NAUI certification is F$550 if you're alone or F$475 per person for two or more. Snorkeling trips are possible. They pick up clients regularly from all of the Nananu-i-Ra resorts and their equipment is first rate. Ra Divers uses the aluminum *Bligh Explorer* to take as many as 16 divers to Bligh Waters and Vatu Passage, while the smaller *Phantom* frequents Sailstone Reef.

Papoo Divers (tel. 944-4726), operated by Papu Pangalau, is based at Sekoula Estate on the southeast side of Nananu-i-Ra.

The diving close to Nananu-i-Ra is spectacular only if you observe the small details—there's not the profuse marine life or huge reefs you'll find elsewhere, though the underwater photographer will like it. This area is good for wreck diving, though, as the 33-meter *Papuan Explorer* was scuttled in 1990 in 22 meters of water off the west side of Nananu-i-Ra, 150 meters off a 189-meter jetty that curves out into the sheltered lagoon. The interisland ferry *Ovalau* is 26 meters down in the open sea off northern Nananu-i-Ra.

Accommodations

Accommodation prices on Nananu-i-Ra have crept up in recent years, and the number of beds is limited. With the island's growing popularity, it's best to call ahead to one of the resorts and arrange to be picked up at Ellington Wharf. None of the innkeepers will accept additional guests when they're fully booked, and camping is usually not allowed. This is especially true June–August, the peak windsurfing season. There's no public telephone at Ellington Wharf, but the staff of Adventure Water Sports on the wharf will make local calls for you at F$1 each.

If you want an individual room or *bure,* make 100 percent sure one is available; otherwise you could end up spending a few nights in the dormitory waiting for one to become free. All the budget places have cooking facilities, and a few also serve snacks and meals. MacDonald's and Betham's have mini-marts with a reasonable selection of groceries (including beer). Also take the opportunity to buy groceries in Vaileka on the way to Nananu-i-Ra. Bring enough cash, as most places don't accept credit cards.

Near the middle of Nananu-i-Ra are several nice budget places to stay, all offering cooking facilities. They usually have free beds in the dorms, but advance bookings are necessary if you want your own room. The bay here is well protected from the wind, so it's actually a better place to swim and snorkel.

(MacDonald's Nananu Beach Cottages (tel. 628-3118, www.macsnananu.com) offers two attractive beach houses and one garden house, all with bath and fridge, at F$135 single or double, plus F$12 per additional person to four maximum. A duplex is F$90 for each of the two units, while a larger two-story house accommodating up to six is F$145 for the first two. The four-bunk dorm is F$25 per person. All units have access to cooking facilities, and a three-meal package is available at F$40 per person. Mabel MacDonald's Beachside Café serves excellent grilled cheese sandwiches and pizzas, as well as selling groceries. Dinner must be ordered by 1500. A Fijian *lovo* feast is arranged once a week. It's peaceful and attractive, with excellent snorkeling (lots of parrot fish) from the long private wharf off their beach. Ryan MacDonald takes guests on a snorkeling trip to

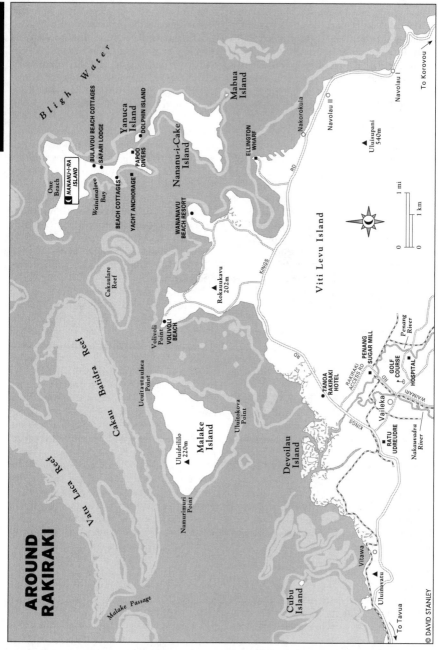

AROUND RAKIRAKI

© DAVID STANLEY

the outer reef, and kayaks are available for rent. The atmosphere at MacDonald's is excellent.

Right next to MacDonald's and facing the same white beach is **Betham's Beach Cottages** (tel. 628-0400, www.bethams .com.fj). They have four units in two cement-block duplex houses, each sleeping up to six, at F$135 single or double. The one wooden beachfront bungalow costs the same. The mixed dormitory with four ancient beds is F$25 per person. There's no hot water, but cooking facilities and a fridge are provided. Noisy parties are actively discouraged here, and the electric generator is switched off at 2200 (as is also the case at MacDonald's). A paperback lending library is at your service. Betham's impressive grocery store also sells alcohol, and their well-stocked beachfront bar serves dinner, though the food is better at MacDonald's.

Sharing the same high sandy beach with Mc-Donald's and Betham's is **Charlie's Cottages** (tel. 623-1188, www.charliescottages.com). Each of the two houses on the hillside has a three-bed dorm (F$25 pp) in the same area as the kitchen and one double room with shared bath (F$80). You can watch the sunrise on one side of the hill and the sunset on the other. Charlie's also rents another house at F$110 double.

Just a few minutes' walk across the peninsula via a 200-meter right-of-way next to Charlie's is **Safari Island Lodge** (tel. 669-3333, www .safarilodge.com.fj). The two-story lodge has a four-bed dorm upstairs and two bunks in the common room downstairs at F$30 per person. Also upstairs is a room with shared bath at F$110 double. A bare beachfront *bure* with private bath is F$220 while a two-bedroom "villa" is F$395. Three meals a day in the restaurant/bar are F$65 per person. Organized activities (at additional cost) include windsurfing, sea kayaking, catamaran sailing, snorkeling trips, water skiing, kitesurfing, and fishing. Snorkeling gear and kayaks are loaned free. The beach here isn't as good as the one in front of MacDonald's and Betham's. Verify all prices carefully and ask if they're quoting in Fijian dollars or Australian dollars. Add 5 percent to anything you pay by credit card. You should avoid prepaying accommodations at Safari Island Lodge until you've actually seen the property with your own eyes.

A better choice would be **Bulavou Beach Bungalows** (tel. 628-3103, www.bulavou beachbungalowsfiji.com), which opened in 2007 just 50 meters up the mile-long picture-postcard beach from Safari Island Lodge. Each of the three buildings at Bulavou has two floors. Confusingly, the managers refer to each floor as a "bungalow." Each two-bedroom floor/bungalow accommodates up to six people at F$150 for up the first four persons, then F$25 for each additional person, taxes included. Each floor/bungalow also has a large fridge you're welcome to stock with drinks, but cooking facilities are not provided so add F$55/70 per person for the meal plan (two/three meals).

Far more upscale than any of the places on Nananu-i-Ra is **Dolphin Island** (tel. 378-5791, www.dolphinislandfiji.com), which opened on neighboring Yanuca Island in 2004. Only two couples can be accommodated here at one time (F$4,000 for one or F$5,000 for two all inclusive, plus 17.5 percent tax, three-night minimum stay). You pay for the luxury and exclusivity.

Getting There

Boat transfers from Ellington Wharf to Nananu-i-Ra are F$25–40 per person round-trip (20 minutes), though the resorts may levy a surcharge for one person alone. Check prices when you call to book your accommodation. Take an express bus from Lautoka to Vaileka, then a taxi to the landing at F$15 for the car (or a bit less if they use the meter). Otherwise, all of the express buses will drop you on the highway, a two-kilometer walk from Ellington Wharf. Coming from Nadi, you will have to change buses in Lautoka.

RAKIRAKI

This part of northern Viti Levu is known as Rakiraki, but the main town is called **Vaileka**

on Kings Road, near Rakiraki

© MARK HEARD / WWW.FLICKR.COM/HEARDSY

(population 5,000). The Penang Sugar Mill was erected here in 1881. The main business district is at Vaileka, a kilometer off Kings Road. There are three banks, a Western Union Currency Exchange, and a large produce market in Vaileka, but most visitors simply pass through on their way to/from Nananu-i-Ra Island.

Right beside Kings Road, just 100 meters west of the turnoff to Vaileka, is the **grave of Ratu Udreudre,** the cannibal king of this region, who is alleged to have consumed 872 corpses. A rocky hill named **Uluinavatu** (stone head), a few kilometers west of Vaileka, is reputed to be the jumping-off point for the disembodied spirits of the ancient Fijians. A fortified village and temple once stood on its summit. Uluinavatu's triangular shape is said to represent a man, while a similar-looking small island offshore resembles a woman with flowing hair.

The **Nakauvadra Range,** towering south of Rakiraki, is the traditional home of the Fijian serpent-god Degei, who is said to dwell in a cave on the summit of Mount Uluda (866 m). This "cave" is little more than a cleft in the rock. To climb the Nakauvadra Range, which the local Fijians look upon as their primeval homeland, permission must be obtained from the chief of Vatukacevaceva village, who will provide guides. A *sevusevu* must be presented.

Accommodations and Food

The **Tanoa Rakiraki Hotel** (Kings Rd., tel. 669-4101, www.tanoarakiraki.com), a couple of kilometers north of Vaileka, has 36 air-conditioned rooms with fridge and private bath at F$85/148 single or double standard/superior in the new blocks, and 10 rather musty fan-cooled rooms at F$60 single or double in the old wing. Reduced rates are sometimes offered on the air-conditioned rooms. The 16-bed dorm is F$38 per person. The reception area, restaurant, and old wooden wing occupy the core of the original hotel, which dates

© DAVID STANLEY

Flying Prince buses serve villages in northern Viti Levu from Vaileka.

back to 1945; the two-story accommodations blocks were added much later. Extensive gardens surround the hotel, and the Rakiraki's outdoor bowling green draws middle-aged lawn-bowling enthusiasts from Australia and New Zealand. Those folks like old-fashioned "colonial" touches, such as the typed daily menu featuring British-Indian curry dishes, and gin and tonic in the afternoon. The Tui Ra (or king of Ra) lives in the village across the highway from the hotel. Only the local or "stage" buses will drop you off on Kings Road right in front of the hotel (the express buses will take you to Vaileka). A taxi from Vaileka is F$3.

Ady's Travellers Motel, behind the Bank of Baroda in Vaileka, provides backpacker accommodations.

A number of restaurants near the bus station at Vaileka serve basic local meals. The Sunbeam express buses stop at **Gafoor & Sons Restaurant** (tel. 669-4225), which serves

takeaway meals for F$3.50 from a glass-covered warmer at the rear counter. The **Cosmopolitan Club** (tel. 669-4330), two blocks from Vaileka bus station, is the local drinking place.

Getting There and Around

A taxi from Vaileka to Ellington Wharf, where outboard motorboats from the Nananu-i-Ra resorts pick up guests, will run F$15. Otherwise take a local bus east on Kings Road to the turnoff and walk two kilometers down to the wharf. All buses from Lautoka and Suva stop at this turnoff.

Sunbeam Transport has express buses from Vaileka to Lautoka (108 km, F$8.40) at 1035, 1230, 1605, 1730, and 2105, and to Suva (157 km, F$12.90) at 0830, 0900, 1100, 1440, and 1850. Flying Prince buses to Suva leave Vaileka at 0745, 0845, and 1230. Vatukoula Express buses to Suva pass through Vaileka at 0545, 0730, 0830, and 1230. More frequent local buses also operate.

Northwestern Viti Levu

West of Rakiraki, Kings Road passes the government-run Yaqara Cattle Ranch, where Fijian cowboys keep 5,500 head of cattle and 200 horses on a 7,000-hectare spread enclosed by an 80-kilometer fence. In 1996, an ultramodern artesian water bottling plant owned by Canadian businessman David Gilmour opened here, and plastic bottles of Fiji Water are now the country's fastest-growing export. In 2003, an Australian company leased 5,000 hectares of land around Yaqara, with the intention of creating a Studio City for foreign film producers.

TAVUA

Tavua (population 2,400), an important junction on the north coast, is the gateway to the gold mine at nearby Vatukoula. Of the three banks in Tavua, the ANZ Bank has a Visa/MasterCard ATM. Western Union Currency Exchange (Mon.–Fri. 0730–1730, Sat. 0730–1530) is across the street from the Total service station.

The two-story **Tavua Hotel** (Nabuna St., tel. 668-0522, www.tavuahotel.com), a wooden colonial-style building on a hill, is a 10-minute walk from the bus stop. Dating from 1938 and fully renovated in 2002, the 11 air-conditioned rooms with bath are now a reasonable value at F$68 single or double. Family rooms are F$100/115/135 for 3/4/5 persons. The seven-bed dormitory is F$27 per person. All rooms are air-conditioned except the dorm. Dinner is F$10–20 here. This hotel looks like it's going to be noisy due to the large bar downstairs, but all is silent after the bar and restaurant close at 2100. It's a good base from which to explore Vatukoula or break up a trip across northern Viti Levu.

New China Restaurant (tel. 668-1401), opposite the Total service station, serves fast food from the warmer at F$4 or made to order meals from the menu on the wall at F$5–10.

Nairs Restaurant (no phone, closed Sun.), on Leka Street near the post office, serves a cheap fish-and-chips lunch.

The Tavua Hotel has been serving visitors to the nearby goldfields since 1938.

© DAVID STANLEY

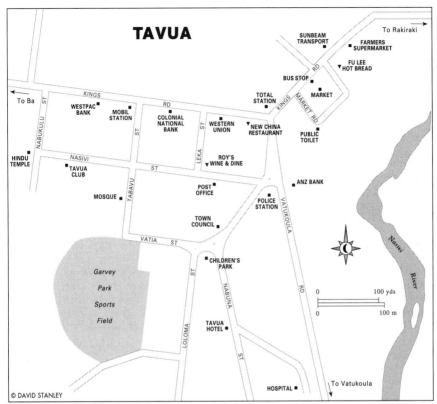

© DAVID STANLEY

Socialize at the **Tavua Club** (tel. 668-0265) on Nasivi Street.

Getting There and Around

Sunbeam Transport has express buses from Tavua to Suva (198 km, F$15.95) at 0725, 0750, 1000, 1340, and 1750, and to Lautoka (67 km, F$5.20) at 1105, 1130, 1320, 1655, 1825, and 2200. Local buses from Tavua to Vaileka (41 km), Vatukoula (8 km), Ba (F$2.40), and Lautoka are frequent. A truck from Tavua Market to Nadrau via Nadarivatu leaves around 1600 (F$5).

VATUKOULA

In 1932, an old Australian prospector named Bill Borthwick discovered gold at Vatukoula, eight kilometers south of Tavua. Two years later, Borthwick and his partner, Peter Costello, sold their stake to an Australian company, and in 1935 the Emperor Gold Mine opened. In 1977, there was a major industrial action at the mine, and the government had to step in to prevent it from closing. In 1983, the Western Mining Corporation of Australia bought a 20 percent share and took over management. Western modernized the facilities and greatly increased production, but after another bitter strike in 1991, they sold out, and the Emperor Gold Mining Company took over again. The Emperor was controlled by the South African mining company Durban Roodepoort Deep (DRD), which closed the mine in December 2006 after sustaining huge losses during the final three years of operations. In April 2007, the Australian group Westech Gold bought the mine for A$1 and resumed production later in the year.

The ore comes up from underground through the Smith Shaft near "Top Gate." It is washed, crushed, and roasted, then fed into a flotation process and the foundry, where gold and silver are separated from the ore. Vatukoula Gold Mines Limited produces tens of thousands of ounces of gold from hundreds of thousands of metric tons of ore extracted both underground and at an open pit. Silver is also produced, and waste rock is crushed into gravel and sold. Between 1935 and 2006, the Emperor produced seven million ounces of gold worth over US$4 billion at today's prices. Proven recoverable ore reserves at Vatukoula are said to be sufficient for another 20 years of mining, with another five million ounces of gold awaiting extraction underground. In 1999, the Smith Shaft was deepened to allow easier access to high-grade ores, followed by work on the Cayzer Shaft in 2000 and the Philips Shaft in 2002. Westech is increasing production with a new plant and machinery plus diversification into surface mining.

The Emperor is one of Fiji's largest private employers, and Vatukoula is a typical company town with education and social services under the jurisdiction of the mine. Several thousand miners are employed here, most of them indigenous Fijians who live in World War II–style Quonset huts in racially segregated ghettos. In contrast, tradespeople and supervisors, usually Rotumans and part-Fijians, enjoy much better living conditions, and senior staff and management live in colonial-style comfort.

VATIA POINT

Noted photographer Jim Siers operates a sport-fishing lodge at Vatia Point between Ba and Tavua. **Angler's Paradise** (tel.

668-1612, www.fijifishing.com) has a three-room guesthouse (F$188 pp a day for room and board), a couple of fast fishing boats (F$1,540 a day for up to four anglers), and good giant trevally fishing. Fishing rods, reels, and line are F$135 per set per day. Bring your own lures (lost poppers are F$67 each, lost jigs F$48). Fishing trips to the Yasawa Islands are easily arranged but longer trips involve a F$190 per day fuel surcharge.

BA

The large Indo-Fijian town of Ba (population 18,500) on the Ba River is seldom visited by tourists. Nearly half of Fiji's Muslims live in Ba Province, and there's an attractive mosque in the center of the town of Ba. Small fishing boats depart from behind the service station opposite the mosque, and it's fairly easy to arrange to go along on all-night trips. A wide belt of mangroves covers much of the river's delta. Ba's original town site was on the low hill where the post office is today, and the newer lower town is often subjected to flooding. Ba is well known in Fiji for the large Rarawai Sugar Mill, built

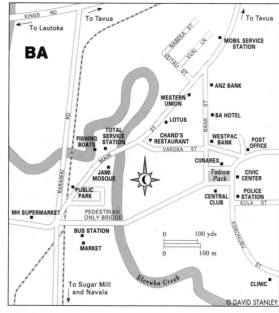

Of the many places along Main Street serving Indian and Chinese meals, your best choice is probably **Chand's Restaurant** (tel. 667-0822, Mon.–Sat. 0800–2100, Sun. 1200–1500), just across the bridge from the mosque. Their upstairs dining room serves an Indian vegetarian *thali* for F$8.75.

The **Ciinarex** (tel. 667-4048), on Tabua Park just up the hill from the hotel, shows mostly Bollywood films in Hindi.

For drinks, it's the **Central Club** (tel. 667-4348) on Tabua Park. The Central Club Kitchen (Mon.–Tues. 1100–2100, Wed.–Sat. 1100–2100, Sun. 1100–1900), downstairs at the club, serves reasonable meals at F$4.

The ANZ and Westpac banks on Bank Street both have Visa/MasterCard ATMs outside facing the street. Otherwise, it's better to go to Western Union/Money Exchange (tel. 667-0766, Mon.–Fri. 0730–1730, Sat. 0730–1530) or Lotus Foreign Exchange (tel. 667-8155), beside Chand's Restaurant around the corner on Main Street.

Important express buses leaving Ba daily are the regular Sunbeam Transport buses to Suva via Tavua at 0655, 0715, 0915, 1300, and 1715 (227 km, five hours, F$17.95). Via Sigatoka, Pacific Transport has a bus to Suva at 0615 (259 km, six hours, F$20) and Sunbeam Transport has buses at 1015 and 1130. Local buses to Tavua (29 km, F$2.40) and Lautoka (38 km, F$5.20) are frequent.

© DAVID STANLEY

Jame Mosque is a landmark in Ba. Half of Fiji's Muslim population lives in this province.

by the Colonial Sugar Refining Co. in 1886. In 2002, the transnational company Nestlé established a large food-processing plant at Ba.

The **Ba Hotel** (110 Bank St., tel. 667-4000, padarethgroup@connect.com.fj) has 13 air-conditioned rooms with bath at F$75/80/100 single/double/triple. It's very pleasant, with a swimming pool, bar, and restaurant.

Lautoka and Vicinity

Fiji's second city, Lautoka (population 52,000), is the focus of the country's sugar and timber industries, a major port, and the Western Division and Ba Province headquarters. It's a likable place with a row of towering royal palms lining the main street and a lovely seaside walk along Marine Drive. Although Lautoka grew up around the Fijian village of Namoli, the temples and mosques standing prominently in town today reflect the large Indo-Fijian population. In recent years, things have changed somewhat,

with many Indo-Fijians abandoning Fiji as indigenous Fijians move in to take their place, and Lautoka's population is now almost evenly balanced between the groups. Yet in the countryside, Indo-Fijians still comprise a majority.

The **Lautoka Sugar Mill,** one of the largest in the Southern Hemisphere, was founded in 1903. It's busiest June–December, with trains and trucks constantly depositing loads of cane to be fed into the crushers. Mill tours are not offered, but you can get a good view of the

NORTHERN VITI LEVU

© DAVID STANLEY

LAUTOKA

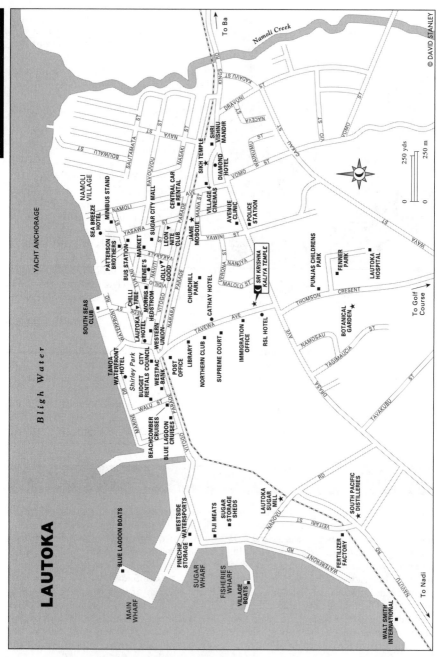

Bligh Water

YACHT ANCHORAGE

To Ba

Namoli Creek

250 yds
250 m

NAMOLI VILLAGE

SEA BREEZE HOTEL
MINIBUS STAND

SHRI VISHNU MANDIR
SIKH TEMPLE
DIAMOND HOTEL

VILLAGE 4 CINEMAS

CENTRAL CAR RENTAL

AVENUE CLINIC
POLICE STATION

PATTERSON BROTHERS
BUS STATION
MARKET

SUGAR CITY MALL
LEON NITE CLUB
JAME MOSQUE

CHILLI TREE
RENEE'S
MORRIS HEDSTROM
LAUTOKA HOTEL
JOLLY GOOD

WESTERN UNION

CHURCHILL PARK

CATHAY HOTEL

SRI KRISHNA KALIYA TEMPLE

PUNJAS CHILDRENS PARK
FENNER PARK
LAUTOKA HOSPITAL

SOUTH SEAS CLUB

TANOA WATERFRONT HOTEL

Shirley Park

BUDGET CITY RENTALS COUNCIL
WESTPAC BANK

POST OFFICE
LIBRARY
NORTHERN CLUB
SUPREME COURT

IMMIGRATION OFFICE
RSL HOTEL

BOTANICAL GARDEN

To Golf Course

BEACHCOMBER CRUISES
BLUE LAGOON CRUISES

BLUE LAGOON BOATS

WESTSIDE WATERSPORTS

PINECHIP STORAGE

FIJI MEATS

SUGAR STORAGE SHEDS

LAUTOKA SUGAR MILL

SOUTH PACIFIC DISTILLERIES

SUGAR WHARF
FISHERIES WHARF
VILLAGE BOATS

MAIN WHARF

FERTILIZER FACTORY

WALT SMITH INTERNATIONAL

To Nadi

HOW A SUGAR MILL WORKS

The sugarcane is fed through a shredder toward a row of huge rollers that squeeze out the juice. The crushed fiber (bagasse) is burned to fuel the mill or is processed into paper. Lime is then added to the juice, and the mixture is heated. Impurities settle in the clarifier, and mill mud is filtered out to be used as fertilizer. The clear juice goes through a series of evaporators, in which it is boiled into steam under partial vacuum to remove water and create a syrup. The syrup is boiled again under greater pressure in a vacuum pan, and raw sugar crystals form. The mix then enters a centrifuge, which spins off the remaining syrup (molasses — used for distilling or animal feed). The moist crystals are sent on to a rotating drum, where they are tumble-dried using hot air. Raw sugar comes out in the end.

operation from the main gate on the south side of the complex. South Pacific Distilleries, on Navutu Road south of the mill, bottles Bounty rum, Regal gin, Royal whiskey, and Tribe vodka. Molasses from the sugar mill, of course, is the distillery's main raw material. The fertilizer factory, across the highway from the distillery, uses mill mud from the sugar-making process. To the north, just beyond the conveyor belts used to load raw sugar onto the ships, is a veritable mountain of pine chips ready for export to Japan, where they are used to make paper.

This is the main base for Blue Lagoon cruises to the Yasawa Islands, yet because Lautoka doesn't depend on tourism, you get a truer picture of ordinary life than you would in Nadi, and the city has a rambunctious nightlife. There's some shopping, but mainly this is just a pleasant place to wander around on foot. Beware of sword sellers and other scam artists who seem to have migrated to the Lautoka waterfront after being run out of Nadi.

SIGHTS

Begin at Lautoka's big, colorful **market,** next to the bus station, which is busiest on Saturday

© DAVID STANLEY

fruit and vegetables for sale outside Lautoka Market

(open Mon.–Fri. 0700–1730, Sat. 0530–1600). Handicrafts are sold at stalls along the Naviti Street side of the market. From the market, walk south on Yasawa Street to the photogenic **Jame Mosque**, a prominent symbol of Lautoka's large Indo-Fijian population. Five times a day, local Muslim males direct prayers toward a small niche known as a *mihrab*, where the prayers fuse and fly to the Kaaba in Mecca, and thence to Allah. You can visit the mosque outside of prayer times if you're conservatively dressed and willing to remove your shoes. During the crushing season (June–Nov.), narrow-gauge trains rattle past the mosque along a line parallel to Vitogo Parade, bringing cane to Lautoka's large sugar mill.

Follow the line east to the **Sikh Temple**, rebuilt after a smaller temple was burned by arson in 1989. To enter, you must wash your hands and cover your head (kerchiefs are provided at the door), and cigarettes and liquor are forbidden inside the compound. The teachings of the 10 Sikh gurus are contained in the Granth, a holy book prominently displayed in the temple. Sikhism began in the 16th century in the Punjab region of northwest India as a reformed branch of Hinduism much influenced by Islam: For example, Sikhs reject the caste system and idolatry. The Sikhs are easily recognized by their beards and turbans.

◖ Sri Krishna Kaliya Temple

Follow your map west along Drasa Avenue to the Sri Krishna Kaliya Temple on Tavewa Avenue, the most prominent Krishna temple in the South Pacific (open daily until 1800). The images on the right inside are Radha and Krishna, while the central figure is Krishna dancing on the snake Kaliya to show his mastery over the reptile. The story goes that Krishna chastised Kaliya and exiled him to the island of Ramanik Deep, which Indo-Fijians believe to be Fiji. (Curiously, the indigenous Fijian people have also long believed in a serpent-god, named Degei, who lived in a cave in the Nakauvadra Range.) The two figures on the left are incarnations of Krishna and Balarama. At the front of the temple is a representation of His Divine Grace A. C. Bhaktivedanta Swami Prabhupada, founder

© DAVID STANLEY

an altar at Lautoka's Sri Krishna Kaliya Temple

© DAVID STANLEY

Lautoka's botanical garden is a pleasant place to stroll.

of the International Society for Krishna Consciousness (ISKCON). Interestingly, Fiji has the highest percentage of Hare Krishnas in the population of any country in the world. The temple gift shop (tel. 666-4112, daily 0900–1600) sells stimulating books, compact discs, cassettes, and posters, and it's possible to rent videos. On Sunday, there's a lecture at 1100, *arti* or prayer *(puja)* at 1200, and a vegetarian feast at 1300, and visitors are welcome to attend.

Botanical Garden

Opposite the hospital, half a kilometer south of Sri Krishna Kaliya Temple on Thomson Crescent, is the entrance to Lautoka's botanical garden (weekdays 0700–1700, admission free). It's a pleasant shady spot with a varied array of plants. There are numerous birds in the gardens, and picnic tables are provided. **Punjas Children's Park** (daily 1000–1800, admission free), across the street from the gardens, is perfect if you're with children under 12, and it has a snack bar.

ENTERTAINMENT

Lautoka has a mega-theater called **Village 4 Cinemas** (25 Namoli Ave., tel. 666-3555, www.damodarvillage.com.fj). It costs F$5 to view a film on one of the four screens.

Lautoka's nightclubs cater almost exclusively to locals, and they're surprisingly down-market. The **Hunter's Inn** (tel. 666-0388, closed Sun., admission free), next to the Lautoka Hotel, is rough and dark. Also at the Lautoka Hotel is the **Ashiqi Nite Club** (Fri.–Sat. 2000–2400, F$3 cover charge). Ashiqi caters to the city's Indo-Fijian residents, whereas Hunter's Inn is patronized mostly by indigenous Fijians. Because access to Ashiqi is off the hotel's inner courtyard, it's more secure and thus a better bet for foreign visitors.

Similar to Hunter's Inn are **The Zone Night Club** (26 Naviti St., tel. 665-1199, Wed.–Sat. 2000–0100), upstairs in a building almost opposite the Chilli Tree Café, and **Leon Nite Club,** opposite the market.

The **South Seas Club** (tel. 666-0784, daily 0900–2200), on Nede Street, is a safe,

Village 4 Cinemas offers a choice of four films several times a day.

© DAVID STANLEY

predominately male drinking place where you'll be welcome. The club's restaurant (weekdays 0930–1900, weekends 1000–2000) in the rear courtyard has tasty Indian dishes at around F$6.

The more exclusive **Northern Club** (tel. 666-2469 or 666-0184, Mon.–Sat. 1000–2300, Sun. 1200–2200) on Tavewa Avenue has an atmospheric colonial-style bar. The club restaurant (daily 1000–1500 and 1700–2130) serves excellent meals in the F$7–13 range. Tourists can sign in at the door for a single visit or pay F$11 for a one-week pass, which entitles you to use the large swimming pool and to play tennis.

Sunday *Puja*

The big event of the week is the Sunday *puja* (prayer) at the Sri Krishna Kaliya Temple (5 Tavewa Ave., tel. 666-4112). The noon service is followed by a vegetarian feast at 1300, and visitors may join in the singing and dancing, if they wish. Take off your shoes and sit on the white marble floor, men on one side, women on the other. Bells ring, drums are beaten, conch shells blown, and stories from the Vedas, Srimad

© DAVID STANLEY

The Sunday afternoon festival and feast at Lautoka's Hare Krishna temple, the largest in the South Pacific, is worth attending.

Bhagavatam, and Ramayana are acted out as everyone chants, *Hare Krsna, Hare Krsna, Krsna Krsna, Hare Hare, Hare Rama, Hare Rama, Rama, Rama, Hare, Hare.* It's a real celebration of joy and a most moving experience. At one point, children will circulate with small trays covered with burning candles, on which it is customary to place a donation; you may also drop a small bill in the yellow box in the center of the temple. You'll be readily invited to join the vegetarian feast later, and no more money will be asked of you.

SPORTS AND RECREATION

There aren't any dive shops in Lautoka, although **Westside Watersports** (tel. 666-1462, www.fiji-dive.com) has an office on Wharf Road that handles bookings for their Yasawa operations.

The **Lautoka Golf Club** (no phone), a nine-hole, par-69 course, charges F$10 greens fees. The clubhouse and bar are open only on Saturdays. If you come early on Saturday with your own clubs, you'll be very welcome to join local members in the competition. Other days you can play for free if you bring your own clubs, although it might not be safe to go alone (muggings are not unknown here). It's a scenic location on a ridge above the city. Vijay Singh was a member of this club before turning professional. A taxi from the market should cost about F$3–4.

Lautoka is a sports city, and all day Saturday you can catch exciting rugby (Apr.–Sept.) or soccer (Feb.–Oct.) games at the stadium in Churchill Park. Ask about league games.

ACCOMMODATIONS
Under US$25
Renee's Backpackers Golden Arch Hotel (17 Naviti St., tel. 666-0033, homenaway@connect.com.fj) opened in 2006. The 11 rooms are F$35/45 single/double, or F$60 for a family room accommodating five. Most (but not all) of the rooms are air-conditioned but none have private bath. The hotel's restaurant serves Chinese dishes.

To be close to the action, stay at the 38-room **Lautoka Hotel** (2 Naviti St., tel. 666-0388, www.lautokahotelfiji.com), which has a nice swimming pool. Room prices vary from F$35 single or double for a spacious fan-cooled room with shared bath to F$60 single or double with air-conditioning, TV, and private bath, or F$80 with fridge in the new wing. It's F$18 per person in the 10-bed dorm. The rooms with private bath are good, but the shared-bath rooms above the reception in the old building are subjected to a nocturnal rock beat from nearby discos most nights.

The 14 rooms with bath and fan at the disreputable **Diamond Hotel** (Nacula St., tel. 666-6721) are F$45 single or double until 1000 or F$20 an hour. This place is not recommended for female travelers.

US$25-50

A good choice is the clean, quiet, three-story ◖ **Sea Breeze Hotel** (5 Bekana Ln., tel. 666-0717, www.seabreezefiji.com), on the waterfront near the bus station. They have four rooms with private bath and fan at F$52/58 single/double, 13 air-conditioned rooms at F$62/68, and five air-conditioned sea-view rooms at F$68/74. A good breakfast is F$9 extra. The pleasant lounge has a color TV, and a swimming pool overlooks the lagoon. It's Lautoka's best value and is often full.

The upscale **Northern Club** (Tavewa Ave., tel. 666-2469 or 666-0184) rents six self-catering studios in a two-story block at F$90 single or double. The club has a large bar, swimming pool, and tennis courts just up the hill.

The 40-room **Cathay Hotel** (Tavewa Ave., tel. 666-0566, www.fiji4less.com) almost opposite the Northern Club features a swimming pool, TV room, and bar. The charge is F$55 single or double with fan and private bath, F$67 with air-conditioning. The renovated rooms are F$74. Ask the receptionist if there will be a towel in the room. Some of the rooms in less desirable locations have been divided into backpacker dormitories, with 3–6 beds or bunks for F$22/24 per person with fan/air-conditioning. Each dorm has its own toilet and shower. You can't check in until after 1000.

There's a swimming pool, and the Cathay offers free luggage storage for guests.

Owned by the Fiji Ex-Servicemen League, the **R.S.L. Hotel** (Tavewa Ave., tel. 665-1679, rslhotel@connect.com.fj) is opposite the Sri Krishna Kaliya Temple. There are six clean rooms with bath at F$70 single or double per night or F$45 for three hours, and there's a large public bar on the premises.

US$50-100

Lautoka's top city hotel is the **Tanoa Waterfront Hotel** (Marine Dr., tel. 666-4777, www.tanoawaterfront-fiji.com), a two-story building erected in 1987. The 47 air-conditioned rooms are F$135 single or double (children under 12 are free if no extra bed is required). The 26 "executive" rooms are F$168 single or double, and are equipped with Internet connections at F$8/40 per hour/day. Phone calls from the rooms and the minibar items are expensive. There's an attractive swimming pool. The Waterfront's Fins Restaurant serves dinner mains at F$15–22.

Saweni Beach Apartment Hotel (tel. 666-1777, www.fiji4less.com), a kilometer off the main highway south of Lautoka, caters to seniors, families, and couples looking for quiet, inexpensive beach accommodations. It offers two rows of flats, each with six self-catering apartments at F$95/120 double fan-cooled/air-conditioned. One apartment has two four-bed dorm rooms at F$21 per person. A renovated four-bedroom "beach house" (tel. 330-8644, www.fiji-beach-house.com) with full kitchen, air-conditioned bedrooms, living room, and TV is F$400 for up to four, then F$50 per additional person to a maximum of eight (minimum stay three nights). Guests unwind by the pool. Bird-watchers can observe waders on the flats behind the hotel. The so-so beach comes alive on weekends, when local picnickers arrive from Lautoka. A concrete platform here is all that remains of an American flying boat base from 1942. During the season, it's typical to have more than a dozen yachts anchored offshore, and the crews often come ashore here for curry dinners in the restaurant in the main

building. A bus from bay No. 14 at Lautoka Bus Station runs right to the hotel six times a day. Otherwise, any of the local Nadi buses will drop you off a 10-minute walk away (a taxi from Lautoka is F$8 for the 18 km).

US$150-250

In 2008, the **Fiji Orchid** (Saweni Beach Road, tel. 664-0099, www.fijiorchid.com) boutique resort opened near Saweni Beach in an orchid garden formerly owned by actor Richard Burr. The six luxurious *bure* are F$555 plus 17.5 percent tax, while two rooms with private bath in the main house are F$275 plus tax. A restaurant, bar, and swimming pool are on the premises. Airport transfers are included.

FOOD

Chandra's Town End Restaurant (15 Tukani St., tel. 666-5877, Mon.–Sat. 0630–1800, Sun. 0800–1700), on the ocean side of the bus station, serves cheap meals like fish and chips (F$3) or meat and rice (F$4).

Jolly Good Fast Foods (60 Naviti St., tel. 666-9980, daily 0800–2200, mains F$6–12), at Vakabale Street opposite the market, is a great place to sit and read a newspaper over a coffee. Their best dishes are listed on the "made to order" menu on the wall beside the cashier. Beef and pork are not offered, so have fish, chicken, mutton, or prawns instead—the portions are large. Eating outside in their covered garden is fun, and the only drawback is the lack of beer.

Hometown Restaurant (27 Naviti St., Mon.–Sat. 0730–1800) is an excellent breakfast or lunch place with inexpensive Chinese specialties.

Morris Hedstrom (tel. 666-2999, Mon.–Sat. 0800–1800, Sun. 0800–1300), at Vidilio and Tukani Streets, is Lautoka's largest supermarket. At the back of the store is a food court that offers the usual fish or chicken and chips, hot pies, ice cream, and breakfast specials. It's clean and only a bit more expensive than the market places.

More upscale is the air-conditioned **Chilli Tree Café** (tel. 665-1824, Mon.–Sat. 0730–1600), at the corner of Nede and Tukani

South Indian specialties can be tasted at unpretentious Minaxi Hot Snax.

Streets. They serve a good, filling breakfast for F$11, plus cakes and specially brewed coffee. You can "build your own" salad and sandwich from the menu.

The **Nanyang Restaurant** (4 Nede St., tel. 665-2668), across the street from the Chilli Tree, dishes out Lautoka's top Chinese meals (F$12–30) in gaudy surroundings.

The **Pizza Inn** (2 Naviti St., tel. 666-4592) in the Lautoka Hotel serves pizzas for F$7–35. Also known as the Seaview Restaurant, this pleasing spot has a good bar.

Unpretentious **Minaxi Hot Snax** (56 Naviti St., tel. 666-1306, Mon.–Fri. 0830–1730, Sat. 0830–1600), just down from Jolly Good, may be the number-one place in Fiji to sample South Indian dishes. The *masala dosai,* a rice pancake with coconut chutney, makes a nice light lunch, and there are also *samosas, iddili,* and puri. The deep-fried puri are great for breakfast, and you can also get ice cream and sweets. Most dishes are around F$5 and on Fridays there's *palau.* This spot is recommended.

Gangas Vegetarian Restaurant (42 Vidilio St., tel. 666-0591), in spacious premises diagonally opposite Morris Hedstrom, has small/large Indian *thalis* (plate meals) at F$4.80/8.50. It's also good for fresh juice (F$4.60–6), ice cream, and sweets.

INFORMATION AND SERVICES
Information

The **Western Regional Library** (tel. 666-0091) on Tavewa Avenue is open Monday–Friday 1000–1700, Saturday 0900–1200.

Beachcomber Island Resort (tel. 666-1500) has a sales office upstairs on Wharf Road near Westside Watersports.

Services

ATMs are found at the Westpac Bank branch on Vitogo Parade, a little west of the post office beyond the station, and at the ANZ Bank on Vitogo Parade diagonally opposite the post office. Other ANZ Bank ATMs are found next to Rajendra Prasad Foodtown on Yasawa Street opposite the bus station and at Village 4 Cinemas. Westpac and Colonial National Bank ATMs accessible 24 hours a day are at the Sugar City Mall next to the bus station.

Western Union Currency Exchange (161 Vitogo Parade, tel. 665-1941, Mon.–Fri. 0800–1800, Sat. 0800–1600), just up from the ANZ Bank, changes travelers checks without commission. **Lotus Foreign Exchange** (tel. 666-7855) in the Sugar City Mall is similar.

An unnamed but clearly marked Internet café (Mon.–Sat. 0730–1715) is above PNT Express Courier at Narara Parade and Tavewa Avenue opposite the ANZ Bank. They charge F$1 an hour.

Jeri-Cho Internet Café (tel. 666-4477, daily 0800–2200) at Village 4 Cinemas on Namoli Avenue charges F$1 an hour. It's often full of youths playing online games.

The **Immigration Department** (tel. 666-1706) is on the ground floor of Rogorogoivuda House on Tavewa Avenue almost opposite the Sri Krishna Kaliya Temple. Customs is in an adjacent building.

Free public toilets are next to Bay No. 1A, on the back side of the bus station facing the market, in Shirley Park behind the police post opposite the Lautoka Hotel, and at the botanical gardens.

Health

The emergency room at the **Lautoka Hospital** (tel. 666-0399), off Thomson Crescent south of the center, is open 24 hours a day.

If your problem is not life-threatening, you're better off attending the **Avenue Clinic** (Dr. Mukesh C. Bhagat, 47 Drasa Ave., tel. 665-2955 or 995-2369, weekdays 0830–1800, Sat. 0830–1300). You'll receive good service at this convenient suburban office.

Dr. Suresh Chandra's dental office (tel. 666-0999, Mon.–Fri. 0800–1700, Sat. 0800–1300) is opposite Village 4 Cinemas on Namoli Avenue.

GETTING THERE AND AROUND

Pacific Sun doesn't have an office in Lautoka but their tickets are sold by **Trans World Travel** (159 Vitogo Parade, tel. 666-5466, Mon.–Fri. 0830–1900, Sat. 0900–1200).

Patterson Brothers (15 Tukani St., tel. 666-1173), upstairs and opposite the bus station, should have information on their bus/ferry/bus services (although at last report the through service between Lautoka, Ellington Wharf, Nabouwalu, and Labasa wasn't operating).

Bligh Water Shipping (Waterfront Road, tel. 666-8229, www.blighwatershipping.com .fj), beside Fiji Meats opposite the Fisheries Wharf, operates the MV *Westerland* between Lautoka and Savusavu three times a week. The ship leaves Lautoka Monday, Wednesday, and Friday at 1600 (F$55/95 deck/sleeper, 12 hours).

You can sometimes arrange to be dropped at a Yasawa Islands resort by a village boat from the Fisheries Wharf in Lautoka for around F$40 one-way, but no safety gear will be aboard.

A bus connecting in Nadi with the **Awesome Adventures** (tel. 675-0499) catamaran *Yasawa Flyer II* leaves Lautoka Post Office daily at 0700.

Buses, carriers, taxis—almost everything leaves from the bus stand beside the market. **Pacific Transport** (tel. 666-0499) has express buses to Suva daily at 0630, 0700, 1210, 1550, and 1730 (221 km, five hours, F$17.40) via Sigatoka (Queens Road). **Sunbeam Transport** (tel. 666-2822, www.sunbeamfiji.com) has buses to Suva via Sigatoka at 0830, 0930, 1010, 1110, 1240, 1415, and 1515 (four hours, F$18). Sunbeam Transport also has expresses to Suva via Tavua (Kings Road) at 0615, 0630, 0815, 1215, and 1630 (265 km, six hours, F$20.70), plus two local buses on the same route (nine hours). The northern route is more scenic than the southern, although some of the new Sunbeam buses play insipid videos that detract from the ride. Local buses to Nadi (33 km, F$3) and Ba (38 km, F$3) depart every half hour or so.

Suva minibuses (F$19) belonging to the Viti Minibuses Co-operative Limited use the Mini Bus Stand a block east on Tukani Street.

Car rentals are available in Lautoka from **Central** (75 Vitogo Parade, tel. 666-4511) and **Budget** (4 Walu St., tel. 666-6166).

Into the Interior

Although the picturesque village of Navala receives white-water rafters and sightseers, and regular tours from Nadi visit the Nausori Highlands, the rest of central Viti Levu is seldom visited. The dirt roads are too rough for ordinary rental vehicles, and facilities for tourists don't exist. Yet Fiji's highest mountains and deepest valleys are there, and some spectacular hiking possibilities await self-sufficient backpackers. Nadarivatu is the still undiscovered jewel of central Viti Levu.

▣ KOROYANITU NATIONAL HERITAGE PARK

With help from New Zealand, an ecotourism reserve was created in 1992 between Abaca (am-BA-tha) and Navilawa villages in the Mount Evans Range, 15 kilometers east of Lautoka. Koroyanitu National Heritage Park takes its name from the range's highest peak, 1,195-meter Koroyanitu, and is intended to preserve Fiji's only unlogged tropical montane forest and cloud forest by creating a small tourism business for the local villagers. The village carrier that transports visitors also carries the local kids to and from school, the women earn money by staffing the office or arranging room and board, and the men get jobs as drivers, guides, and wardens. By visiting Koroyanitu, you not only get to see some of Fiji's top sights but support this worthy undertaking.

Four waterfalls are close to the village, and Batilamu, with sweeping views of the western side of Viti Levu and the Yasawas, is nearby. More ambitious hikes to higher peaks beckon. The landscape of wide green valleys set against steep slopes is superb. Doves and pigeons abound in the forests, and you'll also find honeyeaters, Polynesian starlings, Fijian warblers, yellow-breasted musk parrots, golden whistlers, fantailed cuckoos, and wood swallows. It's an outstanding opportunity to see this spectacular area.

The park entry fee is F$8 per person. To explore the various archaeological sites of this area and to learn more about the environment and culture, you should hire a guide (F$10–20 pp, depending on how far you want to go).

Sights

You can swim in the pools at **Vereni Falls,** a five-minute walk from the park lodge. Picnic shelters are provided. From the viewpoint above the falls, it's 15 minutes up the Navuratu Track to **Kokobula Scenic Outlook,** with its 360-degree view of the park and coast. The trail continues across the open grassland to **Savuione Falls,** passing an old village site en route (guide required). From Savuione, there's a trail through the secondary forest directly back to the park lodge (watch for pigeons and doves). You can do all of this in just over two hours if you keep going and don't lose your way.

The finest hike here is to **Mount Batilamu** along a trail that begins at the visitor center in Abaca village. You'll pass large kauri trees *(makadre)* and get a terrific view from on top. This part of the range is also known as the "Sleeping Giant," because that's how it appears from Nadi. Allow half a day round-trip from Abaca to Batilamu. Ask about staying overnight in the Mount Batilumu Hut.

The Batilamu Track continues across the range to **Navilawa** village, from which a six-kilometer road runs south to Korobebe village, where there's regular bus service to/from Nadi. Trekkers can spend the night in Fiji's highest *bure* on Batilamu, although fewer than 100 people a year actually do this walk. An even more ambitious trek is northeast to **Nalotawa** via the site of Navuga, where the Abaca people lived until their village was destroyed by a landslide in the 1930s.

Accommodations

Nase Lodge (no phone), 400 meters from Abaca village, has two six-bunk rooms at F$35 per person. Camping may be possible. Children under 15 are half price, and all prices include the park entry fee. Good cooking facilities are provided, but take food, as there's no shop. Meals can be ordered and a traditional feast with village entertainment can be arranged for groups of four or more.

Otherwise, you can stay with a family in Abaca or Navilawa village at F$44 per person, including meals. On Sunday, avoid entering the village during the church service 1000–1200. Village etiquette should be observed at all times.

Getting There

The closest public bus stop to the park is Abaca Junction on the Tavakuba bus route, but it's 10 kilometers from Abaca village.

At Nadi Airport, **Great Sights Fiji/Tourist Transport Fiji** (tel. 672-3311, www.tourist transportfiji.com), next to the washrooms in the international arrivals area, operates a four-hour Discover Abaca day tour (F$295 for a four-person vehicle) from Nadi upon request. The same company has a half-day four-wheel-drive trip to Navilawa (F$120 pp) every weekday morning.

Round the Island Tours (tel. 664-5431, www.roundtheislandtours.com) in Lautoka also offers Abaca day tours at F$325 for one or two persons, including transportation from Nadi, meals, entry fees, guide, and a gift for the village. This tour can be extended to include a night in Abaca or at the hut on Mount Batilamu. During the rainy season, floods can close the road to Abaca and the trekking possibilities may be limited.

◖ NAUSORI HIGHLANDS

A rough unpaved road runs 25 kilometers southeast from Ba to Navala, a large traditional village on the sloping right bank of the Ba River. It then climbs another 20 kilometers south to Bukuya village in the Nausori Highlands, from whence other gravel roads continue south into the Sigatoka Valley or 40 kilometers due west to Nadi. The Nadi road passes Vaturu Dam, which supplies Nadi with fresh water. Gold strikes near Vaturu may herald a mining future for this area, if the water catch-

ment can be protected. The forests here were logged out in the 1970s, but the open scenery of the grassy highlands still makes a visit well worthwhile.

Bukuya, in the center of western Viti Levu's highland plateau, is far less traditional than Navala, and some of the only thatched *bure* in the village are those used by visitors on hiking/village-stay tours organized by backpacker travel agencies in Nadi. The Tui Magodro, or high chief of the region, resides in Bukuya. During the Colo War of 1876, Bukuya was a center of resistance to colonial rule.

The easiest way to experience the highlands is on a day trip from Nadi. **Rosie Holidays** (tel. 672-2755) operates full-day hiking tours to the Nausori Highlands daily, except Sunday, at F$74 including lunch, tax, and a souvenir *sulu*. **Great Sights/Tourist Transport Fiji** (tel. 672-3311), in the arrivals concourse at Nadi Airport, offers a half-day Nausori Highland Tour by four-wheel-drive vehicle at F$245 for four passengers.

East of Bukuya, a rugged logging track runs along a very high ridge, then drops down to **Nubutautau** on the Sigatoka River. Reverend Thomas Baker, the last missionary to be clubbed and devoured in Fiji (in 1867), met his fate at Nubutautau. Jack London wrote a story, "The Whale Tooth," about the death of the missionary, and the ax that brought about Reverend Baker's demise is still kept in the village (other Baker artifacts are in the Fiji Museum). In 2003, Baker's descendents traveled to Nubutautau from Australia for a *matanigasau* ceremony during which the villagers apologized for this old crime, and a curse that had hung over the village for 136 years was lifted.

NAVALA

Navala, 25 kilometers southeast of Ba, is the last fully thatched village on Viti Levu, and the villagers have made a conscious decision to keep it that way. Its *bure* stand picturesquely above the Ba River against the surrounding hills. When water levels are right, white-water rafters shoot the rapids through the scenic Ba River Gorge near here, and guided hiking or horseback riding can also be arranged. Sightseers are welcome at F$15 per person admission to the village (this fee also applies if you only take photos from across the bridge). Tourists are sometimes asked to pay F$25 per person, plus a F$25 photography fee and another F$20 for a self-appointed guide. A "gift" of kava roots may also be requested! If you get that treatment, insist on being taken to the *turaga-ni-koro* (village herald) and don't be deterred if you're told he is asleep!

Access is fairly easy on the two Sher Ali Khan Transport Ltd. buses that leave Ba at 1230 and 1715 daily except Sunday (F$3). They depart Navala to return to Ba only at 0600 and 0800, so you must stay for the night. **Bulou's Lodge** (tel. 651-0194), one kilometer past Navala, provides accommodations at F$65 per person in a 10-bed dorm, or F$75 per person in the *bure,* meals included. The village entry fee is extra. To hire a taxi from Ba to Navala will cost F$45 one-way or F$60 round-trip, with an hour of waiting time (after bargaining). By rental vehicle, you'll probably need a four-wheel drive.

During the rainy season, the Navala road can be flooded and impassable.

ATS Pacific (tel. 672-2811) and **Great Sights Fiji** (tel. 672-3311), in the arrivals concourse at Nadi Airport, operate full-day tours to Navala at F$207 per person, including lunch.

NADARIVATU AND BEYOND

An important forestry station is at Nadarivatu, a small settlement above Tavua. Its 900-meter altitude means a cool climate and fantastic panorama of the northern coast from the ridge. Beside the road, right in front of the Forestry Training Center is the **Stone Bowl,** official source of the Sigatoka River, and a five-minute walk from the Center is the **Governor-General's Swimming Pool,** where a small creek has been dammed. Go up the creek a short distance to the main pool, though it's dry much of the year and the area has not been maintained. The trail to the fire tower atop **Mount Lomalagi** (Mount Heaven) begins nearby, a one-hour hike each

© MARK HEARD / WWW.FLICKR.COM/HEARDSY

thatching a roof in Navala

way. The tower itself has collapsed and is no longer climbable, but the forest is lovely, and you may see and hear many native birds. Pine forests cover the land.

In its heyday, Nadarivatu was a summer retreat for expatriates from the nearby Emperor Gold Mine at Vatukoula, and until recently, the mine had a 14-bed guesthouse at Nadarivatu. Visitors with tents are allowed to camp at the Forestry Training Center. Ask permission at the Ministry of Forests office as soon as you arrive. Some canned foods are available at a small canteen, but you should bring food from Tavua. Cabin crackers are handy.

Only carriers (trucks) operate between Tavua and Nadarivatu, leaving Tavua in the early afternoon and Nadarivatu in the morning—a spectacular 1.5-hour ride (F$5). They leave from behind Tavua Market at about 1600. It's also possible to hitch. The trucks often originate/terminate in Nadrau village, where Ratu Lemeki Natadria accepts guests at F$80 per person, including meals (you can book this stay through www.fijibure.com/nadrau). A *sevusevu* of kava roots is appropriate.

Mount Victoria

The two great rivers of Fiji, the Rewa and the Sigatoka, originate on the slopes of Mount Victoria (Tomaniivi), the highest mountain in the country (1,323 m). The trail up the mountain begins near the bridge at Navai, 10 kilometers southeast of Nadarivatu. Turn right up the hillside a few hundred meters down the jeep track, then climb up through native bush on the main path all the way to the top. Beware of misleading signboards. There are three small streams to cross; no water after the third. On your way back down, stop for a swim in the largest stream. There's a flat area on top where you could camp—if you're willing to take your chances with Buli, the devil king of the mountain. Local guides (F$20) are available and advisable, but permission to climb the mountain is not required, as this is a nature reserve under the Forestry Department. Allow about six hours for the round-trip. Bright red epiphytic orchids (*Dendrobium mohlianum*) are some-times in full bloom, and if you're very lucky, you might spot the rare red-throated lorikeet or pink-billed parrot finch. Mount Victoria is on the divide between the wet and dry sides of Viti Levu, and from the summit you should be able to distinguish the contrasting vegetation of these zones.

Monasavu Hydroelectric Project

The largest development project ever undertaken in Fiji, this massive F$230 million scheme at Monasavu, on the Nadrau Plateau near the center of Viti Levu, took 1,500 men six years to complete. An earthen dam, 82 meters high, was built across the Nanuku River to supply water to the four 20-megawatt generating turbines at the Wailoa Power Station on the Wailoa River, 625 meters below. The dam forms a lake 17 kilometers long, and the water drops through a 5.4-kilometer tunnel at a 45-degree angle, one of the steepest engineered dips in the world. Overhead transmission lines carry power from Wailoa to Suva and Lautoka. At present, Monasavu is filling 30 percent of Fiji's energy needs, representing millions of dollars in annual savings on imported diesel oil.

The Cross-Island Highway that passes the site was built to serve the dam project. Bus service ended when the project was completed and the construction camps closed in 1985. At the present time, only carriers go from Tavua to Nadrau and buses from Suva to Naivucini. In 1998, there were tense scenes near the dam as landowners set up roadblocks to press claims for land flooded in the early 1980s. In July 2000, during the hostage crisis at Fiji's parliament, landowners occupied the dam and cut off power to much of Viti Levu for almost a month. In October 2005, the courts ordered the Fiji Electricity Authority to pay the landowners compensation of F$52.8 million in installments over the next 99 years.

There's no visitors center or tours at Monasavu, but you can get a view of the lake and dam in the distance from the highway. For more information, contact the Fiji Electricity Authority (tel. 331-3333, www.fea.com.fj) in Suva.

THE LOMAIVITI GROUP

The Lomaiviti (or central Fiji) Group lies in the Koro Sea near the heart of the archipelago, east of Viti Levu and south of Vanua Levu. Of its nine main volcanic islands, Gau, Koro, and Ovalau are among the largest in Fiji. Lomaiviti's climate is moderate, neither as wet and humid as Suva, nor as dry and hot as Nadi. The population is mostly Fijian and engaged in subsistence agriculture and copra making.

The old capital island, Ovalau, is by far the best-known and most visited island of the group, and several small islands south of Ovalau on the way to Suva bear backpacker resorts. Gau, Naigani, and Koro have a couple of upscale resorts, but in general those islands are seldom visited and have few facilities for visitors. Car ferries ply the Koro Sea to Ovalau, while onward ferries run to Vanua Levu a couple of times a week. Ferries between Suva and Savusavu call at Koro.

Lomaiviti has always played a central role in Fijian history. The power base of the last cannibal king, Ratu Seru Cakobau, was on tiny Bau Island off Viti Levu just south of Ovalau. When European traders arrived in the mid-19th century, they established a settlement at Levuka, which became the seat of the first national administration in 1871, then the capital of the British colony in 1874. Though the capital moved to Suva in 1882, Levuka remained an active trading town, and many wooden buildings remain from the time. Today it's the site of Fiji's only tuna cannery.

Both Ovalau and Koro have dive shops, and the Ovalau operation can take you diving off the coast of Wakaya. To dive off Gau or any of

© DAVID STANLEY

HIGHLIGHTS

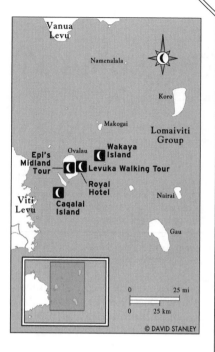

(Levuka Walking Tour: The wooden false-front buildings along Beach Street look like a Wild West movie set, except that it's for real. The old Morris Hedstrom general store building has been converted into one of Fiji's best museums and the local public library (page 205).

(Royal Hotel: Fiji's oldest operating hotel, the Royal hasn't changed much in the past century. The mix of guests and daily routine here are like something out of a Somerset Maugham novel (page 209).

(Epi's Midland Tour: Epi's guided hike across the spine of Ovalau from Levuka to Lovoni is the best guided day hike in Fiji (page 212).

(Caqalai Island: Leleuvia's neighbor, Caqalai, has a great beach, good snorkeling, and just one small backpacker resort (page 217).

(Wakaya Island: Wakaya is the antithesis of Caqalai and Leleuvia: Its exclusive resort is visited only by the rich and famous. Ovalau Watersports can take you scuba diving off Wakaya to see the hammerheads and rays (page 222).

LOOK FOR **(** TO FIND RECOMMENDED SIGHTS, ACTIVITIES, DINING, AND LODGING.

---

the other islands, you'll need to book a cruise on a liveaboard dive boat, such as the *Nai'a*. There's good hiking on all these islands, and the small islands south of Ovalau (Caqalai, Leleuvia, and Yanuca Lailai) have good snorkeling. It's nice to just hang out in Levuka and enjoy the laid-back old South Seas atmosphere.

PLANNING YOUR TIME

Though Levuka can be seen as a day trip from Suva if you fly over in the morning and back in the afternoon, it's much better to spend a few days there. Levuka is a good escape from

Suva on the weekend when the capital is dead. The daily bus-ferry-bus connections between Suva and Levuka make visiting relatively easy. Add a couple of days to your trip if you'd like to stay at any of the small outer-island resorts around Ovalau.

There are no direct connections between Levuka and Koro. You'll need to go back to Suva to catch the ferry. Boats to Koro are only twice a week, so you'll have to stay three or four days. Koro has a few very nice beaches, but it's mostly just a chance to visit an unspoiled island still off the tourist track.

Ovalau Island

Ovalau, a large volcanic island just east of Viti Levu, is the main island of the Lomaiviti Group. Almost encircled by high peaks, the Lovoni Valley in the center of Ovalau is actually the island's volcanic crater and about the only flat land. The crater's rim is pierced by the Bureta River, which escapes through a gap to the southeast. The highest peak is 626-meter Nadelaiovalau ("the top of Ovalau"), behind Levuka. Luckily, Ovalau lacks the magnificent beaches found elsewhere in Fiji, which has kept the package-tour crowd away, and upscale scuba divers have better places to go, so it's still one of the most peaceful, pleasant, picturesque, and historic areas to visit in the South Pacific.

LEVUKA

The town of Levuka on Ovalau's east side was Fiji's capital until the shift to Suva in 1882. Founded as a whaling settlement in 1830, Levuka became the main center for European traders in Fiji, and a British consul was appointed in 1857. The cotton boom of the 1860s brought new settlers, and Levuka quickly grew into a boisterous town, with more than 50 hotels and taverns along Beach Street. Escaped convicts and debtors fleeing creditors in Australia swelled the throng, until it was said that a ship could find the reef passage into Levuka by following the empty gin bottles floating out on the tide. The honest traders felt the need for a stable government, so in 1871 Levuka became the capital of Cakobau's Kingdom of Fiji. The disorders continued, with extremist elements forming a "Ku Klux Klan," defiant of any form of Fijian authority.

On October 10, 1874, a semblance of decorum came as Fiji was annexed by Great Britain, and a municipal council was formed in 1877. British rule soon put a damper on the wild side of the blackbirding. Ovalau's central location seemed ideal for trade, and sailing boats

THE LOMAIVITI GROUP

© DAVID STANLEY

The wooden storefronts lining Levuka's waterfront haven't changed much in a century.

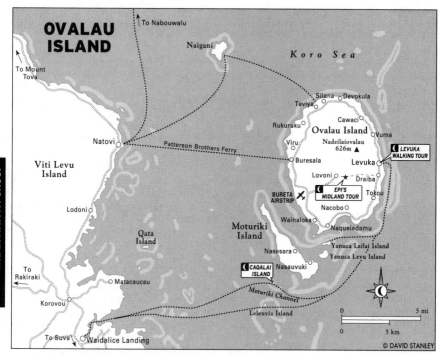

from Lau or Vanua Levu could easily enter the port on the southeast trade winds. Yet the lush green hills that rise behind the town were to be its downfall, as colonial planners saw that there was no room for the expansion of their capital, and in August 1882, Governor Sir Arthur Gordon moved his staff to Suva. Hurricanes in 1888 and 1895 destroyed much of early Levuka, with the north end of town around the present Anglican church almost flattened, and many of Levuka's devastated buildings were not replaced.

Levuka remained the collection center for the Fiji copra trade right up until 1957, and the town seemed doomed when that industry, too, moved to a new mill in Suva. But with the establishment of a fishing industry in 1964, Levuka revived, and today it is a minor educational center, the headquarters of Lomaiviti Province, and a low-key tourist center. Thanks to the tuna cannery, there's a public electricity supply.

It's rather shocking that Levuka still hasn't been approved by UNESCO as a World Heritage Site, because Levuka is to Fiji what Lahaina is to Hawaii: a slice of living history. Each year, another century-old building is lost due to the lack of an internationally sanctioned conservation program. In 2003, the historic Mavida Guesthouse burned to the ground, followed in February 2004 by a supermarket, bank, and airline office on Beach Street. In October 2005, the Levuka Public School was badly damaged by fire. The tuna cannery experienced a major fire in 2008. It doesn't take much imagination to see how the rest of Levuka's old wooden buildings are similarly threatened. To meet this threat, a new Levuka Fire Station was opened in March 2006, just beyond the bridge on the north side of town.

Yet the false-fronted buildings and covered sidewalks that survive along Beach Street still give this somnolent town of 4,400 mostly

Fijian or part-Fijian inhabitants a 19th-century Wild West feel. From the waterfront, let your eyes follow the horizon from left to right to view the islands of Makogai, Koro, Wakaya, Nairai, Batiki, and Gau respectively. Levuka is a perfect base for excursions into the mountains, along the winding coast, or out to the barrier reef a kilometer offshore.

It's customary to say "Good morning," *"Bula,"* or simply "Hello" to people you meet while strolling the backstreets of Levuka, and some locals have been rather put off by tourists who fail to do so. This is one of the little adverse effects of tourism, and a very unnecessary one at that.

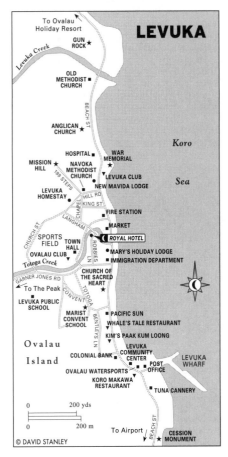

SIGHTS
◖ Levuka Walking Tour

Near Levuka Wharf is the old Morris Hedstrom general store, erected by Percy Morris and Maynard Hedstrom in 1880s, great-granddaddy of today's Pacific-wide Morris Hedstrom chain. The store closed when the lease expired in 1979, and the building was turned over to the National Trust for Fiji. In 1981, the facility reopened as the **Levuka Community Center** (tel. 344-0356, www.nationaltrust .org.fj, weekdays 0800–1300/1400–1630, Sat. 0800–1300) with a museum and library, where cannibal forks vie with war clubs and clay pots for your attention. The many old photos of the town in the museum are fascinating, and a few relics of the mystery ship *Joyita* are on display. The Community Center receives no outside funding, and your F$2 admission fee helps keep this place going. Right next door, Ovalau Watersports can arrange a number of tours, including a historical walking tour and village visits.

Stroll north on **Beach Street** along Levuka's sleepy waterfront past a long row of wooden storefronts that haven't changed much in a century. The sea wall opposite was originally constructed by the Royal Engineers in 1874. Just beyond the wall is the **Church of the Sacred Heart,** erected by French Marist priests who arrived in 1858. The church's square clock tower was added in 1898 to commemorate the first priest, Father Breheret. The green neon light on the stone tower lines up with another green light farther up the hill to guide mariners into port. The tower's French clock strikes the hour twice, with a minute interval in between. Go through the gate behind the church to the formidable **Marist Convent School** (1882), originally a girls' school operated by the sisters and still a primary school.

Totogo Lane leads north from the convent to a small bridge over Totogo Creek and the **Ovalau Club** (1904), adjoining the old **Town Hall** (1898), also known as Queen Victoria Memorial Hall. Next to the town hall is the gutted shell of the **Masonic Lodge building,** erected in 1913. The Little Polynesia chapter of

THE TUNNELS OF LEVUKA

Early on Monday, July 10, 2000, toward the end of the hostage crisis in Suva, a mob from the mountain village of Lovoni sacked and burned Levuka's historic Masonic Lodge. They had first attempted to storm Queen's Wharf, but when the soldiers on duty there fired warning shots, the mob turned its attention to the lodge. Senior members of the Methodist Church in Levuka had been telling their parishioners for years that the lodge was a center of immorality and devil worship. Rumors also abounded of secret tunnels beneath the building that led to the Royal Hotel or to Nasova House near the Cession Monument south of town. A few true believers were even convinced that a tunnel existed through the core of the earth to Scotland, the headquarters of the Masonic movement!

Frustrated at the wharf and unable to take over the nearby police station, the Lovoni mob broke the lodge's windows and poured in gasoline; the lodge was soon set alight. A hysterical throng of 300 cheered and shouted, "Out with the devil!" as the building burned, and it's alleged that the *talatala* (head priest) of the local Methodist Church observed the entire event in ecstasy from Mission Hill. Some looting took place, and among the objects taken by the mob were ceremonial swords and a human skull, a Masonic symbol of equality and mortality. What was never found was any trace of a tunnel, nor any of the ghostly British masons thought to use the passageway to attend secret rites.

All of this happened in support of a demand for amnesty by the George Speight terrorists in Fiji's parliament, and the mob was disciplined by an agitator, who made sure that none of Levuka's shops or other historic monuments were looted (only a few windows had been broken). The same group also invaded Levuka's tuna cannery and occupied it for several days. Later, when the army and police regained control of the town, some 120 people were identified as participants in the sacking of the lodge, most of them eventually discharged by the courts. In recent years, membership in the Masonic order has declined steadily around Fiji, and the Levuka lodge often has had difficulty achieving the required quorum of eight persons at their monthly meetings. The lodge will not be rebuilt, but the building's shell has been left standing as a monument to the folly of mankind. The last sacking of Levuka by the Lovoni folk had been in 1855, and few residents ever dreamed it could happen again.

On July 10, 2000, a superstitious mob set Levuka's old Masonic Lodge on fire.

The tower of the Church of the Sacred Heart in Levuka was erected in 1898.

the Masonic Order was formed here in 1875. In July 2000, the lodge was burned down by a frenzied mob from Lovoni, which had been told by superstitious preachers that it was a center of devil worship.

Follow Garner Jones Road west up the creek to the **Levuka Public School** (1881), the birthplace of Fiji's present public educational system. Before World War I, the only Fijians allowed to attend this school were the sons of chiefs. The building has been rebuilt since the 2005 fire. Other Levuka firsts include Fiji's first newspaper (1869), first Masonic Lodge (1875), first bank (1876), and first municipal council (1877).

Continue straight up Garner Jones Road for about 20 minutes, past the lovely colonial-era houses, and you'll eventually reach a gate at the entrance to the town's water catchment. A trail on the right immediately before the gate leads down to a **pool** in the river below the catchment where you can swim. Overhead, you may see swallows that live in a cave just upstream. The path to **The Peak,** the picturesque green hill

The historic Ovalau Club is Levuka's favorite drinking place.

© DAVID STANLEY

The Marist Convent School (1882) is one of Levuka's largest historic buildings.

that's visible from much of Levuka, branches off to the left between a large steel water tank and the gate at the end of the main trail. It takes about an hour to scale The Peak through the dense bush, and an experienced guide will be required (arranged through your hotel). At the end of the challenging hike, you'll have a view over much of the island's east side.

As you come back down the hill, turn left onto Church Street, and follow it around past Nasau Park sports field (once a Fijian village site) to **Navoka Methodist Church** (1862). From beside this church, 199 concrete steps ascend **Mission Hill** to Delana Methodist High School. The original mission school formed here by Reverend John Binner in 1852 was the first of its kind in Fiji. A stairway leads down through the high school to the hospital.

THE RIDDLE OF THE *JOYITA*

One of the strangest episodes in recent Pacific history is indirectly related to Levuka. On November 10, 1955, the crew of the trading ship *Tuvalu* sighted the drifting, half-sunken shape of the 70-ton MV *Joyita*, which had left Apia on October 3, bound for Fakaofo in the Tokelau Islands north of Samoa, carrying seven Europeans and 18 Polynesians. The *Joyita* had been chartered by Tokelau's district officer to take badly needed supplies to the atolls and pick up their copra, which was rotting on the beach. When the vessel was reported overdue, a fruitless aerial search began, which ended only with the chance discovery by the *Tuvalu* some 150 kilometers north of Fiji. There was no sign of the 25 persons aboard, and sacks of flour, rice, and sugar had been removed from the ship. Also missing were 40 drums of kerosene, seven cases of aluminum strips, and the three life rafts.

The ghost ship was towed to Fiji and beached. Investigators found that the engines had been flooded due to a broken pipe in the saltwater cooling system, the rudder was jammed, and the radio equipment wrecked. The navigation lights and galley stove were switched on. The *Joyita* hadn't sunk, because the holds were lined with eight centimeters of cork. Though several books and countless newspaper and magazine articles have been written about the *Joyita* mystery, no one has learned what really happened, and none of the missing persons was ever seen again. Some relics of the *Joyita* can be seen in the Levuka Community Center.

◖ Royal Hotel

This long wooden building alongside Totoga Creek is Fiji's oldest operating hotel, definitely worth a visit, even if you aren't staying there as a guest. Originally built in 1852, the Royal was rebuilt on its original foundations in 1913 by Captain David Robbie after a fire in the 1890s. Since 1927, it has been run by the Ashley family. The Royal Hotel is the last of the 60 saloons that once lined Levuka's raucous waterfront, and the long wooden bar on the main floor looks like something straight out of an American cowboy movie. In the lounge, ceiling fans revolve above the rattan sofas and potted plants, and Fijian artifacts and historic photos hang from the walls. Generations of Levuka locals have played on the century-old billiard table. Upstairs, the rooms are all unique, some with balconies facing the green mountainsides of Ovalau, others overlooking the Koro Sea. The platform on the roof is a widow's watch, where wives would watch for the overdue return of their husband's ships.

North of Levuka

On a low hill farther north along the waterfront is the **European War Memorial,** which recalls British residents of Levuka who died in World War I. Before Fiji was ceded to Britain, the Cakobau government headquarters was situated on this hill. The 1870s cottage on the hilltop across the street from the monument is called **Sailors Home** for the steamship *Sailors Home,* which worked the England-to-China route in the 1850s. The **Holy Redeemer Anglican Church** (1904) farther north has period stained-glass windows.

Follow the coastal road north from Levuka to a second bridge, where you'll see the **old Methodist church** (1869) on the left. Ratu Seru Cakobau worshiped here, and in the small cemetery behind the church is the grave of the first U.S. consul to Fiji, John Brown Williams (1810–1860). Levuka Creek here marks the town's northern boundary. In the compound across the bridge and beneath a large *dilo* tree is the tomb of an old king of Levuka. The large house in front of the tree is the residence of the present Tui Levuka, customary chief of this area (ask permission before entering the compound).

Directly above this house is **Gun Rock,**

Levuka's Royal Hotel is the oldest operating hotel in Fiji.

© DAVID STANLEY

THE LOMAIVITI GROUP

which was used as a target by the captain of the HMS *Havanah* in 1849. The intention, of course, was to demonstrate to Cakobau the efficacy of a ship's cannon, so that he might be more considerate to resident Europeans. In 1874, Commodore Goodenough pumped a few more rounds into the hill to entertain a group of Fijian chiefs, and the scars can still be seen. Long before that, the early Fijians had a fort atop the rock to defend themselves against the Lovoni hill tribes. Ask permission of the Tui Levuka (the "Roko") or a member of his household to climb Gun Rock for a splendid view of Levuka. If a small boy leads you up and down, it wouldn't be out of place to give him something for his trouble.

Continue north on the road, around a bend and past the ruin of a large concrete building, and you'll reach a cluster of government housing on the site of a cricket field where the Duke of York (later King George V) played in 1878.

There's a beautiful deep pool and waterfall behind **Waitovu village,** about two kilometers north of Levuka. You may swim here, but please don't skinny-dip; this is offensive to the local people and has led to confrontations in the past. Also, avoid arriving on a Sunday.

At Cawaci, a 30-minute walk beyond the Ovalau Holiday Resort, is a small white **mausoleum** (1922) high up on a point, with the tombs of Fiji's first and second Catholic bishops, Bishop Julien Vidal and Bishop Charles Joseph Nicholas. The large coral stone church (1893) of **St. John's College** is nearby. This is the original seat of the Catholic Church in Fiji, and the sons of the Fijian chiefs were educated here from 1894 onwards. The French-style church's walls are three meters thick around the buttresses.

South of Levuka

The **Pacific Fishing Company** tuna cannery (tel. 344-0055, www.pafcofiji.com) is just south of Queen's Wharf. A Japanese cold-storage facility opened here in 1964, followed by the cannery in 1975. After sustaining losses for four years, the Japanese company involved in the joint venture pulled out in 1986, turning the facility over to the government, which now owns the cannery. Major improvements to the wharf, freezer, storage, and other facilities were completed in 1992. The plant is supplied by Taiwanese fishing boats. In 2002, an agreement was signed with the U.S. seafood company Bumble Bee to supply tuna loins to a cannery in San Diego, California, now Pafco's largest market. In November 2009, Bumble Bee announced it was investing US$20 million to upgrade the cold storage facilities here. Nearly 1,000 residents of Ovalau (85 percent of them women) have jobs directly related to tuna canning, and the government has heavily subsidized the operation.

A little farther along is the **Cession Monument,** where the Deed of Cession, which made Fiji a British colony, was signed by Chief Cakobau in 1874. The traditional *bure* on the other side of the road was used by Prince Charles during his 1970 visit to officiate at Fiji's independence. The huge traditional-style building with a blue roof next door is the venue of provincial council meetings. A nearby European-style bungalow is **Nasova House** (1869), the former Government House or residence of the governor.

One of Fiji's most rewarding hikes begins at Draiba village, a kilometer south of the Cession Monument. A road to the right, around the first bend and just after a small bridge, marks the start of the 4.5-hour hike through enchanting forests and across clear streams to **Lovoni village.** Go straight back on this side road until you see pig pens on your right, at the end of the road. The unmarked Lovoni trail begins at the foot of the hill, just beyond the pens.

The Lovoni trail is no longer used by the locals and requires attentiveness to follow, so consider taking Epi's Midland Tour or hiring a guide if you're not a very experienced hiker. Be sure to reach Lovoni before 1500 to be able to catch the last carrier back to Levuka.

In 1855, the fierce Lovoni tribe, the Ovalau, burned Levuka, and they continued to threaten the town right up until 1871, when they were finally captured during a truce and sold to European planters as laborers. In 1875, the

On this spot in 1874, Chief Cakobau signed the Deed of Cession, making Fiji a British colony.

British government allowed the survivors to return to their valley, where their descendants live today. In July 2000, a Lovoni mob again ran amok through Levuka during the George Speight coup attempt.

If you forgo this hike and continue on the main road, you'll soon come to the old **Town Cemetery,** a little south of Draiba. Many of the graves here date back to the early colonial period. A few kilometers farther along is the **Devil's Thumb,** a dramatic volcanic plug towering above **Tokou village,** one of the scenic highlights of Fiji. Catholic missionaries set up a printing press at Tokou in 1889 to produce gospel lessons in Fijian, and in the center of the village is a sculpture of a lion made by one of the early priests. It's five kilometers back to Levuka.

Wainaloka village on the southwest side of Ovalau is inhabited by descendants of Solomon Islanders from the Lau Lagoon region who were blackbirded to Fiji more than a century ago. The present inhabitants have never visited the Solomon Islands and know nothing about it!

ENTERTAINMENT

You're welcome to enter the **Ovalau Club** (tel. 344-0507, Mon.–Thurs. 1600–2230, Fri. 1400–midnight, Sat. 1000–midnight, Sun. 1000–2100), just across Totoga Creek from the police station, said to be the oldest membership club in the South Pacific. You'll meet genuine South Seas characters here, and the place is brimming with atmosphere. The original billiard table is still in use. Ask the bartender to show you the framed letter from Count Felix von Luckner, the World War I German sea wolf. Von Luckner left the letter and some money at the unoccupied residence of a trader on Katafaga Island in the Lau Group, from which he took provisions. In the letter, Count von Luckner identifies himself as Max Pemberton, an English writer on a sporting cruise through the Pacific.

During the colonial period, the **Levuka Club** on Beach Street served the needs of Indo-Fijians who weren't allowed into the Ovalau Club. At last report it was closed.

A disco called simply **The Club** (tel. 344-0429)

operates in a back room at Levuka Pizza Thursday and Friday until 0100, Saturday until midnight. It's a youth hangout.

SPORTS AND RECREATION

Ovalau Watersports (tel. 344-0166, www .owlfiji.com), across the street from the Westpac Bank, is run by Nobi and Andrea Dehm with help from Ned Fisher, all of whom worked as Divemasters at Leleuvia Island Resort for many years. They offer diving around Levuka daily at 0900 at F$170 for two tanks, plus F$20 for gear (minimum of two divers). An Open Water certification course is F$650 (taught in English or German). They also take out snorkelers at F$50 per person for two sites—just show up at their dive shop around 0845. You'll visit the two sites used by the divers that day. Ask Andrea about whale-watching trips May–September.

At high tide, the river mouth near the Royal Hotel is a popular swimming hole for the local kids (and some tourists). The rest of the day, some locals cool off by just sitting in the water fully dressed.

Tours

The two-hour **Historical Town Tour** (F$10) from the Levuka Community Center operates Monday–Friday at 1000 and 1400, Saturday at 1000.

Ovalau Watersports (tel. 344-0166, www .owlfiji.com, weekdays 0800–1600, Sat. 0800–1300), beside the Levuka Community Center, arranges a variety of tours including walking tours around Levuka (F$10–25 pp, two-person minimum) with Noa Vueti, nicknamed Nox, a longtime Levuka resident.

Ovalau Watersports also organizes three-hour visits to Silana village with handicraft demonstrations and the chance to swim (F$40 pp, minimum of six). If you'd like to add a three-hour hike to the ruins of the ancient village of Aravudi to the Silana tour, it's F$25 per person in total (minimum of two). You can also stay in the village at F$25/35 dorm/cottage per person and participate in activities like fishing, trolling, canoeing, rafting, and snorkeling at

additional cost. Three meals are F$19 per person extra.

If you wish to organize your own tour, it costs F$120 to hire a five-person minibus around the island (or F$150 with an extension to Lovoni).

A taxi tour to Cawaci with stops along the way should cost F$20–25 for a four-passenger car.

◖ Epi's Midland Tour

Epi's Midland Tour (tel. 362-4174) is a guided hike to Lovoni that departs Monday–Saturday at about 1100 (F$50 pp including lunch and transportation, minimum of four). You must reserve by phone before 0800. Epi is an enthusiastic guy and is very knowledgeable about Fiji's forest plants. At Lovoni, you may go for a swim in the river or meet the village chief. You hike over and return by truck (or you can just go both ways by truck if you don't wish to walk). The route up and over Ovalau's central spine is steep, and rugged footwear is essential. Take along a water bottle. Epi's tour is highly recommended as a way of becoming familiar with the geography and flora of the island, while meeting local residents and having an enjoyable day.

ACCOMMODATIONS
Levuka

There are a couple of budget places to stay around Levuka (but thankfully, no luxury resorts). **Mary's Holiday Lodge** (Beach St., tel. 344-0013) occupies a large wooden house on the waterfront. The 12 basic fan-cooled rooms with shared bath are F$35/50 single/double, or F$20 per person in a three-bed dorm. A sandwich-and-tea breakfast (served 0700–0900) is included. Check your mosquito net and fan upon arrival. Laundry is F$9 a load.

For the full Somerset Maugham flavor, stay at the ◖ **Royal Hotel** (Robbies Lane, tel. 344-0024, www.royallevuka.com). The 15 fan-cooled rooms with private bath upstairs in the original colonial building are pleasant, with much-needed mosquito nets provided. Each room in the main building is in a different style, including six singles (F$29), six doubles (F$43), and one four-person family room (F$67). The section between the hotel and Beach Street contains five cottages, of which only the three closer to the ocean have kitchens (F$84/94 single/double). The garden section beside the main building includes the Captain Robbie duplex with two air-conditioned apartments (F$95), the air-conditioned Captain Kaad cottage with two rooms (F$127 for up to five people), and the Captain Volk house with four rooms with shared bath at F$122. Checkout time is 1000, but you can arrange to stay until 1500 by paying another 50 percent of the daily rate (payment by credit cards is 5 percent extra). The bar, beer garden, snooker tables, dart boards, swimming pool, gym, and videos (at 2000) are strictly for guests only. An English breakfast (F$7.50) is served Monday–Saturday 0800–1100 and Sunday 0900–1200 in the atmospheric dining room on the main floor (open to the public). The anachronistic prices, interesting mix of guests, and uncut colonial atmosphere make the Royal one of the best values in Fiji.

The popular **Levuka Homestay** (Church St., tel. 344-0777, www.levukahomestay.com), behind the Royal Hotel, is a better choice than the Royal for the fussy traveler. The four well-appointed rooms with bath and fridge are F$140/160 single/double, including a hearty breakfast and tax. A 5 percent discount is offered if you pay in cash. The three lower air-conditioned rooms in this custom-built house, which climbs the hillside on five levels, are preferable to the fourth room tucked away directly below the owners' apartment. John and Marilyn will make you feel right at home.

The **New Mavida Lodge** (Beach St., tel. 344-0477, newmavidalodge@connect.com.fj) reopened in 2006, totally rebuilt in solid concrete after a fire in 2003. The nine clean air-conditioned rooms with TV and modern bathrooms are F$80 double. The two oceanview rooms upstairs are F$120, and there's also a 10-bed dorm with separate male/female washrooms at F$25 per person. All rates include an ample breakfast and you can order dinner. There's also a communal kitchen and fridge.

The folks at Ovalau Watersports (Beach St., tel. 344-0166, www.owlfiji.com) rent the **Levuka Holiday Cottage** in front of Gun Rock, a 15-minute walk north of Levuka. This

The New Mavida Lodge offers spotlessly clean accommodations in Levuka.

self-catering bungalow (F$85/550 double per day/week) is ideal for couples who want to melt into the local scene for a while.

Around the Island

The **Ovalau Holiday Resort** (tel. 344-0329, ohrfiji@connect.com.fj) is a quiet place opposite a rocky beach at Vuma, four kilometers north of Levuka. The five two-room bungalows with kitchen, fridge, hot shower, and sitting area are F$79 single or double, F$89 for 3–5 persons, or F$119 for 6–8 persons. There's also a dorm for F$25 per person. If you plan to use the cooking facilities, make sure your groceries are protected from mice. Given sufficient advance notice, the resort's restaurant does some fine cooking. Their Bula Beach Bar, in a converted whaler's cottage, adjoins the swimming pool, and the snorkeling off their beach is okay. It's a nice place for an afternoon at the beach, even if you prefer to stay in Levuka.

Bobo's Farm (tel. 344-0166, www.owlfiji.com), near Rukuruku, provides accommodations for four people in a two-room garden bungalow at F$40/60 single/double, plus F$10/12/16 for breakfast/lunch/dinner (real Fijian food) and 5 percent tax. There's no electricity in the bungalow. Bobo's is a great place to relax. You can hike to a waterfall for a swim or snorkel at Rukuruku on the coast. For F$20 per person, Bobo can take you to a sandbank where the snorkeling is even better. Bobo's is an excellent choice for families—children love this place. It could be the best place in the country to get a feel for rural Fiji without staying in a village. Ovalau Watersports books this homestay. If you come by carrier from Levuka on Monday, Wednesday, or Friday, you'll need to hire a four-wheel-drive vehicle (same owner as the carrier) for F$10 one-way for the four kilometers from Taviya to Bobo's. Tuesday, Thursday, and Saturday, the Rukuruku truck comes within 200 meters of Bobo's for F$3. A taxi direct from Levuka will cost F$30.

FOOD

Kim's Paak Kum Loong Wine and Dine (tel. 344-0059, Mon.–Sat. 0700–1400 and 1800–2100, Sun. 1800–2100), upstairs in a building near Court's Furniture Store, is

The front tables upstairs at Kim's Paak Kum Loong Wine and Dine have nice harbor views.

© DAVID STANLEY

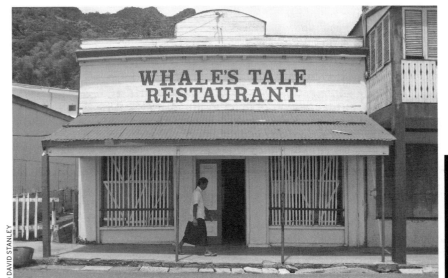

© DAVID STANLEY

The Whale's Tale Restaurant on Beach Street offers good home cooking.

Levuka's most popular restaurant. A full breakfast is F$9. A curry or roast chicken lunch from the glass warmers near the door is around F$5, while the dinner menu features Chinese dishes for F$8–13.50 (meals ordered from the menu are individually prepared). Sundays from 1800, there's a buffet (F$25), which includes salad and ice cream, but only if at least 10 people reserve. Beer is available. If you can get a table, dine on the breezy front terrace with a view of the waterfront.

The ◖ **Whale's Tale Restaurant** (tel. 344-0235, Mon.–Sat. 1100–2000) on Beach Street is also popular. Buttered pasta for lunch costs F$11, and the three-course dinner special, with a choice from among three main plates, is F$18–20. They're licensed, so you can get a beer with your meal, and their specially percolated coffee is the best in town. They also sell bags of pounded kava (F$1) as well as the popular Rukuruku chili salt (F$2).

The **Sea Breeze Restaurant** (no phone, Mon.–Sat. 0730–1700), formerly known as Shivneels Curry House, between Whale's Tale and Emily, serves various fish and chicken dishes for F$4.50. On Sunday mornings, you may be able to get tea and cakes here.

The **Sea Site Restaurant** (tel. 344-0553, closed Sun.), a bit north of Whale's Tale, is basic, but decent for ice cream.

Emily Café (tel. 344-0382), between the Sea Site and the Church of the Sacred Heart, is a good place for coffee, cakes, and rotis.

The thatched **Levuka Pizza** (tel. 344-0429, Mon.–Sat. 0930–1400 and 1800–2100, Sun. 1800–2100), also known as the Koro Makawa Restaurant, is the place with the high wire fence around it across the street from Ovalau Watersports. It's a pleasant, airy spot once you're inside. They bake 13 varieties of a rather unusual thin-crust pizza (F$9/13 small/large). There are also chicken, fish, beef, and pork dishes for under F$10 or prawns at F$14–15 and the beer is cold. A cooked breakfast here will be F$7.50.

INFORMATION AND SERVICES

The **Levuka Tourism Association** has a useful website at www.levukafiji.com.

The **Levuka Community Center** (tel.

344-0356) may have information on the off-shore island resorts and various land tours around Ovalau. You can borrow one or two books from the Community Center library for a refundable F$10 deposit or become an annual member for F$25. Ovalau Watersports has a second-hand book exchange.

Liza at the Whale's Tale Restaurant (tel. 344-0235) will be happy to give you her frank opinion of the offshore resorts—invaluable when planning a trip. Andrea at Ovalau Watersports is also very helpful.

The Westpac Bank and commission-free Colonial National Bank, adjacent on Beach Street, change travelers checks and both have ATMs.

Ovalau Watersports provides Internet access at F$0.10 a minute (no minimum). The Royal Hotel charges F$6 an hour for sluggish Internet access.

VM Narsey and Sons (Mon.–Sat. 0900–1800, Sun. 0900–1000), next door to the Whale's Tale Restaurant, provides very fast Internet connections at their four terminals (F$0.10 a minute or F$5 an hour).

Public toilets are available across the street from the Colonial National Bank and behind the post office. Ovalau Watersports does laundry at F$10 a load, while the Royal Hotel charges F$9 a bag.

Levuka's sub-divisional hospital (tel. 344-0088) is on the north side of town.

GETTING THERE

Pacific Sun (tel. 977-6582), next to the Church of the Sacred Heart, has three flights a day between Bureta Airport and Suva (F$88). The minibus from Levuka to the airstrip is F$10 per person. A taxi to the airport will run F$35.

Inquire at **Patterson Brothers Shipping** (tel. 344-0125, patterson@connect.com.fj), beside the market on Beach Street, about the ferry *Spirit of Harmony* from Ovalau to Nabouwalu, Vanua Levu, via Natovi. The connecting bus departs Levuka daily except Wednesday and Sunday at about 0500. At Nabouwalu, there's an onward bus to Labasa, but bookings must be made in advance (F$60 straight through).

Patterson Brothers Shipping also operates the "Sea-Road" bus/ferry/bus service between Suva and Levuka. It should take just less than five hours right through, and costs F$30. The

The Patterson Brothers "Sea-Road" service connects Levuka to Suva.

© DAVID STANLEY

Patterson Brothers combination involves an express bus from Levuka to Buresala, departing daily at 0500, a 45-minute ferry ride from Buresala to Natovi, then the same bus on to Suva (change at Korovou for Lautoka). In the opposite direction, the bus to Natovi leaves Suva at 1300 daily except Wednesday and Sunday. Bicycles are carried free on the ferry. Advance bookings are recommended on the Patterson Brothers bus/ferry/bus services, although they do sell tickets at their waterfront office in Levuka just before the bus is due to leave.

The people at the Levuka Community Center (tel. 344-0356) may know about other local boats from Levuka to Suva. Their carriers usually pick up passengers in front of the Community Center Monday–Saturday at 0730.

Ask about the car ferry *Sinu-i-wasa Tolu* of **Venu Shipping Ltd.,** which in past has run overnight trips from Levuka to Suva.

The small resort islands off Ovalau are not served by ferry but each is linked to Viti Levu by small boat. The boats to Caqalai and Leleuvia leave from Waidalice Landing between Nausori and Korovou. Ask the driver of the bus from Nausori to drop you off immediately after crossing the Waidalice River. The boat to Naigani is from Natovi and the Patterson Brothers bus or any bus to Nataleira will take you there. Caqalai, Leleuvia, and Yanuca Lailai have regular boats to Levuka. If you just show up at the Levuka Wharf around 1000, you should be able to find a boat leaving for one of the islands and may be able to arrange a room on the spot.

GETTING AROUND

Both taxis and carriers park across the street from the Church of the Sacred Heart in Levuka. Due to steep hills on the northwest side of Ovalau, there isn't a bus all the way around the island. Carriers leave Levuka for Taviya (F$3) near Rukuruku village Monday–Saturday at 0730, 1145, and 1600 along a beautiful, hilly road. During the school holidays, only the 1145 trip may operate. Occasional carriers to Bureta, Lovoni, and Viru park across the street from Kim's Paak Kum Loong Restaurant. To Lovoni, they leave Levuka at 0630, 1100, and 1700, Saturday at 1100 only. There's no service on Sunday.

A truck direct to Rukuruku (F$3) leaves Levuka at 1130 on Tuesday, Thursday, and Saturday, and it's possible to do a round-trip for F$6, as the carrier returns immediately to Levuka. Monday–Saturday, you can have a day at the beach at Rukuruku by taking the 0730 carrier to Taviya, then walking the remaining kilometer to Rukuruku (from the top of the hill, turn right down the side road to the beach). A vanilla plantation and beautiful verdant mountains cradle Rukuruku on the island side. Return to Levuka on the 1500 carrier from Taviya (check all of this with the driver).

Islands off Ovalau

◖ CAQALAI ISLAND

Caqalai (THANG-ga-lai) is a palm-fringed isle owned by the Methodist Church of Fiji, which operates a small backpacker resort, **Caqalai Island Accommodation** (tel. 362-0388 or 942-1586, caqalairesort@yahoo.com). The 12 simple *bure* are F$60 per person, the 10-bed dorm F$50 per person, and camping space F$40 per person, three meals included. Flush toilets and a shower shed are provided. You must bring your own alcohol, as none is sold on the island.

Caqalai is primitive but adequate, and the island and people are great. Dress up for Sunday service in the village church, and enjoy the *lovo* that afternoon. The Sunday choir singing and kava ceremony are an authentic Fiji experience. There's excellent snorkeling all around the island, especially along the edge of Snake Island where banded sea snakes congregate. You can wade to Snake Island at low tide. Enter the water to the left just before reaching the island and swim around the island to the coral. Viti Watersports (www.vitiwatersports.com) offers scuba diving here at F$100/150 for one/two tanks.

Information is available at the Royal Hotel in Levuka (boat from Ovalau or Waidalice F$30 pp each way). The Royal Hotel also arranges day trips to Caqalai. Those already staying on Caqalai can make shopping trips to Levuka at F$10 per person each way.

LELEUVIA ISLAND

Leleuvia is a lovely, isolated, 17-hectare reef island with nothing but coconut trees, fine sandy beaches, and a ramshackle assortment of tourist huts scattered around. The small backpacker Leleuvia Island Resort (tel. 368-0721, www.leleuvia.com), originally built in the 1980s, is well maintained with running water and electricity when the generator is on. Late at night, you'll need to use a flashlight.

Accommodations run F$50 per person in a dorm of four, six, or eight beds; F$60 per person in a double room or thatched hut; and F$55 per person in a duplex family lodge with a double and two single beds. Children under 10 are half price, under five free. Meals are included in all rates (good food, small portions). Toilets and showers are shared. You can lock your door if you brought your own padlock, otherwise your room will remain unlocked.

A few activities are available, and the snorkeling here is fine, although the sea is sometimes cold. For F$10 per person, they'll drop you off on "Honeymoon Island," where the corals are just lovely. Scuba diving can be arranged through Ovalau Watersports in Levuka. Once or twice a week, they'll have a *lovo* dinner. Later, if you want to join the musicians and staff at the kava bowl, having a nice bundle of kava roots in your backpack will ensure you a warm welcome. Otherwise, beer and soft drinks are for sale.

Getting there from Levuka costs F$30 per person each way (two-person minimum). Book through Ovalau Watersports. To arrange a transfer from Suva, call the island direct for instructions. You'll transfer to the Leleuvia boat (F$30 pp) at Waidalice.

MOTURIKI ISLAND

In 2002, a 2,600-year-old female skeleton was discovered on the southeast coast of Moturiki Island. The burial style and fragments of Lapita pottery found nearby suggest a connection with Santa Cruz in the Solomon Islands dating back as far as 3,170 years.

Small outboards to Moturiki Island depart Naqueledamu Landing on Ovalau most afternoons. The finest beaches are on the east side of Moturiki. Camping is officially discouraged, but possible.

NAIGANI ISLAND

Naigani, 11 kilometers off Viti Levu, is a lush tropical island near Ovalau at the west end of the Lomaiviti Group. It's just the right size for exploring on foot, with pristine beaches and only one Fijian village in the southwest corner.

Naigani Island Resort (tel. 331-2433, www.naiganiresort.com), also known as "Mystery Island," is on a shallow beach on the southeast side of Naigani. Naigani offers 12 two-bedroom villas at F$150 for a four-person garden villa or F$250 for a five-person beachfront villa, continental breakfast included. The meal plans are F$60/75 per person for two/three meals, or you can order à la carte (no cooking facilities). Children under 13 are charged half price for meals and transfers. The electric generator is switched off in the middle of the night, causing fans to stop and the rooms to heat up uncomfortably. Internet usage is F$15 an hour.

There's a swimming pool with a water slide and special activities for children, but no TVs in the villas. Some non-motorized water sports are free, but fishing trips cost extra. The day trip to Picnic Beach on Canabuli Bay at the north end of the island is F$25 per person (good snorkeling if you swim straight out). Scuba diving, to sites like Nursery and Swim Through, costs F$135 for four tanks. At high tide, when the sea is calm, some of Fiji's best snorkeling is here. At the south end of the two-hole golf course is a sign indicating the start of a trail to the top of the southern hill on the island. There's a good view of the resort's bay 300 meters beyond the summit.

The dive staff at Naigani is very professional but the resort management is a little disorganized. Clarify exactly what your package includes early on in your stay. You may be the only guests. A taxi from Suva to Natovi landing will cost around F$80 one-way for the car, then it's another F$70 per person round-trip for the boat to Naigani. From Levuka, call them up and arrange to be collected by the speedboat at Taviya or Rukuruku villages on the northwest side of Ovalau at F$50 per person.

YANUCA LAILAI ISLAND

It was on tiny Yanuca Lailai Island, just off the south end of Ovalau, that the first 463 indentured Indian laborers to arrive in Fiji landed from the ship *Leonidas* on May 14, 1879. To avoid the introduction of cholera or smallpox into Fiji, the immigrants spent two months in quarantine on Yanuca Lailai. Later, Nukulau Island off Suva became Fiji's main quarantine station.

It's possible to stay on Yanuca Lailai at **Lost Island Resort.** *Bure* accommodations are F$58 per person, the dorm F$45 per person, camping F$30 per person, meals included. Current information should be available from the Levuka Community Center (tel. 344-0356) or Ovalau Watersports (tel. 344-0166, www.owlfiji.com). Expect to pay F$25 per person each way for the boat from Levuka. A day trip from Levuka will be F$65 per person (1000–1600).

Other Islands of the Lomaiviti Group

BATIKI ISLAND

Batiki has a large interior lagoon of brackish water flanked by mudflats and is surrounded by a broad barrier reef. Four Fijian villages are on Batiki, and you can walk around the island in four hours. Waisea Veremaibau of Yavu village, on the north side of the island, has accommodated guests in past. Fine baskets are made on Batiki. Due to hazardous reefs, there's no safe anchorage for ships.

GAU ISLAND

Gau is the fifth-largest island in Fiji, with 16 villages and 13 settlements. There's a barrier reef on the west coast, but only a fringing reef on the east. A hot-spring swimming pool is close to the Public Works Department depot at **Waikama.** From Waikama, hike along the beach and over the hills to **Somosomo village.** If you lose the way, look for the creek at the head of the bay, and work your way up it until you encounter the trail. There's a bathing pool in Somosomo with emerald-green water.

A road runs from Somosomo to **Sawaieke village,** where the Takalaigau (high chief of Gau) resides. The remnants of one of the only surviving pagan temples *(bure kalou)* in Fiji is beside the road at the junction in Sawaieke. The high stone mound is still impressive.

It's possible to climb **Delaico** (760 m), highest on the island, from Sawaieke in three or four hours. The first hour is the hardest. From

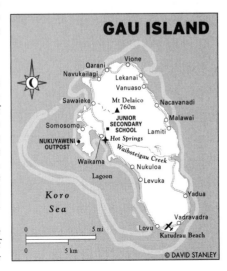

GAU ISLAND

Vione
Qarani
Navukailagi
Lekanai
Vanuaso
Sawaieke
Mt Delaico
760m
Nacavanadi
Somosomo
JUNIOR
SECONDARY
SCHOOL
Malawai
Lamiti
NUKUYAWENI
OUTPOST
Hot Springs
Waiboteigau Creek
Waikama
Nukuloa
Lagoon
Levuka
Koro
Sea
Yadua
Lovu
Vadravadra
Katudrau Beach
0   5 mi
0   5 km
© DAVID STANLEY

CORAL REEF ADVENTURE

Since 1993, the liveaboard *Nai'a* (www.naia. com.fj) has been the flagship of Fiji's diving industry, discovering and naming many remote sites now regularly visited by other boats. In addition to *Nai'a*'s regular cruises around Fiji, its humpback whale tours to Tonga and scientific expeditions to the shark-rich waters of Kiribati are annual events. During late 2000 and early 2001, the MacGillivray Freeman Films IMAX production *Coral Reef Adventure* was filmed in Fiji by Howard Hall, who selected *Nai'a*'s Cat Holloway and Rob Barrel as his guides, both topside and underwater. And *Nai'a* Divemaster Rusi Vulakoro has a starring role in the film. *Nai'a* passengers will recognize their favorite dive sites on the giant screen, as well as the sharks, turtles, manta rays, sea snakes, gobies, and shrimp that they have come to love. One of the highlights of every *Nai'a* voyage is an afternoon spent in a village on the island of Gau. So impressed were Howard and Michelle Hall when they first visited Gau as *Nai'a* passengers that the whole village visit is captured in *Coral Reef Adventure*.

the summit is a sweeping view. The Fiji petrel, a rare seabird of the albatross family, lays its eggs underground on Gau's jungle-clad peaks. Only two specimens have ever been taken: one by the survey ship *Herald* in 1855, and a second by local writer Dick Watling in 1984.

The co-op and government station (hospital, post office, etc.) are at **Qarani** at the north end of Gau. Two ships a week arrive here from Suva on an irregular schedule, but there is no wharf, so they anchor offshore. The wharf at Waikama is used only for government boats.

There are a number of waterfalls on the east coast. The most impressive are behind **Lekanai** and up Waiboteigau Creek, both an hour's walk off the main road. Look for the "weather stone" on the beach, a five-minute walk south of **Yadua village**. Bad weather is certain if you step on it or hit it with another stone.

The **Nuku Resort** (tel. 603-0818, www .nukuresort.com), formerly known as the Nukuyaweni Outpost, stands on a lovely golden sand beach on the Bay of Angels a couple of kilometers southwest of Somosomo. This place has been under development since the 1990s and it looks like it may open soon. The four handcrafted, solar-powered *bure* should cost around F$1,000 per person including meals, non-alcoholic drinks, non-motorized activities, and tax. Aside from the swimming pool, guests will be able to enjoy great snorkeling off the 500-meter beach.

There's extraordinary scuba diving in Nigali Passage, just 15 minutes away by boat (large schools of big fish and manta rays).

The airstrip is on Katudrau Beach at the south end of Gau. At last report the weekly flights to/from Suva were not operating. Check with Pacific Sun (tel. 977-6582) for current information.

KORO ISLAND

Koro is an 8- by 16-kilometer island shaped like a shark's tooth. A ridge traverses the island from northeast to southwest, reaching 561 meters near the center. High jungle-clad hillsides drop sharply to the coast. The top beach is along the south coast, between Mundu and the lighthouse at Muanivanua Point. Among Koro's 14 large Fijian villages is **Nasau,** the government center, with post office, hospital, and schools.

The road to **Vatulele village** on the north coast climbs from Nasau to the high plateau at the center of the island. The coconut trees and mangoes of the coast are replaced by great tree ferns and thick rainforest.

The track south between Nacamaki and Tua Tua runs along a golden palm-fringed beach. There's a cooperative store at **Nagaidamu** where you can buy *yaqona* and supplies. Koro kava is Fiji's finest. A 30-minute hike up a steep trail from the co-op brings you to a waterfall and an idyllic swimming hole. Keep left

© DAVID STANLEY

It's unlikely you'll meet another tourist on this deserted beach north of Tua Tua, Koro Island.

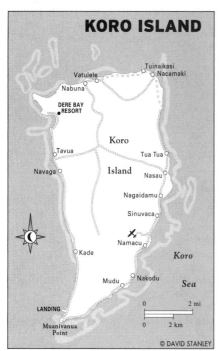

if you're on your own (taking a guide would be preferable).

The **Koro Beach Resort** (tel. 331-1075, www.korobeachresort.com) is on a long white beach at the northwestern tip of Koro. The six *bure* are F$100 per person per day plus tax, including meals. Four cottages and homes available by the week are listed on the website. When the Koro Beach Resort is full, guests are accommodated across the bay in three spacious bungalows at the **Dere Bay Resort** (tel. 331-1075, www.derebayresort.com), which the company also owns. It's F$200 per person to stay there. Otherwise, the Dere Bay remains closed, although the dive shop is open. The Koro Beach crowd is also marketing residential sites behind the Dere Bay Resort under the name Koro Seaview Estates (www.koro seaviewestates.com). Actor Clint Eastwood owns a 325-hectare estate adjacent to this property, although it's still virgin rainforest and Eastwood has never been to Koro.

Since 2007, Linda Blue has rented out a house at **(Blue Waitui** (www.bluewaitui .com) on a hill between the Koro Beach Resort and Dere Bay. It's just a five-minute walk down to the white sand beach and there are sweeping sea views. The guesthouse can sleep up to six and costs F$100/500 a day/week plus tax, with cooking facilities provided. Upstairs is a large bedroom with private covered screened porch overlooking Dere Bay. Guests are welcome to pick fruits and vegetables from the extensive organic gardens. It is a five-minute walk through the rain forest to the beach.

Koro has an unusual inclined **airstrip** on the east side of the island near Namacu village. You land uphill, take off downhill. At last report, the weekly Pacific Sun flights were not operating. Northern Air (tel. 340-0449) operates charter flights from Suva. Chartering a four-seat aircraft from Suva to Koro will cost around F$1,200 one-way.

The **Consort Shipping Line** (www.consortshipping.com.fj) ferry, *Spirit of Fiji Islands*, plies between Suva and Savusavu/Taveuni and ties up to the wharf near Muanivanua Point. The ship calls northbound in the middle of the night on Wednesdays; the southbound trips stop at Koro Thursdays at 0200. The fare to/from Suva is F$48 deck one-way. To Savusavu, it's F$36. Inquire about transfers from the airport or wharf when making your accommodations bookings.

The Dere Bay/Koro Beach Marina has a boat available for charter to Savusavu.

MAKOGAI ISLAND

Makogai shares a figure-eight-shaped barrier reef with neighboring Wakaya. The anchorage is in Dalice Bay on the northwest side of the island. From 1911 to 1969, this was a leper colony staffed by Catholic nuns, and many of the old hospital buildings still stand. Over the years, some 4,500 patients were sheltered here, including many from various other Pacific Island groups.

Among the 1,241 souls interred in the patients' cemetery on the hill is Mother Marie Agnes, the "kindly tyrant" who ran the facility for 34 years. Both the British and French governments honored her with their highest decorations, and upon retiring at the age of 80, she commented that "the next medal will be given in heaven." Also buried here is Maria

Filomena, a Fijian sister who had worked at the colony from its inception. After contracting leprosy in 1925, she joined her patients and continued serving them for another 30 years. Only in 1948 was an effective treatment for leprosy introduced, allowing the colony to be phased out over the next two decades.

Today, Makogai is owned by the Department of Agriculture, which runs an experimental sheep farm here, with some 2,000 animals. A new breed intended as a source of mutton and bearing little wool was obtained by crossing British and Caribbean sheep.

NAIRAI ISLAND

Seven Fijian villages are found on this 336-meter-high island between Koro and Gau. The inhabitants are known for their woven handicrafts. Hazardous reefs stretch out in three directions, and in 1808 the brigantine *Eliza* was wrecked here. Among the survivors was Charles Savage, who served as a mercenary for the chiefs of Bau for five years, until he fell into the clutches of Vanua Levu cannibals.

In 2007, the **Natauloa Beach Resort** (tel. 395-2885, www.natauloabeachresort.com.au) opened on Nairai. The 12 modern bungalows are F$2,850 per person for five nights, including meals and transfers. Two children under 12 are accommodated free if sharing with their parents. This resort caters to well-healed scuba divers with packages of 5/10/20 dives at F$650/1,300/2,400. Game fishing is also offered. A swimming pool and tennis courts are provided.

◖ WAKAYA ISLAND

A high cliff on the west coast of Wakaya is known as Chieftain's Leap, for a young chief who threw himself over the edge to avoid capture by his foes. In those days, a hill fort sat at Wakaya's highest point, so that local warriors could scan the horizon for unfriendly cannibals. Chief Cakobau sold Wakaya to Europeans in 1840, and it has since had many owners. In 1862, David Whippy set up Fiji's first sugar mill on Wakaya.

The German raider Count Felix von Luckner was captured on Wakaya during World War I. His ship, the *Seeadler,* had foundered on a reef at Maupihaa in the Society Islands on August 2, 1917. The 105 survivors (prisoners included) camped on Maupihaa, while on August 23, von Luckner and five men set out in an open boat to capture a schooner and continue the war. On September 21, 1917, they found a suitable ship at Wakaya. Their plan was to go aboard pretending to be passengers and capture it, but a British officer and four Indian soldiers happened upon the scene. Not wishing to go against the rules of chivalry and fight in civilian clothes, the count gave himself up and was interned at Auckland as a prisoner of war. He later wrote a book, *The Sea Devil,* about his experiences.

In 1973, Canadian industrialist David Harrison Gilmour bought the island for US$3 million, and in 1990 he and wife Jill opened **The Wakaya Club & Spa** (tel. 344-8128, www .wakaya.com), with nine spacious cottages starting at F$3,610 double plus 17.5 percent tax, all-inclusive (five-night minimum stay). A three-bedroom hilltop villa called "Vale O" is F$14,440 plus tax per night. Children under 16 are not accommodated. The snorkeling is superb, and there's scuba diving, a nine-hole golf course, a swimming pool, wireless Internet, and an airstrip for charter flights (around F$2,000 round-trip per couple from Nadi).

Only game fishing and massage cost extra. As you might expect at these prices (Fiji's highest!), it's all very tasteful and elegant—just ask Pierce Brosnan, Carol Burnett, Russell Crowe, Tom Cruise, Céline Dion, Bill Gates, Nicole Kidman, Michelle Pfeiffer, or Burt Reynolds. It's a sort of country club for the rich and famous, rather than a trendy social scene. Despite this, the service is not flawless. Since no Fijian villages are anywhere nearby, this is one of the only places in Fiji where it's possible to swim discreetly nude. Picnics on absolutely private beaches are arranged. A third of Wakaya has been subdivided into 100 parcels, which are available as homesites; red deer imported from New Caledonia run wild across the rest.

Only resort guests may set foot on these ritzy shores, but everyone can snorkel or scuba dive from a boat on Wakaya's glorious reefs. Ovalau Watersports in Levuka offers diving here and liveaboard dive boats often pass this way. Among the many dive sites are Blue Ridge on the northern side of the island's outer reef, named for its blue ribbon eels. The marine life here is profuse, as it is at the Lion's Den nearby, where lionfish are common. Wakaya Passage off the island's south point is the place for manta ray and hammerhead shark encounters.

master bedroom of the Vale O villa at The Wakaya Club & Spa, on Wakaya Island

VANUA LEVU

Though only half as big as Viti Levu, 5,587-square-kilometer Vanua Levu (Great Land) has much to offer. The transport is good, the scenery is varied, and people are warm and hospitable. Far fewer visitors visit the "friendly north" than heavily promoted western Fiji. Fijian villages are numerous all the way around the island—here you'll be able to experience real Fijian life, so it's well worth making the effort to visit Fiji's second-largest island.

The drier northwest side of Vanua Levu features sugarcane fields and pine forests, while on the damper southeast side, copra plantations predominate, with a little cocoa around Natewa Bay. Toward the southeast, the scenery is more bucolic beauty, with coconut groves dipping down toward the sea. Majestic bays cut into the island's south side, and one of the

world's longest barrier reefs flanks the north coast. There are some superb locations here just waiting to be discovered, both above and below the waterline.

Indo-Fijians still form a majority in the cane-growing area surrounding the large market town of Labasa, while Savusavu is racially balanced and most of the rest of Vanua Levu is predominately Fijian. Between 1996 and 2007, the number of Indo-Fijians living in rural areas of around Labasa fell 25 percent as cane farmers departed as their land leases expired. Together Vanua Levu, Taveuni, and adjacent islands form Fiji's Northern Division (often called simply "the north"), which is subdivided into three provinces: The west end of Vanua Levu is Bua Province; most of the north side of Vanua Levu is Macuata Province; and

HIGHLIGHTS

◖ Natewa Bay and Udu Point: Natewa is the South Pacific's largest bay, viewable on a scenic seven-hour bus ride between Savusavu and Labasa (page 235).

◖ Waisali Rainforest Reserve: Just off the highway between Savusavu and Labasa, this mountain forest offers unexploited stands of native trees and 21 recorded species of birds (page 241).

◖ Namenalala Island: Namenalala is a nature reserve island south of Vanua Levu, accessible only to guests at the one small upscale resort and liveaboard dive boat passengers. The snorkeling and diving are superb (page 248).

◖ Vanaira Bay: The Dolphin Bay Divers Retreat on Vanaira Bay at Vanua Levu's east end is the closest resort to the fabulous Rainbow Reef. The usual access is from Taveuni (page 251).

◖ Rabi Island: Seldom-visited Rabi is unique in Fiji for its Micronesian people and way of life (page 252).

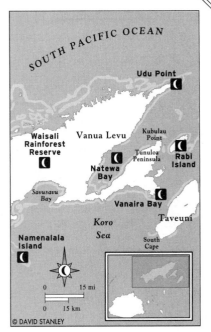

LOOK FOR ◖ TO FIND RECOMMENDED SIGHTS, ACTIVITIES, DINING, AND LODGING.

the southeast side of Vanua Levu and Taveuni make up Cakaudrove Province.

In recent years, Savusavu has become an important tourist destination, with several upscale resorts and a growing expatriate population. It's also the transportation hub of the island, with large car ferries from Suva; flights from Nadi, Suva, and Taveuni; and buses from everywhere to Labasa and the east end of the island. Savusavu itself is wonderfully picturesque—a pleasant place to hang out. You won't regret touring this area.

PLANNING YOUR TIME

Savusavu is well worth a couple of days, or longer if you've booked a stay at one of the resorts. You can go sailing or scuba diving, visit the pearl farm, hang out at the marinas, and join tours to local villages and nature areas. There's a good selection of restaurants, cafés, and bars.

At the very least, you should do a day trip from Savusavu to Labasa by public bus to see the other side of the island. A better plan would be to spend a night in Labasa and return to Savusavu on the bus that travels via Natewa Bay. If you're going on to Taveuni, there's a bus/ferry/bus connection from both Labasa and Savusavu five times a week.

Contrarian travelers might consider visiting Labasa before Savusavu. There are direct flights to Labasa from Nadi and Suva, and

VANUA LEVU

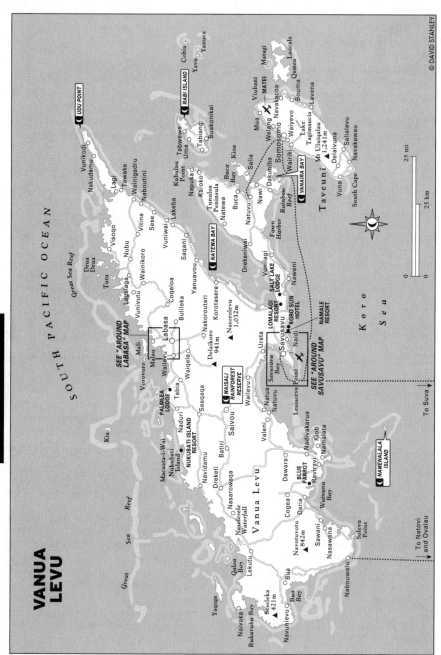

VANUA LEVU

© DAVID STANLEY

SOUTH PACIFIC OCEAN

Great Sea Reef

◧ UDU POINT

Vunikodi
Nakudamu
Lagi
Tawake
Wainigadru
Naboutini

Drea
Visoqo
Drua
Tutu
Nubu
Vitina
Sese
Lagalaga
Wainikoro
Vuniwai
Vunivutu
Cogeloa
Buileka
Nakoroutari
Yanuavou
Korotasere
Nasorolevu
1,032m ▲

Malau
Labasa
Mali
SEE "AROUND LABASA" MAP
Wailevu
Vorovoro
Waiqele
Delaikoro
941m ▲
Urata
NATEWA BAY ◧

PALMLEA LODGE ●
Tabia
Naduri
Seaqaqa
Saivou
Wailevu
Natua
Lesiaceva Point
SEE "AROUND SAVUSAVU" MAP

Macuata-i-Wai ●
Nukubati Island
NUKUBATI ISLAND RESORT
Batiri
Navidamu
Dreketi
Valeni
Natuvu

Kia
Navasoroloa
Wainunu Bay

Great   *Sea*   *Reef*

Vanua Levu

Naselesele Waterfall
Cogea
Daria
Nadivakarua
Namalata
Klob
Ravitavi
BLUE PARROT
Dawara

Navotuvotu
842m ▲
Sawani
Nasawana
Solevu Point

Galoa Bay
Lekutu
Bua
◧ NAMENALALA ISLAND

Yaqaga
Naivaka
Rukuruku Bay
Navuhievu
Nabouwalu

Seseleka
421m ▲
Bua Bay

To Natovi and Ovalau

To Suva

Lomalagi Resort
SALT LAKE LODGE
Vumlagi
Naweni
Drekeniwai
Fawn Harbor
Savusavu
KORO SUN HOTEL
Naidi
NAMALE RESORT
Savusavu Bay

Vunivau
Natewa
Buca Bay
Natuvu
Nawi
Dakuniba
Wairiki
VANAIRA BAY ◧
Rainbow Reef

Kubulau Point
Napuka
Karoko
Tunuloa Peninsula
Buca
Kioa
Salia

Tabwewa
Uma
Tabiang
Buakonikai

Napuka
RABI ISLAND ◧
Cobia

Yavu
Yanuca

Magi
Navacoa
Bouma
Laucala
Qamea

Mua
Viubani
Welagi
MATEI ✈
Waiyevo
Waiyevo
Tagimaucia
Lake
Tagimaucia

Somosomo
Mt Uluiqalau
1,241m ▲
Delaivuna
Vuna
Salialevu
Navakawau
South Cape

T a v e u n i

K o r o
S e a

WAISALI RAINFOREST RESERVE ◧

25 mi
25 km

0
0

another bus/ferry/bus route from Suva via Nabouwalu. However, unless you're a bit of a sociologist, you probably won't want to hang around Labasa long, especially with Savusavu beckoning just across Vanua Levu's central mountain range.

GETTING THERE

Air Pacific (tel. 330-4388) has daily flights to Labasa and Savusavu from Nadi and Suva. By boat, the Patterson Brothers (tel. 331-5644, patterson@connect.com.fj) ferry *Spirit of Harmony* plies between Natovi on Viti Levu and Nabouwalu on Vanua Levu five times a week with bus connections to Suva and Labasa. Ships operated by the Consort Shipping Line and Bligh Water Shipping Ltd. call at Savusavu between Suva and Taveuni two or three times a week. Bligh Water Shipping also has a ship between Lautoka and Savusavu three times a week. Natuvu at the east end of Vanua Levu is connected to Taveuni by small boat daily except Sunday with bus connections to/from Savusavu and Labasa. Details of all of these services are provided in the respective sections of this chapter.

Labasa and Vicinity

Labasa is a busy Indian market town that services Vanua Levu's major cane-growing area. It's Fiji's fifth-largest town, with 28,000 inhabitants, four banks, and the Northern Division and Macuata Province headquarters. Vanua Levu's only sugar mill is here. Labasa was built on a delta where the shallow Labasa and Qawa Rivers enter the sea; maritime transport is limited to small boats. The Qawa River has been heavily polluted by wastes from the mill. Large ships must anchor off Malau, 11 kilometers north, where Labasa's sugar output is

VANUA LEVU

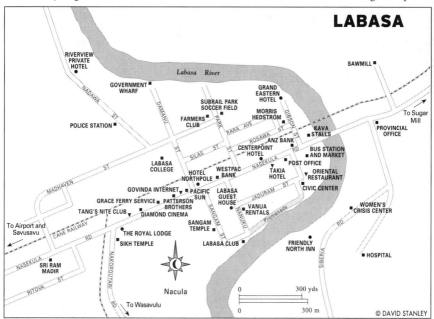

© DAVID STANLEY

VIDI VIDI

Vidi vidi is a game similar to billiards, except that the ball is propelled by a flick of the finger, rather than the tap of a cue. Two or four players position themselves around a rectangular "cram board," with holes in the four corners. The eight or nine brown balls are placed in the center of the board, and the players try to knock them into the holes by using a striker ball. The red "king ball" must go in last, and if a player knocks it in prematurely, all the balls he has sunk must come out and be knocked in again. First played in India, *vidi vidi* was brought to Fiji by Indian immigrants.

Tribe Wanted (www.tribewanted.com) gets to spend time on Vorovoro, which has been leased from the native landowners. The success of this project illustrates vividly the power of social networking in the Internet age.

Other than providing a fine base from which to explore the surrounding countryside, as well as a good choice of places to spend the night, Labasa has little to interest the average tourist. That's its main attraction: Since few visitors come, there's adventure in the air, inexpensive food in the restaurants, and fun places to drink (though female travelers might attract unwelcome attention). Labasa's not beautiful, but it is real, and the bus ride that brings you here is great.

SIGHTS

Labasa has an attractive riverside setting, with one long main street lined with shops and restaurants. The park along the river's left bank near the Labasa Club is quite pleasant. Visitors are most welcome at the North Indian–style **Sangam Temple** nearby, which

loaded. Labasa's lack of an adequate port has hindered development.

In 2006, tiny Vorovoro Island, next to Mali Island near the port of Malau, became the site of a unique social experiment. Each of the 5,000 members of the Internet community

the North Indian-style Sangam Temple

© DAVID STANLEY

contains colorful idols of Vishnu, Ganesha, and others.

The **Labasa Sugar Mill,** beside the Qawa River two kilometers east of town, opened in 1894. At the height of the crushing season (May–Dec.), there's usually a long line of trucks, tractors, and trains waiting to unload cane at the mill. From the road here, you get a view of **Three Sisters Hill** to the right.

Around Labasa

The **Snake Temple** (Naag Mandir) at Nagigi, 12 kilometers northeast of Labasa, contains a large rock shaped like a cobra that Hindu devotees swear is growing. Frequent buses pass Naag Mandir.

On your way back to Labasa from Nagigi, ask to be dropped at Bulileka Road, just before the sugar mill. Here you can easily pick up a yellow-and-blue bus to the **hanging bridge,** a suspension footbridge at Bulileka, six kilometers east of Labasa. Get off the Bulileka bus at Boca Urata where it turns around. The hanging bridge is 150 meters down the road from that point (ask). Cross the bridge, and continue through the fields a few hundred meters to the paved road, where you can catch another bus back to Labasa. The main reason for coming is to see this picturesque valley, so you may wish to walk part of the way back.

Indian **firewalking** takes place once a year, sometime in July or August, at

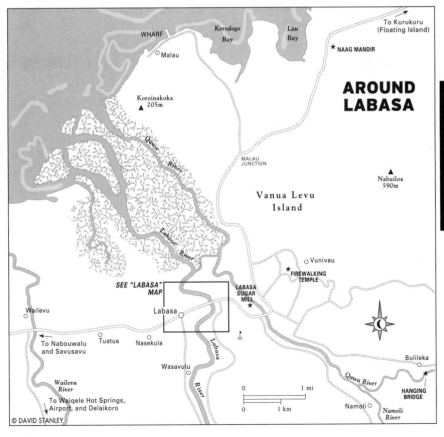

Many Hindu devotees believe this cobra-shaped rock at the Snake Temple is growing.

Agnimela Mandir, also known as the Sangam Mahamariamman Firewalking Temple, at Vunivau, five kilometers northeast of Labasa. This temple was established in 1940.

The **Waiqele hot springs,** located 14 kilometers southwest of town, are near a Hindu temple called Shiu Mandir, about four kilometers beyond Labasa airport (green-and-yellow Waiqele bus). Again, the only reason to come is to see a bit of the countryside.

You can get a view of much of Vanua Levu from the telecommunications tower atop **Delaikoro** (941 m), 25 kilometers south of Labasa, farther down the same road past the airport. Only a four-wheel-drive vehicle can make it to the top.

Farther afield is the **Floating Island** in a circular lake at Kurukuru, between Wainikoro and Nubu, 44 kilometers northeast of Labasa (accessible on the Dogotuki, Kurukuru, and Lagalaga buses). It's a 45-minute walk from the turnoff at Lagalaga to Kurukuru. In late 2006, the 14th season of the American television series *Survivor* was filmed at Vunivutu Bay near Lagalaga. North of Labasa, the pavement ends at Coqeloa.

If you're a surfer, ask about hiring a boat out to the **Great Sea Reef** north of Kia Island, 40 kilometers northwest of Labasa.

ENTERTAINMENT

Elite Cinema (tel. 881-1260) has films in English and Hindi Saturdays at 1000 only. **Diamond Theater** (tel. 881-1471, admission F$3) has shows at 1000 and 1300.

The **Labasa Club** (tel. 881-1304, daily 1000–2200) on Nanuku Street serves cheap beer in a congenial, male-oriented atmosphere. There are two large snooker tables inside and a nice terrace out back facing the river.

The **Bounty Nightclub** (tel. 881-1655, Wed.–Sat. 2200–0100) at the Takia Hotel is accessible via an orange stairway on the side of the building.

A much rougher place frequented mostly by indigenous Fijians is **Tang's Nite Club** (66 Nasekula Rd., Mon.–Sat. 2030–0100) near Diamond Cinema. There's a F$5 cover charge.

inside Agnimela Mandir, the firewalking temple, near Labasa

The Takia Hotel in Labasa contains Bounty, the city's top nightclub.

ACCOMMODATIONS
Under US$25

The 10-room 【 **Riverview Private Hotel** (Nadawa St., tel. 881-1367) is in a quiet two-story concrete building beyond the police station. The four fan-cooled rooms with shared bath are F$25/30 single/double, while another four rooms with private bath are F$45/55. There are also two deluxe air-conditioned rooms with TV, fridge, and hot plate at F$70/80. The breezy five-bed dormitory with a terrace overlooking the river is F$20 per person (one of the nicest dorms in Fiji). Communal cooking facilities are available. There's a very pleasant riverside bar here. The gate closes at 2200.

The **Labasa Guest House** (Nanuku St., tel. 881-2155) has eight fan-cooled rooms at F$20/25 single/double. Some rooms have a toilet and shower, while others don't, but the price of all is the same (the two back rooms with private bath are the best). You can put your own padlock on your door. The doors are locked at 2200, and you'll hear a lot of

The colonial-style Grand Eastern is Labasa's most imposing hotel.

© DAVID STANLEY

dog and rooster noise through the night. This place is extremely basic, but cheap.

US$25-50

The Royale Lodge (47 Nasekula Road, tel. 881-8816, www.theroyale.net), upstairs in the B. S. Lal Building almost opposite Diamond Theater, has four air-conditioned singles with bath at F$55 and three doubles at F$65. Some rooms have no windows and it's overpriced for what it is.

The claustrophobic **Centerpoint Hotel** (24 Nasekula Rd., tel. 881-1057, cenhotel@ connect.com.fj) has four fan rooms at F$50/70 single/double and seven air-conditioned rooms at F$70/90, including breakfast.

The four-story **Takia Hotel** (10 Nasekula Rd., tel. 881-1655, hoteltakia@connect.com .fj), next to the post office, has seven fan-cooled rooms at F$54/64 single/double, 26 air-conditioned rooms at F$96/106, and one family suite at F$136/146, all with private bath. Children under 12 are free. The

fan rooms are along the corridor between the disco and the bar, and will only appeal to party animals (free admission to the disco for hotel guests).

The splendid **(Grand Eastern Hotel** (Gibson St., tel. 881-1022, www.hexagon fiji.com) overlooks the river, just a few minutes' walk from the bus station. It's a classic colonial-style hotel owned by the Charan Jeath Singh Group (www.cjsgroupfiji.com) and managed by the Hexagon Group. The 10 standard rooms with terraces in the wing facing the river are F$85 single or double, while the 10 larger deluxe rooms facing the swimming pool are F$113. There are also four suites upstairs in the main two-story building at F$140 double (children under 12 free). All rooms have air-conditioning, fridge, and private bath. The Grand Eastern's atmospheric dining room and bar are brimming with vintage charm.

Opened in 1996, the **Friendly North Inn** (Siberia Rd., tel. 881-1555, fni@connect.com.fj)

© DAVID STANLEY

The Hotel Northpole in Labasa has a very good restaurant/bar.

opposite the hospital is about a kilometer from the bus station (F$3 by taxi). They have six air-conditioned rooms with TV and fridge at F$60/70 single/double, plus four with cooking facilities and two more with two beds at F$75 single or double. All rooms have private bath. The Inn's large open-air bar (Mon.–Fri. 1600–2000, Sat. and Sun. 1200–2200) is a pleasant place for a beer.

US$50-100

A stylish place to stay in downtown Labasa is the **Hotel Northpole** (tel. 881-8008, north pole@connect.com.fj) in a new purpose-built building on Nasekula Road near the Pacific Sun office. The 17 air-conditioned rooms with bath are F$75/95 single/double, including breakfast. The double rooms have wireless Internet. Special reduced rates are often offered Friday–Sunday. The Northpole caters mostly to business travelers but it's a good mid-priced choice. The Good Times Bar and Grill downstairs has Fiji Bitter on tap.

FOOD

The **Oriental Restaurant & Bar** (2 Jaduram St., tel. 881-7321, Mon.–Sat. 1000–1500 and 1830–2200, Sun. 1830–2200), next to the bus station, is surprisingly reasonable, with Chinese food, grilled meats, vegetarian dishes, and curries at around F$8, or lobster at F$39. Cold bottles of "long-neck" Fiji Bitter are served. Thankfully, there's no smoking inside, only out on the balcony.

Simple Fijian, Chinese, and Indian meals are available for F$4–5 at many places along Nasekula Road, such as the **Jie Ning Restaurant** (tel. 881-8620) below the Centerpoint Hotel.

The **Kwong Tung Restaurant** (18 Nasekula Rd., tel. 881-1980, Mon.–Sat. 0730–1930, Sun. 1000–1500), opposite the Takia Hotel, is hugely popular for breakfast and lunch, with large crowds of locals (no beer served).

Another good Indian place with *thali,* sweets, and ice cream is **Gopals Restaurant** (tel. 881-8749) near the Centerpoint Hotel on Nasekula Road.

Breakfast is hard to find in Labasa, although several places along the main street serve buttered cakes and coffee. The egg sandwiches (F$1.50) at **Popular Tea Room** opposite the post office are good.

Morris Hedstrom Supermarket (Rosawa St., tel. 881-1211, Mon.–Thurs. 0800–1730, Fri. 0800–1900, Sat. 0800–1630), next to the entrance to the Grand Eastern Hotel, has a clean, inexpensive food bar perfect for a fast lunch.

OTHER PRACTICALITIES
Information and Services

The **Northern Regional Library** (tel. 881-2894, Mon.–Fri. 0900–1300 and 1400–1700, Sat. 0900–1200) is in the Civic Center near Labasa Bus Station.

The **Post Shop** at the Labasa Post Office sells large colored topographical maps of the main islands of Fiji.

The ANZ Bank is opposite the bus station, and the Westpac Bank is farther west on Nasekula Road. Both provide ATMs outside their offices. **Western Union Money Exchange** (tel. 881-4147, weekdays 0715–1715, Sat. 0715–1515), on Nasekula Road near the Centerpoint Hotel, charges no commission but their rate isn't the best.

You can check your email at the **Govinda Internet Café** (tel. 881-8492, www.govinda internetcafe.com, Mon.–Sat. 0800–1900, Sun. 1500–1900) next to the Pacific Sun office on Nasekula Road at F$2 an hour.

Public toilets are behind the market.

Health

The **Northern District Hospital** (tel. 881-1444), northeast of the river, is open 24 hours a day for emergencies.

Less serious medical problems should be taken to a private doctor, such as Dr. Pardeep Singh (tel. 881-3824, weekdays 0800–1300 and 1400–1600, Sat. 0800–1300) in Savilla House next to the Civic Center. Otherwise, Dr. Rajesh Kumar (15 Nanuku St., tel. 881-1461) is across the street from the Labasa Club.

The **Labasa Women's Crisis Center** (tel. 881-4609, www.fijiwomen.com, weekdays 0830–1500), in Bayly House on Siberia Road near the hospital, offers free and confidential counseling for women.

My Chemist (tel. 881-4611) is on Nasekula Road opposite the post office.

GETTING THERE AND AROUND
By Air

Pacific Sun (tel. 881-1454, Mon.–Fri. 0800–1700, Sat. 0800–1200), at Northern Travel on the corner of Nasekula Road and Damanu Street, flies to Nadi (F$212) three times a day and to Suva (F$182) twice daily. Flights to Nadi via Suva are more expensive than nonstop flights. Ask inside their office about special reduced fares.

To get to the airport, 10 kilometers southwest of Labasa, take a taxi (F$8) or the hourly green-and-yellow Waiqele bus (F$1.15).

By Boat

Patterson Brothers Shipping (tel. 881-2444) has an office near Pacific Sun on Nasekula Road where you can book your bus/ferry/bus ticket through to Suva via Nabouwalu and Natovi (10 hours, F$55). This bus leaves Labasa at 0600 fives times a week, and passengers arrive in Suva at 1830. Another service is straight through to Levuka (F$60).

Consort Shipping Line (tel. 881-1454, www.consortshipping.com.fj) has a combined office with Pacific Sun at the corner of Nasekula Road and Damanu Street where you can book passage on the *Spirit of Fiji Islands* from Savusavu to Suva and Taveuni.

Blight Water Shipping (tel. 881-8471, www.blighwatershipping.com.fj) has an office opposite Pacific Sun on Nasekula Road booking passage to Suva (F$61 economy) on the *Suilven*.

Two bus/boat ferry services link Labasa to Taveuni. Gulam Nabi (tel. 881-2580), near Patterson Brothers, books the **Grace Ferry Service** bus/boat to Taveuni, departing Tuesday, Thursday, Friday, and Saturday at 0500 (seven hours, F$30). Star Cake Restaurant (tel. 823-1617), just down from Gulam Nabi, sells tickets for **KaraMal Ferry Services,** formerly known as the *Raja* ferry. Their bus leaves Labasa on Monday, Wednesday, Friday, and Saturday at 0500 (F$30).

To be dropped off on Kia Island on the Great Sea Reef, negotiate with the fishing boats tied up near the Labasa Club. Village boats from Kia and Udu Point sometimes unload at the Government Wharf on the other side of town.

By Road

Buses from Labasa to Savusavu (94 km, three hours, F$6.25) leave at 0700, 0800, 0930, 1230, and 1615, a very beautiful ride on an excellent paved highway over the Waisali Saddle between the Korotini and Valili mountains and along the palm-studded coast. The bus from Labasa to Savusavu via Natewa Bay leaves at 0900.

There are four regular buses a day to Nabouwalu (210 km, F$13.50), a dusty, tiring six-hour trip. Other buses are Labasa to Kubulau via Wailevu at 1400 and Labasa to Daria (F$14.45) via Nabouwalu.

Rental cars are available from **Carpenters Rentals** (Rosawa St., tel. 881-1522, www.carpenters.com.fj), beside the entrance to the Grand Eastern Hotel, starting at F$202 a day including insurance for a twin-cab four-wheel-drive vehicle (F$500 deposit). You must reserve, as they're in short supply. **Vanua Rentals,** in the Mobil service station on the corner of Nanuku and Jadaram Streets, charges F$100 a day with a F$500 deposit. **Avis** (tel. 881-5892, www.avis.com.fj), at Asco Motors next to Jame Mosque just outside town, has cars from F$115. Nearby, **Budget Rent A Car** (tel. 881-1999, www.budget.com.fj) is at Niranjan's Mazda dealership on Zoing Place up Ivi Street from opposite the Jame Mosque west of town. Budget cars start at F$122 plus F$22 insurance. Obtaining gasoline outside the two main towns is difficult, so tank up.

Labasa taxis have meters that start at F$1.50 flag fall (or F$2 from 2200–0600), then F$0.50 a kilometer.

◖ NATEWA BAY AND UDU POINT

Natewa Bay is the largest bay in the South Pacific, almost bisecting the island of Vanua

VANUA LEVU

the Labasa-Savusavu-Labasa express bus at Labasa Bus Station

Levu. It's an area seldom visited by tourists, although daily bus service between Labasa and Savusavu makes it easily accessible. The sea kayaking is often good along this coast.

Unique to Natewa Bay are "dolphin-calling" trips, during which a Fijian boatman "calls" dolphins by using traditional magic. It's said that when the bay is flat and calm, two pods totaling as many as 100 dolphins can be seen! Trips can be organized through the Lomalagi Resort (tel. 828-4585, www.lomalagi.com) at the south end of Natewa Bay.

At Udu Point, Vanua Levu's northeastern-most tip, a Meridian Wall was built in 1999 just west of Vunikodi village to mark the spot where the 180-degree longitudinal meridian and international date line cut across the island. Both sunset and sunrise can be observed from the wall. To get there, you must "charge" (charter) or hire a boat from Wainigadru, where the Natewa Bay buses call.

Getting There

A Vishnu Holdings (tel. 885-0276) bus between Labasa and Savusavu takes the roundabout route via Natewa Bay, departing both ends at 0900 every morning (seven hours, F$18). Other Natewa Bay buses from Savusavu may finish their runs at Yanuavou or Wainigadru.

WESTERN VANUA LEVU

Most people pass through western Vanua Levu in transit between Viti Levu and Labasa. However, it's worth spending a night in the tidy little government station of Nabouwalu, where the ferry from Natovi ties up, to get a taste of small-town life seldom experienced by foreign visitors. Unless you have your own transportation, it's not easy to follow the south coast from Nabouwalu to Savusavu and almost everyone rides a bus along the dusty north coast highway nonstop to Labasa.

Nabouwalu

The Patterson Brothers ferry from Viti Levu ties up to a wharf in this friendly little government station (the headquarters of Bua Province), near the southern tip of Vanua Levu. The view from the wharf is picturesque, with Seseleka (421 m) and, in good weather, Yadua

---

THE CRESTED IGUANA

In 1979, a new species of lizard, the crested iguana (*Brachylophus vitiensis*), was discovered on uninhabited Yaduatabu Island, a tiny 70-hectare dot in Bligh Water off the west end of Vanua Levu. These iguanas are similar to those of the Galapagos Islands, and they may have arrived thousands of years ago on floating rafts of vegetation. The same species was later found on some islands in the Yasawa and Mamanuca Groups.

Both sexes are shiny emerald green with white stripes, and the animals turn black when alarmed. The females have longer tails, growing up to 90 centimeters long. Both sexes have a yellow snout. They're not to be confused with the more common banded iguana found elsewhere in Fiji, the male of which is also green with white stripes, while the female is totally green.

Yaduatabu is separated from neighboring Yadua Island by only 200 meters of shallow water, and upon discovery the iguanas were being threatened by a large colony of feral goats that was consuming their habitat. Fortunately, the National Trust for Fiji Islands took over management of the island, created an iguana sanctuary with an honorary warden from the Fijian village on Yadua, and eliminated the goats.

About 6,000 lizards are present, basking in the sun in the canopy during the day and coming down to the lower branches at night. It's possible to visit Yaduatabu by taking the ferry to Nabouwalu, then hiring a local boat to Yadua, where guides can be arranged. Prior permission must be obtained from the National Trust for Fiji Islands office in Suva.

Island visible to the northwest. Nabouwalu has a high-tech, 24-hour electricity supply system based on windmills and solar panels, installed in early 1998. Most of the 600 residents of this area are indigenous Fijians.

Fijian women in the small market on the corner of the coastal and wharf roads serve a good lunch of fish in *lolo* (coconut milk). Small stores nearby sell groceries.

The lovely **Government Resthouse,** near the police station on the hillside above the wharf at Nabouwalu, has two rooms with shared cooking facilities at F$20 per person. Try to make advance reservations with the district officer of Bua, in Nabouwalu (tel. 883-6027, weekdays 0800–1700). Upon arrival, check in at the administrative offices in the provincial headquarters, a kilometer up the road from the post office. If you already have a booking, you can check in with the caretaker at the Resthouse itself Saturdays 0800–1200, but it's not possible to check in on Saturday afternoons, Sundays, or after 1700.

The Patterson Brothers car ferry sails from Natovi on Viti Levu to Nabouwalu Monday, Tuesday, Thursday, Friday, and Saturday at about 0800 (four hours, F$45), returning from Nabouwalu to Natovi at 1230. At Natovi, there are immediate bus connections to/from Suva, and the boat continues to Buresala on Ovalau Island, where it spends the night. Getting a car onto the 20-vehicle *Spirit of Harmony* without reservations can be difficult, as more than a dozen trucks are often lined up waiting to go. The schedule often varies. Patterson Brothers runs an express bus between Nabouwalu and Labasa for ferry passengers only (must be booked in conjunction with a ferry ticket). This bus takes only four hours to cover the 137 kilometers to Labasa, compared to the six hours required by the two regular buses, which make numerous detours and stops.

East of Nabouwalu

There's a 141-kilometer road along the south coast of Vanua Levu from Nabouwalu to Savusavu, but occasional eastbound carriers

from Nabouwalu reach only as far as Daria, while westbound buses go as far as Kiobo beyond the former Mount Kasi Gold Mine (Kubulau bus). There also a bus to Daria from Labasa. At Cogea, five kilometers north of Daria, are some small hot springs the local people use for bathing.

The **Mount Kasi Gold Mine** near Dawara, in the hills above the west end of Savusavu Bay, 70 kilometers from Savusavu, produced 60,000 ounces of gold between 1932 and 1946. Beginning in 1979, several companies did exploratory work in the area in hope of reviving the mine, and in 1996, it was recommissioned by Pacific Island Gold, which began extracting about 40,000 ounces a year from the mine. In 1998, the mine was forced to close again, and the 170 workers were laid off due to low gold prices on the world market.

The Wainunu River area is a virtually untouched wilderness with a tropical rainforest that has never been logged. Wainunu has a lot of history. Tea, coffee, rubber, and copra were produced here and loaded on tall ships for Levuka in the 19th century. David Whippy of Nantucket, the founder of Levuka, is buried here and his descendants live on the estate today.

Joe Whippy runs 【 **Blue Parrot Bures** (tel. 829-0290, blueparrotbures@yahoo.com) at Wainunu Bay, a half-day walk from Daria. The two thatched *bure* with bath are F$150 per person, while the four-bed dorm in the main building is F$120 per person. The rates include all meals (mostly vegetarian) and a boat trip on the Wainunu River. Fishing trips are possible. Joe is a bit of a character and a few days with him would be an in-depth introduction to the history and environment of this part of Fiji. The Kubulau buses from Labasa and Savusavu stop 10 kilometers short of here and arrive after dark, but you can hire a carrier from Savusavu for the 2.5-hour trip direct to Blue Parrot at F$200.

The Road to Labasa

The twisting, tiring north coast bus ride from

suspension bridge at Bua village

Nabouwalu to Labasa takes you past Fijian villages, rice paddies, and cane fields. The early sandalwood traders put in at **Bua Bay.** At Bua village on Bua Bay is a large suspension bridge. Dry open countryside stretches west of Bua to Seseleka (421 m). Much of this part of the island has been reforested with pine.

Farther east, the road passes a major rice-growing area and runs along the **Dreketi River,** Vanua Levu's largest. A rice mill at Dreketi and citrus project at Batiri are features of this area. The pavement begins at Dreketi but older sections, beyond the junction with the road from Savusavu, are in bad shape. In the Seaqaqa settlement area between Batiri and Labasa, about 60 square kilometers of native land were cleared and planted with sugarcane and pine during the 1970s.

(Palmlea Lodge and Bures (tel. 828-2220, www.palmleafarms.com) is on an organic farm four kilometers off the highway from Tabia School, 14 kilometers west of Labasa. Palmlea styles itself as Fiji's "Oceanside Eco Hideaway" with two one-bedroom *bure* at F$179–219 double and one two-bedroom *bure* at F$289–329 for up to four guests. Taxes, breakfast, and transfers from Labasa Airport are included. There's an attractive restaurant (mains F$17–28) and a 25-meter lap swimming pool. They also have a speedboat for surfing and fishing trips. There's a secluded golden sand beach 10 minutes by rowboat from the resort jetty. The managers pack a picnic lunch and beverages for their guests to have the beach all to themselves. A half-day boat trip to a good snorkeling spot is $65 per person (minimum of two) and boat trips to the Great Sea Reef are also possible. A taxi from Labasa will be about F$20 one-way. Aside from through buses on the highway, three daily yellow and blue buses to Naduri and Nasea/Nugumu (F$1.70) pass within one kilometer of Palmlea.

Nukubati Island

The luxury-category **Nukubati Island Resort** (tel. 603-0919, www.nukubati.com) sits on tiny Nukubati Island, one kilometer off the north shore of Vanua Levu, 40 kilometers west of Labasa. The four fan-cooled beachfront suites are F$1,150/1,350 single/double, while the three honeymoon *bure* are F$1,450/1,520, plus 17.5 percent tax. There's a five-night minimum stay. Children are not allowed. Meals (emphasis on seafood, especially lobster), drinks, and non-motorized activities are included, but sportfishing and scuba diving (certified divers only) are extra. Access is via Nukubati Landing, a one-hour drive west of Labasa Airport (transfer included in the price). This is the closest upscale resort to the Great Sea Reef, the fifth-longest barrier reef in the world. And while other reefs around Fiji have been seriously damaged by coral bleaching, this area is less affected. No swimming pool is provided, but the beach consists of white coral sand.

Savusavu and Vicinity

Savusavu (www.fiji-savusavu.com) is a picturesque little town opposite Nawi Island on Savusavu Bay. The view from here across to the mountains of southwestern Vanua Levu and down the coast toward Nabouwalu is superlatively lovely. In the 1860s, Europeans arrived to establish coconut plantations. They mixed with the Fijians, and even though the copra business went bust in the 1930s, their descendants and the Fijian villagers still supply copra to a coconut-oil mill, eight kilometers west of Savusavu, giving this side of Vanua Levu a pleasant agricultural air. In 2000, the first black pearl farm was established on the far side of Nawi Island, and J. Hunter Pearls are now available at Prouds outlets throughout Fiji.

Savusavu's urban population of 7,000 is almost evenly split between Indo-Fijians and indigenous Fijians, with many part-Fijians here too. One of Fiji's largest white expatriate communities is also present, including many Americans who have bought property here.

Savusavu is Vanua Levu's main port, and cruising yachts often rock at anchor offshore, sheltered from the open waters of Savusavu Bay by Nawi Island. The surrounding mountains and reefs also make Savusavu a well-protected hurricane refuge. The diving possibilities of this area were recognized by Jean-Michel Cousteau in 1990, when he selected Savusavu as the base for his Project Ocean Search. Access to good snorkeling is difficult, however, as the finest beaches are under the control of the top-end resorts and much other shore access is over extremely sharp karst. The nicest public beach near town is on Lesiaceva Point, just outside the Jean-Michel Cousteau Fiji Islands Resort. Although much smaller than Labasa, Savusavu is the administrative center of Cakaudrove Province and has three banks. In recent years, tourism has taken off around Savusavu, with

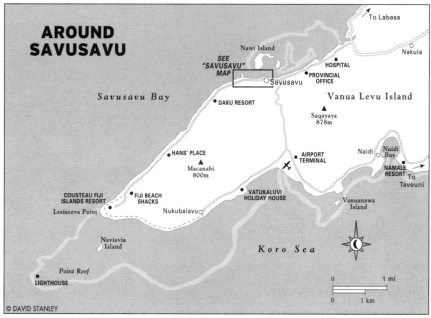

AROUND SAVUSAVU

To Labasa

Nawi Island

Nakula

SEE "SAVUSAVU" MAP

HOSPITAL

PROVINCIAL OFFICE

Savusavu

Savusavu Bay

DAKU RESORT

Vanua Levu Island

Saqayaya 878m

HANS' PLACE

Macanabi 800m

AIRPORT TERMINAL

Naidi

Naidi Bay

NAMALE RESORT

To Taveuni

COUSTEAU FIJI ISLANDS RESORT

FIJI BEACH SHACKS

VATUKALUVI HOLIDAY HOUSE

Lesiaceva Point

Nukubalavu

Vanuanawa Island

Naviavia Island

Koro Sea

Point Reef

LIGHTHOUSE

0   1 mi

0   1 km

© DAVID STANLEY

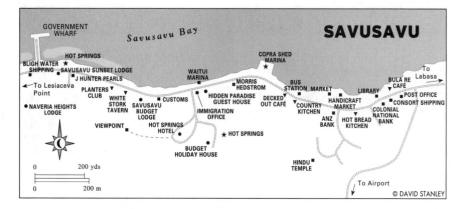

SAVUSAVU

Savusavu Bay

GOVERNMENT WHARF

HOT SPRINGS

BLIGH WATER SHIPPING ★
SAVUSAVU SUNSET LODGE
J HUNTER PEARLS

WAITUI MARINA

COPRA SHED MARINA ★

← To Lesiaceva Point

PLANTERS CLUB

MORRIS HEDSTROM

BUS STATION MARKET

BULA RE CAFÉ

To Labasa →

POST OFFICE

● NAVERIA HEIGHTS LODGE

WHITE STORK TAVERN

CUSTOMS

HIDDEN PARADISE GUEST HOUSE

DECKED OUT CAFÉ

LIBRARY

HANDICRAFT MARKET

CONSORT SHIPPING

SAVUSAVU BUDGET LODGE

IMMIGRATION OFFICE

COUNTRY KITCHEN

ANZ BANK

HOT BREAD KITCHEN

COLONIAL NATIONAL BANK

VIEWPOINT

HOT SPRINGS HOTEL

★ HOT SPRINGS

BUDGET HOLIDAY HOUSE

HINDU TEMPLE

0   200 yds

0   200 m

To Airport

© DAVID STANLEY

new resorts springing up, though the town is far from spoiled.

SIGHTS

The one main street through Savusavu consists of a motley collection of Indian and Chinese shops, parked taxis, loitering locals, and a clutch of tourists. The **market** in the center of town always bustles but is biggest early Saturday morning. Notice the kava dens at the back of the market. Nearby, the **Handicraft Center** (weekdays 0730–1700, Sat. 0730–1500), behind the Savusavu Town Council opposite the ANZ Bank, displays numerous grotesque masks with a few good objects mixed in.

The **Copra Shed Marina** is like a small museum, with map displays and historical photos, information boards, fancy boutiques, and many of Savusavu's tourist services. Tako

The Copra Shed Marina in Savusavu contains many facilities for visitors.

VANUA LEVU

© DAVID STANLEY

© DAVID STANLEY

Locals often use the Savusavu hot springs to cook food.

Handicrafts and The Art Gallery at the marina carry some very nice handicrafts and works of art. In front of the marina is a stone dated to 1880, which is said to be from Fiji's first copra mill. To the west is Savusavu's second yachting center, the **Waitui Marina.** A wonderful scenic viewpoint (and romantic spot to watch a sunset) is on the hill just above and west of the Hot Springs Hotel, above the Waitui Marina.

Visit the small **hot springs** boiling out among fractured coral below and behind the Hot Springs Hotel. Residents use the springs to cook native vegetables; bathing is not possible. These and smaller hot springs along the shore of Savusavu Bay, across the street from J. Hunter Pearls near the main wharf, are reminders that the whole area was once a caldera.

For a good circle trip, take a bus or taxi from Savusavu past the airport to **Nukubalavu** village (six km, F$8) at the end of the road along the south side of the peninsula. Buses leave Savusavu for Nukubalavu at 0930, 1300, and 1700 (F$1.15). From here you can walk west along the beach to the Cousteau Fiji Islands

Resort on **Lesiaceva Point** in about an hour at low tide. Try to avoid cutting through the resort at the end of the hike, as the Cousteau management disapproves (all beaches in Fiji are public up to two meters above the high-tide mark). From Lesiaceva, it's six kilometers by road back to Savusavu.

◖ Waisali Rainforest Reserve

For some mountain hiking, ask one of the Labasa bus drivers to drop you at the entrance to the Waisali Rainforest Reserve (Mon.–Sat. 0900–1500, admission F$8/2 adult/student, www.nationaltrust.org.fj), established by the National Trust for Fiji in 1991, about 25 kilometers northwest of Savusavu. This 116-hectare reserve protects one of Vanua Levu's last unexploited tropical rainforests, with native species such as the *dakua, yaka,* and *yasi* well represented. Some of Fiji's few remaining giant kauri trees are here. The rare red-breasted musk parrot and orange dove are among the 21 bird species recorded here. A short nature trail leads to viewpoints offering sweeping views. In all, two hours of hiking is available. Swimming in the rock pool near the waterfall is no longer permitted but there's a *bure* where you can relax.

ENTERTAINMENT

Drinkers can repair to the **Planters Club** (tel. 885-0233, Mon.–Thurs. 1100–2100, Fri. and Sat. 1100–2200, Sun. 1000–2000) toward the wharf—this place never runs out of Fiji Bitter. The weekend dances at the club are local events. Despite the Members Only sign, visitors are welcome. It's a vintage colonial club.

The **White Stork Tavern,** next to the Planters Club, is a rough public bar open Thursday–Saturday from 1900–midnight.

The **Waitui Marina** (tel. 885-3031 or 997-2558, waituimarina.bebi-electronics.com, daily 1000–2200) has a pleasant bar that occasionally organizes *lovo* or barbecue nights.

The bar at the **Copra Shed Marina** (daily 1100–2200) is rather hidden in the northeast corner of the building—ask. Happy hour is 1730–1830. Remove your hat as you enter.

The **Uro's Nite Club** (tel. 885-0366 or 923-8422), upstairs in the building beside the Bula Re Café, is "the place to be" on Thursday, Friday, and Saturday nights.

SPORTS AND RECREATION

Rock'n Downunder Divers (tel. 885-3447, www.dive-savusavu.com, Mon.–Fri. 0830–1600, Sat. 0900–1300) at the Waitui Marina offers one-/two-tank dives at F$110/195, including gear. Snorkeling trips are F$50/70 for two/three locations, including gear. They rent bicycles at F$35 a day and kayaks at F$25/40 single/double for half a day. The friendly staff can also organize land-based village sightseeing tours if enough people are interested.

The Jean-Michel Cousteau Fiji Islands Resort and Koro Sun Resort also have dive shops.

Deep sea game fishing is offered by **Ika Levu Fishing Charters** (tel. 994-8506, www.fishinginfiji.com) at F$900 a half day (0700–1200) or F$1,500 a full day (0700–1600) for up to six anglers. You can book through Trip'N

The Planters Club offers food and drink in pleasant surroundings.

VANUA LEVU

© DAVID STANLEY

Tour Travel (tel. 885-3154, tripntour@connect. com.fj) in the Copra Shed Marina.

Tours

J. Hunter Pearls (tel. 885-0821, www.pearls fiji.com) runs tours to their pearl farm beside Nawi Island weekdays at 0930 and 1330 (F$25). Bring along a mask and snorkel if you want to swim between the clam racks. Inquire at their pearl salesroom just past the Planters Club.

Cruises to Taveuni and adjacent islands on the three-masted schooner *Tui Tai* can be booked at **Tui Tai Adventure Cruises** (tel. 885-3032, www.tuitai.com) beside the Planters Club. The five-day cruises begin at F$6,300 per person, plus 17.5 percent tax.

ACCOMMODATIONS
Under US$25

Rachel Lal's six-room **(** **Budget Holiday House** (tel. 885-0149) is just behind the Hot Springs Hotel. The five clean rooms with shared bath cost F$30/40 single/double. You might be allowed to camp here for F$8. The rooms are nicer than those at Hidden Paradise but breakfast is not provided. There's a well-equipped common kitchen. A cacophony of dogs, roosters, and the neighbor's kids will bid you good morning.

US$25-50

Hidden Paradise Guest House (tel. 885-0106, hiddenparadise@connect.com.fj), just beyond Morris Hedstrom, has six rather hot wooden rooms at F$30 per person with fan and shared bath (F$40 pp with air-conditioning), including a good breakfast. A seven-bed dorm in back is used for overflows. Cooking and washing facilities are provided.

Savusavu Budget Lodge (tel. 885-3127, www.savusavubudgetlodge.com), a two-story concrete building on the main street, has five standard rooms with bath at F$40/50 single/double and eight air-conditioned rooms at F$61/70, breakfast included. Their restaurant (Mon.–Sat. 0800–2000, Sun. 0800–1800) serves curry meals in the F$5 range and beer is available.

Savusavu Sunset Lodge (tel. 885-2171), a two-story guest house near the Government Wharf, offers good views from the upper deck. The four fan-cooled rooms with shared bath are F$35/45/55 single/double/triple, including breakfast. The four air-conditioned rooms with fridge and TV are F$70 single or double.

Hans' Place (tel. 885-0621, www.fiji-holiday .com), on the Savusavu peninsula three kilometers southwest of town, is built on a hillside with good sunset views. The two self-catering units are F$60/250/750 double a day/week/ month or F$80/350/950. It's a good choice for a couple wishing to spend a week or more in this area, but the cottages are too small for families.

The **Bayside Bure** next to the Jean-Michel Cousteau Fiji Islands Resort is a one-room self-catering cabin with TV and deck at F$50/60 single/double, plus tax. A nice beach with great snorkeling is just across the road. Book through Trip'N Tour Travel (tel. 885-3154, tripntour@ connect.com.fj) at the Copra Shed Marina.

US$50-100

The **Copra Shed Marina Apartments** (tel. 885-0457, coprashed@connect.com.fj), above the Captain's Café in the Copra Shed Marina, has three apartments for rent. One is F$95 for up to three persons with the shower downstairs; the other two are F$165 accommodating four with private bath. Both have cooking facilities.

The **Hot Springs Hotel** (tel. 885-0195, www.savusavufiji.com), on the hillside overlooking Savusavu Bay, is named for the nearby thermal springs and steam vents. There are 48 rooms, all with balconies offering splendid views. Fan rooms on the second floor are F$100 single or double, including breakfast, while the air-conditioned rooms on the third and fourth floors are F$132. All rooms have a mini-fridge. The four-bed dormitories on the first floor are F$37 per person and popular among divers. This former Travelodge is beginning to show its age and some of the rooms could use a cleaning. Even so, the price is right. No beach is nearby, but the swimming pool terrace is pleasant. The Mahi Bar on the deck above the pool is open daily. Catch the sunset here.

The fussy visitor may be better served at **❰ Naveria Heights Lodge** (tel. 885-0348, www.naveriaheightsfiji.com), a bright cheery place with three bungalows perched on a hilltop a kilometer above the Government Wharf. There's a wonderful view from the swimming pool. It's F$160 single or double, including a tasty breakfast, tax, and airport transfers with special packages for seven nights. The lodge has an active fitness program with healthy food and exercise activities. They also organize hiking, bird-watching, and mountain biking tours for guests. Only four-wheel-drive vehicles can climb the gravel road to Naveria Heights. A few four-wheel-drive taxis do exist in Savusavu (F$8) or you can call and ask to be picked up from the main road.

The **Daku Resort** (tel. 885-0046, www.dakuresort.com), one kilometer west of the ferry landing, was managed by the Beachcomber Island crowd from Lautoka until 2004. Before then it was an Anglican Church retreat. Today this friendly "upscale budget" property offers a variety of room types. The four tin-roofed garden *bure* with fan and fridge (but no cooking) on the nicely landscaped grounds just below the pool go for F$180 single or double, while two larger family bungalows above the restaurant rent for F$250. If you want a kitchen, there's a cottage (F$240) and villa (F$300) on the hill and a house (F$240) next to the pool. A self-catering, three-bedroom "beach house" next to the entrance is F$280. Add the 5 percent hotel tax to these rates. The mediocre beach just across the dusty road has some snorkeling possibilities, though the visibility isn't the best (and you shouldn't leave valuables unattended).

The **Vatukaluvi Holiday House** (tel. 862-1783, geofftaylor@connect.com.fj), on the south side of the peninsula, one kilometer west of Savusavu airport, accommodates five people at F$120 for the whole breezy house (or a reduced rate for two weeks). Cooking facilities and fridge are provided, and there's good snorkeling off the beach. Ask for Geoff

Taylor, vice-commodore of the Savusavu Yacht Club, at the Copra Shed Marina. A taxi to Vatukaluvi will cost F$4 from the airport or F$6 from Savusavu (or perhaps less if the driver uses the meter).

The folks at the Bula Re Café (tel. 920-2161) rent a **Waterfront Apartment** above the café with TV and cooking facilities at F$112 a night. Weekly and monthly rates are available.

US$150-250

❰ Fiji Beach Shacks (tel. 885-1002, www.fijibeachshacks.com) is a two-bedroom "House of Bamboo" on the hillside near the Cousteau Fiji Islands Resort at Lesiaceva. The wonderful view makes the 120 steps up from the beach worth the climb. This luxury dwelling includes a full kitchen, lounge, two bathrooms, laundry, and private plunge pool at F$295 double, plus 17.5 percent tax (minimum stay three nights). Each extra person is only F$20 a night, making this a fine choice for families or small groups. Transfers from Savusavu Airport are included.

Tropic Splendor Beachfront Cottage (tel. 851-0152, www.tropic-splendor-fiji.com), on the north shore of Savusavu Bay west of town, offers honeymooners and adventure travelers the chance to have their own private cottage with a wrap-around deck overlooking the beach and garden. Inside there's a kitchen and fridge, DVD library, TV, king-size bed, and tiled bathroom. Laundry facilities are available. It's F$360 double plus 17.5 percent tax, including a daily fruit basket and transfers from Savusavu Airport (minimum stay three nights). Sea kayaks and snorkeling gear are provided. Your friendly hosts will make you feel right at home.

Over US$250

In 1994, oceanographer Jean-Michel Cousteau, son of the famous Jacques Cousteau, purchased a hotel on Lesiaceva Point, six kilometers southwest of Savusavu. The **Jean-Michel Cousteau Fiji Islands Resort** (tel. 885-0188, www.fijiresort.com) stylishly re-creates a Fijian village with 25 small thatched *bure.* The ecotourism theme is used to justify the lack of air-conditioning, TVs, radios, and telephones in the rooms. Bring insect repellent. Garden accommodations, airport transfers, and meals begin at F$912/1,310 single/double, plus 17.5 percent tax (minimum stay three nights). Alcohol and fancy coffees are extra (don't accept any "complimentary" drinks unless you're prepared to pay for them). There's also pressure to contribute to various causes and funds. The restaurant is built like a towering pagan temple, and non-guests wishing to dine there *must* reserve (be aware, it's pricey). Arrive on time for breakfast, please. Up to two children under 13 eat and sleep free when sharing with their parents (children over 12 are F$400 each). A Bula Camp for those aged 3–9 functions 0900–2100 and kids and adults have separate little swimming pools. This resort also caters to the romantic-couples market with spa and massage treatments (beginning at F$130), private island picnics (F$75 per couple), and pier dining by candlelight (F$70 per couple for the set-up). Free activities include sailing, kayaking, glass-bottom boat trips, tennis, yoga, water aerobics in the pool, videos, slide shows, tours and evenings with the on-site marine biologist or cultural host, rainforest trips, and visits to a local Fijian village. In addition, the outstanding on-site dive operation, L'Aventure Cousteau, offers scuba diving (F$150/250 for one/two tanks plus tax and gear) and PADI scuba instruction (F$1,000 plus tax and gear for full certification). Cousteau himself is in residence occasionally, and he joins guests on the morning dive when he's in the mood. To avoid damaging the reef, they use 21 buoyed dive sites off southern Vanua Levu. There's good snorkeling off their mediocre beach (ask about Split Rock), though the resort's large Private Property signs warn non-guests to keep out. A taxi from Savusavu shouldn't be over F$6.

FOOD

The breakfast buffet at the **Seaview Restaurant** (tel. 885-0106, daily 0700–1000), at Hidden Paradise Guest House near the Waitui Marina, is a good value. You can get an excellent curry lunch here as well (Mon.–Sat. 0900–1600).

Savusavu's top restaurant is **Surf and Turf** (tel. 885-3033, daily 1000–1430 and 1730–2130) on the back side of the Copra Shed Marina with a deck overlooking the bay. This is a good place to sample traditional Fijian fare. Try the pumpkin soup, *kokoda,* green curry tuna, sirloin steak, or cinnamon ice cream with banana fritters. Dinner is in the F$15–25 range, lobster F$40. In the evening, the outdoor seating on the wharf is nice.

The less formal **Captains Café** (tel. 855-0511) on the front side of the Copra Shed Marina serves enchiladas (F$8.50), fajitas (F$9.50), quesadillas (F$8), burgers (F$10), chicken (F$10.50), fish and chips (F$9.50), and *laksa* (F$13.50). Unlike Surf and Turf, the Captains Café is alcohol-free.

The **Decked Out Café** (tel. 885-2929, Mon.–Thurs. 0800–1600, Fri. 0800–2300, Sat. 0800–2100), just east of the Copra Shed Marina and across the street, has a large deck outside where you can consume your beer, specialty coffee (F$4), shake (F$5), or kai-loma fruit smoothie (F$5). Their menu also includes burgers (F$9.50), steak sandwich (F$8), *kokoda* (F$9.50), fish fillet (F$15), and pizza (F$15–20).

The **Country Kitchen** (tel. 822-2071, daily 0730–1700), opposite the bus station, offers large servings of curries, chop suey, and fried rice at F$6.

The spacious **Chong Pong Restaurant** (tel. 885-0588), above a supermarket opposite Savusavu Market, serves unpretentious Chinese chicken, pork, beef, mutton, seafood, and vegetarian meals at F$5–8. The decor is basic but the chef is from China and it's excellent value. You can even order a beer!

The **Blue Water Restaurant** (tel. 885-0810, daily 0900–2200), opposite the market, has chicken and lamb dishes at F$6.50–7.50, fish F$7.50, prawns F$9.50, pizza F$12–23, and vegetables F$5. It's a bit more attractive than the Chong Pong and beer is also served here.

The **Bula Re Café** (tel. 920-2161, Mon.–Sat.

0900–1700), opposite the post office, serves a full range of drinks, including specialty coffees, wines, and beers, and there's a nice seaside patio in back overlooking the bay. Try the ice cream with coffee.

Emanuels Restaurant (tel. 828-3053) at the north end of town has filling local meals for F$5.

OTHER PRACTICALITIES
Information and Services
The **Savusavu Branch Library** (tel. 885-0154, Mon.–Thurs. 0900–1630, Fri. 0900–1600) is opposite the Colonial National Bank.

The Yacht Shop (tel. 885-0040) at the Copra Shed Marina sells local nautical charts (F$22.50) and British charts (F$95).

The ANZ Bank and Westpac Bank branches in Savusavu charge F$5 commission on exchanges whereas the **Colonial National Bank** charges none. All three banks have ATMs outside. **Express Currency Exchange** (tel. 885-1566), just beyond the Colonial National Bank on Main Street, charges no commission but gives a rather poor rate. Use them for changing small amounts.

Internet access is available at the **Savusavu Internet Café** (tel. 885-3250, Mon.–Fri. 0830–1700, Sat. 0830–1700) in front of the Bula Re Café for F$0.07 a minute.

Free public toilets are behind the Town Council office opposite the ANZ Bank.

Yachting Facilities
The **Copra Shed Marina** (tel. 885-0457, copra shed@connect.com.fj) near the bus station allows visiting yachts to moor at F$10 a day. This includes use of the facilities by the whole crew, but a F$10 refundable key deposit is required for the shower. You can have your laundry done for F$9 (wash and dry).

Waitui Marina (tel. 885-3031 or 997-2558, waituimarina.bebi-electronics.com) offers similar services.

Yachts can clear Fiji customs in Savusavu. Arriving yachts should contact the Copra Shed Marina over VHF 16. The customs office (tel. 885-0727, weekdays 0800–1300 and

Savusavu has one of Fiji's favorite yacht anchorages just offshore.

1400–1600), where yachties must report after the quarantine check, is next to Savusavu Budget Lodge west of the Waitui Marina. After clearing quarantine and customs controls, yachties can proceed to the Immigration Department (tel. 885-0800), across the street from the Waitui Marina. If you check in after 1630 or on weekends or holidays, there's an additional charge on top of the usual quarantine fee.

Health
The **District Hospital** (tel. 885-0444, 0830–1600) is two kilometers east of Savusavu on the road to Labasa.

Dr. Joeli Taoi's **Private Clinic** (tel. 885-0721, Mon.–Thurs. 0900–1300 and 1400–1630, Fri. 0900–1300/1400–1500) is in the back of the Palm Court Mall opposite the Waitui Marina. There's also a pharmacy here.

GETTING THERE AND AROUND
By Air
Pacific Sun (tel. 885-0141), in the Copra Shed Marina, has flights to Savusavu three times a day from Nadi (F$195) and daily to Suva (F$169), but there are no flights between Savusavu and Taveuni. The airstrip is beside the main highway, three kilometers east of town. Local buses to Savusavu pass the airport about once an hour, or take a taxi for F$5.

By Boat
Consort Shipping Line Ltd. (tel. 885-0279, www.consortshipping.com.fj), above Express Currency Exchange, runs the large car ferry MV *Spirit of Fiji Islands* between Suva and Savusavu (14 hours, F$50/85 deck/four-bed cabin). The ferry leaves Savusavu southbound Wednesday at 2200 and Sunday at 1800, calling at Koro on the way to Suva. Wednesday at 0700 and Saturday at 1800, the *"Sofi"* leaves Savusavu for Taveuni (F$32). These schedules often change.

The MV *Suilven* of **Bligh Water Shipping Ltd.** (tel. 885-3191, www.blighwatershipping.com.fj), next to Morris Hedstrom Supermarket,

---

FIJI'S FINEST BUS RIDE
The scenic seven-hour bus ride between Labasa and Savusavu via Natewa Bay is like a trip through two distinct countries. For the first few hours, you're among sugar fields or dry barren hills, and the bus passengers around you will be mostly Indo-Fijian. Then you climb through a thickly forested area with few farms, and as the road drops again, extensive coconut plantations begin to appear. You look over your shoulder and notice that most of the bus passengers are now indigenous Fijians. Then comes the spectacular ride down Natewa Bay, climbing over lush headlands or roaring along the beach. Your first glimpse of Savusavu Bay as the old bus lumbers slowly over the hill beyond the airport is a thrilling culmination to this fascinating trip.

---

departs Savusavu for Suva (F$55/95 economy/first-class sleeper) Tuesday, Thursday, and Sunday at 2000, arriving at 0700 the next morning. Bligh Water Shipping operates the MV *Westerland* between Savusavu and Lautoka on Tuesday and Thursday at 2100 and Sunday at 1000 (F$55/95 deck/sleeper, 12 hours).

The Country Kitchen (tel. 885-0680) opposite the bus station sells tickets on the **Grace Ferry** bus/boat to Taveuni, departing Tuesday, Thursday, Friday, and Sunday at 0700 (F$25). The small store facing the bus station waiting room sells tickets on tickets for the KaraMal Ferry Service (ex-Raja) service to Taveuni, leaving Savusavu Monday, Wednesday, Friday, and Saturday at 0700 (F$25).

If you're interested in getting aboard a cruising yacht as unpaid crew, put up a notice advertising yourself at both yacht clubs and ask around.

By Road
Regular buses leave Savusavu for Labasa at 0700, 0930, 1330, 1430, and 1530 (92 km,

© RODBLAND

on the bus headed to Savusavu from the ferry

three hours, F$6.25). This ride over the Waisali Saddle is one of the most scenic in Fiji.

Otherwise, there's the seven-hour bus ride from Savusavu to Labasa via Natewa Bay (F$18), more than twice as long but even more intriguing. It departs each end daily at 0900. To go to Nabouwalu, you must change buses at Seaqaqa.

Buses along the Hibiscus Highway from Savusavu to Buca Bay and Napuka leave weekdays at 1030, 1300, and 1430 and weekends at 1030 and 1400 (three hours, F$7). Shorter runs to villages like Naweni are more frequent.

Buses leave Savusavu for Lesiaceva Point at 0730, 1200, and 1600 (F$1.15). For more information on buses headed south or east of Savusavu, call Vishnu Holdings (tel. 885-0276).

Numerous taxis congregate at Savusavu market; they're quite affordable for short trips in the vicinity, especially if they use the meter.

Trip'N Tour Travel (tel. 885-3154, tripn tour@connect.com.fj) in the Copra Shed Marina rents four-wheel-drive vehicles starting at F$110 a day, plus F$22 insurance. UTV buggies are F$95 per day, plus insurance. Bicycles are F$25, scooters F$45. They also have cottages and houses for rent.

Carpenters Rentals (tel. 885-0274, www .carpenters.com.fj) is at Carpenters Motors beside the Mobil service station at Morris Hedstrom Supermarket. **Budget Rent A Car** (tel. 881-1999, www.budget.com.fj) is next to the Bula Re Café.

James Rental Cars (tel. 885-0455) at the Total service station near the post office has cars at F$110 a day, including tax and insurance (F$500 deposit).

Avis (tel. 885-0960, www.avis.com.fj) at the Hot Springs Hotel has cars from F$125 all inclusive.

◖ NAMENALALA ISLAND

On a narrow high island southwest of Savusavu in the Koro Sea, ◖ **Moody's Namena** (tel. 828-0577, www.moodysnamenafiji.com) is one of Fiji's top hideaways. In 1984, Tom and Joan Moody leased Namenalala from the Fiji government, which needed a caretaker to protect the uninhabited island from poachers. Their present resort occupies less than 10 percent of Namenalala's 45 hectares, leaving the rest as a nesting ground to great flocks of red-footed boobies, banded rails, and Polynesian starlings. Giant clams proliferate in the surrounding waters within the 24-kilometer Namena Barrier Reef. November–March, hawksbill turtles haul themselves up onto the island's golden sands to lay their eggs (Namenalala is the last important nesting site for hawksbills left in Fiji). The corals along the nearby drop-offs are fabulous, and large pelagic fish glide in from the Koro Sea. Sea snakes abound. The Moodys have fought long and hard to protect Namenalala's fragile reefs from liveaboards that sometimes use them for high-impact night diving. In 2004, the Namena Marine Reserve was created, and divers must now pay F$25 per person per year to dive there. Only resort guests are allowed to come ashore.

Each of the Moody's six bamboo-and-wood hexagonal-shaped *bure* are perched on cliff tops, allowing panoramic views, while still well tucked away in the lush vegetation to ensure maximum privacy. Illuminated by romantic gas lighting, each features a private hardwood terrace with 270-degree views. Alternative energy is used as much as possible to maintain the atmosphere (though a diesel generator is used to do the laundry and recharge batteries).

The cost to stay here is F$2,900 per person double occupancy for five nights, including meals and transfers from Savusavu Airport. Add 17.5 percent tax. Singles pay F$220 a day extra. Children under 16 are not accepted. The food is excellent, thanks to Joan's firm hand in the kitchen and Tom's island-grown produce—though one reader found the food too "American" and would have preferred more fresh fish. The ice water on the tables and in the *bure* is a nice touch, but they don't sell liquor, so bring your own. In the evening, it's very quiet. Namenalala is in a rain shadow, so insects are not a problem.

This resort is perfect for bird-watching, fishing, and snorkeling, and scuba diving is available at F$570 plus tax for six tanks (certification card required). The soft corals at Namenalala are among the finest in the world, and the diversity of species is greater than on the Barrier Reef. If you want a holiday that combines unsullied nature with interesting characters and a certain elegance, you won't go wrong here. The remoteness is reflected in the price. Moody's closes in March and April every year.

Buca Bay and Rabi

ALONG THE HIBISCUS HIGHWAY

This lovely coastal highway runs 75 kilometers east from Savusavu to Natuvu on Buca Bay, then up the east coast of Vanua Levu to the Catholic mission station of **Napuka** at the end of the peninsula. In 2001, the first 20 kilometers or so east of Savusavu were paved but the rest is still rough. The tiring bus ride from Savusavu to Natuvu takes 2.5 hours.

Old frame mansions from the heyday of the 19th-century planters and 21st-century homes of newly arrived foreigners can be spotted among the palms, and offshore you'll see tiny flowerpot islands where the sea has undercut the coral rock. Buca Bay is a recognized "hurricane hole," where ships can find shelter during storms. Former Prime Minister Rabuka hails from Drekeniwai village on Natewa Bay.

Buses to Savusavu leave Buca Bay at 0800 and 1600 (75 km, three hours, F$5). Small passenger ferries leave Natuvu for Taveuni Monday–Saturday at 1030 (F$15). It's a beautiful boat trip, but can be rough if the wind is up.

Accommodations

The fanciest place around Savusavu is the **Namale Fiji Resort** (tel. 885-0435, www .namalefiji.com) on a beach nine kilometers east of Savusavu. The 16 thatched *bure* begin at F$1,568/1,850 single/double, and rise to F$4,370 for four people in the Dream House, which has a private plunge pool on its deck (add 17.5 percent tax to these nightly rates). Included are meals, drinks, airport transfers, and all activities other than scuba diving, sport fishing, and spa services. Motivational seminars with owner Tony Robbins in a 60-seat conference center are Namale's stock in trade and it gets crowded during these events. Namale caters only to in-house guests—there's no provision for sightseers who would like to stop in for lunch. Children under 12 are also banned.

In 2009, a Namale imitator opened on an adjacent island connected to Vanua Levu by a causeway. The two secluded oceanfront villas at **Savasi Island** (tel. 850-1192, www.savasi island.com) start at F$1,050 single or double including meals, airport transfers, bicycles, and kayaks. The 17.5 percent tax is extra. As a honeymoon hideaway, it's hard to beat.

The **Yau Kolo Campground** (tel. 885-3089, www.yaukolo.com), on the inland side of the road 13 kilometers east of Savusavu, offers tent sites at F$18 per person (own tent). The four-bed dorm is F$30 per person. A light breakfast and tax are included. Yau Kolo's café serves a variety of tasty, budget-priced dishes and the coldest beer around Savusavu (self-catering facilities are not provided). Activities include snorkeling, kayaking, fishing, and hiking. The garden setting is nice with fine lagoon views, and there's a natural swimming hole with cascades a five-minute hike up the creek.

The **Koro Sun Resort** (tel. 885-0262, www .korosunresort.com) is 14 kilometers east of Savusavu on the Hibiscus Highway. The eight garden bungalows start at F$610/740 single/double, while the eight two-bedroom hillside bungalows are F$630/760. Several more upscale units are also available. These inflated prices include all meals but 17.5 percent tax is extra. The resort's main building was reconstructed after a serious fire in February 2009. Set in a coconut grove, the Koro Sun has many interesting caves, pools, trails, falls,

ponds, and lakes nearby to explore. The resort's Rainforest Spa offers massage and body treatments. There are two swimming pools, a waterslide, two tennis courts, sportfishing, sea kayaking, mountain biking, and many other activities (non-motorized sports are included). The nine-hole golf course is pitted with crab holes and gets swampy after rains, but it's picturesque. It's too hilly for golf carts to be used. The snorkeling is fine as well, but the nearest swimmable beach is a kilometer away. Scuba diving is with Koro Sun Dive (tel. 885-2452, www.korosundive.com) at F$195 plus tax and gear for two tanks. Underwater weddings are possible! A dive site known as Dream House (a deep-water pinnacle) is right at Koro Sun's front door.

Collin McKenny from Seattle owns and operates the upscale **Lomalagi Resort** (tel. 828-4585, www.lomalagi.com) on Natewa Bay, three kilometers west of Nasinu village. It's three kilometers off the Hibiscus Highway up unpaved Salt Lake Road, about 25 kilometers from Savusavu airport. The six fan-cooled villas start at F$950 double including VAT, airport transfers, laundry, and meals (children under 12 not admitted, three-night minimum stay). The 5 percent hotel tax and alcohol are extra. Dining nightly with the owners at a common table is fun or you can request private candlelit dining on your deck. The villas are well spaced along the hillside above the sandy beach, and each has an excellent view. Two artificial waterfalls drop into the S-shaped saltwater swimming pool. Kayaks, mountain bikes, and snorkeling gear are loaned free. Beatle George Harrison is well remembered at Lomalagi for an evening of song he shared with local villagers during his stay. Non-guests are welcome to stop by for drinks, but call ahead to say you're coming if you'd like to order a meal.

Salt Lake Lodge (tel. 828-3005, www .saltlakelodgefiji.com) is on Salt Lake Road, just a five-minute walk from the junction with the Hibiscus Highway. It's right on the tidal Qaloqalo River with water access to both the picturesque Salt Lake and the Koro Sea.

The decks of the two *bure* face a private river beach and swimming pontoon. You can borrow a *bilibili* and pole yourself around. The two units together are F$200 double or F$275 for a group or family of up to six persons, plus 17.5 percent tax (minimum stay two nights). Only one party of guests is accepted at a time. The owners live on a large organic farm across the street, which means abundant fresh fruit and vegetables in season. The fishing is also good and an outboard is available for hire. A communal kitchen, gas barbecue, and fire pit are provided.

La Dolce Vita Holiday Villas (tel. 851-8023, www.ladolcevitafiji.com) occupies both sides of the road 30 kilometers east of Savusavu. The five spacious, air-conditioned units are F$665 plus 17.5 percent tax, including meals, non-motorized water sports, and laundry service. The electricity operates 1730–2300 only. There's a swimming pool and a six-hole golf course.

Hannibal's Resort (tel. 828-0830, www.hannibalsresortfiji.com), at Fawn Harbor 62 kilometers east of Savusavu, has five self-catering bungalows at F$118 double, including tax. The electricity comes from solar panels, water is recycled into their organic garden, and wastes are composted.

🄲 Vanaira Bay

Vanaira Bay is a wonderfully remote spot with a fine coral beach with good snorkeling. Even if you're not a diver, it's a great place to go on lovely walks along the palm-ringed sands in perfect solitude. You can enjoy it by staying at friendly 🄲 **Dolphin Bay Divers Retreat** (tel. 828-3001, www.dolphinbaydivers.com), at the far east end of Vanua Levu, directly across Somosomo Strait from Taveuni. The accommodations are in two rustic *bure* with solar electricity at F$95 single or double and three large safari tents without electricity at F$55, plus F$70 per person for all meals (and the food is good). The resident PADI diving instructor offers boat dives at F$190/550/890 for 2/6/10 tanks, including gear. Dolphin Bay offers night dives at F$80. Dolphin Bay is the only dive resort right on the famous Rainbow Reef. Their four-day scuba certification course (taught in English or German) costs F$650. You'll enjoy meeting Dolphin Bay's resident owners, Viola and Roland, who pioneered tourism to this little corner of Fiji. Boat transfers from Taveuni wharf are F$35 per person one-way. The regular supply boat often goes to Taveuni on Friday afternoon, and they may take you for free if they're going anyway, so call ahead. It's also possible to be picked up at Buca Bay if you're coming from Savusavu (this must be arranged in advance).

On Sau Bay in the same general area, **Almost Paradise** (tel. 828-3000, www.almostparadisefiji.com) has three bungalows with bath and deck at F$150/195/270 single/double/triple, including all meals. Free activities include kayaking, sailing, rowing, snorkeling, and hiking. The accommodations here are better than those at Dolphin Bay Divers and you can still dive with them. Boat transfers from Taveuni or Natuvu in Buca Bay are F$40 per person each way.

KIOA ISLAND

The Taveuni ferry passes between Vanua Levu and Kioa, home to some 300 Polynesians from Vaitupu Island, Tuvalu (the former Ellice Islands), 1,000 kilometers north. Captain Owen of the ship *Packet* obtained Kioa from the Tui Cakau in 1853, and since then it was operated as a coconut plantation. In 1946, it was purchased by the Ellice Islanders, who were facing overpopulation on their home island.

The people live at **Salia** on the southeast side of 21-square-kilometer Kioa. The women make baskets for sale to tourists in Savusavu, while the men go fishing alone in small outrigger canoes. If you visit, try the coconut toddy *(kaleve)* or the more potent fermented toddy *(kamanging)*.

There are no facilities for tourists on Kioa, but it's possible to arrange paying-guest accommodations in a private home by contacting the Kioa Island Council (tel. 850-3976, www.kioaisland.org).

◖ RABI ISLAND

In 1855, at the request of the Tui Cakau on Taveuni, a Tongan army conquered some Fijian rebels on Rabi. Upon the Tongans' departure a few years later, a local chief sold Rabi to Europeans to cover outstanding debts, and until World War II, the Australian firm Lever Brothers ran a coconut plantation here. In 1940, the British government began searching for an island to purchase as a resettlement area for the Micronesian inhabitants of Ocean Island (Banaba) in the Gilbert Islands (presently part of Kiribati), whose home island was being ravaged by phosphate mining. At first,

THE BANABANS

The people of Rabi Island, between Vanua Levu and Taveuni in northern Fiji, are from Banaba, a tiny, six-square-kilometer raised atoll 450 kilometers southwest of Tarawa in the Micronesian Gilbert Islands. Like Nauru, Banaba was once rich in phosphates, but from 1900 through 1979, the deposits were exploited by British, Australian, and New Zealand interests in what is perhaps the best example of a corporate/colonial rip-off in the history of the Pacific Islands.

After the Sydney-based Pacific Islands Company discovered phosphates on Nauru and Banaba in 1899, a company official, Albert Ellis, was sent to Banaba in May 1900 to obtain control of the resource. In due course, "King" Temate and the other chiefs signed an agreement granting Ellis's firm exclusive rights to exploit the phosphate deposits on Banaba for 999 years in exchange for £50 a year. Of course, the guileless Micronesian islanders had no idea what the scheme would truly cost them.

As Ellis rushed to have mining equipment and moorings put in place, a British naval vessel arrived on September 28, 1901, to raise the British flag, joining Banaba to the Gilbert and Ellice Islands Protectorate. The British government reduced the term of the lease to a more realistic 99 years, and the Pacific Phosphate Company was formed in 1902.

Things ran smoothly until 1909, when the islanders refused to lease any additional land to the company, after 15 percent of Banaba had been stripped of both phosphates and food trees. The British government arranged a somewhat better deal in 1913, but in 1916 it changed the protectorate into a colony so the Banabans could not withhold their land again. After World War I, the company was renamed the British Phosphate Commission (BPC), and in 1928 the resident commissioner, Sir Arthur Grimble, signed an order expropriating the rest of the land, against the Banabans' wishes. The islanders continued to receive their tiny royalty right up until World War II.

On December 10, 1941, with a Japanese invasion deemed imminent, the order was given to blow up the mining infrastructure on Banaba, and on February 28, 1942, a French destroyer evacuated company employees from the island. In August, some 500 Japanese troops and 50 laborers landed on Banaba and began erecting fortifications. The six Europeans they captured eventually perished as a result of ill treatment, and all but 150 of the 2,413 local mine laborers and their families were eventually deported to Tarawa, Nauru, and Kosrae. As a warning, the Japanese beheaded three locals and used another three to test an electrified fence.

Meanwhile the BPC decided to take advantage of this situation to rid itself of the island's original inhabitants once and for all. In March 1942, the commission purchased Rabi Island off Vanua Levu in Fiji for £25,000 as an alternative homeland for the Banabans. In late September 1945, the British returned to Banaba, with Albert Ellis the first to step ashore. Only surrendering Japanese troops were found on Banaba; the local villages had been destroyed.

Two months later, an emaciated and wild-eyed Gilbertese man named Kabunare Koura emerged from three months in hiding and told his story to a military court:

We were assembled together and told that the war was over and the Japanese

Wakaya Island in the Lomaiviti Group was considered, but the outbreak of war and the occupation of Ocean Island by the Japanese intervened. Back in Fiji, British officials decided Rabi Island would be a better homeland for the Banabans than Wakaya, and in March 1942, they purchased Rabi from Lever Brothers using £25,000 of phosphate royalties deposited in the Banaban Provident Fund.

Meanwhile, the Japanese had deported the Banabans to Kosrae in the Caroline Islands to serve as laborers, and it was not until December 1945 that the survivors could be brought to Rabi, where their 4,500 descendants live today.

would soon be leaving. Our rifles were taken away. We were put in groups, our names taken, and then marched to the edge of the cliffs where our hands were tied and we were blindfolded and told to squat. Then we were shot.

Kabunare either lost his balance or fainted, and fell over the cliff before he was hit. In the sea, he came to the surface and kicked his way to some rocks, where he severed the string that tied his hands. He crawled into a cave and watched the Japanese pile up the bodies of his companions and toss them into the sea. He stayed in the cave two nights and, after he thought it was safe, made his way inland, where he survived on coconuts until he was sure the Japanese had left. Kabunare said he thought the Japanese had executed the others to destroy any evidence of their cruelties and atrocities on Banaba. After a postwar trial on Guadalcanal, the Japanese commander of Banaba, Suzuki Naoomi, was hanged for his crimes.

As peace returned, the British implemented their plan to resettle all 2,000 surviving Banabans on Rabi, which seemed a better place for them than their mined-out homeland. The first group arrived on Rabi on December 14, 1945, and in time they adapted to their mountainous new home and traded much of their original Micronesian culture for that of the Fijians. There, they and their descendants live today.

During the 1960s, the Banabans saw the much better deal Nauru was getting from the BPC. Mainly through the efforts of Hammer De-Roburt and the "Geelong Boys," who had been trapped in Australia during the war and thus received an excellent education and understanding of the white people's ways, the Nauruan leadership held its own against colonial bullying. Meanwhile, the Banabans were simply forgotten on Rabi.

In 1966, Tebuke Rotan, a Banaban Methodist minister, journeyed to London on behalf of his people to demand reparations from the British for laying waste to their island. After some 50 visits to the Foreign and Commonwealth offices, he was offered £80,000 compensation, which he rejected. In 1971, the Banabans sued for damages in the British High Court. After lengthy litigation, the British government in 1977 offered the Banabans an ex gratia payment of A$10 million, in exchange for a pledge that there would be no further legal action.

In 1975, the Banabans asked that Banaba be separated from the rest of Kiribati and joined to Fiji, their present country of citizenship. Gilbertese politicians, anxious to protect their fisheries zone and wary of the dismemberment of the country, lobbied against this, and the British rejected the proposal. The free entry of Banabans to Banaba was guaranteed in the Kiribati constitution, however. In 1979, Kiribati obtained independence from Britain and mining on Banaba ended the same year. Finally, in 1981, the Banabans accepted the A$10 million compensation money, plus interest, from the British, though they refused to withdraw their claim to Banaba. (Much of the money "disappeared" between 1989 and 1991, during a period of corruption in the Rabi Council of Leaders.) The present Kiribati government rejects all further claims from the Banabans, asserting that they should be settled with the British. The British are simply trying to forget the whole thing.

VANUA LEVU

Contemporary Banabans are citizens of Fiji and live among Lever Brothers' former coconut plantations in the northwest corner of the island. The nine-member Rabi Island Council administers the island.

Rabi lives according to a different set of rules than the rest of Fiji; in fact, about all they have in common are their monetary, postal, and educational systems, kava drinking (a Fijian implant), and Methodism. The local language is Gilbertese, and the social order is that of the Gilbert Islands. Most people live in hurricane-proof concrete-block houses devoid of furniture, with personal possessions kept in suitcases and trunks. The cooking is done outside in thatched huts. The islanders fish with handlines from outrigger canoes.

Alcoholic beverages are not allowed on Rabi, so take something else as gifts. On Friday nights, the local *maneaba* (community hall) in Tabwewa village rocks to a disco beat, and dancing alternates with sitting around the omnipresent kava bowl, but on Sunday virtually everything grinds to a halt. Another charming feature: Adultery is a legally punishable offense on Rabi.

The island reaches a height of 472 meters and is well wooded. The former Lever Brothers headquarters is at Tabwewa, while the disused airstrip is near Tabiang at Rabi's southwest tip. Rabi's other two villages are Uma and Buakonikai. At Nuku, between Uma and Tabwewa, is a post office, Telecom office, clinic, handicraft shop, and general store. The hill behind the Catholic mission at Nuku affords a good view. Enjoy another fine view from the Methodist church center at Buakonikai.

Accommodations

Up on the hillside above the post office at Nuku is the four-room **Rabi Island Council Guest House.** This colonial-style structure is the former Lever Brothers manager's residence, and it is little changed since the 1940s, except for the extension now housing the dining area and lounge. View superb sunsets from the porch. One of the rooms is reserved for island officials; the rest are used mostly by contract workers. Other guests pay F$50 per person a night, which includes three meals. The facilities are shared (no hot water) and the electric generator operates 1800–2200 only—just enough time to watch a video (the library next to the courthouse rents *Go Tell It to the Judge,* a documentary about the Banaban struggle for compensation).

Considering the limited accommodations and the remoteness of Rabi, it's important to call the **Rabi Island Council** (tel. 881-2913, ext. 30, www.banabans.com.fj) for guesthouse bookings and other information before setting out. Foreign currency cannot be changed on Rabi, and even Fijian bills larger than F$10 may be hard to break. Insect repellent is not sold locally.

Getting There and Around

To get to Rabi, catch the daily Napuka bus at 1030 from Savusavu to Karoko. A chartered speedboat from Karoko to the wharf at Nuku on the northwest side of Rabi costs F$70 each way, less if people off the Napuka bus are going over anyway.

Motorized transport on Rabi consists of two or three island-council trucks plying the single 23-kilometer road from Tabwewa to Buakonikai weekdays and Saturday mornings.

TAVEUNI

Long, green, coconut-covered Taveuni is Fiji's fourth-largest island. It's 42 kilometers long, 15 kilometers wide, and 442 square kilometers in area. Only eight kilometers across the Somosomo Strait from Vanua Levu's southeast tip, Taveuni is known as the Garden Island of Fiji because of the abundance of its flora. About 60 percent of the land is tropical rainforest, and virtually all of Fiji's coffee is grown here. Its surrounding reefs and those off nearby Vanua Levu are among the world's top dive sites. The strong tidal currents in the strait nurture the corals, but can make diving a tricky business for the unprepared.

Because Taveuni is free of mongooses, there are many wild chickens, *kula* lorikeets, red-breasted musk parrots, honeyeaters, silktails, fern-tails, goshawks, and orange-breasted doves, making this a special place for bird-watchers. Here you'll still find the jungle fowl, banded rail, and purple swamp hen, all extinct on Viti Levu and Vanua Levu. The Fiji flying fox and mastiff bat are also seen only here. The Taveuni longhorn beetle is the largest beetle in Australasia.

The island's 16-kilometer-long, 1,000-meter-high volcanic spine causes the prevailing trade winds to dump colossal amounts of rainfall on the island's southeast side, as well as considerable quantities on the northwest side. Southwestern Taveuni is much drier. At 1,241 meters, Uluiqalau in southern Taveuni is the second-highest peak in Fiji, and Des Voeux Peak (1,195 m) in central Taveuni is the highest point in the country accessible by road. The European discoverer of Fiji,

© BARRY PETERS

HIGHLIGHTS

Rainbow Reef: This famous scuba-diving venue is actually off the south side of Vanua Levu, but most divers arrive from Taveuni. The soft corals of the Great White Wall here are awesome (page 260).

Bouma National Heritage Park: This is one of Fiji's most famous and most accessible nature reserves, with three waterfalls and good hiking (page 265).

Lavena: Lavena village, at the end of the road down Taveuni's east coast, is the start of a lovely coastal hiking trail to a river where you can swim (page 266).

Des Voeux Peak: The eight-kilometer climb to the telecommunications tower on Taveuni's second-highest peak can be a bumpy ride or an all-day grind on foot. It's one of Fiji's most productive bird-watching venues, and you may get a view of legendary Lake Tagimaucia (page 268).

LOOK FOR ◖ TO FIND RECOMMENDED SIGHTS, ACTIVITIES, DINING, AND LODGING.

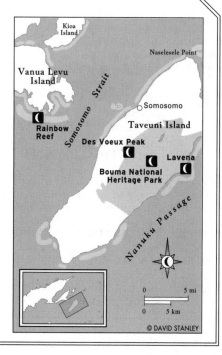

Abel Tasman, sighted this ridge on the night of February 5, 1643. Vuna in southwestern Taveuni is dormant now, but it's considered Fiji's most active volcano, having erupted within the past 350 years. The almost inaccessible southeast coast features plummeting waterfalls, soaring cliffs, and crashing surf. The 12,000 inhabitants live on the island's gently sloping northwest side. Indigenous Fijians make up the bulk of the population, but Indo-Fijians run many of the shops, small hotels, buses, and taxis.

The deep, rich volcanic soil nurtures indigenous floral species, such as *Medinilla spectabilis*, which hang in clusters like red sleigh bells, and the rare *tagimaucia (Medinilla waterhousei)*, a climbing plant with red-and-white flower clusters 30 centimeters long. *Tagimaucia* grows only around Taveuni's 900-meter-high crater lake and on Vanua Levu. It cannot be transplanted and blossoms only October–January. The story goes that a young woman was fleeing from her father, who wanted to force her to marry a crotchety old man. As she lay crying beside the lake, her tears turned to flowers. Her father took pity on her when he heard this and allowed her to marry her young lover.

Taveuni is a popular destination for scuba divers, and the nature reserves of northeastern Taveuni make it an ideal ecotourism destination. In 1991, the producers of the film *Return to the Blue Lagoon* chose Taveuni for their remake of the story of two adolescents on a desert isle. This is a beautiful, scenic, and friendly island on which to hang out, so be sure to allow yourself enough time there.

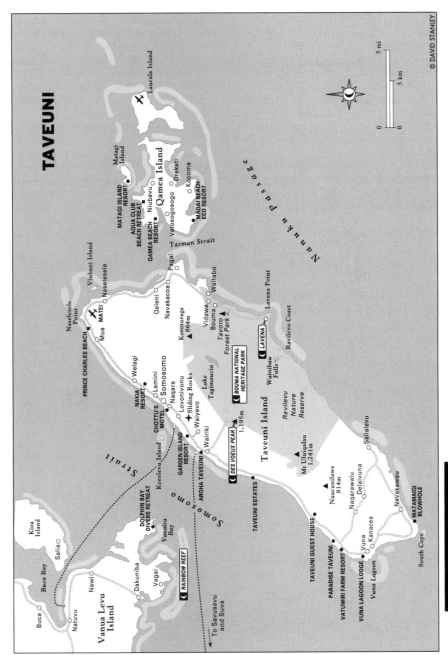

TAVEUNI

© DAVID STANLEY

PLANNING YOUR TIME

Taveuni is as far east as most tourists go in Fiji. And since it takes a bit of effort to get here, many visitors spend a week on the island. The minimum stay would be two nights and three days. It's not worth going for less time.

There's lots to see and do, especially scuba diving in the Somosomo Strait to the west or hiking in the nature reserves to the east. Bus routes go east to Lavena and south to Vuna, two obligatory day trips.

Most visitors on package tours stay somewhere along the tourist strip near Matei Airport, but there are also good places to stay in Naqara near the Vanua Levu ferry landing, in Waiyevo where the Suva ferry docks, and at Vuna in the south. If you can, it's worthwhile to use Vuna and Lavena as bases for exploring their areas. The islands of Matagi and Qamea are accessible only to pre-packaged resort tourists.

GETTING THERE

Matei Airstrip at the north tip of Taveuni is served by **Pacific Sun** (tel. 888-0461), which flies to Taveuni from Nadi (F$230) three times a day and from Suva (F$182) daily. Flights to/from Taveuni are often heavily booked, so reconfirm to avoid being bumped. The Pacific Sun office is at the airport. You get superb views of Taveuni from the plane: Sit on the right side going up, the left side coming back.

Consort Shipping (tel. 888-0036, www.consortshipping.com.fj, weekdays 0730–1700, Sat. 0730–1500) is represented by the grocery store below the First Light Inn in Waiyevo. The *Spirit of Fiji Islands* departs Taveuni southbound Wednesday at 1600 and Sunday at 1100. The trip from Taveuni to Suva (23 hours, F$58 deck) is via Koro and Savusavu. A bed in a four-bed cabin is F$95 while a two-person suite is F$160/250 single/double. The fare from Taveuni to Savusavu is F$32 deck.

Blight Water Shipping (tel. 888-0261, www.blighwatershipping.com.fj, weekdays 0800–1600, Sat. 0800–1200), in the market opposite the First Light Inn, operates the MV *Suilven* from Taveuni to Savusavu (F$28 economy) and Suva (F$65 economy) Tuesday, Thursday, and Sunday at 1400. Aside from the

The car ferry *Suilven* links Taveuni to Savusavu and Suva twice a week.

© DAVID STANLEY

TAVEUNI

economy lounge with airline-style seating and videos blasting, you can get a curtained bunk to Suva adjacent to the first-class lounge for F$104, a two-person cabin for F$136, or the Prime Minister's Cabin for F$359. Ask about special trips from Taveuni to Vanua Balavu on the *Suilven* at the end of every month. Although fares on the *Spirit of Fiji Islands* are slightly lower, the *Suilven* is a better ship more likely to adhere to its timetable.

The small passenger boat MV *Amazing Grace* departs Taveuni for Natuvu on Tuesday, Thursday, Friday, and Saturday at 0830 (two hours, F$15). Through boat/bus tickets with a bus connection at Natuvu are available to Savusavu (four hours, F$25) and Labasa (six hours, F$30). Information on the *Amazing Grace* is available at **Grace Shipping** (tel. 888-0320) in a large purple building at the south end of Naqara. On the Taveuni side, arrive at the wharf a little early as the ferry does fill up occasionally.

KaraMai Ferry Services (ex-Raja) operates between Taveuni and Vanua Levu on Monday, Wednesday, Friday, and Saturday.

The **Suncity Ferry Service** (tel. 820-9205) to Natuva on Vanua Levu departs Taveuni daily except Wednesday at 0700.

All of the large car ferries from Suva tie up at Wairiki Wharf, a kilometer south of the First Light Inn. The smaller ferries to Natuvu on Vanua Levu use the Korean or Government Wharf at Lovonivonu village, midway between Waiyevo and Naqara.

GETTING AROUND

Monday–Saturday at 0900 and 1630, **Pacific Transport** (tel. 888-0278) buses leave Waiyevo and Naqara northbound to Lavena. Southbound to Vuna buses leave Naqara Monday to Saturday at 0900, 1100, and 1630. Both the northbound and southbound 1630 buses stop and spend the night at their turn-around points, Lavena and Navakawau, heading back to Naqara the next morning at 0600 (at 0700 on Sun.). Sunday service is infrequent, although there are buses to Lavena and Vuna at around 1530. Check the current schedule carefully as soon as you arrive, and beware of buses leaving a bit early. The buses begin

The open sides of Pacific Transport buses offer sweeping views of Taveuni.

their journeys at the Pacific Transport garage at Naqara, but they all go to Waiyevo hospital and Wairiki to pick up passengers before heading north or south. Fares average F$5 one-way to either end of the island.

The sporadic bus service and expensive taxi fares make getting around rather inconvenient. Taveuni's minibus taxis don't run along set routes, picking up passengers at fixed rates as they do on other islands, but only operate on an individual charter basis. The taxi fare from Waiyevo to Naqara is reasonable at F$3, but from the airport to Waiyevo, it's expensive at F$18. In general, the taxi fare will be about 10 times the corresponding bus fare. Save money by using the buses for long rides and taxis for shorter hops. Hitchhiking also works fine (drivers often expect you to give them the equivalent of bus fare).

You could hire a minibus taxi and driver for the day. Prepare a list of everything you want to see, then negotiate a price with a driver.

Budget Rent a Car has closed their Taveuni office and none of the other chains operate here. Instead, you can hire a car and driver for the day.

Northern Taveuni

Many of Taveuni's tourist facilities, including accommodations, restaurants, and dive shops, are within walking distance of the airport at Matei. It's a good area in which to stay if you're arriving by air, although boat passengers and those planning to use public transportation for sightseeing will find central Taveuni more convenient. When selecting a place to stay, be aware that the beach east of Matei Point is a broad mud flat at low tide and the best places for swimming are west of the airport in the vicinity of Beverly's Campground.

Peckham Pearls Ltd. (tel. 888-2789, peckhampearls@connect.com.fj, weekdays 0800–1700) has a sales room behind Sonal Shopping Center in Matei. On weekdays they offer guided tours of their offshore pearl farm at F$25 per person whenever the tide is high.

SPORTS AND RECREATION
C Rainbow Reef
Taveuni and its surrounding waters have earned a reputation as one of Fiji's top diving areas. The fabulous 32-kilometer Rainbow Reef off the south coast of eastern Vanua Levu abounds in turtles, fish, overhangs, crevices, and soft corals, all in 5–10 meters of water. Favorite dive sites here include Annie's Bommie, Blue Ribbon Eel Reef, Cabbage Patch, Coral Garden, Jack's Place, Jerry's Jelly, Orgasm, Pot Luck, the Ledge, the Zoo, and White Sandy Gully. At the Great White Wall, a tunnel in the reef leads past sea fans to a magnificent drop-off and a wall covered in awesome white soft coral. Unfortunately, the hard corals of the Rainbow Reef have been heavily impacted by coral bleaching. The soft corals are still okay, and the White Wall is as spectacular as ever. Beware of strong currents in the Somosomo Strait.

Snorkelers should be aware that shark attacks are not unknown on northern Taveuni. Never snorkel out to the edge of the reef alone anywhere around Matei. This is less of a problem elsewhere on the island, although one should always seek local advice. Northern Taveuni is one of the few places in Fiji where sharks are a problem. Also beware of getting run over by a passing speedboat.

Diving Guides
Jewel Bubble Divers (tel. 888-2080, www.jeweldivers.com), next to Beverly's Campground, is run by an experienced local diver named Qiolele Morisio. He and his capable staff know these waters. Their boat *Clarissa* goes out at 0830, charging F$230 for two tanks, plus 12.5 percent tax and F$35 for gear.

Vunibokoi Divers (tel. 888-0560, www

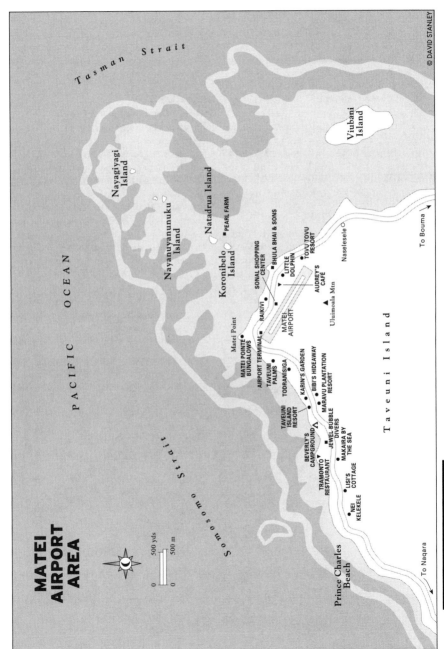

© DAVID STANLEY

MATEI AIRPORT AREA

0 — 500 yds
0 — 500 m

Tasman Strait

PACIFIC OCEAN

Nayagiyagi Island

Nayanuyanunuku Island

Natadrua Island

Koronibelo Island

■ PEARL FARM

■ BHULA BHAI & SONS

Viubani Island

SONAL SHOPPING CENTER

LITTLE DOLPHIN

TOVU TOVU RESORT

AUDREY'S CAFÉ

Naselesele

RAIKIVI

Uluimoala Mtn

To Bouma

Matei Point

MATEI AIRPORT

MATEI POINTE BUNGALOWS

AIRPORT TERMINAL

TAVEUNI PALMS

TODRANISIGA

KARIN'S GARDEN

BIBI'S HIDEAWAY

MARAVU PLANTATION RESORT

Taveuni Island

TAVEUNI ISLAND RESORT

BEVERLY'S CAMPGROUND

JEWEL BUBBLE DIVERS

TRAMONTO RESTAURANT

MAKAIRA BY THE SEA

LISI'S COTTAGE

NEI KELEKELE

Prince Charles Beach

Somosomo Strait

To Naqara

.tovutovu.com), based at the Tovu Tovu Resort, is run by Tyrone Valentine and Samu Matana, former Divemasters at the Taveuni Island Resort. To dive with them costs F$150/250 for one/two tanks, plus F$29 for gear. Their Open Water certification course is F$890.

Matei Game Fishing (tel. 888-0371, www.taveunisportfishing.com), at "Raikivi" opposite Sonal Shopping Center at Matei, does game-fishing trips on the *Lucky Strike.*

Sportfishing is also offered by **Makaira Charters** (tel. 888-0680, www.fijibeachfrontatmakaira.com), above the Tramonto Restaurant, at F$685/1,235 a half/full day.

ACCOMMODATIONS

Places to stay are scattered all around Taveuni, with a cluster within walking distance of Matei Airport. There are several places to eat out in this vicinity, so avoid prepaying all your meals. When deciding where to stay, beware of misleading resort websites and the glowing reports of travel agents and glossy magazine writers who came on freebie trips.

Taveuni still doesn't have a public electricity supply, but most of the places to stay have their own generators, which typically run 1800–2100 only. The intermittent electric supply makes food storage a challenge and cases of food poisoning are not unknown.

Under US$25

Beverly's Campground (tel. 888-0684) is on a good beach a little over a kilometer south of the airport. Run by Bill Madden, it's a peaceful, shady place, adjacent to Maravu Plantation's beach. It's F$15 per person to camp or F$17 per person in a set tent, and there's also a dorm with six beds at F$20 per person and two basic doubles at F$40. The toilet and shower block is nearby. Cooking facilities are available, but bring groceries (Bill provides free fresh fruit from his garden daily). The kitchen shelter by the beach is a nice place to sit and swap traveler's tales with the other guests, and the clean white beach is just seconds from your tent. Don't expect clean linens or fancy furnishings. If you're camping, be prepared for a nocturnal visit from the land crabs.

Over the hill a few hundred meters south

Taveuni's least expensive accommodations are the set tents at Beverly's Campground.

is **Lisi's Accommodation,** in a small village across the highway from Prince Charles Beach. It's F$10 per person to camp or F$40 single or double in a four-room bungalow with shared cooking and bathing facilities. Your friendly hosts Mary and Lote Tuisago serve excellent Fijian meals upon request. Horseback riding can be arranged here (F$10 an hour).

US$25-50

The **Tovu Tovu Resort** (tel. 888-0560, www.tovutovu.com) is just east of Bhula Bhai & Sons Supermarket at Matei. It's across the road from a shallow beach with murky water, and guests often walk the two kilometers to Beverly's Campground to swim. The two front *bure* capable of sleeping three are self-catering at F$95 single or double. Just behind are another two *bure* with private bath but no cooking at F$85. A larger self-catering bungalow sleeping four is F$130. The three-meal plan is F$40 per person. The restaurant terrace is a nice place to sit and something of a local hangout. Unfortunately, Tovu Tovu is poorly managed with uneven standards of food and accommodations.

Little Dolphin (tel. 888-0130), opposite Bhula Bhai & Sons Supermarket, less than a kilometer east of the airport, has an airy, two-story cottage with cooking facilities called the "treehouse." At F$90 plus tax single or double a night, it's a good value, and the view from the porch is great. A kayak and snorkeling gear are loaned free. Be sure to reserve in advance by phone.

(Bibi's Hideaway (tel. 888-0443), about 600 meters south of the airport, has some of the gracious atmosphere of neighboring properties, but without the sky-high prices. A variety of accommodations is available. The film crew making *Return to the Blue Lagoon* stayed here for three months, and with the extra income, the owners built a honeymoon *bure* with a picture window, which is F$90 double. Nearby is a two-room house at F$55 per room or F$110 for the whole house. A small cottage is F$80 double. There's also a larger family unit accommodating six at F$110. All units have access to cooking facilities and fridge. Electricity is daily 1800–2100. Bibi's is located on lush, spacious grounds, and James, Victor, and Pauline Bibi will make you feel right at home. It's an

© DAVID STANLEY

the treehouse at Little Dolphin in Matei, Taveuni

excellent mid-priced choice, if you don't mind being a bit away from the beach.

US$100-150

Todranisiqa (tel. 941-3985, todrafj@yahoo. com), between the airport terminal and Karin's Garden, has one self-catering unit available at F$295 single or double, plus a double room at F$265, including breakfast. Your host May Goulding will cook lunch and dinner for you at F$75 for two people. Local rate discounts are sometimes available. There's a great view from this hill.

Karin's Garden (tel. 888-0511, www.karins gardenfiji.com) is almost opposite Bibi's Hideaway 650 meters south of the airport. The one two-room self-catering bungalow with fan facing the owner's home is F$260/290/310 double/triple/quad, including tax. They serve a three-course dinner for F$40–45 but reservations are required. Their big dogs will greet you at the gate.

US$150-250

Matei Pointe Bungalows (tel. 888-0422, www.fijilodging.com), right on the point at the end of the driveway opposite the airport access road, has three self-catering villas from F$285 double, plus 17.5 percent tax. A larger three-bedroom unit is F$500 plus tax. The location and grounds are lovely but the units can be a little grubby. Still, it's always worth a try straight off the plane as you can get a 50 percent discount on a walk-in basis if a unit happens to be available when you arrive. Weekly rates are available.

Makaira by the Sea (tel. 888-0680, www .fijibeachfrontatmakaira.com) is something of a misnomer as it's actually located on a high bluff across the road from the water. It's directly above the noisy Tramonto Restaurant, and has some of the best views on the island. The two self-catering *bure* on spacious grounds are F$295 double for the smaller and F$400 for the larger, plus 17.5 percent tax. Discounts are possible through their website. A two-person kayak and snorkeling gear are provided. Non-smokers may not enjoy this place.

Over US$250

Taveuni Palms (tel. 888-0032, www.taveuni palms.com), near the airport at Matei, has two luxury villas on a high plateau above a white-sand beach. Each two-bedroom villa has its own plunge pool and spa. It's over the top at F$2,250 double plus 17.5 percent tax, meals included (five-night minimum stay). Extra persons for a maximum of four are F$475 each. Scuba diving is arranged through Taveuni Dive. The constant attention from staff detracts from the advertised privacy.

Maravu Plantation Resort (tel. 332-4303, www.maravu.net), 600 meters south of the airport, is a village-style resort on a 20-hectare copra-making plantation. The beach is quite a distance down the hill and across the road. Maravu caters mostly to American honeymooners. It consists of five "planters" *bure* at F$345/495 single/double and five "honeymoon" *bure* at F$475/760. The four "honeymoon suites," each with a private spa and sundeck, are F$540/895. Several other categories of rooms also exist and the minimum stay is four nights. When space is available, you might get a lower local walk-in rate. Included are breakfast, transfers, horseback riding, bicycles (in poor shape), kayaks, nocturnal rooster noise, and some other activities, but tax is 17.5 percent extra. Of the optional meal plans, you might be better off taking the dinner plan only (F$57) as the buffet lunch down by the beach won't be worth F$38 after the staff have finished eating. Maravu's wine menu is way overpriced, and drinks at the manager's weekly cocktail party are added to your bill. On the landscaped grounds are an elegant bar, spa (extra charge), and swimming pool. The resort often arranges a *meke* to go with dinner on Wednesday or Thursday. If you're not staying there, you must reserve meals in advance. Unfortunately this place is rather disorganized and you should check your bill carefully. Bring insect repellent.

Almost across the street from Maravu Plantation is **Taveuni Island Resort** (tel. 888-0441, www.taveuniislandresort.com), run by the Cammick family. This upscale resort started out in the 1970s as a low-budget scuba camp known as Ric's Place, but today it's patronized by an eclectic mix of upscale divers, anglers, honeymooners, and "romantic couples" who arrive on prepaid package tours. The 10 *bure* range F$1,577–2,840 single or double, including meals and transfers. The 17.5 percent tax and drinks are extra. Unlike Maravu, which encourages visits by families, children under 15 are not accepted here and the minimum stay is four nights. The open terrace dining area and swimming pool merge scenically with the sea on the horizon. This resort no longer has a dive shop of its own and you must use one of the outside operators. Be aware that only registered house guests are welcome on this property, as the "Beware of the Dog" sign on the gate reminds passersby. Despite this, thefts from the rooms have been reported. It's hard to understand how people can pay the outlandish prices charged at Taveuni Island Resort and Taveuni Palms when there are so many other resorts in Fiji (including the Garden Island Resort at Waiyevo) that offer a comparable experience for a fraction of the price.

FOOD

The nicest place to eat out around Matei is the **Vunibokoi Restaurant** (tel. 888-0560) at the Tovu Tovu Resort, east of Bhula Bhai & Sons Supermarket. You can get traditional Fijian dishes here. From 1800–2000, upscale dinners (F$15–20) prepared by Mareta are served on a terrace overlooking the sea. A local string band accompanies the Friday-night *lovo* buffet (F$25) here. Reservations are recommended.

(Audrey's Island Café & Pastries (tel. 888-0039, daily 1000–1800), run by a charming American woman at Matei, serves afternoon tea (F$12 pp) to guests who also enjoy the great view from the terrace. Audrey has various homemade goodies to take away.

The snack bar at **Matei Airport** (daily 0830–1600) sells tasty curry rotis for F$1.80. They're kept under the counter, so ask. The supermarkets in this area also sell roti packets.

The **Tramonto Restaurant** (tel. 888-2224, closed Sun.), on a hilltop at the southwest end of the Matei tourist strip, serves meals in the F$20 range. The portions tend to be small here. If you can get a group of at least six persons together, the Tramonto lays out an excellent smorgasbord dinner at F$25 per person (every Sunday night, there's a F$25 buffet). Happy hour is Thursday 1700–1900 with F$10 jugs and F$20 pizza. The Friday curry specials are F$15. Saturday it's surf and turf at F$20 and the Sunday roast dinner is F$25. The view of the beach and Somosomo Strait from the open terrace is superb.

Groceries

Those staying at Matei will appreciate the well-stocked **Bhula Bhai & Sons Supermarket** (tel. 888-0462, Mon.–Sat. 0730–1800, Sun. 0800–1100) at the Matei Postal Agency between the airport and Naselesele village. A second grocery store, **Sonal Shopping Center** (tel. 888-0431, Mon.–Sat. 0700–1900, Sun. 0700–1200 and 1400–1900), is between Bhula Bhai and the airport. There's also **Jagdish Singh and Sons Store** (tel. 888-0748) opposite Karin's Garden.

Eastern Taveuni

(BOUMA NATIONAL HERITAGE PARK

This important nature reserve between Bouma and Lavena in northeastern Taveuni has been developed with New Zealand aid money. In 1990, an agreement was signed with the communities of Waitabu, Vidawa, Korovou, and Lavena putting this area in trust for 99 years, and the Tavoro Forest Park at Bouma was established a year later. The Lavena Coastal Walk, Vidawa Rainforest Hike, and Waitabu Marine Park are other features of the park, and the various admission fees and tour charges are used for local community projects, to provide residents with an immediate practical reason for preserving their natural environment.

There are three lovely **waterfalls** just south of Bouma (admission F$12). From the information kiosk on the main road, it's an easy 10-minute walk up a broad path along the river's right bank to the lower falls, which plunge 20 meters into a deep pool. You can swim here, and changing rooms, toilets, picnic tables, and a barbecue are provided. A well-constructed trail leads up to a second falls in about 30 minutes, passing a spectacular viewpoint overlooking Qamea Island and Taveuni's northeast coast. You must cross the river once, but a rope is provided for balance. Anyone in good physical shape can reach this second falls with ease, and there's also a pool for swimming. The muddy, slippery trail up to the third and highest falls involves two river crossings with nothing to hold onto, and it would be unpleasant in the rain. But this trail cuts through the most beautiful portion of the rainforest with the richest birdlife, and these upper falls are perhaps the most impressive of the three, as the river plunges over a black basalt cliff, which you can climb and use as a diving platform into the deep pool. The water here is very sweet.

A new activity in this area is the six-hour **Vidawa Rainforest Hike,** during which local guides introduce the birdlife, flora, and archaeological sites of the area to visitors. You scramble over volcanic ridges offering spectacular views and explore old village sites with their temple platforms and ring ditches still clearly visible. Your guide brings it all to life with tales of the old ways of his people. A picnic lunch is served by a spring-fed stream deep in the interior. The trek ends at **Bouma Falls,** where hikers are rewarded with a refreshing swim. The F$40 per-person cost includes park entry fees, a guide, and lunch (call 822-0361 the day before to book). Be aware that Vidawa Rainforest Hike is rigorous and even the guides have been known to get lost!

Similar is the **Waitabu Marine Park** (tel. 820-1999., www.waitabu.org), where a lagoon area two kilometers before Bouma has been declared a "no fishing" sanctuary for fish and snorkelers. The dive shops at Matei sometimes organize snorkeling trips here. The F$40–50 per-person tour price includes snorkeling gear, transportation, and food. Discounts for children are available. A snorkeling tour arranged on the spot is F$30 per person. The departure time varies according to tide and weather conditions.

Bouma is difficult to visit by public bus. If you depart Waiyevo or Naqara on the 0900 bus, you can make a round-trip to Lavena, six kilometers south. This bus returns to Naqara immediately and there won't be another public bus until very early the next morning. A taxi from Matei to Bouma will cost F$60 roundtrip. A minibus based at Maravu Plantation Resort makes day trips to Bouma and Lavena. Call 888-0555 for times and rates.

◖ LAVENA

The **Lavena Coastal Walk** officially opened in 1993. You pay your F$12 admission fee (separate from the F$12 fee charged at Bouma) at the Lavena Lodge Visitor Center, right at the end of the road at Lavena. Guides are available at F$15. From the Visitor Center, you can hike the five kilometers down the Ravilevo Coast to **Wainibau Falls** in about 1.5 hours. You'll pass Naba village, where the descendants of blackbirded Solomon Islanders live to this day, and a suspension bridge over the Wainisairi River, which drains Lake Tagimaucia in Taveuni's interior. The last 15 minutes is a scramble up a creek bed, which can be very slippery as you wade along. Two falls here plunge into the same deep basalt pool, and during the rainy season you must actually swim a short distance to see the second pool. Diving into either pool is excellent fun. Be on guard, however, as flash flooding often occurs. Keep to the left near the base of the falls. Several lovely beaches and places to stop are along the trail (allow four hours there and back from Lavena with plenty of stops). It's a great walk, even in the rain.

If you also want to see **Savulevu Yavonu Falls,** which plummet off a cliff directly into the sea, you must hire a boat at F$200 for up to five people. Intrepid ocean kayakers sometimes

the Lavena coast

paddle down this back side of Taveuni, past countless cliffs and waterfalls. The steep forested area south of Wainibau Stream forms part of the Ravilevu Nature Reserve.

It's not possible to visit Lavena as a day trip by public bus (taxis charge F$90 round-trip to bring you here). Buses depart Lavena for Naqara Monday–Saturday at 0600 and 1100, and Sunday at 0700—beware of their leaving a bit early.

ACCOMMODATIONS

At Bouma, visitors can camp by the river behind the park information kiosk (tel. 820-4709) at F$15 per head. Toilets and showers are provided. Meals can be ordered, or you can cook your own in a communal kitchen. There's a campground just 200 meters off the main road at the **Waitabu Marine Park** (tel. 820-1999), charging F$15 per person in your own tent or F$20 per person in a set tent. You can order meals at F$10 each or cook for yourself.

◖ Lavena Lodge (tel. 820-3639), next to Lavena village at the end of the bus route, is a pleasant European-style building with running water and lantern lighting. The four rooms (two doubles and two three-bed dorms) are F$30 per person the first night including the Lavena Coastal Walk fee, then F$20 per person additional nights. Sinks are provided in the rooms, but the bath is shared. Good cooking facilities are provided, and you can eat at a picnic table on a hill overlooking the beach or on the lodge's terrace. Dinner can be ordered for F$10. The lodge is often full but overflow guests are accommodated in the village at the same rates. A small village store is opposite the lodge, and two other tiny trade stores are nearby (however, it's much better to bring groceries with you). Mosquito coils are essential (the flies are a nuisance too). An excellent golden beach is right in front of the lodge, and at Ucuna Point, a five-minute walk away, is a picnic area where you can spend an afternoon (be careful with the currents if you snorkel). It's a great place to hang out for a few days—the film *Return to the Blue Lagoon* was filmed here.

TAVEUNI

Central Taveuni

WAIYEVO AND WAIRIKI

Taveuni's police station, hospital, and government offices are on a hilltop at **Waiyevo**, above the Garden Island Resort. On the coast below are the island's post office, largest hotel, and wharf.

The 180th degree of longitude passes through a point marked by a display called **Taveuni's Time Line** at Waiyevo, 500 meters up the road from the shops near the Garden Island Resort. It's said that one early Taveuni trader overcame the objections of missionaries to his doing business on Sunday by claiming the international date line ran through his property. According to him, when it was Sunday at the front door, it was already Monday around back. Similarly, European planters got their native laborers to work seven days a week by having Sunday at one end of the plantation, and Monday at the other. An 1879 ordinance ended this by placing all of Fiji west of the date line, so you're no longer able to stand here with one foot in the past and the other in the present. Despite this, it's still the most accessible place in the world that is crossed by the 180th meridian.

To get to the **Waitavala Sliding Rocks,** walk north from the Garden Island Resort about five minutes on the main road, then turn right onto Waitavala Road. Take the first road to the right up the hill, and when you see a large metal building on top of a hill, turn left and go a short distance down a road through a plantation to a clearing on the right. The trail up the river to the sliding rocks begins here. The waterslide in the river is especially fast after heavy rains, yet the local kids go down standing up! Admission is free. Take your bathing suit.

At **Wairiki,** two kilometers south of Waiyevo, are a few stores and the picturesque Catholic mission, with a large stone church containing interesting sculptures and stained glass. There are no pews: The congregation sits on the floor Fijian-style. From Wairiki Secondary School, you can hike up a tractor track to the large

The Waitavala Sliding Rocks on the west side of the island are a favorite swimming hole.

© DAVID STANLEY

concrete cross on a hill behind the mission (30 minutes each way). You'll be rewarded with a sweeping view of much of western Taveuni and across Somosomo Strait. A famous 19th-century naval battle occurred here when Taveuni warriors turned back a large Tongan invasion force, with much of the fighting done from canoes. The defeated Tongans ended up in Fijian ovens, and the French priest who gave valuable counsel to the Fijian chief was repaid with laborers to build his mission.

Des Voeux Peak

A jeep road from Wairiki climbs to the telecommunications station on Des Voeux Peak. At 1,195 meters, Des Voeux is Taveuni's second-highest mountain. This is an all-day trip on foot, with a view of the crater containing Lake Tagimaucia as a reward (clouds permitting).

The lake itself is not accessible from here. This peak is one of Taveuni's best bird-watching venues, and the rare monkey-faced fruit bat *(Pteralopex acrodonta)* survives only in the mist forest around the summit. Virtually all of Taveuni's endemic species of birds have been seen here. Unless you hire a four-wheel-drive vehicle to the viewpoint, it will take four arduous hours to hike the eight kilometers up and another two to walk back down. Take an adequate supply of water with you or you'll never make it. The first five kilometers pass open areas with varied views, while the upper three kilometers are through largely undisturbed forest.

AROUND SOMOSOMO

Somosomo, four kilometers north of Waiyevo, is the chiefly village of Cakaudrove and the seat of the Tui Cakau, Taveuni's "king"; the late Ratu Sir Penaia Ganilau, last governor-general and first president of Fiji, hailed from here. The two distinct parts of the village are divided by a small stream where women wash their clothes. The southern portion called **Naqara** is the island's commercial center, with several large stores, the island's bank, and a couple of places to stay. Pacific Transport has its bus terminus here.

Somosomo, to the north of Naqara, is the chiefly quarter, with the personal residence of the Tui Cakau on the hill directly above the bridge (no entry). Beside the main road below is the large hall built for the 1986 meeting of the Great Council of Chiefs. Missionary William Cross, one of the creators of today's system of written Fijian, who died at Somosomo in 1843, is buried in the attractive new church next to the meeting hall. There's even electric street lighting in this part of town!

Lake Tagimaucia

The challenging trail up to lovely Lake Tagimaucia, 823 meters high in the mountainous interior, begins at the south end of Naqara. The first half is the hardest. You'll need between six hours and a full day to do a round-trip, and a guide will be necessary, as there are many trails to choose from. You must wade for a half hour through knee-deep mud in the crater to reach the lake's edge. Much of the lake's surface is covered with floating vegetation, and the water is only five meters deep. From October to January, you have a chance of seeing the rare red-and-white *tagimaucia* flower blossoming near the lake.

A SKELETON IN BRITAIN'S NUCLEAR CLOSET

In 1957 and 1958, some 300 Fijian soldiers and sailors were employed by the British during hydrogen-bomb testing in the Line Islands, now called Kiribati (between Hawaii and Tahiti). Three particularly dirty atmospheric tests took place off Malden Island in May and June 1957, with another six tests on Christmas Island in November 1957 and September 1958.

The troops were exposed to significant levels of radiation, and many instances of test-related health problems have been documented among veterans. The most notorious case involves Ratu Penaia Ganilau, later knighted and made president of Fiji, who landed barefoot on Malden immediately after a test in May 1957. Sir Penaia died of leukemia in 1993 after a long illness and was buried on Taveuni. Other Fijians were used to clear away thousands of sea birds killed by the blasts, or to dump drums of nuclear waste into the sea. Few protective measures were taken, and there have been accusations that the troops were deliberately exposed to radiation so they could be used as guinea pigs. Litigation against the British government began in 1997, but to date no compensation has been paid by the British to the Fijian victims of their tests.

© DAVID STANLEY

the office of Taveuni Dive at Wairiki

SPORTS AND RECREATION

Garden Island Diving (tel. 888-0286), at the Garden Island Resort, does daily dives at F$185/545/890 for two/six/10 dives, plus F$30 a day for gear. The multi-dive packages cannot be shared between two divers. Night diving is F$110 and PADI scuba certification costs F$700. Add 17.5 percent tax to these rates. You'll find cheaper dive shops, but Garden Island's facilities are first-rate. This is the closest dive shop to the famous Rainbow Reef.

Taveuni Dive (tel. 828-1063, www.taveuni dive.com, weekdays 1000–1700) has a dive shop on the main road in Wairiki, plus bases at Taveuni Estates and Paradise Taveuni. They charge F$120/240 for one-/two-tank dives, plus F$30 for gear. Snorkeling trips are F$90 per person (minimum of two).

ACCOMMODATIONS
Under US$25

A friendly Indo-Fijian family runs **Kool's Accommodation** at Naqara. The four renovated rooms with bath in a long block facing the eating area are F$25/35 single/double.

There's also an eight-bed dorm at F$15 per person. Communal cooking facilities are provided (but no fridge).

Sunset Accommodation (tel. 888-0229) behind Sunset Store, on a busy corner near the Korean Wharf at Lovonivonu, has two self-catering rooms with bath in a separate bungalow at F$20/30 single/double. Beware of ants if you have food with you. It's a great deal and often full.

US$25-50

The original budget hotel on Taveuni was **Chottu's Motel** (tel. 888-0233, chottus@ connect.com.fj), at Naqara, which charges F$38/50/61 single/double/twin in one of four double rooms with shared facilities in the guesthouse. The cooking facilities are very good. The newer motel section is F$59/71 double/twin for one of the six larger units with kitchenette, fridge, fan, and private bath. An extra person is F$22. The water is solar-heated, so cold showers are de rigueur in overcast weather (ask for a discount in that case). Many supermarkets are just up the street. No check-ins are accepted after 1800. Naqara is a convenient place to stay for catching buses, but at night there's nothing much to do other than watch the BBC on TV. Most of their guests are local.

The **First Light Inn** (tel. 888-0339, first light@connect.com.fj), near the Garden Island Resort at Waiyevo, was built in late 1999, just in time for the millennium celebrations. This large, two-story concrete building has 11 fan-cooled rooms at F$56/66 double/triple and nine air-conditioned rooms at F$66/76. Cooking facilities are provided in the fan rooms only. The inn's generator makes a lot of noise and local contract workers sometimes book rooms here on the weekends to watch the football games on TV and have fun, so be prepared.

The **Dolphin Bay Divers Retreat** (tel. 828-3001, www.dolphinbaydivers.com) is located on Vanua Levu (on Vanaira Bay at Vanua Levu's east end) but is most easily accessible from Taveuni.

US$50-100

In 2009, **Aroha Taveuni** (tel. 888-1882, www.arohataveuni.com) opened on a reasonable beach just south of Wairiki Wharf. The two duplex units with bathroom, kitchen, fridge, and outdoor showers are F$180 single or double. There's a pool in front of the owner's house next door and the snorkeling offshore is good on an incoming tide. It's a good value. Two grocery stores, two restaurants, and Taveuni Dive are in Wairiki, a five-minute walk to the south.

US$100-150

The **Garden Island Resort** (tel. 888-0286, www.gardenislandresort.com) is by the sea at Waiyevo, three kilometers south of Naqara. Formerly known as the Castaway, this was Taveuni's premier (and only) hotel when it was built by the Travelodge chain in the 1960s. From 1996 to 2008, the scuba operator Aqua Trek USA ran the property. The new owners, Hong Kong–based CHI International, spent a large sum on renovations in 2009, adding flashy international decor in the public areas. The 30 air-conditioned rooms in an attractive two-story building are F$240/270 single/double, plus 17.5 percent tax, continental breakfast included. Children under 12 are free when

© DAVID STANLEY

a waterfront bungalow at Aroha Taveuni near Wairiki Wharf

The Garden Island Resort arranges trips to tiny Korolevu Island, a popular snorkeling spot.

sharing with adults. The buffet meal plan is overpriced at F$100 per person and ordering from the menu might work better (dinner reservations before 1700 required). The house band is pretty good! Notice the fruit bats hanging in the trees overlooking the swimming pool. There's no beach, but the Garden Island offers evening entertainment, a swimming pool, excursions, sportfishing, and water sports. Snorkeling trips (F$25 pp including snorkeling gear) are arranged to Korolevu Island, and a dive shop is on the premises. Airport transfers are F$45 per person round-trip (unless you're alone, a taxi will be cheaper). The Garden Island is an okay place to hang out—and a better value than the high-end places around Matei.

US$150-250

The **Nakia Resort** (tel. 888-1111, www.nakia fiji.com) sits on a bluff overlooking Somosomo Strait between Somosomo and Matei Airport. The four *bure* are F$428 double or F$713 for up to eight, plus 17.5 percent tax. Seven-night packages are available. This eco-resort uses solar energy, artesian spring water, and organic produce grown on the estate. There's a 15-meter freshwater swimming pool but no beach.

FOOD

Frank Fong's **Waci-Pokee Restaurant** (tel. 888-0036, Mon.–Fri. 0700–1800, Sat. 0700–1400), just down from the post office in Waiyevo (no sign), serves tasty Chinese and local meals for about F$6. You can eat outside in the thatched Cannibal Café directly behind the Waci-Pokee, a terrace overlooking Vanua Levu. Their slogan is "we'd love to have you for dinner." Ask to see the regular menu (which is not on display) for dinner listings (F$4–8.50) and order dinner beforehand, if possible. A piece of chocolate cake is F$1.

The **First Light Bar** (tel. 888-0339), upstairs in a building adjacent to the First Light Inn at Waiyevo, has beer on tap and a nice deck over the sea where you could consume takeaway food from the Waci-Pokee. They also have a pool table.

The **Trio Restaurant** (no phone, weekdays 0900–1500), in the fish market opposite the First Light Inn, serves a picnic-table lunch of fish in coconut milk at F$5.

Dinner mains at the elegant restaurant of the

Garden Island Resort (tel. 888-0286) will set you back F$25–35. The hotel organizes a *meke* and *lovo* (F$35 pp) if enough paying guests are present to make it worth their while.

Shivam's Curry House (tel. 850-0200, Mon.–Sat. 0700–2000) in Wairiki dishes out local meals at F$5–6.50.

More upscale is the **Bakery Bistro** (tel. 888-1212, Wed.–Sat.), next to Taveuni Dive across the street from Shivam's in Wairiki, with pizza from F$10. It's popular among local expats.

Kumar's Restaurant (tel. 888-1005, Mon.–Sat. 0730–1700), beside Chandra's Supermarket at Naqara, serves curries in the F$4–6 range. For breakfast, order an egg sandwich with coffee for under F$3.

Your best bet at Naqara is **Ma's Restaurant** (no phone, weekdays 0700–1700, Sat. 0700–1400), in the passageway adjacent to the Colonial National Bank. You can get a good curry or chop suey lunch for F$5.50. Some of the vegetable vendors at the bus stop in Naqara sell takeaway meals.

Groceries

A cluster of grocery stores is in Naqara. The large **Morris Hedstrom** supermarket (tel. 888-0053), a bit north in Somosomo, has a food court. Grocery stores also exist at Matei, Wairiki, and Waiyevo.

SERVICES

Traveler's checks can be changed at the **Colonial National Bank** (tel. 888-0433, weekdays 0900–1600) in Naqara. This bank has an ATM.

Taveuni's main post office is below the First Light Inn at Waiyevo.

Card phones are at Matei Airport, at Bhula Bhai & Sons Supermarket in Matei, at Naqara, outside the post office in Waiyevo, and at several other locations.

Lani's Digital Services (Mon.–Sat. 0730–1730), opposite the Colonial National Bank in Naqara, has Internet access at F$4 an hour.

The island's **hospital** (tel. 888-0444) is up on the hill at Waiyevo.

Southern Taveuni

The southern end of Taveuni is one of the island's most beautiful areas, but transportation is spotty, with bus service from Naqara Monday–Saturday at 0900, 1100, and 1645 only. Since the 1645 bus spends the night at Vuna and doesn't return to Naqara until the next morning, the only way to really see southern Taveuni is to spend the night there. If this isn't possible, the four-hour round-trip bus rides, which leave Naqara at 0900 and 1100, are still well worth doing with the possibility of a two-hour stopover.

One of the only stretches of paved road on southern Taveuni is at **Taveuni Estates** (tel. 888-0044, www.taveuniestates.com), formerly known as Soqulu Plantation, about eight kilometers south of Waiyevo. This upscale residential development features an attractive nine-hole golf course (greens fees F$40) by the sea, tennis courts, and a bowling green.

The Taveuni Estates Club House, behind the bowling green, prepares the best oven-baked pizza on the island. It's perfect at happy hour. A taxi from Waiyevo to Taveuni Estates will run F$10.

The bus from Naqara continues south along the coast to Paradise Taveuni, where it turns inland to Delaivuna. There it turns around and returns to the coast, which it follows southeast cutting directly across some hills to Navakawau. On the way back, it goes via South Cape to Kanacea and continues up the coast without going to Delaivuna again. Southeast of Kanacea, there is very little traffic.

A hike around southern Taveuni provides an interesting day out for anyone staying in the area. From Paradise Taveuni, a road climbs east to the top of the island to **Delaivuna,** where the bus turns around. Private Property signs on the road beyond are mainly intended to

TAVEUNI

the southwest coast of Taveuni at Vuna Lagoon Lodge

ward off miscreants who create problems for the plantation owners by leaving open cattle gates. Visitors with enough sense to close the gates behind themselves may proceed.

You hike one hour down through the coconut plantation to a junction with two gates, just before a small bridge over a (usually) dry stream. If you continue walking 30 minutes down the road straight ahead across the bridge, you'll reach **Salialevu,** site of the Bilyard Sugar Mill (1874–1896), one of Fiji's first. In the 1860s, European planters tried growing cotton on Taveuni, turning to sugar when the cotton market collapsed. Later, copra was found to be more profitable. A tall chimney, boilers, and other equipment remain below the school at Salialevu.

After a look around, return to the two gates at the bridge and follow the other dirt road southwest for an hour through the coconut plantation to **Navakawau village** at the southeast end of the island. Some of Fiji's only Australian magpies (large black-and-white birds) inhabit this plantation.

Just east of South Cape as you come from Navakawau is the **Matamaiqi Blowhole,** where waves, driven by trade winds, crash into the

unprotected black volcanic rocks, sending geysers of sea spray soaring skyward, especially on a southern swell. The viewpoint is just off the main road.

At **Vuna,** lava flows have formed pools beside the ocean, which fill up with fresh water at low tide and are used for washing and bathing.

SPORTS AND RECREATION

In 2008 **Taveuni Dive** (tel. 828-1063, www .taveunidive.com) and **Pro Dive** (www.prodive .com.au) of Australia joined forces, and from their base at Paradise Taveuni, they offer scuba diving at F$250 for two dives, plus F$30 for gear. A dive package including 10 boat dives, one night dive, and unlimited shore diving is F$1,250 (or F$1,400 including gear). They do daily trips to the Vuna Reef and other dive sites off southern Taveuni. They will also take you to the Great White Wall and Rainbow Reef across Somosomo Strait if you press them, but it's a 35-minute boat ride each way.

ACCOMMODATIONS
Under US$25
◖ **Vuna Lagoon Lodge** (tel. 888-0627), on

© DAVID STANLEY

a dive boat at Paradise Taveuni at the south end of the island

the Vuna Lagoon near Vuna village, three kilometers south of Vatuwiri Farm, consists of two European-style houses just back from a black lava coastline highlighted by small golden beaches. A room with shared bath is F$35 single or double, the two with private bath F$65, and the four-bed dorm is F$22 per person. Cooking facilities are provided but you'll need to bring groceries if you want to use them as the tiny stores in the village have little more than a few rusty cans. A better plan is to order dinner at F$12–15 (fish and curries mostly). Namoli Beach, a 10-minute walk away, is good for swimming and snorkeling (better at low tide, as the current picks up appreciably when the tide comes in). The friendly proprietor, Adi Salote Samanunu, is a daughter of the chief of Vuna. It's one of the best deals on Taveuni and is often full, so call ahead for reservations.

US$25-50

The **Taveuni Guest House** (tel. 888-0531, www.dolphinbaydivers.com), next to a supermarket three kilometers north of Paradise Taveuni, is operated by Dolphin Bay Divers Retreat. Rooms in this single-story house with

a large porch overlooking the strait are F$60 single or double or F$20 per person in a shared room. A black-sand beach is across the road and down the hill. The bus from Naqara passes the door.

Over US$250

Taveuni Dive (tel. 828-1063, www.taveuni dive.com) has three luxury villas for rent at Taveuni Estates, costing F$475 for a two- or three-bedroom or FF950 for a deluxe four-bedroom villa. These upscale residences must be booked in advance through the website.

Paradise Taveuni (tel. 888-0125, www.par adiseinfiji.com) is on beautifully landscaped grounds just north of Vuna Point at the south end of Taveuni. This property was a backpacker resort called Susie's Plantation until 2005, when new owners came in and upgraded the entire operation. The resort's thatched *bure* are pricey at F$950 double for one of the four back units or F$1,000 for one of the five front units. Breakfast is included but lunch and dinner meal plan is F$60 per person extra. You can also order à la carte. The resort's generator is rather noisy and this place has insect problems. Guests are treated

TAVEUNI

© DAVID STANLEY

visitor accommodations at Paradise Taveuni

to a free snorkeling safari by boat. Jet Skiing (F$400), wild boar hunting (F$200), game fishing (F$1,500 per boat), and four-wheel-drive tours (F$150–250) are among the activities offered. Taveuni Dive is based here, but even if you're not a diver, you'll enjoy snorkeling off Paradise Taveuni's rocky beach. Airport transfers are F$50 each way for the car.

The **Vatuwiri Farm Resort** (tel. 888-0316, www.vatuwirifiji.com) at Vuna Point, two kilometers south of Paradise Taveuni, is on a large plantation established in 1871 by James Valentine Tarte. The family's history was the subject of a 1988 novel titled *Fiji* by Daryl Tarte. Currently, Spencer Tarte produces beef, vanilla, cocoa, pigs, and copra, and he rents two two-room cottages to tourists for F$600 single or double, including all meals. The rocky coast here is fine for snorkeling, and horseback riding is available. The Tarte family and their staff are congenial, and this is perhaps your best chance to stay on a real working farm in Fiji.

Islands off Taveuni

QAMEA ISLAND

Qamea (ngga-ME-a) Island, just three kilometers east of Taveuni, is the 12th-largest island in Fiji. It's 10 kilometers long, with lots of lovely bays, lush green hills, and secluded white-sand beaches. At the beginning of the breeding season in late November or early December, land crabs *(lairo)* are harvested in abundance here during their migration to the sea. The birdlife is also rich, due to the absence of mongooses.

In 2001, Dr. Patrick D. Nunn of the University of the South Pacific conducted excavations of settlement sites on Qamea and surrounding islands, and he discovered Lapita-era remains dating back 2600–3000 years. Vatusogosogo, one of six villages on Qamea, is inhabited by descendants of blackbirded Solomon Islanders. Outboards from villages on Qamea land near Navakacoa village on the northeast side of Taveuni. The best times to

TAVEUNI

TABUA

The Fijians share *yaqona* (or kava) with the Polynesians, but the *tabua*, or whale's tooth, is significant only in Fiji. The *tabua*, obtained from the sperm whale, has always played an important part in Fijian ceremonies. In the 19th century, they were hung around the necks of warriors and chiefs during festivals. Even today they are presented to distinguished guests and are exchanged at weddings, births, deaths, and reconciliations, and also when personal or communal contracts or agreements are entered into. *Tabua*, contrary to popular belief, have never been used as a currency and cannot be used to purchase goods or services. It is a great honor to be presented with a *tabua*.

COURTESY OF THE FIELD MUSEUM OF NATURAL HISTORY, CHICAGO

try for a ride over are Thursday and Friday afternoons.

The upscale **Qamea Beach Resort** (tel. 888-0220, www.qamea.com), on the west side of Qamea, has 11 air-conditioned *bure* at F$1,310 double, plus 17.5 percent tax, and one split-level honeymoon villa at F$1,570 (children under 16 not accepted), meals included. Airport Transfers (F$143 per person round-trip) are extra. All units have a ceiling fan, mini-fridge, giant outdoor shower, lawn furniture, and hammock-equipped front deck, but they're rather dark inside. Meals are served in a tall central dining room and lounge designed like a *burekalou* (temple), and a trio sings around dinnertime. Drink prices are astronomical, so bring along a duty-free bottle.

Gay and lesbian travelers will feel comfortable at Qamea but young honeymooners are the resort's cash cows. You can swim in the lava pools that emerge off Qamea's beach at low tide and there's also a small freshwater swimming pool. Some activities are included in the basic price but tours to Taveuni, fishing, scuba diving, and spa treatments are extra.

The ☖ **Maqai Beach Eco Resort** (tel. 990-7900, www.maqai.com), at the southern tip of Qamea, is a backpacker-style operation with eight safari tents with private facilities at F$80 single or double and an eight-bed treehouse dorm at F$30 per person. One three-bed dorm is reserved for females only. Camping is also possible. The meal plan is F$30 per person extra and the food is good. Adventurous young travelers love this place. There are two surf breaks within 800 meters of Maqai's sandy beach and boat trips to more remote breaks are available at F$20 per person. Other activities include snorkeling, fishing, and hiking. Scuba diving can be arranged with operators on Taveuni. Transfers from Matei Airport to Qamea are F$25 per person.

MATAGI ISLAND

Matagi is a tiny horseshoe-shaped volcanic island just north of Qamea, its sunken crater forming a lovely palm-fringed bay. The island is privately owned by the Douglas family, which has been producing copra on Matagi for five generations and still does. In 1988, they diversified into the hotel business.

Matangi Island Resort (tel. 888-0260, www.matangiisland.com), 10 kilometers northeast of Taveuni, markets itself as a honeymoon destination by advertising in the U.S. bridal magazines. It tries to do the same as far as scuba diving goes, but the prime dive sites in the Somosomo Strait are a long way from this resort. Matangi's three treehouse *bure* are intended for the recently wed (F$1,710 double). Other guests are accommodated in eight circular *bure* scattered among the coconut palms below Matagi's high jungle interior. An oceanview *bure* is F$1,160 single or double, while a beachfront *bure* goes for F$1,310. Prices include meals, snacks, laundry, and some activities, but 17.5 percent tax, drinks, and return boat transfers from Taveuni (F$220 pp plus tax) are extra. Children under 16 are not accepted. To compensate for the weedy, muddy beach, a swimming pool was added in 2008. Scuba diving is F$250 for two tanks plus pricey gear and taxes.

LAUCALA ISLAND

Laucala Island, which shares a barrier reef with Qamea, was depopulated and sold to Europeans in the mid-19th century by the chief of Taveuni, after the inhabitants sided with Tongan chief Enele Ma'afu in a local war. In 1972, the late billionaire businessman and New York publisher Malcolm Forbes bought 12-square-kilometer Laucala from the Australian company Morris Hedstrom for US$1 million. He then spent additional millions on an airstrip, wharf, and roads. Forbes replaced the leaky thatched *bure* of the 300 Fijian inhabitants with 40 red-roofed houses with electricity and indoor plumbing. In 1984,

Forbes opened a small resort called Fiji Forbes on Laucala. After his death in 1990, he was buried on the island. His former private residence stands atop a hill overlooking the native village, the inhabitants of which make copra. During the turbulence following the Speight coup attempt in mid-2000, Laucala Island was invaded by local thugs with scores to settle, and the resort managers were beaten and held captive for 24 hours. In 2003, the island was sold to Dietrich Mateschitz, the Austrian founder of the energy-drink producer Red Bull, for US$10 million and in 2008 the resort reopened.

Laucala Island Resort (tel. 888-0077, www.laucala.com) offers 25 luxurious *bure* with one to three bedrooms with private pools starting at F$7,220 a day, plus 17.5 percent tax. Meals, drinks, a spa treatment, scuba diving, tennis, golf, horseback riding, laundry, and just about everything else is included. The direct charter flight from Nadi will be extra. This place is so exclusive you have to request clearance just to visit their website.

THE LAU GROUP AND ROTUMA

The Lau Group is Fiji's most remote region by far, its 57 islands scattered over a vast area of ocean between Viti Levu and Tonga. Roughly half of the islands are inhabited. Though all are relatively small, they vary from volcanic islands to uplifted atolls and some combination of the two. Tongan influence has always been strong in Lau, and due to intermarrying with Polynesians, the people have a somewhat lighter skin color than other Fijians. The westward migrations continue today: More than 40,000 Lauans live on Viti Levu, while less than 13,000 still live on their home islands. Historically, the chiefs of Lau have always had a political influence in Fiji far out of proportion to their economic or geographical importance.

Vanua Balavu (52 square km) and Lakeba (54 square km) are the largest and most important islands of the group. These are also the only islands with organized visitor accommodations, and Vanua Balavu is the more rewarding of the two. Lakeba and Vanua Balavu enjoy government-subsidized air service, but the other islands are accessible only after a long sea voyage from Suva. Copra-collecting ships circulate through Lau every couple of weeks, usually calling at five or six islands on a single trip.

Rotuma is on the opposite side of the country from Lau, 600 kilometers north of Viti Levu. This isolated 5-by-14-kilometer volcanic island is surrounded on all sides by more than 322 kilometers of open sea. There's a saying in Fiji that if you can find Rotuma on a map, then it's a fairly good map. Rotuma's climate is damper and hotter than other parts of Fiji. The Rotumans are a Polynesian people linked

HIGHLIGHTS

◖ **Vanua Balavu Island:** Vanua Balavu is the most popular island of Lau and Rotuma, though it doesn't get more than a handful of visitors a year. The island's small resort makes a good base for snorkelers, hikers, and explorers (page 281).

◖ **Lakeba Island:** After Vanua Balavu, Lakeba is one of the only islands of Lau open to visitors. Lakeba's numerous limestone caves will appeal to speleologists (page 284).

◖ **Ono-i-Lau Island:** Ono-i-Lau is one of Fiji's remotest islands. The diving and snorkeling are fine if you can find a liveaboard dive boat to take you there (page 287).

◖ **Sisilo Hill:** This hill is the burial place of the last kings of Rotuma, and a few historic relics can still be seen (page 289).

LOOK FOR ◖ TO FIND RECOMMENDED SIGHTS, ACTIVITIES, DINING, AND LODGING.

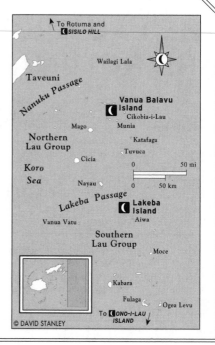
© DAVID STANLEY

to Melanesian Fiji by historical and geographical chance.

Few of these islands are prepared for tourism, so it really helps to know someone before you go. Individual tourists don't need a special permit or invitation to visit Lau or Rotuma—you can just get on a plane and go. (Cruising yachties do need a permit.) And since the best accommodations are on Vanua Balavu in northern Lau, that's the logical place to head first. Words like pristine, untouched, and idyllic all seem to have been invented for Lau and Rotuma, and the unconditional friendliness of the local people is renowned. This is one area where you don't need to worry about bumping into a McDonald's! There are no banks in Lau, so you must bring all the Fijian currency you think you'll need.

PLANNING YOUR TIME

Getting to Vanua Balavu or Lakeba isn't cheap, so you wouldn't want to go for less than a few days. Not that you'll have any choice, as Pacific Sun only flies to Vanua Balavu and Lakeba once a week. The boat from Suva takes several days just to get to Vanua Balavu, Lakeba, or Rotuma.

These three islands are the only ones with guest houses. There are no regular hotels, restaurants, bars, dive shops, or tourist shops anywhere in these islands, but your hosts should be able to arrange small boats for snorkeling or island visits. Hiking is the easiest activity to arrange, as you can walk anywhere. The main reason to go is to experience life on a remote island seldom seen by outsiders.

Northern Lau

◖ VANUA BALAVU ISLAND

The name Vanua Balavu means the "long land." The southern portion of this unusual, seahorse-shaped island is mostly volcanic, while the north is uplifted coral. This unspoiled environment of palm-fringed beaches backed by long grassy hillsides and sheer limestone cliffs is a wonderful area to explore. Varied vistas and scenic views appear on all sides. To the east is a 130-kilometer barrier reef enclosing a 37-by-16-kilometer lagoon. The scenic Bay of Islands at the northwest end of Vanua Balavu is a recognized hurricane shelter. The villages of Vanua Balavu are impeccably clean, the grass cut and manicured. Large mats are made on the island, and strips of pandanus can be seen drying in front of many houses.

In 1840, Commodore Wilkes of the U.S. Exploring Expedition named Vanua Balavu and its adjacent islands within the barrier reef the "Exploring Isles." In the days of sail, Lomaloma, the largest settlement, was an important Pacific port. The early trading company Hennings Brothers had its headquarters here. The great Tongan warlord Enele Ma'afu conquered northern Lau from the chiefs of Vanua Levu in 1855 and made Lomaloma the base for his bid to dominate Fiji. A small monument flanked by two cannons on the waterfront near the wharf recalls this event. Fiji's first public botanical garden was laid out here more than a century ago, but nothing remains of it. History has passed Lomaloma by. Today, it's only a big sleepy village, with a small hospital and a couple of general stores. Some 400 Tongans live in Sawana, the south portion of Lomaloma village, and many of the houses have the round ends characteristic of Lau. Fiji's first prime minister and later president, Ratu Sir Kamisese Mara, was born in Sawana. Former prime minister Laisenia Qarase lives in exile in Mavana village.

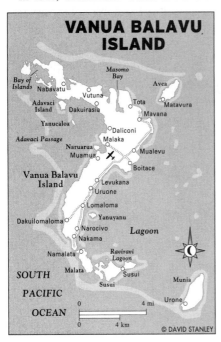

Sights

Copra is the main export, and there's a small coconut-oil mill at **Lomaloma.** A road runs inland from Lomaloma up and across the island to **Dakuilomaloma.** From the small communications station on a grassy hilltop midway, there's an excellent view.

Follow the road south from Lomaloma three kilometers to **Narocivo village,** then continue two kilometers beyond to the narrow passage that separates Vanua Balavu and Malata islands. At low tide, you can easily wade across to **Namalata village.** Alternatively, work your way around to the west side of Vanua Balavu, where there are isolated tropical beaches. There's good snorkeling in this passage.

A guide can show you **hot springs** and **burial caves** among the high limestone outcrops between Narocivo and Namalata. This can be easily arranged at Nakama, the tiny collection of houses closest to the cliffs, upon payment of F$10 per group. Small bats inhabit some of the caves. You can get right in the hot springs and soak, which is reputed to be very therapeutic.

Rent a boat to take you over to the **Raviravi Lagoon** on Susui Island, the favorite picnic spot near Lomaloma for the locals. The beach and snorkeling are good, and there's a lake where sea turtles are kept.

Events

A most unusual event occurs from time to time at Masomo Bay, west of **Mavana village,** usually around Christmas. For a couple of days, the Mavana villagers, clad only in skirts of *drauniqai* leaves, enter the waters and stir up the muddy bottom by swimming around clutching logs. No one understands exactly why, and magic is thought to be involved, but this activity stuns the *yawa* (mullet fish) that inhabit the bay, rendering them easy prey for waiting spears. Peni, the *bete* (priest) of Mavana, controls the ritual. No photos are allowed. A Fijian legend tells how the *yawa* were originally brought to Masomo by a Tongan princess.

Accommodations

Moana's Guesthouse (tel. 820-1125 or 822-1148, www.moanasguesthouses.com), on the beach about a kilometer from Sawana village, is run by Tevita and Carolyn Fotofili, with the help of daughter Moana. Their two large thatched *bure* are F$95 per person with shared bath, all meals and snacks included (children under 12 half price). The food is outstanding and plentiful, with lots of fresh fruit. To snorkel here, you swim out 100 meters to a point where the bottom drops down to 10 meters. A motorboat is for hire for trips around Vanua Balavu or even to nearby islands like Kanacea. There's also a Fijian outrigger sailing canoe. If you enjoy peace and solitude and aren't too worried about amenities, this is the place. Moana's

© CAROLYN FOTOFILI

Simple island accommodations are available at Moana's Guesthouse.

THE COCONUT PALM

Human life would not be possible on most of the Pacific's far-flung atolls without this all-purpose tree. It reaches maturity in eight years, then produces about 50 nuts a year for 60 years. Aside from the tree's aesthetic value and usefulness in providing shade, the water of the green coconut provides a refreshing drink, and the white meat of the young nut is a delicious food. The harder meat of more mature nuts is grated and squeezed, which creates a coconut cream that is eaten alone or used in cooking. The oldest nuts are cracked open and the hard meat removed, then dried, to be sold as copra. It takes about 6,000 coconuts to make a ton of copra. Copra is pressed to extract the oil, which in turn is made into candles, cosmetics, and soap. Scented with flowers, the oil nurtures the skin.

The juice or sap from the cut flower spathes of the palm provides toddy, a popular drink; the toddy is distilled into a spirit called arrack, the whiskey of the Pacific. The sap can also be boiled to make candy. "Millionaire's salad" is made by shredding the growth cut from the heart of the tree. For each salad, a fully mature tree must be sacrificed.

The nut's hard inner shell can be used as a cup and makes excellent firewood. Rope, cordage, brushes, and heavy matting are produced from the coir fiber of the husk. The smoke from burning husks is an effective mosquito repellent. The leaves of the coconut tree are used to thatch the roofs of the islanders' cottages or are woven into baskets, mats, and fans. The trunk provides timber for building and furniture.

---

accepts cash only (also take insect repellent, sunscreen, and a half kilo of kava).

Getting There

Pacific Sun flies to Vanua Balavu once a week from Suva (F$205 one-way). These flights are heavily booked, so reserve your return journey before leaving Suva. Even then, if it has been raining too hard, the soggy airstrip may be closed. You can hitch a ride from the airstrip to Lomaloma with the Pacific Sun agent for a small fee or hire a carrier from the airport to Moana's for F$20. After checking in at the airstrip for departure, you might have time to scramble up the nearby hill for a good view of the island.

Boat service from Suva on the *Sea-Link* is only once a month. Check with **Bligh Water Shipping** (www.blighwatershipping.com.fj) about special trips from Taveuni to Vanua Balavu (F$55/95 economy/sleeper) on the MV *Suilven* around the end of the month.

Several carriers a day run from Lomaloma north to Mualevu, and some continue on to Mavana.

OTHER ISLANDS OF NORTHERN LAU

After setting himself up at Lomaloma in 1855, Chief Ma'afu encouraged the establishment of European copra and cotton plantations in Lau, and several islands are freehold land to this day. **Kanacea,** to the west of Vanua Balavu, was sold to a European by the Tui Cakau in 1863, and the Kanacea people now reside on Taveuni. In 2004, **Mago** (20 square km), a copra estate formerly owned by English planter Jim Barron, was purchased by actor Mel Gibson for US$14.8 million. Gibson's residence on Mago includes a private golf course and swimming pool, and the actor keeps a small plane on the island that he uses to commute to Suva.

Naitauba is a circular island about 186 meters high, with high cliffs on the north coast. Once owned by Hennings Brothers, in 1983 it was purchased from TV star Raymond Burr for US$2.1 million by the California spiritual group Johannine Daist Communion, currently known as Adidam (www.adidam.org). Adidam holds four-to-eight-week meditation retreats on Naitauba for longtime members of the group.

Adidam's founder and teacher, Adi Da Samraj, the former Franklin Albert Jones, who attained enlightenment in Hollywood in 1970, lived on the island until his death in 2008.

There's a single Fijian village and a gorgeous white-sand beach on **Yacata Island.** Right next to Yacata and sharing the same lagoon is 260-hectare **Kaibu Island,** where a small adults-only luxury resort opened in 1987. The Kaimbu Island Resort featured the three spacious octagonal guest cottages and a private airstrip but in 2007 the resort closed. Following this, Kaibu Island was listed on the Internet for sale at US$38 million and in 2010 specialist private island realtor Boehm GmbH reported that Kaibu had been sold. Information about the new owners was unavailable at press time.

Vatu Vara to the south, with its soaring interior plateau, golden beaches, and azure lagoon, is privately owned and unoccupied most of the time. The circular, 314-meter-high central limestone terrace, which makes the island look like a hat when viewed from the sea, gives it its other name, Hat Island. There is reputed to be buried treasure on Vatu Vara. In 2010, specialist realtor Boehm GmbH reported that this freehold island had been sold for US$75 million.

Katafanga, to the southeast of Vanua Balavu, was at one time owned by Harold Gatty, the famous Australian aviator who founded Fiji Airways (later Air Pacific) in 1951. A 1,034-meter runway extends halfway up the east side of the island. In 2004, construction began on a deluxe resort with a dining pavilion and spa on a coral cliff and 20 air-conditioned villas with individual hot tubs and dipping

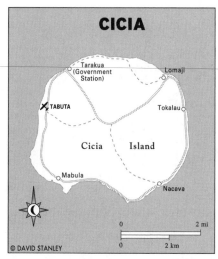

pools along a white lagoon beach. A nine-hole golf course would have separated Katafaga's airstrip from the rest of the resort. At last report, work on the resort had stopped and the island was for sale at US$25 million.

Cicia (pronounced Thithia), between northern and southern Lau, has five Fijian villages. Much of the 34-square-kilometer island is covered by coconut plantations. Fiji's only black-and-white Australian magpies have been introduced to Cicia and Taveuni. There's an airstrip on Cicia but at last report there were no scheduled flights.

Wailagi Lala, northernmost of the Lau Group, is a coral atoll bearing a lighthouse, which beckons to ships entering Nanuku Passage, the northwest gateway to Fiji.

Southern Lau

◖ LAKEBA ISLAND

Lakeba is a rounded volcanic island reaching a height of 215 meters. The fertile red soils of the rolling interior hills have been planted with pine, but the low coastal plain, with eight villages and all of the people, is covered with coconuts. To the east is a wide lagoon enclosed by

a barrier reef. In the olden days, the population lived on Delai Kedekede, an interior hilltop well suited for defense.

The original capital of Lakeba was Nasaqalau, on the north coast, and the present inhabitants of Nasaqalau retain strong Tongan influence. When the Nayau clan conquered the island, their paramount chief, the Tui Nayau, became ruler of all of southern Lau from his seat at Tubou. From the 1970s to the 1990s, the Tui Nayau, the late Ratu Sir Kamisese Mara, served as prime minister and later as president of Fiji.

Many forestry roads have been built throughout the interior of Lakeba. You can walk across the island from Tubou to Yadrana in a couple of hours, enjoying excellent views along the way. A radio station operates on solar energy near the center of the island. **Aiwa Island,** which can be seen to the southeast, is owned by the Tui Nayau and is inhabited only by flocks of wild goats.

Tubou and Vicinity

A 29-kilometer road runs all the way around Lakeba. From the Catholic church, you get a good view of Tubou, an attractive village and one of the largest in Fiji, with a hospital, wharf, several stores, and the Lau provincial headquarters. Tubou was originally situated at Korovusa just inland, where the foundations of former houses can still be seen. Farther inland on the same road is the forestry station and a nursery.

The Tongan chief Enele Ma'afu (died 1881) is buried on a stepped platform behind the Provincial Office near Tubou's wharf. In 1847,

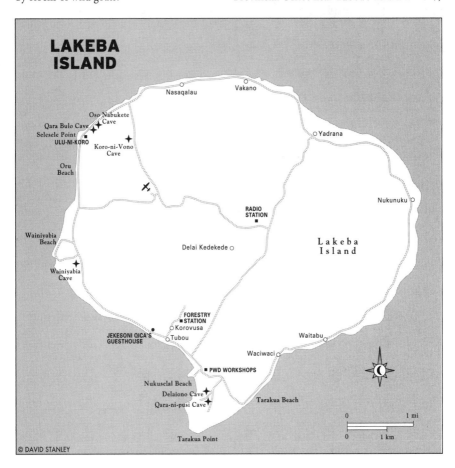

LAKEBA ISLAND

Nasaqalau
Vakano
Oso Nabukete Cave
Qara Bulo Cave
Selesele Point
ULU-NI-KORO
Koro-ni-Vono Cave
Yadrana
Oru Beach
Nukunuku
RADIO STATION
Wainiyabia Beach
Delai Kedekede
Lakeba Island
Wainiyabia Cave
FORESTRY STATION
Korovusa
JEKESONI QICA'S GUESTHOUSE
Tubou
Waitabu
Waciwaci
PWD WORKSHOPS
Nukuselal Beach
Delaiono Cave
Qara-ni-pusi Cave
Tarakua Beach
0 1 mi
0 1 km
Tarakua Point

© DAVID STANLEY

© DAVID STANLEY

the tombs of Ma'afu and Ratu Sukuna at Tubou, Lakeba Island

Ma'afu arrived in Fiji with a small Tongan army, ostensibly to advance the spread of Christianity, and by 1855 he dominated eastern Fiji from his base at Vanua Balavu. In 1869, Ma'afu united the group into the Lau Confederation and took the title Tui Lau. Two years later, he accepted the supremacy of Cakobau's Kingdom of Fiji, and in 1874 he signed the cession to Britain. Alongside Ma'afu is the grave of Ratu Sir Lala Sukuna (1888–1958), an important figure in the development of indigenous-Fijian self-government. David Cargill and William Cross, the first Methodist missionaries to arrive in Fiji, landed on the beach just opposite the burial place on October 12, 1835. Here they invented the present system of written Fijian. Fiji's first prime minister, Ratu Sir Kamisese Mara (1920–2004), is also buried here.

The number-one beach near Tubou is **Nukuselai,** which you can reach by walking east along the coastal road as far as the Public Works Department workshops. Turn right onto the track, which runs along the west side of the compound to Nukuselai Beach.

Nasaqalau and Vicinity

The finest **limestone caves** on the island are near the coast on the northwest side of Lakeba, 2.5 kilometers southwest of Nasaqalau. **Oso Nabukete** is the largest; the entrance is behind a raised limestone terrace. You walk through two chambers before reaching a small, circular opening about one meter in diameter, which leads into a third chamber. The story goes that women attempting to hide during pregnancy are unable to pass through this opening, thus giving the cave its name, the "Tight Fit to the Pregnant" Cave.

Nearby is a smaller cave, **Qara Bulo** (Hidden Cave), which one must crawl into. Warriors used it as a refuge and hiding place in former times. The old village of Nasaqalau was located on top of the high cliffs behind the caves at Ulu-ni-koro. The whole area is owned by the Nautoqumu clan of Nasaqalau, and they will arrange for a guide to show you around for a fee. Take a flashlight and some newspapers to spread over the openings to protect your clothing.

Each October or November, the Nasaqalau people perform a shark-calling ritual. A month before the ritual, a priest *(bete)* plants a post with a piece of tapa tied to it in the reef. He then keeps watch to ensure that no one comes near the area, while performing a daily kava ceremony. When the appointed day arrives, the caller wades out up to his neck and repeats a chant. Not long after, a large school of sharks led by a white shark arrives and circles the caller. He leads them to shallow water, where all but the white shark are formally killed and eaten.

Accommodations

Jekesoni Qica's Guesthouse (tel. 882-3188) in Tubou offers room and board at F$65 per person; baths are shared. The locals at Tubou concoct a potent homebrew *(uburu)* from cassava—ask the owner, Jack, where you can get some.

Getting There

Pacific Sun flies to Lakeba once a week from Suva (F$205 each way). A bus connects the airstrip to Tubou, and buses run around the island several times a day.

OTHER ISLANDS OF SOUTHERN LAU

Unlike the islands of northern Lau, many of which are freehold and owned by outsiders, the isles of southern Lau are communally owned by the Fijian inhabitants. This is by far the most remote corner of Fiji. In a pool on **Vanua Vatu** are red prawns similar to those of Vatulele and Vanua Levu. Here the locals can summon the prawns with a certain chant.

Oneata is famous for its mosquitoes and tapa cloth. In 1830, two Tahitian teachers from the London Missionary Society arrived on Oneata and were adopted by a local chief who had previously visited Tonga and Tahiti. The men spent the rest of their lives on the island, and there's a monument to them at Dakuloa village.

Moce is known for its tapa cloth, which is also made on Namuka, Vatoa, and Ono-i-Lau. **Komo** is famous for its dances *(meke),* which are performed whenever a ship arrives. Moce, Komo, and Olorua are unique in that they are volcanic islands without uplifted limestone terraces.

The **Yagasa Cluster** is owned by the people of Moce, who visit it occasionally to make copra. Fiji's finest *tanoa* (ceremonial bowls) are carved from *vesi* (ironwood) at **Kabara,** the largest island in southern Lau. The surfing is also said to be good at Kabara, if you can get there.

Fulaga is known for its wood carvings; large outrigger canoes are still built on Fulaga, as well as on **Ogea.** More than 100 tiny islands in the Fulaga lagoon have been undercut into incredible mushroom shapes. The water around them is tinged with striking colors by the dissolved limestone, and there are numerous beaches. Yachts can enter this lagoon through a narrow pass.

◖ Ono-i-Lau Island

Ono-i-Lau, far to the south, is closer to Tonga than to the main islands of Fiji. It consists of three small volcanic islands, remnants of a single crater, in an oval lagoon. A few tiny coral islets sit on the barrier reef. The highest point on Ono-i-Lau is 113 meters and total area is 7.9 square kilometers. The population of approximately 350 is almost entirely indigenous Fijian. The people of Ono-i-Lau make the best *magi magi* (sennit rope) and *tabu kaisi* mats in the country. Only high chiefs may sit on these mats. Ono-i-Lau once had air service from Suva, but although the airstrip is maintained for emergency use, there are no regular flights and the only access is occasional visits by vessels such as the barge *Sea-Link* or the copra boat *Adi Lomai.* For information on departures, inquire at Muaiwalu Wharf in Suva.

The Moala Group

Structurally, geographically, and historically, the high volcanic islands of Moala, Totoya, and Matuku have more to do with Viti Levu than with the rest of Lau. In the mid-19th century, the Tongan warlord Enele Ma'afu conquered the islands, and today they're still administered as part of the Lau Group. All three islands have varied scenery, with dark green rainforests above grassy slopes, good anchorage, many villages, and abundant food. Their unexplored nature yet relative proximity to Suva by boat make them an ideal escape for adventurers. No tourist facilities of any kind exist in the Moala Group.

Triangular **Moala** is an intriguing 68-square-kilometer island, the ninth-largest in

MOALA

(Government Station) Naroi

Maloku

Vunuku

Delai Moala ▲ 467m

Moala

Nuku

Navatu

Vadra

Namoala

Narukua

Keteira
Cakova

Nasoki

0   2 mi
0   2 km

© DAVID STANLEY

Fiji. Two small crater lakes on the summit of Delai Moala (467 m) are covered with matted sedges, which will support a person's weight. Though the main island is volcanic, an extensive system of reefs flanks the shores. Ships call at the small government station of Naroi, also the site of a disused airstrip.

Totoya is a horseshoe-shaped high island enclosing a deep bay on the south. The bay, actually the island's sunken crater, can only be entered through a narrow channel known as the Gullet, and the southeast trade winds send high waves across the reefs at the mouth of the bay, making this a dangerous place. Better anchorage is found off the southwest arm of the island. Five Fijian villages are found on Totoya, while neighboring **Matuku** has seven. The anchorage in a submerged crater on the west side of Matuku is one of the finest in Fiji.

Rotuma

Rotuma is a little piece of Polynesia in Melanesian Fiji. This is mostly a place for those who want to go where few tourists have ever gone. Most visitors to Rotuma are relatives or friends of local residents, and the number of foreign tourists arriving here is negligible.

According to legend, lushly vegetated Rotuma was formed by Raho, a Samoan folk hero who dumped two basketfuls of earth here to create the twin islands, joined by the Motusa Isthmus. Tongans from Niuafo'ou conquered Rotuma in the 17th century and ruled from Noa'tau until they were overthrown.

The first recorded European visit was by Captain Edwards of HMS *Pandora* in 1791, while he was searching for the *Bounty* mutineers. Tongan Wesleyan missionaries introduced Christianity in 1842, followed in 1847 by Marist Roman Catholics. Their followers fought pitched battles in the religious wars of 1871 and 1878, with the Wesleyans emerging victorious. Tiring of strife, the chiefs asked Britain to annex the island in 1879. Cession officially took place in 1881, and Rotuma has been part of Fiji ever since. European traders ran the copra trade from their settlement at Motusa, until local cooperatives took over. A 2004 film, *The Land Has Eyes,* directed by Vilsoni Hereniko, explores the stifling conformism of Rotuman society.

On Rotuma today, the administration is in the hands of a district officer responsible to the

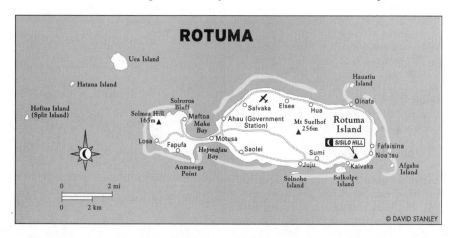

district commissioner at Levuka. Most decisions of the 15-member Rotuma island council pertain to local concerns. The island remains remote from the rest of Fiji, and a desire for independence is felt among some Rotumans. Some 2,800 Rotumans presently inhabit the island, and another 4,700 live in Suva and Naitasiri. The lighter-skinned Polynesian Rotumans are easily distinguished from Fijians. The women weave fine white mats. Fiji's juiciest oranges are grown here, and Rotuma kava is noted for its strength.

SIGHTS

Ships arrive at a wharf on the edge of the reef, connected to Oinafa Point by a 200-meter coral causeway, which acts as a breakwater. There's a lovely white beach at **Oinafa.** The airstrip is to the west, between Oinafa and Ahau, the government station. Look for the fine stained-glass windows in the Catholic church at **Sumi** on the south coast. Inland near the center of the island is Mount Suelhof (256 m), the highest peak; climb it for the view.

Maftoa, across the Motusa Isthmus, has a graveyard with huge stones brought here long ago. It's said that four men could go into a trance and carry the stones with their fingers. The yacht anchorage in Hopmafau Bay is well protected from northern winds.

Sororoa Bluff (218 m), above Maftoa, can be climbed, though the view is obstructed by vegetation. Deserted **Vaioa Beach,** on the west side of Sororoa Bluff, is one of the finest in the Pacific. A kilometer southwest of Vaioa Beach is **Solmea Hill** (165 m), with an inactive crater on its north slope. On the coast at the northwest corner of Rotuma is a natural **stone bridge** over the water. A cave with a swimmable freshwater pool is at **Fapufa** on the south coast.

Hatana, a tiny islet off the west end of Rotuma, is said to be the final resting place of Raho, the demigod who created Rotuma. A pair of volcanic rocks before a stone altar surrounded by a coral ring are said to be the King and Queen stones. Today, Hatana is a refuge for seabirds. **Hofiua,** or Split Island, looks like

it was cut in two with a knife; a circular boulder bridges the gap.

Visitors are expected to request permission before visiting sites like Sisilo or the cave at Fapufa. Inquire at Ahau about whom to ask (permission will always be given unless something peculiar has come up). It's a courtesy expected by the Rotumans and will avoid unpleasant misunderstandings.

(Sisilo Hill

This archaeological site near Noa'tau features the massive Kine'he'he Platform and the burial place of the *sau* (kings) of yore. In 1824, 20 well-maintained stone tombs were recorded here. Each consisted of four coral slabs, including a large one at the head, a smaller one at the foot, and two long slabs along the sides. Traditional feasts would be held here, with kava poured on the kings' graves. The last *sau* to be interred here was a man named Maraf who was killed during a battle between the island clans in 1845. He was buried with a defective cannon as his headstone. The old burial ground on Sisilo Hill is now overgrown with brush, and a local guide will be necessary if you want to see anything. In any case, it's important to ask permission of the elders in Noa'tau before visiting a sacred spot such as this.

ACCOMMODATIONS

Though the airport opened as far back as 1982, places to stay on Rotuma are few. Many Rotumans live in Suva, however, and if you have a Rotuman friend, he/she may be willing to send word to his/her family to expect you. Ask your friend what you should take along as a gift. It's appropriate to make a financial contribution to your host family soon after you arrive, in order to compensate them for your stay (F$50 a day per couple is the minimum you should offer). When deciding on the amount, bear in mind that groceries purchased in the small stores around Rotuma cost about double what they would on Viti Levu.

The only official place to stay is **Mojito's Barfly** (tel. 889-1144) across the street from Motusa Primary School. The four rooms with shared bath in two Polynesian-style houses are used to accommodate government workers, who pay F$65 per person, including meals and laundry (no cooking facilities provided). Despite the name, there's no bar.

There's no bank on Rotuma, or anywhere else in Lau, so be sure to change enough money to cover all local expenditures before leaving Suva. In emergencies, you might be able to have someone wire money to you via Western Union, care of the Post Shop at Ahau.

GETTING THERE

At last report the weekly Pacific Sun flights from Suva to Rotuma were not operating. Check with the airline to see if this has changed. Ships operate from Suva to Rotuma once a month, a two-day trip. (Turn to *Ships to Kadavu, Lau, and Rotuma* in the *Suva* chapter for more information.) Bligh Water Shipping (www.bligh watershipping.com.fj) occasionally has a ship to Rotuma from Lautoka.

Be aware that transportation to and from Rotuma, either by boat or plane, can be erratic, and you should be as flexible as possible. It's not uncommon for the boat from Suva to be delayed two weeks with engine trouble, and even when operating, the plane has also been known not to go on schedule or flights can be canceled.

BACKGROUND

The Land

Fiji lies 5,100 kilometers southwest of Hawaii and 3,150 kilometers northeast of Sydney, astride the main air route between North America and Australia. Nadi is the hub of Pacific air routes, while Suva is a regional shipping center. The 180th meridian cuts through Fiji, but the international date line swings east so the entire island group can share the same day.

THE FIJI ISLANDS

The name Fiji is a Tongan corruption of the indigenous name "Viti." The Fiji Islands are arrayed in a horseshoe configuration, with Viti Levu (great Fiji) and adjacent islands on the west, Vanua Levu (great land) and Taveuni to the north, and the Lau Group on the east. This upside-down-U-shaped archipelago encloses the Koro Sea, which is relatively shallow and sprinkled with the Lomaiviti (central Fiji) group of islands. Together the Fiji Islands are scattered over 1,290,000 square kilometers of the South Pacific Ocean with less than 1.5 percent dry land.

If every single island was counted, the isles of the Fiji archipelago would number in the thousands. However, a mere 322 are judged large enough for human habitation, and of

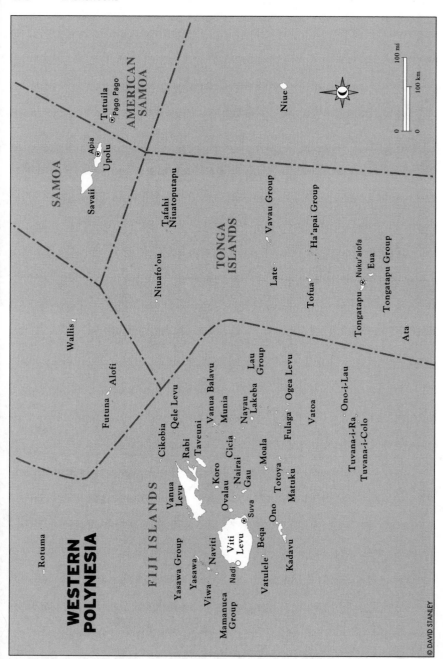

WESTERN POLYNESIA

© DAVID STANLEY

FIJI ISLANDS

Rotuma

Mamanuca Group

Yasawa Group

Yasawa

Viwa

Naviti

Nadi

Viti Levu

Suva

Vatulele

Beqa

Kadavu

Ono

Vanua Levu

Rabi

Cikobia

Qele Levu

Taveuni

Koro

Ovalau

Nairai

Gau

Cicia

Totoya

Matuku

Moala

Vanua Balavu

Munia

Navau

Lakeba

Lau Group

Fulaga

Ogea Levu

Vatoa

Tuvana-i-Ra

Tuvana-i-Colo

Ono-i-Lau

Futuna

Alofi

Wallis

SAMOA

Savaii

Apia

Upolu

Tutuila

Pago Pago

AMERICAN SAMOA

Niuafo'ou

Tafahi

Niuatoputapu

TONGA ISLANDS

Vavau Group

Late

Ha'apai Group

Tofua

Tongatapu

Nuku'alofa

Eua

Ata

Tongatapu Group

Niue

100 mi

100 km

0

those, only 106 are inhabited. That leaves 216 uninhabited islands, most of them prohibitively isolated or lacking fresh water.

Most of the Fiji Islands are volcanic oceanic islands. All of Fiji's volcanoes are presently dormant or extinct, although both Vuna on Taveuni and Nabukelevu on Kadavu, classified as dormant, have erupted within the past 2,000 years. There are as many as 50 groups of hot springs. The two largest islands, Viti Levu and Vanua Levu, together account for 87 percent of Fiji's 18,272 square kilometers of land. Viti Levu has 57 percent of the land area and 75 percent of the people, while Vanua Levu, with 30 percent of the land, has 18 percent of the population. Viti Levu alone is bigger than all five archipelagos of French Polynesia. In fact, Fiji has more land and people than all of Polynesia combined.

Viti Levu

Oval-shaped Viti Levu (10,531 square km) is about 150 by 100 kilometers in size. The 1,000-meter-high Nadrau Plateau in central Viti Levu is cradled between Tomaniivi (1,323 meters) on the north and Monavatu (1,131 meters) on the south. On different sides of this elevated divide are the Colo-East Plateau drained by the Rewa River, the Navosa Plateau drained by the Ba, the Colo-West Plateau drained by the Sigatoka, and the Navua Plateau drained by the Navua. Some 29 well-defined peaks rise above Viti Levu's interior; most of the inhabitants live in the river valleys or along the coast.

The Nadi River slices across the Nausori Highlands, with the Mount Evans Range (1,195 meters) towering above Lautoka. Other highland areas of Viti Levu are cut by great rivers like the Sigatoka, the Navua, the Rewa, and the Ba, navigable far inland by outboard canoe or kayak. White-water rafters shoot down the Navua and occasionally the Ba, while the lower Sigatoka flows gently through Fiji's market-garden "salad bowl." Fiji's largest river, the Rewa, pours into the Pacific through a wide delta just below Nausori. After a hurricane, the Rewa becomes a dark torrent—worth a special visit to Nausori to see. Sharks have been known to enter both the Rewa and the Sigatoka and swim far upstream.

Vanua Levu

Vanua Levu (5,587 square km) has a peculiar shape, with two long peninsulas pointing northeastward. Natewa Bay, the South Pacific's largest bay, almost cuts the island in two. A mountain range between Labasa and Savusavu reaches 1,032 meters at Nasorolevu. Navotuvotu (842 meters), east of Bua Bay, is Fiji's best example of a broad shield volcano, with lava flows built up in layers. The mountains are closer to the southeast coast, and a broad lowland belt runs along the northwest. Of the rivers, the Dreketi is the largest, flowing west across northern Vanua Levu; navigation on the Labasa River is restricted to small boats. The interior of Vanua Levu is lower and drier than Viti Levu, yet scenically superb: The road from Labasa to Savusavu is a visual feast.

Other Islands

Vanua Levu's bullet-shaped neighbor Taveuni soars to 1,241 meters, its rugged southeast coast battered by the trade winds. Taveuni, the garden island, and Kadavu, with its contorted shape, are known as the finest islands in Fiji for their scenic beauty and agricultural potential. Geologically, the uplifted limestone islands of the Lau Group have more in common with Tonga than with the rest of Fiji. Northwest of Viti Levu is the rugged volcanic Yasawa Group.

Coasts and Reefs

More than a quarter of the South Pacific's coral reefs are in Fiji. Fringing reefs are common along most of the coastlines, and Fiji is outstanding for its 33 barrier reefs. The Great Sea Reef off the north coast of Vanua Levu is the fourth-longest in the world, and the Great Astrolabe Reef north of Kadavu is one of the most diverse. Countless other unexplored barrier reefs are found off northern Viti Levu and elsewhere. The many cracks, crevices, walls,

GAU ISLAND CROSS-SECTION

The difference between barrier and fringing reefs is illustrated in the southwest-northwest cross-section of Gau Island. The vertical scale has been exaggerated. The barrier reef of Gau's southwestern shore is separated from the main island's coast by a deep lagoon, while only a tidal flat lies between Gau's northeastern coast and the edge of the fringing reef.

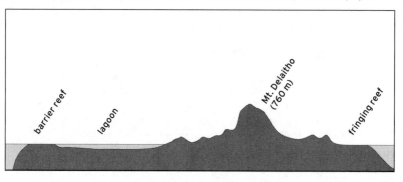

and caves along Fiji's reefs are guaranteed to delight the scuba diver.

The configuration of the Great Astrolabe Reef off Ono and Kadavu islands confirms Darwin's theory of atoll formation. The famous formulator of the theory of natural selection surmised that atolls form as high volcanic islands subside into lagoons. The original island's fringing reef grows up into a barrier reef as the volcanic portion sinks. When the last volcanic material finally disappears below sea level, the coral rim of the reef/atoll remains as an indicator of how big the island once was.

Of course, all this takes place over millions of years, but deep below every atoll is the old volcanic core. Darwin's theory is well illustrated here, where Ono and the small volcanic islands to the north remain inside the Great Astrolabe Reef. Return in 25 million years, and all you'll find will be the reef itself.

CORAL REEFS

Coral reefs are the world's oldest ecological system and cover some 200,000 square kilometers worldwide, between 25 degrees north and 25 degrees south latitude. A reef is created by the accumulation of millions of calcareous skeletons left by myriad generations of tiny coral polyps, some no bigger than a pinhead. A small piece of coral is a colony composed of large numbers of polyps. Though the reef's skeleton is usually white, the living polyps are of many different colors. The individual polyps on the surface often live a long time, continuously secreting layers to the skeletal mass beneath the tiny layer of flesh.

Coral polyps thrive in clear salty water where the temperature never drops below 18°C nor goes over 30°C. They require a base not more than 50 meters below the water's surface on which to form. The coral colony grows slowly upward on the consolidated skeletons of its ancestors until it reaches the low-tide mark, after which development extends outward on the edges of the reef.

Polyps extract calcium carbonate from the water and deposit it in their skeletons. All limy reef-building corals also contain microscopic algae within their cells. The algae, like all green plants, obtain energy from the sun and contribute this energy to the growth of the reef's skeleton. As a result, corals behave (and look) more like plants than animals, competing for sunlight just as terrestrial plants do. Many polyps are also carnivorous; they use their minute, stinging tentacles to capture tiny planktonic animals and organic particles at night. Sunlight is critical for coral growth. Colonies grow quickly on the ocean side, especially the windward side, due to clearer water and a greater abundance of food. A strong, healthy reef can grow 4–5 centimeters a year. Fresh or cloudy water inhibits coral growth, which is why villages and ports all across the Pacific are located at the reef-free mouths of rivers. Hurricanes can kill coral by covering the reef with sand, which prevents light and nutrients from getting through. Erosion caused by logging or urban development can have the same effect. In Fiji, the hard corals have been seriously impacted by coral bleaching related to surges in water temperatures during hurricanes or otherwise; the soft corals are less affected.

Coral Types

Corals belong to a broad group of stinging creatures, which includes polyps, soft corals, stony corals, sea anemones, sea fans, and jellyfish. Only those types with hard skeletons and a single hollow cavity within the body are considered true corals. Stony corals such as brain, table, staghorn, honeycomb, and mushroom corals have external skeletons and are important reef builders. Soft corals, black corals, and sea fans have internal skeletons. The fire corals are recognized by their smooth, velvety surface and yellowish brown color. The stinging toxins of this last group can easily penetrate human skin and cause swelling and painful burning that can last up to an hour. The many varieties of soft, colorful anemones gently waving in the current might seem inviting to touch, but beware, because many are also poisonous.

The corals, like most other forms of life in the Pacific, colonized the ocean from the fertile seas of Southeast Asia. Therefore the number of species declines as you move east. More than 800 species of reef-building coral make their home in the Pacific, compared to only 48 in the Caribbean. The diversity of coral colors and forms is endlessly amazing. This is our most unspoiled environment, a world of almost indescribable beauty.

Exploring a Reef

Until you've explored a good coral reef, you haven't experienced one of the greatest joys of nature. While one cannot walk through pristine forests due to a lack of paths, it's quite possible to swim over untouched reefs. Coral reefs are the most densely populated living space on earth—the rainforests of the sea! It's wise to bring along a high-quality mask you've tested thoroughly beforehand, as there's nothing more disheartening than a leaky, ill-fitting mask. Also, many dive shops and resorts in Fiji rent snorkeling gear.

Conservation

Coral reefs are one of the most fragile and complex ecosystems on earth, providing food and shelter for countless species of fish, crustaceans (shrimps, crabs, and lobsters), mollusks (shells), and other animals. The coral reefs of the South Pacific protect shorelines during storms, supply sand to maintain the islands, furnish food for the local population, form a living laboratory for science, and are major tourist attractions. Reefs worldwide host more than two million species of life. Without coral, the South Pacific would be immeasurably poorer.

Hard corals grow only about 10–25 millimeters a year, and it can take 7,000–10,000 years for a coral reef to form. Though corals look solid, they're easily broken. By standing on them, breaking off pieces, or carelessly dropping anchor, you can destroy in a few minutes what took millennia to form. Once a piece of coral breaks off, it dies, and it may be years before the coral reestablishes itself and even longer before the broken piece is replaced. The "wound" may become infected by algae, which can multiply and kill the entire coral colony.

CORALS OF THE PACIFIC

Acropora

staghorn fire coral
(Millepora accicornis)

table coral

mushroom coral
(Fungia fungites)

elkhorn fire coral
(Millepora platyphylla)

brain coral
(Meandrina)

honeycomb coral (Favia matthaii)

When this happens over a wide area, the diversity of marine life declines dramatically.

We recommend that you not remove seashells, coral, plant life, or marine animals from the sea. Doing so upsets the delicate balance of nature, and coral is much more beautiful underwater anyway! This is a particular problem along shorelines frequented by large numbers of tourists, who can completely strip a reef in very little time. Also think twice about purchasing jewelry or souvenirs made from coral or seashells. Genuine traditional handicrafts that incorporate shells are one thing, but by purchasing unmounted seashells or mass-produced coral curios, you are contributing to the destruction of the marine environment. The triton shell, for example, helps keep in check the reef-destroying crown-of-thorns starfish.

The anchors and anchor chains of private yachts can do serious damage to coral reefs. Pronged anchors are more environmentally friendly than larger, heavier anchors, and plastic tubing over the end of the anchor chain helps minimize the damage. If at all possible, anchor in sand. A longer anchor chain makes this easier, and a good windlass is essential for larger boats. A recording depth sounder will help locate sandy areas when none are available in shallow water. If you don't have a depth sounder and can't see the bottom, lower the anchor until it just touches the bottom and feel the anchor line as the boat drifts. If it grumbles, lift it up, drift a little, and try again. Later, if you notice your chain grumbling, motor over the anchor, lift it out of the coral, and move. Not only do sand and mud hold better, but your anchor will be less likely to become fouled. Try to arrive before 1500 to be able to see clearly where you're anchoring—polarized sunglasses make it easier to distinguish corals.

Stricter government regulation of the marine environment is urgently needed, and in some places coral reefs are already protected. Legislators must write stricter laws and impose fines. If you witness dumping or any other marine-related activity that you think may be illegal, don't become directly involved, but do take a few notes and calmly report the incident to the local authorities or police at the first opportunity. You'll learn something about their approach to these matters, and you'll make them aware of your concerns.

Resort developers can minimize damage to their valuable reefs by providing public mooring buoys so yachts don't have to drop anchor and pontoons so snorkelers aren't tempted to stand on coral. Licensing authorities can make such amenities mandatory whenever appropriate, and, in extreme cases, endangered coral gardens should be declared off-limits to private boats. As consumerism spreads, once-remote areas become subject to the problems of pollution and overexploitation, and the garbage is visibly piling up on many shores. As a guest in Fiji, it's appropriate to take a conservationist approach. For as Marshall McLuhan said, "On Spaceship Earth, there are no passengers; we are all members of the crew."

CLIMATE

Along the coast the weather is warm and pleasant, without great variations in temperature. The southeast trade winds prevail June–October, the best months to visit. In February and March, the wind often comes directly out of the east. These winds dump 3,000 millimeters of annual rainfall on the humid southeast coasts of the big islands, increasing to 5,000 millimeters inland. The drier northwest coasts, in the lee, get only 1,500–2,000 millimeters.

The official dry season (June–Oct.) is not always dry at Suva, although much of the rain falls at night. In addition, Fiji's winter (May–Nov.) is cooler and less humid, the preferred months for mountain trekking. During the drier season, the reef waters are clearest for the scuba diver. Yet even during the rainy summer months (Dec.–Apr.), bright sun often follows the rains, and the rain is only a slight inconvenience. The refreshing trade winds relieve the high humidity. Summer is hurricane season, with Fiji, Samoa, and Tonga receiving up to five tropical storms annually.

In Fiji you can obtain recorded weather

FIJI CLIMATE CHART

LOCATION		JAN.	FEB.	MAR.	APR.	MAY	JUNE	JULY	AUG.	SEPT.	OCT.	NOV.	DEC.	ALL YEAR
Nadi airport, Viti Levu	C	27.0	26.9	26.7	26.2	25.0	24.0	23.3	23.8	24.5	25.2	25.9	26.6	25.4
	mm	294	291	373	195	99	78	51	62	88	73	137	181	1,922
Yasawa Island	C	27.0	26.9	26.6	26.4	26.0	25.3	24.6	24.8	25.1	25.7	26.1	26.7	25.9
	mm	281	287	344	168	110	106	45	68	90	78	187	165	1,929
Ba, Viti Levu	C	27.2	27.1	26.9	26.5	25.3	24.1	23.3	23.8	24.7	25.5	26.1	26.1	25.6
	mm	322	409	387	203	101	67	46	65	72	91	126	228	2,117
Nadarivatu, Viti Levu	C	21.6	22.0	21.5	21.0	20.0	18.9	18.3	18.8	19.0	20.1	20.6	21.1	20.2
	mm	599	668	689	362	181	99	89	125	126	136	220	400	3,694
Rakiraki, Viti Levu	C	27.6	27.6	27.3	26.8	25.9	24.9	24.2	24.6	25.1	25.9	26.6	27.1	26.2
	mm	307	371	372	236	122	66	47	68	74	83	140	221	2,107
Suva, Viti Levu	C	26.8	26.9	26.8	26.1	24.8	23.9	23.1	23.2	23.7	24.4	25.3	26.2	25.1
	mm	314	299	386	343	280	177	148	200	212	218	268	313	3,158
Vunisea, Kadavu I.	C	26.4	26.8	26.1	25.4	24.2	23.2	22.4	22.6	23.1	23.9	24.7	26.1	24.6
	mm	239	225	313	256	208	102	112	121	122	126	151	177	2,152
Nabouwalu, Vanua Levu	C	26.9	27.1	26.7	26.3	25.5	24.7	23.9	24.0	24.4	25.2	25.4	26.3	25.6
	mm	328	354	352	275	198	130	96	114	139	164	208	279	2,637
Labasa, Vanua Levu	C	26.8	26.8	26.6	26.2	25.3	24.4	23.8	24.2	24.7	25.4	25.9	26.4	25.6
	mm	449	457	465	236	97	86	38	60	77	96	210	263	2,534
Vunikodi, Vanua Levu	C	26.6	26.7	26.6	26.3	26.0	25.3	24.6	24.7	25.0	25.6	25.9	26.6	25.8
	mm	302	377	409	225	143	131	92	90	114	132	264	220	2,499
Rotuma Island	C	27.4	27.3	27.2	27.4	27.2	26.8	26.4	26.5	26.7	26.8	27.0	27.2	27.0
	mm	358	390	430	278	262	244	207	230	277	283	327	331	3,617
Matuku, Lau Group	C	26.8	27.0	26.8	26.3	25.1	24.1	23.1	23.6	24.2	25.0	25.7	26.4	25.3
	mm	231	230	265	192	151	116	114	78	110	97	139	152	1,875
Ono-i-Lau, Lau Group	C	26.3	26.5	26.4	25.7	24.3	23.4	22.4	22.4	22.7	23.6	24.5	25.3	24.4
	mm	201	199	266	196	144	109	90	94	106	114	128	145	1,792

information updated every five hours by dialing 330-1642 or 673-6080. The same information is available online at www.met.gov.fj.

Currents and Winds

The Pacific Ocean has a greater impact on the world's climate than any other geographical feature on earth. By moving heat away from the equator and toward the poles, it stretches the bounds of the area in which life can exist. Broad, circular ocean currents flow from east to west across the tropical Pacific, clockwise in the North Pacific, counterclockwise in the South Pacific. North and south of the horse latitudes, just outside the tropics, the currents cool and swing east. The prevailing winds push the same way: the southeast trade winds south of the equator, the northeast trade winds north of the equator, and the low-pressure doldrums in between. Westerlies blow east above the cool currents north and south of the tropics. This natural air-conditioning system brings warm water to Australia and Japan, cooler water to Peru and California.

The climate of the high islands is closely related to these winds. As air is heated near the equator, it rises and flows at high altitudes toward the poles. By the time it reaches about 30 degrees south latitude, it will have cooled enough to cause it to fall and flow back toward the equator near sea level. In the southern hemisphere, the rotation of the earth deflects the winds to the left to become the southeast trades. When these cool, moist trade winds hit a high island, they are warmed by the sun and forced up. Above 500 meters elevation they begin to cool again and their moisture condenses into clouds. At night the winds do not capture much warmth and are more likely to discharge their moisture as rain. The windward slopes of the high islands catch the trades head-on and are usually wet, while those on the leeward side may be dry.

ENVIRONMENTAL ISSUES

Fiji's forests and reefs are poorly protected. Large tracts of virgin rainforest were cleared and replanted in mahogany in the 1960s, leading to a serious loss of biodiversity. (Compounding this tragedy, there were other areas of degraded forest where the mahogany plantations could have

HURRICANES IN THE TROPICS

The official hurricane (or cyclone) season south of the equator is November–April, although hurricanes have also occurred in May and October. Since the ocean provides the energy, these low-pressure systems can form only over water with a surface temperature above 27°C; during years when water temperatures are high (such as during an El Niño), their frequency increases. The rotation of the earth must give the storm its initial spin, and this occurs mostly between latitudes 5 and 20 on either side of the equator.

As rainfall increases and the seas rise, the winds are drawn into a spiral that reaches its maximum speed in a ring around the center. In the South Pacific, a cyclone develops as these circular winds, rotating clockwise around a center, increase in velocity: force 8-9 winds blowing at 34-47 knots are called a gale, force 10-11 at 48-63 knots is a storm, force 12 winds revolving at 64 knots or more is a hurricane. Wind speeds can go as high as 100 knots, with gusts to 140 knots on the left side of the storm's path in the direction it's moving.

The eye of the hurricane can be 10-30 kilometers wide and surprisingly clear and calm, although at sea, contradictory wave patterns continue to wreak havoc. In the South Pacific, most hurricanes move south at speeds of 5-20 knots. As water is sucked into the low-pressure eye of the hurricane and waves reach 14 meters in height, coastlines can receive a surge of up to four meters of water, especially if the storm enters a narrowing bay or occurs at high tide.

CLIMATE CHANGE

The gravest danger facing the atolls and reefs of Oceania is the greenhouse effect, a gradual warming of the earth's environment due to fossil fuel combustion and the widespread clearing of forests. By the year 2030, the concentration of carbon dioxide in the atmosphere will have doubled from preindustrial levels, and as infrared radiation from the sun is absorbed by the gas, the trapped heat melts mountain glaciers and the polar ice caps. In addition, seawater expands as it warms up, so water levels could rise almost a meter by the year 2100, destroying shorelines created 5,000 years ago.

A 1982 study demonstrated that sea levels had already risen 12 centimeters in the previous century; in 1995, 2,500 scientists from 70 countries involved in the Intergovernmental Panel on Climate Change (IPCC) commissioned by the United Nations completed a two-year study with the warning that over the next century air temperatures may rise as much as 5°C and sea levels could go up 95 centimeters by 2100. Not only will this reduce the growing area for food crops, but rising sea levels will mean saltwater intrusion into groundwater supplies – a troubling prospect if accompanied by the increasing frequency of droughts that have been predicted. Coastal erosion will force governments to spend vast sums on road repairs and coastline stabilization.

Coral bleaching occurs when the organism's symbiotic algae are expelled in response to environmental stresses, such as when water temperatures rise as little as 1°C above the local maximum for a week or longer. Bleaching is also caused by increased radiation due to ozone degradation, and widespread instances of bleaching and reefs being killed by rising sea temperatures took place in Fiji during the El Niño event of 1998. A "hot spot" over Fiji in early 2000 caused further damage. The earth's surface has warmed 1°C over the past century, and by 2080 water temperatures may have increased 5°C. Acidification of the world's oceans is also gaining pace with sea waters absorbing up to half of the world's carbon dioxide emissions. Corals and shellfish cannot tolerate highly acidic waters. In Fiji,

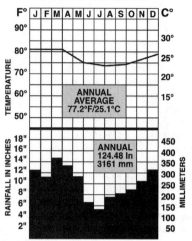

SUVA'S CLIMATE

ANNUAL AVERAGE 77.2°F/25.1°C

ANNUAL 124.48 In 3161 mm

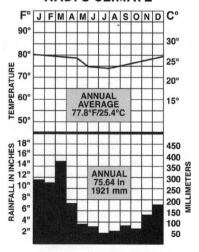

NADI'S CLIMATE

ANNUAL AVERAGE 77.8°F/25.4°C

ANNUAL 75.64 In 1921 mm

coral bleaching will become an annual event by 2050, effectively killing all of the region's reefs. Reef destruction will reduce coastal fish stocks and lead to whole shorelines being swept away.

Increasing temperatures may already be contributing to the dramatic jump in the number of hurricanes in the South Pacific. For example, Fiji experienced only 12 tropical hurricanes from 1941 to 1980, but 10 from 1981 to 1989, and in the face of devastating hurricanes, insurance companies are withdrawing coverage from some areas. In 1997 and 1998, the El Niño phenomenon brought with it another round of devastating hurricanes. Hurricane Ami in January 2003 was the worst storm to hit Fiji in a decade.

Unfortunately, those most responsible for the problem, the industrialized countries led by the United States (and including Australia and Canada), have strongly resisted taking any action to significantly cut greenhouse-gas emissions, and new industrial polluters such as India and China are making matters much worse. And as if that weren't bad enough, the hydrofluorocarbons (HFCs) presently being developed by corporate giants like DuPont to replace the ozone-destructive chlorofluorocarbons (CFCs) used in cooling systems are far more potent greenhouse gases than carbon dioxide.

In February 2007, the Fourth Assessment Report by the IPCC concluded that "warming of the climate system is unequivocal, as is now evident from observations of increases in global average air and ocean temperatures, widespread melting of snow and ice and rising global average sea level...most of the observed increase in globally averaged temperatures since the mid-20th century is very likely due to the observed increase in anthropogenic greenhouse gas concentrations." The word anthropogenic means simply "caused or produced by humans." Climate change deniers take note.

What to expect? A similar increase in temperature of just 6°C at the end of the Permian period 250 million years ago eventually wiped out 95 percent of species alive on earth at the time, and it took 100 million years for species diversification to return to previous levels.

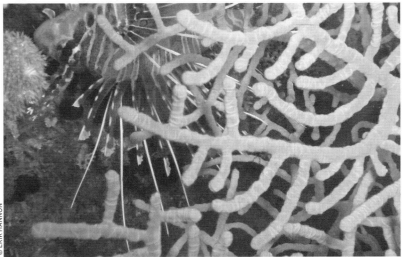

© ERIK HANNON

Coral reefs, one of the most fragile ecosystems on earth, are harmed by climate change.

been established with far less impact, and the existing rainforest could have been harvested sustainably.) The logging of native species goes on today with little government control.

In the agricultural areas, land ownership issues have led to soil degradation and erosion, as little effort is made to conserve or improve the land long-term. Runoff of fertilizer and mill wastes has polluted some coastal waters off western Viti Levu and Vanua Levu. The waters of Nadi Bay are murky for a reason. Suva Harbor has been partly contaminated by poor waste management practices and sewer seepage. Industrial wastes have had an impact at Suva, Lautoka, and Labasa.

National parks have been created in western Viti Levu and on Taveuni most notably, but these are based on partnerships with local landowning clans rather than government management of state lands. The protection of reefs also depends on the cooperation of resorts, tour operators, Fijian clans, and individual tourists, groups whose interests do not always coincide. This has left even the protected areas of Fiji vulnerable with limited resources for conservation.

Flora and Fauna

FLORA

The flora of Fiji originated in the Malaysian region; in the two regions, ecological niches are filled by similar plants. More than 2,000 species of plants grow in Fiji, of which 476 are indigenous to Fiji; 10 percent of those are found only here. Taveuni is known for its rare climbing *tagimaucia* flower. The absence of leaf-eating animals in Fiji allowed the vegetation to develop largely without the protective spines and thorns found elsewhere, and one of the only stinging plants is the *salato,* a shrub or tree bearing large, heart-shaped leaves with purple ribs and ragged edges that inflict painful wounds when touched. Hairs on the leaves break off in the skin, and the intense stinging pain begins half a minute later. This soon diminishes into an itch that becomes painful again if scratched. The itch can recur weeks and even months later.

Patterns of rainfall are in large part responsible for the variety of vegetation here. The wetter sides of the high islands are heavily forested, with occasional thickets of bamboo and scrub. Natural forests cover 40 percent of Fiji's total land area, and about a quarter of these forests are classified as production forest suitable for logging. The towering *dakua* or kauri tree, once carved into massive Fijian war canoes, has already disappeared from Viti Levu, and the last stands are now being logged on Vanua Levu. Since the 1960s, much replanting has been done in mahogany, a hardwood originating in Central America. The native *yaka* is a conifer whose wood has an attractive grain.

Coconut groves fill the coastal plains. On the drier sides, open savanna *(talasiga)* of coarse saw grasses predominates where the original vegetation has been destroyed by slash-and-burn agriculture. Sugarcane is now cultivated in the lowlands here, and Caribbean pine has been planted in many dry hilly areas, giving them a Scandinavian appearance in contrast to the palm-fringed shorelines. Around Christmas, poinciana, or flame trees, along the roads bloom bright red. The islands of the Lau Group are restricted to a few hardy, drought-resistant species such as coconuts and pandanus. Well-drained shorelines often feature ironwood, or *nokonoko,* a casuarina appreciated by woodcarvers.

Mangroves are commonly found along high island coastal lagoons. The cable roots of the saltwater-tolerant red mangrove anchor in the shallow upper layer of oxygenated mud, avoiding the layers of hydrogen sulfide below. The tree provides shade for tiny organisms dwelling in the tidal mudflats—a place for birds to nest and for fish or shellfish to feed and spawn. The mangroves also perform the same task as land-building coral colonies along the reefs. As sediments are trapped between the roots, the trees extend farther into the lagoon, creating a unique natural environment. The past decade has seen widespread destruction of the mangrove forests as land is reclaimed for agricultural use in northwest Viti Levu and around Labasa.

Many of Fiji's forest plants have medicinal applications, which have recently attracted the attention of patent-hungry pharmaceutical giants. The sap of the tree fern *(balabala)* was formerly used as a cure for headaches by Fijians, and its heart was eaten in times of famine.

Though only introduced to Fiji in the late 1860s, sugarcane probably originated in the South Pacific. On New Guinea the islanders have cultivated the plant for thousands of years, selecting vigorous varieties with the most colorful stems. The story goes that two Melanesian fishermen, To-Kabwana and To-Karavuvu, found a piece of sugarcane in their net one day. They threw it away, but, after twice catching it again, they decided to keep it and painted the stalk a bright color. Eventually the cane burst, and a woman came forth. She cooked food for the men but hid herself at night. Finally she was captured and became the wife of one of the men. From their union sprang the whole human race.

FAUNA

Some Fijian clans have totemic relationships with eels, prawns, turtles, and sharks, and are able to summon these creatures with special chants. Red prawns are revered on Vanua Vatu in southern Lau, on a tiny island off Naweni in southern Vanua Levu, and on Vatulele Island. The Nasaqalau people of Lakeba in southern Lau call sharks, and villagers of Korolevu in central Viti Levu call eels. The women of Namuana on Kadavu summon giant sea turtles with their chants. Turtle-calling is also practiced at Nacamaki village, in the northeast corner of Koro. Unfortunately sea turtles are becoming so rare that the turtle callers are having less and less success each year.

Mammals

The first Fijians brought with them pigs, dogs, chickens, and gray rats. The only native mammals are the monkey-faced fruit bat, or flying fox, called *beka* by the Fijians, and the smaller, insect-eating bat. Dolphins and whales ply the waters offshore.

The Indian mongoose was introduced by planters in the 1880s to combat rats, which were damaging the plantations. Unfortunately, no one realized at the time that mongooses

Mongooses were introduced by planters in the 1880s.

© ERIK HANNON

hunt by day, whereas rats are nocturnal, so the two seldom meet. Today, the mongoose is the scourge of chickens, native ground birds, iguanas, and other animals, though Kadavu, Koro, Gau, Ovalau, and Taveuni are mongoose-free (and thus the finest islands for bird-watching). Feral cats do the same sort of damage.

Birds

Of the 57 breeding species of land birds, 26 are endemic. Some 150 bird species have been recorded in Fiji, including broadbills, cuckoos, doves, fantails, finches, flycatchers, fruitdoves, hawks, herons, honeyeaters, kingfishers, lorikeets, owls, parrots, pigeons, rails, robins, silktails, swallows, thrushes, warblers, whistlers, and white-eyes. The Fijian names of some of these birds, such as the *kaka* (parrot), *ga* (gray duck), and *kikau* (giant honeyeater), imitate their calls. Red and green *kula* lorikeets are often seen in populated areas collecting nectar and pollen from flowering trees or feeding on fruit. Of the seabirds, boobies, frigate birds, petrels, and tropic birds are present.

The best time to observe forest birds is in the very early morning—they move around a lot less in the heat of the day. Kadavu and Taveuni are the best islands for bird-watching, with Colo-i-Suva Forest Park outside Suva the most accessible spot.

More in evidence is the introduced Indian mynah, with its yellow legs and beak, the Indian bulbul, and the Malay turtledove. The hopping common mynah bird *(Acridotheres tristis)* was introduced to many islands from Indonesia at the turn of the 20th century to control insects, which were damaging the citrus and coconut plantations. The mynahs multiplied profusely and have become major pests, inflicting great harm on the very trees they were brought in to protect. Worse still, many indigenous birds are forced out of their habitat by these noisy, aggressive birds. This and rapid deforestation by humans have made the South Pacific the region with the highest proportion of endangered endemic bird species on earth.

Reptiles and Amphibians

Three of the world's seven species of sea turtles nest in Fiji: the green, the hawksbill, and the leatherback. Nesting occurs between November and February, on nights when there is a full moon and a high tide. Sea turtles lay their eggs on the beach from which they themselves hatched. The female struggles up the beach and lays as many as 100 eggs in a hole, which she digs and then covers with her hind flippers. Female turtles don't commence this activity until they are 20 years old, thus a drop in numbers today has irreversible consequences a generation later. It's estimated that breeding females already number in the hundreds or low thousands, and all species of these magnificent creatures (sometimes erroneously referred to as "tortoises") now face extinction due to ruthless hunting, egg harvesting, and beach destruction. Turtles are often choked by floating plastic bags they mistake for food, or they drown in fishing nets. The Fiji Fisheries Department estimates that between 1980 and 1989 more than 10,000 hawksbill turtle shells were exported to Japan. The turtles and their eggs are now protected by law in Fiji (maximum penalty of six months in prison for killing a turtle). Sadly, this law is seldom enforced.

Geckos and skinks are small lizards often seen on the islands. The skink hunts insects by day; its tail breaks off if you catch it, but a new one quickly grows. The gecko is nocturnal and has no eyelids. Adhesive toe pads enable it to pass along vertical surfaces, and it changes color to avoid detection. Unlike the skink, which avoids humans, geckos often live in people's homes, where they eat insects attracted by electric lights. Its loud clicking call may be a territorial warning to other geckos.

One of the more unusual creatures found in Fiji and Tonga is the banded iguana, a lizard that lives in trees and can grow up to 70 centimeters long (two-thirds of which is tail). The iguanas are emerald green, and the male is easily distinguished from the female by his bluish-gray cross stripes. Banded iguanas change color to control their internal temperature, becoming darker when in the direct sun. Their

© MARK HEARD / WWW.FLICKR.COM/HEARDSY

a banded black-and-white sea snake

millipedes are the poisonous centipedes found in Fiji. While the millipede will roll up when touched, the centipede may inflict a painful sting through its front legs. The two types are easily distinguished by the number of pairs of legs per body segment: centipedes one, millipedes two. Fiji's largest centipedes grow up to 18 centimeters long and can have anywhere from 15 to 180 pairs of legs. These nocturnal creatures feed on insects and may be found in houses, while the two species of scorpions dwell only in the forest.

Sea Life

Fiji's richest store of life is found in the silent underwater world of the pelagic and lagoon fishes. It's estimated that half the fish remaining on our globe are swimming in the Pacific. The Pacific reefs provide a habitat for more than 4,000 fish species, 5–10 times the diversity of temperate oceans.

Coral pinnacles on the lagoon floor provide a safe haven for angelfish, butterfly fish, damselfish, groupers, soldierfish, surgeonfish, triggerfish, trumpet fish, and countless more. These fish seldom venture more than a few meters away from the protective coral, but larger fish such as barracuda, jackfish, parrot fish, pike, stingrays, and small sharks range across lagoon waters that are seldom deeper than 30 meters. The external side of the reef is also home to many of the above, but the open ocean is reserved for bonito, mahimahi, swordfish, tuna, wrasses, and the larger sharks. Passes between ocean and lagoon can be crowded with fish in transit, offering a favorite hunting ground for predators.

In the open sea, the food chain begins with phytoplankton, which flourish wherever ocean upwelling brings nutrients such as nitrates and phosphates to the surface. In the western Pacific this occurs near the equator, where massive currents draw water away toward Japan and Australia. Large schools of fast-moving tuna ply these waters feeding on smaller fish, which consume tiny phytoplankton drifting near the sunlit surface. The phytoplankton also exist in tropical lagoons where mangrove

nearest relatives are found in Central America, and how they could have reached Fiji remains a mystery. In 1979, a new species, the crested iguana, was discovered on Yaduataba, a small island off the west coast of Vanua Levu. It's estimated that 6,000 crested iguanas are presently on Yaduataba.

Two species of snakes inhabit Fiji: the very rare, poisonous *bolo loa* and the harmless Pacific boa, which can grow up to two meters long. Venomous sea snakes are common on some coasts, but they're docile and easily handled. Fijians call the common banded black-and-white sea snake the *dadakulaci*.

Land- and tree-dwelling native frogs are noteworthy for the long suction discs on their fingers and toes. Because they live deep in the rainforests and feed at night, they're seldom seen.

In 1936, the giant toad was introduced from Hawaii to control beetles, slugs, and millipedes. When this food source is exhausted, they tend to eat each other. At night, gardens and lawns may be full of them.

Insects and Arachnids

Not to be confused with the inoffensive

leaves, sea grasses, and other plant material are consumed by far more varied populations of reef fish, mollusks, and crustaceans.

Sharks

Human activities threaten deepwater shark species with extinction. Tens of thousands of sharks are harvested in the central and western Pacific each year, with the vast majority taken only for their fins. These are used to make soup at Asian restaurants, and the rest of the carcass is dumped back into the sea, a cruel, wasteful practice that is gradually removing this top predator from the ecosystem. The consequences of these depredations are as yet unknown.

In contrast, the danger from sharks to swimmers has been exaggerated. Of some 300 species, only 28 are known to have attacked humans. Most dangerous are the white, tiger, and blue sharks. Fortunately, all of these inhabit deep water far from the coasts. An average of 70–100 shark attacks a year occur worldwide with 10 fatalities, so considering the number of people who swim in the sea, your chances of being involved are about one in a million. In the South Pacific, shark attacks on snorkelers or scuba divers are extremely rare, and the tiny mosquito is a far more dangerous predator.

Sharks are not aggressive where food is abundant, but they can be very nasty far offshore. You're always safer if you keep your head underwater (with a mask and snorkel), and don't panic if you see a shark—you might attract it. Even if you do, they're usually only curious, so keep your eye on the shark and slowly back off. The swimming techniques of humans must seem very clumsy to fish, so it's not surprising if they want a closer look.

Sharks are attracted by shiny objects (a knife or jewelry, for example), bright colors (especially yellow and red), urine, blood, spearfishing, and splashing (divers should ease themselves into the water). Sharks normally stay outside the reef, but get local advice. White beaches are safer than dark, and clear water safer than murky. Avoid swimming in places where sewage or edible wastes enter the water, or where

fish have just been cleaned. Slaughterhouses sometimes attract sharks to an area by dumping offal into the nearby sea. You should also exercise care in places where locals have been fishing with spears or even with a hook and line that day.

Never swim alone if you suspect the presence of sharks. If you see one, even a supposedly harmless nurse shark lying on the bottom, get out of the water calmly and quickly, and go elsewhere. Studies indicate that sharks, like most other creatures, have a "personal space" around them that they will defend. Thus an attack could be a shark's way of warning someone to keep his distance, and it's a fact that more than half the victims of these incidents are not eaten but merely bitten. Sharks are less of a problem in the South Pacific than in colder waters, because small marine mammals (commonly hunted by sharks) are rare here, so you won't be mistaken for a seal or an otter.

Let common sense be your guide, not irrational fear or carelessness. Many scuba divers come to actually *look* for sharks, and local Divemasters seem able to swim among them with impunity. If you're in the market for some shark action, many dive shops can provide it. Just be aware that getting into the water with feeding sharks always entails some danger, and the Divemaster who admits this and lays down some basic safety guidelines (such as keeping your hands clasped or arms folded) is probably a safer bet than the macho man who just says he's been doing it for years without incident. Never snorkel on your own (without an experienced guide) near a spot where sharks are fed regularly, since you never know how the sharks will react to a surface swimmer without any food for them. Like all other wild animals, sharks deserve to be approached with respect.

Sea Urchins

Sea urchins (living pincushions) are common in tropical waters. The black variety is the most dangerous: Their long, sharp quills can go right through a snorkeler's fins. Even the small ones, which you can easily pick up in your hand, can pinch you if you're careless. They're found on

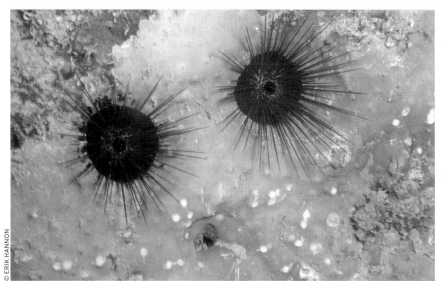

© ERIK HANNON

black sea urchins

rocky shores and reefs, never on clear, sandy beaches where the surf rolls in.

Most sea urchins are not poisonous, though quill punctures are painful and can become infected if not treated. The pain is caused by an injected protein, which you can eliminate by holding the injured area in a pail of very hot water for about 15 minutes. This will coagulate the protein, eliminating the pain for good. If you can't heat water, soak the area in vinegar or urine for 15 minutes. Remove the quills if possible, but as they are made of calcium, they'll decompose in a couple of weeks anyway—not much of a consolation as you limp along in the meantime. In some places sea urchins are considered a delicacy: The orange or yellow urchin gonads are delicious with lemon and salt.

Other Hazardous Creatures

Although jellyfish, stonefish, crown-of-thorns starfish, cone shells, eels, and poisonous sea snakes are dangerous, injuries resulting from any of these are rare. Gently apply methylated spirits, alcohol, or urine (but not water, kerosene, or gasoline) to areas stung by jellyfish. Inoffensive sea cucumbers (bêche-de-mer)

punctuate the lagoon shallows, but stonefish also rest on the bottom and are hard to see due to camouflaging; if you happen to step on one, its dorsal fins inject a painful poison, which burns like fire in the blood. Fortunately, stonefish are not common.

It's worth knowing that the venom produced by most marine animals is destroyed by heat, so your first move should be to soak the injured part in very hot water for 30 minutes. (Also hold the opposite foot or hand in the same water to prevent scalding due to numbness.) Other authorities claim the best first aid is to squeeze blood from a sea cucumber scraped raw on coral directly onto the wound. If a hospital or clinic is nearby, go there immediately.

Never pick up a live cone shell; some varieties have a deadly stinger dart coming out from the pointed end. The tiny blue-ring octopus is only five centimeters long but packs a poison that can kill a human. Eels hide in reef crevices by day; most are harmful only if you inadvertently poke your hand or foot in at them. Of course, never tempt fate by approaching them (fun-loving Divemasters sometimes feed the big ones by hand and stroke their backs).

History and Government

HISTORY
The Pre-European Period

The first people to arrive in Fiji were members of a light-skinned Austronesian-speaking race, probably the Polynesians. They originated in Taiwan or insular Southeast Asia and gradually migrated east past the already occupied islands of Melanesia. Distinctive Lapita pottery, decorated in horizontal geometric bands and dated from 1290 B.C., has been found in the sand dunes near Sigatoka, indicating they had reached here by 1500 B.C. or earlier. Much later, about 500 B.C., Melanesian people arrived, bringing with them their own distinct pottery traditions. From the fusion of these primordial peoples was the Fijian race born.

The hierarchical social structure of the early Fijians originated with the Polynesians. Status and descent passed through the male line, and power was embodied in the *turaga* (chief). The hereditary chiefs possessed the mana of an ancestral spirit or *vu*. Yet under the *vasu* system, a chiefly woman's son could lay claim to the property of his mother's brothers, and such relationships, combined with polygamy, kept society in a state of constant strife. This feudal aristocracy combined in confederations, or *vanua*, which extended their influence through war. Treachery and cannibalism were an intrinsic part of these struggles; women were taken as prizes or traded to form alliances. For defense, villages were fortified with ring ditches, or built along ridges or terraced hillsides.

The native aristocracy practiced customs that today seem barbarous and particularly cruel. The skull cap of a defeated enemy might be polished and used as a *yaqona* (kava) cup to humiliate a foe. Some chiefs even took delight in cooking and consuming body parts as their agonized victims looked on. Men were buried alive to hold up the posts of new houses, war canoes were launched over the living bodies of young girls, and the widows of chiefs were strangled to keep their husbands company in the spirit world. The farewells of some of these women are remembered today in dances and songs known as *meke*.

These feudal islanders were, on the other hand, guardians of one of the highest material cultures of the Pacific. They built great ocean-going double canoes *(drua)* up to 30 meters long; built and adorned large solid thatched houses *(bure)*; performed marvelous song-dances called *meke*; made tapa, pottery, and sennit (coconut cordage); and skillfully plaited mats. For centuries the Tongans came to Fiji to obtain great logs for making canoes and sandalwood for carving.

European Exploration

In 1643 Abel Tasman became the European discoverer of Fiji when he sighted Taveuni, although he didn't land. Tasman was searching for *terra australis incognita*, a great southern continent believed to balance the continents of the north. He also hoped to find new markets and trade routes. Unlike earlier Spanish explorers, Tasman entered the Pacific from the west rather than the east. He was the first European to see Tasmania, New Zealand, and Tonga, as well as Fiji. By sailing right around Australia from the Dutch East Indies, he proved New Holland (Australia) was not attached to the elusive southern continent.

In 1774, Captain Cook anchored off Vatoa in southern Lau. Like Tasman, he failed to proceed farther or land. It was left to Captain William Bligh to give Europeans an accurate picture of Fiji for the first time. After the *Bounty* mutiny in May 1789, Bligh and his companions were chased by canoe-loads of Fijian warriors just north of the Yasawa Islands as they rowed through on their escape route to Timor. Some serious paddling, a timely squall, and a lucky gap in the Great Sea Reef saved the Englishmen from ending up as the main course at a cannibal feast. The section of sea where this happened is now known as Bligh Water. Bligh cut directly across the center of

Fiji between the two main islands, and his careful observations made him the first real European explorer of Fiji, albeit an unwilling one. Bligh returned to Fiji in 1792, but once again he stayed aboard his ship.

Beachcombers and Chiefs

All of these early explorers stressed the perilous nature of Fiji's reefs. This, combined with tales told by the Tongans of cannibalism and warlike Fijian natives, caused most travelers to shun the area. Then, in 1800, a survivor from the shipwrecked American schooner *Argo* brought word that sandalwood grew in abundance along the Bua coast of Vanua Levu. This precipitated a rush of traders and beachcombers to the islands. A cargo of sandalwood bought from the islanders for $50 worth of trinkets could be sold to the Chinese in Canton for $20,000. By 1814 the forests had been stripped to provide joss sticks and incense, and the trade collapsed.

During this period Fiji was divided among warring chieftains. The first Europeans to actually mix with the Fijians were escaped convicts from Australia, who showed the natives how to use European muskets and were thus well received. White beachcombers such as the Swedish adventurer Charles Savage and the German Martin Bushart acted as middlemen between traders and Fijians and took sides in local conflicts. In one skirmish, Savage was separated from his fellows, captured, and eaten. With help from the likes of Savage, Naulivou, the cannibal chief of tiny Bau Island just off eastern Viti Levu, and his brother Tanoa extended their influence over much of western Fiji.

In his book *Following the Equator,* Mark Twain had this to say about the beachcombers:

They lived worthless lives of sin and luxury, and died without honor – in most cases by violence. Only one of them had any ambition; he was an Irishman named Connor. He tried to raise a family of fifty children and scored forty-eight. He died lamenting his failure. It was a foolish sort of avarice. Many a father would have been rich enough with forty.

From 1820 to 1850, European traders collected bêche-de-mer, a sea cucumber which, when smoked and dried, also brought a good price in China. While the sandalwood traders only stayed long enough to take on a load, the bêche-de-mer collectors set up shore facilities where the slugs were processed. Many traders, such as David Whippy, followed the example of the beachcombers and took local wives, establishing the part-Fijian community of today. By monopolizing the bêche-de-mer trade and constantly warring, Chief Tanoa's son and successor, Ratu Seru Cakobau (tha-kom-BAU), became extremely powerful in the 1840s and proclaimed himself Tui Viti, or king of Fiji.

The beginnings of organized trade brought a second wave of official explorers to Fiji. In 1827 Dumont d'Urville, from France, landed on Bau Island and met Tanoa. The Frenchmen caused consternation and confusion by refusing to drink *yaqona* (kava), preferring their own wine. The American Exploring Expedition of 1840, led by Commander Charles Wilkes, produced the first recognizable map of Fiji. When two Americans, including a nephew of Wilkes, were speared in a misunderstanding on a beach at Malolo Island, Wilkes ordered the offending fortified village stormed, and 87 Fijians were killed. The survivors were made to water and provision Wilkes's ships as tribute. Captain H. M. Denham of the HMS *Herald* prepared accurate navigational charts of the island group in 1855–1856, making regular commerce possible.

European and Tongan Penetration

As early as the 1830s, an assortment of European and American beachcombers had formed a small settlement at Levuka on the east coast of Ovalau Island just northeast of Bau, which whalers and traders used as a supply base. In 1846, John Brown Williams was appointed American commercial agent, one step below a consul. On July 4, 1849, Williams's home on Nukulau Island near present-day Suva burned down. Though the conflagration was caused by the explosion of a cannon during Williams's own fervent celebration of

FIJI ISLANDS CHRONOLOGY

1500 B.C.	Polynesians reach Fiji	1858	first British consul arrives in Fiji
500 B.C.	Melanesians reach Fiji	1860	founding of the town of Levuka
1643	Abel Tasman sights Taveuni	1862	Britain refuses to annex Fiji
1774	Captain Cook visits southern Lau	1865	confederacy of Fijian chiefs formed
1789	Captain Bligh and crew paddle past the Yasawas	1867	American warship threatens to shell Levuka
1797	Captain Wilson visits northern Lau		
1800	sandalwood discovered on Vanua Levu	1868	Polynesia Company granted the site of Suva
1820	bêche-de-mer trade begins	1871	Cakobau and Thurston form a government
1827	Dumont d'Urville visits Bau	1874	Fiji becomes a British colony
1830	Tahitian missionaries arrive in southern Lau	1875	measles epidemic kills a third of Fijians
1835	Methodist missionaries arrive at Lakeba	1879	first indentured Indian laborers arrive
1840	American Exploring Expedition visits Fiji	1881	first large sugar mill built at Nausori
1847	Tongan invasion of Lau led by Enele Ma'afu	1881	Rotuma annexed to Fiji
1849	home of John Brown Williams burns	1882	capital moved from Levuka to Suva
		1904	first elected Legislative Council
1851	first visit by hostile American gunboats	1916	Indian immigration ends
		1920	indenture system terminated
1854	Chief Cakobau accepts Christianity	1928	first flight from Hawaii lands at Suva
1855	Cakobau puts down the Rewa revolt	1939	Nadi Airport built

his national holiday, he objected to the way Fijian onlookers carried off items that they rescued from the flames. A shameless swindler, Williams had purchased Nukulau for only $30, yet he blamed the Tui Viti for his losses and sent Cakobau a $5,001.38 bill. American claims for damages eventually rose to $45,000, and in 1851 and 1855 American gunboats called and ordered Cakobau to pay up. This threat hung over Cakobau's head for many years, the 19th-century equivalent of 20th-century third-world debt. Increasing American involvement in Fiji led the British to appoint a consul, W. T. Pritchard, who arrived in 1858.

The early 1830s also saw the arrival from Tonga of the first missionaries. Though Tahitian pastors were sent by the London Missionary Society to Oneata in southern Lau as early as 1830, it was the Methodists based at Lakeba after 1835 who made the most lasting impression by rendering the Fijian language into writing. At first Christianity made little headway among the islanders—only after converting the powerful chiefs were the missionaries successful. Methodist missionaries David Cargill and William Cross were appalled by what they saw during a visit to Bau in 1838. A white missionary, Reverend Thomas Baker, was clubbed and eaten in central Viti Levu by the *kai colo* (hill people) as late as 1867.

1940	Native Land Trust Board established		1987	Rabuka declares Fiji a republic
1942	Fijian troops sent to the Solomon Islands		1987	Fiji expelled from British Commonwealth
1951	Fiji Airways (later Air Pacific) formed		1990	racially weighted constitution promulgated
1953	Queen Elizabeth II visits Fiji		1992	Rabuka elected under 1990 constitution
1963	women and Fijians enfranchised		1997	constitution revised to allow common roll voting
1965	Constitutional Convention held in London		1997	Fiji readmitted to the Commonwealth
1966	internal self-government achieved		1998	revised constitution comes into effect
1968	University of the South Pacific established		1999	Labor Party under Mahendra Chaudhry elected
1970	Fiji's first constitution adopted		2000	civil coup in May topples government
1970	Fiji becomes independent			
1973	sugar industry nationalized		2001	Qarase elected under 1997 constitution
1977	governor-general overturns election results		2003	South Pacific Games held in Suva
1978	Fijian peacekeeping troops sent to Lebanon		2006	military coup topples Qarase government
1981	Fijian troops sent to the Sinai		2009	InterContinental Resort Fiji opens
1983	Monasavu Hydroelectric Project opens		2009	1997 constitution abrogated
1987	Labor defeats Alliance Party		2009	Fiji suspended from the Commonwealth
1987	two military coups led by Colonel Rabuka		2010	30-year land leases converted to 99 years

In 1847, Enele Ma'afu, a member of the Tongan royal family, arrived in Lau and began building a personal empire under the pretense of defending Christianity. In 1853, King George of Tonga made Ma'afu governor of all Tongans resident in Lau. Meanwhile, there was continuing resistance from the warlords of the Rewa River area to Cakobau's dominance. In addition, the Europeans at Levuka suspected Cakobau of twice ordering their town set afire and were directing trade away from Bau. With his power in decline, in 1854 Cakobau accepted Christianity in exchange for an alliance with King George, and, in 1855, with the help of 2,000 Tongans led by King George

himself, Cakobau was able to put down the Rewa revolt at the Battle of Kaba. In the process, however, Ma'afu became the dominant force in Lau, Taveuni, and Vanua Levu.

During the early 1860s, as Americans fought their Civil War, the world price of cotton soared, and large numbers of Europeans arrived in Fiji hoping to establish cotton plantations. In 1867, the USS *Tuscarora* called at Levuka and threatened to bombard the town unless the still-outstanding American debt was paid. The next year an enterprising Australian firm, the Polynesia Company, paid off the Americans in exchange for a grant from Cakobau of 80,000 hectares of choice land, including the site of modern Suva. The British government later refused to recognize this grant, though they refunded the money paid to the Americans and accepted the claims of settlers who had purchased land from the company. Settlers soon numbered about 2,000 and Levuka boomed. It was a lawless era, and a need was felt for a central government. An attempt at national rule by a confederacy of chiefs lasted two years until failing in 1867, then three regional governments were set up in Bau (western), Lau (eastern), and Bua (northern), but these were only partly successful. With prices for Fiji's "Sea Island" cotton collapsing as the American South resumed production, a national administration under Cakobau and planter John Thurston was established at Levuka in 1871.

However, Cakobau was never strong enough to impose his authority over the whole country, so with growing disorder in western Fiji, infighting between Europeans and Fijian chiefs, and a lack of cooperation from Ma'afu's rival confederation of chiefs in eastern Fiji, Cakobau decided he should cede his kingdom to Great Britain. The British had refused an invitation to annex Fiji in 1862, but this time they accepted, rather than risk seeing the group fall into the hands of another power, and on October 10, 1874, Fiji became a British colony. A punitive expedition into central Viti Levu in 1876 brought the hill tribes (kai colo) under British rule. In 1877, the Western Pacific High Commission was set up to protect British interests in the surrounding unclaimed island groups as well. In 1881, Rotuma was annexed to Fiji. At first Levuka was the colony's capital, but in 1882 the government moved to a more spacious site at Suva.

The Making of a Nation

The first British governor, Sir Arthur Gordon, and his colonial secretary and successor, Sir John Thurston, created modern Fiji almost single-handedly. They realized that the easiest way to rule was indirectly, through the existing Fijian chiefs. To protect the communal lands on which the chieftain system was based, they ordered that native land could not be sold, only leased. Not wishing to disturb native society, Gordon and Thurston ruled that Fijians could not be forced to work on European plantations. Meanwhile the blackbirding of Melanesian laborers from the Solomon Islands and New Hebrides had been restricted by the Polynesian Islanders Protection Act of 1872.

By this time sugar had taken the place of cotton, and there was a tremendous labor shortage on the plantations. Gordon, who had previously served in Trinidad and Mauritius, saw indentured Indian workers as a solution. The first arrived in 1879, and by 1916, when Indian immigration ended, there were 63,000. To come to Fiji, the Indians had to sign a labor contract (girmit), in which they agreed to cut sugarcane for their masters for five years. During the next five years, they were allowed to lease small plots of their own from the Fijians and plant cane or raise livestock. More than half the Indians decided to remain in Fiji as free settlers after their 10-year contracts expired, and today their descendants form over a third of the population, many of them still working small leased plots.

Though this combination of European capital, Fijian land, and Indian labor did help preserve traditional Fijian culture, the Fijians became envious onlookers passed over by European and (later) Indian prosperity. Installed by the British more than a century ago, the separate administration and special rights for indigenous Fijians continue today.

In early 1875, Cakobau and two of his sons returned from a visit to Australia infected with measles. Though they survived, the resulting epidemic wiped out a third of the Fijian population. As a response to this and other public health problems, the Fiji School of Medicine was founded in 1885. At the beginning of European colonization, there were about 200,000 Fijians—then approximately 114,748 in 1881, and just 84,000 by 1921.

The Colonial Period

In 1912 a Gujarati lawyer, D. M. Manilal, arrived in Fiji from Mauritius to fight for Indian rights, just as his contemporary Mohandas Gandhi was doing in South Africa. Several prominent Anglican and Methodist missionaries also lobbied actively against the system. Indentured Indians continued to arrive in Fiji until 1916, but the protests led to the termination of the indenture system throughout the empire in 1920 (Manilal was deported from Fiji after a strike that year).

Although Fiji was a political colony of Britain, it was always an economic colony of Australia: The big Australian trading companies Burns Philp and W. R. Carpenters dominated business. (The ubiquitous Morris Hedstrom is a subsidiary of Carpenters.) Most of the Indians were brought to Fiji to work for the Australian-owned Colonial Sugar Refining Company, which controlled the sugar industry from 1881 right up until 1973, when it was purchased by the Fiji government for $14 million. After 1935, Fiji's gold fields were also exploited by Australians. Banking, insurance, and tourism are largely controlled by Australian companies today.

Under the British colonial system, the governor of Fiji had far greater decision-making authority than his counterparts in the French Pacific colonies. Whereas the French administrators were required to closely follow policies dictated from Paris, the governors of the British colonies had only to refer to the Colonial Office in London on special matters such as finance and foreign affairs. Otherwise they had great freedom to make policy decisions.

No representative government existed in Fiji until 1904, when a legislative council was formed with six elected Europeans and two Fijians nominated by the Great Council of Chiefs (Bose Levu Vakaturaga), itself an instrument of colonial rule. In 1916, the governor appointed an Indian member to the council. A 1929 reform granted five seats to each of the three communities: three elected and two appointed Europeans and Indians, and five nominated Fijians. The council was only an advisory body, and the governor remained in complete control. The Europeans generally sided with the Fijians against any demands for equality from the Indians—typical colonial divide and rule.

During World War II, Fijians were outstanding combat troops on the Allied side in the Solomon Islands campaign. In 1952–1956, Fijians helped suppress Malaya's national liberation struggle. So skilled were the Fijians at jungle warfare against the Japanese that it was never appropriate to list a Fijian as "missing in action"—the phrase used was "not yet arrived." The war years saw the development of Nadi Airport. Until 1952, Suva, the present Fijian capital, was headquarters for the entire British Imperial Administration in the South Pacific.

In 1963, the Legislative Council was expanded (though still divided along racial lines), and women and indigenous Fijians got the vote for the first time. Wishing to be rid of the British, whom they blamed for their second-class position, the Indians pushed for independence, but the Fijians had come to view the British as protectors and were somewhat reluctant. A Constitutional Convention was held in London in 1965 to move Fiji toward self-government, and after much discussion a constitution was adopted in 1970. Some legislature members were to be elected from a common roll (voting by all races), as the Indians desired, while other seats remained ethnic (voting in racial constituencies) to protect the Fijians. On October 10, 1970, Fiji became a fully independent nation, and the first Fijian governor-general was appointed in 1973—none other than Ratu Sir George Cakobau, great-grandson of the chief who had ceded Fiji to Queen Victoria 99 years before.

SINCE INDEPENDENCE
Political Development

During the 1940s, Ratu Sir Lala Sukuna, paramount chief of Lau, played a key role in the creation of a separate administration for indigenous Fijians, with native land (83 percent of Fiji) under its jurisdiction. In 1954, he formed the Fijian Association to support the British governor against Indian demands for equal representation. In 1960 the National Federation

Party (NFP) was formed to represent Indian cane farmers.

In 1966, the Alliance Party, a coalition of the Fijian Association, the General Electors' Association (representing Europeans, part-Fijians, and Chinese), and the Fiji Indian Alliance (a minority Indian group) won the legislative assembly elections. In 1970, Alliance Party leader Ratu Sir Kamisese Mara led Fiji into independence, and in 1972 his party won Fiji's first post-independence elections. Ratu Mara served as prime minister almost continuously until the 1987 elections.

The formation of the Fiji Labor Party (FLP), headed by Dr. Timoci Bavadra, in July 1985 dramatically altered the political landscape. Fiji's previously nonpolitical trade unions had finally come together to back a party that campaigned on bread-and-butter issues rather than race. Late in 1986, Labor and the NFP formed the Coalition with the aim of defeating the Alliance in the next election. In the April 1987 elections, the Coalition won 28 of 52 House of Representatives seats; 19 of the 28 elected Coalition members were Indo-Fijians. What swung the election away from Alliance was not a change in Indo-Fijian voting patterns but support for Labor from urban Fijians and part-Fijians, which cost Alliance four previously "safe" seats around Suva.

The Coalition cabinet had a majority of Indo-Fijian members, but all cabinet positions of vital Fijian interest (Lands, Fijian Affairs, Labor and Immigration, Education, Agriculture and Rural Development) went to indigenous Fijian legislators, though none of them was a traditional chief. Coalition's progressive policies marked quite a switch from the conservatism of the Alliance—a new generation of political leadership dedicated to tackling the day-to-day problems of people of all races, rather than dedicated to perpetuating the privileges of the old chiefly oligarchy. Given time, the Coalition might have required the high chiefs to share the rental monies they received for leasing lands to Indo-Fijians more fairly with ordinary Fijians. Most significant of all, the Coalition would have transformed Fiji from a pluralistic society where only indigenous Melanesian Fijians were called Fijians into a truly multiracial society where all citizens would be Fijians.

The First Coup

After the election, the extremist Fiji-for-Fijians Taukei (landowners) movement launched a destabilization campaign by throwing barricades across highways, organizing protest rallies and marches, and carrying out firebombings. On April 24, 1987, Senator Inoke Tabua and former Alliance cabinet minister Apisai Tora organized a march of 5,000 Fijians through Suva to protest "Indian domination" of the new government. Mr. Tora told a preparatory meeting for the demonstration that Fijians must "act now" to avoid ending up as "deprived as Australia's aborigines." (In fact, under the 1970 constitution, the Coalition government would have had no way of changing Fiji's land laws without indigenous Fijian consent.)

At 1000 on Thursday, May 14, 1987, Lieutenant Colonel Sitiveni Rabuka (ram-BU-ka), an ambitious officer whose career was stalled at number three in the Fiji army, and 10 heavily armed soldiers dressed in fatigues, their faces covered by gas masks, entered the House of Parliament in Suva. Rabuka ordered Dr. Bavadra and the Coalition members to follow a soldier out of the building, and when Dr. Bavadra hesitated the soldiers raised their guns. The legislators were loaded into army trucks and taken to Royal Fiji Military Forces headquarters. There was no bloodshed, though Rabuka later confirmed that his troops would have opened fire had there been any resistance. At a press conference five hours after the coup, Rabuka claimed he had acted to prevent violence and had no political ambitions of his own.

Australia and New Zealand promptly denounced the region's first military coup. Governor-General Ratu Sir Penaia Ganilau attempted to reverse the situation by declaring a state of emergency and ordering the mutineers to return to their barracks. They refused to obey. The next day Rabuka named a 15-member Council of Ministers, which he chaired, to govern Fiji, with former Alliance Prime Minister Ratu Mara as foreign minister. Significantly, Rabuka was the only military officer on the council; most of the others were members of Ratu Mara's defeated administration. Rabuka claimed he had acted to "safeguard the Fijian land issue and the Fijian way of life."

On May 19, Dr. Bavadra and the other kidnapped members of his government were released after the governor-general announced a deal negotiated with Rabuka to avoid the possibility of foreign intervention. Rabuka's Council of Ministers was replaced by a 19-member caretaker Advisory Council appointed by the Great Council of Chiefs. The council would govern until new elections could take place. Ratu Ganilau would head the council, with Rabuka in charge of Home Affairs and the security forces. Only two seats were offered to Dr. Bavadra's government, and they were refused.

Until the coup, the most important mission of the Royal Fiji Military Forces was service in South Lebanon and the Sinai with peace-keeping operations. Half of the 2,600-member Fiji army was on rotating duty there, the Sinai force financed by the United States, the troops in Lebanon by the United Nations. During World War II, Indo-Fijians refused to join the army unless they received the same pay as European recruits; indigenous Fijians had no such reservations and the force has been 95 percent Fijian ever since. Service in the strife-torn Middle East gave the Fiji military a unique preparation for its often political role in Fiji today. (After Australia and New Zealand, Lebanon is the foreign country most familiar to indigenous Fijians.)

The Second Coup

In July and August 1987, a committee set up by Governor-General Ganilau studied proposals for constitutional reform, and, on September 4, talks began at Government House in Suva between Alliance and Coalition leaders under the chairmanship of Ratu Ganilau. With no hope of a consensus on a revised constitution, the talks were aimed at preparing for new elections.

Then, on September 26, 1987, Rabuka struck again, just hours before the governor-general was to announce a government of national unity to rule Fiji until new elections could be held. The plan, arduously developed over four months and finally approved by veteran political leaders on all sides, would probably have resulted in Rabuka being sacked. Rabuka quickly threw out the 1970 constitution and pronounced himself "head of state." Some 300 prominent community leaders were arrested, and Ratu Ganilau was confined to Government House. Newspapers were shut down, trade unions repressed, the judiciary suspended, the public service purged, the activities of political opponents restricted, a curfew imposed, and the first cases of torture reported.

At midnight on October 7, 1987, Rabuka declared Fiji a republic. Rabuka's new Council of Ministers included Taukei extremists Apisai Tora and Filipe Bole, Fijian Nationalist Party leader Sakeasi Butadroka, and other marginal figures. Rabuka appeared to have backing from the Great Council of Chiefs, which wanted a return to the style of customary rule, now threatened by the Indian presence and Western democracy. Regime ideologists trumpeted traditional culture and religious fundamentalism to justify their actions. Ratu Mara himself was annoyed that Rabuka's second coup had destroyed an opportunity to restore the reputations of himself and Ratu Ganilau. On October 16, Ratu Ganilau resigned as governor-general, and two days later Fiji was expelled from the British Commonwealth.

The Republic of Rabuka

Realizing that Taukei-plus-military rule was a recipe for disaster, on December 5, 1987, Rabuka appointed Ratu Ganilau president and Ratu Mara prime minister of the new republic. The 21-member cabinet included 10 members of Rabuka's military regime, four of them army officers. Rabuka himself (now a self-styled brigadier) was once again Minister of Home Affairs. This interim government set itself a deadline of two years to frame a new constitution and return Fiji to freely elected representative government. By mid-1988, the army had been expanded into a highly disciplined 6,000-member force loyal to Brigadier Rabuka, who left no doubt he would intervene a third time if his agenda was not followed. The Great Council of Chiefs was to decide on Fiji's republican constitution.

The coups transformed the Fijian economy. In 1987, Fiji experienced 11 percent negative growth in the gross domestic product. To slow the flight of capital, the Fiji dollar was devalued 33 percent in 1987, and inflation was up to nearly 12 percent by the end of 1988. At the same time, civil servants (half the workforce) had to accept a 25 percent wage cut as government spending was slashed. Food prices skyrocketed, causing serious problems for many families. At the end of 1987, the per capita average income was 11 percent *below* what it had been in 1980. Between 1986 and 1996, some 58,300 Indo-Fijians left Fiji for Australia, Canada, New Zealand, and the United States. Nearly three-quarters of Fiji's administrators and managers, and a quarter of all professional, technical, and clerical workers departed, taking tens of millions of dollars with them, a crippling loss for a country with a total population of less than 750,000.

On the other hand, the devaluations and wage-cutting measures, combined with the creation of a tax-free exporting sector and the encouragement of foreign investment, brought about an economic recovery by 1990. At the expense of democracy, social justice, and racial harmony, Fiji embarked on a standard International Monetary Fund/World Bank–style structural adjustment program. In 1992, the imposition of a 10 percent value-added tax (VAT) shifted the burden of taxation from rich to poor, standard IMF dogma. In effect, Rabuka and the old oligarchs had pushed Fiji squarely back into the third world.

In November 1989, Dr. Bavadra died of spinal cancer at age 55, and 60,000 people attended his funeral at Viseisei; it was the largest funeral in Fijian history. Foreign journalists were prevented from covering the event. The nominal head of the unelected interim government, Ratu Mara, considered Rabuka an unpredictable upstart and insisted that he choose between politics or military service. Thus in late 1989, the general and two army colonels were dropped from the cabinet, though Rabuka kept his post as army commander.

On July 25, 1990, President Ganilau promulgated a new constitution approved by the Great Council of Chiefs, which gave the chiefs control of the presidency and Senate. Of the 70 seats in Parliament, 37 were reserved for ethnic Fijians. Christianity was made the official religion, and Rabuka's troops were granted amnesty for any crimes committed during the 1987 coups. The Coalition promptly rejected this supremacist constitution as undemocratic and racist.

Not satisfied with control of the Senate, in early 1991 the Great Council of Chiefs decided to project their power into the lower house through the formation of the Soqosoqo ni Vakavulewa ni Taukei (SVT), commonly called the Fijian Political Party. Meanwhile Fiji's multiethnic unions continued to rebuild their strength by organizing garment workers and leading strikes in the mining and sugar industries.

Return to Democracy

The long-awaited parliamentary elections took place in late May 1992, and the SVT captured 30 of the 37 indigenous Fijian seats. Another five went to Fijian nationalists, while the 27 Indian seats were split between the NFP with 14 and the FLP with 13. The five other races' seats went to the General Voters Party (GVP).

Just prior to the election, Ratu Mara retired from party politics and was named vice-president of Fiji by the Great Council of Chiefs. An intense power struggle then developed in the SVT between Ratu Mara's chosen successor as prime minister, former finance minister Josevata Kamikamica, and ex-general Rabuka, who had resigned from the army to rejoin the cabinet in late 1991. Since the SVT lacked a clear majority in the 70-seat house, coalition partners had to be sought, and in a remarkable turn of events, populist Rabuka gained the support of the FLP by offering concessions to the trade unions and a promise to review the constitution and land leases. Thus, Rabuka became prime minister thanks to the very party he had ousted from power at gunpoint exactly five years earlier!

The SVT formed a coalition with the GVP, but in November 1993 the Rabuka government was defeated in a parliamentary vote of no confidence over the budget, leading to fresh elections in February 1994. In these elections, Rabuka's SVT increased its representation to 31 seats. Many Indo-Fijians had felt betrayed by FLP's backing of Rabuka's prime ministership in 1992, and FLP representation dropped to seven seats, compared to 20 for the NFP.

Ratu Ganilau died of leukemia in December 1993, and Ratu Mara was sworn in as president in January 1994. Meanwhile, Rabuka cultivated a pragmatic image to facilitate his international acceptance in the South Pacific, and within Fiji itself he demonstrated his political prowess by holding out a hand of reconciliation to the Indo-Fijian community. The 1990 constitution had called for a constitutional review before 1997, and in 1995 a three-member commission was appointed, led by Sir Paul Reeves, a former governor-general of New Zealand, together with Mr. Tomasi Vakatora, representing the Rabuka government, and Mr. Brij Lal for the opposition.

The report of the commission, titled *Towards a United Future,* was submitted in September 1996. It recommended a return to the voting system outlined in the 1970 constitution, with some members of parliament elected from racially divided communal constituencies and others from open ridings on a common roll of racially mixed electorates. The commissioners suggested that the post of prime minister no longer be explicitly reserved for an indigenous Fijian but simply for the leader of the largest grouping in parliament of whatever race.

The report was passed to a parliamentary committee for study, and in May 1997 all sides agreed to a power-sharing formula to resolve Fiji's constitutional impasse. The number of guaranteed seats for indigenous Fijians in the lower house was reduced from 37 to 23, and voting across racial lines was instituted in another third of the seats. The prime minister was to be required to form a cabinet composed of ministers from all parties in proportion to their representation in parliament—a form of power sharing unique in modern democracy. The country's president and nearly half the members of the senate would continue to be appointed by the Great Council of Chiefs. Human rights guarantees were included. The Constitution Amendment Bill passed both houses of parliament unanimously, and was promulgated into law by President Mara on July 25, 1997. In recognition of the rare national consensus that had been achieved, Fiji was welcomed back into the British Commonwealth in October 1997. The new constitution formally took effect in July 1998.

For many years it was unfashionable to look upon Fiji as a part of Melanesia, and the nation's Polynesian links were emphasized. The 1987 coups had a lot to do with rivalry between the eastward-looking chiefs of Bau and Lau and the Melanesian-leaning western Fijians. Ironically, some of the political friction between the dark-skinned commoner Rabuka and the tall aristocrat Ratu Mara can also be seen in this light. The latter was always networking among Fiji's smaller Polynesian neighbors, and it was only in 1996 that Rabuka brought Fiji into the Melanesian Spearhead Group that had existed since 1988. Of course, the pragmatist Rabuka was merely acknowledging the vastly greater economic potential of Melanesia, but he was clearly much more comfortable socializing with the other Melanesian leaders at regional summits than Ratu Mara ever would have been.

People's Coalition Government

In May 1999, Fiji's 419,000 eligible voters participated in the first election under the 1997 constitution. The IMF-style structural adjustment program of the previous government and a strong desire for change were key issues, and although Rabuka himself was elected, his SVT Party took only eight of the 71 parliamentary seats. The NFP allied with Rabuka was wiped out entirely by the Labor Party, which won all 19 Indo-Fijian seats, plus 18 of the 25 common roll seats elected by all voters. Two indigenous Fijian parties, the Fijian Alliance and the Party of National Unity, won a total of 14 seats. They formed an alliance with Labor's 37 members to give "People's Coalition" an overwhelming 51 seats.

Among the seven women elected to parliament were Adi Kuini Vuikaba Speed, widow of former prime minister Timoci Bavadra, and Adi Koila Mara Nailatikau, daughter of President Mara. Labor leader Mahendra Chaudhry was appointed prime minister—the first Indo-Fijian ever to occupy the post. Two-thirds of Chaudhry's cabinet were indigenous Fijians, but it was quite different from the two previous governments, which had included no Indo-Fijians. Rabuka resigned from parliament soon after the election and was made chair of the Great Council of Chiefs. His departure contributed to a feeling among grassroots Fijians that the Indians had taken over. If Dr. Tupeni Baba, Labor's second-in-command and an indigenous Fijian, had become prime minister, the situation might have been different, but Chaudhry's struggle had been long, and his victory was so complete that he insisted on getting the top job. Baba became deputy prime minister. NFP leader Jai Ram Reddy issued a portentous warning at the time: "Fiji is not yet ready for an Indian prime minister."

Fiji's first democratic government in a dozen years survived 365 days. Chaudhry vigorously pushed forward his reforms and applied the brakes to privatization, which won him few friends, and his relations with business and the media were antagonistic. In February 2000, the government introduced a "leadership honesty code" bill that would have required politicians to disclose their personal assets in private to the Ombudsman's office. Corruption had been rife during the Rabuka years, culminating in the collapse of the National Bank of Fiji in 1995 after F$295 million had been siphoned off by politicians and the Fijian chiefs through bad loans and other devices. Mismanagement and cronyism had led to huge losses by the Fiji Development Bank and provincial councils, and kickbacks were routine at Customs & Excise and other government departments. The Chaudhry government's anti-corruption drive was a blast of fresh air.

Reducing poverty was a high priority for the Chaudhry team. People's Coalition attempted to help Fijian villagers through affirmative action programs. The value-added tax and customs duty on basic food items were lowered, utility rates were slashed, and loans were made available for small business.

People's Coalition also bucked the trend toward globalization and lobbied hard for fairer terms of trade. In recognition, Fiji was selected as the venue for the signing of what would have been the Suva Convention, a 20-year successor to the Lomé Agreement governing trade between 77 African, Caribbean, and Pacific (ACP) nations and the 15 European Union states. Dozens of ministers and high officials from these countries were scheduled to be in Suva on June 8, 2000, for the launch of this historic partnership agreement, but it was not to be.

After the May 1999 election, leaders of the defeated SVT party began working on strategies to bring down the People's Coalition government and return to power. In April 2000, the ultra-nationalist Taukei Movement was revived by Apisai Tora, a fringe politician deeply involved in the 1987 coups. Taukei's declared aim was to revise the 1997 constitution to ensure Fijian political supremacy. The SVT supported Taukei, as did some provincial administrations, but the Fiji army declared that it would not be drawn into any attempt to overthrow the government. Taukei agitators tried to make the future of Indo-Fijian land leases an issue, and demonstrations began in Lautoka and Suva.

The Third Coup
On May 19, 2000, a Taukei protest march wound down Victoria Parade in central Suva.

When the thousands of marchers reached the gates of the Presidential Palace, they were told that gunmen had stormed Fiji's parliament, which had been in session, and had taken its members hostage. Many of the marchers rushed to the building, joining terrorists who were only too happy to have willing human shields. In central Suva, gangs of thugs and protesters responded to news of the takeover by looting and burning Indian shops. About 160 shops were emptied or destroyed in the three hours before the police began making arrests.

The initial assault on parliament was led by a failed businessman named George Speight, along with seven renegade members of the army's elite Counter Revolutionary Warfare Unit (also known as the First Meridian Squadron) and 35 ex-soldiers, half of them ex-convicts. The highest-ranking soldier present was retired Major Ilisoni Ligairi, a former British Special Air Services warrant officer who had set up the CRW anti-terrorist unit in 1987. Speight had appeared in the Suva High Court on extortion charges five days before the coup, yet he declared he was acting to defend indigenous Fijian rights. In 1997, Speight had been forced to flee Australia after a pyramid scheme he had a hand in collapsed with A$130 million in losses for gullible investors.

Yet, to understand what was really happening, we have to back up a bit. In early 1999, a bitter struggle was being waged in government circles over who would gain the right to market Fiji's valuable mahogany forests worldwide. The Rabuka government was known to favor a U.S. company called Timber Resources Management, while the incoming Chaudhry government announced they intended to give the contract to the British-based Commonwealth Development Corporation. Speight had previously worked as a consultant for the Americans, and in June 1999 Chaudhry's Forestry Minister removed him from his position as managing director of the state-owned Fiji Hardwood Corporation and Fiji Pine Limited, because Speight had been a political appointee of the former regime. Chaudhry's surprise election in May 1999 had

cost Speight and associates the chance to control the exploitation of mahogany and pine tracts worth hundreds of millions of dollars. Just prior to his assault on parliament, Speight had been trying to foment unrest among landowners by spreading disinformation about the rival bids and the Chaudhry government's intentions. Important figures in the previous Rabuka government were involved in the ongoing mahogany affair, including Rabuka's Minister of Finance and former Speight patron Jim Ah Koy. Speight's coup attempt may have had much more to do with timber rights than indigenous rights.

Among the 45 persons taken hostage by Speight's gang were Prime Minister Chaudhry and the minister of tourism and transport, President Mara's daughter. Ratu Mara immediately declared a state of emergency, and the Fiji Military Forces commander, Commodore Voreqe Bainimarama, ordered his men to surround the parliamentary compound. Unlike the situation during the 1987 coups, the army's high command and the bulk of its troops did not support the coup attempt. Bainimarama declined to use force to free the captives for fear of triggering a bloodbath, and many of the hostages were to spend the next 56 days sitting on mattresses with their lives in the hands of heavily armed thugs.

On May 27, 80-year-old President Mara officially dismissed the elected Chaudhry government after Speight threatened to kill his daughter. The next day a mob of Speight supporters ransacked the offices of Fiji TV to protest coverage critical of the coup. Soon after, a Fijian policeman was shot dead by gunmen near parliament. On May 29, with the situation deteriorating, the army asked President Mara to "step aside" while it restored order. Mara thereupon withdrew to his power base on remote Lakeba in the Lau Group, the ignominious end of a long and distinguished career. That day Bainimarama declared martial law, announced the abrogation of the 1997 constitution, and assumed executive authority. Bainimarama ruled out any return to power by Chaudhry.

© DAVID STANLEY

Parliament building, Suva, Viti Levu

Meanwhile, as the negotiations continued, Speight was constantly making fresh demands. A struggle for power was under way among the Fijian elite. The Great Council of Chiefs wanted to appoint the vice president, Ratu Josefa Iloilo, to replace Mara, but Speight insisted that Ratu Jope Seniloli, a retired schoolteacher with close ties to the chiefly Cakobau family of Bau but no previous political standing, must become vice president. Since the death of Ratu Sir George Cakobau in 1989, the once powerful Cakobaus of eastern Viti Levu had been eclipsed by their historic "Tongan" enemies from Lau, led by Ratu Sir Kamisese Mara. Seven weeks into the crisis, Speight moved to have persons with Cakobau connections granted high positions in an interim administration. His choice for prime minister was Adi Samanunu Cakobau, Fiji's high commissioner in Malaysia and Sir George's eldest daughter.

That was the signal for Bainimarama, a longtime Mara ally, to order his army to tighten the noose around Speight by declaring parliament and nearby streets a "military exclusion zone." The next day (July 3) the Great Council of Chiefs named a civilian cabinet led by the former head of the Fiji Development Bank, Laisenia Qarase. This interim government had the army's blessing, and to win acceptance from the international community, high-profile Speight elements were shut out. These developments triggered widespread disturbances by grassroots Speight supporters throughout the country, including the occupation of a few remote tourist resorts, the blocking of highways, and the burning of the historic Masonic Lodge in Levuka. There was intimidation of Indo-Fijians living in rural areas of northeastern Viti Levu and central Vanua Levu—traditional Cakobau strongholds—with arson, looting, and ethnic cleansing. The military was unable to cope.

Visibly shaken, on July 9 Bainimarama agreed to an amnesty for Speight and the others on the condition that they free the 27 remaining hostages and surrender all arms. The Qarase interim government would be replaced, and Iloilo and Seniloli would become president and vice president. On July 13, the hostage crisis came to a peaceful end at a kava ceremony, when Chaudhry magnanimously stated that he harbored no personal animosity toward Speight, though the army noted that not all of the missing weapons were turned in. Upon his release Chaudhry confirmed that he had been beaten by Speight's thugs early on in the hostage crisis.

It's said that only the threat of a military coup from Bainimarama prevented President Iloilo, who was seen as overly sympathetic to Speight's cause, from accepting Adi Samanunu Cakobau as prime minister. Former prime minister Rabuka (who remained on the sidelines during most of the crisis) remarked that Speight was only a puppet, brought in at the last minute by persons unknown.

Speight is only part-Fijian, and the Taukei extremists represent a small minority of opinion in Fiji. The concerns of indigenous Fijians to protect their lands and culture were and are legitimate, but those interests have been enshrined in all three of Fiji's constitutions and no government would have been able to negate them. As previously in recent Fijian history, the race issue was manipulated by defeated politicians and power-hungry individuals, and rural villagers and marginalized urban Fijians proved effective tools in the hands of rabble-rouser George Speight.

Interim Government

After the hostages were freed, Qarase simply stayed on as prime minister. In late July, he appointed a cabinet consisting mostly of indigenous Fijian civil servants and opposition politicians, without any overt Speight insiders. Qarase announced that his military-backed regime would last 18 months, to give time for a new constitution to be drawn up and fresh elections arranged. However, during the week of July 17, Australia, Britain, and New Zealand announced sanctions against Fiji, because the elected government had not been restored.

Speight's agitating continued, with Bainimarama now the target of choice. On July 27, Speight was arrested at an army checkpoint between Suva and Nausori, and the next day the army rounded up 369 of his followers in a forceful manner. Speight and cohorts were charged with carrying arms in contravention of the amnesty deal, and a week later the charge of treason was added. Speight and a dozen key figures in the coup attempt were sent to await trial on tiny Nukulau Island, a former picnic spot off Suva. In protest, pro-Speight soldiers kidnapped 50 Indo-Fijians at Labasa, but released them quickly when the army threatened to intervene.

In September, the interim government set up a 12-member commission to review the 1997 constitution. Asesela Ravuvu, an academic with a long history of advocating hard-line indigenous Fijian positions, was appointed chair, and among the other members were three Speight supporters. Most Indo-Fijians boycotted the process.

On the afternoon of November 2, 2000, the final act in this tragedy unfolded at Suva's Queen Elizabeth Barracks, as 39 soldiers from the Counter Revolutionary Warfare Unit staged a surprise raid on army headquarters in an attempt to murder Commodore Bainimarama and seize control of Fiji for Speight. Loyal officers helped Bainimarama escape down a gully, and just before dusk the Third Fiji Infantry Regiment launched a fierce counterattack. Five rebels and three government soldiers died in the attempted mutiny, including several rebels who were kicked to death by army troops after being captured. Two-dozen soldiers and civilians were wounded, and the army quickly rounded up the remaining mutineers. The nation was shocked by this unprecedented brutality. The plot thickened when it was revealed that ex-general Rabuka had been present at the barracks during the mutiny. Rabuka claimed he had only gone there to mediate, but Bainimarama ordered him not to re-enter the facility.

After the hostages' release, a number of lawsuits were filed before the Fiji High Court claiming that the change in government was unconstitutional. On November 15, 2000, Chief Justice Anthony Gates issued a ruling in response to a plea brought by an ordinary

Indo-Fijian farmer, Chandrika Prasad, who claimed that his constitutional rights had been violated by the coup. Gates agreed and declared the Speight coup null and void, the interim government illegal, and the 1997 constitution still the law of the land. Gates ruled that Ratu Mara was still the legal president of Fiji and that he had a duty to appoint a new prime minister from among the parliamentarians elected in 1999. Gates suggested that the interim government resign and allow the formation of a government of national unity composed of elected members of parliament. That would get Fiji back on track.

A shocked interim Prime Minister Qarase referred the case to the Fiji Court of Appeal, which upheld Chief Justice Gates' ruling in a historic decision on March 1, 2001. Qarase and Iloilo both announced that the court's decision would be respected. Fiji's top judges had suggested that the president recall parliament, and 40 of the 71 parliamentarians deposed by George Speight signed a petition asking that this be done. Yet instead of recalling parliament, President Iloilo dissolved the old parliament and appointed Qarase to run a caretaker government until fresh elections could be held. Qarase quickly brought back his old 30-minister cabinet, and the unelected government the judges had declared illegal just two weeks before was back in business.

As could be expected, the Fiji Crisis had a disastrous impact on the economy. After positive growth of 7.8 percent in 1999, there was 2.8 percent negative growth in 2000. By the end of 2000, more than 7,400 people had lost their jobs. Tourist arrivals for the three months following the coup were only 37,126, compared to 120,156 for the same period in 1999, and the industry was losing US$1 million a day. Only in 2001 did the economy again begin to grow. The crisis seriously widened the gap between the haves and have-nots in Fiji.

Aftermath and Elections

The judges had ruled that the 1997 constitution remained in force; thus, attempts by the caretaker government to draft a new constitution weighted toward Fijians were halted. The international sanctions against Fiji continued, and in August 2001 Qarase called early elections to legitimize his rule. Qarase's United Fijian Party (SDL) won 32 of the 71 parliament seats, the Labor Party 27 seats, and the pro-coup Conservative Alliance Matanitu Vanua (CAMV) six. Despite being imprisoned, George Speight was elected as the CAMV member from Korovou in northeastern Viti Levu. Qarase formed a government in coalition with the CAMV after it dropped a demand for an amnesty for Speight, who was formally expelled from parliament in December for failing to attend the sessions.

In February 2002, George Speight was sentenced to death for treason, but within hours President Iloilo commuted his sentence to life imprisonment. Speight had entered a guilty plea to avoid a trial that might have revealed the names of those behind the coup. In May 2003, Vice President Jope Seniloli, two cabinet ministers, and the deputy speaker of parliament were charged with taking unlawful oaths to commit capital offenses during the coup. After being sworn in as president by Speight, Seniloli swore in the others as cabinet ministers in Speight's rebel regime. In July 2004, Seniloli and all but one of the others were convicted of treason by Fiji's High Court. Seniloli was sentenced to four years in prison, and the others received sentences ranging from one to six years. In the end, Seniloli was released after serving only three months of his four-year sentence on "medical grounds." Commodore Bainimarama commented that the early release of Seniloli and other convicted traitors made a mockery of the judicial system, and he warned that the army would not allow the Qarase government to halt the prosecutions of coup offenders.

With his eye on the next election, Qarase maneuvered desperately to placate his CAMV allies and shore up support among indigenous Fijians. In October 2004, the government organized a "National Week of Reconciliation" at which many Fijian participants in the coup violence offered verbal apologies and asked forgiveness for their actions in the traditional Fijian way. None of those present offered to give up any of the advantages they had gained from the coup, and their performance was spurned by most coup victims. Qarase himself owed his political prominence to the Speight coup.

In 2005, the government attempted to grant an amnesty to everyone involved in the May 2000 coup through a Reconciliation and Unity Bill. The Fiji Army, Labor Party, Law Society, and many civic organizations objected strongly to the proposed amnesty, and after much debate, the bill was sent back for further study. Meanwhile, by early 2006, some 2,000 people had been investigated for offenses relating to the coup and 728 had been charged.

In February 2006, Qarase's coalition partner, the pro-Speight CAMV, dissolved itself and merged with the SDL. A general election was called in May 2006. Qarase played the race card, and with voting split along racial lines, the SDL won a narrow victory over Labor. The 1997 constitution stipulated that any party winning at least 10 percent of the 71 parliamentary seats had a right to be represented in cabinet, and the SDL and FLP formed a power-sharing cabinet with Laisenia Qarase as prime minister.

The Bainimarama Coup

In 2006, the Qarase government introduced a number of bills designed to favor indigenous Fijians. Since becoming a British colony in 1874, Fiji's shoreline has belonged to the state, and everyone has been allowed free access to Fiji's beaches and reefs. A Customary Fishing Rights Bill would have transferred traditional fishing rights (*qoliqoli*) back to the 410 Fijian clans, giving local chiefs the right to demand payments from anyone wishing to fish, snorkel, scuba dive, or surf in Fiji's coastal waters. A proposed Indigenous Claims Tribunal would have allowed the chiefs to lay claim to much more of Fiji's wealth.

Despite strong protests from the country's tourism industry, Qarase was unwilling to withdraw this legislation. Qarase seemed

eager to reward the CAMV elements that had helped him win the May 2006 election, and he appointed several Speight henchmen as ministers in his cabinet. Not only were many Speight policies being followed and the coup prosecutions soft-pedaled, but the government pressed doggedly ahead with a bill designed to grant an amnesty to Speight and the other coup perpetrators.

The head of the 3,500-member Republic of Fiji Military Forces, Commodore Bainimarama, insisted that the racially motivated legislation be withdrawn and that plans for the amnesty be scrapped. A list of nine "non-negotiable" demands was presented to Qarase by the army with the warning that a "clean-up campaign" would follow if the government failed to comply. To demonstrate that he had the full backing of the military, Bainimarama left on trips to the Middle East and New Zealand while the matter was being considered, and an attempt by Qarase to replace him in his absence failed.

Despite the coup threats, the Qarase government steadfastly refused to withdraw the legislation, offering only to have a committee study its legality. Fiji's chief of police, an Australian named Andrew Hughes, exacerbated the situation by seeking to have Bainimarama charged with sedition. With Qarase unwilling to budge and President Iloilo indisposed to intervene, the Fiji Army under Bainimarama launched a bloodless coup against the elected government on December 5, 2006. Qarase was exiled to his home on remote Vanua Balavu, Hughes fled to Australia, and all government ministers were sacked. The army conducted raids on government offices seeking evidence of corruption, while foreign governments imposed economic and political sanctions on Fiji.

Fiji's fourth coup was different from the previous three in that it was not an attempt to impose indigenous Fijian supremacy over the Indo-Fijians. Nor was religious fundamentalism involved. On the contrary, the Fiji Army claimed to be acting against a clique of corrupt politicians and Fijian chiefs in the name of multiculturalism.

© DAVID STANLEY

The traditional-style seat of the Great Council of Chiefs in Suva was erected in 2003.

Political Transition

In January 2007, a interim government was appointed, with Ratu Iloilo as president, Bainimarama as prime minister, and Mahendra Chaudhry as minister of finance. The interim cabinet was half the size of Qarase's last cabinet. A state of emergency was in place for six months after the coup and press freedoms were restricted, but by mid-2007 all soldiers had been withdrawn from the streets and the roadblocks removed. Life continued normally in Fiji throughout 2007 and petty crime was greatly reduced, making the country much safer for residents and visitors alike.

In April 2007, the Great Council of Chiefs was shut down after it rejected the appointment of former army commander Ratu Epeli Nailatikau as vice president. The GCC had backed the Qarase government and lost much of its influence with the 2006 coup. Many of the high chiefs had become wealthy as members of powerful statutory bodies and came to be viewed as corrupt by ordinary Fijians, so the Council's closing caused few

misgivings. In June 2007, the New Zealand High Commissioner to Fiji was expelled for making speeches critical of the regime at public events in Fiji. The governments of Australia and New Zealand issued travel advisories claiming Fiji was unsafe due to the coup but these were widely recognized as politically motivated and erroneous. However the sanctions and scare tactics did have an effect and Fiji's economy contracted 6.6 percent in 2007. After recovering slightly in 2008, it fell another 2.5 percent in 2009. On April 15, 2009, the Fiji dollar was devalued 20 percent.

Throughout 2007 and 2008, the National Council for Building a Better Fiji, with representation from many levels of society, drafted a People's Charter to establish guidelines for future public policy in Fiji. This document gained central importance in 2009. In April 2009, the Fiji Court of Appeal, presided over by a panel of Australian judges, ruled that 2006 coup was unconstitutional and elections must be held immediately under the 1997 constitution. The next day President Iloilo abrogated the 1997 constitution, fired all of the judges, and reappointed Bainimarama and his cabinet. The president announced that democratic parliamentary elections would be held in September 2014. The postponing of elections originally scheduled for 2010 led to Fiji being suspended from the Pacific Islands Forum in May 2009 and the Commonwealth of Nations in September 2009.

In July 2009, Prime Minister Bainimarama announced that a new constitution would be ready by 2013 based on the principles of the People's Charter. The key reform is that the ethnically based voting system handed down by the British colonial regime will be replaced by a modern one-person-one-vote system with no racially based voting. All of Fiji's previous constitutions have required voters to register by race and vote for candidates of their own race. The hereditary chiefs and the Methodist Church told ethnic Fijians how to vote, cementing in place a corrupt system. If the ideas expressed in the People's Charter do bear fruit, a most remarkable political transition will have been achieved. Prime Minister Bainimarama has announced that politicians active in government after 1987—including himself—will not be allowed to run in the 2014 elections in order to give Fiji a completely fresh start.

GOVERNMENT

As this book goes to press, Fiji is ruled by a caretaker prime minister and cabinet appointed by the president. The government elected in May 2006 was removed by a military coup in December 2006. In July 2009, 88-year-old President Iloilo retired for health reasons and was succeeded by Vice President Nailatikau.

The abrogated 1997 constitution provided for a parliamentary system of government with

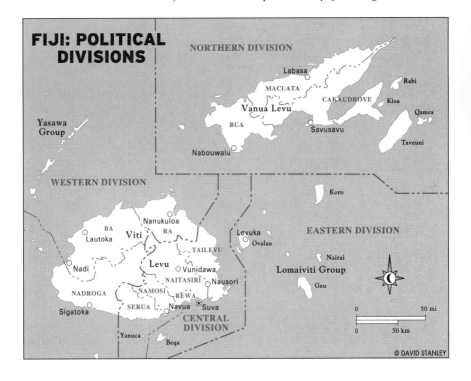

FIJI: POLITICAL DIVISIONS

© DAVID STANLEY

FIJI IN A COCONUT SHELL

DIVISION/ PROVINCE	HEADQUARTERS	AREA (SQUARE KM)	POPULATION (2007)	PERCENT FIJIAN
Central Division	**Suva**	**4,293**	**342,386**	**62.1**
Naitasiri	Vunidawa	1,666	160,760	57.9
Namosi	Navua	570	6,898	89.3
Rewa	Nausori	272	100,787	61.5
Serua	Navua	830	18,249	61.0
Tailevu	Korovou	955	55,692	72.3
Western Division	**Lautoka**	**6,360**	**319,611**	**47.6**
Ba	Lautoka	2,634	231,760	41.8
Nadroga	Sigatoka	2,385	58,387	60.1
Ra	Nanukuloa	1,341	29,464	68.8
Northern Division	**Labasa**	**6,198**	**135,961**	**55.4**
Macuata	Labasa	2,004	72,441	38.9
Bua	Nabouwalu	1,378	14,176	78.9
Cakaudrove	Savusavu	2,816	49,344	72.9
Eastern Division	**Levuka**	**1,422**	**39,313**	**90.6**
Kadavu	Vunisea	478	10,167	98.0
Lau	Lakeba	487	10,683	98.7
Lomaiviti	Levuka	411	16,461	91.3
Rotuma	Ahau	46	2,002	0.04
TOTAL FIJI	**SUVA**	**18,272**	**837,271**	**56.8**

a 71-seat House of Representatives, or "lower house," consisting of 46 members from communal ridings and 25 from multiracial ridings with elections every five years. Twenty-three communal seats were reserved for indigenous Fijians, 19 for Indo-Fijians, three for general electors (part-Fijians, Europeans, Chinese, etc.), and one for Rotumans. The leader of the largest party or coalition of parties in parliament was the head of government, or prime minister. The structure of the 2013 constitution is still unknown.

The 32-member "upper house," or Senate, had 14 members appointed by the Great Council of Chiefs, nine by the prime minister, eight by the leader of the opposition, and one by the Council of Rotuma. Any legislation affecting the rights of indigenous Fijians had to be approved by nine of the 14 senators appointed by the chiefs. The Great Council of Chiefs also chose Fiji's head of state, the president, for a five-year term. All of this will change with the new constitution. The function and membership of the Great Council of Chiefs is being reconsidered.

Aside from the national government, there's a well-developed system of local government. On the Fijian side, the basic unit is the village *(koro)* represented by a village herald *(turaga-ni-koro)*, who is chosen by consensus. The 1,169 villages and 483 settlements are grouped into 189 districts *(tikina),* the districts into 14 provinces *(yasana).* The executive head of each provincial council is the *roko tui,* appointed by the Fijian Affairs Board.

The national administration is broken down into four divisions (central, eastern, northern, and western), each headed by a commissioner. These civil servants and the 19 district officers work for the Ministry of Regional Development. The Micronesians of Rabi and Polynesians of Rotuma govern themselves through island councils of their own. Ten city and town councils also function at the local level.

Fiji has a High Court, a Fiji Court of Appeal, and a Supreme Court. The president appoints the chief justice and eight other judges after consulting the prime minister. After both the 2000 and 2006 coups, the courts emerged as the last bastion of legality in Fiji's national system of government. Criminal and civil cases of lesser importance are handled in magistrates' courts.

Economy

Fiji has a diversified economy based on tourism, sugar production, fishing, mineral water, garment manufacturing, timber, gold mining, vegetables, and coconut products. Although eastern Viti Levu and the Lau Group have long dominated the country politically, western Viti Levu remains Fiji's economic powerhouse with tourism, sugar, mining, and timber all concentrated there.

Aside from the cash economy, subsistence agriculture is important to indigenous Fijians in rural areas, where manioc, taro, yams, sweet potato, and corn are the principal subsistence crops. Coastal subsistence fishing is twice as important as commercial fishing in terms of actual catch.

AGRICULTURE AND INDUSTRY
Sugar

It's estimated that a quarter of Fiji's population relies on sugar for its livelihood. Although the F$250 million a year Fiji earns from sugar is far less than it makes on tourism, more people

rely on sugar for their livelihood. Almost all of Fiji's sugarcane is grown by small, independent Indo-Fijian farmers on contract to the government-owned Fiji Sugar Corporation (FSC). Some 22,000 farmers cultivate cane on holdings averaging four hectares leased from around 2,000 indigenous Fijian landowners. For many years the corporation has used 595 kilometers of 0.610-meter narrow-gauge railway to carry the cane to mills at Lautoka, Ba, Rakiraki, and Labasa, and the current shift to truck transport is hurting farmers by increasing costs. Fiji's four aging, inefficient sugar mills are in urgent need of modernization, yet major new investments are unlikely, as the FSC has been operating at a loss since 1997. The Government of India is currently providing technical support to keep Fiji's sugar mills going. A distillery at Lautoka produces rum and other liquors from the byproducts of sugar.

Around a quarter of a million metric tons of sugar are exported annually to Britain, Japan, and other countries, providing direct or indirect employment for 45,000 people. Some 17,000

© DAVID STANLEY

The sugar mill at Labasa is one of four in Fiji.

seasonal workers cut the cane, which is transported by 2,000 truck drivers and processed by another 2,000 mill workers. Around 190,000 tons of Fiji sugar is sold to the European Union each year at fixed rates based on import quotas set forth in the Cotonou Agreement. The EU uses this agreement as a way of providing aid to 77 former colonies in Africa, the Caribbean, and the Pacific. Until recently, the subsidies were three times above market value and worth F$100 million a year to Fiji. However, big producers like Australia, Brazil, and Thailand have used the World Trade Organization to pressure the EU into phasing out the subsidies, and in July 2006 the EU reduced the price it was paying Fiji by 36 percent. In late 2009, the EU went further and suspended some sugar-related subsidies after the promised 2010 election was delayed. Already reeling from antiquated production methods, Fiji's sugar industry is in real danger of collapse.

Other Crops and Water

In the past, Fiji has grown almost half its own requirements of rice, but the industry has been damaged by competition from imported rice. Much of Fiji's rice is grown around Nausori and Navua, and on Vanua Levu.

Most of Fiji's copra is produced in Lau, Lomaiviti, Taveuni, and Vanua Levu, half by European or part-Fijian planters and the rest by indigenous Fijian villagers. Copra production has slipped from 40,000 tons a year in the 1950s to about 10,000 tons today due to the low prices paid to producers. Things started looking up in 2010 after a local company began buying copra for biodiesel production.

In 1998, F$35 million worth of kava root was exported to Germany, the United States, and other countries, where it was used by pharmaceutical firms to make antidepressants and muscle relaxants. In late 2001, kava exports plummeted after the European Union imposed import restrictions on the roots after allegations that kava-based medicines might cause liver damage. In 2008, only F$4.7 million worth of kava was exported.

Another unique export is natural artesian water drawn from a well at Yaqara on northwestern Viti Levu and bottled in a modern plant set up by Canadian David Gilmour, owner of the Wakaya Club. In 2004, Gilmour sold his interest to Roll International Corporation of Los Angeles. Fiji Water (www.fijiwater.com) has grown into the second-largest selling imported water brand in the United States. In 2008, Fiji sold almost F$110 million of water, the third-largest export. The indigenous landowners of the watershed have a 25 percent interest in the local company, making them the richest clan in Fiji.

Timber

In the late 1970s, more than 40,000 hectares of softwood were planted by Fiji Pine and private landowners in western Viti Levu and Vanua Levu. The mature trees are now milled and marketed by Tropik Timber, a Fiji Pine subsidiary. Processing facilities for the 16,000 hectares of pine on Vanua Levu are inadequate, and the round logs must be transported to Viti Levu by truck and ferry at great expense.

In addition to softwood, tens of thousands

© DAVID STANLEY

chipped pine being prepared for export at Lautoka

of hectares of hardwood (74 percent of it mahogany) planted by the British after 1952 are mature and ready for harvesting. With buyers in Europe and elsewhere increasingly averse to natural rainforest timber, Fiji is in the enviable position of possessing the world's largest "green" mahogany forest. The government-controlled Fiji Hardwood Corporation was set up in 1997 to manage this asset, which has been valued as high as F$400 million. Thus far, squabbling between the various stakeholders has delayed exploitation of this resource. Fiji already exports about F$60 million a year in sawed softwood lumber, wood chips, and other wood products (the export of raw logs was banned in 1987).

Yet outside the managed plantations, Fiji's native forests are poorly protected from the greed of foreign logging companies and short-sighted local landowners, and each year large tracts of pristine rainforest are lost. Now that all of the lowland forests have been cleared, attention has turned to the highlands. The planted pine and mahogany have had the corollary benefit of reducing pressure on the natural forests to supply Fiji's timber needs.

Fishing

Commercial fishing is important, with a government-owned tuna processing plant at Levuka supplied in part by Fiji's own fleet of longline vessels. Only about 6 percent of the skipjack and albacore tuna is now canned, and most of the rest is chilled and sent to canneries in the United States. Chilled yellowfin tuna is flown to Hawaii and Japan to serve the sashimi (raw fish) market. Fish is now Fiji's second-largest export, and overfishing has resulted from too many fishing licenses being issued to foreign companies by the government.

Related to fishing is the marine-aquarium industry, which exports tropical fish and live coral. Walt Smith International (www .waltsmith.com) behind Pride Mahogany on Navutu Road in Lautoka is a world leader in coral farming, with thousands of living rocks currently growing on iron racks in undersea farms off western Viti Levu.

Mining

Mining activity centers on gold from Vatukoula on northern Viti Levu. The Emperor Gold Mine at Vatukoula closed in late 2006 after losing money for several years, but a year later Westech Gold purchased the property and reopened the mine. In 2008, gold exports were worth F$27 million, still far below the F$88 million exported in 2004 but recovering. Elsewhere on Viti Levu, a rich gold deposit is at Tuvatu, unfortunately within the Nadi water-catchment area and thus an environmental hazard. In 1998, the Mount Kasi gold mine on Vanua Levu closed due to low world prices, and the development of other gold fields has been frozen.

Beginning in 1984, Placer Pacific spent US$10 million exploring the extensive low-grade copper deposits at Namosi, 30 kilometers northwest of Suva, but in 1997, despite offers of near tax-free status from the government, the company put the US$1 billion project on hold, saying it was not economical.

Garment Industry

Garments produced by a hundred companies are Fiji's fourth-largest export. Some foreign manufacturers have moved their factories to Fiji to take advantage of the low labor costs, and the South Pacific Regional Trade and Economic Cooperation Agreement (SPARTECA) allows Fijian products with at least 35 percent local content partial duty- and quota-free entry into Australia and New Zealand. The value of SPARTECA is gradually eroding and garment exports seem to have peaked. In 2008, Fiji exported textiles worth F$100 million, a decline of more than 50 percent from 2004 as companies closed due to competition from low-cost producers in Asia. The garment industry still employs 8,000 mostly female workers (down from 20,000 at its peak). Women working in the industry have complained of body searches and sexual harassment; those who protest or organize industrial action are often fired and blacklisted. Asian workers are also employed in the factories.

Other Manufacturing

Companies that process food or make furniture, toys, or shoes are also prominent in the tax-free exporting sector. Until recently, it was believed that manufacturing would eventually overtake both sugar and tourism as the main source of income for the country, but the globalization of trade and the progressive reduction of tariffs worldwide are cutting into Fiji's competitiveness. SPARTECA's local-content rule discourages local companies from reducing costs by introducing labor-saving technology, condemning them to obsolescence in the long term.

ECONOMIC PROBLEMS

In spite of all the potential, unemployment is a major social problem in Fiji. The economy generates only 2,000 new jobs a year, but 17,000 young people leave school every year, and unemployment is high. A retirement age of 55 has been implemented in the civil service to create opportunities for young people and reduce labor costs. To stimulate industry, firms based in Fiji that export 95 percent of their production are granted 13-year tax holidays, the duty-free import of materials, and the freedom to repatriate capital and profits. An increasing list of incentives is being added to the books.

In 1995, Fiji's financial standing was severely shaken when it was announced that the government-owned National Bank of Fiji was holding hundreds of millions of dollars in bad debts resulting from politically motivated loans to indigenous Fijians and Rotumans. The subsequent run on deposits cost the bank another F$20 million, and the government was forced to step in to save the bank. Vast sums were diverted from development projects to cover the losses, an indication of systemic corruption not usually noticed by visitors. In 1999, Colonial Life Insurance paid F$9.5 million for a 51 percent interest in what was left of the National Bank.

Cronyism and corruption, which the Chaudhry government attempted to control, returned full force after the May 2000 coup. Bribery by American business interests trying to obtain contracts to harvest Fiji's mahogany reserves may have played a major role in the Speight coup itself, and during the administration of Laisenia Qarase, government officials were accused of accepting bribes to grant fishing licenses to Asian companies. It became a standard practice to provide "gifts" to officials when bidding for government contracts or investment approvals, and a desire to stamp out official corruption was a central objective of the 2006 military coup. The Fiji Independent Commission Against Corruption was established soon after coup.

Before the 2006 coup, foreign reserves fell as the Qarase government borrowed tens of millions from the World Bank and Asian Development Bank to cover budget deficits. Fiji's government debt is currently 52 percent of the gross domestic product and rising. Over half this money is owed to Fiji's National Provident Fund, which provides pensions to workers. Under the Qarase government, debt, deficit spending, and corruption were obstacles to aid and investment in Fiji. The Bainimarama Coup has created additional problems due to economic and political sanctions.

TRADE AND AID

Although Fiji imports more than twice as much as it exports, some of the imbalance is resold to tourists and foreign airlines that pay in foreign exchange. Raw sugar is the nation's largest visible export earner, followed by fish, mineral water, garments, wood products, fruits and vegetables, gold, biscuits, molasses, flour, fabrics, coconut oil, and kava, in that order. Large trade imbalances exist with Australia, New Zealand, and most Asian countries.

Mineral fuels eat up much of Fiji's import budget, despite the Monasavu Hydroelectric Project and other self-sufficiency measures that came online in the 1980s. Petroleum products, manufactured goods, food, chemicals, motor vehicles, and textiles account for most of the import bill.

Fiji is the least dependent South Pacific nation. Development aid comes from Australia, the European Union, Japan, New Zealand, and China. European Union aid to Fiji totals F$400 million a year, mostly in the form of subsidized

purchases of sugar. The New Zealand government has devoted much of its limited aid budget to the creation of national parks and reserves. North American aid to Fiji is negligible.

Aside from conventional aid, Fiji's army is financed through its participation in multinational forces. In 2002, the last 600 Fiji soldiers returned from service in Lebanon, but the army has 300 peacekeeping troops in Sinai. In late 2003, some 400 Fijian ex-soldiers and police were sent to Iraq by a private British security firm to serve as security guards. Some 3,500 people serve in Fiji's armed forces, costing the country more than is spent on any other public institution. As many as 1,000 Fijians also serve in the British Army.

Remittances from Fijians working or serving abroad bring in F$300 million a year, the country's second-highest source of foreign exchange. Other new industries Fiji is trying to introduce to take the place of declining exports include movie production, call centers, and data processing centers.

TOURISM

Tourism has been the leading moneymaker since 1989, accounting for three-quarters of Fiji's export earnings or one sixth of Fiji's economy. In 2009, some 540,000 tourists visited Fiji—twice as many as visited French Polynesia and over 10 times more than visited Tonga. Things appear in better perspective, however, when Fiji is compared to Hawaii, which is about the same size in surface area. Overpacked Hawaii gets more than seven million tourists, 13 times as many as Fiji. About 42 percent of Fiji's tourists come from Australia, 17 percent from New Zealand, 12 percent from the United States, 6 percent from Britain, 5 percent from continental Europe, 4 percent from Japan, and 3 percent from Canada.

Gross receipts figures from tourism are often misleading, as two-thirds of every tourist dollar is repatriated overseas by foreign investors or used to pay for tourism-related imports. Because of this, sugar is more profitable for Fiji than tourism. The hotel industry employs around 10,000 people with an estimated 50,000 jobs in all sectors related to tourism. While the sugar industry is run mostly by mostly Indo-Fijians, ethnic Fijians predominate in the tourist industry. Management of the top hotels is usually expatriate, with Indo-Fijians filling technical positions such as maintenance, cooking, and accounting, and indigenous Fijians working in more visible positions such as receptionists, waiters, guides, and housekeepers. With an eye to profitability, the resorts try to use as many part-time workers as possible.

Fiji has just under 300 licensed hotels with a total of around 8,000 rooms, more than a third of the South Pacific's tourism plant. Most of Fiji's upmarket tourist resorts are centered along the Coral Coast of Viti Levu, Nadi and Denarau Island, and in the Mamanuca Islands off Nadi. Backpacker tourism focuses on the Yasawa Islands, Coral Coast, and Nadi. Quite a few people also visit Suva but tourism to Vanua Levu and Taveuni is relatively small.

Investment by U.S. hotel chains has increased with major developments around Nadi. Big names like Accor, Hilton, Holiday Inn, InterContinental, Outrigger, Radisson, Shangri-La, Sheraton, Sofitel, Warwick, and Westin are all well represented in Fiji. Most of the large resort hotels in Fiji are foreign-owned (the Cathay, Hexagon, and Tanoa hotel chains are Fiji-based exceptions).

The Fiji government is trying to promote

ISLAND ECOTOURISM

Ecotourism has become popular, and with increasing concern in Western countries over the damaging effects of solar radiation, more and more people are looking for active recreation as an alternative to lying on the beach. This trend is being fueled by baby boomers who are eager to spend their disposable income on "soft-adventure travel" in exotic locales. In Fiji, the most widespread manifestation of the ecotourism/adventure phenomenon is the scuba-diving boom, and tours by chartered yacht, ocean kayak, raft, surfboard, bicycle, and even on foot, are proliferating.

This presents both a danger and an opportunity. Income from visitors wishing to experience nature gives local residents and governments an incentive to preserve the environment, although tourism can quickly degrade that environment through littering, the collection of coral and shells, and the development of roads, docks, and resorts in natural areas. Means of access created for tourists often end up being used by local residents whose priority is not conservation. Perhaps the strongest argument in favor of the creation of national parks and reserves in tropical countries is the ability of such parks to attract visitors from industrialized areas, while at the same time creating a framework for the preservation of nature. For the final analysis, it is governments that must enact regulations to protect the environment — market forces usually do the opposite.

Too often today, what is called ecotourism is actually packaged consumer tourism with a green coating, or just an excuse for high prices. A genuine ecotourism resort is built of local materials using natural ventilation. That means no air conditioning and only limited use of fans. The buildings fit into the natural landscape and do not restrict access to customary lands or the sea. Local fish and organic vegetables enjoy preference over imported meats on tourist tables, and wastes are minimized and properly treated. The use of motorized transport is kept to an absolute minimum. Cultural sensitivity can be enhanced by profit-sharing with the landowning clans and local participation in ownership.

Real ecotourism is a people-oriented form of tourism that benefits the islanders themselves. At smaller, locally owned businesses, visitors get to meet locals on a more personal basis, while contributing to local development. This kind of tourism offers excellent employment opportunities for island women as proprietors, *and* it's exactly what most visitors want. Appropriate tourism requires little investment, there's less disruption, and full control remains with the people themselves.

luxury-hotel development by offering 20-year tax holidays on new projects. Yet in 2007, the US$200 million JW Marriott Fiji Resort & Spa project south of Nadi collapsed after the Fiji Islands Revenue and Customs Authority suddenly altered its taxation policies with construction was half complete. Foreign investors take note.

The country's tourism marketing slogan, "Fiji Me," appears intended to encourage young Australians to come to Fiji and get "Feejeed." The previous slogan, "the truly relaxing tropical getaway," was directed at romantic couples. And before that, there was "the way the world should be," which was knocked out by the Rabuka coup. A benefit of the December 2006 coup is that it has ended plans to privatize Fiji's coastlines for the benefit of a few Fijian chiefs.

People and Culture

ETHNIC GROUPS
The Fijians

Fiji is a transitional zone between Polynesia and Melanesia. Indigenous Fijians bear a physical resemblance to the Melanesians, but like the Polynesians, they have hereditary chiefs, patrilineal descent, a love of elaborate ceremonies, and a fairly homogeneous language and culture. Fijians have interbred with Polynesians to the extent that they have lighter skin and larger stature than other Melanesians. In the interior and west of Viti Levu, where there was not as much contact with Polynesians, the people tend to be somewhat darker and smaller than the easterners.

The Fijians have always lived in villages along the rivers or coast, with anywhere from 50 to 400 people led by a hereditary chief. In the past, to see a Fijian family living in an isolated house in a rural area was uncommon. The traditional thatched *bure* is fast disappearing from Fiji as villagers rebuild in tin and panel (often following destructive hurricanes). Grass is not as accessible as cement, takes more time to repair, and is less permanent.

Away from the three largest islands, the population is almost totally Fijian. *Mataqali* (clans) are grouped into *yavusa* (tribes) of varying rank and function. Several *yavusa* form a *vanua*, a number of which make up a *matanitu*. Chiefs of the most important *vanua* are known as high chiefs. In western Viti Levu, the groups are smaller, and outstanding commoners can rise to positions of power and prestige reserved for hereditary chiefs in the east. The three traditional Fijian confederacies are Burebasaga, Kubuna, and Tovata.

Fijians work communal land individually, not as a group. Each Fijian is assigned a piece of native land. They grow most of their own food in village gardens, and only a few staples, such as tea, sugar, and flour, are imported from Suva and sold in local co-op stores. A visit to one of these stores will demonstrate just how little they import and how self-sufficient they are. Fishing, village maintenance work, and ceremonial presentations are done together. While village life provides a form of collective security, individuals are discouraged from rising above the group. Fijians who attempt to set up a business are often stifled by the demands of relatives and friends. The Fijian custom of claiming favors from members of one's own group is known as *kerekere*. This pattern makes it difficult for Fijians to compete with Indo-Fijians, for whom life has always been a struggle. Only a small fraction of companies operating in Fiji are owned and operated by indigenous Fijians.

The Indo-Fijians

Most of the Indo-Fijians now in Fiji are descended from indentured laborers recruited in Bengal and Bihar more a century ago. In the first year of the system (1879), some 450 Indians arrived in Fiji to work in the cane

© DAVID STANLEY

A small rural mosque in southern Taveuni: 20 percent of Indo-Fijians are Muslim.

fields. By 1883, the total had risen to 2,300, and in 1916, when the last indentured laborers arrived, 63,000 Indians were present in the colony. In 1920, the indenture system was finally terminated, the cane fields were divided into four-hectare plots, and the Indian workers became tenant farmers on land owned by Fijians. Indians continued to arrive until 1931, though many of these later arrivals were Gujarati or Sikh businesspeople.

In 1940, the Indian population stood at 98,000, still below the Fijian total of 105,000, but by the 1946 census Indians had outstripped Fijians 120,000 to 117,000—making Fijians a minority in their own homeland. In the wake of the 1987 coups, the relative proportions changed as tens of thousands of Indians emigrated to North America and Australia, and by early 1989 indigenous Fijians once again outnumbered Indo-Fijians. The 2007 census reported that Fiji's total population was 837,271, of which 56.8 percent were Fijian, while 37.5 percent were Indian (at the 1986 census, 46 percent were Fijian and 48.7 percent

Indian). Between 1986 and 2007, the number of Indians in Fiji decreased by 34,906, with the heaviest falls in rural areas. Between 1996 and 2007, the number of Indo-Fijians living in rural areas declined by 20 percent while in urban areas it increased 6 percent. Aside from emigration, the more widespread use of contraceptives by Indian women has led to a lower fertility rate. Based on current trends it's projected that ethnic Fijians will account for almost 70 percent of the population by 2030 and Indo-Fijians only about 25 percent.

Unlike the village-based Fijians, a majority of Indo-Fijians are concentrated in the cane-growing areas and live in isolated farmhouses, small settlements, or towns. Many Indo-Fijians also live in Suva, as do an increasing number of Fijians. Within the Indo-Fijian community there are divisions of Hindu (80 percent) versus Muslim (20 percent), north Indian versus south Indian, and Gujarati versus the rest. The Sikhs and Gujaratis have always been somewhat of an elite, as they immigrated freely to Fiji outside the indenture system.

The different groups have kept alive their ancient religious beliefs and rituals. Hindus tend to marry within their caste, although the restrictions on behavior, which characterize the caste system in India, have disappeared. Indo-Fijian marriages are often arranged by the parents, while Fijians generally choose their own partners. Rural Indo-Fijians still associate most closely with other members of their extended patrilineal family group, and Hindu and Muslim religious beliefs continue to restrict Indo-Fijian women to a position subservient to men.

Fiji's laws prevent Indo-Fijians, or anyone else, from purchasing native communal land, driving other ethnic groups to find different means of economic survival. Today, Indo-Fijian business interests dominate the country's service and retail sectors, including the lucrative duty-free outlets around Nadi, small general stores, and road transportation throughout the country. As a group, they earn 70 percent of the income and pay 80 percent of the taxes in Fiji. The perceived economic disparity between indigenous Fijians and Indo-Fijians is a source—though by no means the only source—of tension between the two groups. In reality, however, the average household income of indigenous Fijians is higher than that of Indo-Fijians. Info-Fijian farmers have been especially hard-hit by changes in the sugar industry and most would happily emigrate to North America, Australia, or New Zealand if they could only find a way.

Other Groups

The 3,000 Fiji-born Europeans, or *kaivalagi,* are descendants of Australians and New Zealanders who came to build cotton, sugar, or copra plantations in the 19th century. Many of these planters married Fijian women, and the 12,000 part-Fijians, or *kailoma,* of today are the result. There is little intermarriage between Fijians *(kaiviti)* and Indo-Fijians *(kaihidi),* though Fijians intermarry freely with Chinese and Solomon Islanders.

Many of the 5,000 Chinese in Fiji are descended from free settlers who came to set up small businesses a century ago, although since 1987 there has been an influx of Chinese from mainland China who were originally admitted to operate market gardens, but who have since moved into the towns. Small numbers of Chinese workers and entrepreneurs continue to arrive. Fiji Chinese tend to intermarry freely with the other racial groups.

The 10,000 Rotumans, a majority of whom now live in Suva, are Polynesians. On neighboring islands off Vanua Levu are the Micronesians of Rabi (from Kiribati) and the Polynesians of Kioa (from Tuvalu). The descendants of Solomon Islanders blackbirded during the 19th century still live in communities near Suva, Levuka, and Labasa. The Tongans in Lau and other Pacific Islanders who have immigrated to Fiji make this an ethnic crossroads of the Pacific.

Social Conditions

Some 98 percent of the country's population was born in Fiji. The emphasis placed on ethnicity since 1987 has been a tragedy for Fiji, though racial antagonism has been exaggerated. At the grassroots level, the different ethnic groups have always gotten along remarkably well, with little animosity. Unfortunately race relations in Fiji have been manipulated by agitators with hidden agendas unrelated to race. As important as race are the variations between rich and poor, or urban and rural.

Although Fiji's economy grew by 124 percent between 1970 and 2000, the number of people living in poverty increased by two-thirds over the same period. The imposition in 1992 of a value-added tax (VAT), combined with reductions in income tax and import duties, shifted the burden of taxation from the haves to the have-nots. Over a third of the population now lives in poverty, and contrary to the myth of Indian economic domination, Indo-Fijians are more likely to be facing abject poverty than members of other groups. Eighty percent of cane farmers now live below the poverty line. Single-parent urban families cut off from the extended-family social safety net are the specific group

schoolchildren in Navala Village in the Nausori Highlands of northern Viti Levu

© MARK HEARD / WWW.FLICKR.COM/HEARDSY

most affected, especially women trying to raise families on their own. A 2003 government survey counted 183 squatter settlements containing 13,725 households and 82,350 people, about 10 percent of Fiji's population. Sixty percent of the squatters live in Suva's northeastern suburbs, nearly half of them without assets of any kind.

Literacy is high at 87 percent. Although education is not compulsory at any level, 98 percent of children age 6–14 attend school. Many schools are racially segregated. More than 100 church-operated schools receive government subsidies. The Fiji Institute of Technology was founded at Suva in 1963, followed by the University of the South Pacific in 1968. The university serves the 12 Pacific countries that contribute to its costs. Medical services in Fiji are heavily subsidized. The divisional hospitals are at Labasa, Lautoka, and Suva, and there are also 19 subdivisional or area hospitals, 74 health centers, 100 nursing stations, and 409 village clinics scattered around the country. The most common infectious diseases are influenza, gonorrhea, and syphilis.

LAND RIGHTS

When Fiji became a British colony in 1874, the land was divided between white settlers who had bought plantations and the *taukei ni gele,* the Fijian "owners of the soil." The government assumed title to the balance. Today the alienated (privately owned) plantation lands are known as "freehold" land—about 10 percent of the total. Another 7 percent is Crown land, 80 percent of it currently leased for periods of up to 99 years. The remaining 83 percent is inalienable Fijian communal land, which can be leased (about 30 percent is) but may never be sold. Compare this 83 percent (much of it not arable) with only 3 percent Maori land in New Zealand and almost zero native Hawaiian land. Land ownership has provided the Fijians with a security that allows them to preserve their traditional culture, unlike indigenous peoples in most other countries.

Communal land is administered on behalf of some 6,600 clan groups *(mataqali)* by the Native Land Trust Board, an inept government agency established in 1940. The NLTB retains 25 percent of the lease money to cover administration, and a further 10 percent is paid directly to regional hereditary chiefs. In 1966, the British colonial administration established a system that allowed native land to be leased for 10 years, and in 1976 the Agricultural Landlord and Tenants Act (ALTA) increased the period to 30 years. In 1997, the 30-year leases began coming up for renewal. Thousands of Indo-Fijian farmers were evicted and properties began to deteriorate.

In 2010, the interim government announced that ALTA would be revoked under a new Land Reform program and the 30-year leases would be converted to 99-year leases. Ownership of the land would not change but rents would be reviewed to ensure that they reflected economic realities. Fiji's 22,000 Indo-Fijian sugarcane farmers were relieved, the country's sugar industry was given a reprieve, and an explosive social situation was avoided. Indo-Fijians have always accepted Fijian ownership of the land, provided they were granted satisfactory leases.

GENDER ISSUES

Traditionally, indigenous Fijian women were confined to the home, while men handled most matters outside the immediate family. The clear-cut roles of the woman as homemaker and the man as defender and decision-maker gave stability to village life. Western education has caused many Fijian women to question their subordinate position, and the changing lifestyle has made the old relationship between the sexes outmoded. Women's liberation has arrived as paid employment expands and access to family planning better enables women to hold jobs.

THE FLAG OF FIJI

Fiji's current national flag was adopted in 1970 when the country achieved independence from Great Britain. The Union Jack in the upper left corner recalls Fiji's 96 years as a British colony. On the right side of the flag is a shield with gold-colored royal lion on a red background holding a cocoa pod between its paws. The red cross below the lion divides the lower part of the shield in four with stalks of sugarcane, a palm tree, a bunch of bananas, and a dove of peace in the four white boxes created by the cross. The flag's light blue background represents the Pacific Ocean. Though Fiji has been a republic since 1987, the symbolism of British royalty remains on its flag and currency.

Fijian women are more emancipated than their sisters in other Melanesian countries, though men continue to dominate public life throughout the region. Tradition is often manipulated to deny women the right to express themselves publicly on community matters.

Cultural barriers hinder women's access to education and employment, and the proportion of girls in school falls as the grade level increases. Female students are nudged into lower-paying fields such as nursing or secretarial services; in Fiji and elsewhere, export-oriented garment factories exploit women workers, paying low wages amidst poor working conditions. Levels of domestic violence vary greatly, though it's far less prevalent among indigenous Fijians than it is among Indo-Fijians, and in Fiji's Macuata Province women have a suicide rate seven times above the world average, with most of the victims being Indo-Fijian. Those little signs on buses reading "real men don't hit women" suggest the problem. Travelers should take an interest in women's issues.

© MARK HEARD / WWW.FLICKR.COM/HEARDSY

church in Navala, on northern Viti Levu

RELIGION

The main religious groups in Fiji are Methodists (290,000), Hindus (233,500), Catholics (76,500), Muslims (52,500), Assemblies of God (47,500), and Seventh-Day Adventists (32,500). About 35 percent of the total population is Hindu or Muslim due to the large Indo-Fijian population, and only 2 percent of Indo-Fijians have converted to Christianity despite Methodist missionary efforts dating back to 1884. About 78 percent of indigenous Fijians are Methodist, and 8.5 percent are Catholic.

After the 1987 military coups, an avalanche of well-financed American fundamentalist missionary groups descended on Fiji, and membership in the Assemblies of God and some other new Christian sects has grown at the expense of the Methodists. While the Methodist Church has long been localized, the new evangelical sects are dominated by foreign missionaries, ideas, and money.

The Assemblies of God (AOG) is a Pentecostal denomination founded in Arkansas in 1914 and presently headquartered in Springfield, Missouri. It emphasizes the practice of glossolalia, or "speaking in tongues." Although the AOG carries out some relief work, it doesn't involve itself in social reform, in the belief that only God can solve humanity's problems. In Fiji, the number of AOG adherents increased twelve-fold between 1966 and 1992. A large AOG Bible College operates in Suva, and from Fiji the group has spread to other Pacific countries.

The Seventh-Day Adventist Church is a politically ultraconservative group that grew out of the 19th-century American Baptist movement. The SDA Church teaches the imminent return of Christ, and Saturday (rather than Sunday) is observed as the Lord's Day. SDAs regard the human body as the temple of the Holy Spirit, thus much attention is paid to health matters. Members are forbidden to partake of certain foods, alcohol, drugs, and tobacco, and the church expends considerable energy on the provision of medical and dental services. They are also active in education and local economic development.

The ecumenical Pacific Conference of

Churches began in 1961 as an association of the mainstream Protestant churches, but since 1976 many Catholic dioceses have been included as well. Both the Pacific Theological College (founded in 1966) and the Pacific Regional Seminary (opened in 1972) are in southern Suva, and the South Pacific is one of the few areas of the world with a large surplus of ministers of religion.

LANGUAGE

Fijian, a member of the Austronesian family of languages, spoken from Easter Island to Madagascar, has more speakers than any other indigenous Pacific language. Fijian vowels are pronounced as in Latin or Spanish, while the consonants are similar to those of English. Syllables end in a vowel, and the next-to-last syllable is usually the one emphasized. Where two vowels appear together they are sounded separately. In 1835, two Methodist missionaries, David Cargill and William Cross, devised the form of written Fijian used in Fiji today. Since all consonants in Fijian are separated by vowels, "mb" is spelled as b, "nd" as d, "ng" as g, "ngg" as q, and "th" as c.

Though Cargill and Cross worked at Lakeba in the Lau Group, the political importance of tiny Bau Island just off Viti Levu caused the Bauan dialect of Fijian to be selected as the "official" version of the language, and in 1850 a dictionary and grammar were published. When the Bible was translated into Bauan, that dialect's dominance was assured, and it is today's spoken and written Fijian. From 1920 to 1970, the use of Fijian was discouraged in favor of English, but since independence there has been a revival.

Hindustani or Hindi is the household tongue of most Indo-Fijians. Fiji Hindi has diverged from that spoken in India, with the adoption of many words from English and other Indian languages such as Urdu. Though a quarter of Indo-Fijians are descended from immigrants from southern India, where Tamil and Telegu are spoken, few use those languages today, even at home. Fiji Muslims speak Hindi out of practical considerations, though they might consider Urdu their mother tongue. In their spoken forms, Hindi and Urdu are very similar.

English is the second official language in Fiji and is understood by almost everyone. All schools teach exclusively in English after the fourth grade. Indo-Fijians and indigenous Fijians usually communicate with one another in English. Gilbertese is spoken by the Banabans of Rabi.

Arts and Entertainment

It's cheap to go to the movies in towns such as Ba, Labasa, Lautoka, Nadi, Nausori, and Suva, if a repertoire of romance, horror, and adventure is to your liking (only in Suva and Lautoka can you see the latest Hollywood films). Most Indian films are in Hindi, sometimes with English subtitles. These same towns have local nightclubs where you can enjoy as much drinking and dancing as you like without spending an arm and a leg. When there's live music, a cover charge is collected.

A South Pacific institution widespread in Fiji is the old colonial club that offers inexpensive beer in safe, friendly surroundings. Such clubs are found in Labasa, Lautoka, Levuka, Nadi, Savusavu, Sigatoka, Suva, and Tavua, and although they're all private clubs with Members Only signs on the door, foreign visitors are allowed entry (except at the pretentious Union Club in Suva). Many of these are male domains, although foreign women are not refused entry. The yacht clubs in Savusavu and Suva also have good bars. Many bars and clubs in Fiji refuse entry to persons dressed in flip-flops, boots, rugby jerseys, shorts, tank tops, or T-shirts. Guests must remove their hats at the door—the penalty for not complying is to buy a round of drinks for the house.

Fiji's unique spectacle is the **Fijian firewalking** performed several times a week at the large hotels along the southwest side of Viti Levu: Shangri-La's Fijian Resort (Fri.), Outrigger on the Lagoon (Tues.), Rydges Hideaway Resort (Thurs.), the Naviti (Wed.), the Warwick (Mon. and Fri.), and the Pacific Harbor Arts Village (Wed.–Sat.). A fixed admission price is charged, but it's well worth going at least once. The same hotels that present firewalking usually stage a Fijian dancing show *(meke)* on an alternative night.

FIJIAN DANCING *(MEKE)*

The term *meke* describes the combination of dance, song, and theater performed at feasts and on special occasions. Brandishing spears, their faces painted with charcoal, the men wear frangipani leis and skirts of shredded leaves. The war-club dance reenacts heroic events of the past. Both men and women perform the *vakamalolo*, a sitting dance, while the *seasea* is danced by women flourishing fans. The *taralala*, in which visitors may be asked to join, is a simple two-step shuffle danced side-by-side (early missionaries forbade the Fijians from dancing face-to-face). As elsewhere in the Pacific, the dances tell a story, though the music now is strongly influenced by Christian hymns and contemporary pop. Less sensual than Polynesian dancing, the rousing Fijian dancing evokes the country's violent past. Fijian *meke* are often part of a *magiti* (feast) performed at hotels.

TRADITIONAL CUSTOMS

Fijians and Indo-Fijians have retained a surprising number of their ancestral customs, despite the flood of conflicting influences that have swept the Pacific over the past century. Rather than a melting pot where one group assimilated another, Fiji is a patchwork of varied traditions.

The obligations and responsibilities of Fijian village life include not only the construction and upkeep of certain buildings, but personal participation in the many ceremonies that give lives meaning. Hindu Indians, on the other hand, practice firewalking and observe festivals such as Holi and Diwali, just as their forebears in India did for thousands of years.

Fijian Firewalking

In Fiji, both Fijians and Indo-Fijians practice firewalking, with the difference being that the Fijians walk on heated stones instead of hot embers. Legends tell how the ability to walk on fire was first given to a warrior named Tui-na-viqalita from Beqa Island, just off the south coast of Viti Levu, who had spared the life of a spirit god he caught while fishing for eels. The freed spirit gave to Tui-na-viqalita the gift of immunity to fire. Today his descendants act as *bete* (high priests) of the rite of *vilavilairevo* (jumping into the oven). Only members of his tribe, the Sawau, perform the ceremony. The Tui Sawau lives at Dakuibeqa village on Beqa, but firewalking is now only performed at the resort hotels on Viti Levu.

Fijian firewalkers (men only) are not permitted to have sex or to eat any coconut for two weeks prior to a performance. A man whose wife is pregnant is also barred. In a circular pit about four meters across, hundreds of large stones are first heated by a wood fire until they are white-hot. If you throw a handkerchief on the stones, it will burst into flames. Much ceremony and chanting accompanies certain phases of the

Fijian firewalking

© ERIK HANNON

ritual, such as the moment when the wood is removed to leave just the white-hot stones. The men psych themselves up in a nearby hut, then emerge, enter the pit, and walk briskly around it once. Bundles of leaves and grass are then thrown on the stones, and the men stand inside the steaming pit again to chant a final song. They seem to have complete immunity to pain, and there is no trace of injury. The men appear to fortify themselves with the heat, gaining some psychic power from the ritual.

Indian Firewalking

By an extraordinary coincidence, Indo-Fijians brought with them the ancient practice of religious firewalking. In southern India, firewalking occurs in the pre-monsoon season as a call to the goddess Kali (Durga) for rain. Indo-Fijian firewalking is an act of purification, or fulfillment of a vow to thank the god for help in a difficult situation.

In Fiji there is firewalking in most Hindu temples once a year, at full moon sometime between May and September according to the Hindu calendar. The actual event takes place on a Sunday in July or August at the Mahadevi Sangam Temple on Howell Road, Suva, and at Agnimela Mandir in Vunivau near Labasa, Vanua Levu. During the 10 festival days preceding the walk, participants remain in isolation, eat only unspiced vegetarian food, and spiritually prepare themselves. There are prayers at the temple in the early morning and group singing of religious stories evenings from Monday through Thursday. The yellow-clad devotees, their faces painted bright yellow and red, often pierce their cheeks or other body parts with spikes or three-pronged forks as part of the purification rites. Their faith is so strong they feel no pain.

The event is extremely colorful; drumming and chanting accompany the visual spectacle. Visitors are welcome to observe the firewalking, but since the exact date varies from temple to temple according to the phases of the moon (among other factors), you just have to keep asking to find out where and when it will take place. To enter the temple, you must remove your shoes and any leather clothing.

The *Yaqona* Ceremony

Yaqona (yang-GO-na) is a tranquilizing, nonalcoholic drink that numbs the tongue and lips. Better known as kava, it's made from the *waka* (dried root) of the pepper plant *(Macropiper methysticum)*. This ceremonial preparation is the most honored feature of the formal life of Fijians, Tongans, and Samoans. It is performed with the utmost gravity according to a sacramental ritual to mark births, marriages, deaths, official visits, the installation of a new chief, and other significant occasions.

There are several forms of the full *yaqona* ceremony, which is performed only for high chiefs, and abbreviated versions are put on for tourists at the hotels.

New mats are first spread on the floor, on which a hand-carved *tanoa* (a wooden bowl nearly a meter wide) is placed. A long fiber cord decorated with cowrie shells leads from the bowl to the guests of honor. At the end of the cord is a white cowrie, which symbolizes a link to ancestral spirits. As many as 70 men take their places before the bowl. The officiates are adorned with tapa, fiber, and croton leaves, their torsos smeared with glistening coconut oil, their faces usually blackened.

The guests present a bundle of *waka* to the hosts, along with a short speech explaining their visit, a custom known as a *sevusevu*. The *sevusevu* is received by the hosts and acknowledged with a short speech of acceptance. The *waka* are then scraped clean and pounded in a *tabili* (mortar). Formerly they were chewed. Nowadays the pulp is put in a cloth sack and mixed with water in the *tanoa*. In the ceremony the *yaqona* is kneaded and strained through *vau* (hibiscus) fibers.

The mixer displays the strength of the grog (kava) to the *mata ni vanua* (master of ceremonies) by pouring out a cupful into the *tanoa*. If the *mata ni vanua* considers the mix too strong, he calls for *wai* (water), then says *"Lose"* (mix), and the mixer proceeds. Again he shows the consistency to the *mata ni vanua* by pouring out a cupful. If it appears right, the *mata ni vanua* says *"Loba"* (squeeze). The mixer squeezes the remaining juice out of the pulp,

© MARK HEARD / WWW.FLICKR.COM/HEARDSY

kava ceremony at Bulou's Lodge, Navala

puts it aside, and announces, *"Sa lose oti saka na yaqona, vaka turaga"* (the kava is ready, my chief). He runs both hands around the rim of the *tanoa* and claps three times.

The *mata ni vanua* then says *"Talo"* (serve). The cupbearer squats in front of the *tanoa* with a *bilo* (half coconut shell), which the mixer fills. The cupbearer then presents the first cup to the guest of honor, who claps once and drains it, and everyone claps three times. The second cup goes to the guests' *mata ni vanua*, who claps once and drinks. The man sitting next to the mixer says *"Aa,"* and everyone answers *"Maca"* (empty). The third cup is for the first local chief, who claps once before drinking, and everyone claps three times after. Then the *mata ni vanua* of the first local chief claps once and drinks, and everyone says *"Maca."* The same occurs for the second local chief and his *mata ni vanua*.

After these six men have finished their cups, the mixer announces, *"Sa maca saka tu na yaqona, vaka turaga"* (the bowl is empty, my chief), and the *mata ni vanua* says *"Cobo"* (clap). The mixer then runs both hands around the rim of the *tanoa* and claps three times. This terminates the full ceremony, but then a second bowl is prepared and everyone drinks. During the drinking of the first bowl, complete silence must be maintained.

Social Kava Drinking

Fijian villagers have simplified grog sessions almost daily. Kava drinking is an important form of Fijian entertainment and a way of structuring friendships and community relations. Some say the Fijians have *yaqona* rather than blood in their veins. Excessive kava drinking over a long period can make the skin scaly and rough, a condition known as *kanikani*.

Individual visitors to villages are invariably invited to participate in informal kava ceremonies, in which case it's customary to present a bunch of kava roots to the group. Do this at the beginning, before anybody starts drinking, and make a short speech explaining the purpose of your visit (be it a desire to meet the people and learn about their way of life, an interest in seeing or doing something in particular on their island, or just a holiday from work). Don't hand the roots to anyone, just place them on the mat in the center of the circle. The bigger the bundle of roots, the bigger the smiles. (The roots are easily purchased at any town market for about F$30 a kilo.)

Clap once when the cupbearer offers you the *bilo,* then take it in both hands and say *bula* just before the cup meets your lips. Clap three times after you drink. Remember, you're a participant, not an onlooking tourist, so don't take photos if the ceremony is formal. Even though you may not like the appearance or taste of the drink, do try to finish at least the first cup. Tip the cup to show you are done.

It's considered extremely bad manners to turn your back on a chief during a kava ceremony, to walk in front of the circle of people when entering or leaving, or to step over the long cord attached to the *tanoa*. During a semiformal ceremony, you should remain silent until the opening ritual is complete, signaled by a round of clapping.

Presentation of the *Tabua*

The *tabua* is a tooth of the sperm whale. It was once presented when chiefs exchanged delegates at confederacy meetings and before conferences on peace or war. In recent times, the *tabua* is presented during chiefly *yaqona* ceremonies as a symbolic welcome for a respected visitor or guest or as a prelude to public business or modern-day official functions. On the village level, *tabuas* are still commonly presented to arrange marriages, to show sympathy at funerals, to request favors, to settle disputes, or simply to show respect.

Old *tabuas* are highly polished from continual handling. The larger the tooth, the greater its ceremonial value. *Tabuas* are prized cultural property and may not be exported from Fiji. Endangered-species laws prohibit their entry into the United States, Australia, and many other countries.

Stingray Spearing and Fish Drives

Stingrays are lethal-looking creatures with caudal spines up to 18 centimeters long. To catch them, eight or nine punts are drawn up in a line about a kilometer long beside the reef. As soon as a stingray is sighted, a punt is paddled forward with great speed until close enough to hurl a spear.

Another time-honored sport and source of food is the fish drive or *yavirau,* in which an entire village participates. Around the flat surface of a reef at rising tide, sometimes as many as 70 men and women group themselves in a circle a kilometer or more in circumference. All grip a ring of connected liana vines with leaves attached. While shouting, singing, and beating long poles on the seabed, the group slowly contracts the ring as the tide comes in. The shadow of the ring alone is enough to keep the fish within the circle. The fish are finally directed landward into a net or stone fish trap.

The Rising of the *Balolo*

This event takes place only in Samoa and Fiji. The *balolo (Eunice viridis)* is a thin, segmented worm of the Coelomate order, considered a culinary delicacy throughout these islands— the caviar of the Pacific. It's about 45 centimeters long and lives deep in the fissures of coral reefs. Twice a year it releases an unusual "tail" that contains its eggs or sperm. The worm itself returns to the coral to regenerate a new reproductive tail. The rising of the *balolo* is a natural almanac that keeps both lunar and solar times, and has a fixed day of appearance—even if a hurricane is raging—one night in the last quarter of the moon in October, and the corresponding night in November. It has never failed to appear on time for more than 100 years now, and you can even check your calendar by it.

Because this rising occurs with such mathematical certainty, Fijians wait in their boats to scoop the millions of writhing, reddish brown (male) and moss-green (female) spawn from the water when they rise to the surface before dawn. Within an hour after the rising, the eggs and sperm are released to spawn the next generation of *balolo*. The free-swimming larvae seek a suitable coral patch to begin the cycle again. This is one of the most bizarre curiosities in the natural history of the South Pacific, and the southeast coast of Ovalau is a good place to observe it.

ARTS AND CRAFTS

The traditional art of Fiji is closely related to that of Tonga. Fijian canoes, too, were patterned after the more-advanced Polynesian type, although the Fijians were timid sailors. War clubs, food bowls, *tanoas* (kava bowls), eating utensils, clay pots, and tapa cloth *(masi)* are considered Fiji's finest artifacts.

There are two kinds of wood carvings: the ones made from *vesi (Intsia bijuga)*—ironwood in English—or *nawanawa (Cordia subcordata)* wood are superior to those of the lighter, highly breakable *vau (Hibiscus tiliaceus)*. In times past, it often took years to make a Fijian war club, as the carving was done in the living tree and left to grow into the desired shape. The finest *tanoas* are carved in the Lau Group.

If you want to buy top-quality handicrafts, visit the Fiji Museum in Suva to see what is authentic before visiting the handicraft markets. To learn what's available and to become familiar with prices, browse one of the half-dozen outlets of **Jack's Handicrafts** (www.jacksfiji.com) around Viti Levu. You'll find them in downtown Nadi, Sigatoka, and Suva. The four-pronged cannibal forks available in most souvenir stores make unique gifts.

Locally made handicrafts are always a better buy than imported luxury goods, but avoid the "tikis" and mock New Guinea masks smeared with black shoe polish to look like ebony. Also avoid crafts made from endangered species such as sea turtles (tortoiseshell) and marine mammals (whales' teeth, etc.). Prohibited entry into most countries, these will be confiscated by customs if found.

Pottery Making

Fijian pottery-making is unique, in that it's a Melanesian art form. The Polynesians forgot how to make pottery thousands of years ago. Today the main center for pottery making in Fiji is the Sigatoka Valley on Viti Levu. Here, the women shape clay by pressing a wooden paddle against a rounded stone held inside the future pot. The potter's wheel was unknown in the Pacific.

A saucer-like section forms the bottom; the sides are built up using slabs of clay, or coils and strips. These are welded and battered into shape. When the form is ready, the pot is dried inside the house for a few days, then heated over an open fire for about an hour. Resin from the gum of the *dakua* (kauri) tree is rubbed on the outside while the pot is still hot. This adds a varnish that brings out the color of the clay and improves the pot's water-holding ability.

This pottery is extremely fragile, which accounts for the quantity of potsherds found on ancient village sites. Smaller, less breakable pottery products such as ashtrays are now made for sale to visitors.

Weaving

Woven articles are the most widespread handicrafts. Pandanus fiber is the most common, but coconut leaf and husk, vine tendril, banana stem, tree and shrub bark, the stems and leaves of water weeds, and the skin of the sago palm leaf are all used. On some islands the fibers are passed through a fire, boiled, and then bleached in the sun. Vegetable dyes of very lovely mellow tones are sometimes used, but gaudier store dyes are much more prevalent. Shells are occasionally utilized to cut, curl, or make the fibers pliable.

Tapa Cloth

This is Fiji's most characteristic traditional product. Tapa is light, portable, and inexpensive, and a piece makes an excellent souvenir to brighten up a room back home. It's made by the women on Vatulele Island off Viti Levu, on Taveuni, and on certain islands of the Lau Group.

To produce tapa, the inner, water-soaked bark of the paper mulberry (*Broussonetia papyrifera*) is stripped from the tree and steeped in water. Then it's scraped with shells and pounded into a thin sheet with wooden mallets. Four of these sheets are applied one over another and pounded together, then left to dry in the sun.

While Tongan tapa is decorated by holding a relief pattern under the tapa and overpainting the lines, Fijian tapa (*masi kesa*) is distinctive for its rhythmic geometric designs applied with stencils made from green pandanus and banana leaves. The stain is rubbed on in the same manner in which temple rubbings are made from a stone inscription.

The only colors used are red, from red clay, and a black pigment obtained by burning candlenuts. Both powders are mixed with boiled gums made from scraped roots. Sunlight deepens and sets the colors. Each island group had its characteristic colors and patterns, ranging from plantlike paintings to geometric designs. Sheets of tapa feel like felt when finished. On some islands, tapa is still used for clothing, bedding, and room dividers, and as ceremonial red carpets. Tablecloths, bedcovers, place mats, and wall hangings of tapa make handsome souvenirs.

HOLIDAYS AND FESTIVALS

Public holidays in Fiji include New Year's Day (January 1), Good Friday and Easter

Monday (March/April), Prophet Mohammed's Birthday (April), Queen Elizabeth's Birthday (a Monday around June 14), Fiji Day (a Monday or Friday around October 10), Diwali (October or November), and Christmas Days (December 25 and 26).

Check the Tourism Fiji website (www.fijime.com) to see if any festivals are scheduled during your visit. The best known are the Bula Festival in Nadi (July), the Farmers Carnival in Lautoka (mid-July), the Hibiscus Festival in Suva (August), the Sugar Festival in Lautoka (September), the Bougainvillea Festival in Ba (September), and the Back to Levuka Festival (early October). Around the end of June, there's the President's Cup Yacht Series at Nadi. Before Diwali, the Hindu festival of lights, Hindus clean their homes, then they light lamps or candles to mark the arrival of spring. Fruit and sweets are offered to Lakshmi, goddess of wealth. There are often great clothing sales just before Diwali, and specials on sweets at all the Indian restaurants. Holi is an Indian spring festival in February or March.

The International Triathlon at Nadi is in May. One of the main sporting events of the year is the International Bula Marathon held in June. The main event involves a 42-kilometer run from Lautoka to the Sheraton at Nadi.

Spectator Sports

The soccer season in Fiji is February–October, while rugby is played almost year-round. The main rugby season is April–September, when there are 15 players on each side. From November–March, rugby is played as "sevens," with seven team members to a side. (The Fijians are champion sevens players and in 1997 they defeated South Africa to take the Rugby World Cup Sevens in Hong Kong. In 2005, they defeated New Zealand to win the Melrose Cup for a second time.) Rugby is typically played only by Fijians, while soccer teams are both Fijian and Indo-Fijian. Cricket is played November–March, mostly in rural areas. Lawn bowling is popular in Suva. Saturday is the big day for team sports (only soccer and lawn bowling are practiced on Sunday).

© DAVID STANLEY

queen of the Farmers Carnival parade, Lautoka

ESSENTIALS

Getting There

Fiji's geographic position makes it the hub of transportation for the entire South Pacific, and Nadi is the region's most important international airport, with long-haul service to points all around the Pacific Rim. Thirteen international airlines fly into Nadi: Aircalin, Air New Zealand, Air Niugini, Air Pacific, Air Vanuatu, Continental Airlines, Jetstar, Korean Air, Our Airline, Pacific Blue, Qantas Airways, Solomon Airlines, and V Australia, some of them on code shares. Air Pacific also uses Suva's Nausori Airport for regional flights. The websites of all these carriers are linked to www.southpacific.org/air.html.

Fiji's national airline, **Air Pacific,** was founded in 1951 as Fiji Airways by Harold Gatty, an Australian aviator who set a record with American Willy Post in 1931 by flying around the world in eight days. In 1972, the airline was reorganized as a regional carrier and the name changed to Air Pacific. The carrier flies from Nadi to Apia, Auckland, Brisbane, Christchurch, Hong Kong, Honiara, Honolulu, Kiritimati, Los Angeles, Melbourne, Port Vila, Sydney, Tarawa, and Tongatapu, and from Suva to Auckland, Funafuti, and Tongatapu.

Qantas owns 46.5 percent of Air Pacific (the Fiji government owns the rest), and all Qantas

© DAVID STANLEY

flights to Fiji are actually code shares with the Fijian carrier. Qantas is Air Pacific's general sales agent in Europe, and you'll fly Air Pacific to Fiji if you booked with Qantas.

BOOKING TIPS
Preparations
First decide when you're going and how long you wish to stay away. Your plane ticket will be your biggest single expense, so spend some time considering the options. If you're online, your first step should be to check the websites of the airlines. The sites of Air Pacific and Air New Zealand often list web specials that will give you an idea of how much you'll have to spend. Then call the airlines on their toll-free 800 numbers to hear the sort of fare information they're providing. **Air Pacific** (tel. 800/227-4446, www.airpacific.com) and **Continental Airlines** (tel. 800/231-0856, www.continental.com) operate flights to Fiji from North America. **Air New Zealand** (tel. 800/262-1234, www.airnewzealand.com) and **Qantas** (tel. 800/227-4500, www.qantas.com .au) code share on the Air Pacific flights.

Call them all and say you want the *lowest possible fare.* Cheapest are the excursion fares, but these usually have limitations and restrictions, so be sure to ask. Some have an advance-purchase deadline, which means it's wise to begin shopping early. If you're not happy with the answers you get, call back later and try again. Many different operators take calls on these lines, and some are more knowledgeable than others. The numbers are often busy during peak business hours, so call first thing in the morning, after dinner, or on the weekend. *Be persistent.*

Cheaper Fares
You can often get a better deal through a consolidator, a specialist travel agency that deals in bulk and sells seats and rooms at wholesale prices. Many airlines have more seats than they can market through normal channels, so they sell their unused long-haul capacity to discounters or "bucket shops" at discounts of 40–50 percent off the official tariffs. The discounters buy tickets on this gray market and pass the savings along to you. Many such companies run ads in the Sunday travel sections of newspapers like the *San Francisco Chronicle, New York Times,* and *Toronto Star,* or in major entertainment weeklies.

Despite their occasionally shady appearance, most discounters and consolidators are perfectly legitimate, and your ticket will probably be issued by the airline itself. Most discounted tickets look and are exactly the same as regular full-fare tickets, but they're usually nonrefundable. There may also be other restrictions not associated with the more expensive tickets, as well as penalties if you wish to change your routing or reservations. Such tickets may not qualify for frequent-flier miles. The web specials of the airlines also carry many restrictions, which you should review carefully. Some consumer protection is obtained by paying by credit card.

Internet Bookings
For an exact fare quote that you can book instantly online, simply access an online travel agency. You type in your destination and travel dates, then watch as the site's system searches its database for the lowest fare. You may be offered complicated routings at odd hours, but you'll certainly get useful information.

Try a couple of sites for comparison, such as **Cheap Flights** (www.cheapflights.com), **Cheap Tickets** (www.cheaptickets.com), **Lowestfare.com** (www.lowestfare.com), **Expedia** (www.expedia.com), **OneTravel.com** (www.onetravel.com), **Orbitz** (www.orbitz .com), **Priceline** (www.priceline.com), and **Travelocity** (www.travelocity.com).

All these companies are aimed at the U.S. market, and a credit card with a billing address outside the United States may not be accepted. For the South Pacific, you'll sometimes need a paper ticket, and it's unlikely the agency will agree to send it to an address that is different from the one on your card. So despite the global reach of the Internet, you'll probably have to use a website based in your own country.

Flight Network (www.flightnetwork.com) in Canada allows you to search for specials online. **Travelocity.ca** (www.travelocity.ca) and **Expedia.ca** (www.expedia.ca) also serve Canada, and **Expedia.co.uk** (www.expedia.co.uk) is in the United Kingdom. Travelocity and Expedia have branches in many other countries. In Australia, it's **Travel.com.au** (www.travel.com.au) and **Flightcentre.com** (www.flightcentre.com.au). Flightcentre.com links to similar sites in nine other countries.

If you live in Europe, turn to **Flightbookers** (www.ebookers.com) in the United Kingdom and many other European countries. **Cheapestflights.co.uk** (www.cheapestflights.co.uk) and **Travel Bag** (www.travelbag.co.uk) are also in Britain. **Opodo** (www.opodo.com) operates in numerous European countries. **Flights.com** (www.flights.com) is in Frankfurt, Germany, while **Travel Overland** (www.travel-overland.de) is in Munich.

When comparing prices, note whether taxes, processing fees, fuel or security surcharges, and shipping are charged extra. Check beforehand to see if you're allowed to change your reservations or refund the ticket. After booking, print out your confirmation. If you're reluctant to place an order on an unfamiliar site, look for a contact telephone number and give them a call to hear how they sound (a listing here is not a recommendation). At all of these sites, you'll be asked to pay by credit card over a secure server.

Student Fares

Students and people under 26 years old can sometimes benefit from lower student fares by booking through **STA Travel** (www.statravel.com), with branches around the world. In the United States, call the toll-free number (tel. 800/781-4040) for information. **Student Universe** (230 Third Avenue, Waltham, MA 02451, USA, tel. 617/321-3100 or 800/272-9676, www.studentuniverse.com) allows you to get quotes and purchase student tickets online. Canada's largest student travel organization is **Travel Cuts** (www.travelcuts.com).

Round-the-World

The major airlines have combined in global alliances to compete internationally. Thus Qantas is part of the Oneworld family (www.oneworldalliance.com), comprising American Airlines, British Airways, Cathay Pacific, Finnair, Iberia, LanChile, and others, while Air New Zealand is a member of the Star Alliance (www.staralliance.com) of Air Canada, Lufthansa, SAS, Singapore Airlines, Thai, United Airlines, and many others. This is to your advantage, as frequent-flier programs are usually interchangeable within the blocks, booking becomes easier, flight schedules are coordinated, and through fares exist.

It's now possible to design some extremely wide-ranging trips by accessing the network of one of the two competing groups. For example, Air Pacific flights can be included in Oneworld's **Global Explorer** round-the-world ticket, which is mileage based. You can make up to 15 stopovers on a trip of 39,000 miles maximum. However, Fiji cannot be included in the Oneworld Explorer pass, which is continent based. Qantas offices worldwide sell the Global Explorer ticket.

Similar is the **Round-the-World Fare** valid on flights operated by the members of the Star Alliance. You're allowed 29,000, 34,000, or 39,000 miles with a minimum of three and a maximum of 15 stops. One transatlantic and one transpacific journey must be included, but the ticket is valid for one year, and backtracking is allowed. Fiji can be visited on this fare. Call the airline to check the cost of these tickets, as prices vary considerably from country to country.

Circle-Pacific

The Star Alliance's **Circle-Pacific Fare** provides a trip around the Pacific (including Asia) on Air New Zealand and other Star Alliance carriers. You get 22,000 or 26,000 miles with all the stops you want (minimum of three). Travel must begin in Honolulu, Los Angeles, San Francisco, Seattle, or Vancouver (no add-ons). It's valid for six months, but you must travel in a continuous circle without any backtracking. No date changes are allowed for the outbound sector, but subsequent changes are free. To reissue the ticket (for example, to add additional stops after departure) costs extra, so plan your trip carefully.

Qantas and Air Pacific also have Circle-Pacific fares, so compare. The **World Travelers' Club** (237 Estudillo Ave. Suite 205, San Leandro, CA 94577, USA, tel. 510/895-8495 or 800/693-0411, www.around-the-world.com) is very good on circle-the-Pacific fares.

AIR SERVICES
From North America

Air Pacific is the major carrier serving Fiji out of Los Angeles, with a round-trip costing US$1,100–1,300 from Los Angeles or CDN$1,600–1,900 from Vancouver via Los Angeles. You can often get a discount by calling Air Pacific at 800/227-4446 but the cheapest fares may involve a two-week advance purchase, 50 percent cancellation fee, and a US$100 penalty for date changes. As the quota for each discounted class of service is sold out, you have to move up to the next higher category to get on the flight, even though all economy seats are exactly the same. Thus it pays to book well ahead if you want one of the cheaper tickets. Ask if taxes and fees are included.

Air Pacific flies nonstop from Los Angeles to Nadi four times a week (10.5 hours) and from Honolulu three times a week (six hours). Scheduled Air New Zealand and Qantas flights between Los Angeles and Fiji are code shares with Air Pacific and you'll ride an Air Pacific plane if you booked with them. Often Qantas still has seats on flights that are sold out at Air Pacific.

In 2009, Continental Airlines launched direct flights to Nadi from Honolulu and Guam twice

AIRPORT CODES

AKL – Auckland	**LKB** – Lakeba	**SIN** – Singapore
APW – Apia/Faleolo	**MEL** – Melbourne	**SUV** – Suva
BNE – Brisbane	**MFJ** – Moala	**SVU** – Savusavu
CHC – Christchurch	**MNF** – Mana	**SYD** – Sydney
FGI – Apia/Fagalii	**NAN** – Nadi	**TBU** – Tongatapu
FUN – Funafuti	**NGI** – Gau	**TRW** – Tarawa
HIR – Honiara	**NOU** – Nouméa	**TVU** – Taveuni
HNL – Honolulu	**OSA** – Osaka	**TYO** – Tokyo
ICI – Cicia	**POM** – Port Moresby	**VBV** – Vanua Balavu
INU – Nauru	**PPG** – Pago Pago	**VLI** – Port Vila
IUE – Niue	**PPT** – Papeete	**WLG** – Wellington
KDV – Kadavu	**PTF** – Malololailai	**WLS** – Wallis
KXF – Koro	**RAR** – Rarotonga	**YVR** – Vancouver
LAX – Los Angeles	**RTA** – Rotuma	**YYZ** – Toronto
LBS – Labasa	**SEA** – Seattle	
LEV – Levuka	**SFO** – San Francisco	

a week. Numerous connections to Japan and the U.S. mainland are available. With the merger of Continental Airlines and United Airlines in 2010, the combined entity is expected to launch new services to Nadi from Los Angeles and perhaps other North American cities.

Canada is poorly served by Air Pacific; the direct flight from Vancouver to Nadi via Honolulu was canceled in early 2007 and all Vancouver passengers must now fly Alaska Airlines to Los Angeles and change planes. Air New Zealand has a nonstop flight from Vancouver to Auckland that avoids U.S. routings.

No flights operate between Fiji and the Cook Islands or French Polynesia on any airline. To get between the two, you must transit Auckland. If you're starting from Los Angeles and want to combine Tahiti and Fiji in a single ticket, Qantas will work best as they have code share agreements with both Air Pacific and Air Tahiti Nui via Auckland. Some Air Pacific flights between Honolulu and Nadi stop in Apia allowing you combine Samoa with Fiji very easily.

North American Ticket Agents

Some of the cheapest round-trip tickets to Fiji are sold by **Fiji Travel** (15727 South Western Ave., Suite C, Gardena, CA 90247, USA, tel. 310/512-6430 or 800/500-3454, www.fiji travel.com).

Goway Travel (5757 West Century Blvd., Suite 807, Los Angeles, CA 90045, USA, tel. 800/387-8850, www.goway.com), with additional offices in Sydney, Toronto, and Vancouver, also offers competitive fares to Fiji.

A leading Canadian specialist travel agency is **Pacesetter Travel** (3284 Yonge St., Suite 301, Toronto, ON M4N 3M7, Canada, tel. 416/322-1031 or 800/387-8827, www.pace settertravel.com), with offices in Ottawa, Toronto, Vancouver, and Victoria.

For circle-Pacific or round-the-world fares, try **Airtreks** (tel. 877/247-8735, www.air treks.com) or **Air Brokers International** (tel. 800/883-3273, www.airbrokers.com), both based in San Francisco, or **JustFares.com** (tel. 800/766-3601, www.justfares.com) in Seattle. In Canada, there's **Long Haul Travel** (www.longhaultravel.ca) in Toronto.

From Australia

Air Pacific offers daily nonstop flights to Nadi from Brisbane, Melbourne, and Sydney (all Qantas flights to Fiji are operated by Air Pacific planes). **Pacific Blue** (www.flypaci ficblue.com), owned by Sir Richard Branson's Virgin Blue, began flying to Nadi from Brisbane and Sydney in 2004. Direct flights to Fiji from Adelaide and Melbourne were added in 2009. Round-trip fares from Sydney to Nadi on Pacific Blue start as low as A$320 including tax with tons of restrictions, or A$639 with fewer restrictions. The lowest fares are available through the website, and competition from Pacific Blue has forced Air Pacific to lower its fares. Pacific Blue's no-frills service means that food costs extra on the plane, so bring along a sandwich or have something to eat before boarding. (Air Pacific is a full-service carrier, which means they'll feed you and do other things Pacific Blue won't.)

V Australia (www.vaustralia.com.au) flies from Sydney to Nadi with connections from numerous Australian cities on Virgin Blue Airlines. Similarly, **Jetstar** (www.jetstar.com) is a Qantas-owned discount airline with flights to Nadi from Sydney. Immediate connections to/from Melbourne are available. The websites of both V Australia and Jetstar often list seat sales to Fiji.

You can sometimes get a better price by working through a travel agent specializing in bargain airfares, such as Flight Centre (www .flightcentre.com.au). If you're looking for a more complicated ticket involving a number of stops, try **Trailfinders** (8 Spring St., Sydney, NSW 2000, Australia, tel. 02/9276-4200, www.trailfinders.com.au).

The cheapest tickets must be bought 14 days in advance and heavy cancellation penalties apply. Shop around, as you can often find much better deals than the published fares, especially during the off months.

From New Zealand

Air New Zealand and Air Pacific fly from Auckland to Nadi once or twice a day, and Air Pacific also flies from Christchurch once a week. In addition, Air Pacific flies nonstop between Auckland and Suva twice a week.

It's sometimes almost as cheap to buy a package tour to Fiji with airfare, accommodations, and transfers included, but these are usually limited to seven nights on one island and you're stuck in a boring tourist-oriented environment. Ask if you can extend your return date and still get the tour price. Agents to call include STA Travel (www.statravel.com) and Flight Centre International (www.flightcentre.co.nz).

From Europe

Since no European carriers reach Fiji, you'll have to use a gateway city such as Los Angeles, Honolulu, Sydney, or Seoul. Air New Zealand offers daily nonstop flights London–Los Angeles, with connections in Los Angeles direct to Fiji. From Germany, it may be cheaper, faster, and easier to travel via Seoul on Korean Air. Cathay Pacific code shares Air Pacific's twice weekly Hong Kong–Nadi flights, allowing you to plus into Cathay Pacific's large network in Asia and Europe. Also call your local British Airways or Qantas office and ask what connections they're offering to Fiji on Air Pacific.

The British specialist in South Pacific itineraries is **Trailfinders** (tel. 0845/050-5886, www.trailfinders.com), in business since 1970. Its 24 offices around the United Kingdom and Ireland offer a variety of discounted round-the-world tickets through Fiji, which are often much cheaper than the published fares. If you're in the United Kingdom, it's easy to order a free copy of their magazine, *Trailfinder,* and brochures online.

Western Air Travel (Bickham, Totnes, Devon TQ9 7NJ, United Kingdom, tel. 0845/680-1298, www.westernair.co.uk) is also good on round-the-world tickets. Check the ads in the London entertainment magazines for other such companies. **Round the World Flights** (102 Islington High Street, Islington,

London N1 8EG, United Kingdom, tel. 020/7704-5700, www.roundtheworldflights .com) allows you to build your own flights online.

Barron Travel (Noordermarkt 16, 1015 MX Amsterdam, the Netherlands, tel. 020/625-8600, www.barrontravel.com) specializes in the Pacific islands. In Sweden, there's **Tour Pacific** (Sundstorget 3, SE-25110 Helsingborg, Sweden, tel. 042/179500, www.tourpacific .se).

In Switzerland, try **Globetrotter Travel Service** (www.globetrotter.ch) with offices in 15 Swiss cities.

In Germany, one of the most efficient travel agencies selling tickets to Fiji is **Jet-Travel** (Buchholzstr. 35, D-53127 Bonn, Germany, tel. 0228/284315, www.jet-travel.de). The website of **Travel Overland** (www.travel-overland .de) with five offices in Germany quotes exact fares on flights to Nadi.

REGIONAL AIRLINES

A number of regional carriers fly to and from Fiji. **Aircalin** (tel. 800/254-7251, www.air calin.nc) flies to Fiji from Nouméa and Wallis. From Suva, **Air Pacific** (www.airpacific.com) flies to Funafuti in Tuvalu and Nuku'alofa on Tongatapu. From Nadi, there are Air Pacific flights to Apia, Honiara, Kiritimati, Port Vila, Tarawa, and Tongatapu. **Air Niugini** (www .airniugini.com.pg) code shares with Air Pacific between Nadi and Port Moresby via Honiara. **Air Vanuatu** (www.airvanuatu .com) also partners with Air Pacific on flights from Port Vila. **Solomon Airlines** (www.fly solomons.com) code shares with Air Pacific to Honiara. **Our Airline** (www.ourairline.com .au) has a weekly flight from Tarawa to Nadi operated by Air Kiribati. Keep in mind that few regional flights operate daily, and many are only once or twice a week.

Air Pacific

Air Pacific offers a Pacific Bula Pass as an add-on to their tickets to Fiji from Australia, New Zealand, and the United States. For only US$99 you can fly roundtrip from Nadi to

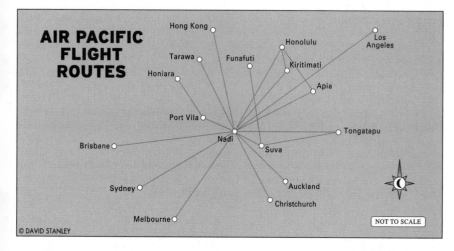

AIR PACIFIC
FLIGHT
ROUTES

Hong Kong
Tarawa
Honiara
Funafuti
Honolulu
Kiritimati
Los Angeles
Apia
Port Vila
Nadi
Brisbane
Suva
Tongatapu
Sydney
Auckland
Melbourne
Christchurch

© DAVID STANLEY

NOT TO SCALE

Apia, Honiara, Nuku'alofa, Tarawa, or Port Vila. To fly to all of them is US$299. This pass can only be purchased in Australia, New Zealand, and the United States prior to travel to Fiji. Only "M" class economy seats can be used, date changes cost US$50, and the pass is non-refundable.

Obtainable locally are Air Pacific's special Bula Fares, which are based on two one-way fares at different levels, starting at F$598 round-trip to Apia, F$438 to Tongatapu, F$508 to Port Vila, F$848 to Honiara, and F$898 to Tarawa. Tax is extra. Only a few seats on each flight are available at the lowest price, and once they're sold, you must move up a level or two to get on the plane.

PROBLEMS

When planning your trip, allow a minimum two-hour stopover between connecting flights at U.S. airports, although with airport delays on the increase, even this may not be enough. In the islands, allow at least a day between flights. Try to avoid flying on weekends and holidays, when the congestion is at its worst.

If your flight is canceled due to mechanical problems with the aircraft, the airline will cover your hotel bill and meals. If they reschedule the flight on short notice for reasons of their own or you're bumped off an overbooked

flight, they should also pay. They may not feel obligated to pay, however, if the delay is due to weather, a strike by another company, or security alerts.

To compensate for no-shows, most airlines overbook their flights. To avoid being bumped, ask for your seat assignment when booking, check in early, and go to the departure area well before flight time. Of course, if you *are* bumped by a reputable international airline at a major airport, you'll be regaled with free meals and lodging and sometimes even free flight vouchers or cash payments (don't expect anything like this from Pacific Sun). Some airlines require you to reconfirm your onward reservations whenever you break your journey for more than 72 hours, while others (such as Air New Zealand) don't.

Baggage

International airlines generally allow economy-class passengers 20 kilograms of baggage. On Air Pacific flights to Honolulu, the limit is 30 kilograms. However, if Los Angeles is included in your ticket, the allowance is two pieces not more than 32 kilograms each for all of your flights on that carrier. Under the piece system, neither bag must have a combined length, width, and height of more than 158 centimeters (62 inches), and the two pieces together must not exceed 272 centimeters (107 inches). On most long-haul tickets to/from the continental United States or Europe, the piece system should apply to all sectors, but check this with the airline and look on your ticket. Many U.S. domestic airlines now charge extra for all checked baggage. The frequent-flier programs of some airlines allow participants to carry up to 10 kilograms of excess baggage free of charge. In Fiji, Pacific Sun restricts you to 15 kilograms total, although Los Angeles passengers connecting to Pacific Sun are allowed two pieces. Overweight luggage costs 1 percent of the full business-class fare per kilogram—watch out, this can be a lot! Pack according to the lowest common denominator.

Bicycles, folding kayaks, golf clubs, and surfboards can usually be checked as baggage (sometimes for an additional "oversize" charge), but sailboards may have to be shipped airfreight. If you do travel with a sailboard, call it a surfboard at check-in. Air Pacific charges US$22 each for bulky items, plus any applicable overweight baggage charge.

Tag your bags with name, address, and phone number inside and out. Stow anything that could conceivably be considered a weapon (scissors, sewing needles, razor blades, nail clippers, etc.) in your checked luggage. Metal objects, such as flashlights and umbrellas, that might require a visual inspection should also be packed away. If in doubt, ask the person at the check-in counter if you'll be allowed to carry a certain item aboard the plane. As you're checking in, look to see if the three-letter city codes on your baggage tag receipt and boarding pass are the same. If you're headed to Nadi, the tag should read NAN (Suva is SUV).

Check your bag straight through to your final destination; otherwise the airline staff may disclaim responsibility if it's lost or delayed at an intermediate stop. If your baggage is damaged or doesn't arrive at your destination, inform the airline officials *immediately* and have them fill out a written report; otherwise future claims for compensation will be compromised. Keep receipts for any money you're forced to spend to replace missing items.

On flights touching the United States, you'll be told to leave your baggage unlocked. In that case, consider loosely fastening the zippers together with nylon cable ties, available at any hardware store. Upon arrival, if you notice that the ties have been cut or that the bag has been mysteriously patched up with tape, carefully examine the contents right away. This could be a sign that baggage handlers have pilfered items, and you must report the theft before leaving the customs hall in order to be eligible for compensation.

Claims for lost luggage can take weeks to process. Keep in touch with the airline to show your concern, and hang on to your baggage tag until the matter is resolved. If you feel you did not receive the attention you deserved, write the airline an objective letter outlining the case. Get the names of the employees you're dealing with, so you can mention them in the letter. Of course, don't expect any pocket money or compensation on a remote outer island. Report the loss, then wait until you get back to their main office.

ORGANIZED TOURS
Packaged Holidays

Any travel agent worth their commission would rather sell you a package tour instead of only a plane ticket, and it's a fact that some vacation packages actually cost less than regular round-trip airfare! While packaged travel certainly isn't for everyone, reduced group airfares and discounted hotel rates make some tours an excellent value. For two people with limited time and a desire to stay at first-class hotels, this is the cheapest way to go.

The wholesalers who put these packages together get their rooms at bulk rates far lower than what individuals pay, and the airlines also give them deals. If they'll let you extend your return date to give you some time to yourself, this can be a great deal, especially with the hotel thrown in for "free." Special-interest tours are very popular among people who want to be sure they'll get to participate in the activities they enjoy.

The main drawback to the tours is that

you're on a fixed itinerary in a tourist-oriented environment, out of touch with local life. You may not like the hotel or meals you get, and singles pay a healthy supplement. You'll probably get prepaid vouchers to turn in as you go along and won't be escorted by a tour conductor. Do check all the restrictions.

What follows is a list of North American companies that make individualized travel arrangements or offer package tours to Fiji. Spend some time surfing through their websites, and crosscheck the resorts they offer using the listings in this guide.

- **Fiji Travel,** 15727 South Western Ave., Suite C, Gardena, CA 90247, USA, tel. 310/512-6430 or 800/500-3454, www.fijitravel.com

- **Fiji Vacations,** 711 West 17th St., Suite H-1, Costa Mesa, CA 92627, USA, tel. 800/927-1923, www.fijivacations.com

- **Goway Travel,** 5757 West Century Blvd., Suite 807, Los Angeles, CA 90045, USA, tel. 800/387-8850; 3284 Yonge St., Suite 300, Toronto, Ontario M4N 3M7, Canada, tel. 416/322-1034; 1200 W. 73rd Ave., Suite 1050, Vancouver, BC V6P 6G5, Canada, tel. 604/264-8088, www.goway.com

- **Islands in the Sun,** 300 Continental Blvd., Suite 350, El Segundo, CA 90245, USA, tel. 310/536-0051, www.islandsinthesun.com

- **Jetabout Vacations,** 300 Continental Blvd., Suite 350, El Segundo, CA 90245, USA, tel. 800/348-8151, www.jetaboutfijivacations.com

- **McCoy Travel,** P.O. Box 275, Kahului, Maui, HI 96733, USA, tel. 800/256-4280, www.mccoytravel.com

- **Pacific Destination Center,** 18685 Main St., Suite 622, Huntington Beach, CA 92648, USA, tel. 714/960-4011 or 800/227-5317, www.pacific-destinations.com

- **Pacific for Less,** 1993 S. Kihei Rd., #21-130, Kihei, HI 96753, USA, tel. 800/915-2776, www.pacific-for-less.com

- **South Pacific Holidays,** 10906 N.E. 39th St., Suite A-1, Vancouver, WA 98682-6789, USA, tel. 877/733-3454, www.tropical fiji.com

- **Sunspots International,** 1918 N.E. 181st, Portland, OR 97230, USA, tel. 800/266-6115, www.sunspotsintl.com

Rascals in Paradise (500 Sansome St., Suite 601, San Francisco, CA 94111, USA, tel. 415/273-2224, www.rascalsinparadise. com) has been organizing personalized tours to Fiji for families since 1987. They have been instrumental in initiating numerous children's programs.

Margi Arnold's **Creative Travel Adventures** (8500 E. Jefferson Ave., Unit 5H, Denver, CO 80237, USA, tel. 888/568-4432, www.honeymoonfiji.com) specializes in honeymoon travel.

Impulse Fiji (P.O. Box 10000, Nadi Airport, Fiji Islands, tel. 679/672-0600, www. impulsefiji.com), based in Nadi, also caters for couples, honeymoons, and weddings, plus last-minute travel.

From Australia

Hideaway Holidays (Val Gavriloff, Newington Technology Park, Unit 14A/8 Avenue of Americas, Newington, NSW 2127, Australia, tel. 02/8799-2500, www.hideawayholidays. com.au) specializes in packages to Fiji and the South Pacific. It's been in the business since 1977.

Other Australian wholesalers and tour operators involved in Fiji include:

- **ATS Pacific Ltd.,** Level 10, 130 Elizabeth St., Sydney, NSW 2000, Australia, tel. 02/9268-2111, www.atspacific.com.au

- **Coral Seas Travel,** 141 Walker Street, North Sydney, NSW 2060, Australia, tel. 1800/641-803, www.coralseas.com.au

- **Essence Tours,** P.O. Box 1367, Maroochydore, QLD 4558, Australia, tel. 1300/762-901, www.essencetours.com.au

- **Goway Travel,** 350 Kent St., 8th Fl., Sydney, NSW 2000, Australia, tel. 02/9262-4755, www.goway.com

- **Pacific Holidays,** Floor 11, 815 George St., Sydney, 2000, Australia, tel. 02/9080-1600, www.pacificholidays.com.au

- **Talpacific Holidays,** Level 5, 11 Finchley Street, Milton, QLD 4064, Australia, tel. 1300/665-737, www.talpacific.com

From New Zealand

Ginz Travel (Level 1, 538 Wairakei Rd., Christchurch, New Zealand, tel. 03/357-0010, www.ginz.com) arranges flights, accommodations, rental cars, and package deals to Fiji. **Go Holidays** (Gen-I Tower, Level 4, 66 Wyndham St., Auckland, New Zealand, tel. 09/914-4000, www.goholidays.co.nz) lists cheap packages and flights.

Pacific Destinationz (Unit 7, 6 Omega St., North Harbour, Albany, Auckland, New Zealand, tel. 09/915-8888, www.pacificdesti nationz.co.nz) has its own representative office at Nadi International Airport.

From Europe

Austravel (3 Barton Arcade, Deansgate, Manchester, M3 2BB, United Kingdom, tel. 0844/826-0840, www.austravel.com), with offices in Manchester and Edinburgh, is a South Pacific–oriented tour company owned by the TUI Travel Group. **Tailor Made Travel** (18 Port St., Evesham, Worchestershire, WR11 6AN, United Kingdom, tel. 0800/988-5887, www.tailor-made.co.uk) specializes in upscale South Pacific tours.

In Germany, the **Pacific Travel House** (Schwanthalerstrasse 100, 80336 München, tel. 089/543-2180, www.pacific-travel-house .com) and **Adventure Holidays** (Brüsselerstr. 37, 50674 Köln, Germany, tel. 0221/530-3590, www.adventure-holidays.com) offer a variety of package tours.

In Austria, the South Pacific specialist is **Coco Weltweit Reisen** (Eduard-Bodem-Gasse 8, A-6020 Innsbruck, tel. 0512/365-791, www .coco-tours.at).

Scuba Tours

Fiji is one of the world's prime scuba locales, and most of the islands have excellent facilities for divers. Although it's not that difficult to make your own arrangements as you go, you should consider joining an organized scuba tour if you want to cram in as much diving as possible. To stay in business, the dive-travel specialists mentioned here are forced to charge prices comparable to what you'd pay on the beach, and the convenience of having everything prearranged is often worth it. Before booking, find out exactly where you'll be staying and diving, and ask if daily transfers and meals are provided. Of course, diver certification is mandatory.

Before deciding, carefully consider booking a cabin on a "liveaboard" dive boat. Liveaboards are a bit more expensive than hotel-based diving, but you're offered up to five dives a day and a total experience. Some repeat divers won't go any other way.

Companies specializing in dive tours to Fiji include:

- **Caradonna Dive Adventures,** 2101 W. State Road 434, Suite 221, Longwood, FL 32779, USA, tel. 407/774-9000 or 800/328-2288, www.caradonna.com

- **Dive Discovery,** P.O. Box 9807, San Rafael, CA 94912, USA, tel. 415/444-5100 or 800/886-7321, www.divediscovery.com

- **Island Dreams,** 1309 Antoine Dr., Houston, TX 77055, USA, tel. 713/973-9300 or 800/346-6116, www.islandream.com

- **Poseidon Dive Adventures,** 14 Winterbranch, Irvine, CA 92604, USA, tel. 800/854-9334, www.poseidondiveadven tures.com

- **Sea Fiji Travel,** P.O. Box 944, Niwot, CO 80544, USA, tel. 303/652-0751 or 800/854-3454, www.seafiji.com

- **South Pacific Island Travel,** 10701 Aurora Ave. North, Seattle, WA 98133, USA, tel. 206/367-0956 or 877/773-4846, www .spislandtravel.com

- **World of Diving,** 215 Pier Ave., Ste. C, Hermosa Beach, CA 90254, USA, tel. 800/463-4846, www.worldofdiving.com

Aqua-Trek (P.O. Box 337, Moss Beach, CA 94038, USA, tel. 800/541-4334, www.aquatrek.com) is unique in that they operate their own dive shops in Fiji at Mana Island and Pacific Harbor.

In Australia, try **Dive Adventures** (Unit 607, 379 Pitt St., Sydney, NSW 2000, Australia, tel. 02/9299-4633, www.diveadventures.com), a scuba wholesaler with an office in Port Melbourne. **Allways Dive Expeditions** (168 High St., Ashburton, Melbourne, VIC 3147, Australia, tel. 03/9885-8863, www.allwaysdive.com.au) organizes dive expeditions to Fiji.

Dive, Fish, Snow Travel (39A, Apollo Dr., Mairangi Bay, Auckland, New Zealand, tel. 09/479-2210, www.divefishsnow.co.nz) arranges scuba and game-fishing tours to Fiji at competitive rates.

In Europe, **Schöner Tauchen** (Hastedter Heerstr. 211, D-28207 Bremen, Germany, tel. 0421/450-010, www.schoener-tauchen.com) specializes in dive tours to Fiji.

Dive the World (Soi Hat Patong, 188/2 Thaweewong Road, Patong Beach, Phuket, 83150 Thailand, tel. 66-83/505-7794, www.divetheworldfiji.com) has a website with lots of information about diving around Fiji, and they promise to beat everyone else's prices.

Alternatively, you can make your own arrangements directly with island dive shops.

Kayak Tours

Ocean kayaking is experiencing a boom in Fiji, with kayaking tours now offered in the Yasawas, Kadavu, Viti Levu, and Lau. Most islands have a sheltered lagoon ready-made for the excitement of kayak touring, and this effortless transportation mode can convert you into an independent 21st-century explorer! Many international airlines accept folding kayaks as checked baggage at no additional charge.

Among the most exciting tours to Fiji are the eight-day kayaking expeditions offered May–October by **Southern Sea Ventures** (P.O. Box 641, St. Ives, NSW 2075, Australia, tel. 02/8901-3287, www.southernseaventures.com). Their groups (limited to 12 people) paddle stable expedition sea kayaks through the sheltered tropical waters of the northern Yasawa chain. Accommodations are tents on the beach, and participants must be in reasonable physical shape, as three or four hours a day are spent on the water. The A$1,995 price doesn't include airfare. **World Expeditions** (Level 5, 71 York St., Sydney, NSW 2000, Australia, tel. 02/8270-8400, www.worldexpeditions.com) offers similar trips.

Tamarillo Tropical Expeditions (Anthony Norris, P.O. Box 9869, Wellington, New Zealand, tel. 04/239-9885, www.tamarillo.co.nz) organizes one-week kayaking trips to Ono and Kadavu year-round at NZ$2,295 all-inclusive from Nadi. Two support boats carry the luggage and food. Nights are spent at small island resorts and in local villages, not in tents. Every third or fourth trip, Tamarillo offers a more rigorous "classic extreme" expedition for experienced kayakers who want to push the envelope a little further.

Surfing Tours

For information on tours to Tavarua Island and the famous Cloudbreak, contact **Tavarua Island Tours** (P.O. Box 60159, Santa Barbara, CA 93160, USA, tel. 805/686-4551, www.tavarua.com). Tavarua is often sold out six months in advance.

Waterways Surf Adventures (1828 Broadway, Suite D, Santa Monica, CA 90404, USA, tel. 310/584-9900, www.waterwaystravel.com) handles bookings for Tavarua's neighbor, Namotu Island Resort. Seven-night package tours from Los Angeles with airfare, meals, and boat transfers included are from US$3,703 per person. Only group bookings for 20 or more persons are accepted March–December (individual bookings accepted Jan.–Feb.). However, they do keep a waiting list of people who wish to be informed of vacancies at any time of year.

Quiksilver Travel (15202 Graham St., Huntington Beach, CA 92649, USA, tel.

877/217-1091, www.quiksilvertravel.com) also has surfing tours to Fiji.

In Australia, **Surf the Earth** (33 Dominions Rd., Ashmore, QLD 4214, Australia, tel. 07/5527-9855, www.surftheearth.com.au) books a variety of surfing trips to Fiji.

Tours for Naturalists

Reef and Rainforest Adventure Travel (400 Harbor Dr., Suite D, Sausalito, CA 94965, USA, tel. 415/289-1760 or 800/794-9767, www.reefrainforest.com) books diving, cruises, and other adventure tours to Fiji.

Outdoor Travel Adventures (2927-A Canon St., San Diego, CA 92106, USA, tel. 619/523-2137 or 800/554-9059, www.otadventures.com) offers a variety of adventure tours to Fiji.

Hiking Tours

Year-round **Adventure Fiji,** a division of Rosie Holidays (tel. 672-2755, www.rosiefiji.com) at Nadi Airport, runs adventuresome hiking trips in central Viti Levu south of Rakiraki. Horses carry trekkers' backpacks, so the trips are feasible for almost anyone in good condition. Accommodation is in Fijian villages. The F$828/1,147 price per person for three/five nights includes transport to the trailhead, food and accommodations at a few of the 11 Fijian villages along the way, guides, and a bamboo raft ride on a tributary of the Wainibuka River. A minimum of two people is required for such a tour. Trekkers hike about five hours a day, allowing lots of time to get to know the village people. You'll probably be required to ford rivers along the way, so have along a pair of cheap canvas shoes to avoid ruining your expensive hiking boots.

Bus Tours

Feejee Experience (tel. 672-5950 or 672-3311, www.feejeeexperience.com), represented by Tourist Transport Fiji at Nadi Airport, offers organized backpacker bus tours around Fiji. The "Hula Loop" travel pass around Viti Levu is F$485 and includes activities such as rafting, hiking, kayaking, village visits, and beach stops (food and accommodations not included). For F$725 total, you can add one night on Beachcomber Island. The minimum time required to do such a trip is four days, but the nonrefundable passes are valid for six months of continuous travel (without backtracking). Reservations are required. A good plan is to confirm only your starting date with Feejee Experience and book everything else as you go. Always say you just want to stay one night at a stop and book a seat on the bus for the next day. After having a look around if you decide you like the resort and want to stay longer, inform the representative at dinner. Otherwise if you don't like the place, you might not be able to leave the following day if the bus is full. Although some people like the organized program and party atmosphere Feejee Experience provides, you can do about the same thing on your own for less than half the price.

Tours for Students

Rustic Pathways (P.O. Box 1150, Willoughby, OH 44096, USA, tel. 440/975-9691 or 800/321-4353, www.rusticpathways.com) operates a variety of summer programs (June–Aug.) in Fiji for high school students. Most involve some form of community service combined with travel and adventure sports. All tours are conducted by experienced leaders, and prices are reasonable, starting at US$1,295 for 10 days, plus airfare.

Tours for Seniors

Since 1989, the **Pacific Islands Institute** (3566 Harding Ave., Suite 202, Honolulu, HI 96816, USA, tel. 808/732-1999, www.explorethepacific.com) has operated educational tours to most of the South Pacific countries in cooperation with Hawaii Pacific University. Their **Elderhostel** people-to-people study programs are designed for those aged 55 or over (younger spouses welcome).

CRUISES AND CHARTERS

Tourist Cruises

Blue Lagoon Cruises Ltd. (6 Nuqa Place,

Lautoka, Fiji, tel. 666-1622, www.bluelagoon cruises.com) has been offering luxury mini-cruises from Lautoka to the Yasawa Islands since its founding by Captain Trevor Withers in 1950. The 68-passenger *Fiji Princess* and 72-passenger *Mystique Princess* operate weekly two-night (from F$1,567), three-night (from F$2,090), and six-night (from F$6,033) cruises. Prices are per cabin (two persons) and include meals (but not alcohol), entertainment, shore excursions, and tax (no additional "port charges" and no tipping). Single occupancy is less. Children under 15 can share the cabin with their parents for a nominal price and reduced family rates for two cabins are available. Saloon or A deck is about 50 percent more expensive than the main deck, but you have the railing outside your cabin door instead of a porthole window. The meals are often beach-barbecue affairs, with Fijian dancing. You'll have plenty of opportunities to snorkel in the calm, crystal-clear waters (bring your own gear). Blue Lagoon Cruises has an excellent reputation. Reservations are essential.

Captain Cook Cruises (Denarau Marina, Nadi, Fiji, tel. 670-1823, www.captaincook .com.fj) operates out of Nadi's Denarau Marina rather than Lautoka. They offer cruises to the Yasawa Islands aboard the aging 60-state-room MV *Reef Escape* and the newer 75-state-room MV *Reef Endeavour,* departing Nadi on Tuesday and Saturday afternoons. Double-occupancy cabins begin at F$1,799/2,249 per person for three/four nights twin share with bunk beds. The two itineraries vary considerably, and there's a discount if you do both in succession. Six times a year there's a seven-night "Northern Fiji Dateline" cruise to Levuka and Taveuni. Both the 68-meter *Reef Escape* and the 73-meter *Reef Endeavour* were formerly used for cruises along Australia's Great Barrier Reef.

In addition, Captain Cook Cruises operates three-/four-night cruises to the southern Yasawas on the 33-meter topsail schooner *Spirit of the Pacific*—a more romantic choice than the mini-cruise ships. These trips depart Nadi every Monday and Thursday morning and start at F$599/799 per person for two/three nights (children under 12 not accepted). You sleep ashore in a double *bure* at the Barefoot Lodge on Drawaqa Island, the

The *Reef Escape* takes tourists on Yasawa Island cruises from Nadi.

© DAVID STANLEY

food is good (with lots of fresh vegetables and salads), and the staff is friendly and well organized. Captain Cook Cruises also sometimes uses the 27-meter square-rigged brigantine *Ra Marama* on these trips. It's a fine vessel built of teak planks in Singapore in 1957 for a former governor general of Fiji. These trips can be booked through most travel agents in Fiji or via the website; readers who've gone report having a great time.

The 39-meter three-masted schooner *Tui Tai* of **Tui Tai Expeditions** (P.O. Box 474, Savusavu, Fiji, tel. 885-3032, www.tuitai.com), based at Savusavu, caters to the upscale flashpacker market. The five-night cruise departing Natewa Bay starts at US$3,193 plus 17.5 percent tax per person. For seven nights, it's from US$3,900 plus tax. All accommodations have private bathrooms, air-conditioning, and ocean views. Meals, alcohol, spa treatments, and activities (bicycling, snorkeling, scuba diving, surfing, and kayaking) are included. The itinerary focuses on remote islands such as the Ringgold Islands, Kioa, Rabi, and eastern Taveuni. The 22 pampered guests are served by a crew of 18.

Scuba Cruises

Several **liveaboard dive boats** ply Fiji waters. These boats anchor right above the dive sites, so no time is wasted commuting back and forth. All meals are included, and the diving is unlimited. Singles are usually allowed to share a cabin with another diver to avoid a single supplement.

The five-stateroom *Sere Ni Wai* (or "song of the sea") is a 30-meter cruiser based at the Novotel in Suva and operating in the Lomaiviti Group. Captain Greg Lawlor's family has been in Fiji for four generations, but his boat is relatively new, launched in 1995 and refitted in 2009. Formerly marketed as the *Fiji Aggressor*, this boat is now sold in the United States as the *Island Dancer II* by **Dancer Fleet** (15291 NW 60th Ave., Suite 201, Miami Lakes, FL 33014 USA, www.peterhughes.com). Seven-night cruises start at US$2,795 plus tax with up to five dives per day. In Fiji, **Mollie Dean**

Cruises (P.O. Box 3256, Lami, Fiji, tel. 336-1171, www.sere.com.fj) handles bookings on the *Sere Ni Wai.*

Another famous boat is the 34-meter, eight-cabin *Nai'a* which does seven-day scuba cruises to Lomaiviti and northern Lau at US$3,140, or 10 days for US$4,485, excluding airfare. Captain Rob Barrel and Dive Director Cat Holloway have a longstanding interest in dolphins and whales, and whale-watching expeditions to Tonga are organized annually. Long exploratory voyages are occasionally made to places as far afield as the Phoenix Islands of Kiribati (in May or June). Local bookings are accepted when space is available, and you might even be able to swing a discount. **Nai'a Cruises** (P.O. Box 332, Pacific Harbor, Fiji, tel. 345-0382, www.naia.com.fj) has an office in the Arts Village complex at Pacific Harbor, though the *Nai'a* itself is based at Lautoka. In North America call tel. 888/510-1593.

Also based at Pacific Harbor is the 18-meter liveaboard *Beqa Princess,* operated by **Tropical Expeditions** (Charles Wakeham, P.O. Box 129, Pacific Harbor, Fiji, tel. 345-0666, www .tropical-expedition.com). The three spacious air-conditioned cabins accommodate six divers on three-night cruises to the Beqa Lagoon.

The 15-meter catamaran *Republic of Diving* (www.aboardadream.com), based at Savusavu, specializes in diving in the Lomaiviti, Lau, and northern Fiji. Trips of 7/10 days are F$3,650/5,200, plus 5 percent tax with unlimited diving.

Yacht Tours and Charters

Due to the risks involved in navigating Fiji's poorly marked reefs, "bareboat" yacht charters (where you're given a yacht to sail around on your own provided you have the skills) aren't as common in Fiji as they are in Tonga or French Polynesia, but are still possible.

Musket Cove Yacht Charters (P.O. Box 9024, Nadi Airport, Fiji, tel. 666-2215, www .musketcovefiji.com) offers crewed and bareboat yacht charters among the Mamanuca and Yasawa islands from their base at the Musket Cove Marina on Malololailai Island in the

Mamanuca Group. Surfing, diving, and fishing charters are available. For example, their two *Merlin* class yachts can be chartered bareboat or at F$150 for three hours including a crew.

Valentino Sailing Safaris (P.O. Box 10562, Nadi Airport, Fiji, tel. 672-5525, www.sailing fiji.com) offers Mamanuca and Yasawa charters on the crewed 11-meter catamaran *Moana Uli Uli* based at Nadi. Overnight cruises are F$1,550/1,900 for two/four passengers, meals and drinks included (minimum of two nights).

Larger groups could consider the 27-meter ketch *Tau* at the Novotel, Suva, available year-round. For full information, contact **Tau Charter Yacht** (Tony Philp, tel. 336-2128, www.taufiji.com).

One of the classic "tall ships" cruising the South Pacific is the two-masted brigantine *Soren Larsen,* built in 1949. May–November, this 42-meter square-rigged vessel operates 10–22-night voyages to Tonga, Fiji, Vanuatu, and New Caledonia costing NZ$3,495–6,250. The 12-member professional crew is actively assisted by the 22 voyage participants. For information, contact **Tall Ship Soren Larsen** (P.O. Box 60-660, Titirangi, Auckland 0612, New Zealand, tel. 09/817-8799, www.soren larsen.co.nz).

Many overseas yacht brokers arrange charters in Fiji. The American veteran of custom chartering is **Ocean Voyages Inc.** (1709 Bridgeway, Sausalito, CA 94965, USA, tel. 415/332-4681, www.oceanvoyages.com). Trips of a week or more can be arranged in the Yasawas, Mamanucas, Taveuni, and out of Suva. Longer Fiji/Tonga or Fiji/Vanuatu charters of two or three weeks are also possible. In all, Ocean Voyages has over a dozen vessels in the area, and scuba diving is possible at extra cost on some boats.

In Australia, **Paradise Adventures & Cruises** (Heidi Gavriloff, Newington Technology Park, Unit 14A/8 Avenue of Americas, Newington, NSW 2127, tel. 02/8799-2500, www.paradiseadventures.com .au) specializes in privately crewed sailing trips in the Mamanuca and Yasawa Groups. Paradise Adventures also has all-inclusive packages in conjunction with Blue Lagoon Cruises.

In New Zealand, **Sail Connections Ltd.** (tel. 64-9/358-0556, www.sailconnections .co.nz) arranges yacht charters in Fiji.

BY SHIP

Even as much Pacific shipping was being sunk during World War II, airstrips were springing up on the main islands. This hastened the inevitable replacement of the old steamships with modern aircraft, and it's now extremely rare to arrive in Fiji by boat (private yachts excepted). Most islands export similar products, and there's little interregional trade; large container ships headed for Australia, New Zealand, Japan, and the United States usually don't accept passengers. Arrival by cruise ship is also less common in Fiji than it is in places like Vanuatu or French Polynesia.

Those bitten by nostalgia for the slower prewar ways may like to know that a couple of passenger-carrying freighters do still call at the islands, though their fares are much higher than those charged by the airlines. Specialized agencies booking such passages include **TravLtips** (P.O. Box 580188, Flushing, NY 11358, USA, tel. 800/872-8584, www.travltips.com) and **Freighter World Cruises** (180 South Lake Ave., Suite 340, Pasadena, CA 91101, USA, tel. 626/449-3106 or 800/531-7774, www.freight erworld.com).

BY SAILING YACHT
Getting Aboard

It's possible to hitch rides into the Pacific on yachts from California, Panama, New Zealand, and Australia, or around the yachting triangle of Papeete–Suva–Honolulu. If you've never crewed before, consider looking for a yacht already in the islands. In Fiji, the best places to look for a boat are the Royal Suva Yacht Club and Novotel Marina in Suva, the Vuda Point Marina, Port Denarau Marina, and Musket Cove Resort, all near Nadi, and the Copra Shed Marina at Savusavu. Cruising yachts are recognizable by their foreign flags, wind-vane steering gear, sturdy appearance, and laundry hung out to dry. Good captains evaluate crew on personality, attitude, and willingness to learn more than experience, so don't lie. Be honest and open when interviewing with a skipper—a deception will soon become apparent.

It's also good to know what a captain's *really* like before you commit yourself to an isolated week or two with her/him. To determine what might happen should the electronic gadgetry break down, find out if there's a sextant aboard and whether he/she knows how to use it. A boat that looks run-down may often be mechanically unsound too. Also be concerned about a skipper who doesn't do a careful safety briefing early on, or who seems to have a hard time hanging onto crew. If the previous crew has left the boat at an unlikely place, there must have been a reason. Once you're on a boat and part of the yachtie community, it gets easier to hitch rides.

Time of Year

The weather and seasons play a deciding role in any South Pacific trip by sailboat, and you'll have to pull out of many beautiful places, or be unable to stop there, because of bad weather. The prime season for rides in the South Pacific is May–October; sometimes you'll even have to turn one down. Be aware of the hurricane season (November–March in the South Pacific) as few yachts will be cruising at that time.

Also, know which way the winds are blowing; the prevailing trade winds in the tropics are from the northeast north of the equator and from the southeast south of the equator. North of the Tropic of Cancer and south of the Tropic of Capricorn, the winds are out of the west. Thanks to the action of prevailing southeast trade winds, boat trips are smoother from east to west than west to east throughout the South Pacific, so that's the way to go.

Yachting Routes

The common yachting route, or "Coconut Milk Run," across the South Pacific utilizes the northeast and southeast trade winds: from California to Tahiti via the Marquesas or Hawaii, then Rarotonga, Vava'u, Fiji, and New Zealand. Some yachts continue west from Fiji to Port Vila. Cruising yachts average about 150 kilometers a day, so it takes about a month to get from the west coast of the United States to Hawaii, then another month from Hawaii to Tahiti.

To enjoy the finest weather, many yachts clear the Panama Canal or depart California in February to arrive in the Marquesas in March. From Hawaii, yachts often leave for Tahiti in April or May. Many stay on for the *Heiva i Tahiti* festival, which ends on July 14, at which time they sail west to Vava'u or Suva, where you'll find them in July and August. From New Zealand, the Auckland-to-Fiji yacht race in June brings many boats north.

By late October, the bulk of the yachting community is sailing south via New Caledonia to New Zealand or Australia to spend the southern summer there. In April or May on alternate years (2011, 2013, etc.), there's a yacht race from Auckland and Sydney to Suva, timed to coincide with the cruisers' return after the hurricane season. Jimmy Cornell's website, www.noonsite.com, provides lots of valuable information for cruising yachties.

Life Aboard

To crew on a yacht, you must be willing to wash and iron clothes, cook, steer, keep watch at night, and help with engine work. Other jobs might include changing and re-setting sails, cleaning the boat, scraping the bottom, pulling up the anchor, and climbing the mainmast to watch for reefs. Do more than is expected of you. As a guest in someone else's home, you'll want to wash your dishes promptly after use and put them, and all other gear, back where you found them. Tampons must not be thrown in the toilet bowl. Smoking is usually prohibited as a safety hazard.

Anybody who wants to get on well under sail must be flexible and tolerant, both physically and emotionally. Expense-sharing crew members pay US$70 or more a week per person. After 30 days, you'll be happy to hit land

MARITIME COORDINATES

ISLAND GROUP/ ISLAND	LAND AREA (SQUARE KM)	HIGHEST POINT (METERS)	LATITUDE	LONGITUDE
Viti Levu Group				
Beqa	36.0	439	18.40°S	178.13°E
Vatulele	31.6	34	18.50°S	177.63°E
Viti Levu	10,531.0	1,323	17.80°S	178.00°E
Yasawa Group				
Naviti	34.0	388	17.13°S	177.25°E
Yasawa	32.0	244	16.80°S	177.50°E
Kadavu Group				
Dravuni	0.8	40	18.78°S	178.53°E
Kadavu	450.0	838	19.05°S	178.25°E
Ono	30.0	354	18.88°S	178.50°E
Lomaiviti Group				
Gau	140.0	747	18.00°S	179.30°E
Koro	104.0	522	17.30°S	179.40°E
Makogai	8.4	267	17.43°S	178.98°E
Ovalau	101.0	626	17.70°S	178.80°E
Wakaya	8.0	152	17.65°S	179.02°E
Vanua Levu Group				
Namenalala	0.4	105	17.11°S	179.10°E
Qamea	34.0	304	16.77°S	179.77°W
Rabi	69.0	463	16.50°S	180.00°E
Taveuni	442.0	1,241	16.85°S	179.95°E
Vanua Levu	5,587.0	1,032	16.60°S	179.20°E
Yaduatabu	0.7	100	16.84°S	178.28°E

ISLAND GROUP/ ISLAND	LAND AREA (SQUARE KM)	HIGHEST POINT (METERS)	LATITUDE	LONGITUDE
Lau Group				
Cicia	34.0	165	17.75°S	179.33°W
Fulaga	18.5	79	19.17°S	178.65°W
Kabara	31.0	143	18.95°S	178.97°W
Kanacea	13.0	259	17.25°S	179.17°W
Lakeba	54.0	215	18.20°S	178.80°W
Ogea Levu	13.3	82	19.18°S	178.47°W
Ono-i-Lau	7.9	113	20.80°S	178.75°W
Vanua Balavu	53.0	283	17.25°S	178.92°W
Vuaqava	7.7	107	18.83°S	178.92°W
Wailagi Lala	0.3	5	16.75°S	179.18°W
Moala Group				
Matuku	57.0	385	19.18°S	179.75°E
Moala	62.5	468	18.60°S	179.90°E
Totoya	28.0	366	18.93°S	179.83°W
Ringgold Isles				
Qelelevu	1.5	12	16.09°S	179.26°W
Rotuma Group				
Conway Reef	0.1	2	21.77°S	174.52°E
Rotuma	47.0	256	12.50°S	177.13°E

for a freshwater shower. Give adequate notice when you're ready to leave the boat, but *do* disembark when your journey's up. Boat people have few enough opportunities for privacy as it is. If you've had a good trip, ask the captain to write you a letter of recommendation; it'll help you hitch another ride.

Food for Thought

When you consider the big investment, depreciation, cost of maintenance, operating expenses, and considerable risk (most cruising yachts are not insured), travel by sailing yacht is quite a luxury. The huge cost can be surmised from charter fees. International law makes a clear distinction between passengers and crew. Crew members paying only for their own food, cooking gas, and part of the diesel are very different from those who charter, who do nothing and pay full costs. The crew is there to help operate the boat, adding safety, but like passengers, they're very much under the control of the captain. Crew has no say in where the yacht will go.

The skipper is personally responsible for crew coming into foreign ports: He or she is entitled to hold their passports and to see that they have onward tickets and sufficient funds for further traveling. Otherwise the skipper might have to pay their hotel bills and even return airfares to the crew's country of origin. Crew may be asked to pay a share of third-party liability insurance. Possession of drugs can result in seizure of the yacht. Because of such considerations, skippers often hesitate to accept crew. Crew members should remember that at little cost to themselves, they can learn a bit of sailing and visit places nearly inaccessible by other means. Although not for everyone, it's *the* way to see the real South Pacific, and folks who arrive by yacht are treated differently from other tourists.

AIRPORTS
Nadi International Airport

Nadi Airport (NAN) is between Lautoka and Nadi, 22 kilometers south of the former and eight kilometers north of the latter. There are frequent buses to these towns until about 2200. To catch a bus to Nadi, cross the highway; buses to Lautoka stop on the airport side of the road. Pacific Transport and Sunbeam express buses stop right outside the departures hall. Sunbeam Transport buses to Suva (F$16) via the Coral Coast leave the airport daily at 0900, 1000, 1040, 1140, 1310, 1445, and 1545. Pacific Transport express buses to Suva (F$15.40) stop here at 0700, 0725, 1240, 1620, and 1800. Coral Sun Fiji inside the arrivals terminal sells tickets for the air-conditioned Fiji Express bus to Suva (F$22), departing at 0730 and 1300 with scheduled stops at all major resorts. A taxi from the airport should be F$10 to downtown Nadi or F$32 to Lautoka.

An ANZ Bank "Currency Express" window in the baggage-claim area opens for all international flights. An ATM is there, and another is next to the 24-hour ANZ Bank branch in the first arrivals hall just beyond the customs controls (Visa and MasterCard accepted). These banks deduct a F$5 commission on exchanges. A third ANZ banking counter (for changing leftover Fiji dollars back into other currencies) is in the departure lounge.

You can avoid the ANZ Bank's F$5 commission and get a slightly better rate at Western Union/City Forex (www.citygroupintl.com) in the middle of the second arrivals hall. This office opens for all international arrivals. Upon departure from Fiji, you can again avoid the F$5 commission by using the Western Union/GlobalEX office in the departures hall before the immigration and security controls. The commission-happy ANZ Bank controls all exchanges within the departure lounge itself.

As you come out of customs, uniformed tour guides will ask you where you intend to stay, in order to direct you to a driver from that hotel. Most Nadi hotels offer free transfers upon arrival (ask), but you ought to change money before going. Just after customs, the Fiji Islands Backpackers Association has a display listing their members with free phones to call for reservations. The Tourist Transport stand in the first arrivals hall arranges free transfers for the flashpacker resorts and tour companies,

© DAVID STANLEY

Most visits to Fiji begin and end at Nadi International Airport.

and the Rosie Holidays and ATS Pacific stands handle the more upscale tours.

If you don't have an advance booking, airport-based travel agents will try to sign you up for the commission they'll earn. The people selling stays at the outer-island backpacker resorts can be persistent, so be polite but defensive in dealing with them.

All the major tour companies have regular offices in the second arrivals hall, including Destination World, Pacific Destinationz, Sun Vacations, Adventure Fiji, Musket Cove, Rosie Holidays, Southern World, Bounty Island, Beachcomber Island, Anchorage Beach Resort, Coral Sun Fiji, Turtle Island, Tourist Transport Fiji (Feejee Experience), and ATS Pacific, anticlockwise around the hall.

The offices of the backpacker travel agencies and resorts are in lower-rent premises upstairs from the second arrivals hall. These include Western Travel Services in office No. 4, Sunset Tours in office No. 21, Rabua's Travel Agency in office No. 23, Ratu Kini of Mana Island in office No. 26, and David's Place of Tavewa

Island in office No. 31. The Turtle Island office downstairs handles Oarsman's and Safe Landing resorts.

Many car rental companies are also located in the arrivals arcades. In the first arrivals hall after customs you'll find Budget, Hertz, Europcar, and Avis. In the second arrivals hall are Sharmas (not recommended), Thrifty, Central, and Roxy. Upstairs from here are Khan's and Tanoa.

Most of the international airlines flying into Nadi have offices in the arrivals terminal. Air Pacific is in the first arrivals hall, Aircalin in the second, and Air New Zealand, Korean Airlines, Qantas, and Solomon Airlines upstairs. Pacific Blue is in downtown Nadi.

Unfortunately, Tourism Fiji isn't represented at the airport, and the Airport Information Desk just inside the first arrivals hall has only general information about the airport but no tourist information.

If you'd like to rent a cell phone, Vodafone (www.vodafonerental.com.fj) has an obvious office next to the ANZ Bank. To use the public telephones at the airport, you must buy a phone card at one of the gift shops in the terminal. The prepaid Internet kiosks scattered around the airport take cards costing F$5 (50 minutes) and $10 (100 minutes), which are sold at Tappoo souvenir shops and some of the airport cafés. The airport post office is across the parking lot from the arrivals terminal (ask).

The reliable left-luggage service in the domestic departures area just down from the Pacific Sun check-in counter is open 24 hours (bicycles or surfboards F$6.15 a day, suitcases and backpacks F$4.10 a day, other smaller luggage F$3.10 a day). Most hotels around Nadi will also store luggage, often for free. A three-dog sniffer unit checks all baggage passing through NAN for drugs.

Several places to eat are in the departures terminal, including Café Aurora (daily 0500–2100) near the domestic check-in counters and the more expensive Café International just before the international departures gate. The best coffee is served at Esquires Coffee House on the right near the departures gate, and they also offer wireless Internet access at F$5 for 30 minutes. There are no drinking fountains in the departure lounge.

To save money, visit the open-air food market under a large tree between the guard post at the entrance to the airport compound and the bus stop on the main highway. The women there sell excellent potato rotis and fish in *lolo* for lunch only.

The duty-free shops in the departure lounge have a good selection of products at reasonable prices. If you're arriving for a pre-booked stay at a deluxe resort, grab two bottles of Fiji rum at the duty free in the arrivals area next to the baggage-claim area, as drinks at the resort bars are expensive (you can usually get mixers at the hotel shops). You can spend leftover Fijian currency on duty-free items just before you leave Fiji (the famous Bounty Rum brewed in Lautoka costs around F$27). Keep in mind that if you'll be transiting Honolulu or Los Angeles on your way to a final destination elsewhere in North America or Europe, any duty-free alcohol in your hand luggage will be confiscated at U.S. security checkpoints. Also for security reasons, souvenir cannibal forks and war clubs are not sold at the departure lounge shops, so buy these beforehand and pack them in your suitcase.

The international departure tax is usually included in the ticket price. Otherwise, it's F$75, although transit passengers connecting within 12 hours and children under the age of 12 are exempt (no airport tax on domestic flights). Nadi International Airport never closes. NAN's 24-hour flight arrival and departure information number is tel. 673-1615 (www.ats.com.fj).

Nausori Airport

Nausori Airport (SUV) is on the plain of the Rewa River delta, 23 kilometers northeast of downtown Suva. After Hurricane Kina in January 1993, the whole terminal was flooded by Rewa water for several days. In July 2010, Air Pacific began twice weekly nonstop flights between Auckland and SUV after the airstrip was upgraded to receive Boeing 737-700 aircraft.

There's no special airport bus, and a taxi direct to/from Suva will run about F$25. You can save money by taking a taxi from the airport only as far as Nausori (4 km, F$3.50), then a local bus to Suva from there (19 km, with service every 10 minutes until 2100 for F$2.10). It's also possible to catch a local bus to Nausori (F$0.70) on the highway opposite the airport about every 15 minutes. When going to the airport, catch a local bus from Suva to Nausori, then a taxi to the airport.

The ANZ Bank agency at the airport has an ATM. Avis (tel. 337-8361) and Budget (tel. 330-2450) have car rental desks in the terminal, and a lunch counter provides light snacks. You're not allowed to sleep overnight at this airport. No departure tax is levied on domestic flights. The information number at Nausori Airport is tel. 347-8344.

Getting Around

Traveling around Fiji's main islands is easy by small plane, inter-island catamaran, car ferry, local cargo boat, outboard canoe, open-sided bus, and air-conditioned coach. You can move as quickly or slowly as you like in Fiji. The more time you have, the fewer inter-island flights you'll need to catch. Boats sail almost everywhere between the islands, although some of the services intended for locals may be considered less than safe by visitors. Fortunately, safer, faster, and more expensive vessels also ply these waters.

BY AIR

Pacific Sun (tel. 672-0888, www.pacificsun .com.fj) flies from Nadi to Suva (F$193) six or seven times a day; to Labasa (F$212), Savusavu (F$195), and Taveuni (F$230) three times a day; and to Kadavu (F$165) daily. Also from Nadi, the resort islands of Malololailai (F$82) and Mana Island (F$96) get three flights a day. From Suva, Pacific Sun has flights to Levuka (three times a day, F$88), Labasa (twice daily, F$182), Kadavu (daily, F$147), Savusavu (daily, F$169), Taveuni (daily, F$182), Lakeba (weekly, F$205), and Vanua Balavu (weekly, F$205). Reduced "Bula Flexi" and "Bula Saver" fares with certain restrictions are available on some flights. Pacific Sun flights are often heavily booked and it's best to reserve in advance through their website to be sure of a seat if your time is limited. Pacific Sun was founded in 1981 as Sunflower Airlines, which later became Sun Air. In 2006, the company

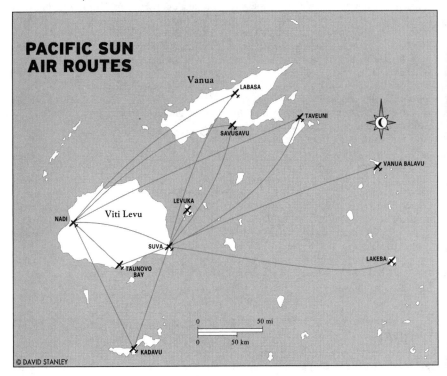

was purchased by Air Pacific, which began operating as Pacific Sun in February 2007. Their only competitor, Air Fiji, went bankrupt in mid-2009. Flying in Pacific Sun's six-passenger Britten-Norman Islanders, 44-passenger ATR 42-500s, and versatile 16-passenger Twin Otters is sort of fun.

Turtle Airways Ltd. (tel. 672-1888, www .turtleairways.com), owned by Richard Evanson of Turtle Island Resort, flies their five four-seat Cessna 206 floatplanes and one seven-seat DeHaviland Beaver from Nadi to Castaway and Mana Islands (F$225 one-way, minimum of two). Turtle Airways also serves the Yasawas (F$299 one-way, minimum of two). The Beaver is a classic aircraft, performing remarkable white-water takeoffs and landings.

Because only Nadi and Nausori airports have electric lighting on their runways, all flights are during daylight hours. The gravel outer-island runways and vintage planes are part of the fun of flying here. Those unaccustomed to island flying should prepare themselves for abrupt landings on short airstrips cut out of the bush or aircraft carrier–style takeoffs over the sea. The views from these low-flying planes can be exceptional. Don't be surprised if one of the pilots opens a window during the flight to get a bit of air. What may seem scary to you is just routine for them. Always reconfirm your return flight immediately upon arrival at an outer island, as the reservation lists are sometimes not sent out from Nadi. Failure to do this could mean you'll be bumped without compensation.

Student discounts are for local students only, and there are no standby fares. Children 12 and under pay 50 percent, and infants two and under carried in arms pay 10 percent. Pacific Sun allows passengers with tickets purchased prior to arrival in Fiji to carry 20 kilograms of baggage, while tickets issued in Fiji cover only 15 kilograms. The allowance on Turtle Airways is always 15 kilograms.

BY BOAT

The best established local company is **Patterson Brothers Shipping,** set up by Levuka copra planter Reg Patterson and his brother just after World War I. Patterson's 385-passenger car ferry *Spirit of Harmony* operates on the Buresala–Natovi–Nabouwalu run. Patterson Brothers also operates the "Sea Road" service from Suva to Levuka via Buresala. (Two previous Japanese-built car ferries used by Patterson Brothers have sunk in recent years. In August 2003, the *Ovalau* sank off Nananu-i-Ra, followed by *Princess Ashika* off Tonga in August 2009. Fortunately no lives were lost on the *Ovalau* but almost 100 people went down with the *Princess Ashika*.)

Consort Shipping Line (www.consort shipping.com.fj) runs the large car ferry *Spirit of Fiji Islands* from Suva to Koro, Savusavu, and Taveuni twice a week. **Bligh Water Shipping Ltd.** (www.blighwatershipping.com.fj) operates the *Suilven,* a former Norwegian ferry, along the same route, and the *Westerland* between Lautoka and Savusavu. **Venu Shipping Ltd.** operates the *Sinu-i-wasa* from Suva to Kadavu and Levuka.

From Nadi, **South Sea Cruises** (www.ssc .com.fj) operates fast catamaran shuttles to the Mamanuca Group on the *Tiger IV* and *Cougar,* and to the Yasawa Islands on the *Yasawa Flyer II.* A sea voyage is an essential part of any authentic Fiji experience.

BY BUS

Scheduled bus service is available all over Fiji, and the fares are low. Most long-distance bus services operate several times a day, and the bus stations are usually adjacent to local markets. Buses with a signboard in the window reading Via Highway are local "stage" buses that will stop anywhere along their routes and can be excruciatingly slow on a long trip. Express buses are faster, but they'll only stop in a few towns, and some won't let you off at resorts along the way. Strangely, the times of local buses are not posted at the bus stations, and it's often hard to find anyone to ask about buses to remote locations. The people most likely to know are the bus drivers themselves, but you'll often receive misleading or incorrect information about local buses. Express bus times *are*

an air-conditioned Sunbeam Transport express bus used on Viti Levu

posted at some stations, and it's sometimes possible to obtain printed express bus timetables from bus drivers.

On Viti Levu, the most important routes are between Lautoka and Suva, the biggest cities. If you follow the southern route via Sigatoka, you'll be on Queens Road, the smoother and faster of the two. Kings Road via Tavua is longer, and it can be rough and dusty, but you get to see a bit of the interior. Fares from Suva are F$5.40 to Pacific Harbor, F$11.25 to Sigatoka, F$15.70 to Nadi, F$16 to Nadi Airport, F$18 to Lautoka, and F$20 to Ba. Fares average just more than F$3 for each hour of travel.

Pacific Transport Ltd. (tel. 330-4366) has six buses a day along Queens Road, with expresses leaving from across the street from the Flea Market in Suva for Lautoka at 0645, 0830, 0930, 1210, 1500, and 1730 (221 km, five hours). Eastbound, the expresses leave Lautoka for Suva at 0630, 0700, 1210, 1550, and 1730. An additional Suva-bound express leaves Nadi at 0900. These buses stop at Navua, Pacific Harbor, Sigatoka (coffee break), Nadi, and Nadi Airport, plus major

resorts upon request (ask). The 1500 bus from Suva continues to Ba. Sunbeam Transport operates seven daily express buses between Lautoka and Suva (F$18), stopping at many Coral Coast resorts along the way.

Sunbeam Transport Ltd. (tel. 666-2822, www.sunbeamfiji.com) also services the northern Kings Road from Suva to Lautoka five times a day, with expresses leaving Suva at 0600, 0645, 0815, 1200, 1330, and 1715 (265 km, six hours). From Lautoka, they depart at 0615, 0630, 0815, 1215, and 1630. A Sunbeam express bus along Kings Road is a comfortable way to see Viti Levu's picturesque back side, though some of the new Sunbeam buses play insipid videos, which is distracting. The expresses stop at Nausori, Korovou, Ellington, Vaileka (Rakiraki), Tavua, Ba, and a few other places. If time doesn't matter, there's also a "stage" bus that leaves Suva at 0750 and Lautoka at 0835, spending nine fun-filled hours on Kings Road. Sunbeam fares from Suva on the northern road are F$2.10 to Nausori, F$4.35 to Korovou, F$12.90 to Vaileka, F$15.95 to Tavua, F$17.95 to Ba, and F$20.70 to Lautoka.

In addition to Sunbeam, a **Reliance Transport** bus to Lautoka via King's Road leaves Suva at 0930. **Vatukoula Express** has buses from Suva to Vaileka (Rakiraki) at 1030, 1445, and 1640.

Coral Sun Fiji (tel. 672-3105 or 672-2177, www.coralsunfiji.com) operates a twice-daily air-conditioned coach called the Fiji Express between Nadi Airport and Suva via the Coral Coast resorts. It costs a bit more than the regular expresses but is more comfortable. The Fiji Express departs Nadi Airport at 0730 and 1300. From the Holiday Inn in Suva, it leaves at 0715 and 1530.

There are many local buses, especially closer to Suva or Lautoka, some with big open windows with roll-down canvas covers, which give you a panoramic view of Viti Levu. The local buses often show up late, but the long-distance buses are usually right on time. Bus service on Vanua Levu and Taveuni is also good, but there are no buses on Kadavu and most outer islands. In rural areas, passenger trucks called "carriers" charge set rates to and from interior villages.

Minibuses and Running Taxis

Minibus service between Suva, Nadi, and Lautoka operates several times an hour. Shared "running" taxis and minibuses also shuttle back and forth between Suva, Nadi, and Lautoka, leaving when full and charging only a few dollars more than the bus. Look for them in the markets around the bus stations. They'll often drop you exactly where you want to go; drawbacks include the less-than-safe driving style and lack of insurance coverage. In a speeding minibus, you miss out on much of the scenery, and tourists have been killed in collisions.

Often the drivers of private or company cars and vans try to earn a little extra money by stopping to offer lifts to persons waiting for buses beside the highway. They ask the same as you'd pay on the bus but are much faster, and you'll probably be dropped off exactly where you want to go. Many locals don't understand hitchhiking, and it's probably only worth doing on remote roads where bus service is inadequate. In such places, almost everyone

will stop. Be aware that truck drivers who give you a lift may also expect the equivalent of bus fare; locals pay this without question. It's always appropriate to offer the bus fare.

TAXIS

Fiji's taxis are plentiful and among the cheapest in the South Pacific, affordable even for low-budget backpackers. In all of the towns, the taxis are required by law to have meters and you should ask the driver to turn it on when you get in if he doesn't do so automatically. A short ride across town might cost F$2, a longer trip into a nearby suburb about F$3. The meters are not used for journeys over 16 kilometers and you must agree on a flat fare beforehand. Taxis parked in front of luxury hotels may not wish to use their meters and it may be worth walking a short distance and flagging one down on the street. Taxis returning to their stand after dropping off other passengers will often pick up people waiting at bus stops and charge something approaching the regular bus fare (ask if it's the "returning fare"). All taxis have their home base painted on their bumpers, so it's easy to tell if it's a returning car. Don't tip your driver; tips are neither expected nor necessary.

CAR RENTALS

Rental cars are expensive in Fiji, due in part to high import duties on cars and the 12.5 percent value-added tax, so with public transportation as good as it is here, you should think twice before renting a car. By law, third-party public-liability insurance is compulsory for rental vehicles and is included in the basic rate, but collision damage waiver (CDW) insurance is F$10–22 per day extra. Even with CDW, you're still responsible for a "nonwaivable excess," which can be as high as the first F$4,000 in damage to the car (ask). Many cars on the road have no insurance, so you could end up paying for damage even if you're not responsible for the accident.

Your home driver's license is recognized for your first three months in Fiji, provided it's readable in English. Driving is on the left (as in

Britain and Australia), and you should request an automatic if you might be uncomfortable shifting gears with your left hand. Seat belts must be worn in the front seat, and the police are empowered to give roadside breath-analyzer tests. Around Viti Levu, they routinely employ handheld radar. Speed limits are 50 kph in towns, 80 kph on the highway. Pedestrians have the right-of-way at crosswalks.

Unpaved roads can be very slippery, especially on inclines. Fast-moving vehicles on the gravel roads throw up small stones, which can smash your front window (and you'll have to pay the damages). As you pass oncoming cars, hold your hand against the windshield just in case. When approaching a Fijian village, slow right down, as poorly marked speed bumps usually cross the road. Also beware of narrow bridges, and take care with local motorists, who sometimes stop in the middle of the road, pass on blind curves, and drive at high speeds. Cane-hauling trains have the right of way at level crossings. Driving can be an especially risky business at night. Many of the roads are atrocious (check the spare tire). The 486-kilometer road around Viti Levu is now fully paved except for a 45-kilometer stretch on the northeast side, which is easily passable if you go slowly. Luckily, there isn't a lot of traffic.

If you plan on using a rental car to explore the rough country roads of Viti Levu's mountainous interior, think twice before announcing your plans to the agency, as they may suddenly decline your business. The rental contracts all contain clauses stating that the insurance coverage is not valid under such conditions. Budget and a few others have four-wheel-drive vehicles that may be driven into the interior. You're usually not allowed to take the car to another island by ferry. Tank up on Saturday, as many gas stations are closed on Sunday, and always keep the tank more than half full. If you run out of gas in a rural area, small village stores sometimes sell fuel from drums. At regular gas stations, expect to pay about F$2.25 a liter (or F$8.50 per U.S. gallon).

Several international car rental chains are represented in Fiji, including Avis (www.avis .com.fj), Budget (www.budget.com.fj), Hertz (www.hertzfiji.net), and Thrifty (www.rosiefiji .com). Local companies like Carpenters Rentals (www.carpenters.com.fj), Central Rent-a-Car (www.central-rent-car.com.fj), Dove Rent-a-Car, Kenns Rent-a-Car, Khan's Rental Cars (www.khansrental.com.fj), Quality Rent-a-Car (www.qualityrental.com.fj), Satellite Rentals (www.satelliterentacar.com.fj), and Tanoa Rent-a-Car are often cheaper, but check around as prices vary. The international companies rent only new cars, while the less expensive local companies may offer second-hand vehicles. If in doubt, check the vehicle carefully before driving off. The international franchises generally provide better support should anything go wrong. Budget, Central, Kenns, and Khan's won't rent to persons under age 25, while most of the others will, as long as you're over 21. Sharmas Rent-a-Car is not recommended.

The main companies have offices in the arrivals concourse at Nadi Airport, and several are also at Nausori Airport. Agencies with town offices in Suva include Avis, Budget, Carpenters, Central, Dove, Hertz, and Thrifty. Satellite Rentals has an office in the West Point Arcade (tel. 670-1911) in downtown Nadi, while Budget is at the Port Denarau Retail Center. In Lautoka, you'll find Budget and Central. Avis and Thrifty also have desks at or near many resort hotels on Viti Levu. In northern Fiji, Avis, Budget, and Carpenters have offices at Labasa and Savusavu, but rental cars are not available on the other islands.

Both unlimited-kilometer and per-kilometer rates are offered. **Thrifty** (tel. 672-2755), run by Rosie Holidays, has unlimited-kilometer prices from F$138/828 daily/weekly, which include CDW (F$2,000 nonwaivable) and tax. **Budget** (tel. 672-2735) charges F$123/686 for their cheapest mini including insurance (F$1,000 nonwaivable). **Avis** (tel. 672-2233) begins at F$125/610 including insurance (F$4,000 nonwaivable). Prices at Avis and Budget may be lower if you book ahead from abroad. Though more expensive, the international chains are more likely to deliver what they promise.

The insurance plans used by all the local companies have high nonwaivable excess fees, which makes renting from them more risky. Also beware of companies like Satellite and Tanoa that add the 12.5 percent value-added tax later (most of the others include it in the quoted price). Of the local companies, **Khan's Rental Cars** (tel. 672-3506), in office No. 10 upstairs from arrivals at Nadi Airport, charges F$450–500 a week including insurance (F$2,000 nonwaivable) for their cheapest car. **Central** (tel. 331-1866 or 672-2771), in the second concourse at Nadi Airport and in Suva and Lautoka, charges F$110/500 a day/week including insurance (F$2,000 nonwaivable) for their cheapest car.

Many of the local car rental agencies offer discounts on their brochure prices for weekly rentals, and you shouldn't hesitate to bargain, as there's lots of competition. Some companies advertise low prices with the qualification in fine print that these apply only to rentals of three days or more. Ask how many kilometers

are on the odometer, and beware of vehicles above 50,000 kilometers as they may be unreliable. On a per-kilometer basis, you'll only want to use the car in the local area. Most companies charge a delivery fee if you don't return the vehicle to the office where you rented it. If you want the cheapest economy subcompact, reserve ahead. Also be prepared to put up a cash deposit on the car.

If you rent a car, remember those sudden tropical downpours, and don't leave the windows open. Also avoid parking under coconut trees (a falling nut might break the window), and never go off and leave the keys in the ignition. Lock everything in the trunk.

Taking into consideration the price of fuel, it's often cheaper to rent a taxi by the day than it is to rent a car. Show the driver a list of everything you might want to see before setting out and be sure the price is clearly understood. If your driver is well chosen, you'll have a relaxing day with a local guide for free.

Visas and Officialdom

Everyone needs a passport that is valid at least three months beyond the date of entry. No visa is required of visitors from 101 countries (including Western Europe, North America, Japan, Israel, and most Commonwealth countries) for stays of up to four months. A complete list of exempt nationalities is on www.fijime.com. Tickets to leave Fiji are officially required but are not usually checked upon arrival (they *will* be verified by the airline as you check in). The obligatory vaccination against yellow fever or cholera only applies if you're arriving directly from an infected area, such as the Amazon jungles or the banks of the Ganges River (no vaccinations necessary if you're arriving from North America, New Zealand, or Australia).

Extensions of stay are given out by the immigration offices at Lautoka, Nadi Airport, Savusavu, and Suva. You must apply before

your current permit expires. After the first four months, you can obtain another two months to increase your total stay to six months by paying a F$93 fee. Bring your passport, onward or return ticket, and proof of sufficient funds. After six months, you must leave and stay away at least four days, after which you can return and start on another four months. An exception is made for yachties, who can obtain extensions for up to one year.

Fiji has four ports of entry for yachts: Lautoka, Levuka, Savusavu, and Suva. The Ports Authority can be contacted over VHF channel 16. Calling at an outer island before clearing customs is prohibited. Levuka is the easiest place to check in or out, as all of the officials have offices right on the main wharf, and Savusavu is also convenient. Lautoka is the most inconvenient, as the popular yacht anchorages off western Viti Levu are far from

DIPLOMATIC OFFICES

Permanent Mission to the United Nations: 801 Second Ave., 10th Floor, New York, NY 10017, USA; tel. 212/687-4130, www.fijiprun.org

Embassy of Fiji: 2000 M Street NW, Suite 710, Washington, DC 20036, USA; tel. 202/337-8320, www.fijiembassydc.com

High Commission of Fiji: 19 Beale Cres., Deakin, ACT 2600, Australia; tel. 61-2/6260-5115

Consulate-General of Fiji: 100 Walker St., North Sydney, NSW 2060, Australia; tel. 61-2/9900-0700, www.fijihighcom.com

High Commission of Fiji: 31 Pipitea St., Thorndon, Wellington, New Zealand; tel. 64-4/473-5401, www.fiji.org.nz

High Commission of Fiji: Defense House, 4th Floor, Champion Parade, Port Moresby NCD, Papua New Guinea; tel. 675/321-1914

High Commission of Fiji: 34 Hyde Park Gate, London SW7 5DN, United Kingdom; tel. 44-20/7584-3661, www.fijihighcommission.org.uk

Embassy of Fiji: 92-94 Square Plasky, 1030 Brussels, Belgium; tel. 32-2/736-9050, www.fijiembassy.be

Embassy of Fiji: Noa Building, 14th Floor, 3-5, 2-Chome, Azabudai, Minato-Ku, Tokyo 106, Japan; tel. 81-3/3587-2038, www.fijiembassy.jp

Embassy of Fiji: 1-15-2 Ta Yuan Diplomatic Building, Sanlitun, Chaoyang District, Beijing 100600, China; tel. 8610/6532-7305, www.fijiembassy.org.cn

High Commission of Fiji: Level 2, Menara Chan, 138 Jalan Ampang, 50450 Kuala Lumpur, Malaysia; tel. 60-3/2732-3335

High Commission of Fiji: N-87, Panchsheel Park, New Delhi 110 017, India; tel. 91-11/4175-1092

Lautoka. To visit the outer islands, yachts require a letter of authorization from the Ministry of Foreign Affairs in Suva, or the commissioner (at Labasa, Lautoka, or Nausori) of the division they wish to visit. Yacht clubs in Fiji can advise on how to obtain permission. Yacht Help Fiji (www.yachthelp.com) also has useful information for yachties.

Conduct

Foreign travel is an exceptional experience enjoyed by a privileged few. Too often, tourists try to transfer their lifestyles to tropical islands, thereby missing out on what is unique to the region. Travel can be a learning experience if approached openly and with a positive attitude. So read up on the local culture before you arrive and become aware of the social and environmental problems of the area. A wise traveler soon graduates from hearing and seeing to listening and observing. Speaking is good for the ego and listening is good for the soul.

The path is primed with packaged pleasures, but pierce the bubble of tourism and you'll encounter something far from the schedules and organized efficiency: a time to learn how other

VILLAGE ETIQUETTE IN FIJI

- It's a Fijian custom to smile when you meet a stranger and say something like "Good morning," "Bula," or at least "Hello." Of course, you needn't do this in large towns, but you should do so almost everywhere else. If you meet someone you know, stop for a moment to exchange a few words. As you shake hands, tell the person your name.

- Fijian villages are private property, and you should only enter after you've been welcomed. Of course it's okay to continue along a road that passes through a village, but make contact before leaving the road. Wait until someone greets you, and then say you wish to be taken to the *turaga-ni-koro* (village herald). This village spokesperson will accept your *sevusevu* of kava roots and grant you permission to look around, unless something important is happening, such as a funeral, celebration, feast, or church service (avoid arriving on a Sunday). A villager will be assigned to act as your guide and host. Yet even after this, you should still ask before taking pictures of individuals or inside buildings.

- If you wish to surf off the coast of a village, picnic on a village beach, or fish in the lagoon near a village, you should also ask permission. You'll almost always be made most welcome and granted any favors you request if you present a *sevusevu* to the village herald or chief. If you approach the Fijians with respect, you're sure to be treated the same way in return.

- Take off your footwear before entering a *bure*, and stoop as you walk around inside. Fijian villagers consider it offensive to walk in front of a person seated on the floor (pass behind) or to fail to say *tulou* (excuse me) as you go by. Clap three times when you join people already seated on mats on the floor. Shake hands with your hosts.

- In a *bure*, men should sit cross-legged, women with their legs to the side. Sitting with your legs stretched out in front or with your knees up during presentations is dis-respectful. After a meal or during informal kava drinking, you can stretch your legs out, but never point them at the chief or the kava bowl. Don't sit in doorways or put your hand on another's head.

- If offered kava *(yaqona)*, clap once with cupped hands, take the bowl, say *bula*, and drink it all in one gulp. Then hand the bowl back to the same person and clap three times saying *vinaka* (thanks). Don't stand up during a *sevusevu* to village elders – remain seated. When you give a gift, hold it out with both hands, not one hand. Otherwise just place the bundle on the floor before them.

- It's good manners to take off your hat while walking through a village, where only the chief is permitted to wear a hat. Objects such as backpacks, handbags, and cameras should be carried in your hands rather than slung over your shoulders.

- Dress modestly in the village, which basically means a shirt for men and covered shoulders and thighs for women. Short shorts are not the best attire for men or women (long shorts okay), and bikinis are analogous to nudity (this also applies when swimming in a village river, pool, or beach). Wrapping a *sulu* around you will suffice.

- Don't point at people in villages. Do you notice how the Fijians rarely shout? In Fiji, raising your voice is a sign of anger. Don't openly admire a possession of someone, as he or she may feel obligated to give it to you. If sharing a meal, wait until grace has been said before eating. Alcohol is usually forbidden in villages.

- Fijian children are generally very well behaved. There's no running or shouting as you arrive in a village, and they'll leave you alone if you wish. Most Fijians love children, so don't hesitate to bring your own. You'll never have to worry about finding a babysitter. Just make sure your children understand the importance of being on their best behavior in the village.

people live. Walk gently, for human qualities are as fragile and responsive to abuse as the brilliant reefs. The islanders tend to be soft-spoken and reserved. Often they won't show open disapproval if their social codes are broken, but don't underestimate them. Consider that you're only one of thousands of visitors to their country, so don't expect to be treated better than anyone else. Respect is one of the most important aspects of Pacific life, and humility is also greatly appreciated.

If you're alone, you're lucky, for the single traveler is everyone's friend. Get away from other tourists and meet the people. There aren't many places on earth where you can still do this meaningfully, but Fiji is one of them. If you do meet people with similar interests, keep in touch by writing. This is no tourist's paradise, though, and local residents are not exhibits or paid performers. They have as many or more problems than you, and if you see them as real people, you are less likely to be viewed as a stereotypical tourist. You may have come to escape your civilization, but keep in mind that you're just a guest in theirs.

Most important of all, try to see things their way. Take an interest in local customs, values, languages, challenges, and successes. If things work differently than they do back home, give thanks that you are experiencing this different culture. Reflect on what you've experienced, and you'll return home with a better understanding of how much we all have in common, outwardly different as we may seem.

DRESS

It's important to know that the dress code in Fiji is strict. Wearing short shorts, halter tops, and bathing suits in public shows a lack of respect. In Fijian villages, it's considered offensive to reveal too much skin. Wrap a *sulu*

around you to cover up. Men should always wear a shirt in town, and women should wear dresses that adequately cover their legs while seated. Nothing will mark you so quickly as a tourist, nor make you more popular with street vendors, than scanty dress. Of course, it is acceptable to wear skimpy clothing on the beach in front of a resort hotel. Yet in a society where even bathing suits are considered extremely risqué for local women, public nudity is unthinkable, and topless sunbathing by women is also banned in Fiji (except at isolated island resorts).

QUESTIONS

Phrase questions carefully. Polite islanders may simply answer yes or no according to what they think you want to hear—don't suggest the answer in your question. If you want to be sure of something, ask several people the same question in different ways. Also don't ask negative questions, such as "you're not going to Suva, are you?" Invariably the answer will be "yes," meaning "yes, I'm not going to Suva." It also could work like this: "Don't you have anything cheaper?" "Yes." "What do you have that is cheaper?" "Nothing." Yes, he doesn't have anything cheaper.

PHOTOGRAPHY

Get consent before photographing individuals. If you're asked for money (rare), you can always walk away—give your subjects the same choice. At markets, smile and say something friendly to the vendors before and after taking photos to establish a rapport. Show them their pictures on your screen and always keep a promise to mail the photos you take of them. There is probably no country in the world where the photographer will have as interesting and willing subjects as in Fiji.

Accommodations

We don't solicit freebies from the hotel chains; our only income derives from the price you paid for this guide. So we don't mind telling you that some of the luxury resorts are just not worth the exorbitant prices they charge. Many simply re-create Hawaii at twice the cost. Even worse, they tend to isolate you from the Fiji you came to experience. Large consumer tourism resorts are always worth visiting as sightseeing attractions, watering holes, or sources of entertainment, but be selective if you're paying top dollar.

When things are slow, many resorts offer specials and some prices become negotiable. Occasionally you'll pay a third less than the "rack rates" quoted in this guide. This is most likely to happen in February, March, and November, the lowest tourist seasons. Otherwise, prices are usually the same year-round without seasonal variations. Christmas is a busy time in Fiji, and December and January can be busy with young Australians and New Zealanders enjoying their summer school holidays. Their parents are more likely to come in July and August to escape the cold winter weather Down Under.

Many mid-priced hotels around Fiji have reduced "local walk-in rates," which are usually also available to foreign tourists already in Fiji who book direct. The back section of the *Fiji Times* often advertises local rate deals, and although the ads often say they're for local residents only, they'll often give them to you if you call and say you saw it in the *Times*. Needless to say, always ask the price of your accommodations before accepting them.

The word "resort" is rather loosely applied in Fiji. A backpacker resort may consist of little more than a cluster of thatched huts with communal bathing and eating facilities to one side. At the other end of the market are the designer resorts that offer en suite bathrooms with marble floors, personal butlers and maids, and chefs capable of pleasing the most demanding gourmet. Most Fijian resorts lie somewhere in between, providing cleanliness and adequate comfort while keeping costs in line. You won't find any high-rise hotels on Fiji's beaches; rather, the emphasis is on two- and three-story blocks at the larger properties and strings of bungalows elsewhere.

When picking a hotel, bear in mind that although a thatched bungalow is cooler and more aesthetic than a concrete box, it's also more likely to have insect problems. If in doubt, check the window screens and carry mosquito coils and repellent. Hopefully there'll be a resident lizard or two to feed on the bugs. Don't automatically accept the first room offered; if you're paying good money, look at several, then choose.

If you have to choose a meal plan, take only breakfast and dinner (Modified American Plan or MAP) and have fruit for lunch. Dormitory or other backpacker accommodations are available on many islands, with communal cooking facilities sometimes provided. If you're young and single, the dorms are just the place to meet

ACCOMMODATION PRICE RANGES

Throughout this guide, accommodations are loosely grouped in the price categories that follow, based on the price of a double room without meals. The arbitrary exchange rate employed is indicated below, and of course, currency fluctuations and inflation can lead to variations.

• Under US$25	Under F$45
• US$25-50	F$45-90
• US$50-100	F$90-180
• US$100-150	F$180-270
• US$150-250	F$270-450
• Over US$250	Over F$450

other travelers. Couples can usually get a double room at a hostel or backpacker camp for a price only slightly above two dorm beds.

Increasingly popular in Fiji are the "flashpacker" resorts aimed at business-class backpackers willing to spend considerably more than traditional low-budget travelers. ATMs feed the flashpackers money and their credit cards pay for expensive sporting activities and soft-adventure tours. The flashpacker resorts are fully air-conditioned, and many have compulsory meal plans. It's yuppie paradise.

A 17.5 percent government tax (12.5 percent VAT plus a 5 percent hotel tax) is added to all accommodations prices. The inexpensive hotels usually include the tax in their quoted rates, but the expensive hotels often don't. Note carefully whether a quoted rate is "inclusive" or "exclusive" of VAT and pay attention to the currency as some places quote in U.S. rather than Fijian dollars.

RESERVING AHEAD

Booking accommodations in advance often works to your disadvantage, as overseas travel agents will begin by trying to sell you their most expensive properties (which pay them the highest commissions) and work down from there. The quite adequate midrange and budget places included in this guidebook often aren't on their screens, or are sold at highly inflated prices. Few hotels charging less than US$80 have the accounting wherewithal to process agency commissions. Herein we provide the rates for direct bookings, and if you book through a travel agent abroad, you could end up paying considerably more as multiple commissions are tacked on. Discounted local rates are never available to people who book through travel agents.

There aren't many hotels in the medium to lower price ranges where it's to your advantage to book ahead, but you can often obtain substantial discounts at the upscale hotels by including them in a package tour. If you intend to spend most of your time at a specific first-class hotel, you'll benefit from bulk rates by purchasing a package rather than paying the higher "rack rates" the top resorts and hotels charge to individuals who just walk in off the beach or street. Almost everyone staying on Denarau Island and at most of the smaller boutique hotels around Fiji will have arrived on a prepaid package tour.

Always check the resort's own website for online specials before booking anything as many offer deep discounts or free nights. Also consider the hotel's cancellation policy, which you should expect to be rigorously applied. At many hotels you'll be charged the full amount for your entire stay unless you cancel 30 days in advance.

PacificBedBank.com (www.pacificbed bank.com) and **Fijiagent.com** (www.fijiagent .com) book rooms online via a secure server, though only wholesalers and travel agents can use these services. **Wotif.com** (www.wotif .com) is accessible to the general public, and **TravelMaxia.com** (www.travelmaxia.com) allows you to make direct contact with the resorts.

ACCOMMODATION CATEGORIES

Fiji offers a wide variety of places to stay, from low-budget to world-class. Standard international hotels are found in Nadi and Suva, while many of the upmarket beach resorts are on small islands in the Mamanuca Group off Nadi or along the Coral Coast on Viti Levu's sunny southern side. The Mamanuca resorts are secluded, with fan-cooled *bure* accommodations, while at the Coral Coast hotels you often get an air-conditioned room in a main building. The Coral Coast has more to offer in the way of land tours, shopping, and entertainment/eating options, while the offshore resorts are preferable if you want a rest or are into water sports. The Coral Coast beaches are only good at high tide, and the reefs are degraded, while on the outer islands the reefs are usually pristine. Some resorts cater almost exclusively to scuba divers or surfers, and these may not be the best places to stay if you aren't interested in those activities.

In recent years, smaller luxury resorts have

multiplied in remote locations, from former plantations near Savusavu and on Taveuni to isolated beach resorts on outlying islands such as Beqa, Kadavu, Matangi, Naigani, Namenalala, Nukubati, Qamea, Toberua, Turtle, Vatulele, Wakaya, and Yasawa. Prices at the "boutique" resorts begin at several hundred dollars a day and rise to four figures, so some care should be taken in selecting the right one. A few, such as Beqa, Kadavu, and Taveuni, are marketed almost exclusively to scuba divers, and Namenalala is a good ecotourism choice. If you delight in glamorous socializing with other upscale couples, Turtle and Vatulele are for you. Families are most welcome at Beachcomber, Castaway, Cousteau, InterContinental, Koro Sun, Malolo, Maravu, Matangi, Naigani, Naviti, Outrigger, Plantation, Shangri-La's Fijian, Sonaisali, Toberua, Treasure, and the Warwick, but children are generally not accepted at all at Lomalagi, Lomani, Matamanoa, Matana, Namale, Namotu, Natadola Beach, Navutu Stars, Nukubati, Qamea, Royal Davui, Taveuni, Tokoriki, Turtle, Vatulele, Wadigi, Wakaya, and Yasawa. The very wealthy will feel at home on Turtle and Wakaya, whereas Mamanuca resorts like Castaway, Mana, and Plantation are designed for larger numbers of guests interested in intensive sporting and group activities.

The low-budget accommodations are spread out, with concentrations in Korotogo, Nadi, Lautoka, Levuka, Suva, and Savusavu. Low-cost outer-island beach resorts exist on Caqalai, Kadavu, Kuata, Leleuvia, Mana, Nacula, Nananu-i-Ra, Nanuya Lailai, Naviti, Tavewa, Waya, Wayasewa, and Yanuca. Flashpacker resorts are on Nadi's Wailoaloa Beach, on the central Coral Coast, and in the Mamanucas and Yasawas. The largest budget chain in Fiji is Cathay Hotels, with properties in Suva, Lautoka, and on the Coral Coast (visit their Fiji For Less website at www.fiji 4less.com). Since 2000, dozens of backpacker resorts of varying quality have appeared in the Yasawa Islands, some under the auspices of the Nacula Tikina Tourism Association (www .fijibudget.com).

A few of the cheapest hotels in Suva, Nadi, and Lautoka double as brothels, making them cheap in both senses of the word. At all of the low-budget hostels and backpacker resorts, women should exercise care in the way they deal with the male staff, as there have been verified cases of harassment. Many hotels, both in cities and at the beach, offer dormitory beds as well as individual rooms. Most of the dorms are mixed. Women can sometimes request a women-only dorm when things are slow, but it's usually not guaranteed. Some budget-priced city hotels lock their front doors at 2300 (or at 2200 in Labasa), so ask first if you're planning a night on the town. Many islands in the Lau and Lomaiviti groups have no regular accommodations for visitors at all.

CAMPING

Camping facilities (bring your own tent) are found at backpacker resorts on Caqalai, Kadavu, Kuata, Leleuvia, Mana, Nacula, Nanua Lailai, Naviti, Ovalau, Taveuni, Tavewa, Waya, Wayasewa, and Yanuca Lailai Islands. Viti Levu beach resorts like Seashell Cove, The Beachouse, and the Coral Coast Christian Center also allow it, but camping isn't possible in cities like Nadi or Suva.

Away from the resorts, get permission before pitching your tent, as all land is owned by someone, and land rights are sensitive issues in Fiji. Some freelance campers on remote beaches have had their possessions stolen, so take care.

In Fijian villages, don't ask a Fijian friend for permission to camp beside his house. Although he may feel obligated to grant the request of a guest, you'll be proclaiming to everyone that his home isn't completely to your liking. If all you really want is to camp, make that clear from the start and get approval to do so on a beach or by a river, but *not* in the village. A *sevusevu* should always be presented in this case. There's really nowhere to camp totally for free in Fiji. Never camp under a coconut tree, as falling coconuts can harm or kill you (actually, coconuts have two eyes so they only strike the wicked).

STAYING IN VILLAGES

The most direct way to meet the Fijian people and learn a little about their culture is to stay in a village for a couple of nights. A number of hiking tours offer overnight stays in remote villages, and it's also possible to arrange it for yourself. **Fiji Holidays** (www.fijibure.com) organizes stays in a dozen villages on Viti Levu and Beqa and on the Yasawas at F$80 per person a night. If you befriend someone from an outlying island, ask them to write you a letter of introduction to their relatives back in the village. Mail a copy of it ahead with a polite letter introducing yourself, then slowly start heading that way.

In places well off the beaten track where there are no regular tourist accommodations, you could just show up in a village and ask permission of the *turaga-ni-koro* (village herald) to spend the night. Both Indo-Fijians and native Fijians will often spontaneously invite you in to their homes. Such kindness should not be taken for granted, however.

All across the Pacific, it's customary to reciprocate when someone gives you a gift—if not now, then sometime in the future. In Fiji, this type of back and forth is called *kerekere.* Visitors who accept gifts (such as meals and accommodations) from islanders and do not reciprocate undermine traditional culture and cause resentment. It's sometimes hard to know how to repay hospitality, but Fijian culture has a solution: the *sevusevu.* This can be money, but it's usually a 500-gram "pyramid" of kava roots *(waka),* which can be easily purchased at any Fijian market for about F$20. *Sevusevu* are more often performed between families or couples about to be married, or at births or christenings, but the custom is a perfectly acceptable way for visitors to show their appreciation.

The *sevusevu* should be placed before (not handed to) the *turaga-ni-koro,* or village herald, so he can accept or refuse. If he accepts (by touching the package), your welcome is confirmed and you may spend the night in the village. Anyone traveling in remote areas of Fiji should be packing kava (take whole roots, not powdered kava).

In addition to the *waka* bundle for the *turaga-ni-koro,* we suggest travelers donate at least

A "pyramid" of kava roots known as a *waka* is often presented as a *sevusevu.*

© DAVID STANLEY

F$50 per person per night to their village hosts (carry sufficient cash in small denominations). If you give the money up front as a *sevusevu*, they'll know you're not a freeloader, and you'll get VIP treatment, though in all cases it's absolutely essential to contribute something.

Your arrival *sevusevu* will invariably be received by the man of the house, and it's also nice to give some money to the lady of the house upon departure, with your thanks. Just say it's your goodbye *sevusevu* and watch the smile. A Fijian may refuse the money, but he or she will not be offended by the offer if it is done properly. Of course, developing interpersonal relationships with your hosts is more important than money, and mere cash or gifts is no substitute for making friends.

If you're headed for a remote outer island without hotels or resorts, you could also take some gifts along. Keep in mind, however, that Seventh-Day Adventists are forbidden to have coffee, cigarettes, or kava, so you might ask if there are any SDAs around in order to avoid embarrassment. One thing *not* to take to a village is alcohol, which is always sure to offend somebody.

Once you're staying with one family, avoid moving to the home of another family in the same village, as this would probably be seen as a slight to the first. Be wary of accepting invitations to meals with villagers other than your hosts, as the offer may only be meant as a courtesy. Don't overly admire any of the possessions of your hosts, or they may feel obligated to give them to you. If you're forced to accept a family heirloom or another item you know you cannot take, ask them to keep it there for you in trust.

Staying in a village is definitely not for everyone. Many houses contain no electricity, running water, toilet, or furniture, and only native food will be available. Water and your left hand serve as toilet paper. You should expect to sacrifice most of your privacy, to stay up late drinking grog, and to sit in the house and socialize when you could be out exploring. On Sunday, you'll have to stay put the whole day. The constant attention and lack of sanitary conditions may become tiresome, but it would be considered rude to attempt to be alone or refuse the food or grog.

With the proliferation of backpacker resorts, staying in villages has become far less a part of visits to the remoter parts of Fiji than it was a decade ago, and relatively few travelers do it today. However, so long as you're prepared to accept all of the above and know beforehand that this is not a cheap (or easy) way to travel, a couple of nights in an outlying village could well be the highlight of your trip. Just don't arrive on a Sunday or overstay your welcome.

Food and Drink

Fiji has many good, inexpensive places to eat. The ubiquitous Chinese restaurants are probably your best bet for dinner, and you can almost always get alcohol with the meal. At lunchtime, look for an Indian place. The Indian restaurants are lifesavers for vegetarians, as all too often a vegetarian meal elsewhere is just the same thing, but with the meat removed.

The service at restaurants is occasionally slow. Trying to make servers do things more quickly is often counterproductive. The friendly personal attention you will usually receive more than compensates. A 12.5 percent tax is added to the bill at some tourist restaurants, although it's usually included in the menu price at ordinary restaurants. Most large shops in Fiji close at 1300 on Saturday, but smaller grocery stores are often open on Sunday. Many restaurants are closed on Sunday.

The Hot Bread Kitchen chain of bakeries around Fiji serves fresh fruit loaves, cheese and onion loaves, muffins, and other assorted breads. The Morris Hedstrom supermarket chain is about the cheapest, and many have milk bars with ice cream and sweets.

© SILKE BARON

cassava, also known as manioc

The famous Fiji Bitter beer is brewed in Suva by Australian-owned Carlton Brewery Ltd., part of the famous Fosters Brewing Group. The 750-milliliter beer bottle is called a "long neck," while the smaller "stubbie" is a "short neck." Another Carlton-owned company, South Pacific Distilleries Ltd., produces Bounty Rum, Regal Whisky, Czarina Vodka, and eight other alcoholic beverages at their plant in Lautoka. If you go local, you may be offered *boro,* a potent home brew made from cassava or taro, yeast, sugar, and water.

In Fiji, beer and other alcohol is available at supermarkets only on weekdays 0800–1800, Saturday 0800–1300. On Sunday, only tourist hotels and private clubs are allowed to sell alcohol. Licensed restaurants can serve alcohol only to those who order meals. Drinking alcoholic beverages on the street is prohibited. The drinking age in Fiji is 18. Unlike Australia and New Zealand, it's not customary to bring your own (BYO) booze into restaurants.

TRADITIONAL FOODS

The traditional diet of the Fijians consists of root crops and fruit, plus lagoon fish and the occasional pig. The vegetables include taro, yams, cassava (manioc), breadfruit, and sweet potatoes. The sweet potato *(kumala)* is something of an anomaly—it's the only Pacific food plant with a South American origin. How it got to the islands is not known.

Taro is an elephant-eared plant cultivated in freshwater swamps. Although yams are considered a prestige food, they're not as nutritious as breadfruit or taro. Yams can grow up to three meters long and weigh hundreds of kilograms. Papaya (pawpaw) is nourishing: A third of a cup contains as much vitamin C as 18 apples. To ripen a green papaya overnight, puncture it a few times with a knife. Don't overeat papaya—unless you *need* an effective laxative.

The ancient Pacific islanders stopped making pottery more than a millennium ago and instead developed an ingenious way of cooking in an underground earth oven known as a *lovo.* First a stack of dry coconut husks is burned in a pit. Once the fire is going well, coral stones are heaped on top, and when most of the husks have burnt away, the food is wrapped in banana leaves and placed on

© DAVID STANLEY

heating stones for a *lovo* or underground oven

FIJIAN AND INDIAN SPECIALTIES

Traditional Fijian food is usually steamed or boiled, instead of fried, and dishes such as baked fish *(ika)* in coconut cream *(lolo)* with cassava *(tavioka)*, taro *(dalo)*, breadfruit *(uto)*, and sweet potato *(kumala)* take a long time to prepare and must be served fresh, which makes it difficult to offer them in restaurants. Many resorts bake fish, pork, and root vegetables wrapped in banana leaves in a *lovo* (earth oven) at least once a week. Don't pass up an opportunity to try *duruka* (young sugar cane) or *vakalolo* (fish and prawns), both baked in *lolo*. *Kokoda* is an appetizing dish made of diced raw fish marinated in coconut cream and lime juice, while smoked octopus is *kuita*. Taro leaves are used to make a dish called *palusami* (often stuffed with corned beef), which is known as *rourou* when soaked in coconut cream. Taro stems are cut into a marinated salad called *baba*. Seasoned chicken *(toa)* is wrapped and steamed in banana leaves to produce *kovu*. *Miti* is a sauce made of coconut cream, oranges, and chilies.

Indian dishes are spicy, often curries with rice and dhal (lentils). Practicing Hindus don't consume beef and Muslims forgo pork. Instead of bread, Indians eat roti, a flat, tortilla-like pancake also called a chapatti. Puri are small, deep-fried rotis. Baked in a stone oven, roti becomes naan, a Punjabi specialty similar to pita bread. *Papadam* is a crispy version of the same. *Palau* is a main plate of rice and vegetables always including peas. Samosas are lumps of potato and other vegetables wrapped in dough and deep-fried. *Pakoras* are deep-fried chunks of dough spiced with chili and often served with a pickle chutney. A set meal consisting of dhal, roti, rice, one or two curries, and chutney, served on a metal plate, is called a *thali*. If meat is included, it's called simply a non-vegetarian *thali*. Yogurt mixed with water makes a refreshing drink called *lassi*. If you have the chance, try South Indian vegetarian dishes like *iddili* (little white rice cakes served with *dhal*) and *masala dosa* (a potato-filled rice pancake served with a watery curry sauce called *sambar*).

the hot stones—fish and meat below, vegetables above. A whole pig may be cleaned, then stuffed with banana leaves and hot stones. This cooks the beast from inside out as well as outside in, and the leaves create steam. The food is then covered with more leaves and stones, and after about two and a half hours everything is cooked.

The *lovo* feasts staged weekly at many large hotels around Nadi or on the Coral Coast offer a good opportunity to taste authentic Fijian food and see traditional dancing. These feasts are usually accompanied by a Fijian *meke,* or song-and-dance performance, in which legends, love stories, and historical events are told in song and gesture. Alternatively, firewalking may be presented.

Tips for Travelers

RESIDENCE AND EMPLOYMENT OPPORTUNITIES

Advance permission is required to reside in Fiji for more than six months or to work. For employment, a sponsor must be found. Application can be made through a Fiji diplomatic mission listed in this guide. Application forms for residence, study, research, and work permits are available on the website of the Fiji Immigration Department (www.immigration .gov.fj), which also provides a list of fees. Police and medical reports, and proof of financial status or qualifications may be required.

Residence permits are difficult to obtain, and the fastest means of obtaining one is to invest F$200,000 or more in the country. For information on business opportunities in your field of expertise, contact the **Fiji Trade and Investment Bureau** (tel. 331-5988, www .ftib.org.fj), Civic Tower, Level 6, directly behind the Suva City Library on Victoria Parade. Foreigners holding professional or technical qualifications in areas required by Fiji also receive preference. Fiji's trade commissioners in Los Angeles, Taiwan, and Australia should be able to assist with the process.

The University of the South Pacific is always in need of qualified staff, so if you're from a university milieu and looking for a chance to live in the South Seas, this could be it. If your credentials are impeccable, you should write to the registrar from home. On the spot, it's better to talk to a department head about his/her needs before going to see the registrar.

Once you've arranged a position, you'll have to leave Fiji and apply for a Permit to Work from abroad.

OPPORTUNITIES FOR STUDY

Students from outside the Pacific islands pay F$1,700–3,000 tuition for each undergraduate course they take at the University of the South Pacific in Suva. Room and board are available at F$6,370 a year, and books will run another F$1,000 or so. There are academic minimum-entry requirements, and applications must be received by December 31 for the following term. The two semesters are late February to the end of June, and late July until the end of November. Many courses in the social sciences have a high level of content pertaining to Pacific culture, and postgraduate studies in a growing number of areas are available. Check the university's website (www.usp.ac.fj) for more information. A Permit to Study (F$136) obtained from an overseas diplomatic office will be required.

The most common form of study practiced by visitors is scuba diving training. Most resort dive shops offer three-day PADI Open Water certification courses at around F$750 per person. The programs combine theory with practice sessions in a swimming pool and the ocean. It's possible to speed the process up by doing a referral course after taking some scuba training at a dive shop near your home before coming to Fiji. Numerous advanced courses are also available, and companies like Subsurface Fiji (www.subsurfacefiji.com) offer training to children as young as eight years old. What better way to combine study with a trip to Fiji! Of course, no student visa is required for this.

ACCESS FOR TRAVELERS WITH DISABILITIES

Facilities for travelers with disabilities are not well developed in Fiji, although things may improve since Fiji ratified the United Nations Convention on the Right of Persons with Disabilities in March 2007. For more information, contact the Fiji Disabled People's Association (3 Brown St., Suva, tel. 331-1203).

Some hotels claim to have special rooms for guests with disabilities, but this may only mean that those rooms are on the first floor and close to the dining room! Generally, however, the resorts are very good about adapting their rooms to special needs if they have plenty of advance notice. If you have a disability, you should inform your travel agent and the airline when making your bookings. It may sound trite, but Fijians often accommodate guests with disabilities by simply picking them up in their arms and carrying them on and off boats, etc.

TRAVELING WITH CHILDREN

Fiji is a safe, family-friendly country. Taking your children along can be a rewarding experience for both them and you, and there are many discounts and facilities for children. Pacific Sun gives a 25 percent discount to children under 12, and the Mamanuca catamaran shuttles and most day cruises out of Nadi are half price for children under 16. Throughout Fiji, most attractions with admission charge half price for children.

Children can stay free at many large resort hotels, provided they share a room with their parents and no extra bedding is required. The same resorts usually offer a deal on children's meals, and most have kids clubs where children aged 3–12 can be dropped off to spend the day playing with their peers under the supervision of a staff member.

Family-friendly resorts offering something like this include Plantation Island Resort, Musket Cove Island Resort, Malolo Island Resort, Beachcomber Island, Bounty Island Sanctuary Resort, Treasure Island Resort, Castaway Island Resort, Navini Island Resort, Mana Island Resort, and Amanuca Island Resort in the Mamanuca Group, Shangri-La's Fijian Resort, Outrigger on the Lagoon, The Naviti Resort, Vakaviti Motel, Rydges Hideaway Resort, and the Warwick Fiji on the Coral Coast, the Novotel and Toberua Island Resort near Suva, Naigani Island Resort in Lomaiviti, and the Grand Eastern Hotel and Jean-Michel Cousteau Fiji Islands Resort on Vanua Levu.

In the cities, the Tokatoka Resort Hotel opposite Nadi International Airport and Suva Motor Inn in Suva have water slides in their swimming pools. The Tanoa International Hotel in Nadi accommodates children under 12 for free.

Most upscale resorts around Fiji catering specifically to "romantic couples" do not accept children. (Isn't it strange how honeymooners are turned off by the end result of their fun and games!) Most backpacker dormitories are also closed to small children, but many of them also have family rooms.

WOMEN TRAVELING ALONE

Women should have few real problems traveling around Fiji on their own, so long as they're prepared to cope with frequent offers of marriage. Female equality and women's rights are recognized by most Fijians and guaranteed by the country's laws. Although a female tourist has less chance of facing sexist violence than a local woman does, it's smart to be defensive and to lie about where you're staying. Cheap videos have created the stereotype of the promiscuous Western woman, and local male dates may be looking for more than you expect. After a night on the town, don't accept a ride back to your hotel unless it's with someone you know very well. The peeping tom is another side of this.

If you want to be left alone, conservative dress and purposeful behavior will work to your advantage. In village situations, seek the company of local women. Women should avoid being by themselves on lonely beaches and trails, and try to choose accommodations where other people are nearby. Fiji's backpacker resorts are great places to meet other travelers, and there's always safety in numbers.

GAY AND LESBIAN TRAVELERS

In March 2010, the interim government issued a decree decriminalizing homosexual conduct in Fiji. However, prejudice against gays and lesbians persists in some circles and same-sex couples will sail smoother seas if they exercise discretion. Public displays of affection should be avoided. Some resorts and nightclubs in Fiji are reputed to be gay-friendly while others are not. Homophobic reactions are less likely to occur in hotels and bars managed by Indo-Fijians. A number of hotels in Fiji advertise on the GLBT website www.purpleroofs.com.

GETTING MARRIED IN FIJI

Most upscale resorts cater to couples wishing to marry in Fiji, and some have constructed special wedding chapels on their grounds. The preferred venue is usually the beach at sunset. Visit www.honeymoonfiji.com or www.resort weddings.com.au or www.fijiweddings.com to get an idea of the wedding packages available. Such arrangements usually include flowers, a photographer, a wedding coordinator, and maybe even singing by the village choir and an escort of Fijian warriors for the bride. You'll need to bring your own rings.

A Fijian wedding is legally binding and recognized in most countries. Required documents include passports, birth certificates, a statutory declaration proving the parties are not already married, a letter of consent from the father of any party under the age of 21, and decrees of divorce or the death certificate of a previous spouse if applicable. Additional requirements may apply if either party is a current or former resident of Fiji.

The couple must purchase a wedding license in person on a weekday at the registry or district office in the province in which they intend to marry. The ceremony can be carried out by a minister of religion who has registered as a marriage officer or by the district registrar. The marriage certificate will list the maiden name of the bride, not a married name.

"Renewal of vows" ceremonies are readily available for romantic tourists who are already married.

WHAT TO TAKE

For maximum mobility, bring only a small wheeled suitcase or a soft medium-size backpack with an internal frame. Try to keep the total weight of bag and contents down to 15 kilograms. For clothes, take loose-fitting cotton washables, light in color and weight, for the tropical climate. Dress is casual in the islands. Stick to clothes you can rinse in your room sink, and don't bring more than two outfits. In midwinter (July and August), it can be cool at night, so a light sweater or windbreaker may come in handy and scuba divers might want to bring a light wetsuit. You'll also need a sun hat or visor, and maybe a small umbrella.

A **mask** and **snorkel** are essential equipment—you'll be missing half of Fiji's beauty without them. **Reef shoes** can also be very handy. If you bring a tent, don't bother bringing a foam pad, as the ground is seldom cold here. You won't need a sleeping bag in the tropics, so that's another item you can easily cut. Other items to consider taking include a portable radio, compass, pocket flashlight, plastic cup, can and bottle opener, spoon, and water bottle.

Bring an adequate supply of any personal **medications,** plus your prescriptions (in generic terminology), as even basics such as aspirin can be unobtainable in the islands. Aside from the obvious toiletries, you might want to bring wax earplugs, insect repellent, sunscreen, lip balm, a motion-sickness remedy, a diarrhea remedy, a cold remedy, Alka-Seltzer, aspirin, antibacterial ointment, and antiseptic cream. Baby powder prevents and treats prickly heat rash.

Everyone needs a passport to enter Fiji, but don't bother getting an international driver's license, as your regular license is all you need to drive here. **Traveler's checks** are recommended, and in Fiji, American Express is the most efficient company when it comes to providing refunds for lost checks. The best plastic to have is Visa and MasterCard.

Carry your valuables in a money belt worn around your waist or neck under your clothing; most camping stores have these. Make several photocopies of the information page of your passport, personal identification, driver's license, scuba certification card, credit cards, airline tickets, receipts for purchase of traveler's checks, etc.—you should be able to get them all on both sides of one page. On the side of the photocopies, write the phone numbers you'd need to call to report lost documents.

The digital revolution has made bulky film cameras a thing of the past for most travelers. The memory cards of **digital cameras** are unaffected by airport X-ray machines, and you can use them over and over again. Camera stores in Nadi and Suva can burn your photos onto CDs, although it's easier to carry a couple of spare memory cards. You'll need a 240 volt-compatible battery charger, plus an adapter with two flat plugs at angles. A spare battery will come in handy; many of the smaller resorts have limited electricity.

Health and Safety

Fiji's climate is a healthy one, and the main causes of death are non-communicable diseases such as heart disease, diabetes, and cancer. The sea and air are clear and usually pollution-free. The humidity nourishes the skin, and the local fruit is brimming with vitamins. If you take a few precautions, you'll never have a sick day. The information provided below is intended to make you knowledgeable, not fearful. If you have access to the Internet, check wwwnc.cdc.gov/travel for up-to-the-minute information.

Health care is good, with an abundance of hospitals, health centers, and nursing stations scattered around the country. The largest hospitals are in Labasa, Lautoka, Levuka, Ba, Savusavu, Sigatoka, Suva, and Taveuni. The crowded government-run medical facilities provide free medical treatment to local residents but have special rates for foreigners. It's usually no more expensive to visit a private doctor or clinic, where you'll receive much faster service since everyone is paying. We've tried to list private doctors and dentists throughout the guidebook, but in emergencies and outside clinic hours, you can always turn to the government-run hospitals.

To call an ambulance dial 911. There's a dive recompression chamber (tel. 321-5525) at the Colonial War Memorial Hospital in Suva.

TRAVEL INSURANCE

The sale of travel insurance is a big business, but the value of the policies themselves is often questionable. If your regular group health insurance also covers you while you're traveling abroad, it's probably enough, as medical costs are generally low in Fiji. Most policies only pay the amount above and beyond what your national or group health insurance will pay and are invalid if you don't have any health insurance at all. You may also be covered by your credit card company if you paid for your plane ticket with the card. Buying extra travel insurance is about the same as buying a lottery ticket: There's always the chance it will pay off, but it's usually money down the drain.

If you do opt for the security of travel insurance, make sure emergency medical evacuations are covered. Some policies are invalid if you engage in "dangerous activities," such as scuba diving, parasailing, surfing, or even riding a motor scooter, so be sure to read the fine print. Some companies will pay your bills directly, while others require you to pay and collect receipts, which may be reimbursed later.

Some policies also cover travel delays, lost baggage, and theft. In practice, your airline probably already covers the first two adequately, and claiming something extra from your insurance company could be more trouble than it's worth. Theft insurance never covers items left on the beach while you're swimming. All said, you should weigh the advantages and decide for yourself if you want a policy. Just don't be too influenced by what your travel agent says, as they'll only want to sell you coverage to earn another commission.

ACCLIMATIZING

Don't go from winter weather into the steaming tropics without a rest before and after. Minimize jet lag by setting your watch to local time at your destination as soon as you board the flight. Westbound flights to Fiji from North America or Europe are less jolting, since you follow the sun and your body gets a few hours extra sleep. On the way home, you're moving against the sun, and the hours of sleep your body loses cause jet lag. Airplane cabins have low humidity, so drink lots of juice or water instead of carbonated drinks, and don't overeat in-flight. It's also wise to forgo coffee, as it will only keep you awake, and alcohol, which will dehydrate you.

Scuba diving on departure day can give you a severe case of the bends. Before flying, there should be a minimum of 12 hours surface interval after a non-decompression dive and a minimum of 24 hours after a decompression dive. Factors contributing to decompression sickness include a lack of sleep and/or the excessive consumption of alcohol before diving.

If you start feeling seasick on board a ship, stare at the horizon, which is always steady, and try to stop thinking about it. Anti-motion-sickness pills are useful to have along; otherwise, ginger helps alleviate seasickness. Travel stores sell AcuBands that find a pressure point on the wrist and create a stable flow of blood to the head, thus miraculously preventing seasickness.

The tap water in Fiji is usually drinkable, except immediately after a cyclone or during droughts, when care should be taken. If in doubt, boil it or use purification pills. Natural artesian water in plastic bottles is widely available. Tap water that is uncomfortably hot to touch is usually safe. Allow it to cool in a clean container. Don't forget that if the tap water is contaminated, the local ice will be too. Avoid brushing your teeth with water unfit to drink, and wash or peel fruit and vegetables if you can. Cooked food is less subject to contamination than raw.

SUNBURN

Though you may think a tan will make you look healthier and more attractive, it's actually very damaging to the skin, which becomes dry, rigid, and prematurely old and wrinkled, especially on the face. Begin with short exposures to the sun, perhaps a half-hour at a time, followed by an equal time in the shade. Avoid the sun from 1000 to 1500, the most dangerous time. Clouds and beach umbrellas will not protect you fully. Wear a T-shirt while snorkeling to protect your back. Drink plenty of liquids to keep your pores open. Sunbathing is the main cause of cataracts to the eyes, so wear sunglasses and a wide-brimmed hat, and beware of reflected sunlight.

Use a sunscreen lotion containing PABA rather than oil, and don't forget to apply it to your nose, lips, forehead, neck, hands, and feet. Sunscreens protect you from ultraviolet rays (a leading cause of cancer), while oils magnify the sun's effect. A 15-factor sunscreen provides 93 percent protection (a more expensive 30-factor sunscreen is only slightly better at 97 percent protection). Apply the lotion *before* going to the beach to avoid being burned on the way, and reapply every couple of hours to replace sunscreen washed away by perspiration. Swimming also washes away your protection. After sunbathing, take a tepid shower rather than a hot one, which would wash away your natural skin oils. Stay moist, and use a vitamin E evening cream to preserve the youth of your skin. Calamine ointment soothes skin already burned, as does coconut oil. Pharmacists recommend Solarcaine to soothe burned skin. Rinsing off with a vinegar solution reduces peeling, and aspirin relieves some of the pain and irritation. Vitamin A and calcium counteract overdoses of vitamin D received from the sun. The fairer your skin, the more essential it is to take care.

As earth's ozone layer is depleted due to the commercial use of chlorofluorocarbons (CFCs) and other factors, the need for protection from ultraviolet radiation is becoming more urgent. Previously, UV-related cancers didn't develop until age 50 or 60, but now much younger people are affected.

AILMENTS

Cuts and scratches become infected easily in the tropics and take a long time to heal. Prevent infection from coral cuts by immediately washing wounds with soap and fresh water, then rubbing in vinegar or alcohol (rum will do)—painful but effective. Use an antiseptic like hydrogen peroxide and an antibacterial ointment such as Neosporin, if you have them. Islanders usually dab coral cuts with lime juice. All cuts turn septic quickly in the tropics, so try to keep them clean and covered.

For bites, burns, and cuts, an antiseptic such as Solarcaine speeds healing and helps prevent infection. Pure aloe vera is good for sunburn, scratches, and even coral cuts. Bites by sand flies itch for days and can become infected. Not everyone is affected by insect bites in the same way. Some people are practically immune to insects, while traveling companions experiencing exactly the same conditions are soon covered with bites. You'll quickly know which type you are.

Prickly heat, an intensely irritating rash, is caused by wearing heavy clothing that is inappropriate for the climate. When sweat glands are blocked and the sweat is unable to evaporate, the skin becomes soggy, and small red blisters appear. Synthetic fabrics like nylon are especially bad in this regard. Take a cold shower, apply calamine lotion, dust with talcum powder, and take off those clothes! Until things improve, avoid alcohol, tea, coffee, and any physical activity that makes you sweat. If you're sweating profusely, increase your intake of salt slightly to avoid fatigue, but not without concurrently drinking more water.

Use antidiarrheal medications such as Lomotil or immodium sparingly. Rather than take drugs to plug yourself up, drink plenty of unsweetened liquids like green coconut or fresh fruit juice to help flush yourself out. Egg yolk mixed with nutmeg helps diarrhea, or eat rice and drink tea for the day. Avoid dairy products. Most cases of diarrhea are self-limiting and require only simple replacement of the fluids and salts lost in diarrheal stools. If the diarrhea is persistent or you experience high fever, drowsiness, or blood in the stool, stop traveling, rest, and consider seeing a doctor. For constipation, eat pineapple or any peeled fruit.

Dengue Fever

There's no malaria in Fiji, but a mosquito-transmitted disease known as dengue fever is endemic. In early 1998, a major outbreak in Fiji resulted in an estimated 25,000 cases and 14 deaths. Signs are headaches, sore throat, and pain in the joints, fever, chills, nausea, and rash. This painful illness, also known as "breakbone fever," can last anywhere from five to 15 days. Although you can relieve the symptoms somewhat, the only real cure is to stay in bed, drink lots of water, and wait it out. Avoid aspirin, as this can lead to complications. No vaccine exists, so just try to avoid getting bitten (the *Aedes aegypti,* or black-and-white-striped mosquito, bites only during the day). Dengue fever can kill infants, so extra care must be taken to protect them if an outbreak is in progress.

STDs and AIDS

The number of AIDS cases in Fiji is still modest but growing. Other sexually transmitted diseases (STDs) such as syphilis are more common among sex workers in Nadi and Suva, and it's essential to practice safe sex at all times if you want to avoid infection. A pack of condoms costs under a dollar at any pharmacy in Fiji. Abstinence is even more effective.

SAFETY

Fiji is a perfectly safe country to visit so long as you take normal precautions. If you dress modestly, act purposefully, and remain aware of your surroundings, your chances of being mugged are low. After dark, stick to well-lit streets, and take a taxi back to your hotel after a night on the town. Avoid becoming inebriated. It's wise to use a money belt or to lock your valuables in your bag in your hotel room before stepping out. On the beach, keep an eye on your stuff. Clothes hung out to dry or shoes outside your door could also disappear. Lock your room or car and keep valuables out of sight. All of this is only common sense.

Steer clear of strangers who accost you on the street for no reason. In Suva, beware of the seemingly friendly Fijian men (usually with a small package or canvas bag in their hands) who will greet you with a hearty *Bula!* These are "sword sellers" who will ask your name, quickly carve it on a mask, and then demand F$20 for a set that you could buy at a Nadi curio shop for F$5. Other times they'll try to engage you in conversation and may offer a "gift." Just say "thank you very much" and walk away from them quickly without accepting anything, as they can suddenly become unpleasant and aggressive. Their grotesque swords and masks themselves have nothing to do with Fiji.

Another popular scam involves someone who asks you to give them a F$50 banknote in exchange for one F$10 and two F$20 notes. If you comply, the person will switch your F$50 for a F$5 note as you are examining the three notes they gave you and will demand their F$50.

On the streets of Nadi, beware of high-pressure touts who may try to lure you into their shops, and self-appointed guides who offer to help you find the "best price." Never ever allow strangers to accompany you on shopping expeditions. Also, don't be fooled by anyone on the street who claims to work at your resort and offers to show you around. They only want to sell you something.

Similarly, overly sociable people at bars may expect you to buy them drinks and snacks. This may not be a problem in the beginning, but know when to disengage. In the main tourist centers, such as Nadi and Suva, if a local invites you to visit his home, you may be seen mainly as a source of beer and other goods.

The reverse of this is under-friendly tourists who feel they're on some sort of charter holiday rather than traveling. No hellos, no talking to strangers, etc. If this puts you off, imagine how it affects the Fijians. Outside of the towns, it's customary to smile and say hello to people passing by. Only tourists look the other way.

Indigenous Fijians may demand money of you for scuba diving, snorkeling, surfing, and even swimming in *qoliqoli* areas where they claim to own the traditional fishing rights. If you're with a local scuba operator or tour company, you should let your guide handle the situation and refuse to pay anything directly yourself. If you're there on your own, you should tell the person(s) that you weren't aware of the situation and try to leave the area immediately. Even though all of Fiji's beaches and reefs are owned by the state and *qoliqoli* rights are not enshrined in law, it's best to accept de facto situations. Take seriously any warnings you may hear about this sort of thing, as matters can turn ugly very quickly.

When snorkeling beware of speedboats, which may not see you. In November 2009, a male tourist drowned after being hit by a speedboat at a resort off Taveuni while snorkeling close to shore.

Don't react if offered drugs. Marijuana is an important cash crop in central Viti Levu, but it's strictly illegal in Fiji and the penalties are severe. Prostitution is also illegal in Fiji.

Information and Services

MONEY

The currency is the Fiji dollar, which is a bit under two to one to the U.S. dollar in value. To obtain the current rate, visit www.xe.com/ucc. The Fiji dollar is a stable currency, pegged to a basket of the U.S., New Zealand, and Australian dollars, the yen, and the pound. In April 2009, the Fiji dollar was devalued 20 percent and inflation as of press time is running over 6 percent.

The first Fijian coins were minted in London in 1934, but British currency continued to circulate in Fiji until 1969, when dollars and cents were introduced (at the rate of two Fiji dollars to one pound). There are coins of F$0.05, F$0.10, F$0.20, F$0.50, and F$1, and bills of F$2, F$5, F$10, F$20, F$50, and F$100 (be careful as the F$5 and F$50 notes, as well as the F$2 and F$20 notes, are confusingly similar).

The ANZ Bank, Colonial National Bank, and Westpac Banking Corporation have branches in all the main towns. Normal banking hours are Monday–Thursday 0930–1500, Friday 0930–1600, and there are several 24-hour banks and exchange offices at Nadi Airport. It's a good idea to plan ahead and

change enough money to see you through the weekends. It's usually not possible to change traveler's checks or foreign banknotes in rural areas or on the outer islands. Carry sufficient Fijian cash to the outer islands and always have an ample supply of small Fijian banknotes in your wallet or purse.

For security the bulk of your liquid assets should be in traveler's checks. If your American Express checks or card are lost or stolen, call 004/890-1001, then 888/937-2639, or the number you were given when you bought the checks. Traveler's checks have the added advantage of attracting a higher exchange rate than cash. Overseas banks don't earn much on traveler's checks and may try to convince you that they're a thing of the past. In fact, traveler's checks are still readily accepted in Fiji and the fees and rates associated with them are transparent.

The Colonial National Bank changes traveler's checks without commission, whereas the ANZ Bank and Westpac Bank each take a F$5 commission on traveler's checks (but not on cash exchanges). Numerous private exchange offices around Fiji change traveler's checks at the same rate as the banks without

Fijian banknotes feature Queen Elizabeth II.

WIKIMEDIA COMMONS

© DAVID STANLEY

In Fiji, private exchange offices give better rates than the banks, with no commission or line.

commission, and you'll avoid the long bank lines while saving money by dealing with them. Take care when changing money at the luxury hotels, as they often give a rate much lower than the banks.

Most banks have automated teller machines (ATMs) outside their branches accessible 24 hours a day, and these provide local currency at good rates against most debit cards. Be aware, however, that both your bank and the one providing the ATM may charge a stiff service fee for each transaction. If you don't have an account with the Westpac, ANZ Bank, or Colonial National Bank, either in Fiji or abroad, you'll be charged an extra fee every time you use their ATMs. Ask your own bank how much they'll charge if you use an ATM in Fiji, what your daily limit will be, and if you'll need a special personal identification number (PIN). Occasionally the machines don't work due to problems with the software. To avoid emergencies (such as if a machine were to "eat" your card), it's unwise to be totally dependent on ATMs.

Credit cards are strictly for the cities and

resorts. The most useful cards to bring are MasterCard and Visa, as many tourism operators don't accept American Express. The ANZ Bank gives cash advances on MasterCard and Visa, but remember that cash advances are considered personal loans and accrue interest from the moment they are paid. If you're forced to get a cash advance through a large supermarket or resort, they'll probably add 10 percent commission for the favor. Many tourist facilities levy a 5 percent surcharge on credit card payments (Turtle Airways adds 10 percent). MasterCard and Visa also levy surcharges of around 2.5 percent on foreign currency conversions associated with their cards. These fees do add up, hence our recommendation of traveler's checks. Small wonder the banking community promotes plastic!

The import of foreign currency is unrestricted but "negotiable bearer instruments" over F$10,000 most be declared on a Border Currency Report Form. Only F$500 in Fiji banknotes may be imported or exported but you should avoid taking any Fiji banknotes out of the country at all, as Fiji dollars are difficult to change and heavily discounted outside Fiji. Also, don't consider buying Fiji dollars at exchange offices outside Fiji as the spreads between their buying and selling rates are too great and you'll get a better deal in Fiji. Officially you're only allowed to export a maximum of F$5,000 in foreign cash, but this is seldom an issue.

If you need rescue money sent in a hurry, Western Union can receive fast transfers from anywhere in the world at their offices in Suva, Nadi, and Lautoka, and at most post offices in Fiji. The sender can complete the transaction online in a few minutes at www.western union.com (the sender pays the fee). Western Union outlets around Fiji are also some of the best places to change traveler's checks (no commission charges), so watch for the familiar yellow signs.

In 1992, Fiji introduced a value-added tax (VAT), currently 12.5 percent, which is usually (but not always) included in quoted prices. Among the few items exempt from VAT are unprocessed local foods, books printed in Fiji, and bus fares. Fiji's "duty-free" shops such as Prouds or Tappoo are not really duty-free, as all goods are subject to various fiscal duties, plus the 12.5 percent value-added tax. An additional 5 percent hotel turnover tax is charged, to bring it up to 17.5 percent total at hotels. Despite VAT and the hotel tax, Fiji is still one of the least expensive countries in the South Pacific. Fiji isn't cheap the way Indonesia and Guatemala are cheap, and you might consider it medium priced. Anything imported into Fiji will cost much more than goods produced here. Similarly, top-end resorts, tours, and sporting activities run by Europeans will be a lot more expensive than services provided by Fiji nationals.

Tipping isn't customary in Fiji, although some visitors are working hard to change that. A few resorts have staff Christmas funds to which contributions are always welcome. Maybe have a quality baseball cap or a small bottle of nice perfume in your bag to give to anyone who has really gone out of their way for you.

Bargaining is the order of the day in smaller shops. Once purchased, items cannot be returned, so don't let yourself be talked into anything. If you're buying from an Indo-Fijian merchant, always bargain hard and consider all sales final. Indigenous Fijians usually begin by asking a much lower starting price, in which case bargaining isn't as important.

COMMUNICATIONS
Post
Post offices are open weekdays 0800–1600, and they hold general delivery mail two months. Postcard postage is inexpensive, so mail lots of them from here! Consider using air mail for parcels, since surface mail takes up to six months. The weight limit for overseas parcels is 10 kilograms. Post Fiji's *fast* POST service guarantees that your letter or parcel will get on the first international airline connection to your destination for a small surcharge. Express mail service (EMS) is more expensive but faster, and up to 20 kilograms may be sent. Main post offices around Fiji accept EMS mail.

When writing to Fiji, use the words "Fiji Islands" in the address (otherwise the letter might go to Fuji, Japan) and underline Fiji (so it doesn't end up in Iceland). Also include the post office box number, as there's no residential mail delivery in Fiji. If it's a remote island or small village you're writing to, the person's name will be sufficient. Sending a picture postcard to an islander is a very nice way of saying thank you.

Aside from EMS, the other major courier services active in Fiji are **CDP** (tel. 331-3077) at Ba, Labasa, Lautoka, Levuka, Nadi, Savusavu, Sigatoka, and Suva; **DHL** (tel. 337-2766) with offices at Nadi, Savusavu, and Suva; **TNT** (tel. 330-8677) at Nadi and Suva; and **UPS** (tel. 324-9431) at Lautoka, Nadi, and Suva.

Telecommunications
Card telephones are very handy, and if you're staying in Fiji more than a few days and intend to make your own arrangements, it's wise to purchase a local telephone card upon arrival, as coin telephones don't exist. In this guide we

provide all the numbers you'll need to make hotel reservations, check restaurant hours, find out about cultural events, and compare car rental rates, saving you a lot of time and inconvenience.

By using a telephone card to call long distance, you limit the amount the call can possibly cost and won't end up overspending should you forget to keep track of the time. On short calls, you avoid three-minute minimum charges. International telephone calls placed from hotel rooms are always more expensive than the same calls made from public phones using telephone cards (ask the receptionist for the location of the nearest public phone). What you sacrifice is your privacy, as anyone can stand around and listen to your call, which often happens. Public phones are usually found outside post offices or large stores. Check that the phone actually works before bothering to arrange your numbers and notes, as it seems like quite a few of the public phones in Fiji are out of order at any given time.

Tele Cards issued by TransTel (www.trans tel.com.fj) are sold at all post offices and many shops in denominations of F$3, F$5, F$10, and F$20 (foreign phone cards cannot be used in Fiji). It's wiser to get a F$3 or F$5 card rather than one of the higher values in case you happen to lose it. With a Tele Card, you scratch off a strip on the back of the card to reveal a code number. On hearing a dial tone, dial 101 and follow the voice prompts. The Tele Card can be used from all types of phones, but you must enter the code numbers slowly, one by one, otherwise you'll get message telling you the code is invalid.

As far as telephone charges go, Fiji is divided into three regions. Western includes all of Viti Levu west of Rakiraki and Sigatoka, plus the Yasawas. Eastern is all of Viti Levu east of Korolevu, plus Ovalau and Kadavu. Northern is Vanua Levu and Taveuni. Calls within a region are F$0.36 for the first 20 minutes, while inter-regional calls are F$0.34 a minute. Calls to mobile phone cost F$0.64 a minute.

Direct dial international calls with a Tele Card cost anywhere from F$0.81 to F$1.83

per minute. All operator-assisted international calls cost an additional F$2.25 connection fee. Direct dial international calls made using telephone cards have no minimum or connection fees and the charges are broken down into flat six-second units (telephone cards with less than F$3 credit on them cannot be used for international calls).

Fiji's international access code from public telephones is 00, so insert your card, dial 00, the country code, the area code, and the number (to Canada and the United States, the country code is always 1). To call overseas collect (billed to your party at the higher person-to-person rate), dial 031, the country code, the area code, and the number. If calling Fiji from abroad, dial your own international access code, Fiji's telephone code is **679**. There are no area codes in Fiji. If the line is inaudible, hang up immediately and try again later.

You can search for any telephone number in Fiji at www.whitepages.com.fj and www.yel lowpages.com.fj. Within Fiji, domestic directory assistance is 011, international directory assistance 022, the domestic operator 010, the international operator 012. In emergencies, dial 911.

Trunk Radio System (TRS) calls can be direct-dialed from inside Fiji, but must go through an operator from overseas. All such seven-digit numbers have 11 in the first three numbers, and many are only answered at certain times of day (usually 0800–1000 and 1400–1600). Many resorts in the Yasawa Islands or the interior of Viti Levu have VHF radio telephone connections. In these cases, dial the number provided in this guide, wait for two beeps, then key in the extension number. Be aware that only one person at a time can speak over radio telephone hookups.

If you have a calling card or phone pass issued by your own telephone company, you can access an operator or automated voice prompt in your home country by dialing a "country direct" number from any touch-tone phone in Fiji. Such calls are billed to your home telephone number at the full non-discounted rate that an operator-assisted call to Fiji would cost from your country, which in Fiji works out to several times more than using a local telephone card. (Don't be fooled by misleading advertisements implying that "direct" calls are cheaper.) Still, if you don't mind paying extra for the convenience, the "country direct" numbers to dial include:

- TNZ New Zealand 004/890-6401

- Telstra Australia 004/890-6101

- Optus Australia 004/890-6102

- AT&T United States 004/890-1001

- MCI United States 004/890-1002

- Sprint United States 004/890-1003

- Teleglobe Canada 004/890-1005

Even though the phone companies have the cheek to suggest it, never use a "direct" number to place a domestic call within a single foreign country or an international call to a country other than your own. The call will be routed through your home country, and you'll be shocked when you see the bill.

Mobile Phones

Because rural telephone services in Fiji are poor, many people carry mobile phones. Mobile numbers always begin with a nine, and you should avoid using them if possible, as such calls cost a minimum of F$0.64 a minute and your phone card will soon be devoured.

Vodafone (tel. 990-2123, www.vodafone .com.fj) has a sales office in the arrivals area at Nadi International Airport, to the left as you come out of customs. If you have a GSM dual-band or tri-band mobile phone that operates on a 900 Mhz frequency, you can easily connect to Vodafone, provided you set up roaming service before leaving home. However, this can be unexpectedly expensive with local calls charged at international rates, and you should consider renting a cell phone from Vodafone and using a Vodafone SIM card. Within Fiji, mobile-to-mobile calls are F$0.52 a minute, while mobile-to-landline is F$0.95 a minute. Text messages are F$0.55 each. Incoming calls are free.

The Internet

Fiji is the most advanced country in the South Pacific as far as the Internet goes. Most tourism-related businesses in Fiji now have email addresses and websites, making communication from abroad a lot cheaper and easier. In this guide, we've embedded the website addresses in the listings whenever possible, but we only list an email address if a website is not currently available. Email addresses tend to change over time, whereas Web addresses are more permanent. Most websites list the current email address of the company, and it's a good idea to check the site beforehand anyway, as your question may be answered there.

Many resorts now have Facebook pages, which are excellent sources of photos and insider tips. The reviews on Tripadvisor (www .tripadvisor.com) are also very useful. The company's own website may provide useful information but you should be aware that the photos on resort sites are often misleading. Resort booking sites should also be considered as suspect, as their object is to sell you a room and not to help you make the best choice.

When sending email to Fiji, never include attachments such as Excel or Word files or photos with your message unless they have been specifically requested, as the recipient may be forced to pay stiff long-distance telephone charges to download them.

In Fiji, public Internet access is available in Nadi, Lautoka, Sigatoka, Pacific Harbor, Suva, Savusavu, Labasa, and a few other places (only Suva has 24-hour Internet cafés). Some resorts also provide computers at rates higher than the public Internet cafés. If your Internet service provider doesn't offer an electronic mailbox you can use on the road, you should open a free online email account at www.yahoo.com or www.hotmail.com before leaving home.

If you brought your own laptop computer, you can set up an unlimited-access dial-up account with **Connect Internet Services** (tel. 330-0100, www.connect.com.fj) for a monthly rate, plus a one-time setup fee. Before plugging in, ask your hotel if any service charges apply when using your connection from your room.

Unwired Fiji (tel. 0800/327-5040, www.un wired.com.fj) offers Wi-Fi Internet access at many points around Suva. You'll have to purchase a wireless broadband modem from them and pay a monthly service fee.

MEDIA
Print Media

The *Fiji Times* (tel. 330-4111, www.fijitimes .com), "the first newspaper published in the world today," was founded at Levuka in 1869 but is currently owned by the Rupert Murdoch News Ltd. group. The Fiji government has a controlling 44 percent interest in the *Daily Post* (tel. 327-5176, www.fijidailypost.com), which is also partly owned by Colonial Mutual Insurance. The more critical *Fiji Sun* (tel. 330-7555) was established in 1999.

The region's leading newsmagazines is *Islands Business* (tel. 330-3108, www.islands business.com), published monthly in Suva. There's also a fortnightly Fijian news and business magazine called *The Review.*

TV

Television broadcasting began in Fiji in 1991. Fiji 1 (tel. 330-5100) is on the air daily 1430–midnight, with Australian programming rebroadcast at other hours. Fiji 1 gives the Fiji news daily at 1800 and 2200, and the BBC World News weekdays at 2230. Government-owned Yasana Holdings has a majority interest in the station. In addition to this free station, there's a paid service for which a decoder must be rented. The three paid channels are Sky Plus (English-language programming), Sky Entertainment (Hindi programming from India), and Star Sports. The daily papers provide program guides.

Radio

A great way to keep in touch with world and local affairs is to take along a portable radio. Your only expense will be the radio itself and batteries. In this section, we provide the names and frequencies of all the local stations, so set your tuning buttons as soon as you arrive.

The public **Fiji Broadcasting Corporation** (tel. 331-4333, www.radiofiji.com.fj) operates six AM/FM radio stations: **Radio Fiji Gold** in English for older listeners, **2day FM** in English for younger listeners, Radio Fiji One (RF1) in Fijian for older listeners, Bula FM in Fijian for younger listeners, Radio Fiji Two (RF2) in Hindi for older listeners, and Radio Mirchi in Hindi for younger listeners. The public-service Radio Fiji stations are supported by a government grant, while the other stations are funded by commercial advertising.

In addition, **Communications Fiji Ltd.** (tel. 331-4766, www.fijivillage.com), owned by Fiji TV, operates four lively commercial FM stations, which broadcast around the clock throughout the country: **FM 96** (www .fm96.com.fj) and **Legend** in English, Viti FM in Fijian, and Sargam and Radio Navtarang in Hindi. FM 96 caters to the under-30 age group, while Legend is aimed at a more mature audience.

Bula Namaste FM is an independent station broadcasting in Fijian, Hindi, and English.

In **Suva,** you can pick up the local stations at the following frequencies: FM 96 at 96.0 MHz, Radio Mirchi at 98.0 MHz, Navtarang at 98.8 MHz, Bula Namaste FM at 99.4 MHz, Radio Fiji Gold at 100.4 MHz, Bula FM at 102.0 MHz, Viti FM at 102.8 MHz, 2day FM at 104.0 MHz, Sargam 104.6 MHz, RF2 at 105.2 MHz, Legend at 106.8 MHz, RF1 at 107.6 MHz, RF1 at 558 kHz AM, and RF2 at 774 kHz AM.

At **Nadi** and **Lautoka,** check the following frequencies: RF1 at 92.2 MHz, Radio Fiji Gold at 94.6 MHz, FM 96 at 95.4 MHz, Navtarang at 97.4 MHz, Radio Mirchi at 98.4 MHz, FM 96 at 99.2 MHz, Viti FM at 99.6 MHz, Radio Fiji Gold at 100.0 MHz, Bula FM at 102.4 MHz, Sargam at 104.2 MHz, RF2 at 105.4 MHz, Legend at 106.4 MHz, 2day FM at 107.4 MHz, and RF1 at 639 kHz AM.

On the **Coral Coast,** it's FM 96 at 96.6 MHz, Radio Mirchi at 98.2 MHz, Radio Fiji Gold at 100.6 MHz, Navtarang at 101.6 MHz, Bula FM at 103.0 MHz, Viti FM at 103.8 MHz, RF2 at 105.0 MHz, Sargam at 105.8 MHz, Legend at 107.2 MHz, and RF1 at 927 kHz.

Around **Rakiraki,** look for RF2 at 89.8 MHz, Bula FM at 91.4 MHz, RF1 at 92.2 MHz, Radio Mirchi at 93.0 MHz, Radio Fiji Gold at 94.6 MHz, Navtarang at 97.0 MHz, Radio Fiji Gold at 100.0 MHz, Viti FM at 104.8 MHz, RF1 at 1152 kHz, and RF2 at 1467 kHz. At **Ba,** you can get MixFM at 88.6 MHz, Bula FM at 91.4 MHz, Radio Fiji Gold at 94.6 MHz, Radio Mirchi at 98.2 MHz, FM 96 at 99.2 MHz, Navtarang at 101.6 MHz, Radio Pachin at 103.2, Viti FM at 103.8 MHz, RF2 at 105.0 MHz, and RF1 at 639 kHz AM.

On Vanua Levu, check the following frequencies at **Labasa:** FM 96 at 95.4 MHz, Navtarang at 97.4 MHz, Radio Mirchi at 98.4 MHz, Viti FM at 99.6 MHz, Radio Fiji Gold at 100.0 MHz, Bula FM at 102.4 MHz, Sargam at 104.2 MHz, RF2 at 105.4 MHz, Legend at 106.4 MHz, RF1 at 684 kHz, and RF2 at 810 kHz. At **Savusavu,** it's FM 96 at 96.6 MHz, Radio Mirchi at 98.4 MHz, Radio Fiji Gold at 100.0 MHz, Navtarang at 101.6 MHz, Bula FM at 102.4 MHz, Viti FM at 103.8 MHz, RF2 at 105.4 MHz, Sargam at 105.8 MHz, Legend at 107.2 MHz, and RF2 at 1152 kHz. On **Taveuni,** you may hear Radio Mirchi at 98.2 MHz, Radio Fiji Gold at 100.6 MHz, and Bula FM at 103.0 MHz.

The local stations broadcast mostly pop music and repetitive advertising with very little news or commentary (the presenters sometimes get things hilariously mixed up). Radio Fiji Gold broadcasts local news and a weather report weekdays at 0700 and 1700. Radio FM 96 broadcasts news and weather on the hour weekdays 0600–1900, Saturdays and Sundays at 0700–1900.

Fiji doesn't have a shortwave broadcaster, but the **BBC World Service** is rebroadcast over 88.2 MHz FM in Suva, Nadi, and Lautoka 24 hours a day. In Suva, you can also get Radio France International (RFI) in French at 91.8 MHz FM.

TOURIST INFORMATION
Information
Government-funded **Tourism Fiji** (tel. 330-2433, www.fijime.com), formerly known as the Fiji Visitors Bureau, mails out general

TOURIST OFFICES

Fiji Islands: Tourism Fiji, P.O. Box 9217, Nadi Airport, Fiji Islands; tel. 679/672-2433, www.fijime.com

United States: Tourism Fiji, 5777 West Century Blvd., Suite 220, Los Angeles, CA 90045, USA; tel. 310/568-1616, www.bulafijinow.com

Australia: Tourism Fiji, Level 12, St. Martin's Tower, 31 Market St., Sydney, NSW 2000, Australia; tel. 61-2/9264-3399, www.bulafiji-au.com

New Zealand: Tourism Fiji, P.O. Box 47056, Ponsonby, Auckland, New Zealand; tel. 64-9/376-2533, www.bulafiji.co.nz

Korea: Tourism Fiji, Suite 301, 740-19, Gurodong, Gurong, Seoul, Korea; tel. 82-2/363-7955, www.bula-fiji.com

Japan: Tourism Fiji, 14th floor, NOA Bldg., 3-5, 2-Chome, Azabudai, Minato-ku, Tokyo 106, Japan; tel. 81-3/3587-2561, www.bulafiji-jp.com

United Kingdom: Tourism Fiji, Lion House, 111 Hare Lane, Claygate, Surrey KT10 0QY, United Kingdom; tel. 44-1372/475-772

Germany: Tourism Fiji, Karl Marx Alee 91a, 10243 Berlin, Germany; tel. 49-30/4225-6285, www.bulafiji.de

brochures, free upon request. Since the closing of their Suva office in 2009, they don't provide any walk-in tourist information offices in Fiji, only an administration office in Nadi. Their overseas offices are listed on www.southpacific .org/info.html. Ask for free copies of the *Jasons Fiji Islands Map* and *Jasons Visitors Guide*, both of which only promote their advertisers.

Travel Agencies

If you like the security of advance reservations but aren't interested in joining a regular packaged tour, several Fiji-based companies specialize in booking cruises, hotel rooms, airport transfers, sightseeing tours, rental cars, etc. Only the Captain Cook and Blue Lagoon mini-cruises need to be booked far in advance from abroad; upon arrival you'll have dozens of hotels and resorts competing for your business. So rather than risk being exiled to one of Fiji's most expensive resorts by some agent thinking only of his/her commission, consider waiting to make most of your ground arrangements upon arrival at Nadi Airport.

Fiji's largest in-bound tour operator is **Rosie Holidays** (tel. 672-2755, www.rosiefiji.com), with a 24-hour office in the arrivals arcade at Nadi Airport and 16 branches around Viti Levu. This guide will give you an idea of what's out there, and upon arrival in Fiji, Rosie can make your accommodations bookings for you on the spot. Of course, you run the risk of finding that your place of choice is fully booked. This locally owned business has provided efficient, personalized service since 1974.

Rosie's main competitor is **ATS Pacific** (tel. 672-2811, www.atspacific.com.fj), or Allied Tours Services, with an office at Nadi Airport and tour desks at many Nadi and Coral Coast hotels. **Coral Sun Fiji** (tel. 672-3105, www .coralsunfiji.com) at Nadi Airport is also very reliable. **Sun Vacations** (tel. 672-4273, www.sunvacationsfiji.com) at Nadi Airport is a smaller company offering personalized service. Numerous other private travel agencies have offices at Nadi Airport and in town, many of them oriented toward backpackers or budget travelers.

TIME AND MEASUREMENTS
Time

The international date line generally follows 180 degrees longitude and creates a difference of 24 hours in time between the two sides. It swings east at Tuvalu to avoid slicing Fiji in two. Everything in the Eastern Hemisphere west of the date line is a day later, while everything in the Western Hemisphere east of the line is a day earlier (or behind). Air travelers lose a day when they fly west across the date line and gain it back when they return. Keep track of things by repeating to yourself, *If it's Sunday in Seattle, it's Monday in Manila.*

Fiji time is Greenwich Mean Time (GMT) plus 12 hours. When it's noon in Fiji, it will be 1000 in Sydney, 1200 in Auckland (same time), 1300 in Tonga, 1400 the day before in Hawaii, 1600 the day before in Los Angeles, 1900 the day before in Toronto, and midnight in London, England. To look at it another way, Fiji is 20 hours ahead of California and two hours ahead of Sydney, Australia. Daylight saving time is in effect from late October to late March. You can check the exact time locally in Fiji by dialing 014.

You're better telephoning Fiji from North America in the evening, as it will be mid-afternoon in the islands (plus you'll probably benefit from off-peak telephone rates). From Europe, call very late at night. In the other direction, if you're calling from Fiji to North America or Europe, do so in the early morning, as it will already be afternoon in North America and evening in Europe.

In this guide, all clock times are rendered according to the 24-hour system, so that, for example, 0100 is 1:00 A.M., 1300 is 1:00 P.M., 2330 is 11:30 P.M. There isn't much twilight in the tropics, and when the sun begins to go down, you've got less than half an hour before nightfall.

The islanders operate on "coconut time"— the nut will fall when it is ripe. In the languid air of the South Seas, punctuality takes on a new meaning. Appointments are approximate and service casual. Even the seasons are fuzzy: sometimes wetter, sometimes drier, but almost always hot. Slow down to the island pace, and get in step with where you are.

Measurements

The metric system is used in Fiji. Most distances herein are quoted in kilometers—they become easy to comprehend when you know that one kilometer is the distance that a normal person walks in 10 minutes. A meter is slightly more than a yard, and a liter is just more than a quart.

Electric Currents

If you're taking along a plug-in razor, radio, computer, camera battery charger, electric immersion coil, or other electrical appliance, be aware that Fiji uses 240 AC voltage, 50 cycles.

Most appliances require a converter to change from one voltage to another. You'll also need an adapter to cope with the three-pronged socket plugs (with the two top prongs at angles). Pick up both items before you leave home, as they can be hard to find here.

Videos

Commercial travel videotapes make nice souvenirs, but always keep in mind that there are three incompatible video formats in the world: NTSC (used in North America), PAL (used in Britain, Germany, Japan, Australia, New Zealand, and Fiji), and SECAM (used in France and Russia). Don't buy prerecorded tapes abroad unless they're the same kind used in your country. The same applies to DVDs.

RESOURCES

Glossary

A$ Australian dollars

adi the female equivalent of *ratu*

archipelago a group of islands

ATM automated teller machine

atoll a low-lying, ring-shaped coral reef enclosing a lagoon

balabala tree fern

balawa pandanus, screw pine

balolo in Fijian, a reef worm *(Eunice viridis)*

bark cloth see tapa

barrier reef a coral reef separated from the adjacent shore by a lagoon

bêche-de-mer sea cucumber; an edible sea slug

beka flying fox

bete a traditional priest of the old religion

bilibili a bamboo raft

bilo a kava-drinking cup made from a coconut shell

blackbirder A 19th-century European recruiter of island labor, mostly ni-Vanuatu and Solomon Islanders taken to work on plantations in Queensland and Fiji

Bose vaka-Turaga Great Council of Chiefs

Bose vaka-Yasana Provincial Council

breadfruit a large, round fruit with starchy flesh, often baked in the *lovo*

bula **shirt** a colorful Fijian aloha shirt

buli Fijian administrative officer in charge of a *tikina;* subordinate of the *roko tui*

bure a Fijian house

BYO Bring Your Own (used to refer to restaurants that allow you to bring your own alcoholic beverages)

C Celsius

caldera a wide crater formed through the collapse or explosion of a volcano

cassava manioc; the starchy edible root of the tapioca plant

CDW collision damage waiver

chain an archaic unit of length equivalent to 20 meters

ciguatera a form of fish poisoning caused by microscopic algae

codeshare a system whereby two or more airlines own seats on a single flight

coir coconut-husk sennit used to make rope, etc.

confirmation A confirmed reservation exists when a supplier acknowledges, either orally or in writing, that a booking has been accepted.

copra dried coconut meat used in the manufacturing of coconut oil, cosmetics, soap, and margarine

coral a hard, calcareous substance of various shapes, composed of the skeletons of tiny marine animals called polyps

coral bank a coral formation more than 150 meters long

coral bleaching the expulsion of symbiotic algae by corals

coral head a coral formation a few meters across

coral patch a coral formation up to 150 meters long

cyclone Also known as a hurricane (in the Caribbean) or typhoon (in Japan). A tropical storm that rotates around a center of low atmospheric pressure, it becomes a cyclone when its winds reach force 12 or 64 knots. At sea, the air will be filled with foam and driving spray, and the water surface will be completely white with 14-meter-high waves. In the Northern Hemisphere, cyclones spin counterclockwise, while south of the equator they move clockwise. The winds of cyclonic storms are deflected toward a low-pressure area at the center, although the "eye" of the cyclone may be calm.

dalo see taro

Degei the greatest of the pre-Christian Fijian gods

desiccated coconut the shredded meat of dehydrated fresh coconut

direct flight a through flight with one or more stops, but no change of aircraft, as opposed to a nonstop flight

drua an ancient Fijian double canoe

dugong a large plant-eating marine mammal; called a manatee in the Caribbean

EEZ Exclusive Economic Zone; a 200-nautical-mile offshore belt of an island nation or seacoast state that controls the mineral exploitation and fishing rights

endemic native to a particular area and existing only there

expatriate a person residing in a country other than his/her own; in the South Pacific, such persons are also called "Europeans" if their skin is white, or simply "expats."

F$ Fiji dollars

FAD fish aggregation device

fissure a narrow crack or chasm of some length and depth

FIT foreign independent travel; a custom-designed, prepaid tour composed of many individualized arrangements

4WD four-wheel drive

fringing reef a reef along the shore of an island

GPS Global Positioning System, the space-age successor of the sextant

guano manure of seabirds or bats, used as a fertilizer

guyot a submerged atoll, the coral of which couldn't keep up with rising water levels

hurricane see cyclone

ika fish

ivi the Polynesian chestnut tree (Inocarpus edulis)

jug a cross between a ceramic kettle and a pitcher, used to heat water for tea or coffee in Australian-style hotels

kai freshwater mussel

kaihidi an Indo-Fijian

kaisi a commoner

kaivalagi a European

kaiviti an indigenous Fijian

kava a Polynesian word for the drink known in the Fijian language as yaqona and in English slang as "grog." This traditional beverage is made by squeezing a mixture of the grated root of the pepper shrub (Piper methysticum) and cold water through a strainer of hibiscus-bark fiber.

kerekere asking or borrowing something from a member of one's own group

km kilometer

knot about three kilometers per hour

kokoda chopped raw fish and sea urchins marinated with onions and lemon

koro village

kph kilometers per hour

kumala sweet potato (Ipomoea batatas)

kumi stenciled tapa cloth

lagoon an expanse of water bounded by a reef

lali a hollow-log drum hit with a stick

lapita pottery pottery made by the ancient Polynesians from 1600–500 B.C.

LDS Latter-day Saints; the Mormons

leeward downwind; the shore (or side) sheltered from the wind; as opposed to windward

liveaboard a tour boat with cabin accommodation for scuba divers

LMS London Missionary Society; a Protestant group that spread Christianity from Tahiti (1797) across the Pacific

lolo coconut cream

lovo an underground, earthen oven (called an umu in the Polynesian languages); after A.D. 500, the Polynesians had lost the art of making pottery, so they were compelled to bake their food rather than boil it.

magiti feast

mahimahi dorado, Pacific dolphin fish (no relation to the mammal)

mana authority, prestige, virtue, "face," psychic power, a positive force

mangrove a tropical shrub with branches that send down roots forming dense thickets along tidal shores

manioc cassava, tapioca, a starchy root crop

masa kesa freehand painted tapa

masi see tapa

mata ni vanua an orator who speaks for a high chief

mataqali a landowning extended family

matrilineal a system of tracing descent through the mother's familial line

meke traditional song and dance

Melanesia the high island groups of the western Pacific (Fiji, New Caledonia, Vanuatu, Solomon Islands, Papua New Guinea); from *melas* (black)

Micronesia chains of high and low islands mostly north of the Equator (Carolines, Gilberts, Marianas, Marshalls); from *micro* (small)

mm millimeters

MV motor vessel

mynah an Indian starling-like bird (*Gracula*)

NAUI National Association of Underwater Instructors

NGO nongovernmental organization

NFIP Nuclear-Free and Independent Pacific movement

N.Z. New Zealand

overbooking the practice of confirming more seats, cabins, or rooms than are actually available to insure against no-shows

Pacific Rim the continental landmasses and large countries around the fringe of the Pacific

PADI Professional Association of Dive Instructors (also Put Another Dollar In, or Pay And Dive Immediately)

palusami a Samoan specialty of coconut cream wrapped in taro leaves and baked

pandanus screw pine with slender stem and prop roots. The sword-shaped leaves are used for plaiting mats and hats.

parasailing a sport in which participants are carried aloft by a parachute pulled behind a speedboat

pass a channel through a barrier reef, usually with an outward flow of water

passage an inside passage between an island and a barrier reef

patrilineal a system of tracing descent through the father's familial line

pawpaw papaya

pelagic relating to the open sea, away from land

Polynesia divided into Western Polynesia (Tonga and Samoa) and Eastern Polynesia (French Polynesia, Cook Islands, Hawaii, Easter Island, and New Zealand); from *poly* (many)

pp per person

punt a flat-bottomed boat

qoliqoli traditional fishing rights claimed by Fijian clans

Quonset hut a prefabricated, semicircular, metal shelter popular during World War II; also called a Nissen hut

rain shadow the dry side of a mountain, sheltered from the windward side

rara a grassy village square

ratu a title for Fijian chiefs, prefixed to their names

reef a coral ridge near the ocean surface

roko tui senior Fijian administrative officer

roti a flat Indian bread

sailing the fine art of getting wet and becoming ill while slowly going nowhere at great expense

salusalu garland, lei

scuba self-contained underwater breathing apparatus

SDA Seventh-Day Adventist

self-catering see self-contained

self-contained a room with private facilities (a toilet and shower not shared with other guests); the brochure term "en suite" means the same thing; as opposed to a "self-catering" unit with cooking facilities

sennit braided coconut-fiber rope

sevusevu a formal presentation of *yaqona*

shifting cultivation a method of farming involving the rotation of fields instead of crops

shoal a shallow sandbar or mud bank

shoulder season a travel period between high/peak and low/off-peak seasons

SPREP South Pacific Regional Environment Program

subduction the action of one tectonic plate wedging under another

subsidence geological sinking or settling

sulu a wraparound skirt or loincloth similar to a sarong

symbiosis a mutually advantageous relationship between unlike organisms

tabu taboo, forbidden, sacred, set apart, a negative force

tabua a whale's tooth, a ceremonial object

takia a small sailing canoe

talanoa to chat or tell stories

tanoa a special wide wooden bowl in which yaqona (kava) is mixed; used in ceremonies in Fiji, Tonga, and Samoa

tapa a cloth made from the pounded bark of the paper mulberry tree (Broussonetia papyrifera). It's soaked and beaten with a mallet to flatten and intertwine the fibers, then painted with geometric designs; called siapo in Samoan, masi in Fijian.

tapu see tabu

taro a starchy elephant-eared tuber (Colocasia esculenta), a staple food of the Pacific Islanders; called dalo in Fijian

tavioka tapioca, cassava, manioc, arrowroot

teitei a garden

tel. telephone

tiki a humanlike sculpture used in the old days for religious rites and sorcery

tikina a group of Fijian villages administered by a buli

timeshare part ownership of a residential unit with the right to occupy the premises for a certain period each year, in exchange for payment of an annual maintenance fee

trade wind a steady wind blowing toward the equator from either northeast or southeast

trench the section at the bottom of the ocean where one tectonic plate wedges under another

tridacna clam eaten everywhere in the Pacific, its size varies between 10 centimeters and one meter

tropical storm a cyclonic storm with winds of 35–64 knots

tsunami a fast-moving wave caused by an undersea earthquake; sometimes erroneously called a tidal wave

tui king

turaga chief

turaga-ni-koro village herald or mayor

U.S. United States

US$ U.S. dollars

vakaviti in the Fijian way

vale lailai toilet

vanua land, region

vigia a mark on a nautical chart indicating a dangerous rock or shoal

VSO Volunteer Service Overseas, the British equivalent of the Peace Corps

waka a bundle of whole kava roots

windward the point or side from which the wind blows, as opposed to leeward

yam the starchy, tuberous root of a climbing plant

yaqona see kava

yasana an administrative province

zories rubber shower sandals, thongs, flip-flops

Phrasebook

BASIC FIJIAN

Although most people in Fiji speak English fluently, mother tongues include Fijian, Hindi, and other Pacific languages. Knowledge of a few words of Fijian, especially slang words, will make your stay more exciting and enriching. Fijian has no pure *b*, *c*, or *d* sounds, as they are known in English. When the first missionaries arrived, they invented a system of spelling, with one letter for each Fijian sound. The reader should be aware that the sound "mb" is written *b*, "nd" is *d*, "ng" is *g*, "ngg" is *q*, and "th" is *c*.

Au lako mai Kenada. I come from Canada.
Au ni lako mai vei? Where do you come from?
Au sa lako ki vei? Where are you going?
bula a Fijian greeting
bure a Fijian thatched house
Daru lako! Let's go!
dua one
dua oo said by males when they meet a chief or enter a Fijian dua
io yes
kaivalagi foreigner
kana eat
kauta mai bring
kauta tani take away
Kocei na yacamu? What's your name?
koro village
lailai small
lako mai come
lako tani go
levu big, much
lima five
Loloma yani Please pass along my regards.
magimagi coconut rope fiber
magiti feast
maleka delicious
marama madam
mataqali a clan lineage
moce goodbye
Na cava oqo? What is this?
ni sa bula Hello, how are you? (can also say *sa bula* or *bula vinaka*; the answer is *an sa bula vinaka*)

ni sa moce good night
ni sa yadra good morning
qara cave
rua two
sa vinaka it's okay
sega no, none
sega na leqa you're welcome
sota tale see you again
talatala reverend
tale once more
tolu three
tulou excuse me
turaga sir, Mr.
uro a provocative greeting for the opposite sex
va four
vaka lailai a little, small
vaka levu a lot, great
vaka malua slowly
vaka totolo fast
vale house
vale lailai toilet
vanua land, custom, people
vinaka thank you
vinaka vakalevu thank you very much
vu an ancestral spirit
wai water
yadra good morning
yalo vinaka please
yaqona kava, grog

BASIC HINDI

aao come
accha good
bhaahut julum very beautiful (slang)
chota small (male)
choti small (female)
dhanyabaad thank you
ek aur one more
haan yes
hum jauo I go (slang)
jalebi an Indian sweet
jao go
kab when
kahaan where

Kahaan jata hai? Where are you going?
Kaise hai? How are you?
khana food
Kitna? How much?
kya what
laao bring
maaf kijye ga excuse me
nahi no
namaste hello, goodbye

pani water
rait okay
ram ram same as *namaste*
roti a flat Indian bread
seedhe jauo go straight
Theek bhai I'm fine
Yeh kia hai? What's this?
yihaan here

Suggested Reading

DESCRIPTION AND TRAVEL

Geraghty, Craig, Glen, and Paul. *Children of the Sun.* Gympie, Australia: Glen Craig Publishing, 1996. This photo book is like one big Fiji family picture album in glorious color.

Gravelle, Kim. *Romancing the Islands.* Suva: Graphics Pacific, 1997. In these 42 stories, ex-American, now-Fiji resident Kim Gravelle shares a quarter-century of adventures in the region. A delightfully sympathetic look at the islands and their characters.

Nimmerfroh, Achim. *Fiji's Wild Beauty.* Germany: Nimmerfroh Dive Productions, 2006. A photographic guide to the coral reefs of the South Pacific with more than 750 images of marine creatures.

Stephenson, Dr. Elsie. *Fiji's Past on Picture Postcards.* Suva: Fiji Museum, 1997. Some 275 old postcards of Fiji from the Caines Jannif collection.

Theroux, Paul. *The Happy Isles of Oceania: Paddling the Pacific.* London: Hamish Hamilton, 1992. The author of classic accounts of railway journeys sets out with kayak and tent to tour the Pacific.

Traditional Handicrafts of Fiji. Suva: Institute of Pacific Studies, 1997. The significance and history of Fijian handicrafts.

Troost, J. Maarten. *Getting Stoned with Savages.* New York: Broadway Books, 2006. An amusing trip through the islands of Fiji and Vanuatu by the author of *The Sex Lives of Cannibals.*

Wright, Ronald. *On Fiji Islands.* New York: Penguin Books, 1986. Wright relates his travels to Fijian history and tradition in a most pleasing and informative way.

GEOGRAPHY

Derrick, R. A. *The Fiji Islands: Geographical Handbook.* Suva: Government Printing Office, 1965. Derrick's earlier *History of Fiji* (1946) was a trailblazing work.

Donnelly, Quanchi, and Kerr. *Fiji in the Pacific: A History and Geography of Fiji.* Australia: Jacaranda Wiley, 1994. A high school text on the country.

Nunn, Patrick D. *Oceanic Islands.* Cambridge, Mass.: Blackwell, 1994. A basic text on island formation, coral reefs, and sea-level change.

Nunn, Patrick D. *Pacific Island Landscapes.* Suva: Institute of Pacific Studies, 1998. A leading geographer demystifies the geology and geomorphology of Fiji, Samoa, and Tonga, with emphasis on the origin of the islands.

NATURAL SCIENCE

Allen, Gerald R., and Roger Steene. *Indo-Pacific Coral Reef Field Guide*. El Cajon, Calif.: Odyssey Publishing, 1998. Essential for identifying the creatures of the reefs.

Lebot, Vincent, Lamont Lindstrom, and Mark Marlin. *Kava—the Pacific Drug*. New Haven, Conn.: Yale University Press, 1993. A thorough examination of kava and its many uses.

Randall, John E., Gerald Robert Allen, and Roger C. Steene. *Fishes of the Great Barrier Reef and Coral Sea*. Honolulu: University of Hawaii Press, 1997. An identification guide for amateur diver and specialist alike.

Ryan, Paddy. *Fiji's Natural Heritage*. Auckland: Exisle Publishing, 2000. With 500 photos and 288 pages of text, this is probably the most comprehensive popular book on any Pacific island ecosystem.

Ryan, Paddy. *The Snorkeler's Guide to the Coral Reef*. Honolulu: University of Hawaii Press, 1994. An introduction to the wonders of the Indo-Pacific reefs. The author spent 10 years in Fiji and knows the country well.

Veron, J. E. N. *Corals of Australia and the Indo-Pacific*. Honolulu: University of Hawaii Press, 1993. An authoritative, illustrated work.

Watling, Dick. *A Guide to the Birds of Fiji & Western Polynesia*. Suva: Environmental Consultants, 2001. The guide has detailed species accounts for the 173 species with confirmed records in the region, and notes a further 22 species with unconfirmed records. Copies can be ordered through www.pacificbirds.com.

Watling, Dick. *Mai Veikau: Tales of Fijian Wildlife*. Suva: Fiji Times, 1986. A wealth of easily digested information on Fiji's flora and fauna. Copies are available in Fiji bookstores.

Wheatley, Nigel. *Where to Watch Birds in Australasia and Oceania*. Princeton University Press, 1998. The descriptions of nature reserves and forested areas will interest any ecotourist.

Whistler, W. Arthur. *Flowers of the Pacific Island Seashore*. Honolulu: University of Hawaii Press, 1993. A guide to the littoral plants of Hawaii, Tahiti, Samoa, Tonga, Cook Islands, Fiji, and Micronesia.

HISTORY

Clunie, Fergus. *Yalo i Viti*. Suva: Fiji Museum, 1986. An illustrated catalog of the museum's collection, with lots of intriguing background information provided.

Derrick, R. A. *A History of Fiji*. Suva: Government Press, 1946. This classic work, by a former director of the Fiji Museum, deals with the period up to 1874 only. It was reprinted in 1974 and should be available at bookstores in Fiji.

Ewins, Rory. *Colour, Class and Custom: The Literature of the 1987 Fiji Coup*. 2nd ed., 1998. Available online at http://speedysnail.com/pacific/fiji_coup.

Field, Michael, Tupeni Baba, and Unaisi Nabobo-Baba. *Speight of Violence: Inside Fiji's 2000 Coup*. Honolulu: University of Hawaii Press, 2005. A powerful account of events that continue to haunt Fiji, as told by a former hostage, the hostage's wife on the outside, and a veteran Pacific reporter.

Fraenkel, Jon, and Stewart Firth, eds. *From Election to Coup in Fiji*. Suva: IPS Publications, 2007. A panel of political observers discusses the 2006 election campaign and its aftermath.

Howard, Michael C. *Fiji: Race and Politics in an Island State*. Vancouver: University of British Columbia Press, 1991. Perhaps the best scholarly study of the background and root causes of the first two Fiji coups.

Lal, Brij V. *Broken Waves: A History of the Fiji Islands in the 20th Century.* Honolulu: University of Hawaii Press, 1992. Lal is a penetrating writer who uses language accessible to the layperson.

Thomson, Peter. *Kava in the Blood.* Auckland: Tandem Press, 1999. Thomson served as permanent secretary to Fiji's governor-general at the time of the 1987 Rabuka coups. His behind-the-scenes account helps explain the complicated political situation in Fiji.

Wallis, Mary. *Life in Feejee: Five Years Among the Cannibals.* First published in 1851, this book is the memoir of a New England sea captain's wife in Fiji. It's a charming, if rather gruesome, firsthand account of early European contact with Fiji and has some fascinating details of Fijian customs. You'll find ample mention of Cakobau, who hadn't yet converted to Christianity. Reprinted by the Fiji Museum, Suva, in 1983, but again out of print. A rare South Seas classic!

Wallis, Mary. *The Fiji and New Caledonia Journals of Mary Wallis, 1851–1853.* Suva: Institute of Pacific Studies, 1994. This reprint of the sequel to *Life in Feejee* offers many insights, and the editor, David Routledge, has added numerous notes.

Waterhouse, Joseph. *The King and People of Fiji.* Honolulu: University of Hawaii Press, 1997. The Reverend Joseph Waterhouse witnessed Fijian life at the earliest stages of the 19th century. His work offers an excellent insight into the traditional Fijian way of life.

SOCIAL SCIENCE

Colpani, Satya. *Beyond the Black Waters: A Memoir of Sir Sathi Narain.* Suva: Institute of Pacific Studies, 1996. Having migrated from southern India with his family, Sir Sathi Narain (1919–1989) became a leader in the construction industry and an influential figure in the country's life.

Norton, Robert. *Race and Politics in Fiji.* St. Lucia, Australia: University of Queensland Press, 1990. A revised edition of the 1977 classic. Norton emphasizes the flexibility of Fijian culture, which was able to absorb the impact of two military coups without any loss of life.

Ravuvu, Asesela. *Development or Dependence: The Pattern of Change in a Fijian Village.* Suva: Institute of Pacific Studies, 1988. Highlights the unforeseen negative impacts of development in a Fijian village.

Roth, G. Kingsley. *Fijian Way of Life.* 2nd ed. Melbourne: Oxford University Press, 1973. A standard reference on Fijian culture.

LANGUAGE AND LITERATURE

Capell, A. *A New Fijian Dictionary.* Suva: Government Printer, 1991. A Fijian-English dictionary invaluable for anyone interested in learning the language. Scholars generally have a low opinion of this work, which contains hundreds of errors, but it's still a handy reference. Also see C. Maxwell Churchward's *A New Fijian Grammar.*

Griffen, Arlene, ed. *With Heart and Nerve and Sinew: Post-coup Writing from Fiji.* Suva: Marama Club, 1997. An eclectic collection of responses to the first coups and life in Fiji thereafter.

Hereniko, Vilsoni, and Teresia Teaiwa. *Last Virgin in Paradise.* Suva: Institute of Pacific Studies, 1993. The Rotuman Hereniko has written a number of plays, including *Don't Cry Mama* (1977), *A Child for Iva* (1987), and *The Monster* (1989).

Kikau, Eci. *The Wisdom of Fiji.* Suva: Institute of Pacific Studies, 1981. This extensive collection of Fijian proverbs opens a window to understanding Fijian society, culture, and philosophy.

London, Jack. *South Sea Tales.* New York: Random House (Modern Library Classics), 2002. Stories based on London's visit to Tahiti, Samoa, Fiji, and the Solomon Islands in the early 20th century.

Lynch, John. *Pacific Languages: An Introduction.* Honolulu: University of Hawaii Press, 1998. The grammatical features of the Oceanic, Papuan, and Australian languages.

Tarte, Daryl. *Islands of the Frigate Bird.* Suva: Institute of Pacific Studies, 1999. A novel about the struggle for survival of Central Pacific peoples.

Veramu, Joseph C. *Moving Through the Streets.* Suva: Institute of Pacific Studies, 1994. A fast-moving novel providing insights into the lifestyles, pressures, and temptations of teenagers in Suva. Veramu has also written a collection of short stories called *The Black Messiah* (1989).

Wendt, Albert, ed. *Nuanua: Pacific Writing in English Since 1980.* Honolulu, University of Hawaii Press, 1995. This worthwhile anthology of contemporary Pacific literature includes works by 10 Fijian writers including Prem Banfal, Sudesh Mishra, Satendra Nandan, and Som Prakash.

REFERENCE BOOKS

Crocombe, Ron. *The South Pacific.* Suva: University of the South Pacific, 2001. Parameters, patterns, perceptions, property, power, and prospects in the 28 nations and territories of Oceania.

Douglas, Ngaire, and Norman Douglas, eds. *Pacific Islands Yearbook.* Suva: Fiji Times, 1994. First published in 1932, this is the 17th edition of the original sourcebook on the islands. Although the realities of modern publishing have led to the demise of both the *Yearbook* and its cousin, *Pacific Islands Monthly,* this final edition remains an indispensable reference work for students of the region.

Gorman, G. E., and J. J. Mills. *Fiji: World Bibliographical Series, Volume 173.* Oxford: Clio Press, 1994. Critical reviews of 673 of the most important books about Fiji.

Lal, Brig V., and Kate Fortune, eds. *The Pacific Islands: An Encyclopedia.* Honolulu: University of Hawaii Press, 2000. This important book combines the writings of 200 acknowledged experts on the physical environment, peoples, history, politics, economics, society, and culture of the South Pacific. The accompanying CD-ROM provides a wealth of maps, graphs, photos, biographies, and more.

BOOKSELLERS AND PUBLISHERS

Some of the books listed here are out of print and not available at bookstores. Major research libraries should have a few; otherwise, check the specialized antiquarian booksellers or regional publishers listed in this section for hard-to-find books on Fiji. Sources of detailed topographical maps or navigational charts are provided in the following section. Many titles can be ordered online through www.south pacific.org/books.html.

Bibliophile, 103 Adelaide Parade, Woollahra, Sydney, NSW 2025, Australia (tel. 02/9387-1154, www.bibliophile.com.au). An antiquarian bookstore specializing in books about Oceania. View their extensive catalog online.

Book Bin, 215 SW 4th St., Corvallis, OR 97333, USA (tel. 541/752-0040, www.book bin.com). Their searchable catalog of books on the Pacific Islands at Abe Books lists hundreds of rare titles.

Pacific Island Books, 2802 East 132nd Circle, Thornton, CO 80241, USA (tel. 303/920-

8338, www.pacificislandbooks.com). One of the best U.S. sources of books about Fiji. They stock many titles originally published by the Institute of Pacific Studies.

Serendipity Books, P.O. Box 1244, West Leederville, WA 6901, Australia (tel. 08/9382-2246, www.serendipitybooks.com.au). The largest stocks of antiquarian, secondhand, and out-of-print books on the Pacific in Western Australia.

University Book Centre, University of the South Pacific, P.O. Box 1168, Suva, Fiji Islands (tel. 323-2500, www.uspbookcentre.com). An excellent source of books written and produced in the South Pacific itself.

University of Hawaii Press, 2840 Kolowalu St., Honolulu, HI 96822-1888, USA (tel. 808/956-8255, www.uhpress.hawaii.edu). Their *Hawaii and the Pacific* catalog is well worth requesting if you're trying to build a Pacific library.

MAPS

Bier, James A. *Reference Map of Oceania.* Honolulu: University of Hawaii Press, 2007. A fully indexed map of the Pacific Islands with 51 detailed inset maps of individual islands. Useful details such as time zones are included.

Bluewater Books & Charts, 1811 Cordova Rd., Fort Lauderdale, FL 33316, USA (tel. 954/763-6533 or 800/942-2583, www.bluewaterweb.com). An outstanding source of navigational charts and cruising guides to the Pacific.

Fiji Hydrographic Office, P.O. Box 362, Suva, Fiji Islands (tel. 331-5457). Produces navigational charts of the Yasawas, Kadavu, eastern Vanua Levu, and the Lau Group. The U.S. agent is Captains Nautical Supplies, 2500 15th Ave. West, Seattle, WA 98119, USA (tel. 800/448-2278, www.captainsnautical.com).

International Maps. Hema Maps Pty. Ltd., P.O. Box 4365, Eight Mile Plains, QLD 4113, Australia (tel. 07/3340-0000, www.hemamaps.com.au). Maps of the Pacific, Fiji, Solomon Islands, Vanuatu, and Samoa.

Lands and Surveys Department. Plan and Map Sales, P.O. Box 2222, Government Buildings, Suva, Fiji Islands (tel. 321-1460, www.lands.gov.fj). The main publisher of topographical maps of Fiji with a 1:50,000 series covering most of the country.

PERIODICALS

Commodores' Bulletin. Seven Seas Cruising Assn., 2501 East Commercial Blvd., Suite 201, Fort Lauderdale, FL 33308, USA (tel. 954/771-5660, www.ssca.org, US$75 a year worldwide by airmail). This monthly bulletin is chock-full of useful information for anyone wishing to tour the Pacific by sailing boat. All Pacific yachties and friends should be Seven Seas members!

Islands Business. P.O. Box 12718, Suva, Fiji Islands (tel. 330-3108, www.islandsbusiness.com, annual airmailed subscription A$45 to Australia, NZ$65 to New Zealand, US$52 to North America, US$62 to Europe). A monthly newsmagazine, with in-depth coverage of political and economic trends around the Pacific. Travel and aviation news gets some prominence.

Surfer Travel Reports. P.O. Box 1028, Dana Point, CA 92629, USA (www.surfermag.com/travel/pacific). Each month, this newsletter provides a detailed analysis of surfing conditions at a different destination (the last report on Fiji was Issue 7, No. 12). Back issues on specific countries are available at US$7 each. This is your best source of surfing information by far.

The Contemporary Pacific. University of Hawaii Press, 2840 Kolowalu St., Honolulu, HI 96822, USA (www.uhpress.hawaii.edu, published twice a year, US$35 a year). Publishes a good mix of articles of interest to both scholars and general readers; the country-by-country "Political Review" in each number is a concise summary of events during the preceding year. The "Dialogue" section offers informed comment on the more controversial issues in the region, while recent publications on the islands are examined through book reviews. Those interested in current topics in Pacific island affairs should check recent volumes for background information.

Undercurrent. 3020 Bridgeway, Ste. 102, Sausalito, CA 94965, USA (tel. 415/289-0501 or 800/326-1896, www.undercurrent.org, US$20 for six months). An online monthly consumer-protection-oriented newsletter for serious scuba divers. Unlike virtually every other diving publication, *Undercurrent* accepts no advertising or free trips, which allows its writers to tell it as it is. Some back issues can be read online for free.

DISCOGRAPHY

Music lovers will be pleased to know that authentic Pacific music is readily available on compact disc. In compiling this selection we've tried to list noncommercial recordings that are faithful to the traditional music of the islands as it exists today. Island music based on Western pop has been avoided. You can buy many of these CDs at music shops in Suva, or order them online through www.southpacific .org/music.html.

Bula Fiji Bula. New York: Arc Music, 2001. Music of the Fiji Islands, including "Isa Lei."

Fanshawe, David, ed. *South Pacific: Island Music.* New York: Nonesuch Records, 2003. First released in 1981, this recording takes you from Tahiti to the Cook Islands, Tonga, Samoa, Fiji, Kiribati, and the Solomon Islands.

Fanshawe, David, ed. *Spirit of Melanesia.* United Kingdom: Saydisc Records, 1998. An anthology of the music of the five countries of Melanesia, with seven tracks from Fiji. Recorded in 1978, 1983, and 1994.

Linkels, Ad, and Lucia Linkels, eds. *Rabi.* The Netherlands: Pan Records, 2000. Music from Rabi, the new home of the exiled Banabans of Ocean Island, recorded on Rabi in 1997 and 1998.

Linkels, Ad, and Lucia Linkels, eds. *Tautoga.* The Netherlands: Pan Records, 1999. The songs and dances of Rotuma, Fiji, recorded on the island in 1996. It's believed the *tautoga* dance arrived from Tonga in the 18th century.

Linkels, Ad, and Lucia Linkels, eds. *Viti Levu.* The Netherlands: Pan Records, 2000. This unique recording provides 20 examples of real Fijian music, from "Isa Lei" to Bula rock, plus four Indo-Fijian pieces. Recorded between 1986 and 1998, it's the best of its kind on the market.

Magic of the South Seas. New York: Arc Music, 2000. An anthology of music from Tahiti, the Marquesas Islands, Tonga, and Fiji.

Internet Resources

Backpacking Fiji
www.fijibudget.com
An umbrella website for more than a dozen backpacker resorts and dive shops in the central Yasawas.

Bureau of Statistics
www.statsfiji.gov.fj
Provides a wealth of statistical data on Fiji in an accessible format.

Fiji Accommodation and Travel
www.fiji.travelmaxia.com
This Travelmaxia site documents dozens of upscale resorts and hotels, with details on specials and packages, plus maps, photos, and online forms. It's surprisingly precise and up to date.

Fijian Village Homestays
www.fijibure.com
This unique site introduces around a dozen authentic village homestay opportunities around Viti Levu.

Fiji A to Z
www.fijiatoz.com
A "small guide" to Fiji presenting information about the country in a pleasing alphabetical format.

Fiji Government Online
www.fiji.gov.fj
This crisply clear, dynamic site is well worth visiting to taste the image local politicians and bureaucrats try to present to the world. The press releases are often edifying.

Fiji Guide
www.fijiguide.com
An interactive Fiji travel community with an impressive guide section based on Rob Kay's original Lonely Planet guide to Fiji.

Fiji Hotels
www.fiji-hotels.com.fj
Listings of budget, mid-range, and top-end accommodations all around Fiji.

Fiji Islands Backpackers Guide
www.fiji-backpacking.com
A well-organized website full of budget-saving ideas, background on Fiji and the Fijians, accommodations listings, information on transportation and activities, and even a Fijian language section.

Fiji Live
www.fijilive.com
Fiji's largest news and information portal with a wide range of topical content. You must register (free) to access many of the site's features.

Fiji Meteorological Service
www.met.gov.fj
Your top source for Fiji's weather, including a daily Fiji weather bulletin and regional forecasts for eight other Pacific countries.

Fiji Museum Online
www.fijimuseum.org.fj
A virtual tour of the museum with special online exhibitions.

Fiji Times Online
www.fijitimes.com
The site of Fiji's oldest daily newspaper, established in 1869.

Mamanuca Islands
www.fijiresorts.com
Useful information on the resorts, cruises, diving, weddings, and transport, plus a series of picture galleries of the islands off Nadi.

Map South Pacific
www.mapsouthpacific.com
South Pacific maps and travel guides to

Tahiti, Fiji, Samoa, Vanuatu, Easter Island, and more.

National Trust of Fiji Islands
www.nationaltrust.org.fj
Learn about Fiji's natural and cultural heritage here. The eight National Trust protected areas and three community parks are described in detail.

Ovalau Watersports
www.owlfiji.com
This Ovalau-based company can take you diving with sharks and manta rays in the Koro Sea. Aside from describing their dive sites, the site provides an introduction to historic Levuka, Fiji's first capital.

Rivers Fiji
www.riversfiji.com
Provides extensive information on white-water rafting and kayaking on southern Viti Levu.

Rotuma Website
www.rotuma.net
Every niche relating to Rotuma is here, including history, culture, language, maps, population, politics, news, photos, humor, proverbs, recipes, art, and music.

Tourism Fiji
www.fijime.com
This site is used by Fiji's national tourist office to disseminate information about accommodations, activities, transportation, events, and the like.

Index

List of Maps

Acknowledgments

Special thanks to Greek traveler Nicos Hadjicostis for his very detailed feedback, to Philip Felstead for hunting down details around Sigatoka, to Andrea Goerger-Dehm for helping to update Ovalau, to Karen Bower for checking details at Savusavu, and to Soren Vestergaard Hansen and Anne Juhl for precise details of their trip to Suva and the islands around Ovalau.

Thanks to the following readers who took the trouble to write us letters about their trips: Liz Baker, Linda Blue, Mike Boom, Cecily Daroux, Raheman Daya, Paige Foltermann, Ian Heydon, Annemarie Hunter, Lisa J, Greg Kingsley, Annette Metcalf, Carsten Meyer, Jason Nalewabau, George Prasad, Isabel Rieger, Doug Schrader, Adre Sunika, Nic Turrentine, and Wolfgang Weitlaner.

To have your name included here next edition, write: David Stanley, *Moon Fiji,* Avalon Travel, 1700 Fourth St., Berkeley, CA 94710, USA, or feedback@moon.com.

Hotel keepers, tour operators, and Divemasters are also encouraged to send us current information about their businesses. If you don't agree with what we've written, please tell us why—there's never any charge or obligation for a listing.

From the Author

While out researching my books, I find it cheaper to pay my own way, and you can rest assured that nothing in this book is designed to repay "hospitality" from hotels, restaurants, tour operators, or airlines. I don't accept freebies for any sort of coverage, period. I prefer to arrive unexpected and uninvited, and to experience things as they really are. On the road I seldom identify myself to anyone. The essential difference between this book and the myriad travel brochures free for the taking at travel agencies and resorts throughout Fiji is that this book represents you, the traveler, while the brochures represent the travel industry. The companies and organizations included herein are there for information purposes only, and a mention in no way implies an endorsement.

Stay in touch . . .

Southpacific.org

takes you beyond Fiji to Tahiti and French Polynesia, the Cook Islands, Niue, Samoa, Solomon Islands, Tonga, Tuvalu, Vanuatu, and everything in between.

Author David Stanley's personal website provides mini-guides to South Pacific destinations, island maps, listings of films, music, and books, FAQs, and his personal travel blog.

www.moon.com

DESTINATIONS | ACTIVITIES | BLOGS | MAPS | BOOKS

MOON.COM is ready to help plan your next trip! Filled with fresh trip ideas and strategies, author interviews, informative travel blogs, a detailed map library, and descriptions of all the Moon guidebooks, Moon.com is all you need to get out and explore the world—or even places in your own backyard. While at Moon.com, sign up for our monthly e-newsletter for updates on new releases, travel tips, and expert advice from our on-the-go Moon authors. As always, when you travel with Moon, expect an experience that is uncommon and truly unique.

MOON IS ON FACEBOOK—BECOME A FAN!
JOIN THE MOON PHOTO GROUP ON FLICKR

MAP SYMBOLS

▦ Expressway	🅒 Highlight	✗ Airfield	⚓ Golf Course		
▦ Primary Road	○ City/Town	✈ Airport	🅿 Parking Area		
▦ Secondary Road	◉ State Capital	▲ Mountain	▱ Archaeological Site		
▭ Unpaved Road	✸ National Capital	✦ Unique Natural Feature	♠ Church		
------ Trail	★ Point of Interest				
············ Ferry	• Accommodation	⦚ Waterfall	⬡ Glacier		
▰▰▰ Railroad	▼ Restaurant/Bar	▲ Park	▱ Mangrove		
▦ Pedestrian Walkway	▪ Other Location	❸ Trailhead	▱ Reef		
▥ Stairs	⋀ Campground	⚐ Skiing Area	▱ Swamp		

CONVERSION TABLES

$°C = (°F - 32) / 1.8$
$°F = (°C \times 1.8) + 32$
1 inch = 2.54 centimeters (cm)
1 foot = 0.304 meters (m)
1 yard = 0.914 meters
1 mile = 1.6093 kilometers (km)
1 km = 0.6214 miles
1 fathom = 1.8288 m
1 chain = 20.1168 m
1 furlong = 201.168 m
1 acre = 0.4047 hectares
1 sq km = 100 hectares
1 sq mile = 2.59 square km
1 ounce = 28.35 grams
1 pound = 0.4536 kilograms
1 short ton = 0.90718 metric ton
1 short ton = 2,000 pounds
1 long ton = 1.016 metric tons
1 long ton = 2,240 pounds
1 metric ton = 1,000 kilograms
1 quart = 0.94635 liters
1 US gallon = 3.7854 liters
1 Imperial gallon = 4.5459 liters
1 nautical mile = 1.852 km

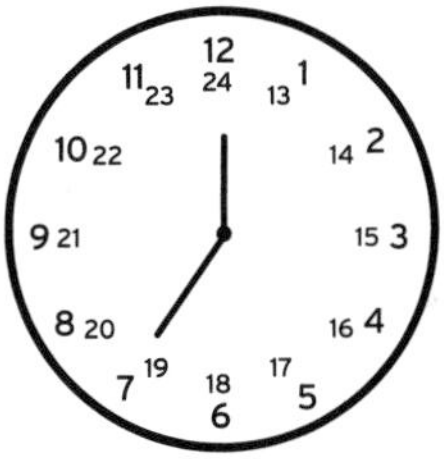

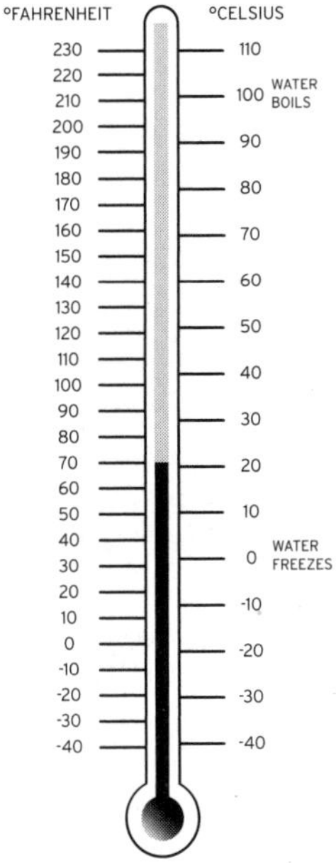

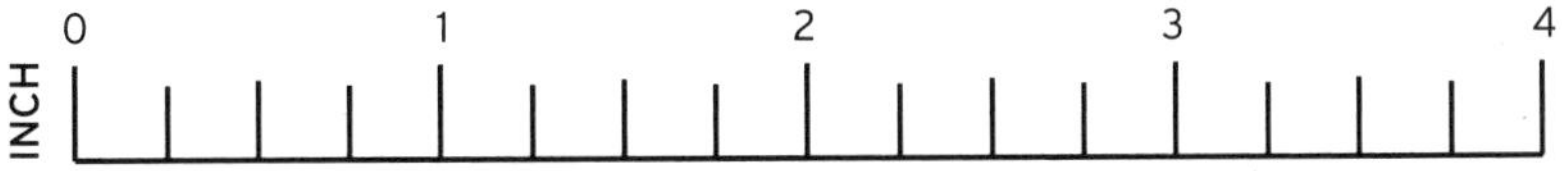

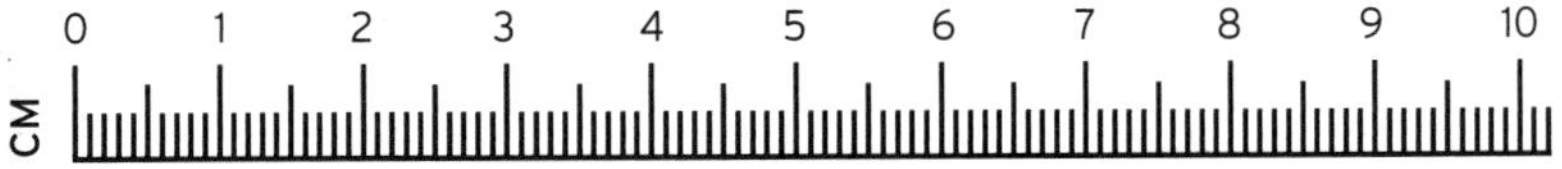

°FAHRENHEIT °CELSIUS

230 / 110
220 / 100 WATER BOILS
210
200 / 90
190
180 / 80
170
160 / 70
150
140 / 60
130
120 / 50
110
100 / 40
90
80 / 30
70
60 / 20
50
40 / 10
30
20 / 0 WATER FREEZES
10
0 / -10
-10
-20 / -20
-30 / -30
-40 / -40

INCH: 0 1 2 3 4

CM: 0 1 2 3 4 5 6 7 8 9 10

MOON FIJI
Avalon Travel
a member of the Perseus Books Group
1700 Fourth Street
Berkeley, CA 94710, USA
www.moon.com

Editor and Series Manager: Kathryn Ettinger
Copy Editor: Ellie Winters
Graphics Coordinator: Elizabeth Jang
Production Coordinator: Elizabeth Jang
Cover Designer: Elizabeth Jang
Map Editor: Mike Morgenfeld
Cartographers: Allison Rawley, Chris Henrick,
  Mike Morgenfeld
Indexer: Greg Jewett

ISBN: 978-1-59880-737-0
ISSN: 1082-4898

Printing History
1st Edition – 1985
9th Edition – February 2011
5 4 3 2 1

Text and maps © 2011 by David Stanley.
All rights reserved.

Front cover photo: A blue and yellow damselfish in a
gorgonian coral © Tim Laman/Getty Images
Title page photo: Women walking in Ba © Mark Heard/
www.flickr.com/heardsy

Color interior photos: p. 6 rock formations adjacent
to the Lavena Coastal Walk, Taveuni Island © Steve
L. Martin; p. 7 (left) driftwood sculpture on Fiji beach
© Valery Shanin/123rf.com; (right) © Erik Hannon; p.
8 (inset) © Tim Parkinson; (bottom) orchid courtesy
Matava Resort; p. 9 (top left) © Tim Parkinson;
(top right) © Erik Hannon; (bottom left) © Barbara
Kraft/The Wakaya Club & Spa; (bottom right) © Tim
Parkinson; p. 10 © Erik Hannon; p. 11, 12 © David
Stanley; p. 13 © Vladimir Ruchkin/123rf.com; p. 15 (top)
© Mark Heard/www.flickr.com/heardsy; (bottom) ©
Erik Hannon; p. 16, 18 © Mark Heard/www.flickr.com/
heardsy; p. 19 © Richard Gifford; p. 20 © adxdopefish;
p. 21 © Erik Hannon; p. 22 © CrashDiver; p. 23 © Ethan
Gordon/The Wakaya Club & Spa; p. 24 © kelpie1

Photos from Flickr Creative Commons members
are used according to the following license: http://
creativecommons.org/licenses/by/2.0/

Printed in Canada by Friesens

KEEPING CURRENT

If you have a favorite gem you'd like to see included in the next edition, or see anything
that needs updating, clarification, or correction, please drop us a line. Send your
comments via email to feedback@moon.com, or use the address above.